A POPULAR HISTORY OF BRITISH INDIA

A POPULAR HISTORY OF BRITISH INDIA

COMMERICAL INTERCOURSE WITH CHINA, AND THE INSULAR POSSESSIONS OF ENGLAND IN THE EASTERN SEAS

By

W. Cooke Taylor, LL.D., &c.,

GYAN

Published by

Gyan Publishing House
5, Ansari Road
Daryaganj, New Delhi-110002
Phone: 011-47034999, 9811692060
E-mail: books@gyanbooks.com

Distribution Network
gyanbooks.com
India, USA, Canada, UK, Australia, France

ISBN : 978-81-212-6753-3 (PB)
First Published, 1842

2nd Impression 2022

Printed at: Gyan Press, Delhi.

A POPULAR HISTORY OF BRITISH INDIA
Author: W. COOKE TAYLOR

A POPULAR HISTORY

OF

BRITISH INDIA,

COMMERCIAL INTERCOURSE WITH

CHINA,

AND THE INSULAR POSSESSIONS OF

ENGLAND

IN

THE EASTERN SEAS.

By W. COOKE TAYLOR, LL.D., &c.,

OF TRINITY COLLEGE, DUBLIN;

AUTHOR OF "THE MANUAL OF ANCIENT AND MODERN HISTORY,"
"THE NATURAL HISTORY OF SOCIETY,"
"ROMANTIC BIOGRAPHY OF THE AGE OF ELIZABETH," &c. &c.

1842

TO

SIR CHARLES FORBES, BART.

THE

HONOURED FRIEND

OF

INDIA AND HER PEOPLE,

THIS WORK IS

BY HIS KIND PERMISSION

MOST

RESPECTFULLY DEDICATED

BY

HIS GRATEFUL AND OBLIGED SERVANTS,

THE PUBLISHERS.

OCTOBER, 1842.

PREFACE.

THE object of this compilation is sufficiently explained by the title; India has now become so important to England, that a convenient manual of its History must be desirable, if not necessary, to all who take an interest in the prosperity of their country. It has been the Author's aim to give a simple narrative of facts, derived from the best authorities, without introducing any opinions of his own, but leaving his Readers to form their own reflections and deduce their own conclusions.

So much confusion exists in oriental orthography, that it would seem as if the sarcasm on philology, might be applied to most attempts made to represent European names by Eastern characters, "the vowels count for nothing and the consonants for very little;" under such circumstances it would be entirely absurd to affect a rigid purity. The system of Sir William Jones has been adopted, as that which most scholars have recognized as nearest to perfection, but it was impossible to adhere to it strictly, because familiarity and usage with other forms of spelling, have rendered other representations of the names both of persons and things too firmly established to be easily altered. It is probable that this necessity of conceding to popular usage, may have led to some inconsistencies in the orthography used in this Work, but it is believed that there are none of any amount to create difficulty to the reader.

An account of British intercourse with China has been subjoined, because that trade was, until lately, connected with the government of India, and must continue to exercise a great influence on the Asiatic relations of this country; but it was not deemed prudent to attempt even an abridged history of the Celestial Empire, as this would have inconveniently increased the size and price of the volume. For the same reason, the notices of the British empire in the East have been made as brief as perspicuity would allow.

It is intended in the successive editions of this Work, to bring down the history of the Indian Empire to the latest period. In such a mass of foreign names and varied dates, some typographical errors could hardly be avoided. Should any such be found, the Reader is requested to send a note of them, or any other deficiencies, to the Publisher.

London, Oct. 1842.

A

POPULAR HISTORY

OF

BRITISH INDIA.

CHAPTER I.

EARLY HISTORY OF HINDUSTAN.

Both in ancient and modern time, historians have been unanimous in regarding the Hindús as one of the earliest, if not the first, civilized nations of the world. Few nations, however, possessing such a claim are more deficient in authentic records of antiquity; instead of histories they possess only vague traditions exaggerated by the imagination of their poets, and monumental remains, which attest, indeed, by their stupendous size, the greatness of their founders, but afford no means of ascertaining the time when their builders existed. Independent of foreign accounts, the chief authorities for the early history of Hindustan, are the eighteen Puranas and the two great epic poems called the Ramayana and Mahabharat. These contain, in their form, decisive evidence of their traditionary origin; nearly all of them are described as repeated by some person who had heard the story from another, and the truths they contain are involved in such a mass of fable, that it is difficult to determine what statements should be received as realities. In the eleventh and twelfth centuries of our era some histories of Kashmír were written, which throw some light on the antiquities of India; and more accurate information respecting the state of the country during the three centuries preceding the Christian era, may be obtained from the Greek writers, who obtained some knowledge of these distant regions in consequence of the conquests of Alexander.

The Hindus appear originally to have possessed only a small portion of India, the country between the rivers Seravoty and Kaggar, which is a tract about 100 miles to the north-west of Delhi, about seventy-five miles in length, and from twenty to forty in breadth. The rest of the peninsula was covered with forests, and tenanted by Mlechas, or barbarians, speaking a rude language. They very soon extended themselves, so that the ancient country of the Hindus may be said to have included the present provinces of Lahore, Delhi, Agra, Oude and Allahabad.

Ayodha, or Oude, appears to have been the first capital of the nation; it was the birth-place of the two principal families, called the dynasties of the Sun and Moon, both of which are said to have issued originally from Brahma (the Supreme Being, according to the mythology of the Hindus) through his sons, the patriarchs Daksha and Atri. Vaivaswat (the sun) had Daksha for his father, and Soma (the moon) was the child of Atri. The first prince of the family of the sun, was named Ikshwaku. He had several sons, one hundred according to the legend, who established themselves in different places; but the direct line resided at Ayudha, or Oude, in which Ikshwaku was succeeded by his grandson, named Kakutstha. From fifty to seventy generations of the solar race followed, distinguished only by legends, purely mythological, from each other. After these we come to the most celebrated hero of the solar line, Rama, the son of Damarantha, whose marvellous exploits and adventures form the subject of one of the great epic poems, the Ramayama. Stripped of its fabulous and romantic decorations, his story merely relates that Rama established a powerful kingdom in Hindustan, that he invaded the Dekkan, and conquered the island of Ceylon. But on this simple basis the Hindu poets have erected a structure of adventure, so wildly supernatural that it is almost without a parallel in the whole range of fiction. A brief abstract of the poem will serve to show the nature of the legends which the Hindus have substituted for history, and also help to illustrate the nature both of the mythology and literature of this singular people.

Dasaratha, king of Oude, would have been the most fortunate of monarchs had he not long been childless. By the advice of the Brahmins he determined to propitiate the benevolent deities by the sacrifice of a horse, the most solemn of the religious ceremonies used by the Hindus, and one which requires the labour of years to be bestowed on its preparation. Princes and Brahmins were invited to attend this important rite from afar, and its complete success ensured Dasaratha the blessing of male children. The Devas and heavenly sages who had assisted at the sacrifice, proceeded to the mansion of Brahma, the chief of the Hindu gods, and informed him that the benevolent deities were worsted by certain evil genii, called Rakshasas, commanded by prince Ravanas, and that the good spirits were unable to make a successful resistance, having bound themselves by a promise to render their adversaries invulnerable. The god Vishnu "the illustrious lord of the universe," arrived during the discussion; he was "clad in vestments of yellow, ornamented with golden bracelets and riding on the eagle Vainataya, like the sun on a cloud, and holding his discus and mace in his hand." At the request of the deities, Vishnu consented to become incarnate in the persons of four sons of Daranatha; and, as notwithstanding these incarnations he still retained his dignity and station in heaven, the Indian fable ascribes to Vishnu five separate existences at the same time. Rama is born, and on the demand of Vishnu, is furnished with an army of supernatural monkeys to aid him in the approaching war.

When Rama and his brothers had attained a marriageable age, a sage named Visva Mitra appeared at the court of Daranatha, and obtained from the king a promise of whatever boon he desired. He had made a solemn vow of offering a particular sacrifice, but had hitherto been prevented by the opposition of the Rakshasas from performing the ceremony in a manner acceptable to the deities; he, therefore, implored Daranatha to give him the aid of his gallant son, Rama, against those impious demons. The aged monarch was unwilling to expose his beloved son in so perilous a war; Visva Mitra severely upbraided him for breach of promise, and "at the wrath of the sage the earth trembled, and fear seized even the gods." Daranatha yielded; Rama and his brothers set forth for the war, and "at their departure a shower of odorous flowers signified the approbation of heaven, and the celestial inhabitants themselves celebrated the event with songs of joy." In the course of the expedition Visva Mitra instructed Rama in the history and nature of every important object they passed; he also presented him with a suit of celestial armour, even more valuable than that which Thetis brought to Achilles, for each separate piece came without hands when summoned by its master, and was even able to enter into conversation with the hero.

Having slain the sorceress Taraka, Rama, his brothers and the sage, traverse the countries bordering on the Ganges, and at length reach the palace of a king named Janaka, who possessed an enormous bow which no person had yet been able to bend. Janaka received the sage, Visva Mitra, with all the veneration which royalty itself was bound to show to so illustrious a Brahmin. At the sage's request he permitted Rama to essay the bending of the bow, a feat which the king had promised to reward with the hand of his lovely daughter Sita. It required the labour of eight hundred men to draw the carriage which contained the ponderous bow. Rama, notwithstanding, grasped it with one hand, and not only drew it, but broke it in the middle "with an astounding noise like the crash of a falling mountain." Janaka at once consented that Sita should become the bride of the successful hero, and that Rama's three brothers should also be provided with wives. Dasaratha was invited to witness the splendid ceremonials of the marriage; he came with a large train, and when the nuptials were over, he brought Rama back to Ayodha, and associated him with himself in the government of the kingdom.

Kaikeyi, one of the wives of Daranatha, was anxious that her son, Bharata, should succeed to the throne; and to effect this object, she excited such suspicion of Rama in the mind of the king, that he doomed his gallant son to an exile of fifteen years. Rama, followed by his wife Sita, and his brother Lakshman, departed from Ayodha and retired into a forest, where he lived a life of penance. The grief of the father, when he discovered his error, which brought down his grey hairs with sorrow to the grave, is thus powerfully pourtrayed in a passage very faithfully translated by Millman.

"My eye no more my Rama sees—and grief o'erbrims my spirit's sink,
As the swol'n stream sweeps down the trees that grow upon the crumbling brink.

Oh, felt I Rama's touch, or spake one word his home-returning voice,
Again to life should I awake, as quaffing nectar-draughts rejoice.
But what so sad could e'er have been, celestial partner of my heart,
Than Rama's beauteous face unseen, from life untimely to depart?
His exile in the forest o'er, him home return'd to Oude's high town,
Oh, happy those that see once more, like Indra from the sky come down.
No mortal men, but gods I deem, moonlike, before whose wondering sight,
My Rama's glorious face shall beam, from the dark forest bursting bright.
Happy that gaze on Rama's face, with beauteous teeth and smile of love;
Like the blue lotus in its grace, and like the starry king above.
Like to the full autumnal moon, and like the lotus in its bloom,
That youth who sees returning soon, how blest shall be that mortal's doom!"
Dwelling on that sweet memory, on his last bed the monarch lay,
And slowly, softly seemed to die, as fades the moon at dawn away.
"Ah, Rama! Ah, my son!" thus said, or scarcely said the king of men;
His gentle hapless spirit fled, in sorrow for his Rama then.
The shepherd of his people old, at midnight on his bed of death,
The tale of his son's exile told, and breath'd away his dying breath.

After the death of Daranatha his council proffered the vacant throne to Bharata, but he refused to accept it, declaring that he would not usurp the rights of his elder brother. The sages and Brahmins then resolved that Bharata should go in search of his brother; and he, after having settled a regency, departed on the quest. After several wondrous adventures, Bharata reached the forest where Rama and Sita lived in the disguise of penitents. He informed the hero of Daranatha's death, and begged of him to return home and assume the reins of government. Rama steadily refused to comply until his fifteen years of penance should be completed; but to prevent the kingdom from falling into anarchy, he surrendered to Bharata the royal insignia, to wit, the golden slipper and the white umbrella, promising to resume them when his allotted term of penitence should be expired. Bharata, in consequence, returned to Ayodha and administered the kingdom in the name of his brother, while Rama, with his wife and brother, continued their penance in the woods.

In the meantime, Ravana, the prince of those impious dæmons the Rakshasas, having accidentally seen the beautiful Lita, fell violently in love with her; by stratagem and force he succeeded in bearing her off to his city of Lanka, situated in an island of the same name, where he kept her in strict seclusion. Rama, disconsolate for the loss of his lovely spouse, entered into an alliance with Hanuman, the chief of the supernatural monkeys, and engaged him to go in search of Sita. After many vexatious delays and disappointments, Hanuman obtained an interview with the object of his search at Lanka, and after having delivered to her a consoling message from her husband, hasted to rejoin him. Rama and his allies immediately resolved to attack Lanka; they constructed a wondrous bridge across the sea, over which the allied armies of men, angels and monkeys, marched to the siege of the fortress. Fearful were the battles which took place round the city of the dæmons. Earth, water and air, were equally the theatre of engagement, and heaven itself was alarmed by the furious struggle. Rama and Ravana encountered each other in their war-chariots; so furious was the shock of their meeting that the earth trembled for seven days, but at length the prince of the Rakshasas was overthrown, and the gates of his city stormed. Rama and Hanuman made a triumphal entry into Lanka, but the hero after having delivered Sita began to express doubts of her fidelity, and she had to prove her innocence by submitting to the ordeal of fire. Heaven united with earth in the rejoicings occasioned by the establishment of the purity of the princess. Brahma and the other deities descended from heaven to bestow their benediction on her re-union with Rama. The whole party then returned to Ayodha, but Rama, instead of assuming his regal station, resigned the sceptre to his brother Lakshman, and ascended to heaven, his real abode.

After Rama, sixty princes of the same race are said to have ruled in succession over his dominions, none of whom attained any great celebrity. It seems probable that Ayodha ceased to be the capital, and that the seat of government was transferred to Canouj. Another line of the solar kings descended from Nimi, the son of Ikshwaku, by whom the state of Mithila was founded. In this family Janaka was born, the father of Lita, the wife of Rama, and his companion in exile and penitence.

The first prince of the lunar dynasty was Pururavas, the son of Buddha, the son of the moon. His capital was Pratisthana, at the confluence of the Ganges and Jumna. According to the legends, he obtained in marriage Urvasi, one of the *Apsaras* or nymphs of heaven, whose celestial charms were without a parallel. Unfortunately, the king violated the conditions on which alone this unequal union was permitted; his beloved Urvasi was taken from him; and he felt the loss so severely that he was deprived of reason. After many years had elapsed, he discovered her sporting on the banks of a lake, and implored her to return; the nymph refused, but at the same time promised to pay him an annual visit. The fruits of their union were six sons, of whom Ayus, the elder, succeeded to the throne. Pururavas was not satisfied with occasional visits from his celestial bride, he sighed for the permanent enjoyment of her society. Some deities pitying his distress, directed him to perform a sacrifice in a forest, to attain the gratification of his wishes. Fire was wanting to perform this sacred rite, but the king by rubbing two branches of trees together, and reciting over them the holiest verse of the Vedas, generated a flame which enabled him to perform the necessary sacrifice. When this was done he was elevated to the rank of a demi-god, and permitted to enjoy the constant society of his Urvasi in the celestial regions. From this legend it may be concluded that Pururavas was the first who introduced the worship of fire into India, and there are some other traditions which indicate his being the author of some important innovations in the Hindu ritual.

Ayus had two sons, Nahusha, who succeeded him, and Kahetravriddha, who established a separate principality at Kasi or Benares; his grandson, Saunaka, is said to have established the distinction of castes, for in the age of purity all Hindus were equal.

Nahusha was succeeded by Yayati, who had five sons. According to the Puranic legend he married the daughter of an eminent saint, to whom he proved unfaithful. The queen complained to her father, and he inflicted on Yayati the curse of premature decay, with permission, however, to transfer his infirmities to any one who was willing to give him youth and strength in exchange. The king applied to his sons, all of whom refused, except Puru, the youngest. After a brief enjoyment of his renovated constitution, the king restored his youth to Puru, and resumed his own former decrepitude. He made this affectionate son paramount over his elder brothers, each of whom, however, was appointed kings of circles or districts. By their descendants the greater part of southern and western India was colonized, and civilization introduced among the barbarous inhabitants.

Puru continued to reside at Pratisthana, and was the ancestor of several celebrated princes, amongst whom Bharata, the son of Dushyanta, exercised such extensive power that India is sometimes called after his name, Bharata Versha, or the country of Bharata. After about twenty descents from Puru, the crown devolved on Hastin, who removed the capital farther north, to a city which he erected on the banks of the Ganges, and called after his own name, Hastinapur. After having long flourished, the city was finally ruined by the encroachments of the river, but vestiges of its remains may still be discovered. Four descents after Hastin brought the crown to Kuru, "who gave his name to the holy district Kurukshetra," north-west of his capital, an appellation which is still retained. It seems probable that at this time the lunar race had been forced backwards towards the north, by the increasing power of the kingdom of Oude, under Rama and his descendants.

Vichitravirya, the fourteenth in descent from Kuru, died without issue, but his half-brother, Vyasa, married the widow, by whom he had two sons, Pandu and Dhritarashtra. Vyasa is celebrated for having collected the hymns and prayers which constitute the Vedas, or sacred books of the Hindus, and for having arranged them under their present divisions; he also established a school in which they were taught, and the Puranas are sometimes, but erroneously, ascribed to his disciples. He is further described as the original narrator of the Mahabharat, the second great Hindú epic. When his sons attained maturity, Vyasa resigned the government; Pandu retired to the Himalaya mountains, where he had five sons; Dhritarashtra remained in possession of the kingdom, and had a hundred sons, of whom Duryodhan was the eldest.

The Pandavas, or sons of Pandu, came from the mountains to claim a share of their father's kingdom: they were at first regarded as impostors, but a strong party being formed in their favour, a separate principality was assigned them, and they erected a new city for their capital on the banks of the Jumna, which was named Indraprastha. It was on or near the site of Delhi. Frequent dissensions between the kings of Hastinapul and Indraprastha led to the Great War, which forms the subject of the Mahabharat, as the name indicates. Most of the princes of India took a share in this mighty contest, but the chief ally of the Pandavas was Krishna, who having been driven from Mathura, the seat of his family, had founded a new city, Dwaraka in Guzerat. He was, like his allies, one of the lunar race, being a Yadava, or descendant of Yadu, the eldest son of Yayati.

According to the legends, Krishna was an incarnation of the god Vishnu, and as such he is still worshipped by the Hindus. Though of royal birth he was educated in the cottage of a herdsman, where he was concealed from a tyrant who sought his life. The frolics and exploits of the deity in childhood,—his stealing milk, his destroying serpents,—are favourite themes with the pastoral poets, and they love to dwell on his surpassing beauty as a youth, when he captivated the hearts, not only of the female rustics, but of the proudest princesses of Hindustan. As he advanced in years he achieved innumerable adventures; among the rest, he destroyed the tyrant who usurped his inheritance, but was nevertheless unable to defend his native capital, and therefore established himself in Guzerat. It was chiefly by his aid that the Pandavas triumphed in the great battle, which lasted eighteen days; Duryodhan and his host of brethren were slain, the undivided kingdom became the possession of the sons of Pandu, but they were so grieved by the dreadful slaughter which their ambition occasioned, that they resigned their power. The end of Krishna was also unfortunate; he was accidentally killed in a thicket by a hunter, and his sons—driven from their paternal possessions—were forced to seek refuge beyond the Indus. The successors of the Pandavas seem to have transferred the seat of government to Delhi; none of them attained any eminence, and the kingdom of Magadha became the most flourishing in India, a rank which it continued to retain for several centuries.

Jarasandha, who was descended from Puru by a collateral branch, appears to have been the first monarch of Magadha who acquired any remarkable power. He was slain by the Pandavas and Krishna, during the Great War at his capital, Ragaguba, an ancient city which can still be traced by its ruins. For many centuries the kings of Magadha belonged to the warrior caste, and during their dynasty the Buddhist religion was introduced by Sakya, or Gautma, the son of a feudatory prince, who claimed to be an incarnation of the divinity. The last king of the warrior caste was Mahanandi, who was succeeded by Nanda, the son of a Sudia mother, who consequently was deemed one of that caste. Nanda's posterity held the throne for nine generations; the last of the line, who was also named Nanda, was murdered by a Brahmin, who raised a relative of his victim, Chandragupta, to the throne.

We now begin to obtain more accurate information respecting India from the Greek historians, the conquests of Alexander having for a time opened the country to Europeans. Previous to his arrival, the western parts of Hindustan had been conquered by Darius Hystaspes, king of Persia, and his son Xerxes, was attended by a body of Indian troops when he invaded Greece. But the Persian dominion was brief in its duration and limited in its extent; when Alexander crossed the Indus, he found Hindustan divided into several independent states, all of which are declared to have enjoyed a high degree of civilization; the chief state appears to have been the empire of the Prasii, with its capital Palebothra, on the banks of the Ganges. From the accounts which the Hindus gave to the Greeks, it would appear that the Gangetic States had never been attacked by any foreign enemy, during the long interval between the exploits of Rama and the conquests of Alexander. Some perplexity has arisen from the inveterate habit, common to all the Greek historians, of identifying foreign deities with the gods of their own Olympus; thus, they assumed that the achievements of Rama, described in the Ramayana, and the exploits of Krishna, detailed in the Mahabharat, related to their own heroes Bacchus and Hercules, who must of course have invaded India. Alexander did not advance beyond the Hyphasis, one of the five great streams tributary to the Indus; he only knew the great empire of the Prasii by report, having turned back before he reached its western frontier. The kingdom of Bactria which the Greeks founded, probably became the means of introducing some portions of western civilization into Hindustan, but it could not have been the only, or even the principal source of the Sanscrit language and literature, since, as we have seen, the companions of Alexander are unanimous in asserting that they found a system of civilization already established when they came to the frontiers of India, and also since there is not a particle of internal evidence, to show that the Hindus borrowed their systems of poetry and philosophy from foreign sources.

After the retreat of Alexander, there arose a conqueror in India, known to the Greeks by the name of Sandracottus, who has been successfully identified with the Chandra-gupta of Hindu poetry and legend. He was the son of a woman of low extraction, and would therefore have been excluded from all share of power, had not his royal father, Nanda, provoked the hostility of the Brahmins. They united with some prince in the north of India, by whose aid they destroyed Nanda and his legitimate children, after which they raised Chandra-gupta to the throne. The new king not only refused to pay the stipulated reward to the prince, his ally, but procured his assassination. The prince's son led an army to revenge his father's murder, consisting of his own subjects and a body of Greek auxiliaries. Chandra-gupta contrived by crafty intrigues, to excite dissensions between these allies, and thus the invasion was frustrated. He subsequently entered into a treaty with Seleucus Nicator, who after the death of Alexander held for some time the sovereignty of Upper Asia, and probably by the aid of the Greeks extended his empire from the Ganges to the Indus. The descendants of Chandra-gupta were called Mauryas; Asoca, the third of the line, established a commanding influence over the states north of the Nerbudda; he erected columns, inscribed with edicts, for the regulation of the government, which from the remote points of their several positions prove the extent of his government, while their injunctions bear testimony to the civilized character of his policy. The family of Maurya retained possession of the throne for ten generations, and were succeeded by three other Sudra dynasties, under whom the prosperity of the kingdom of Magadha gradually declined.

Though the kingdom of Avanti, or Oujein, cannot claim equal antiquity with those already mentioned, it is the first of which we possess any authentic date. The Samvat era, still current in the countries north of the Nerbudda, dates from Vicramaditya, B. C. 56. This prince was a great patron of learning and learned men; nine of the sages whom he protected were called the Nine Gems of Science, and were scarcely less celebrated than the Seven Wise Men of Greece. Vicramaditya rendered a still more important service to India, by arresting the conquests of the Sakkas, or Scythians, who had overturned the Greek kingdom of Bactria, the modern Balkh. From his numerous wars against these barbarians, he was named Sakari, or the Foe of the Sakkas. It is probable, however, that some tribes or wandering clans of this race, settled in northern India, and became the progenitors of the Najput tribes between Oude and Marwar.

The celebrity of Avanti ceased with Vicramaditya, and the next prince of any note is Salivahana, king of Pratisthana in the Dekkan. The Daka era is reckoned from him, (A. D. 76,) but little is known of him beyond his name. From this time India appears to have been severed into a number of small principalities, distracted both by political and religious feuds, until it was invaded and brought under subjection by the Mohammedans, in the tenth century of our era.

Modern investigations have shown that the Hindus were not the original natives of India, but that they came at some unknown age, from countries west of the Indus, bringing with them the Sanscrit language and the religion of the Vedas; that they established themselves in the eastern part of the Punjáb, or the country inclosed by the Indus and its tributary streams; and that they gradually acquired dominion over the barbarous tribes in their neighbourhood. It is probable that the original immigrants were a colony of priests, a religious and philosophical community rather than a political body, and that having established an ascendancy by their superiority of knowledge, they introduced the system of caste to secure the same advantages for their posterity. It is generally conceded, that the distinction of caste was not so rigidly observed in the more ancient periods of Hindu history, as it was in later times; the Brahmins are described, as having been forced to share their exclusive privilege of teaching the Vedas, with members of the warrior class, and both appear sometimes engaged in fierce contests both for spiritual and temporal supremacy. Caste is the fundamental principle of the Hindu polity, and the maintenance of its purity appears to be the main object of the great code of legislation ascribed to Menu. There are four original castes, the Brahmins or priests, the Kshatriyas or warriors, the Vaisyas or merchants, and the Sudras or vulgar.

The Brahmins possessed the exclusive privilege of explaining the Vedas, and as these sacred books are the source of all Hindu learning, whether religious or scientific, the possession of knowledge was confined exclusively to their caste. They were the only physicians, because diseases were regarded as a punishment for sin, which could only be removed by religious expiations.

They were the judges, for they alone possessed a knowledge of law, and they were the national priests, having the exclusive right of offering sacrifice. Sovereigns were obliged to treat them with respect, as being of a supernatural order; it was deemed impious to refuse their requests, their estates were free from impost, and it was unlawful to put them to death even when convicted of the most atrocious crimes. On the other hand, they were bound to perform ascetic duties, which, with the single exception of celibacy, are as rigid as those of the strictest monastic order in Europe; for without such austerities, the belief in their superior sanctity could not long have been maintained. It is impossible that such a system could have developed itself within any nation, but the example of the Jesuits in Paraguay, shows that there are no limits to the authority which a learned and judicious community, can establish over the minds of simple barbarians. The Kshatriyas or warrior caste ranked next to the Brahmins, with whom they, as well as the Varsyas, shared the privilege of reading the Vedas, but were forbidden to make any comment or interpretation of the Sacred Books. It is exceedingly probable that the first immigrants found it necessary to defend the supremacy they had acquired, and that they therefore trained a body of warriors, whose allegiance they hoped to secure by communicating to them a portion of their own privileges, while at the same time, they took every precaution to prevent these soldiers from ever becoming rivals to the Brahminical power. In fact, we know that the warriors made more than one effort to overthrow the power of the priests, and hence the laws regulating the Kshatiryas, are better calculated to make monks than soldiers. To the jealousy of the Brahmins must be attributed the great want of warlike spirit among the Hindus, and the ease with which they were subdued by foreign conquerors. The Brahmins assert that the old warrior caste is annihilated, and the institutes of Menu relate that several of their tribes were expelled from their caste, for neglecting to observe holy customs, and pay proper respect to their spiritual superiors.

Agriculture, trade and commerce, occupied the attention of the Vaisyas, who were probably the most numerous of all the castes. They, like the preceding classes, were permitted to wear the sacred cord, which was the symbol of regeneration; but this privilege was refused to the Sudras, who, according to the Hindù expression, were only born once. The Sudras were absolutely forbidden all knowledge of the Vedas; they were liable to be punished with death, if detected reading one of the sacred books. It was declared that they were born to be servants; that their first duty was to wait on a Brahmin, but if they would not obtain a priestly master, they were recommended to enter the service of a Kshatriya or Vaisya. As some consolation for their degraded state, they were allowed to hope, that fidelity to a Brahmin would ensure the transmigration of their soul after death into a body of higher caste. They had also other rights, particularly security of property and personal independence. In spite of all the legal restrictions on marriage, new castes were formed, chiefly by the intermarriage of the Hindus with the descendants of the primitive inhabitants of India. It has been, indeed, asserted that the Brahmins alone retained their original purity. Though the priests were excluded from reigning, they secured the dependance of the rajahs or kings on their order, by rigidly prescribing the routine of his daily occupations, and by insisting on the knowledge of the Vedas, as a qualification for admission into his council. The Brahmins even took upon them to depose kings for impiety and tyranny. In one of the Hindú dramas, Rakshasa, a Brahmin, thus boasts of his share in the destruction of Nanda, to facilitate the elevation of Chandra-gupta as we have already described.

—— " 'Tis known to all the world,
I vowed the death of Nanda and I slew him;
The current of a vow will work its way,
And cannot be resisted. What is done
Is spread abroad, and I no more have power
To stop the tale. Why should I? Be it known
The fires of my wrath alone expire,
Like the fierce conflagration of a forest,
From lack of fuel, not from weariness.
The flames of my just anger have consumed
The branching ornaments of Nanda's stem,
Abandoned by the frightened priests and people,
They have enveloped in a shower of ashes
The blighted tree of his ambitious councils:
And they have overcast with sorrow's clouds
The smiling heaven of those moon-like looks,
That shed the light of love upon my foes."

It has been already mentioned that the Vedas were the first

sacred books which were regarded as the authorities for the religious system of the Brahmins, but it must be added that the religion of the Hindus, in the present day, is very dissimilar from that taught in the Vedas. "The real doctrine of the Indian scripture," says Mr. Colebrook, "is the unity of the deity in whom the universe is comprehended; and the seeming polytheism which it exhibits, offers the elements, and the stars and planets as gods. The three principal manifestations of the divinity, (Brahma, Vishnu and Siva, the persons of the Hindu trinity,) with other personified attributes and energies, and most of the other gods of Hindu mythology, are indeed mentioned, or at least indicated in the Vedas. But the worship of deified heroes is no part of the system; nor are the incarnations of deities suggested in any portion of the text, though such are sometimes hinted at by commentators." "It is true," says Professor Wilson, "that the prevailing character of the ritual of the Vedas, is the worship of the personified elements; of Agni, or fire; Sudra, the firmament; Vayu, the air; Varuna, water; Aditya, the sun; Soma, the moon; and other elementary and planetary personages. It is also true, that the worship of the Vedas is for the most part domestic worship, consisting of prayers and oblations offered in their own houses, not in temples—by individuals for individual good, and addressed to unreal presences, not to visible types. In a word, the religion of the Vedas was not idolatry."

This simple and primitive form of worship, was succeeded in some remote and unknown age, by the adoration of images and types, and of historical personages elevated to the rank of divinities, which swelled into the most cumbrous body of legend and mythology to be found in any pagan nation. It is probable that this religious revolution was the work of the poets; the story of the Ramayana and the Mahabharat turns wholly upon the doctrine of incarnations, all the leading personages being incarnate gods, demigods, and celestial spirits. We know that a similar change was wrought in ancient Greece by Homer and Hesiod, for previous to the appearance of their theogonies, the objects of worship were the Titans, who were purely elementary deities, like the gods of the Asiatic nations. The legends which now constitute the Hindù mythology, are collected in the Puranas, works generally believed to have been written or compiled about the tenth century of our era, when the original religion had been corrupted, and the ancient system of civilization had fallen into decay.

Manu, or Menu, was the legislator of the Hindus; his code of laws was manifestly intended for an early stage of society, but it contains many excellent regulations relating to trade and commerce, marking an era when improvement was progressive. Manu, except when the author of the code is intended, is a generic term, and signifies a sage presiding over a chronological period, called a Manivantara, of whom fourteen. The account given of one of these Manus, Patryavata, bears a striking similarity to the scriptural account of Noah, and it will be interesting to compare the Hindu legend of the flood with the authentic narrative of Scripture. Menu, like Noah, stands alone in an age of universal depravity; he obtains the favour of the deity by the most rigid austerities.

" He in wonder-working penance, sire and grandsire far surpassed.
With his arms on high outstretching, wrought the sovereign of men,
Steadily on one foot standing, penance rigorous and dread,
With his downward head low-drooping, with his fixed unwavering eyes,
Dreed he thus his awful penance, many a long and weary year."

At length Brahma appeared to him in the shape of a little fish, and besought to be saved from some larger fish that threatened to devour him. Menu, without suspecting the presence of a divinity, placed the fish in a crystal vase; Brahma soon became too large for the vessel, and was removed to a lake; he outgrew the lake, and was transferred to the Ganges; and finally was transported by his kind protector to the ocean. Brahma then warned Menu of the approaching deluge, and informed him of the means by which he might escape from its destruction.

" When the awful time approaches—hear from me what thou must do.
In a little time, O blessed!—all this firm and seated earth,
All that moves upon its surface—shall a deluge sweep away.
Near it comes, of all creation—the ablution day is near;
Therefore what I now forewarn thee—may thy highest weal secure.
All the fixed and all the moving—all that stirs, or stirreth not,
Lo, of all the time approaches—the tremendous time of doom.
Build thyself a ship, O Manu—strong, with cables well prepared,
And thyself, with the seven sages—mighty Manu enter in.
All the living seeds of all things—by the Brahmins named of yore,
Place thou first within thy vessel—well secured, divided well.
From thy ship keep watch, O hermit—watch for me, as I draw near;

Horned shall I swim before thee—by my horn thou'lt know me well.
This the work thou must accomplish—I depart ; so fare thee well—
Over those tumultuous waters—none without mine aid can sail.
Doubt thou not, O lofty minded !—of my warning speech the truth."
To the fish thus answered Manu—"All that thou requir'st, I'll do."
Thus they parted, of each other—mutual leave when they had ta'en,
Manu, raja ! to accomplish—all to him the fish had said.
Taking first the seeds of all things—launched he forth upon the sea ;
On the billowy sea, the prudent—in a beauteous vessel rode.
Manu of the fish bethought him ;—conscious of his thought, the fish,
Conqueror of hostile cities ! with his horn came floating by.
King of men, the born of Manu !—Manu saw the sea-borne fish,
In his form foreshewn, the horned—like a mountain huge and high.
To the fish's head his cable, Manu bound—O king of men !
Strong and firm his cable wound he—round and round on either horn ;
And the fish, all conquering raja !—with that twisted cable bound,
With the utmost speed that vessel—dragged along the ocean tide.
In his bark along the ocean—boldly went the king of men :
Dancing with the tumbling billows—dashing through the roaring spray,
Tossed about by winds tumultuous—in the vast and heaving sea,
Like a trembling, drunken woman—reeled that ship, O king of men.
Earth was seen no more, no region—nor the intermediate space ;
All around a waste of water—water all, and air and sky.
In the whole world of creation—princely son of Bharata !
None was seen but those seven Sages—Manu only, and the fish.
Years on years, and still unwearied—drew that fish the bark along,
Till at length it came, where lifted—Himavan its loftiest peak.
There at length it came, and smiling—thus the fish addressed the sage :
"To the peak of Himalaya—bind thou now thy stately ship."
At the fish's mandate quickly—to the peak of Himavan
Bound the sage his bark, and ever—to this day that loftiest peak,
Bears the name of Naubandhana—from the binding of the bark."

The virtue attributed to extravagant penances, of which notice is taken in the preceding extract, led to the promulgation of a new creed, which might be regarded as at once a religious, philosophical and political reform of Brahminism. This religion, which probably possesses more votaries than any existing, is named Buddhism. According to the Brahmins, Buddha was the ninth incarnation of Vishnu, but the Buddhists recognize several successive Buddhas, seven of whom were persons of mortal mould, who, by prayers, penances, and meditation, attained to such excellence of nature as to have been gifted with divine nature, and to have been finally absorbed in the essence of the deity. The doctrine of absorption, or *Nirwana*, may be regarded as the fundamental principle of the Buddhist creed; it holds out the promise that the soul, when sufficiently purified, shall lose all consciousness of separate existence, and be received into the essence of the godhead; and it teaches that this state of bliss is equally attainable by men, angels and demons. It substituted sanctity for sacrifice. "Genuine Buddhism," says Mr. Hodgson, "has no priesthood; the ascetic despises the priest; the saint scorns the aid of mediators." As a consequence, it followed that the Buddhists recognized no distinction of caste, and that, wherever this system existed as a political institution, their creed tended to weaken and destroy its influence. It seems probable that the Buddhists for a time obtained an ascendancy over the Brahmins, particularly in the states of Western India, where symbols of their peculiar creed are found graven on the gigantic cave temples; but in the end they were overcome by the Brahmins, and driven by persecution from the Peninsula. The exiles carried their creed to the vast regions of Asia, which extend beyond the north and east of India; they preached it successfully in Nepaul, Mongolia, China, the farther peninsula, and the island of Ceylon, where it still flourishes with unabated vigour, and is supposed to include among its disciples fully one-third of the human race. It is probably owing to the expulsion of the Buddhists, that so much of the ancient literature of India has been lost, and that such darkness and uncertainty rest upon Hindu history. It was obviously the interest of the Brahmins to destroy every memorial of a contest which had nearly proved fatal to their power, and every record of a creed which struck at the very root of their pretensions.

It is not necessary here, to enter on any discussion of the amount of civilization to which the Hindus had attained, while they continued under the government of their native princes. Professor Wilson's summary of their social state is so complete, and his authority of such weight, that we shall conclude this chapter by quoting his testimony. "The Hindus," says this eminent scholar and enlightened writer, "by the character of their institutions, and by the depressing influence of foreign subjugation, are apparently what they were at least three centuries before the Christian era. Two thousand years have done nothing for them, every thing for us. We must, therefore, in fairness compare them with their cotemporaries, with the people of antiquity; and we shall then have reason to believe that they occupied a very foremost station amongst the nations. They had a religion, less disgraced by idolatrous worship than most of those which prevailed in early times. They had a government, which, although despotic, was equally restricted by law, by institutions and by religion. They had a code of laws, in many respects wise and rational, and adapted to a great variety of relations, which could not have existed except in an advanced state of social organization. They had a copious and cultivated language, and an extensive and diversified literature; they had made great progress in the mathematical sciences; they speculated profoundly on the mysteries of man and nature; and they had acquired remarkable proficiency in many of the ornamental and useful arts of life. Whatever defects may be justly attributed to their religion, their government, their laws, their literature, their sciences, their arts, as contrasted with the same proofs of civilization in modern Europe, it will not be disputed by any impartial and candid critic, that, as far as we have the means of instituting a comparison, the Hindus were, in all these respects, quite as civilized as any of the most civilized nations of the ancient world, and in as early times as any of which records or traditions remain."

CHAPTER II.

THE AFGHAN, AND MONGOLIAN CONQUESTS OF INDIA.

Before the discovery of the passage round the Cape of Good Hope had opened India to European enterprize, the greater part of the country had been subdued by foreign invaders, animate equally by cupidity and religious fanaticism. From the earliest ages, the wealth of India has been the theme of so much exaggeration in western Asia, that the Saracens had scarcely become masters of Persia, before they evinced an anxiety to obtain some portion of the riches, which their native traditions as well as the legends of the countries which they had subdued, led them to believe were accumulated in the countries on the eastern side of the Indus. After the conversion of the Afghans to Mohammedanism, which took place in less than half a century from the first promulgation of that religion, frequent incursions were made into the territories of the Hindus: avarice and bigotry combined to stimulate the marauders to cruelty, for they regarded their victims as at once the most wealthy and the most obstinate of idolators.

After their first great burst of success, the Saracens sunk into indolence and effeminacy; their sovereigns, the Khaliphs, began to recruit their armies from the wild tribes of Turks and Tartars; in a short time, these mercenaries became masters of the empire, and their generals founded independent principalities, limited in their extent and temporary in their duration. The Samanian dynasty, established by a Turkish adventurer, possessed the eastern provinces of the Persian empire, but obtained only a nominal obedience from the military hordes of the Afghans, who have been distinguished by their love of savage independence, from the time that their name first appears in history. To control these dangerous subjects, they entrusted the government of Candahar, or (as it is sometimes called) Ghazní, to one of their officers named Sabektekin, who had risen from the condition of a slave to the highest rank in the army. His extraordinary talents enabled him to unite a great number both of Turkish and Afghan tribes under his government; he soon became so powerful that he not only rendered himself independent of the Samanian sultan, but even crossed the Indus to invade the kingdom of Lahore, (A. D. 997, A. H. 387.) Jeipal, a Brahmin prince who then ruled Lahore, or as it is called from its five rivers, the Punjáb, assembled a powerful army to protect his religion and his country, but was twice defeated with enormous loss, and forced to purchase peace by the sacrifice of a large portion of his dominions. The causes of the success of the invaders, were the discipline of their soldiers, and the weight of their horses. Hindustan was at this time apportioned among various tribes of Rajputs, who were bound to perform a kind of feudal service for their lands; but the Rajput vassals were an ill-equipped and worse-officered body of national militia, suddenly called into the field on moments of emergency; their horses were the feeble race of steeds peculiar to the country, untrained to act in concert. The Turks, like their predecessors the Saracens, had been particularly attentive to the breeding and training of their horses, and hence the Hindus used to describe the dreaded charge of the Ghazni cavalry, as " the burst of a whirlwind."

On the death of Sabektekin, (A. D. 997,) his son, Mahmúd, ascended the throne; he was bigotedly attached to the Sunnite form of the Mohammedan faith, equally proud of his theological skill and military prowess; from his very childhood he believed himself divinely summoned, to extirpate idolatry and establish the creed of Islam beyond the Indus. Jeipal was once more forced to take the field against invasion, and was again defeated; he was taken prisoner after the fight with several of his kinsmen, and the jewels found upon his person have been valued at eighty thousand pounds. The unfortunate prince, believing that his misfortunes arose from some crime which he might expiate by self-sacrifice, resigned his crown to his son, Ananga Pal, and terminated his life on the funeral pile. The renewal of the war by the Rajput chiefs, who refused to obey Ananga Pal, on account of his submission to Mahmúd, led the sultan a second time across the Indus, when he completed the subjugation of the Punjáb, and captured the important city of Multan. A third expedition was undertaken to punish a refractory vassal; but a fourth and more important invasion, was rendered necessary by the revolt of Ananga Pal, who was stimulated by the remonstrances of the priests to make a great effort for throwing off the Mohammedan yoke. The battle which decided the fate of the Punjáb, was fought in the neighbourhood of Peshawur. During forty days the armies remained watching each other: Mahmud at length commenced the battle, but his archers were driven back, and his lines thrown into confusion by the furious charge of the Gakkars, a wild mountain tribe, the ancestors of the modern Jats. The Mohammedans were on the point of being routed, when the elephant, on which Ananga Pal rode, being terrified by the balls of burning naphtha hurled at him by the Afghans, turned and fled: the Hindus, believing themselves deserted by their sovereign, and disheartened by his apparent cowardice, gave way in every direction. A vigorous pursuit was maintained for two days, and more than twenty thousand men are said to have fallen in the battle and the flight.

Mahmúd's fifth invasion of India was undertaken to acquire possession of Nagrakot, a mountain fortress between the sources of the Ravi (Hydraotes) and the Beyah (Hyphasis), celebrated for its strength and reputed sanctity. Its temples were stored with gold and jewels; and that extraordinary spectacle of nature, a burning fountain in its neighbourhood, had from remote ages been regarded with superstitious veneration. Nagrakot yielded after a feeble defence; the treasures, which for many years had been accumulating in its shrines, became the prey of the conquerors, and Mahmúd on his return home proclaimed a solemn festival, that the followers of the Prophet might have an opportunity of admiring his magnificent plunder. The next four expeditions were undertaken to obtain similar treasures, but it is not necessary to recite the particulars; the mind is fatigued and sickened by the sameness of the horrors perpetrated to gratify fanaticism and avarice; towns were burned, temples destroyed, idols broken, and such a multitude of captives driven into slavery, that in the Mohammedan camp the price of a strong man was only ten drachmas, or about five English shillings.

Mahmúd's tenth and most celebrated invasion, was directed against the temple of Somnath. The idol of this shrine was one of the twelve famous Lingams or Phalli erected in Hindustan, and was dedicated to Siva under his title of Swayan Nath, or "the Self-existent." Though situated in Gujerat, water was brought from the distant streams of the holy Ganges for the daily washing of the idols, the revenues of ten thousand villages were assigned for the support of the temple, and princes devoted their daughters to the service of this obscene emblem. Undaunted by the difficulties of the expedition, Mahmúd entered the inhospitable desert, between Multan and Gujerat, his soldiers suffered severely during the march, but they felt that all their toils and perils were rewarded when they beheld the walls of Somnath. The Hindus, animated by the Brahmins, defended themselves with all the rage of fanaticism and despair; but they were unable to resist the enthusiastic fury of the Turks and Afghans, who believed that plunder would would be the reward of life, and paradise the recompense of death. On the second day the fortress was taken by storm, incalculable treasures were found in the temple, which were removed to Ghazni, and the idol was broken to pieces, though the Brahmins offered immense sums for its ransom. Mahmúd did not long survive this brilliant conquest; he died after having raised his kingdom to the highest rank among the states of Upper Asia, and collected in his court the most eminent poets and philosophers who had yet contributed to Persian literature.

A disputed succession weakened the Ghaznevid power after the death of Mahmúd; and when Masúd secured the crown by triumphing over all other competitors, his plans of Indian conquest were frustrated by the increasing power of the Seljukian Turks. Pressed forward by other tribes in their rear, vast hordes of Turks had crossed the Oxus, and among them a warlike sept, commanded by the three sons of Seljuk, had obtained permission from Mahmúd to occupy the vacant pastures of Khorassan. Masúd, jealous of the strangers, wished to drive them back, but Togrul Beg, the grandson of Seljuk, collected the scattered tribes of Turks, defeated the sultan, and wrested from him all his northern provinces. The Seljukians established their empire over all the country between the Euphrates and the Jaxartes, while the Ghaznevids, expelled from their ancestral possessions, removed to their Indian possessions and made Lahore their capital. When once an eastern dynasty begins to decline, nothing can arrest the progress of decay; in a few years the power of the Ghaznevids had become little better than a name; many of the Hindú princes asserted their independence, resumed the practice of their idolatrous rites, and retook several of their ancient fortresses. The Mohammedans, indignant at this proof of their sinking supremacy, became anxious to obtain a new and more prosperous race of sovereigns.

The family of Ghor originally possessed the mountainous district of Ghori, south-eastward of Khorassan ; it had been connected with the royal family of Ghazni by several intermarriages ; but these ties, as is frequently the case in Asia, produced hostility rather than amity ; murders from envy and jealousy laid the foundation of bitter feuds. A series of desultory wars ensued, which ended in placing the Ghorians in possession of the ancestral territories of their rivals. Mohammed Ghori having been appointed by his brother, viceroy of Ghazni, resolved to extend his power over Northern India, he invaded the Punjáb at the head of an Afghán army, which then, as now, was superior in valour to any military body in Asia, laid siege to Lahore, captured the city by treachery, (A. D. 1187) and the last of the Ghuznevid dynasty, Khosran II. terminated his life in prison.

Mohammed Ghori was emulous of the fame of the first great sultan of Ghazni ; he resolved to extend his empire over Hindustan, but he found a formidable opponent in Prithvi Raya, the prince of Ajmir. In the first engagement between the rival sovereigns, the Ghorian monarch was defeated with great loss, and was so depressed by the unexpected result that he remained inactive for several years. At length a pretended saint predicted to him success over the enemies of Islam, and he again marched an army into the territories of Ajmir. Prithvi Raya, lulled into fatal security by his former victory, was surprised in his camp, but he made a desperate though vain resistance. He was at length overcome and taken prisoner. Ajmir, deprived of its monarch, surrendered immediately, and Mohammed, having appointed one of his slaves viceroy of his new dominions, returned to Ghuzni, in order to raise new hordes of Afghans and recruit his army for further conquests. Kuttub, to whom the government had been delegated, was raised from the condition of a slave to that of a general by Mohammed, who was a shrewd judge of merit ; he improved with diligence and ability the advantages which his master had gained ; he reduced the surrounding districts, and after having taken the fort of Merat, laid siege to Delhi. The garrison ventured to meet him in the field ; he defeated them so severely that the citizens refused to continue their defence, and the city was surrendered.

Jaya Chandra, rajah or prince of Kanauj, had remained a tame spectator of Prithri Raya's downfall: but the wanton cruelty of the Mohammedan conquerors inflamed his courage, and he led an army against the Ghorian viceroy, (A. D. 1194.) Information of this movement, which threatened formidable consequences, was sent to Mohammed, at Ghazni; he immediately assembled his Afghans, crossed the Indus, and effected a junction with the troops of Kuttub. After some preliminary skirmishes, a decisive battle was fought on the banks of the Jumna, in which the Hindus were totally defeated, and Jaya Chandra slain. The results of this victory, were the capture of the holy city of Benares, and the subjugation of Hindustan, even to the confines of China. These conquests consolidated the power of the Mohammedans in India, and laid the foundation of the empire of Delhi.

The conquerors next assailed the barbarous Gakkars and reduced them to obedience, but on their return Mohammed Ghori was murdered by two of these mountaineers, who eluded the vigilance of his guards and during the night penetrated to his tent, (A. D. 1206.) As he left no children, the succession to the empire was disputed by his nephews; Kuttub finally prevailed over the other competitors, but resigned himself to sloth and indolence. His son, Aram, exhibited still more deplorable weakness; in less than a year he was deposed by Altmish, originally a slave, whom Kuttub had elevated to the highest dignities, having bestowed upon him the hand of his daughter and declared him his adopted son. The usurper's reign was prosperous, but after his death, his son Feroze dissipated the public treasures and brought the monarchy into such contempt that he was dethroned by his own sister, Ruzia Begum. The queen's feebleness invited rebellion; after a reign of six months she was slain in battle, and the empire remained in confusion until Nassir-ed-dín Mahmúd, the youngest son of Altmish, obtained the crown, (A. D. 1247.)

Mahmúd II. had been consigned to a prison after his father's death, and had been compelled to support himself by his skill in caligraphy; but he never complained of the fatigue of copying books, declaring that "he who would not work for his bread did not deserve it." He was subsequently released, and appointed to the government of a province, where his prudent administration obtained such fame that the Omrahs resolved to entrust him with the fortunes of the empire. In his reign the terrible Mongols, who under the command of Jenghiz Khan and his successors, had carried conquest and devastation from the seas of China to the shores of the Mediterranean, crossed the Indus, but retreated on the approach of Mahmúd. After the death of this excellent monarch, who left no children, the vizier Pulbun or Balin, who like several of his predecessors, had been originally a slave, ascended the throne. His reign was long and prosperous—it may also be termed glorious; for not less than fifteen Mohammedan sovereigns, driven from their thrones by the Mongolian successors of Jenghiz Khan, sought refuge in the court of Delhí, and were supported in a manner worthy of their rank by its generous sovereign. The Mongols made a second attempt to penetrate Hindustan, and the king's favourite son, Mohammed, a prince of great promise, was sent against them, while the monarch proceeded to suppress a dangerous insurrection in Bengal. Mohammed encountered the invaders in the province of Multan, and gained a decisive victory; but following the pursuit with too great eagerness, he fell into an ambuscade and was slain. Decisive as his own triumphs were, they could not console the aged monarch, who had reached his eightieth year, for the loss of his heroic son; he sunk under the calamity, and was succeeded by his grandson, Kai Kobad, (A.D. 1286).

A troubled scene of revolutions, destitute of interest or importance, ended in the elevation of Allah-ed-dín Khilji to the throne. Soon after his accession, the Mongols a third time invaded Hindustan with a countless army; they were met and defeated by Zaffer Khan, a general equally remarkable for his personal courage and skill as a commander. The last great battle was fought almost within sight of Delhí, and the gallant Zaffer Khan fell in the arms of victory. Allah-ed-dín was not sorry for the loss of a general whose ambition he suspected, but the empire at large was filled with sorrow at being deprived of its great hero. "The bravery of Zaffer Khan," says Ferishta, "became so proverbial among the Moguls, that when their horses started, they would ask them if they saw the ghost of Zaffer Khan?" Intoxicated by his victories over the Moguls, Allah-ed-dín began to form the most extravagant projects; he resolved to found a new religion, after the example of Mohammed, and, like Alexander the Great, to intrust his dominions to a viceroy, and undertake the conquest of the world. The very ignorance that led to the formation of designs so insane, prevented the monarch from proceeding any length towards their execution; his first efforts were productive of so many dangers and difficulties that he at once abandoned his ambitious enterprises, but at the same time consulted a holy man as to the means by which he might best transmit his name to posterity. The monarch was fortunate in his choice of an adviser; he was recommended to secure his empire in Hindustan, by subduing the south-eastern provinces of the Peninsula, and to prevent the future incursions of the Moguls, by fortifying Kabul and Kandahar. He engaged with great ardour in the former of these enterprizes, and subdued several Rájáhs, but the remembrance of his follies still rankled in the minds of his nobles, and several conspiracies were formed, from which he escaped with great difficulty. These dangers impressed upon his mind the disadvantages of ignorance; though past the middle age of life he began the study of letters, and, as we are assured by the historians, in a short space of time became eminent for his proficiency. Mallek Kafûr, a general of great reputation, in the mean time carried the Mohammedans' arms into the Dékkan, and gained so many victories, that on his return to Delhí the king himself met him at the gate, and acknowledged that he was his debtor for a new kingdom. An atrocious act of cruelty soon afterwards sullied this generally good reign; the Moguls who had been made prisoners, or who had deserted during the invasions of their countrymen, having become Mohammedans, were enlisted in the royal army; the king from some unknown cause grew jealous of these converts, and disbanded them without pay. In their distress a rebellion was projected; the plot was discovered, and orders issued for the extermination of the Moguls, were obeyed as ruthlessly as they were given. Fifteen thousand of these unhappy men, were seen lying dead on one day in the streets of Delhí, and all their wives and children were enslaved. Allah-ed-dín was poisoned by his favourite general, Mallek Kafûr, (A.D. 1316), who procured the elevation of the king's youngest son, Omar Khilji, to the throne.

The nobles of Delhí, dissatisfied with this arrangement, murdered Mallek, dethroned Omar, and chose his brother Múbarik for their sovereign. Múbarik was a weak debauchee; he placed his entire confidence in a Hindú of the lowest origin, Mallek Khosrau, and thereby disgusted the ancient friends of his family. Mallek treacherously resolved to murder his benefactor; information of his designs was given to the king, but he refused to hear a syllable breathed against his favourite. He became the victim of his infatuation, and all his relatives were involved in his fate. The governors of the provinces on the news of the king's death, took up arms against the usurping Hindú, and having conquered him, put him to a cruel death. (A. D. 1321.) They then raised the most eminent of their own number, Gheias-ed-din Toghluk, to the throne, and their choice was enthusiastically ratified by the people.

Toghluk, like so many of his predecessors, had been originally a slave; he displayed no wish to obtain the crown, for when he entered Delhí after his victory, he proclaimed, "O ye subjects of this great empire! I am no more than one of you who unsheathed my sword to deliver you from oppression, and rid the world of a monster. If, therefore, any of the royal line remain, let him be brought, that we, his servants, may prostrate ourselves before his throne. If not, let the most worthy of the illustrious order be elected among you, and I will swear to abide by your choice." But the people vehemently cried out that none of the royal family remained alive, and that he who had protected the empire from the Mongols, and delivered it from the tyrant, was alone worthy to become its sovereign.

Toghluk's earliest care was to secure his dominions against the formidable Mongols; he erected a chain of forts along the frontiers of Kabul, so judiciously placed, and so well garrisoned, that these invaders were deterred from making any effort to renew their incursions during his reign. He pursued the conquests which his predecessors had begun to make in the Dekkan, or peninsula of Southern India, and he reduced to obedience several Omrahs, who had taken advantage of the former period of confusion to assert their independence. Returning from a victorious campaign, he was crushed to death in a temporary building, in which he had been entertained by his son (A.D. 1323): the fall of the roof, at the moment when the king was left with only a few attendants, has been, by many writers, ascribed to the contrivance of the young prince, who was immediately proclaimed his successor.

Mohammed Toghluk ascended the throne, conscious that he was suspected of parricide; and, to avert the dangerous consequences, he rendered himself popular by excessive liberality. He was the most eloquent and accomplished prince of his time: even at this day, his letters in Arabic and Persian are regarded as the most perfect models of diplomatic correspondence. But literature did not change the native ferocity of his disposition; few princes have rendered themselves more infamous by avarice and cruelty; his eminent abilities only rendered him a greater scourge to his subjects. In the early part of his reign, he subdued several of the southern provinces, especially the greater part of the Carnatic, but the acquisitions of valour were lost by misgovernment. To inordinate taxation, he added the evils of a depreciated currency. Ferishta's account of the result of this expedient is too remarkable to be omitted, for it shews that an oriental writer, two centuries ago, had sounder views in the science of political economy, than many Europeans of our own day.

" The king, unfortunately for his people, adopted his ideas of currency from a Chinese custom, of using paper on the emperor's credit, with the royal seal appended, in lieu of ready money. Mohammed Toghluk, instead of stamped paper, struck a copper coin, which he issued at an imaginary value, and caused it to pass current by a decree throughout Hindustan. The mint was under bad regulations. Bankers acquired large fortunes by coinage. Foreign merchants made their payments in copper to the home manufacturer, though they themselves received for the article they sold silver and gold in foreign markets. There was so much corruption practised in the mint, that for a premium to those persons who had the management of it, merchants had their coin struck considerably below the legal value; and these abuses were connived at by the government. The great calamity, however, consequent upon this debasement of the coin, arose from the known instability of the government. Public credit could not long subsist, in a state so liable to revolutions as Hindustan; for how could the people in the remote provinces receive for money, the base representative of a treasury that so often changed its master? From these evils, the discontent became universal, and the king was at length obliged to call in the copper currency. So great abuses had occurred in the mint, however, that after the treasury was emptied, there still remained a heavy demand. This debt the king struck off, and thousands were ruined. The state, so far from gaining by this crude scheme, had exhausted its treasury; and the bankers and some merchants alone accumulated fortunes, at the expense of their sovereign and the people."

Having heard of the great wealth of China, Mohammed Toghluk resolved to subdue that empire, and assembled a numerous army in the mountainous regions of Nepál. Having made arrangements for securing his communications, the Mohammedan general entered the Chinese frontiers with diminished numbers, and soldiers dispirited by the fatigues and perils of their march. A superior force was ready to meet the invaders, and the Indian army commenced a retreat. But the rainy season surprised them in the mountains; the Nepálese, issuing from their fastnesses, harassed their flanks, the Chinese hung on their rear, and, out of their formidable forces, only a few miserable fugitives escaped to bring intelligence of their ruin.

The next project of the king produced consequences scarcely less calamitous; he resolved to make Dowlatabad the capital of his dominions, and ordered the citizens of Delhí to remove thither, "leaving that noble metropolis a resort for owls, and a dwelling-place for the beasts of the field."

At this time (A.D. 1340) the taxes were so heavy, that the cultivators of the soil, unable to endure the exactions of the revenue officers, abandoned the entire fertile tract between the Jumna and the Ganges, set fire to their houses, and sought refuge in the jungles with their families and cattle. The vanity of the monarch was equal to his cruelty: having lost one of his teeth, he ordered it to be interred with great solemnity at Bír, and erected over it a magnificent tomb, which still exists as a monument of his folly. At length, these excesses drove even the patient Hindús to revolt, and several of the native Rájás recovered their independence. While engaged in subduing one of these insurrections, Mohammed died of a surfeit from fish, in the twenty-eighth year of his cruel reign.

A body of Mongols, in Mohammed's service, had been sent to keep in control the turbulent people of Gujarât; but these barbarians soon set the power of Mohammed at defiance: they withdrew into the Dekkan, seized the strong fortress of Dowlatabad, and proclaimed their independence. The death of the Sultan was propitious to their efforts; it afforded them time for laying the foundation of a new Mohammedan empire, which rose to considerable power, and preserved its existence for several centuries. Its sovereigns are known in history as the Rahmenee dynasty, and they included under their dominion all the provinces which had ever acknowledged the sway of the emperors of Delhí. The governor of Bengal took advantage of the general confusion, to erect his province into an independent state, and several nobles of minor importance shewed themselves ready to take part in the dismemberment of the empire. Amid these commotions, the Omrahs assembled, and resolved to confer the crown on Firoz Toghluk, the cousin of the deceased monarch. His claim was disputed for a time by the citizens of Delhi, who placed a son of Mohammed on the throne. But this competitor was only six years of age, and there was some doubt of his legitimacy. The nobles on both sides, having agreed to discuss what was best to be done in an amicable interview, the boy's claims were set aside, and Feroz was universally acknowledged. But, during these disputes, the revolted provinces had concentrated their strength and consolidated their power, so that the new emperor was compelled to recognize the usurpers of the Dekkan and Bengal as independent sovereigns, and to receive ambassadors from both. Notwithstanding their submission, Feroz seems to have dreaded the hostility of the citizens of Delhí, for he refused to reside within the wall, and erected the new city of Firozabad in the neighbourhood, as the metropolis of his dominions. He was, indeed, so passionately fond of architecture, that he is said to have constructed fifty great aqueducts, or reservoirs of water; forty mosques; thirty schools; twenty caravanserais; a hundred palaces; five hospitals; one hundred tombs; ten baths; ten spires; one hundred and fifty wells; one hundred bridges, and pleasure-gardens without number.

After he had passed his eightieth year, Firoz, finding that the cares of the government pressed too heavily on his advanced age, resigned the crown to his son, Mohammed Toghluk II., who was devoted to pleasure, and slenderly provided with abilities. He gave himself up to debauchery, was deposed in a popular tumult, and the old king was forced to resume the reins of power. On his death, he bequeathed the crown to his grandson, who was, in a few months, assassinated by his cousin, Abu Bekr, and he, in his turn, fell a victim to Mohammed Toghluk III., a younger brother of Firoz (A.D 1387). The six years of Mohammed's reign were spent in quelling the revolts of his principal Omrahs, who aimed at independence, like the sovereigns of the Dekkan and Bengal; their insurrections scarcely allowed him any interval of repose, and the anxiety they occasioned hastened his death. His son, Húmayún, who succeeded, followed his father to the grave in less than two months, and a minor, Mahmúd Toghluk, succeeded to a distracted empire and an exhausted treasury. The government fell into anarchy; civil war raged every where; three claimants for supremacy over the emperor, contended with each other in the streets of Delhí for as many years. Mahmúd became the puppet of whichever obtained a temporary triumph, and the uncertainty of the state was increased by the neutral chiefs, who dreaded the establishment of the power of any of the competitors, and therefore when any one of them was too much depressed, lent him their aid to restore the balance. In the midst of this confusion news arrived of the approach of a formidable enemy, Pír Mohammed Jehanghír, the grandson of the terrible Timúr Lenk, who was sent by that terrible conqueror to subdue Hindustan.

Timúr was a Jagatay Turk, but in consequence of his claim, real or pretended, to descent from Jenghiz Khan, he is commonly called a Mongol, as if all traces of his Mongolian descent would not have disappeared in successive generations. Strongly attached to the Shía creed, he believed that he was employed by Heaven to extirpate heresy as well as idolatry, and to revenge on the Sonnites the murder of Ali. This belief consoled him for the ferocious massacres he had perpetrated, and was craftily encouraged by those who were anxious to conciliate his friendship. In that extraordinary specimen of autobiography, his memoirs, recently published, he shows us how strongly he was influenced by this persuasion. "In the year of the Hejra 771,

(A.D. 1378) when I had driven the Jetes (Uzbek Tartars) out of Tùran (Transoxiana) and mounted the throne, and had directed the royal declaration to be read from all the pulpits, the Syeds, (descendants from the family of Mohammed,) the learned, the prelates, the rich and the poor, all raised their hands in prayer for my prosperity; but Khuaje Abyd, who was the most celebrated prelate of that time, forbade them to pray for me, saying, 'Do not pray for this murderer and blood-thirsty Turk, who has put to death an innumerable number of Mussulmans, nor repeat blessings on him.' On that very night the Khuajè dreamed that he saw me standing in the presence of his holiness the prophet, that he entered, and several times made his obedience to Mohammed, without his salutation being returned; at length he called out, 'O, messenger of God, do you permit this wretch Timúr, who has murdered hundreds of thousands of your followers, and who has destroyed the habitations of so many Mussulmans, to stand before you, whilst you do not return the salutation of me, who am the zealous supporter of your religion, and the establisher of your law?' His holiness replied to him in an angry manner, 'Although Timúr has shed much of the blood of my followers, as he has been the friend, the supporter, and the respecter of my posterity, why dost thou forbid the people to pray for and bless him?' The Khuajè having awoke, came even during the night to me and asked pardon: when this intelligence reached the people, all of them raised their hands in prayer for my prosperity, and, considering me as supported by the divine favour, bore witness to my right. In gratitude for this favour, I day by day showed more attention, respect, and affection to the descendants of Mohammed, and *esteemed myself as the elect of God.*"

Religion afforded Timúr a pretext for invading and conquering the kingdom of Persia. The history of that country from the age of Jenghiz Khan to that of Timúr, is an unvarying repetition of cruelties, usurpations, treasons, and assassinations; the provinces sometimes independent, and sometimes professing a nominal allegiance, were devastated by a ferocious soldiery, and the mosques were either deserted or possessed by ignorant priests, whose doctrines were frequently inconsistent with the creed of Islám. Timúr's conquest of the country was consequently favoured by a large party of the priests, who regarded him as the extirpator of heresy; and it was on the petition of the Imáms and doctors of the law, that he issued his celebrated decree at Shiráz, for the massacre of all the princes of the house of Mûzaffer, as obstinate disturbers of religion and the state.

One great reason which rendered Timúr ambitious of subduing Hindustan, was the great fame which the Sonnite hero, Mahmúd of Ghazí, had obtained by establishing the creed of Islam amongst the idolators beyond the Indus. He, too, aspired to be celebrated as a Gazi, or heroic promulgator of the faith; and hoped, that like Mahmud, he would bequeath a name to be celebrated by history, poetry, and legend. He found, however, great difficulties in persuading his nobles to undertake such an achievement; they were daunted by the severe defeats which the Mongols had suffered on former occasions, and by the fear of the perils and hardships which they would necessarily endure in forcing the mountain passes around Kabul. Timúr's own resolution was shaken, but his courage was restored by a dream, which he thus records in his singular autobiography:—"When I was about to invade Hindustan, and my chiefs by their backwardness rendered me doubtful whether I should proceed, I dreamt that I was in a large garden, and saw a number of people who were pruning the trees, and sowing seeds; that the garden was full of trees, both great and small, on the tops of which the birds had built their nests; I thought that I had a sling in my hand, and that I destroyed the nests with stones from the sling, and drove away all the birds; this dream was realized when I took that country, by expelling all the sultans, and taking possession of the kingdom."

Mirza Pír Mohammed Jehan Ghír was sent to prepare the way for the conquest of Hindustan; he crossed the Indus, defeated the troops sent to oppose him, and took Multan by storm. The solstitial rains, however, compelled him to draw his army within the city, upon which the people of the country blockaded him closely and intercepted his supplies. In the mean time, Timúr, at the head of an immense army, was advancing over the stupendous range of mountains which separates India from the regions of the north. The passage of the Hindu Kúsh, was not effected without great loss and difficulty; the soldiers had to make their way through deep snow, which effaced every trace of a road, and at the same time to defend themselves against the savage mountaineers, who harassed them by continual skirmishes. The invaders, at length, forced their way to Kabul and thence to Attock, the celebrated passage of the Indus. Prince Múbarek, who had revolted, after submitting to Mohammed Jehan Ghír in the preceding year, made a brave attempt to stop the progress of invasion, but he was badly supported by his troops, and with difficulty escaped being made prisoner. Having sent relief to his grandson, Timúr, pursued his march towards Delhí, marking his track by massacre and desolation. Sultan Mahmúd was roused to defend his kingdom; he had a numerous and well-appointed army, attended by a formidable train of war-elephants and a rocket brigade, whose missiles were greatly dreaded. The battle was hot and terrible; but at length, the enervated troops of Delhí, were borne down by the physical superiority of the iron men of the north; the elephants were driven back on their own ranks, and many of them deprived of their guides, rushed wildly over the field, trampling friends and foes alike; a small body of Afghans alone remained firm, and enabled the sultan to effect his retreat, abandoning the remains of his followers to merciless conquerors, who refused to give any quarter. Mahmúd and his ministers fled from the city, which was surrendered to Timúr without further resistance, on the condition of being saved from destruction by the payment of a large ransom. In levying the heavy contribution, some disputes arose between the citizens and the conquerors, which led to blows. The fierce soldiers of Timúr, without waiting for any orders, immediately commenced an indiscriminate massacre and pillage, which continued for three days, until the barbarians were forced to show mercy, because from sheer exhaustion, they were no longer able to continue the work of cruelty. Having sent his plunder back to Samarkand, Timúr led his forces as far as the Ganges, repeating the work of destruction with unvarying ferocity. At length, the intelligence of disorders and rebellions in Western Persia, imperatively recalled Timúr from his sanguinary career; he quitted Hindustan, A.D. 1400, after having converted its fairest provinces into a desert.

Zafir Khan, surnamed Azim Húmayún, had been appointed Governor of Gujarát by Mohammed Toghluk II. (A.D. 1391,

A.H. 794), and had ruled the province with almost regal authority. His son, Mohammed Khan, having been forced to fly from Delhí, where he held the office of Vizier, rebelled against both the Sultan and his father, and proclaimed himself King of Gujarát, just at the time that Timúr invaded India. Mohammed Toghluk, when he fled from Delhí, sought refuge in Gujarát, but not meeting with a very courteous reception, he went to Malwa. Mohammed Khan died soon afterwards, and was buried as a Saint in the city of Patan. Zafir Khan continued his allegiance to the nominal Emperors of Dehli until the family of Firoz became utterly powerless, when he suffered himself to be proclaimed King of Gujarát (A.D. 1407), and took the name of Musaffir Shah. The founder of the Patan dynasty, as the kings of Gujarát are sometimes called, from their capital city, was a wise and virtuous prince. "He continued," says the author of the *Mirat Amadi*, "to dispense justice, to punish the wicked, and to protect the poor, until he was poisoned by his grandson, Ahmed Shah." (A.D. 1410).

After the departure of Timúr, Mahmúd was nominally restored to the empire, but his authority was spurned by his factious nobles; anarchy everywhere prevailed, and the death of the sultan was hailed as a relief by his suffering subjects. With him ended the third dynasty of the Afghan kings of Delhí.

An Afghan noble attempted to usurp the throne, but he was unable to maintain himself against the superior power and popularity of Khizer Khan, a Syed (or descendant of the prophet) who became the founder of a new dynasty. Khizer refused the title of sovereign, pretending that he held the government as viceroy for the house of Timúr, in whose name he ordered all the coins to be struck and all edicts issued. By this expedient, he obviated the jealousies of the Omrahs, whose claims to the crown were superior to his own, and he terrified insurgents by the dread of chastisement from a powerful ruler who had given them such dreadful proof of his merciless disposition. Khizer's administration relieved the empire from many calamities, and the people again began to enjoy the blessings of peace and protection.

After a reign of seven years, Khizer died, and was succeeded by his son Syed Múbarek, who displayed considerable talents for government, and a more than ordinary attention to justice and humanity. But his reign, which lasted thirteen years, was one continued series of wars with the petty principalities which had been formed from fragments of the Delhí empire, and with his own factious nobles. While he was thus engaged, the kingdom of Gujarát was daily increasing in importance, under the wise administration of its second sultan, Ahmed Shah, who extended his conquests to the Dekkan. Múbarek was murdered (A.D. 1435), by a band of assassins, employed by his vizier, who placed the sultan's grandson, Syed Mohammed, on the throne, expecting to reign in his name. But the Omrahs were disgusted with the pretensions of the aspiring ministers; they had recourse to arms; and the king, probably without much reluctance, found it necessary to conciliate them by procuring the assassination of the insolent vizier. This concession, universally attributed to weakness, exposed the monarch to fresh demands, the refusal of which was followed by rebellion. Múbarek's power was reduced to a shadow, and a revolution was only averted by his death. (A.D. 1445.) Four years previous to this, the glorious reign of Ahmed in Gujarát had closed; but his son and successor, Mohammed, though of far inferior abilities, maintained the greatness of the kingdom. Syed Mohammed was succeeded at Delhí by his son Syed Allah-ed-din, who inherited the weakness as well as the throne of his father. After an inglorious reign of seven years, he was compelled to abdicate, (A.D. 1450,) and so little was he feared, that he was permitted to live unmolested in his retirement fourteen years, —a circumstance which can hardly be paralleled in Oriental History.

Beiloli Lodi, an Afghan by birth, became the founder of the fifth dynasty, established by his countrymen in Delhí. His mother was smothered while under the ruins of a falling house, but her husband opening the body, saved the life of an infant destined to be the future emperor of Hindustan. In his early youth a dervish is said to have predicted his future greatness; and this prophecy, by awakening his ambition, may well be believed to have had some influence in working out its own accomplishment. The turbulent Omrahs refused at first to submit to one who had been long their equal, but by uniting firmness with prudent concession, he succeeded in establishing his authority over all the petty principalities round the metropolis.

During his entire reign, he was engaged in a tedious and indecisive war with the Kings of Junpur, whose obstinacy he had bound himself to subdue. Old age had arrived before his darling object was completed, and, feeling his infirmities, he divided his dominions among his children. Soon after the conquest of Junpur, Beiloli died (A.D. 1488), having reigned thirty-eight years. In the mean time, Gujarát was enjoying perfect tranquillity, under the wise administration of Sultan Mahmúd Nizarrah.

On the death of Beiloli, the Omrahs assembled as usual to deliberate on the choice of a successor. While they were debating Sultana Zema, a goldsmith's daughter, raised to the late king's bed on account of her eminent charms and witty conversation, addressed the assembly from behind a curtain, in favour of her son, Sekander Lodi, and thus united all the suffrages for his election. The brothers of the new emperor, dissatisfied by the choice of the Omrahs, refused to recognize Sekander's claims, and thus the early part of his reign was spent in a series of ruinous fraternal wars. One of the most remarkable events in his history, was a public discussion of the doctrine of toleration, the advocates of which, as might be expected, were pronounced guilty of heresy, and punished with death. Sekander's bigotry has rendered him a favourite with Mohammedan authors; not content with extolling him as a saint, they praise him as a hero—though, during his entire reign, he never performed any exploit worthy of being recorded.

The tranquillity which the prudent administration of Mahmúd Bigarrah had established in Gujarát, was disturbed by an event, which, in a future chapter, will engage our attention—the rapid progress of the Portuguese in Southern India. The Sultan of Gujarát joined in the Mohammedan league, formed for the destruction of these Christian intruders (A.D. 1503); but he soon directed his attention exclusively to his domestic affairs, believing that the growing power of the Ottomans would, ere long, compel the Europeans to abandon the Indian seas. Bigarrah was succeeded by his son, Mozaffer II. surnamed, and deservedly, the Merciful.

Syed Ibrahim Lodi succeeded his father in Delhí. A conspiracy was formed to raise his younger brother to the throne, but it was fortunately detected almost at the very moment at which it was about to explode. Sultan Ibrahim punished not only the guilty, but the suspected, with such remorseless cruelty, that he drove most of his nobles into rebellion. Finding himself an object of suspicion to his sovereign, the governor of Lahore invited Baber, the sultan of Ferghana, and the descendant of the illustrious Timúr, to his assistance, by whom Ibrahim was defeated and slain. With him ended the last of the Afghan empires in India. The sovereignty was entrusted to a new race of monarchs, called, by inveterate error, the Great Moguls: but before entering on the history of this revolution, we must briefly direct our attention to the countries west and north of the Indus, and trace the fortunes of the posterity of Timúr.

CHAPTER III.

THE EMPIRE OF DELHI.

WITHIN a very short period after his return from India, Timúr had settled the affairs of Persia; subdued Syria, Asia Minor, and Egypt; defeated the Turkish emperor, Ilderim Payezid on the plains of Galatia, and prepared a vast expedition against China, which he was conducting over the mountains of Tartary, when he was overtaken by the stroke of death (A. D. 1405). He met his fate with the same steady resolution, which had borne him onward through his prosperous career: perceiving his end approach, he convoked his nobles, exhorted them above all things to preserve the unity of his empire, and to secure the supremacy for his favourite grandchild, Pír Mohammed Jehan Ghír. Before the conqueror's body was laid in the grave, active intrigues were commenced for frustrating both his requests. His grandson Khalil, at the instigation of the principal officers of the army, usurped the government, and tried to secure his throne by a lavish distribution of the treasure which Timúr had accumulated; but this great expenditure produced no effect, save the impoverishment of his exchequer. Each chieftain who received his bounty, deemed that he had been underpaid when he learned the amount that had been bestowed on some other leader, whose consequence he underrated as much as he overvalued his own. Khalil succeeded in defeating his cousin, Pír Mohammed, and some other rivals; but he was finally betrayed to Khodadad, the secret enemy of Timúr's family, and, though he retained the name of royalty, he became a passive instrument in the hands of the Shah Rokh, the youngest son of Timúr, who enraged at this insult offered to his family, marched from Khorasan, which was the seat of his government, captured Samarkand, and reduced all the rest of Mawer-al-naher under his obedience. Khodadad was slain by the Moguls, from whom he sought aid. Khalil submitted to his uncle, and was for a brief space treated with great kindness, but finally ended his life by poison

(A.D. 1415, A.H. 817.) Shah Rokh restored the empire founded by his father, nearly to its greatest extent, and ruled his vast dominions with equal firmness and clemency; but his death (A.D. 1446, A.H. 850) was followed by a renewal of the wars that had ensued on the decease of Timúr.

Ulugh Beg succeeded his father, Shah Rokh, in Samarkand: he was a prince of amiable dispositions, fondly attached to scientific pursuits, who has secured an honourable fame by the valuable astronomical tables constructed under his directions, at an observatory which he caused to be erected in Samarkand for the purpose. All his relations, brothers, cousins, and nephews, raised insurrections against this estimable prince; but there were two, more marked in their hostility, from whom far different conduct might have been expected, his own son Abd-al-latif, and Abu-saïd Mirza, whom he had protected in infancy and youth, and had raised to rank and station. Ulugh was defeated and slain by his rebellious son (A.D. 1449, A.H. 853); but the parricide did not long enjoy the fruits of his crime; he was murdered in a mutiny, and his cousin Abdallah was chosen emperor. Abdallah, in a few months, was dethroned by Abu-saïd.

Almost every province of the empire had now been formed into a kingdom by one or other of the descendants of Timúr: Abu-saïd was no sooner established on the throne of Samarkand, than he prepared to extend his dominion over the different principalities formed out of the ancient kingdom of Persia. After a series of desultory wars, and many vicissitudes of fortune, he conquered the greater part of Timúr's ancient empire, and placed his sons over the new provinces. His last expedition was into Persian Irak (A.D. 1467, A.H. 871), where he was defeated, taken prisoner by his enemies, and beheaded.

The dominions of Abu-saïd were divided between his sons after his death. They engaged in mutual wars, barren of any interest, though productive of much misery. Omar Sheikh Mirza received the least of the provinces for his share—the province of Ferghana, on the upper Jaxartes, a river called by the orientals the Sin or Sihun. He was a restless, profuse, good-natured prince, and, on his death (A.D. 1494, A.H. 900), he left his dominions in considerable confusion to his eldest son, Zehir-ed-dín Mohammed, surnamed Baber, or the Tiger.

The state of Central Asia, when the illustrious Baber commenced his reign, must be briefly described. His uncle, Sultan Ahmed Mirza, was king of Bokhara and Samarkand; a second uncle, Mahmúd Mirza, possessed Kunduz and Badakshan; a third, Ulugh Beg Mirza, held Kabúl and Ghazni; Hussein Mirza, a descendant of Timúr, and the most powerful prince of his age, ruled over Khorasan; Mahmúd Khan, a Mogul, and Baber's maternal uncle, possessed Tashkend and Shahrokhia, on the lower Jaxartes, and the chief power over the Moguls of the Desert; finally, Sheibání Khan was collecting in the Desert a horde, compounded of different races, destined in a future day to found a new monarchy. This was two years before the discovery of America by Columbus, and the passage round the Cape of Good Hope by De Gama; the year in which Charles VIII. of France undertook his celebrated expedition against Naples.

No sooner had Baber mounted the throne than his dominions were attacked on every side by his paternal and maternal uncles; he repulsed the several invaders. Two of them, Ahmed and Mahmúd Mirza, died soon afterwards, and their kingdoms were united under Khosrau Sháh, a son of the latter. Khosrau was a weak imprudent prince, but his accidental triumph over the Sultan of Khorasan gave him a temporary importance, of which he knew not how to avail himself. To describe the wars between the petty princes of Transoxiana would be tedious and uninteresting; we shall therefore, for the most part, confine our attention to the progress of Baber, who (A.D. 1497, A.H. 903) made his first great step towards empire by the conquest of Samarkand. Scarcely, however, had he made the acquisition, when he was deprived of it by the desertion of one part of his followers and the revolt of others. Disheartened and weakened by sickness, he sought refuge in Khojend, where he prepared for fresh exertions, and after two years recovered his paternal dominions.

In the mean time Sheibání Khan, at the head of the Uzbeks, as his tumultuary hordes were called, had made himself master of Samarkand and Bokhara. Baber, by a sudden march, surprised the former city, (A.D. 1500, A.H. 906,) and being joined by many of the Begs who had before deserted him, ventured to meet the Uzbeks in the field. He was defeated, and once more driven from the city, apparently a hopeless fugitive.

Baber's sufferings and escapes—his total loss of his hereditary kingdom, and his adventures as the leader of a plundering horde rather than a regular army, have all the interest of romance; but they want the importance of history. After having finally lost his inheritance, Ferghana, which became the prey of the Uzbeks under Sheibání Khan, he seems to have resolved to seek a new kingdom in the south, and entered his cousin Khosrau's dominions in Khorasan. Over this part of Baber's history there rests no little obscurity, our principal authority being his own memoirs; but even from these it appears that having been received by Khosrau as a friend and relation, Baber entered into secret intrigues for depriving his cousin of sovereign power. From Kundúz, Baber marched with the army, which he had enticed from the service of Khosran—against Kabul, which was distracted by civil commotions. He became master of the provinces of Kabul and Ghazni, (A.D. 1504, A.H. 910,) but their superior wealth and power did not console him for the loss of his paternal Ferghana, to which he frequently cast "a longing, lingering look," as the country of his early affections. He shared his new acquisitions among his followers; but finding the plunder exhausted before his troops were satisfied, he resolved on some new exploit, and after long deliberations it was determined to invade Hindustan. This foray, for it does not deserve to be called a campaign, being finished, he returned to tranquillize and consolidate his new kingdom. This proved a very difficult task, principally on account of the complicated claims and pretensions made to sovereignty by the numerous descendants of Timúr; but Baber's power being established by his conquest of Kandahar, he once more turned his attention towards Hindustan. But a new vicissitude awaited him; the army of Kabul revolted, as that of Samarkand had done before, and Baber was for more than two years a partisan chief before he could regain his kingdom.

Scarcely was Baber restored to the throne of Kabul when he heard of the death of his great enemy, Sheibání Khan, and that consequently an opportunity was offered of re-conquering his beloved Ferghana. His enterprise was at first successful; he for the third time became master of Samarkand, but the Uzbeks soon recovered from their dismay, and, being favoured by the natives, compelled Baber to relinquish the country of his ancestors for ever.

The project of invading Hindustan was resumed by the active monarch when he lost all hope of recovering Ma-wer-al-nahár; he crossed the Indus (A.D. 1519, A.H. 925) no longer as a predatory adventurer, but, as he gravely informs us, as a monarch coming to take possession of his right. "The countries among which I now was," he says, "had long been in the possession of the Turks; I regarded them as my own domains, and was resolved to acquire the possession of them either by war or peace."* After some partial successes he returned to Kabul; and though he never resigned his plan, three years had elapsed before he could find a favourable opportunity of renewing his operations. Baber's fourth invasion of India was undertaken, as has been already mentioned, at the instigation of the nobles who were discontented with Ibrahim, the Afghan sultan of Delhí. On this occasion he subdued the whole of the Punjáb, took Lahore by storm, and, enraged at the obstinacy of the resistance which he encountered, burned the city to the ground.

The fifth and final invasion of Hindustan (A D. 1525, A.H. 932) was professedly designed to support Allah-ed-dín's claims to the throne of Delhí; but that prince having intrigued against his ally, Baber no longer deigned to use the pretext of his name, and in his memoirs he never once alludes to Allah-ed-din's pretensions. Ibrahim levied an immense army to protect his crown, and hasted to meet Baber, whose progress had for some time resembled the procession of a monarch through his own dominions, rather than the campaign of an invader in a foreign country. After a severe conflict, Ibrahim was defeated and slain. This single battle decided the fate of the empire; detachments from Baber's army occupied Agra and Delhí without encountering any resistance. His nobles were now anxious to return home and disband their followers,† regarding their conquest merely as a successful inroad; but Baber assembled them, and eloquently pourtrayed the superior advantages of Hindustan, and the glory that would result from founding a new empire. Four years were spent in subduing the Hindu Rájás and the Mohammedan provincial governors, who had established their indepen-

* Memoirs of Baber, 254.

† One vented his feelings in verses, to the following effect:

> If safe and sound I pass the river Sind,
> Deuce take me, if again I 'll visit Hind.

dence during the recent distractions of the empire. These expeditions, some of which were attended with great danger and difficulty, finally proved successful; the Turkish soldiers, reconciled to the climate of India, no longer spoke of returning home, and Baber assumed the title of Pad-sháh or emperor, and Ghazí.

Thus was founded the Empire of Delhi, absurdly called the empire of the Great Mogul, because a doubtful tradition had described one of Baber's very remote ancestors as a Mongolian prince. The error is now so inveterate that it would be vain to expect its cure; we shall however use the name 'emperors of Delhí' for the successors of Baber, which will prevent any mistake, and avoid the difficulty that might arise from the true designation Jagatays.

The great fatigues he had undergone in the various vicissitudes of his shifting fortunes, broke down the strong constitution of Baber, and having arranged the affairs of the empire with great wisdom, he quietly awaited the stroke of death, having appointed his son, Húmayún, his successor. While the emperor was on his death-bed, a plot was formed to procure the crown for his son-in-law, Mehdi Khwájeh, which was defeated by a very singular incident. Mír Khalífeh, Baber's Vizier, was the chief supporter of Khwájeh; he one day, unperceived, stood behind the prince, with whom he had been previously conversing, and Khwájeh, supposing that the vizier had left the apartment, said to himself aloud, "God willing, I will soon flay off your hide, old boy!" At the same moment, turning round, he saw the Vizier's eye sternly fixed upon him. Khwájeh attempted to turn the matter off with a jest, saying, "Ah! my good fellow, the red tongue often gives the green head to the winds;" but Khalífeh was not so easily satisfied, and immediately after placed Khwájeh under arrest, thus securing his inheritance to Húmayún. Baber died on the 26th December, 1530, (A.H. 935), having ruled over his new empire of Hindustan a little more than five years.

In Gujarát, Mozaffer the Clement, displayed equal valour, prudence, and mercy, in the administration of his kingdom. On his death, he bequeathed the government to his son, Sekander, a youth of inferior abilities, and too exclusively attached to those who had been his favourities and companions while a prince. The rich largesses and presents he bestowed on these minions, grievously offended the nobles; a conspiracy was formed, of which the vizier was chief, and Sekander was murdered, after a brief reign of three months. (A.D. 1526). He left behind him a formidable avenger, his brother, the Sultan Bahadar, who marched against the usurping vizier, routed his adherents with little difficulty, and inflicted on him the just penalty of his treason. The new sultan marched against the Portuguese, who had settled at Diu and obtained some advantages, which, however, were not sufficient to compensate him for the expenses of the war; he was more successful against the Hindu Rájás on the frontiers of his kingdom, several of whom he compelled to become tributary. In the midst of his victorious career, he was summoned to defend his own kingdom against the emperor of Delhí, who was preparing for the subjection of Gujarát.

When Húmayún succeeded his father, Baber, on the throne of Delhí, few monarchs could have had fairer prospects of a peaceful and happy reign. He had distinguished himself before his accession as a warrior and a statesman; his superiority was readily acknowledged by his brothers; and his literary attainments gained the respect of his subjects, who were now beginning to cultivate those sciences, which, for a season, rendered the court of Delhí one of the most brilliant and beneficial that ever existed in Asia. Ambition led him to invade Gujarát, where his success was so great that proposals were made for receiving that kingdom as a tributary state, and allowing Sultan Bahadar to reign as the emperor's deputy. Although Húmayún was aware that a dangerous rebellion was on the point of exploding in his hereditary dominions, he rejected this judicious advice and resolved to annex Gujarát as a province to his empire, and appointed his natural brother, prince Askerry, its governor. Scarcely had the emperor returned to Agra, when Sultan Bahadar, assisted by a body of Portuguese mercenaries, recovered his kingdom and compelled Askerry to save himself by a precipitate flight. The Portuguese, relying on the services they had rendered to the sultan, began to extend and secure their dominions by the erection of forts, which gave just offence to Bahadar. He marched with a small army to check their encroachments, but was either slain in a petty skirmish, or, according to the Mahommedan accounts, was treacherously murdered in a conference to which he had been invited by the Portuguese commanders. (A.D. 1536). He was succeeded by his nephew, Mohammed II. who was taken from a prison to ascend the throne. From this time, Gujarát began rapidly to decline; the princes of the Dekkan withheld the tribute they had previously paid to the sultans, and the Portuguese ceased to pay any compensation for the ports of which they had taken possession.

After his return from Gujarát, Húmayún quelled several petty revolts which had broken out in his dominions; but while thus engaged, he received intelligence of a formidable insurrection of the Afghans, headed by Shír Khan, and at the same time obtained private information that the allegiance of his brothers, Hurdal and Kamran, was more than suspicious. Before marching against the Afghan insurgents, Húmayún sent for all the princes of his family, and impressed upon them the necessity of uniting their interests, declaring that their intestine feuds must lead to the disolution of that mighty empire which had cost their father so much pains to acquire. They readily promised him their support, but he had no sooner departed to commence his campaign, than they commenced their treacherous intrigues with renewed vigour.

The emperor's first operations against the Afghan insurgents were crowned with success. Shír Khan, unable to maintain himself in the open field, sought to make peace, and Húmayún, dreading the machinations of his brothers during his absence, readily offered favourable terms. To render the treaty more binding on the insurgents, like all Afghans, more remarkable for their superstition than their fidelity, he employed a celebrated saint, Sheikh Khalil, to conduct the negotiations, and under his auspices, the conditions were speedily and equitably arranged.

The treaty, however, had been scarcely signed, when the treacherous Afghan made secret preparations to surprise the imperial camp, though most of his officers protested against an act which combined perfidy with impiety; a few less scrupulous, however, were found to volunteer; and the choicest of the Afghan troops, with several war-elephants, were secretly drawn together. Sheikh Khalil, suspecting Shír Khan's designs, sent a messenger to warn Húmayún; but the emperor would not believe that Shír Khan would venture on such a breach of honour and religion, and passed the night without taking any precautions. Just as the sun was rising on the following morning, the Afghans attacked the imperial camp in the rear. Completely surprised, imperfectly armed, and unable in the confusion to form their ranks, the soldiers of Delhí made but a faint resistance. Húmayún, after several brave but ineffectual efforts to rally his troops, could only escape captivity by rapid retreat across the Ganges. Though the stream was swollen, he plunged his steed into the river, but the horse sunk exhausted, and the emperor would have been drowned, had not a water-carrier lent him a *musek*, or inflated leathern bag, by the aid of which he reached the opposite bank in safety. On this fatal day eight thousand of the imperial troops were slain or drowned in their efforts to pass the river. A second and still more fatal defeat compelled Húmayún to abandon his capital. He retreated slowly through the Punjáb, where he received unquestionable proofs of prince Kamran's treason. The officers and counsellors of the emperor advised him to inflict condign punishment on the traitor, but he nobly replied,—"No! never for the vanities of this perishable world will I imbue my hands in a brother's blood; for I shall always bear in mind the dying words of our common and respected parent. Almost with his last breath, he said to me, 'O! Húmayún, beware—beware! do not quarrel with your brother, nor ever form evil intentions towards him,'—these words are graven on my heart." Several of his chiefs were displeased by this clemency, so unusual in the East, and withdrew from the imperial standard.

Shír Khan's advance soon compelled the emperor—weakened by desertion—to abandon Lahore, and retire towards the Indus, A new misfortune seemed to await him at every step; the princes of his family abandoned him to consult for their own safety,—the provincial governors refused to send him their contingents, and some whom he had loaded with benefits, attempted to seize him, and send him prisoner to Shír Khan. Thus beset, he was forced to seek refuge with a few faithful followers on the west bank of the Indus. The country through which they fled was a desolate waste; their sufferings from want of water were dreadful—some went mad—others fell down dead. On the fourth day they reached a well, from which they raised water by means of their buckets, and a rudely constructed wheel, put together on the spot by some of the soldiers. "So deep was the well," says Ferishta, "that a drum was beaten to give notice to the driver of the bullocks when the bucket had reached the top. The unhappy followers were so impatient for water, that as soon as the first bucket appeared, several of them threw themselves upon it before it had quite reached the surface, and fell in." During this calamitous retreat, prince Akbar, afterwards emperor, was born; so severe was the pressure of his enemies on the unfortunate emperor, that he was obliged to leave his wife and infant son in his camp, where they were seized by the rebellious prince Askerry, who carried off his nephew to Kandahar. Húmayún had now no resource but to seek refuge in Persia, whither he was invited by the reigning monarch, Shah Tamasp; he accordingly passed the frontiers, and was received by the Shah's orders with the utmost hospitality and kindness.

When the emperor of Delhí entered Persia, he declared his determination of undertaking a pilgrimage to Mecca, if he could not obtain aid to recover his kingdom. Tamasp, however, promised to render him efficient assistance, and revived his courage, by according to the exiled sovereign all the honours of royalty. This generosity has been highly celebrated by all the Persian historians, and by the European writers who have relied upon their statements; but recent investigations have shewn, that Tamasp's conduct was not quite so honourable as it has been hitherto represented. The Memoirs of Húmayún, written by Jouher, one of his confidential servants, shew us that the Persian monarch soon persecuted the royal exile for his adherence to the Sonnite creed, and only granted him assistance at the price of an extensive province. Though Timúr himself was a bigoted Shíah, and made the injuries which the Syrians had inflicted on the house of Alí centuries before, a pretext for the destruction of Damascus, yet most of his descendants embraced the Sonnite creed, and Baber made it the established faith at Delhí. Soon after Húmayún had entered Persia, he received, among other presents from Tamasp, a *taj*, or Persian tiara of crimson silk, which he refused to wear. This *taj* was of a high conical shape, divided into twelve segments, in honour of the twelve Imáms, and was consequently a Shíah cognizance, which no one of the opposite sect could wear without incurring the imputation of apostacy. Tamasp was greatly irritated at Húmayún's refusal of the taj; and, as his biographer informs us, " when a large quantity of wood had been sent to the imperial residence for the use of the followers, Shah Tamasp sent a message to his majesty, saying, unless he and all his followers would become Shíahs, he would make a funeral pile for them with that wood." Nor was this an idle menace; we learn from the same authority, that Tamasp consulted with his brother, Bahram Mírza, respecting the destruction of the royal fugitive, and was with difficulty deterred from such a breach of hospitality, by the unanimous representations of the Persian princes. Húmayún subsequently contrived to inspire the Shah with hopes of his conversion, and told the king's sister, that "he had always been privately well disposed towards the Shiáhs, out of which had partly originated the animosity of his brothers." Soon afterwards, Tamasp levied an army, which he entrusted to the command of one of his sons, and sent to undertake the restoration of Húmayún.

The first operation of the war was the siege of Kandahar, which was obstinately defended by Prince Askerry. But the delay was advantageous to the emperor; it afforded time for those who were weary of Kamran's usurpation, to rally round their lawful sovereign, and it lessened his obligations to the Persians, who seemed well disposed to secure all the fruits of victory for themselves. Kandahar surrendered, and was garrisoned, according to agreement, by a Persian force; but Húmayún seized the first opportunity of securing so strong a place for himself, and having thus provided a place of refuge in case of defeat, he advanced upon Kabul. On his road, he was joined by several deserters from the enemy, and Kamran was forced to abandon Kabul without striking a blow. After a long and desultory war, in which Kabul frequently changed masters, Kamran was finally defeated, and betrayed into his brother's hands by one of his partizans. His life was spared, but he was deprived of his sight, and the effects of this cruel punishment soon brought him to the grave. In the mean time, the Afghan conquerors of Hindustan were engaged in disastrous civil wars, and inflicted such calamities on the country, that the citizens of Agra and Delhí sent pressing messages to Húmayún, entreating him to return and rescue them from the oppressors. Húmayún immediately crossed the Indus, and occupied Lahore, without encountering any serious opposition. Alarmed at this unexpected event, the Afghans laid aside their jealousies to unite against the common enemy, but they were defeated in three general engagements, forced to evacuate their fortresses, and abandon all the conquests they had made. Húmayún made his triumphal entry into Delhí, after an absence of fourteen years, and soon saw every sign of the revolt effaced. But he did not long enjoy his restoration; he accidentally fell down a marble staircase, and was so severely injured that he died within a few days.

Húmayún was succeeded by his favourite son, the illustrious Akbar, by whose abilities the empire of Delhí was raised to the summit of its glory.

Scarcely had he ascended the throne, when a series of insurrections in every quarter deprived him of all his dominions, except the Punjáb; but, though he had not yet attained his fourteenth year, he had sufficient wisdom to appreciate the abilities of Beiram Khan, whom he nominated regent of the empire by the affectionate title of Baba, or "father." This energetic minister, by several timely examples of severity, put an end to the spirit of mutiny which was rapidly spreading through the imperial army. Having thus restored discipline, Beiram Khan and Akbar marched against Hemú, a Hindú prince, who had usurped the throne of Delhí. The armies met at Paniput, and victory was long doubtful. At length Hemú, who was mounted on an elephant of prodigious size, being pierced through the eye with an arrow, fell back into his howda, and was believed to be slain. Notwithstanding the intense agony of the wound, Hemú drew the arrow, and with it the eye, out of the socket, which he wrapped in his handkerchief, and, in spite of his painful situation, attempted to rally his wavering troops. He might have succeeded, had not the cowardly driver of his elephant, terrified by the approach of an imperial lancer, offered to drive the animal wherever he was directed, and consented to bring Hemú within his enemy's lines. The unfortunate prince was dragged from his howda and put to death, while his followers dispersed in every direction. The immediate consequences of this victory were the occupation of Delhí without opposition, and the capture of Mein-at, where Hemú's treasures were deposited. Not long after this victory Beiram Khan began to abuse his power, putting to death those whom he suspected of rivalry, and insulting the prerogatives of royalty. Akbar, sensible of his obligations to the minister, endured several affronts with patience, but his resentment was at length inflamed by a circumstance which is thus related by Abu'l Fazl:—"One day while the king was at Agra, one of the elephants being *must* (*veneris desiderio impulsus*) attacked and killed another of Beiram Khan's, who, at the spur of the moment, commanded the keeper of the royal elephant to be put to death without first speaking to the king. Akbar was highly incensed, the more so on finding that the man was not to blame, having lost all control over the animal." Finding his favour decline, Beiram Khan revolted, but his followers were soon routed by the imperial troops, and he was reduced to such distress that he was forced to throw himself upon the emperor's mercy. The impressive scene of the repentant minister's reception by his generous master, is too illustrative of the character of both to be omitted even in our limited page; it is thus pourtrayed by Ferishta:—"When Beiram Khan entered the court, he hung his turban round his neck, and advancing rapidly threw himself in tears at the foot of the throne. Akbar, stretching forth his hand, caused him to rise, and placed him in his former station at the head of the nobles. A splendid dress was now brought, and the king addressed the fallen minister in the following words:—'If Beiram Khan loves a military life, the governments of Kalpy and Chandery offer a field for his ambition. If he choose rather to remain at court, our favour shall not be wanting to the benefactor of our family; but should he be disposed to seek devotion in retirement, let him perform a pilgrimage to Mecca, whither he shall be escorted in a manner worthy of his rank.' Beiram Khan replied, 'The royal confidence being once shaken, how can I wish to remain in the presence? The clemency of the king is enough, and his forgiveness is more than a reward for my former services. Let me, therefore, avert my thoughts from this world to another, and be allowed to proceed to the holy sepulchre.'" Akbar assented, and granted him a suitable retinue, and a considerable pension. Beiram Khan proceeded to Gujarát to seek means of transport to Arabia, but he was murdered on the road by an Afghan nobleman, whose father he had slain in battle.

Akbar now took the reins of government into his own hands, and by a judicious mixture of firmness and clemency, quelled the turbulent dispositions of the feudatory princes in his diversified dominions, and greatly extended his territories on the side of Bengal. One of his most memorable exploits was the siege of Chaitúr, in which the officers on both sides displayed greater skill in mining and the construction of military works than could have been found in Europe at the same period. This fortress, the strongest in Malwah, was garrisoned by five thousand rajpúts of acknowledged bravery, and plentifully supplied with provisions and the munitions of war; it could not therefore be taken by storm or blockade, and Akbar resolved to assail it by sap. The approaches were made in three lines; batteries were erected to cover the mining operations, and mounted with cannon cast upon the spot, a circumstance which greatly surprised the Hindús, who had greatly relied on the delay and difficulties attending the moving of the emperor's heavy ordnance. At length the miners were conducted under the wall, the chambers heavily loaded with gunpowder, and the trains fired. By some unfortunate accident one of the explosions was delayed until the storming party had mounted the breach; it proved more fatal to the assailants than to the besieged, and the imperialists, thrown into confusion, were beaten back to their entrenchments. A new sap was commenced; it was happily completed, and a lodgement formed at the head of it, calculated to afford ample security against any attempt on the part of the garrison; several breaches were also opened by the batteries, whose fire was incessant, and the garrison was harassed by a series of false attacks, which gave them neither rest nor respite. Notwithstanding these vigorous operations, the besieged maintained an obstinate resistance, until one of the most popular chiefs was shot, while superintending the repairs of the principal breach, by Akbar's own hand. The breach was instantly abandoned: the imperialists gained the walls with little loss, and, opening the gates, gave admission to the war-elephants and cavalry, who rushed furiously through the streets. For some hours, quarter was neither asked nor given; more than thirty thousand of the rajpúts and citizens of Chaitúr were slain; but a body of a thousand sharp-shooters, specially marked out for vengeance, escaped, by the ingenious stratagem of collecting their wives and children together, driving them onwards, as if they had been captives taken in the storm, and representing themselves as a body of imperial foot-soldiers, escorting plunder to the camp.

The fame acquired by the capture of Chaitúr, facilitated Akbar's conquests in Gujarát and Bengal, but it did not abate the hostility of the Afghans, the hereditary enemies of the descendants of Baber. They were, however, defeated in all their efforts, and the emperor gradually extended his sway over the whole of northern Hindustan. Akbar was naturally of a mild and tolerant disposition; he spurned the solicitations of the bigots by whom he was surrounded in the early part of his reign, to persecute those who dissented from the established faith, and he aimed at the formation of a new religion, which might unite into one body Mohammedans, Hindus, the followers of Zoroaster, and even Jews and Christians. Previous, however, to this time, he seems to have been well disposed to adopt the religion of the Gospel in preference to that of the Koran, for he addressed a letter to the King of Portugal, a copy of which has been preserved by Abu'l Fazl, requesting that Christian teachers, and translations of the sacred books of the Christians, should be sent to his court. This mission was entrusted to Xavier, a relation of the celebrated St. Francis Xavier, who presented the emperor with a translation of the Gospels; but, unfortunately, he had mingled with them many of the popular Persian legends, trusting that they might thus be rendered more acceptable. This impious artifice had an effect directly contrary to that which was designed. Akbar was disgusted by meeting with legends of whose falsehood he was previously convinced, and regarded Christianity with suspicion. He now resolved to form an eclectic creed for himself, and, like most Mohammedan sectaries, especially insisted on the great doctrine of the Divine Unity, which he declared was but obscurely revealed to the Prophets. Unlike, however, every other propagator of a new faith, his proceedings were regulated with the utmost caution, and his appeals made solely to the reason. The religion which he endeavoured to introduce was nearly a pure Deism, and his ritual was mainly derived from the forms and ceremonies of the ancient Persians, ascribed to Zoroaster. Many of the Hindús, and a great body of the Shíahs, declared their willingness to embrace the imperial creed; but Akbar introduced an institution, which, though apparently of trifling importance, appears to have been the rock on which his entire system was ultimately shipwrecked. He forbade his subjects to wear beards, and thus gave more offence than had been excited by all his abuse of Mohammed, and ridicule of the incarnations of Vishnu.

The conclusion of Akbar's reign was spent in vain efforts to propagate his new religion, which only spread where the court had influence. His eldest son, Jehan Ghír, strenuously opposed his father's tolerant principles, and attempted to extort from him edicts of persecution, which the emperor not only refused, but endeavoured to convince his son of the folly of bigotry. Akbar had sent a large army into the Dekkan, which had been dismembered on the fall of the Bahmeni dynasty, and had reasonable hopes of extending his empire over the whole of India, when grief for the loss of his favourite son, Daniel, who fell a victim to intemperance, brought him to the grave, (A.D. 1598). Few sovereigns have been more generally or more deservedly lamented than Akbar; he was far the most enlightened monarch that ever ruled over an oriental empire, and he was the only one of the Delhí dynasty who had the wisdom to form a plan for uniting the various races subject to his sway, into an organized and single nation.

Immediately after the death of Akbar became known, the nobles around the court assembled, and agreed to proclaim his eldest son Selim emperor, with the title of Jehan Ghír, which signifies "Conqueror of the World." The first measure adopted by the new sovereign was the restoration of Mohammedanism to its former supremacy, and the removal from office of all who had favoured the religious innovations of Akbar. In the very first year of his reign, Jehan Ghír had to take the field against his own son Khosrú, who was supported in his rebellion by Hassan Bek, the governor of Kabul. The insurrection was suppressed, and eight hundred of the prince's chief supporters punished by the horrible death of impalement. But this did not prevent fresh conspiracies, which kept the emperor in constant anxiety. His chief consolation was derived from the company of the widow of Shír Afghan, a nobleman who had been put to death for treason. The emperor had loved this lady in the lifetime of his father Akbar, and had been grievously afflicted by her marriage with another. He became so deeply enamoured that he named her Núr-mahál, or the "light of the harem,"* and spent every hour he could spare from the affairs of state in her company. In his autobiography the emperor declares, "At the period in which this is written (about the fourteenth year of the emperor's reign) I may say that the whole concern of my household, whether gold or jewels, is under her sole and entire management. Of my unreserved confidence, indeed, this princess is in complete posses-

* She was also called Núr-jehan, or "light of the world."

sion, and I may allege without a fallacy that the whole fortune of my empire has been consigned to this highly endowed family; the father being my finance minister, the son my lieutenant-general, with unlimited powers, and the daughter the inseparable companion of my cares."* During the reign of Akbar immense wealth had been accumulated in the royal treasures, and the Great Mogul, as the emperor of Delhí by pertinacious error continues to be called, was celebrated throughout Europe as the richest monarch in the world. The European ambassadors who visited his court, among whom may be noticed Sir Thomas Roe, sent to negotiate a commercial treaty by the British sovereign, James I., confirmed the reports of the wealth and magnificence of the court of Delhí; but their statements were suspected of exaggeration by many who knew not the value of India while its resources were yet unexhausted. An extract from the "Memoirs of Jehan Ghír" will show that the accounts of his magnificence given by the travellers of the seventeenth century, were not so much overdrawn as is usually supposed: "On the eleventh day of the month of Shábán, of the year (of the Hejra) 1019, (18th of September, 1610), I bestowed the daughter of Mirza Rustam upon my favourite son Parviz, with a marriage portion of one lak of ashrefries, (ninety thousand pounds). On the evening on which the bride was brought to the palace, I presented her with a necklace of sixty pearls, for each pearl of which my father had paid the sum of ten thousand rupees, (consequently the value of the necklace was sixty thousand pounds.) I also presented them with a ruby of the value of two hundred and fifty thousand rupees, (twenty-five thousand pounds); and I finally assigned for her support the annual sum of three laks of rupees, (thirty thousand pounds); and for the establishment of her household one hundred maidens from Surat, who were devoted to her service."†

After the suppression of prince Khosrú's rebellion, Jehan Ghír directed his attention to the affairs of Bengal, and completed the subjugation of that province. His partiality for the relations of his favourite sultana, however, provoked the resentment of the royal family, and a new insurrection was planned by the emperor's third son, Khorrum, better known in history by the name of Shah Jehan, who commenced his career by murdering his

* Memoirs of Jehan Ghír, p. 27. † Ibid, p. 30.

brother Khosrú. The young prince laid siege to Agra, but being repulsed from the walls he hazarded a pitched battle, in which he was completely defeated. He continued, however, to maintain a vigorous struggle, passing with great rapidity from one province to another, while Jehan Ghír, influenced by the jealous councils of the sultana, treated his nobles and ministers so harshly that they were almost driven to rebellion in their own defence. Mohabet Khan, the best general in the emperor's service, having been treacherously attacked by the imperial forces, routed them with great loss, and profited by his victory to make Jehan Ghír a prisoner. The empress was not daunted by this misfortune;—she secretly levied an army, and when she had mustered sufficient strength, contrived a plan for Jehan Ghír's escape, which perfectly succeeded. Mohabet Khan, suddenly deserted by the greater part of his followers, fled to prince Khorrum, and both prepared to renew the war. But the death of the emperor averted the horrors of a new contest; the empress vainly attempted to raise up a rival to prince Khorrum, on whose approach all the nobles flocked to his camp, and saluted him emperor by the title of Shah Jehan, King of the World. (A.D. 1628).

Although the empire of Delhí had reached the summit of its greatness when Shah Jehan ascended the throne, it was at this very period that the signs of its future ruin became most apparent. It was too extensive for its unenlightened rulers: there was no bond of union between its discordant parts, and consequently insurrections were frequent in all the remote provinces. Shah Jehan was, like his father, ruled by his queen, and at her instigation he declared war against the Portuguese, and deprived them of their settlement, Húglí. After the death of his favourite sultana, the emperor abandoned himself to the most profligate debauchery, and exhausted his immense treasures in gratifying the caprices of his favourite mistresses. But his strict administration of justice, and the wisdom of his decisions, which are still quoted with respect, saved him from the contempt which is usually incurred by voluptuous princes. As he grew older avarice succeeded to prodigality, and he made use of the most iniquitous pretexts to forfeit the property of his nobles, and increase the burdens of his people. To save the expense of maintaining his sons at court, he assigned them the government of distant provinces, without any appointments but what they could draw from their subjects, and thus laid the foundation for a new series of calamitous civil wars.

The mutual jealousies of Shah Jehan's four sons prevented them from acting in concert, and through fear of each other they remained quiet until the emperor became so dangerously ill that a report of his death was generally credited. Dara, the eldest, who was at court, hearing that his brothers were levying armies, hastened to assure them that Shah Jehan was not only alive, but was fast recovering. Suján, the second son, refused to credit the report, and took the field with an army which he had been enabled to levy from the wealth he had amassed in his government of Bengal. Aureng-zib, the youngest of the princes, feigning that he had devoted himself to a religious life, took up arms under the pretence of supporting the claims of his brother Morád, and being consequently joined by that prince, steadily advanced towards the capital. In the mean time Suján was defeated by the son of Dara, and forced to retire. Flushed with recent victory, the imperial army marched to drive back Aureng-zib and Morád, but through the treachery of one of the generals it was routed with great loss, and the two princes continued their progress. Dara, enraged at this unexpected failure, and trusting to the vast superiority of his forces, resolved to crush the revolt before it had time to extend further, and marched to encounter his brothers. Aureng-zib baffled Dara by the unexpected rapidity of his movements, and reached a place within five miles of Agra before his advance could be checked by the imperial army. In the battle that ensued, Dara, at the head of the elephants and cavalry, made so furious a charge that he bore down all opposition. Believing the victory secure, he descended from his elephant to mount a horse and pursue the fugitives, but no sooner did his followers miss him from the elephant, than, believing him to have fallen by some sudden blow, they broke their lines and fell into confusion. Aureng-zib, who had contrived by immense exertions to keep a small band together, so ably profited by this sudden turn of fortune, that he gained a decisive victory, and compelled Dara to seek shelter in Agra. Suleímán, the son of Dara, was hastening with a numerous army to his father's aid, when he received news of this calamity. He prepared to remedy the disaster, but his principal generals, gained over by the secret intrigues of Aureng-zib, plotted his arrest, and he was compelled to fly with a few faithful friends to avoid being delivered up to his uncle.

Shah Jehan was well aware of Aureng-zib's crafty and ambitious character, but he thought it best to dissemble his feelings and to throw the whole blame of the war on Dara. The emperor, however, had to deal with a master in the arts of duplicity. Aureng-zib affected to be perfectly satisfied until Shah Jehan was thrown off his guard, when he was suddenly arrested by Aureng-zib's son, Mohammed, and confined a close prisoner to the palace. Soon afterwards he seized his brother Morád, whom he had so long deluded, and confined him in a strong fortress near Delhi. His brothers, Dara and Sujáh, however, still disputed the usurper's power to empire, and his own son, Mohammed, for a time supported the pretensions of the latter. They continued their efforts for two or three years, but they were finally defeated and put to death by Aureng-zib's command. Morád shared their fate, and the entire empire recognised the authority of the crafty usurper. (A.D. 1658).

On his accession Aureng-zib took the proud tittle of Alúmghír, or "Conqueror of the World." From the time that he was firmly established on the throne, the vigilance and steadiness of his administration preserved so much tranquillity in the empire, that historians have recorded few events worthy of notice. But though the prosperity of the empire appeared not to have suffered any diminution, causes were already in operation which menaced its future destruction at no very distant date. The bigotry and intolerance of the emperor revived religious animosities between the varied sects and parties subject to his sway; the perfidy of which he set the example, spread through his court, so that he had neither a minister nor an officer worthy of confidence, and his sons evinced a disposition to emulate him in wars upon their father, and upon each other. Intent on conquest, he sent a large army to invade Assam; but after having obtained several victories, the imperial forces were compelled to return by the violence of the rains, and were almost annihilated in their retreat. Several insurrections were provoked by the rapacity of the imperial tax-gatherers, but only one was formidable, from a general belief that the insurgents were protected by enchantment. Aureng-zib revived the spirits of his soldiers by distributing to them amulets, inscribed with verses from the Koran, and thus, one superstition counteracting the other, the rebels were conquered. An invasion from Persia menaced greater dangers, but it was averted by the death of Shah Abbas, in his camp, before he could reach the scene of action. His successor was too anxious for the security of his throne to commence his reign with an arduous war, and Aureng-zib was more anxious to establish his supremacy over the Dekkan, than to make conquests in Persia.

The power of the Mahrattas in southern India, was now beginning to be formidable under the guidance of Sevaji, who had been originally a leader of banditti, and had gained the chieftaincy of the wild mountain tribes between Canara and Gujarát. Sevaji had acquired great strength during the civil wars which preceded the accession of Aureng-zib, but he had submitted to the conqueror and offered to lead a part of the imperial forces against the Persians. A wanton insult from the emperor drove him to rebellion, and his progress in the south was facilitated by a simultaneous rising of the Afghans, who never forgot that the empire of northern India belonged to them before the arrival of Baber. The Afghan chiefs were invited to a banquet, and treacherously murdered; an act of treachery disavowed by Aureng-zib, but by which he profited without scruple. It was impossible to employ such arts against the Mahrattas: Sevaji and his successor Sambaji were too suspicious to place themselves voluntarily in the emperor's power. Sambaji was, however, surprised and made prisoner while amusing himself in the mountains; he was at once put to death, his capital was forced to surrender, his wives and his infant son were made prisoners.

As Aureng-zib had previously subdued the kingdoms of Golconda and Peijapore, his empire over southern India seemed on the point of being completed; but Rama, the brother of Sambaji, with other Mahratta chieftains, maintained the war, eluding encounter when pursued, and issuing from their fastnesses to devastate the country so soon as the imperial forces were withdrawn. So enriched were they by the spoils they obtained, and so strengthened by the number of desperate adventurers who joined their ranks, that towards the close of Aureng-zib's reign, the advantages of the war had decisively turned in their favour. This contest continued to the emperor's death, which took place in the ninety-fourth year of his age and forty-eighth of his reign.

(A.D. 1707). A civil war ensued on the emperor's death; his three sons took up arms against each other, but the victory finally remained with Bahader Shah, who was recognized by all the provinces of the empire.

The brief reign of this emperor produced nothing worthy of note. His death was followed by a civil war between his children, which ended in favour of the eldest, Moiz-ed-dín, who took the title of Jehander Shah, or " the King who possesses the World." Jehander Shah was a weak prince, and was so foolishly attached to his wife Lal-kúr, a woman of mean birth, that he endeavoured to fill the greatest offices of trust and honour throughout the empire with her relations. This conduct gave such offence to his nobles, that they conspired to raise his nephew to the throne. Ferokh-siar, whose father had already contended for empire, only waited for a favourable moment to assert his claims; he readily obeyed the summons of the conspirators, and routed the imperial forces on the banks of the Jumna. Jehander Shah fled from the field to Delhí, where he was arrested by his own ministers, and given up to the mercy of the conqueror. Ferokh-siar ordered the unfortunate monarch to be slain, and his body to be dragged with shocking indignity through the streets of Dehli. The command was obeyed, and such was the cruelty of the conqueror that the corpse of Jehander Shah was denied a grave. It was during the reign of Ferokh-siar that the Síkhs, now the most formidable native power in India, first rose into importance. They were originally a fraternity of mendicants, founded by Gúrú Nanac, who gave them a code of morals, the basis of which is pure deism, and permitted the reception of converts from all classes of society. They soon increased their numbers, and desolated the province of Lahore, which has since become the seat of their power. About the same time also, the English East India Company obtained a firmân exempting them from the payment of any duties within the emperor's dominions; and this grant was the foundation of the power subsequently acquired by that body in Bengal.

Ferokh-siar owed his elevation to the exertions of two brothers, Abdallah Khan and Hassan Khan, who claimed to be Syeds, or descendants of the Prophet. These powerful nobles seized on all the dignities of the empire, and finding that Ferokh-siar grew jealous of their authority, they openly prepared to set him aside, while the emperor, equally cruel and cowardly, could not be prevailed on to take any precautions for his security. The unfortunate Ferokh-siar was seized in his own harem, blinded with a red-hot iron, and afterwards put to death by cruel tortures. Refí-ed-Derjat, son of Refí-al-Kadr, the nephew of Bahader Shah in the female line, was then placed upon the throne by the Syed brothers, but in less than three months he fell a victim to consumption, or as some say to poison. Refí-ed-Dowlah, the brother and successor of Refí-ed-Derjat, died a few days after his elevation, and the Syeds, who disposed of the empire at their pleasure, proclaimed as their pageant sovereign a grandson of Bahader Shah, who took the title of Nasir-ed-din Mohammed Shah. The nobles were now weary of the yoke imposed upon them by the Syed brothers, and they found no difficulty in inspiring the emperor with the same sentiments. A secret conspiracy was organised; Hassan was murdered in front of the emperor's tent, and Abdallah, who took up arms to avenge his fate, was defeated and taken prisoner. The Syed did not long survive his overthrow, he died in a few months from the effect of his wounds. Though he was a Mohammedan, forty-five of his wives and concubines burned themselves on his decease by setting fire to an apartment in the harem. Nizam-ul-mulk, the governor of the Dekkan, was invited to accept the office of vizier; he refused to accept it, under the pretence that his abilities were inadequate to the task, but in truth because he had resolved upon establishing an independent sovereignty in southern India. He excited the Mahrattas, a warlike race fast rising into importance, to ravage the imperial territories, while the feeble emperor wasted his time in indolent luxury. These freebooters extended their incursions to the very gates of Dehlí, and, though they suffered a defeat, they induced the imperial generals to purchase their future forbearance by a large and dishonourable bribe. Nizam-al-mulk, after much persuasion, was induced to visit the court, but being insulted by the imperial favourites, he engaged the nobles, who were displeased by the disgraceful treaty with the Mahrattas, to invite Nadir Shah to invade the empire; and that conqueror, already indignant at the protection afforded to his Afghan enemies, readily accepted the invitation.

Some historians have expressed doubts of Nizam-al-Mulk's treachery, and it is not easy to comprehend what advantages he could hope to have reaped by betraying his country. Neither did Nadir's avarice or ambition need much prompting, as he must have felt assured of success over a court so degraded that it actually paid tribute to the plundering Mahrattas. The march of Nadir was more rapid than the court of Delhí had anticipated; they were scarcely roused from their state of infatuated security until the conqueror had crossed the Indus. Mohammed Shah then collected an army, and established himself in a fortified camp in the plains of Kamal, near the banks of the Jumna. On Nadir's approach, the emperor having recently received a large re-enforcement, left his camp to encounter his adversary in the open field. After a fierce engagement, which lasted two hours, the imperialists were routed with the loss of 20,000 men, and so completely disheartened, that Mohammed Shah, without making any effort to defend his camp, surrendered himself, his treasures, and his dominions to the conqueror. Nadir received the conquered emperor with great kindness, and promised to restore him to his throne at Delhi. The conquerors advanced to that city in order to receive, as the reward of their victory, the immense treasures of gold and jewels accumulated by the descendants of Baber, and to exact heavy contributions from the nobles and citizens (A. D. 1739). The cruel exactions of those appointed to collect the stipulated sum, were intolerable; a false report of Nadir's death, induced the citizens to take up arms, and even when the mistake was discovered, they persevered in their insane attacks on their resistless conquerors. Nadir was, at length, so provoked, that he gave orders for a general massacre to his troops, who had come up from their encampment. The carnage continued for several hours, during which time Nadir continued in a small mosque, silent, gloomy, and alone. No one dared to interrupt his solitude, until the unhappy Mohammed Shah forced his way to his presence, and in agonizing tones exclaimed "Spare my people!" Nadir immediately gave orders that the massacre should cease, and the promptitude with which he was obeyed, afforded the strongest proof of the strict discipline he had introduced into his army.

Nadir continued at Delhí fifty-eight days; he then returned with a treasure, which some have estimated so high as seventy millions, and none less than thirty millions. Before his departure, he gave Mohammed Shah some judicious advice respecting the administration of his empire, and severely threatened the Omrahs if they failed in their obedience. But the injury which his invasion had inflicted on the empire, was incurable; the army was destroyed, the treasury exhausted, nearly all financial resources cut off: the Mahrattas ravaged the South, and all the provinces which had escaped their devastation were laid waste by Nadir's army. Under the able government of Baji Rav, and his successor, Balaji, the Mahratta power made such rapid progress, that it seemed not very improbable that India might again be formed into a Hindú empire.

Other enemies began to appear in the east and north; an Afghan colony, called the Rohillas, acquired possession of the country east of the Ganges, from Oude to the mountains. Their chief was Ali Mohammed, a Hindú convert adopted by an Afghan officer, in whose character were united the cunning of the Hindú and the courage of the Afghan. He raised the new state of the Rohillas to such importance, that it required an expedition, leaded by the emperor in person, to enforce even a temporary submission.

A far more formidable combination of the Afghans had been formed in their own territories, and the death of Nadir, the worst enemy of India, was but the herald of new invasions and calamities to the unhappy land. Though Nadir had raised the Persian monarchy to the highest pitch of greatness, he had disgusted his subjects by his severe exactions, his excessive cruelties, but, above all, by his alienation from the national religion—the Shiáh form of Mohammedanism. Aware of the hostility he had provoked, Nadir entrusted the guardianship of his person to mercenary Uzbegs and Afghans, who were, like himself, attached to the Sunnite creed. Preparations were in progress for the arrest of all the Persian nobles; but some of them received warning of their danger, and averted it by the assassination of the Shah in his tent (A.D. 1747). Ahmed Khan Abdali, the leader of the Afghans, made a desperate attack on the Persian camp, hoping that he might be in time to rescue his sovereign. Finding himself too late, he made good his retreat to his own frontiers with a large amount of treasure, in spite of all the efforts which the Persians made to intercept him. His fame soon spread abroad among his countrymen, and the Turkish and Tartar tribes north and west of the Himalaya; before the end of the year, he was solemnly crowned king at Kandahar, and his authority was acknowledged, not only in Afghanistan, but also in Balkh, Scinde, Kashmir, and Beluchistan. From some superstitious motive, he changed the name of his tribe from Abdali to Durani, by which it has since been known.

Though the distracted state of Persia might seem to have invited the ambition of the founder of a new dynasty, yet, either from a consciousness of the difficulties which beset such an undertaking, or from feelings of attachment to the family of Nadir, he preferred extending his territories on the eastern side, and led an army to the banks of the Indus, for the purpose of invading the Punjáb. The emperor of Delhi sent his son and his vizier to protect the fords: but Ahmed crossed the river in an unguarded spot, took the Indian army in the rear, and captured Sirhind, where they had deposited their baggage, their stores, and a portion of their artillery. This boldness so intimidated the enemy, that they did not venture to meet him in the field, but fortified themselves in an entrenched camp. The Afghans assaulted their position for ten days, but were finally repelled with great loss, and compelled to retreat. Such, however, was the impression they produced, that the viceroy of the Punjáb consented to pay a permanent tribute.

Mohammed Shah did not long survive this imperfect success; he was succeeded on the throne of Delhi by his son, Ahmed Shah, who bore the same name as his Afghan rival (A.D. 1748). The first efforts of the new emperor were directed against the Rohillas; he entrusted the conduct of the war to his vizier, Safder Jang, who was a very incompetent general, and whose army was in such a miserable state of discipline, that it was formidable to every body except the enemy. Over such a commander, and such forces, the brave Rohillas obtained an easy victory; they took advantage of their success to invade the kingdom of Oude, and Safder Jang had no other resource than to seek assistance from the Mahrattas. By this degrading aid, the vizier triumphed in his turn, and the Rohillas were forced to submit to humiliating conditions of peace.

On his return to Delhí, the vizier heard intelligence of disasters which more than counterbalanced his late imperfect success. The Afghan monarch had again invaded the Punjáb, with an army which the viceroy was not prepared to meet, and having completed its conquest, had sent an envoy to demand the absolute cession of that province. Nadir's visit was too well remembered for compliance to be refused; when the vizier reached the court, he found all arrangements concluded. His discontent was increased by the discovery that a favorite eunuch had superseded him in the confidence of the emperor, and, like a true oriental, he removed this rival by a treacherous assassination. The emperor, enraged at this outrage, applied for help to the powerful Omrah, Ghazi-ed-din, who, with the assistance of the Mahrattas, expelled Safder Jang, and became prime minister in his stead. But Ahmed Shah soon found his new vizier more intolerable than the former, and began to form secret machinations for his removal or destruction. Ghazi-ed-din discovered the intrigue, and sent an armed force against the emperor; Ahmed Shah was taken prisoner by his rebellious minister, who, after depriving him of power, put out his eyes, as well as those of the queen, his mother. Ghazi-ed-din then selected one of the princes of the blood to bear the name of emperor, while he reserved the entire power to himself, and the new sovereign was proclaimed by the title of Alum-Ghír (A.D. 1754).

Ghazi-ed-din maintained tranquillity for a considerable time by the stringent severity of his measures, but he at length provoked a mutiny among the troops, in which he narrowly escaped from destruction. The emperor's conduct, at this crisis, awakened the vizier's suspicions; he resolved to strengthen himself against the probable designs of his master, and, therefore, attempted to obtain possession of the Punjáb, then ruled by the widow of an Afghan noble, to whom Ahmed Shah Durani had entrusted the government during the minority of her son. Ghazi's outrage provoked a third Afghan invasion; Shah Ahmed marched almost without resistance to Delhí, and repeated in that unfortunate capital the massacres and exactions of Nadir Shah. He was much struck by the unhappy position of the emperor; and before returning home appointed a Rohilla chief to command in Delhí, trusting that his influence would be a sufficient counterpoise to the usurped power of the vizier. Ghazi-ed-din applied for assistance to the Mahrattas; by their aid he captured Delhí, wrested the Punjáb from the Afghans, made Alum-Ghír his prisoner, and put him to death (A.D. 1759). Shah Alum, the heir apparent, was fortunately absent, and to him the succession finally devolved.

In the mean time, Ahmed Shah had completed his preparations for his fourth invasion of India; the several Mohammedan states united with him against the Mahrattas, who had now become formidable to them all, and the future fate of India was placed on the hazard of a single battle. The Mahrattas were reluctant to meet the Afghan leader in a fair field, they sheltered themselves in an entrenched camp, where they were soon blockaded by their active enemies, and compelled to endure all the extremities of famine. Thus situated, the Mahratta leaders were forced to come to an engagement on the plains of Paniput; the battle was one of the most sanguinary on record: finally, the fury of the Afghans bore down all opposition; the Mahrattas were refused quarter, and found no safety even in flight, for the peasants whom they had plundered rose on the first news of their calamity, and slaughtered the fugitives without mercy. The wreck of the army retired beyond the Nerbudda, abandoning nearly all their acquisitions in Hindustan Proper; and the government of the Mahratta Peishwa never recovered its former vigour (A.D. 1761). Ahmed Shah returned home without attempting to profit by his victory, and never afterwards took any share in the affairs of India. Shah Alum subsequently recovered Delhí, but afterwards fell into the power of Gholam Khadir, a Rohilla, who put out his eyes. Scindia, a Mahratta chief, having taken Delhí, kept the unfortunate emperor a close prisoner until 1803, when that city was captured by the English, and Shah Alum, after a life of misery and disaster, ended his days a pensioner on the bounty of the East India Company. On his death, his son, Akbar Shah, succeeded to his pension and his title, but the entire power of the race of Timúr remained with the British government.

CHAPTER IV.

EARLY INTERCOURSE BETWEEN EUROPE AND INDIA.

PROGRESS OF DISCOVERY.

LITTLE is known of the Hystapid dynasty in Persia, except what has been communicated to us by the Greeks; and the continuous wars between them and the Persians, from the accession of Darius Hystaspes to the fall of Darius Codomannus, necessarily produced bitter animosities, which prevented the historians of Europe from devoting much attention to the detested despots of Asia. No stronger proof can be given of the little reliance to be placed on the Greek histories of Persia, than the utter inconsistency between the accounts given of Cyrus the Great, by Xenophon and Herodotus: they differ, in almost every particular they record, respecting the birth, the life, and the death, of this mighty conqueror; and, furthermore, neither historian can be successfully reconciled to the incidental notices of Cyrus in the Bible, or to the traditions preserved in Oriental writers. There is, however, little reason to doubt, that commercial intercourse existed, from a very early period, between India and Persia; that the monarchs of the latter country reckoned some princes of Western India among their tributaries; and that caravans connected the trade of the Indus with that of the Euphrates, probably by the great road through Kandahar. The enterprising Phœnicians, and very probably the Egyptians, communicated with the countries of Southern and Eastern Asia, through the Red Sea, the Persian Gulf, and the Indian Ocean. It was for the purpose of procuring his subjects a share of this lucrative trade, that Solomon took possession of the port of Ezion-geber, on the Gulf of Akaba; but his subjects did not share his spirit of enterprize: the Jews never reached such a state of civilization, as would enable them to appreciate the lucrative pursuits of commerce, and the judicious plans of their wisest monarch died with him.

About one hundred and sixty years after the reign of Darius Hystaspes, Alexander the Great undertook his great expedition into India: he did not penetrate farther than the Punjáb—indeed, he did not traverse the whole extent of that country, having been compelled to turn back by a mutiny of his troops on the banks of the Hyphasis. But, both as he advanced and returned, his soldiers were so spread over the country, and acted in so many separate divisions, and all his movements were so exactly measured and delineated by men of science, whom he kept in pay for the purpose, that he acquired a very accurate knowledge of that part of India.

On his return to the banks of the Hydaspes, he found that his officers, during his absence, had assembled a numerous fleet, destined to sail down by that river and the Indus to the Ocean, and thence proceed through the Persian Gulf to the mouth of the Euphrates. The armament thus prepared was so great and magnificent, as to be worthy of such a commander as the conqueror of Asia. It consisted of two thousand vessels, of various sizes, one hundred and twenty thousand men, and two hundred elephants. As the conqueror pursued his course along the streams of these great rivers, the nations on both sides were compelled to submit; but, for the first time in the annals of history, the march of civilization accompanied the progress of military triumph—cities were founded, commercial marts established, and an active intercourse opened with the unknown nations of the remote interior. It took nine months for Alexander to descend to the mouth of the Indus, a distance of more than a thousand British miles; but the delay was occasioned by the prudent determination of Alexander, to leave nothing unexplored or unattempted, which would advance his great and noble project, of uniting the Eastern and Western world by the bonds of mutual trade. On reaching the ocean, Alexander led his army back to Persia by land; the fleet was left under the command of Nearchus, who, after a coasting voyage of seven months, conducted it safely up the Persian Gulf to the Euphrates.

The magnificent schemes of Alexander were frustrated by his early death, and by the destructive civil wars which arose between his successors. They were partially revived by Ptolemy the son of Lagus, who had taken a leading part in the Indian expedition, and who obtained Egypt for his share in the partition of the Macedonian empire. The Seleucidæ might have more effectually carried out the schemes of the great conqueror, had they not been driven from Upper Asia by the Parthians, whose empire soon intervened between the Greeks of Bactria and Europe, thus cutting off the Bactrians from all communication with the western world. The erection of the city of Alexandria on the Nile, and the establishment of the port of Berenice on the Red Sea, made Egypt the high road of communication between India and Europe. From Berenice, Indian goods were brought overland to Coptos, on the Nile, and thence down that river to Alexandria. This became the principal route for Indian commerce, and so continued, during the two hundred and fifty years that Egypt flourished as an independent kingdom, under the paternal government of the Ptolemies.

Two other routes deserve to be noticed; goods destined for northern regions, were sent up the Indus, and thence through the passes of the Hindú Kúsh to the river Oseus; they were conveyed down that river, which then flowed into the Caspian, and either by rivers or by land-carriage, distributed among the populous and opulent nations which then possessed the countries between the Euxine and the Caspian. The commodities of India, intended for the southern and interior provinces of western Asia, proceeded by land from the Caspian gates to some of the great rivers by which they were circulated through every part of the country. This was probably the chief route of trade when Persia was governed by its native princes, and it has not been quite abandoned, even in the present day.

An overland communication between the Syrian coasts and the great rivers of Mesopotamia, appears to have existed from very remote antiquity; it was probably established before the time of Abraham. The journey through the intervening desert, was facilitated by its affording one station abounding with water and capable of cultivation. Solomon appears to have been the first who appreciated the commercial advantages of this favoured spot: he erected there a city, called by the Syrians *Tadmor*, and by the Greeks *Palmyra*, both names, in their respective languages, being descriptive of the Palm-trees, which afford its inhabitants food and shelter. For many centuries this oasis was tenanted by a flourishing and independent community, until its last ruler, the gallant queen Zenobia, was conquered by the emperor Aurelian, and its prosperity blighted for ever by the withering influence of Roman despotism.

The trade between Egypt and India was diminished but not ruined by the Roman conquest, and it soon revived when the increasing taste for luxuries in Italy, produced a demand for the spices, precious stones, pearls, silks, and muslins of the east. An ambassador from the island of Ceylon, presented himself at the court of the Emperor Claudius, and the Chinese records contain an account of an embassy sent to their remote regions from Rome in the reign of the Antonines. When the seat of government was removed from Rome to Constantinople, the intercourse between the empire and the east was necessarily extended, but the Byzantines soon found formidable rivals in the Persians, when they were liberated from the Parthian yoke, and the independence of their country established under the native dynasty of the Sassanides. The Persians, with the usual rapacity of monopolists, raised the price of all Indian and Chinese commodities, particularly silk, and like all monopolists, they were soon punished for their cupidity; the eggs of the silk-worm were brought into Europe, concealed in a hollow cane, by two monks, and the rapidity with which the animals were propagated in Greece and subsequently in Italy, soon rendered the European states independent of the East, for the supply of this valuable material.

The conquests of the enterprising Saracens gave an immense stimulus to Eastern commerce. They established commercial navies on the Persian Gulph, and the city of Bussorah, founded by the Khaliph Omar, at the junction of the Tigris and Euphrates, soon became a place of trade, hardly inferior to Alexandria. The Egyptian trade through the Red Sea, was at the same time revived, and the hardy Arabs, not contented with following in the track of their predecessors, pushed forward their discoveries until they had accurately explored the greater part of the coast-line of south-eastern Asia. It is all but demonstrated that they obtained a knowledge of the mariner's compass from the Chinese, and that through them, this vast improvement in the art of navigation, was made known to Europe.

The religious madness which inspired the crusading spirit, was felt through every part of Christendom; Robert of Gloucester, in his Rhyming Chronicle, declares that it was felt by all the inhabitants

> Of Normandy, of Denmark, of Norway, and Bretagne,
> Of Wales and of Ireland, of Gascony and Spain,
> Of Provence and of Saxony, and of Allemagne,
> Of Scotland and of Greece, of Rome and Aquitaine.

The Crusaders were ignorant and bigoted barbarians; but the capture of the two flourishing cities, Antioch and Tyre, pointed out to them the pleasures of oriental luxuries, and the advantages of oriental commerce. Both were appreciated by the rising republics of Italy, where the arts and industry, the usual concomitants of freedom, had made considerable progress. The Italian States supplied the means of transport to the fanatical soldiers of the Cross, receiving, in return, valuable immunities and privileges in the several cities they subdued. At this time, the glory of the Saracens was gone; they had been trampled down under the feet of their Turkish mercenaries and slaves, who sold or leased out to the spirited merchants of Italy, commercial advantages which they were too proud or too stupid to use themselves. Other revolutions followed, which gave to the Genoese the monopoly of all the Eastern trade, which centred in Constantinople —and to the Venetians, the command of all the commerce which passed through Egypt. Travellers from these States penetrated into the remotest parts of Central Asia; their observations led men to reflect on the geographical consequences resulting from the spherical figure of the earth, for, though the true shape of the globe had been long known, little attention had been paid to the inferences which necessarily followed. By a fortunate blunder, the eastern longitude of Asia had been increased far beyond the reality, and this error led Columbus to conclude, that India might be reached by a voyage undertaken in a westerly direction. He proposed this scheme to the Genoese, and afterwards to the King of Portugal, without success; but, undaunted by these failures, he applied to the court of Spain, and obtained the means of equipping the little armament which discovered a new world.

Ptolemy's undetected error led to the discovery of America; the exposure of another of his mistakes was the chief cause of the first opening of a passage to India round the Cape of Good Hope. The ancient geographer asserted that Africa towards the south, extended its breadth westwards to some unknown and enormous distance. The Portuguese, on the contrary, as they pursued their discoveries along the western coast, not only refuted the prevalent opinion—that the country beyond the tropic of Cancer was uninhabitable on account of the excessive heat, but also found as they advanced, that the continent seemed to contract itself and tend towards the east. Following out this important observation, Bartholomew Diaz, in 1486, actually rounded the southern point of the African continent, but suffering severely by a tempest, he was compelled to return home, after having named the great promontory which he had passed, "The Cape of Storms." John II. King of Portugal, with a more just appreciation of the important discovery which had been made, commanded that it should be called "The Cape of Good Hope." His cousin and successor, Emmanuel, resolved to follow out the important discovery which Diaz had made, and on the 8th of July, 1497, an exploring expedition sailed from the Tagus for this purpose, under the command of Vasco de Gama. On the 22nd of the following May, the bold navigators reached the port of Calicut, on the coast of Malabar. After escaping many plots formed for his destruction by the Zamorin, or monarch of Calicut, Gama returned to Europe, after having freighted his ship with the commodities peculiar to the Malabar coast, and with many of the rich productions of the eastern parts of India.

The hopes and fears of all Europe were roused by this brilliant discovery; it was at once seen that the Venetians, and their agents the Moors, must lose their lucrative monopoly of Indian commerce, and they entered into a treaty with the Sultan of Egypt, to prevent the establishment of Portuguese settlements in the eastern seas. Timber was supplied to him from the forests in Dalmatia to equip a fleet in the Red Sea, where twelve ships of war were soon built, and manned by a gallant body of Mamelukes, under the command of experienced officers. The Portuguese encountered their new enemies with undaunted courage, and after some conflicts they entirely ruined the squadron, and remained masters of the Indian Ocean.

After the overthrow of the dynasty of the Mameluke Sultans

by the Turks, the Venetians easily induced the conquerors of Egypt to join them in a new league for the overthrow of the Portuguese power in India. But the Turks had not the skill and enterprize necessary for undertaking the perilous navigation of the Red Sea, and soon after the power of Venice was irretrievably ruined by the fatal league of Cambray. The Indian trade was consequently transferred from the Mediterranean Sea to the Atlantic Ocean; and Lisbon for a time was in possession of that commerce which had been the source of the wealth and of the glory of Venice.

CHAPTER V.

SKETCH OF THE HISTORY OF THE PORTUGUESE EMPIRE IN INDIA.

EMMANUEL, King of Portugal, was well aware that the Moors would soon make preparations to dispute with him the empire of the Indian Seas; they had indeed, from the first, exerted themselves to drive out the European intruders and menaced them with a formidable war. A fleet therefore of thirteen sail and fifteen hundred men, was fitted out for India, and the command of it given to an experienced officer, Pedro Alvarez de Cabral. His instructions were to enter into a treaty with the Zamorin, and obtain leave to build a fort in the vicinity of Calicut. On his voyage he was driven to the coast of South America, where he made the first discovery of Brazil; he lost several of his sloops in doubling the Cape, but still his forces appeared so imposing at Calicut, that the reluctant Zamorin deemed it prudent to conclude a commercial treaty with the Portuguese, and assign them a house for their factory in the city. Correa, with seventy men, took immediate position of this new acquisition.

Cabral's fleet was to be laden with spicery; the Moorish merchants used every effort to retard the collection of the freight, and in the mean time, the Zamorin requested the admiral to take for him a large vessel belonging to the king of Cochin, with whom he pretended to be at war. Aware of the great importance of producing an impression of European superiority, Cabral sent one of the smallest of his ships against this vessel. The Indians, exulting in their superiority of force, laughed the Portuguese to scorn, but when the battle had once begun, they were unable to endure the sustained fire of the European's guns and were brought in triumph into Calicut. This circumstance not only established the character of the Portuguese for bravery, but gave them a favourable opportunity to display their integrity and honour. When Cabral conversed with the captives, he found that he had been completely deceived by the Zamorin; he therefore restored the sloop to the King of Cochin, and paid for the damage she had sustained. Some other circumstances created dissensions between the new allies, until at length the Zamorin, instigated by the Moors, attacked the Portuguese factory and slaughtered Correa, with most of the garrison. Cabral immediately attacked the Moorish vessels in the harbour, ten of which he plundered and burned; he then bombarded Calicut, and after having slain six hundred of the inhabitants, forced the Zamorin to submit to the new conditions of peace. The intelligence of these events brought ambassadors to Cabral from all the neighbouring powers, and he entered into very close alliances with the rulers of Cochin and Cannanore. Having left factors at some of the principal ports, he returned to Europe, and brought Emmanuel such information, as shewed that there was a necessity for great and continued exertion, in order to establish a Portuguese empire in India.

The Portuguese monarch, in consequence of the information brought by Cabral, fitted out a fleet of twenty ships, the command of which was given to Vasco de Gama. On his arrival in India, Gama, disgusted with the treachery of the Zamorin, proceeded to trade with other states, upon which the sovereign of Calicut, sent out several armed cruizers, to intercept the Portuguese vessels; his ships, however, were all destroyed, and Gama returned home, having left a squadron to protect the ruler of Cochin, whose favours to the Europeans had provoked the resentment of the Zamorin of Calicut. Loche, who had been left in command of the squadron, abandoned his duty, in the hope of obtaining prizes in another quarter. The Zamorin advanced against Cochin, and captured the city. Fortunately, the death of Loche, left the fleet at liberty to return; the brothers Albuquerque arrived nearly at the same time, and Cochin was recovered for its former master.

The command of the Portuguese now devolved upon Pacheco, under whose guidance, the forces of the King of Cochin, though inferior in number, defeated the undisciplined hordes of Calicut in several engagements. But the papal bull, by which all the East was bestowed on the Portuguese, began now to produce its injurious effects. The Portuguese, claimed as matter of right, the submission of the native princes, while they were utterly unable to conceive how an old prelate residing in Rome, could acquire a claim to deprive them of the authority and independence which they had inherited from their ancestors. Almost every port now opposed the entrance of the Portuguese, and the cargo of almost every ship they loaded, was purchased with blood. It was at this time, that Albuquerque was placed at the head of the Portuguese in India, and entered on the career of victory, which has immortalized his name. One of his first visits, was to the island of Ormuz, an island barren by nature, but which commerce had raised to a temporary celebrity, such as has rarely been rivalled. The king of the island had prepared for defence and assembled an army, said to exceed thirty thousand men; yet these were totally defeated, by the discipline and skill of less than five hundred Europeans, and the King of Ormuz submitted to vassalage.

The foundation of the Portuguese empire in the East, may be said to date from the occupation of Goa, by Albuquerque. He fortified it in the best manner, so as to render it impregnable against any attack of the Hindús, or Mohammedans, and having thus discovered the great advantage to be derived from the occupation of cities and harbours, be began to direct his whole course of policy to territorial acquisitions. One of his first conquests was Malacca, and from this, to the island of Ormuz, the coast-line of India was studded with forts and commercial marts, occupied by Portuguese garrisons, or dependent on their power. The financial talents of the governor, were even greater than his military prowess; he raised the revenue by lowering the rate of duties, trade naturally flowing towards those places where it was least exposed to taxation and vexatious interference. After a brilliant regency of five years, he died at the entrance of the harbour of Goa, on his return from the island of Ormuz, which he had rescued from the dangers to which it was exposed by a sudden attack of the Persians. "The princes of India," says an eminent historian, "who viewed Albuquerque as their father, clothed themselves in mourning on his death, for they had experienced the happiness and protection which his friendship gave them. And the sincerity of their grief showed Emmanuel what a subject he had lost. He was buried at Goa, and it became customary for the Mohammedan and Gentoo inhabitants of that city, when injured by the Portuguese, to come and weep at his tomb, utter their complaints to his manes, and call upon his God to revenge their wrongs."*

Under Soarez, the successor of Albuquerque, a system of peculation and corruption was introduced; "the period," say the Portuguese authors, "commenced when the soldier no more followed the dictates of honour, when those who had been captains became traders, and rapacious plunderers of the innocent natives." Many quitted the military service, and became private adventurers; and many who yearly arrived from Portugal, in place of entering into the king's service, followed this example. The courts established by Albuquerque, were either corrupted, or without power, and the petty governor of every petty fort, was arbitrary in his own harbour. After a regency of three years, Soarez was recalled, he left the affairs of his government in a state of the greatest confusion, and the power of the Portuguese perceptibly on the decline: nor was the administration of his successor Sequeyra more beneficial; unmeaning slaughter on the coasts of Madagascar, the Red Sea, India and the Moluccas, comprise the whole history of his regency.

The death of King Emmanuel, produced a change in the Portuguese councils; one of the first acts of the new reign, was to remedy the disorders of India, and for this purpose the government of the Eastern colonies was entrusted to Vasco de Gama, who had been raised to the dignity of Count de Vidigueyra. Though a very old man, Gama displayed equal wisdom, zeal and activity. He delivered Cochin from a siege, with which it was menaced by the Zamorin; his detached squadrons cleared the seas of the Moorish pirates that infested them, and he made preparations for restoring the wise and liberal policy of Albuquerque. His death at the end of three months, soon followed by that of his successor Menezes, again threw affairs into confusion; Sampayo and Mascarene, paying little

* A little before his death, he wrote this manly letter to the King of Portugal. "Under the pangs of death, in the difficult breathing of the last hour, I write this my last letter to your highness; the last of many I have written to you, full of life, for I was then employed in your service. I have a son, Blas de Albuquerque; I entreat your highness to make him as great as my services deserve. The affairs of India will answer for themselves and for me."

attention to the edicts of the distant court of Lisbon, contested the office of chief governor by force of arms. The contest terminated in favour of the former; no sooner had he triumphed over his rival, than he entered on a career of sanguinary conquest, in the midst of which he was arrested by Nunio, who had been commissioned to supersede him, and was sent home a close prisoner to Lisbon.

Nunio soothed and relieved the wrongs of the various princes, whom his predecessors had injured; innocence and industry were again protected; prosperity began to revive. Taking advantage of the war between Bahader, Sultan of Gujarât and Húmayún, Emperor of Delhí, the Portuguese by a promise of aid to the sultan, obtained possession of Diu, which had been long the object of their ambition. When the war was over, Bahader wished to resume his gift, and a desultory war ensued. At length the sultan proposed that all differences should be arranged at a personal interview, to which the Portuguese commanders assented. Suspicions of treachery were entertained and were probably not unfounded at both sides; they led to a squabble in the boats, which ended in the murder of the sultan, whether by accident or by perfidy, it is now impossible to determine. Selim, the Turkish sultan, sent an immense armament to the relief of his Mohammedan brethren in India; Diu was closely invested, and the succours which Nunio had prepared for its relief, were delayed by Noronha, his unworthy successor. The desperate valour of the garrison daunted the Turks; even the women took arms; and the officers' ladies went from rampart to rampart, upbraiding the least appearance of languor. The Turks at length raised the siege, though there were not more than forty men, out of the original garrison of six hundred, who were in a condition to bear arms for the defence of the place.

Although Noronha had made no effort to relieve Diu, he profited by the impression which its brave defence had produced on the princes of India; several of them, including the Zamorin, entered into alliance with Portugal, and thus afforded the governor leisure for extending the limits of the colony in Ceylon. Noronha's administration was sullied by much cruelty and oppression, so that his death gave equal joy to the natives and the settlers.

Stephen de Gama, the son of the great Vasco, succeeded to

the administration, but before he could execute the beneficial plans he had framed, he was superseded by the infamous Souza, who annulled the wise edicts of Nunio, conceding toleration to all religions, and established a system of grinding persecution in the Portuguese dependencies. The temples of Malabar were laid in ashes, and thousands of the unhappy natives, for the crime of idolatry, were slaughtered upon their ruined altars. The Sultan of Gujarát, aided by large bodies of Turkish and Moorish auxiliaries, again laid seige to Diu; the city was as bravely defended as it had been on the former occasion, but it would most probably have fallen, had not the gallant John de Castro, been sent to take the place of the imbecile Souza. Castro not only relieved Diu, but he attacked the enemy in their fortified trenches and routed them with great slaughter. He then carried the war into the hostile country, and so humbled the monarchs of Gujarát and the Dekkan, that they were glad to submit to the terms of peace dictated by the conqueror. The civil government of Castro, merited even greater praise than his military exploits; under his sway, justice was fairly administered and commerce protected, so that Camoens was justified in saying,

> " O'er Indus' banks, o'er Ganges' smiling vales,
> No more the hind his plunder'd field bewails:
> O'er every field, O Peace, thy blossoms glow,
> The golden blossoms of thy olive bough;
> Firm based on wisdom's laws great Castro crowns,
> And the wide East the Lusian empire owns."

Under the administration of Castro, the Portuguese settlements in India touched the highest point of all their greatness. He was succeeded by Gabriel de Sa, whose brief rule is chiefly remarkable for the establishment of the Jesuit missions in the East, under St. Francis Xavier. The Jesuit was very superficial as an apostle; he required from his converts little or no knowledge of the Christian principles; he baptized them, gave them crucifixes to worship, and then told them that they were sure of heaven. Nothing of course could be easier than such conversion, and the many thousands who, on his preaching, assumed the Christian faith, displayed a success which his admirers deemed miraculous. But as a politician, Xavier was far more minute and comprehensive, than as a missionary. Every offer of religious instruction which he made, was attended with the most flattering proposals of alliances;—of alliancies, however, which were calculated to render the natives dependent on the Portuguese, and in fact mere tributaries. In this plan of operations, the great abilities of Xavier were crowned with rapid success. kings and kingdoms, won by his preaching, sued for the friendship of the Portuguese. But while the olive of peace seemed ready to spread its boughs over India, the unrelenting villany of the Portuguese soldiers and merchants, counteracted the labours of Xavier, and several of the newly baptised princes, in resentment of the injuries they received, returned to paganism and hostility. Xavier, who acted as a spy upon the military and civil government of India, not only from time to time laid these abuses before the king of Portugal, but also interested himself greatly, both in the civil and military councils of Portuguese India. He was the intimate friend and counsellor of the great Castro, and his political efforts were only baffled by the hardened corruption of the Portuguese manners.

A series of petty wars, under different governors, followed the death of Castro, but produced no event of marked interest or importance, until the misconduct of Mesquita provoked one of the most desperate insurrections that ever occurred in India. Mesquita, was sent to obtain satisfaction for an insult offered to a Portuguese ship; he scoured the coast of Malabar, seized all the native vessels he could find, and murdered the crews, generally sewing them up in their own sail-cloths, and hurling them into the sea. A woman of rank, whose husband had been among Mesquita's victims, went from place to place among her countrymen, exhorting them to revenge; they flew to arms, vowing never to relax in their efforts, until they had extirpated the Portuguese; a body of the insurgents beset the fort of Cannanore and burned above thirty ships that lay at anchor under its cannon. The natives of Ceylon were driven to arms by similar outrages, and the people of Amboyna, expelled the Portuguese from the island. In the midst of these perilous wars, the death of Don Sebastian, king of Portugal, enabled Phillip II. to annex that country to Spain. This change aggravated the evils of the Indian colonies; so horrible were the cruelties practised by the Inquisition of Goa, that many of the native Christians joined the Pagans and Mohammedans; through the influence of the Jesuits, a bull was obtained, sanctioning a crusade against the infidels, and the subordinate governors were permitted to send out piratical expeditions, to plunder neutral and even allied states.

Houtman, a Dutch merchant, while confined for debt in the jail of Lisbon, acquired some valuable information respecting India; he sent an account of it to his countrymen, then engaged in their glorious struggle against the tyranny of Spain; a subscription was made to pay his debts, and on his return to Holland, the Dutch East India Company was formed. The first appearance of a Dutch fleet in the Indian Seas, gave as much alarm to the Portuguese, as their own arrival had to the Moors; no art was left untried by the Jesuits, to stimulate the Hindús against the Dutch intruders, but the name of the Portuguese was detested in the East, and the machinations of the Jesuits recoiled on their own heads. The English soon appeared, to claim a share in the lucrative commerce of India, where they erected several factories, and the Portuguese became every day less able to compete with their enterprising rivals. The English were however fettered in their operations, by the senseless policy of their imbecile monarch, James I., who was not inaptly described as "the wisest fool in Europe;" he sacrificed the interests of his own subjects, to conciliate the court of Spain. But the Hollanders, who were under a better government, defied the powers of King Phillip; they gained nearly the whole of the spice trade, and annually interrupted the Portuguese commerce with China. To complete the ruin of the Portuguese colonies, an order was sent from the court of Madrid, to the governor-general Agevedo, commanding him to dispose of every employment and office, civil or military, by public sale, in order that money might be raised to support his government. Shipwrecks and dreadful tempests added to the miseries of the Portuguese, and the most remarkable events of the government of the Count de Redondo, who in 1617 superseded Agevedo, were the solemn fasts held at Goa. In some of these, the citizens lay day and night on the floors of the churches, imploring the divine mercy, in the deepest and most awful silence, while not a sound was to be heard in the mournful streets.

In 1632, under the viceroyalty of the Count de Linarez, "our European enemies," says the Portuguese historian, "roved over the seas without opposition, took away many of our ships, and ruined our trade. They also every where incensed the Indian princes against us; for we had no agents at any of their courts to vindicate our cause." Yet, deep as such declension appears, Linarez, on his return to Europe, presented the king of Spain with a hat-band, and the queen with a pair of pendants, valued at one hundred thousand crowns. In 1632, while the Archbishop of Goa was governor, a squadron of nine Dutch vessels rode triumphant in the river of Goa, and burned three galleons in the harbour without opposition; " for the first, " says Feria, " was destitute of both ammunition and men." In 1640, the kingdom of Portugal, by one of the noblest efforts on record, threw off the yoke of Spain, and the Portuguese in India acknowledged the Duke of Braganza as their sovereign. And in 1642, a viceroy was sent to India, by John IV., but though the new monarch paid attention to India, and though the English during their civil wars abandoned the commerce of the east, the Dutch were now so formidable, and their operations so well connected and continued, that every exertion to recover the dominion of India, was fruitless and lost. Soon after the civil wars the English arose to more power and consequence, than even the Dutch in India, and many of the Portuguese became their agents and naval carriers. Towards the end of the seventeenth century, the court of India turned its attention to the Brazils and neglected India. A succession of viceroys was however continued ; but all their numerous settlements on every coast of the eastern world, the ports of Goa and Diu in India and the Isle of Macao in the Bay of Canton, alone remained in possession of the Portuguese. Such was the fall of that power, which once commanded the commerce of Africa and Asia, from the Straits of Gibraltar, to the eastern side of Japan!

Religious intolerance and commercial exclusiveness, combined to overthrow this great empire, and though there is no apparent connexion between freedom of conscience and freedom of trade, it is very common to find them united in history. The Inquisition at Goa was one of the most flagrant exhibitions of bigoted cruelty that ever disgraced a nation, and its ruins, which still exist, contain memorials of its savage barbarities, which fill the minds of visitors with horror. The Portuguese still retain Goa and Macao, but the trade of both has fallen into utter and hopeless insignificance.

CHAPTER VI.

COMMENCEMENT OF INTERCOURSE BETWEEN GREAT BRITAIN AND INDIA.

Soon after the termination of the Wars of the Roses, and the restoration of national tranquillity under the Tudors, the English people began to manifest the spirit of maritime discovery, commercial enterprize, and adventurous colonization, which they had inherited from their Saxon ancestors. This spirit had long been suppressed by the Norman aristocracy, alien to England in lineage, language and feeling; but in the sanguinary struggle between the rival divisions of the Plantagenet family, the Norman nobles had wasted their resources, thinned their ranks, and lost their exclusive possession of political power. Families of Saxon descent began to be raised to the peerage; the forfeiture of monastic lands enabled Henry VIII. to endow the new nobility with estates, and other branches of the same families, emulous of their greatness, sought a road to fame and fortune in the paths which the discoveries of Columbus and Gama had opened to boldness and enterprize. Among all the navigators and adventurers who suddenly appeared under the Tudors, there was scarcely one who could claim affinity with the old Norman nobility; nearly all of them belonged to the class of country gentlemen, the descendants of the Saxon Franklins, men who preferred the paths of honourable industry to the gilded profligacy, which had usurped the name of chivalry.

Previous to the accession of Elizabeth, this country was supplied with Indian commodities from Venice, by an annual ship of great value, and as the Venetians could then charge what price they pleased, the commerce was any thing but lucrative to England. The shipwreck of a rich Venetian carrack, on the Isle of Wight, excited the English merchants and mariners to attempt obtaining a share of the lucrative commerce of the East. Sir William Monson, who witnessed the loss of the vessel, appears to have taken an active part in urging the people of London to attempt to rival the Venetians, and he found the citizens very ready to second his attempts. "They devised," he says, "how such commodities may come into our hands by a more direct way, than to be served as we were at second-hand ; and therefore resolved to make an overture, by favour of the Queen and her letters, to the Great Turk, for an immediate traffic from England to Turkey, and his dominions, and so thence again, with ships of her own subjects, without being beholden to them (the Venetians.) These letters were sent by her Majesty, and received with great humanity and courtesy by the Grand Seignor, as appears by his letters yet extant. In conclusion, the articles were agreed upon, and a grant of great privileges and immunities to her majesty's subjects, which have since continued and been peaceably enjoyed." Thus the first trade between England and India was opened through the Levant, and the Turkey merchants were regarded as the true East India traders.*

A London merchant, named Thorne, who had long resided in Seville, and acquired an extensive knowledge of the East India trade, on his return to England, represented to Henry VIII. the great advantages which the country might derive from Eastern commerce, and suggested that it would be possible to discover a new passage by the north-east or north-west to the Indian Seas, and avoid the tedious navigation round Cape Horn or the Cape of Good Hope. In 1576, some merchants of London, hoping to reap the benefits of this discovery, fitted out two ships under Captain Forbisher, who made three vigorous attempts to effect this passage, but failed as all his successors have done. Sir Francis Drake, on returning from his voyage round the world, gave it as his opinion that the route which Thorne had suggested

* It appears from Hackluyt, that there was a very considerable trade to the Levant in English bottoms, between the years 1512 and 1534. He tells us that several stout ships from London, Southampton, and Bristol, had a constant trade to Candia, China, Cyprus, and Beiroot in Syria. Our imports were silks, camlets, rhubarb, malmsies, muscadels, and other wines; sweet oil, cotton goods, carpets, gall, cinnamon and other spices. Our exports were fine and coarse kerseys, white western dogans, cloths, called statutes, and others called cardinal whites, skins and leather. From a cotemporary document it appears that in this early day Manchester had already acquired some fame as a manufacturing town, particularly for the production of certain woollen cloths, which, singularly enough, were called *cottons*, a corruption of "coatings."

was impracticable. Captain Stephens went from England to the Cape of Good Hope in 1582, and sent home a very full account of his voyage from Goa. Further information was obtained from Ralph Fitch, a merchant of London, who had reached India by a different route. This gentleman, who appears to have been engaged in the Levant trade, travelled from Tripoli in Syria to Ormuz, and thence to Goa. After a short residence amongst the Portuguese, he sailed to Bengal, Pegu, Siam and Molucca, visiting the island of Ceylon, and the cities of Cochin and Calicut; he then returned to Ormuz, whence he proceeded overland to Tripoli, where embarking, he reached England A.D. 1591. The route, however, was still considered precarious until the famous Cavendish opened a certain passage to the East, in his voyage round the world, A. D. 1587. Cavendish was a young man of fortune, who had wasted his property by a life of fashionable extravagance, and hoped to retrieve it by a voyage to the southern seas. He sailed from England, in 1586, with three small ships equipped at his own expense. After having touched at Sierra Leone and the Cape de Verd Islands, he steered for the Straits of Magellan, through which he passed in the January of 1587. Having coasted for some months along the western side of America, he crossed the Pacific to the Indian Archipelago, visited several of the islands and returned by the Cape of Good Hope to England, where he arrived in September, 1588. This voyage was highly instrumental in forwarding the Queen's design of opening a direct trade with the East Indies; the merchants of London were so impressed with the importance of the information communicated by Cavendish, that they formed themselves into a trading company, and applied to the Queen for a charter. Their request was granted, and in December, 1600, the merchant adventurers were incorporated under the title of "The Governor and Company of Merchants of London, trading to the East Indies."*

In this charter, the first governor, Thomas Smythe, and twenty-four directors, were nominated by the crown, but power was vested in the company of proprietors to elect a deputy governor, and also a governor and other members for the future. The

* The subscriptions or shares in this company were at first only £50 each, and the original capital £369,891. 5*s*. In 1676, this capital was doubled by adding the profits to the stock.

privileges granted to them, their successors, their sons on attaining their legal majority, their apprentices, factors and servants who had been employed by the company for fifteen years, are thus stated in the original charter, "freely to traffic and use the trade of merchandise by sea, in and by such ways and passages already discovered or hereafter to be discovered, as they should esteem and take to be fittest, unto and from the East Indies, unto the countries and ports of Asia and Africa, and unto and from all the islands, ports, havens, cities, creeks, rivers and places of Asia, Africa, and America, or any of them, beyond the Cape of Good Hope to the Strait of Magellan, where any trade or traffic may be used, to or from every of them, in such order, manner, form, liberty and condition, as they themselves should from time to time agree upon and determine." They were further empowered to make bye-laws; to inflict punishments either corporal or pecuniary, provided that such punishments did not contravene the laws of England, to export goods free of duty, and afterwards to be allowed a drawback of duty on all exported goods which might be lost on the passage, or so injured as to become unsaleable.

The country had at this time made so much progress in the science of political economy, that doubts were entertained of the prudence of creating new monopolies, and Elizabeth was afraid that the exclusive privileges granted to the new company might be unpopular, and perhaps prejudicial to trade; she therefore inserted a proviso, that if within the space limited by the charter, this monopoly should appear in any respect detrimental to the public, it should then upon two years' warning under the privy seal, become null and void. But if experience proved that this new corporation promoted the weal and benefit of the nation, her majesty pledged her royal word, that she would not only renew the charter, but add such other clauses and graces, as should appear most conducive to the interest of the commerce, the undertakers, and the general advantage of the kingdom.

Five ships under the command of Captain Lancaster, were sent out by the new company; they reached the roads of Achen on the 5th of June, 1602. A commercial treaty was concluded with the king of the country on equitable terms, after which, in order to complete their cargo, the little squadron proceeded to Java. Another commercial treaty was concluded with the king of Bantam, after which the ships returned home, having made a most profitable voyage. This success led to several other voyages, which were generally attended by the same prosperous results.

The rivals of the English were the Portuguese and the Dutch; both nations had established forts and factories along the coast, and had made extensive territorial acquisitions, from which they most carefully excluded all foreign traders. The English company felt this disadvantage very severely, especially as the Dutch equipped armed vessels to attack the English shipping; the Portuguese adopted the same course of policy, and the Company was forced to send larger vessels well armed into the Indian Seas. Sir Henry Middleton was attacked by the Portuguese with a very superior force off Surat, but he inflicted on them a very severe defeat, to the surprise and pleasure of the Indian princes, who had hitherto believed the Portuguese invincible. A second victory over the same jealous foes was obtained by Captain Best, whose valour was reported to the Emperor of Delhí, and produced a most favourable impression on his court.

The governor of the Company wisely resolved to take advantage of these propitious events. In consequence of his application, Sir Thomas Roe was sent as ambassador to the court of Delhí, and nearly at the same time the Shirleys appeared as English envoys in Persia. Several factories were erected and some settlements formed, to the great annoyance of the Dutch, who were firmly resolved to prevent any interference with their lucrative monopoly of the spice trade. Negociations were commenced in Europe to prevent any collision between the Hollanders and the English; but James I. who wanted money to gratify his rapacious and unprincipled favourites, deliberately sacrificed the rights of his subjects and the best interests of the nation over which he unworthily ruled, to the bribes that were offered him by the merchants of Amsterdam.

Although in a great measure deserted by their government, the English under many disadvantages bravely maintained their ground, and at length a treaty was concluded between the East India Companies of England and Holland. Such, however, was the confidence of the Dutch in the mercenary stupidity of the English monarch, that the negociations had been scarcely concluded when every article of the treaty was atrociously violated. At length, under the pretence that the English had stimulated the natives to insurrection, all the Company's agents in Amboyna were arrested, and subjected to the most horrible tortures in order to force them to confession. They were then put to death in the most barbarous manner, and their destruction was followed by a series of public rejoicings and thanksgivings.

When the intelligence of these atrocities arrived in Europe, the indignation of the English was extreme; even James was roused to bestow heavy maledictions on the authors of such cruelties, but his wrath ended in execrations. His successor, Charles I., shewed himself more alive to the honour of the nation, but having been involved at the very commencement of his reign in a struggle with his own subjects, he had not leisure to bestow any attention on foreign affairs. The English trade with India rapidly declined, until the termination of the great civil war, when Oliver Cromwell, who with all his faults possessed a true English spirit, having declared war against the Dutch, so completely humbled them, that they were forced to submit to the terms of peace which he dictated. One of the articles in the treaty concluded April 5th, 1654, was in the following terms, "that the Lords the States General of the United Provinces, shall take care that justice be done upon those who are partakers and accomplices in the massacre of the English at Amboyna, as the Republic of England is pleased to term that fact, provided any of them be living." In consequence of this stipulation the Dutch had to pay a compensation of £82,000 to the English East India Company, and also to give large sums to the families of their victims.

Charles II. on his restoration confirmed and extended the privileges of the Company, and futhermore ceded to them the Island of Bombay, which formed part of the dowry he received on his marriage with the Princess of Portugal. In consequence of the improved aspect of their affairs, the English merchants resolved to attempt the recovery of Bantam, which had been wrested from them by the Dutch. An armament was prepared for that purpose, but when it was on the point of sailing, the Dutch offered a large bribe to the weak and profligate Charles II. who laid an embargo upon the expedition, and finally prohibited the enterprise altogether. Thus were the interests and honour of the kingdom, the rights of a chartered company, and the plighted faith of a government bartered by this mercenary sovereign, for the means of gratifying the rapacity of his minions and his mistresses.

James II., the last of the Stuarts, was the best of the line, so far as trade and commerce were concerned. He afforded every encouragement to the Company, and gave them additional administrative powers. But unfortunately their prosperity was greatly injured by one of their own servants, Sir John Child, Governor of Bombay, whose fraud, ambition, and tyranny brought the settlement to the very verge of ruin. His folly led him to provoke a war with the Emperor of Delhí, who sent a considerable force to attack Bombay. Child's cowardice was as conspicuous as any of his other qualities, and the fort must have fallen, had not his seasonable death relieved the garrison from the greatest of dangers, an imbecile and treacherous commander. On Child's death, the emperor, Aureng-zib, consented to make peace, and granted more favourable terms than the English had a right to expect. Child's successors were little better than himself; so great were their profligacy and rapacity, that from being a populous place, Bombay was almost rendered a desert; it would most probably have been abandoned altogether if the Company's servants could have found means of escaping from the insolence and oppression of their governors by returning to England; but this favour was refused them, and they were detained by their tyrants without a glimmering of hope.

In consequence of this misgovernment abroad, and the peculation introduced by Sir Josiah Child into the management at home, the Company's affairs fell into sad confusion, and the merchants of London proposed either to throw open the trade with India and China, or to form a new commercial association on a wider basis. The matter was brought before the convention parliament, which was assembled on the abdication of James II., and formed one of the many useful projects which the authors of the revolution sacrificed to base and mercenary motives. The directors of the Company found the patriots and statesmen of the day ready to break their pledges to the nation for a share in the wages of iniquity; perhaps, indeed, there never was a parliament in which purity was more loudly professed, and venality more extensively practised, than in that which conferred the crown upon William III. Bribes deferred the danger by which the Company was threatened for three years, but at length the increasing discontent of the commercial and mercantile interests, compelled the House of Commons to interfere, and an address was presented to the King, praying that the Company might be dissolved and its charter revoked. William referred the matter to his privy council, the directors lavishly distributed bribes among its members, and an order for renewing and extending the charter was obtained. The House of Commons had under discussion a bill for imposing taxes on several joint stocks; they inserted a clause, that any company not paying the tax within a specified time, should forfeit its charter. The East India directors were so infatuated as to neglect the first quarterly payment, whereby their charter became void, and new arguments for dissolving the Company were furnished to their adversaries.

The matter was again referred to the privy council; on the one side were the petitions from the merchants of London and the manufacturers of the west of England, on the other were the ready bribes of the directors, and the latter of course prevailed. Great were the astonishment and indignation of the public; the task of enquiry was forced upon the House of Commons, and it appeared from the books of the Company that the sum expended for secret services in one year had amounted to about one hundred thousand pounds, which was confessed to have been spent in "gratifications." It is mortifying to add that the parliamentary investigations stopped at this point; a further prosecution of it would have involved many persons of the highest rank and influence, including the most flaming patriots of the day. The necessities of the government rendered it necessary to raise a loan of two millions; a new association of merchants offered to procure that sum, and in consequence they obtained a charter by which they were incorporated as a New East India Company. The two companies spent a few years in mutual attempts to damage each other, but they soon found that their common interests were thus injured, and they at length formed a coalition. Little attention was now paid to East India affairs; the nation was involved in an arduous war with France, to restrain the unprincipled ambition of Louis XIV., and the readiness with which the united Company negociated loans, recommended them so strongly to the ministry and the parliament, that very large additions were made to their privileges.

From the union of the two Companies in 1708, a great change

was wrought in the management of East India affairs. The courts of directors and proprietors were regularly constituted, and their respective duties and relations clearly defined. In 1726, a charter was granted, by which the Company were permitted to establish a Mayor's Court at each of the three presidencies they had created in India, Madras, Bombay, and Calcutta, consisting of a mayor and nine aldermen, empowered to decide in civil cases of all descriptions; criminal jurisdiction over every offence, except high treason, was given to the court of quarter sessions; and the president and council were erected into a court of appeal. In 1753 this charter was extended, and the authority of European courts finally established.

The revolutions which followed the death of Aureng-zib opened many favourable opportunities for the extension of the Company's power in India. In 1715, an embassy was sent to the court of Delhí to procure additional privileges and protection, and in pursuance of advice received in Calcutta, the envoys gained the favour of Khan Dowran, a nobleman high in the confidence of the emperor, but, unfortunately for that very reason, an object of suspicion to the powerful vizier, Jaffier Khan. As the vizier was also viceroy of Bengal, he looked with a very unfavourable eye on the requests of the English, and it appeared probable that the objects of the embassy would be defeated. At this crisis, the emperor was attacked by a painful disease, which delayed the marriage he was anxious to conclude with the daughter of the Rájá of Jodpore; he was advised to make trial of the skill of a medical gentleman named Hamilton, who had accompanied the English embassy, and under his judicious treatment the emperor's health was soon restored. The grateful monarch desired his restorer to name his reward; Hamilton requested that the privileges solicited by the Company, including freedom of trade and some grants of territory, should be conceded. After some delay, the boon was granted; but the vizier contrived for a considerable time to prevent the Company from profiting by the imperial permission to purchase the villages round Calcutta.

It was about the year 1720 that the French trade with the East Indies become so important as to attract notice, and from that time the English began to look with great jealousy on the flourishing colony of Pondicherry, which their rivals had established on the Coromandel coast. When war was declared between France and England, in 1743, Lord Carteret, who had then the principal management of public affairs, proposed that a squadron should be sent to the East Indies. Three ships of the line and a frigate, were accordingly despatched under the command of Commodore Barnet, who took several rich prizes. The French East India Company proposed that a neutrality should be established in the Indian Seas, but when their terms were rejected by the English, they made the most vigorous preparations to defend their interests, selecting for their commander Labourdonnais, an admiral of high reputation. By the death of Commodore Barnet, the command of the English squadron devolved on Captain Peyton, who wanted both the courage and the skill necessary for such an enterprize. After an indecisive engagement, he fled from the Southern Sea to the Bay of Bengal, abandoning Madras, which was in a scandalously defenceless condition, to the mercy of the enemy.

Labourdonnais made immediate preparations for the attack of this important settlement. On the 14th of September, 1746, he effected a landing about twenty miles south of Madras, and protected by his fleet, which accompanied the march of the army along the coast, advanced to invest the town. Madras was badly garrisoned, and worse defended. After a siege of less than a week, the place capitulated, Labourdonnais stipulating that it should be restored on the payment of a ransom, but this condition was not ratified by the Governor of Pondicherry. Labourdonnais behaved so generously to his prisoners, that at the conclusion of the war, a large present was voted to him by the East India Company. On his return to Europe he was captured by an English cruizer, but his conduct at Madras was remembered; all ranks vied with each other in shewing him respect, and he was liberated by the government on his simple parole. It is melancholy to add, that on his return to France, he was thrown into the Bastile, and detained a prisoner for three years by the machinations of his enemies. His merits, however, were finally established, but the unmerited treatment he received so weakened his mind and body that he did not long survive his liberation.

Admiral Boscawen having arrived with a strong reinforcement to the English, it was resolved to undertake the siege of Pondicherry. Few enterprises have been worse constructed; time was wasted when every moment was valuable; the trenches were opened at a distance from the walls, which rendered the fire of the besiegers ineffectual; finally, the approach of the rainy season rendered it impossible for the army to keep the field, or the fleet to remain on the coast, and Boscawen at length retired, after having suffered a very severe loss in men and stores. Before his efforts could be renewed, intelligence was received of peace having been concluded between France and England at Aix-la-Chapelle; but Boscawen seemed to be still pursued by misfortune; several ships, and about twelve hundred seamen, perished miserably in a storm on the coast of Coromandel.

The peace of Aix-la-Chapelle was little better than a hollow truce in Europe, but in India it scarcely interrupted the operations of war. A passion for territorial acquisitions appears to have seized the French and English Companies simultaneously, and each prepared to take advantage of the political revolutions so common in all oriental governments, to extend their dominions by hiring out their aid to rival competitors. The English were the first to draw the sword, and from no higher inducement than the promise of a trifling fort belonging to the Rájá of Tanjore, on the Coromandel coast. Tanjore was one of the petty kingdoms, into which the Mohammedans found the country divided when they first invaded India; it occupied little more than the space enclosed and intersected by the numerous mouths of the Cavery, being about seventy miles in length, with the same extent of breadth. After several revolutions, it was seized by the brother of Sivajee, the celebrated founder of the Mahratta empire, who bequeathed the throne to his posterity. Sahujee, one of his descendants, was dethroned, in 1741, by his chief minister, who transferred the title of king to Prataup Sing, notwithstanding the stain of illegitimacy attached to his birth. The new monarch reigned quietly for several years, and the English rulers at Madras not only recognized his title, but entered into amicable correspondence with him, and solicited his co-operation against the French. In 1749, the dethroned Sahujee presented himself at Fort St. David, soliciting aid for the recovery of his dominions, promising to reward the assistance of his allies by the cession of the fort of Devi-Cotah, and declaring that many, if not most, of his subjects were ready to take arms in his favour. It was supposed that Coleroon, the northern branch of the Cavery, on which Devi-Cotah stands, would afford the advantage of an excellent harbour, and it was therefore resolved to accept Sahujee's offer. A force of one hundred Europeans and five hundred sepoys was sent under the command of Captain Cope, to take possession of Devi-Cotah, and support any party which might be formed in favour of Sahujee. Artillery and provisions were ordered to be sent round by sea.

Cope experienced no impediment until he had passed the Coleroon, and entered a difficult country covered with wood and jungle. His forces suffered severely from ambuscades of the Tanjorines, and when he came in sight of Devi-Cotah, he was unable to procure any intelligence of the ships, though they were then anchored only four miles off, at the mouth of the river. After having thrown a few shells into the place, the English disgracefully retired; they had found no party formed in favour of Sahujee, and, indeed, they do not appear to have taken the trouble of enquiring whether any such was in existence.

A second expedition was sent out from Madras, under the command of Major Lawrence, to retrieve Cope's disgrace. In this army there was a young lieutenant, named Clive, destined to achieve for himself the most memorable character in the annals of British India, who had been at first employed in the civil service, but had taken the earliest opportunity of exchanging the pen for the sword. Lawrence, who was a shrewd judge of merit, appreciated the talents of this young officer, and often consulted him in the difficulties of the expedition, which were neither few nor trifling. The armament proceeded by sea, a landing was effected on the side of the river opposite to Devi-Cotah, the ground of the bank where the fort stood being so marshy that it would have been impossible to erect breaching batteries on it. Three days after the fire of the artillery had opened, a practicable breach was effected, and preparations for storming were made. It was however necessary to cross the river, a work of some difficulty, for the stream was both wide and rapid, besides which the Tanjorines kept up a smart fire from the thickets which lined the opposite shore. A ship's carpenter, named John Moore, suggested the means for overcoming these difficulties; a raft was constructed sufficient to convey four hundred men, and Moore swam across the river at night, and fastened a rope to a tree, by which it could be pulled across. Having secured the rope and carefully concealed it in the water and bushes, he returned undetected. Before the raft began to move, some pieces of artillery were brought to bear on the part of the bank to which the rope was fixed, which compelled the Tanjorines to remove to some distance. The first detachment having passed over in safety, the transport of the remainder was easy. Major Lawrence resolved to storm immediately, and Clive volunteered to lead the attack. He advanced with a platoon of Europeans and seven hundred sepoys, but rashly allowing himself and the platoon to be separated from the sepoys, he narrowly escaped with his life, and the platoon was all but annihilated. Major Lawrence advanced with his whole force, the soldiers mounted the breach, and after a feeble resistance took possession of the place. A little enquiry showed that there was no hope for Sahujee in Tanjore; an accommodation was therefore made with Prataup Sing, and the English not only abandoned the legitimate monarch, but agreed to detain him prisoner, to prevent his giving any further molestation to the reigning sovereign. It is even asserted that but for the humanity of Boscawen, he would have been delivered into the hands of Prataup Sing.

In the meantime, the French East India Company had engaged in transactions of still higher moment, and a great revolution was accomplished in the Carnatic. The Carnatic is the name given to an extensive district stretching along the Coromandel coast, from the little river Gundigania to the mouths of the Cavery; to this was sometimes added the range of country between the northern branch of the Cavery and Cape Comorin, but this was usually distinguished as the Southern Carnatic. In extending westward from the coast, the Carnatic includes every variety, both of soil and scenery, which is to be met on the great continent of India; that part between the first range of mountains and the sea, was called the Carnatic below the Ghauts; the western district, between the first and second range of mountains, was called Canara or the Carnatic above the Ghauts. When southern India was annexed to the empire of Delhí, the Carnatic was included in the great Subah or vice-royalty of the Dekkan, governed by the Nizam; the great extent of the Dekkan rendered the governors of districts, under the Nizam, persons of great power and influence; they were called nabobs or deputies, and were not unfrequently rivals of the viceroy. When Nizam-al-Mulk was appointed Viceroy of the Dekkan, a chief named Sadatulla was Nabob of the Carnatic, and retained his situation under the Nizam until his death in 1732. Sadatulla's nephew and adopted son, Dost Alí, then seized the nabobship without waiting for the sanction of the viceroy, and to strengthen himself in this position gave his four daughters in marriage to different chiefs, remarkable for their rank and power. One of these, Chanda Sahib, was appointed Dewan, or chief minister of finance to his father-in-law; under pretence of collecting the arrears of the revenue he marched to Trichinopoly, a tributary state governed by a native Hindu. Chanda Sahib's real object was to take advantage of a disputed succession; the Rájá of Trichinopoly died in 1736, leaving a child to succeed him, whose mother exercised the sovereignty under the title of regent. She had to maintain a doubtful struggle against a competitor for the principality, and she therefore cheerfully accepted the proffered aid of Chanda Sahib, which ensured her the victory. Grateful for his support and confiding in his friendship, the princess gave Chanda Sahib free access to the citadel; he abused her confidence by making himself treacherously master of the fortress, and throwing the princess into prison, where she died of grief. Dost Alí rewarded this perfidy by investing his son-in-law with the principality of Trichinopoly.

This ambitious treachery greatly alarmed the Hindu Rájás; they applied to the Mahrattas, as a people of the same origin and religion, to march to their assistance, taking advantage of the struggles in Northern India, which engaged the attention of the Nizam too effectually to allow of his giving any assistance to his feudatory, the Nabob of the Carnatic. A Mahratta army, commanded by Ragojee Bonslah, advanced to the frontiers of the Carnatic in the month of May, 1740. The passes of the mountains might easily have been defended, but a Hindu officer betrayed an important post, and left a free opening to the Mahrattas. Dost Alí then resolved to hazard an engagement; he was defeated and slain; his son, Safder Alí, who was envious of Chanda Sahib, immediately entered into negotiations, paying them a large sum of money, and promising to offer no impediment to their seizure of Trichinopoly. After some delay the Mahrattas invested that city; Chanda Sahib defended himself gallantly for several months, but was finally forced to surrender, and was sent prisoner to Satarah. Fortunately, he had previously secured the safety of his family by sending them to the French settlement at Pondicherry, where they were most kindly treated by the prudent Governor, M. Dupleix, who foresaw that a time would come when he might avail himself of the grateful services of Chanda Sahib.

The descendants of Dost Alí filled the Carnatic with all the confusions of war, murder and assassination, the usual accompaniments of a disputed succession, whether small or great, in Asia. Nizam al Mulk, on his return from Delhí, resolved to arrange the troubled affairs of the Carnatic; and, after several changes conferred the nabobship on Anwar-ed-din Khan, but nominally as regent for the rightful heir, who was a minor. In a short time, however, the young nabob was murdered by a band of Patan soldiers, as the Afghan mercenaries were usually called, who clamoured for arrears of pay due to them, or pretended to be due to them, by his father. It was generally believed that this murder was instigated by Anwar-ed-din, which, combined with the oppressive nature of his government, rendered the people of the Carnatic anxious that he should be dethroned, and the line of Sadatulla restored in the person of Chanda Sahib. M. Dupleix zealously seconded the same course of policy; he corresponded with Chanda Sahib in his captivity, and advanced a considerable portion of the sum which the Mahrattas demanded for his ransom. On being liberated, in 1748, Chanda Sahib raised a body of partisan troops and entered into the quarrels of the petty Rájás between the coasts of Malabar and Coromandel; by this means he collected some treasure and greatly increased his followers, so that at the death of Nizam al Mulk, in 1749, he was at the head of an army of 6,000 men.

Nizam al Mulk was succeeded in the viceroyalty of the Dekkan by his second son, Nazir-Jing, but as he had been in open rebellion against his father, it was affirmed that the Nizam had bequeathed his dominions to a favourite grandson, Murzafa Jing, and, after a brief parade of negociations, an appeal was made to arms. Chanda Sahib immediately tendered his services to Mirzafa Jing, and persuaded him to unite in commencing their operations in the Carnatic, where the memory and interest of the family of Sadatulla would afford them immense advantages.

Dupleix entered into the views of the aspiring chiefs, and supplied them with a valuable auxiliary force. Thus strengthened, they marched against Anwar-ed-din, who had posted himself in an entrenched camp under the fortress of Amhoor. The French offered to storm the entrenchment, and though twice beaten back, at length succeeded in forcing an entrance. Anwar-ed-din, who had attained the uncommon age of one hundred and seven, fell in the engagement; his eldest son was taken prisoner, and his second son, Mohammed Alí, fled with the wreck of the army to Trichinopoly, of which he was governor.

Had the victorious leaders followed up their advantages, and at once advanced against Trichinopoly, that city must have fallen, and the war would have been at an end. They, however, proceeded to Arcot, to make an idle parade of sovereignty, after which they visited Pondicherry, and rewarded the French for their efficient aid by bestowing upon them eighty-one villages in the neighbourhood of that settlement.

So much time was wasted at Pondicherry, that Nazir Jing had time to collect a numerous force and to effect a junction with Mohammed Ali, the governor of Trichinopoly, and a small body of English auxiliaries, under the command of Major Lawrence. The hostile armies were in sight of each other, when thirteen of the French officers, displeased that they had not shared in the expected plunder of Tanjore, the siege of which had been raised by their allies on the approach of Nazir Jing, resigned their commissions, and thus created terror and alarm in the troops they had been destined to command. D'Auteuil, the French commander, immediately commenced his march homewards, leaving his allies in a state of the utmost confusion: Murzafa Jing surrendered to his uncle, by whom he was thrown into chains; Chanda Sahib, with his own troops, made his escape to Pondicherry.

Dupleix did not despair; he was well acquainted with the imbecile character of Nazir Jing, and ventured to send a detachment of only 300 men to attack him in his camp. This enterprise was perfectly successful; the French penetrated more than a mile into the camp, filled it with terror and confusion, slew more than a thousand of the enemy, and returned with the loss of only two or three men. Nazir Jing, not believing himself safe, retired to Arcot, where he quarrelled with and dismissed, his

English auxiliaries. Here he was soon joined by Mohammed Ali, who had been severely defeated by the French at Trivadi, after he had, by similar misconduct, compelled the English to leave his camp. Dupleix took advantage of the crisis to open negotiations with Nazir, and at the same time to concert intrigues for his destruction, with some of the discontented leaders of his Patan auxiliaries. While he thus practised the wiles of diplomacy, he did not neglect the more active operations of war; the French, by an unexpected attack, made themselves masters of the celebrated fort of Gingee, situated on an insulated rock, and justly believed to be the strongest fortress in the Carnatic. After a vain attempt to recover Gingee, Nazir concluded a treaty with Dupleix; but it had scarcely been signed when the governor of Gingee gave the concerted signal to the Patans; they rose in revolt, Nazir was shot by one of the traitors, and Murzafa Jing was brought from his dungeon to assume the viceroyalty of the Dekkan. He was assassinated by the turbulent Patans, and the French, who now disposed of every thing, conferred the vacant dignity on Salabat Jing, the eldest surviving son of Nizam al Mulk (A.D. 1751.)

The activity of the French was advantageously contrasted with the apathy or despair of the English; at this very crisis, Major Lawrence, the commander of the troops, on whose military talents and authority their whole dependence was placed, was permitted to return home to England; and the only exertion made by the authorities at Madras, was to dissuade Mohammed Alí from surrendering Trichinopoly to the French. A detachment was sent to aid this chief; it was met on the road by Chanda Sahib's forces, and shamefully defeated. The European soldiers were the first to fly, and could not be persuaded to rally, though the native troops gallantly stood their ground. In consequence of this victory, Trichinopoly was immediately invested; but a dispute having arisen between M. Law, the commander of the French army, and his superior, M. Dupleix, the siege made very slow progress.

While the war thus lingered at Trichinopoly, Clive, who had been raised to the rank of captain, persuaded the Presidency to send him to create a diversion, by attacking Arcot, the capital of Chanda Sahib. His force consisted of two hundred Europeans and three hundred Sepoys, commanded under him by eight officers, six of whom had never been in action. His artillery amounted only to three field pieces, but two eighteen-pounders were sent after him. On the 31st of August, 1751, he arrived within ten miles of Arcot; it was the day of a fearful storm; thunder, lightning, and rain more terrific than is usual, even in India, seemed to render farther advance impracticable, but Clive, aware of the impression that such hardihood would produce on oriental minds, pushed forward in spite of the elemental strife. Daunted by his boldness, the garrison abandoned both the town and citadel, the latter of which Clive immediately occupied, giving orders that private property should be respected. As a siege was soon to be expected, he exerted his utmost diligence to supply the fort, and made frequent sallies to prevent the fugitive garrison, who hovered round, from resuming their courage.

Chanda Sahib was greatly enraged at the unexpected fall of his capital; he at once sent his son, Rájá Sahib, with a force of four thousand men to expel the English, and this body was joined by one hundred and fifty Europeans from Pondicherry, and about three thousand men who had collected around the fugitive garrison of Arcot. These forces found no difficulty in entering the city. Clive, notwithstanding the enormous disparity of strength, resolved to dislodge them, and sallied from the fort with his artillery. The enemies, however, occupied the houses with their musketry, and he was compelled to retreat with the loss of fifteen men killed, and sixteen badly wounded, the latter including his only artillery officer. On the following day the enemy, reinforced by two thousand men from Vellore, commenced a regular siege of the citadel. One of Clive's eighteen-pounders was soon disabled, the other dismounted and withdrawn; his light guns were, of course, utterly useless; to add to these disadvantages, the enemy occupied some houses which overlooked the ditch, and swept the parapet with a heavy fire of musketry at a distance of thirty yards. Notwithstanding all these disadvantages, Clive, by frequent sallies, so retarded the operations of the besiegers, that, though they were assisted by French officers, it was a fortnight before they could effect a breach. Two of very considerable extent were at length opened, and Clive prepared for their defence, though he had only eighty Europeans and one hundred and twenty Sepoys fit for duty; but he had contrived to infuse into them a portion of his own dauntless spirit, and they resolved to hold out to the last extremity. Rájá Sahib made his assault on the 14th of November, the anniversary of the martyrdom of Alí's family, the festival most reverenced by Mohammedans of the Shíah sect; Clive had prepared for his reception by erecting some works behind the breaches, which commanded them and the traverses beyond. When the assailants advanced, they found themselves exposed to cross-fires, so close and well sustained that they were mowed down by entire ranks. They recoiled from the murderous discharge, but repeated their efforts and were again driven back, until at length they abandoned the attempt, with the loss of four hundred men in killed and wounded. The enemy evacuated the town that night, after having maintained the siege for fifty days. On the following morning, Clive being joined by a detachment from Madras and a body of Mahrattas, commenced an active pursuit, and having overtaken the enemy, inflicted upon them a severe defeat, and recovered Conjeveram, which had been garrisoned by the French. Two wounded officers, who had been taken on their road from Arcot to Madras, were prisoners in the fort, and the French governor threatened to expose them on the ramparts to the fire of their own countrymen, if Clive persevered in his attack, but these gallant men exhorted Clive to disregard their safety; it is pleasing to add that when Conjeveram was taken they were found uninjured.

Clive returned to Fort St. David about the end of December; the enemy took advantage of his absence to resume their operations, and he had to take the field in February to relieve Arcot, which was menaced with a siege. On his road he unexpectedly encountered the enemy, who were vastly superior in number, just as night was beginning to close with the usual rapidity of a tropical climate. A smart but irregular action was fought by moonlight, and the English seemed on the point of being routed, when Lieutenant Keene, who had been sent to attack the rear of the grove in which the enemies were posted, by a sudden charge, got possession of the French guns, and turned them on their former owners. The effect of the surprise was complete; the enemy fled in every direction, and few of the disbanded troops ever returned to their former standards.

Clive would have made use of this success to attempt the capture of Vellore, but he was summoned back to Fort St. David in order to join Major Lawrence, who had now returned from England, in raising the siege of Trichinopoly. Law, who commanded the besiegers, would at once have retired from Trichinopoly but for the pressing and reiterated commands of M. Dupleix ; he was, however, compelled to abandon his camp and take up a new position in the island of Seringham, formed by the branches of the Cavery. Here he was closely besieged by the English, who had been strengthened by contingents from the Rájás of Tanjore and Mysore. Dupleix, aware of the danger to which Law was exposed, sent a large reinforcement to his relief under D'Auteuil, but Clive intercepted the convoy, forced D'Auteuil to retreat, attacked him in the fort to which he retired, and made him prisoner. Law was now in distress for want of provisions, his camp was cannonaded by the English, the troops of Chanda Sahib deserted in whole battalions, and the nabob himself, despairing of escape, yielded himself a prisoner to the Rájá of Tanjore. Chanda Sahib's fate was lamentable ; a dispute arose between the allies respecting the possession of so important a captive, which the Tanjorine ended by causing him to be assassinated. The French army, left without resource, was forced to capitulate, and Mohammed Alí was again recognized as Nabob of the Carnatic.

Lawrence was anxious to recover the rest of the province, especially the strong fortress of Gingee, but he was mortified to find that Mohammed Ali was by no means eager to second his exertions. In fact, the nabob had promised to surrender Trichinopoly to the Raja of Mysore as the price of his timely assistance ; he now refused to fulfil his agreement, and the English sanctioned his breach of faith. This gave so much offence to the rest of the allies, that they returned to their own homes, while the Mysoreans and Mahrattas opened negociations with the French.

There were many circumstances which prevented Dupleix from being so much dispirited by these successive reverses as might have been expected, but none was of greater weight than the influence he possessed in the court of the viceroy of the Dekkan. Salabat-Jing owed his elevation to the French, and particularly to M. Bussy, by whose aid he had been enabled to defeat the machinations of his turbulent nobles. The Omrahs were so enraged against Bussy, that they insisted on his being dismissed ; a treacherous ambuscade was posted to intercept him as he returned to Pondicherry, but he defeated the assassins by his personal strength and valour; when this was told to the Nizam, he ordered Bussy to be recalled to his court, and invested him with the government of the four provinces called the Northern Circars; "thus," says Mr. Orme, "rendering the French masters of the sea-coast of Coromandel and Orissa, in an unintercepted line of six hundred miles, from Medapelly to the pagoda of Juggernaut." These provinces not only afforded large pecuniary resources, but furnished means of receiving reinforcements from Pondicherry and the Mauritius, so as to encourage the French to hope for the establishment of their political supremacy through the whole extent of the Dekkan.

It was resolved, not very wisely, by the Madras Presidency, that the first military operation undertaken should be the reduction of Gingee. Lawrence strenuously opposed the enterprize, but, being forced by ill-health to return to Fort St. David, his successor sent a detachment against the fortress; it was intercepted by the French in the mountainous defiles, and routed with great slaughter. Soon after, a body of Swiss, sent from Madras to strengthen the garrison of Fort St. David in open boats, was met by a French ship of war and forced to surrender. Lawrence, though imperfectly recovered, would no longer remain inactive; he hastened into the field, and on his approach, the enemy, though superior in force, retreated behind the bound-hedge of Pondicherry. This hedge, which commonly forms a part of Indian fortifications, is formed of thorny plants, which grow very rapidly and, twining together, soon make a fence very difficult to be penetrated. Lawrence hesitated to attack the enemy thus protected; he feigned a retreat, and retired in apparent confusion to Bahur. Dupleix gave immediate orders for a vigorous pursuit; Lawrence only waited until they had advanced so far as to render an action inevitable; he then formed his troops into two lines, and charged the hostile ranks with so much impetuosity that they were at once broken. Had the nabob's cavalry done their duty not a man of the enemy would have escaped, but these horsemen of the Carnatic turned aside from the pursuit, for the more agreeable task of plundering the camp, and the remnant of the French obtained time to shelter themselves again behind the bound-hedge of Pondicherry.

In the following campaign some new circumstances brought the hostile armies once more into the neighbourhood of Trichinopoly. Captain Dalton had been left with a garrison in Trichinopoly, but had great difficulty in defending himself from the machinations of the Mysoreans or Mahrattas, who wished to gain possession of the place as perfidiously as they had been deprived of it. Their disputes at length led to open war. Dalton was blockaded in Trichinopoly, and he had the mortification to find that the care of furnishing the magazines which he had entrusted to the Mohammedan governor, had been so grossly neglected that, instead of having provisions for six months, the supply was little more than adequate for twice that number of days. Information of his danger was conveyed to Lawrence, who immediately marched to relieve Trichinopoly, the French army advanced in the same direction, and for more than twelve months, a series of skirmishes and indecisive engagements took place in the vicinity of Trichinopoly, which generally terminated in favour of the English.

The French East India Company had now become weary of the expenses in which they were involved by the ambitious policy of Dupleix; the French and English governments were also displeased that their respective companies should carry on war while they were at peace in Europe; a conference was appointed in London, and there all parties agreed to throw the blame upon Dupleix. The enterprising governor was recalled, and a treaty was then concluded, which threw into the hands of the English all the advantages resulting from the revolutions of the Dekkan. Soon afterwards, Bussy displeased Salabat Jing by his reluctance to carry on war against the Mahrattas, who were in close alliance with the government of Pondicherry. The Nizam was so displeased that he dismissed his French officers and auxiliaries, soliciting the Presidency of Madras to supply their place with an English detachment. Circumstances, however, occurred in a different part of India, which prevented the authorities at Madras from profiting by the favourable dispositions of the Nizam, and led to events which, though threatening in the commencement, finally opened the way for establishing a British empire in India.

CHAPTER VI.

ESTABLISHMENT OF BRITISH SUPREMACY IN BENGAL AND THE CARNATIC.

Notwithstanding the patent rights and privileges which had been conceded to the English by the Emperor of Delhí, they were prevented from extending their power or possessions by the pertinacious opposition of Jaffier Khan, the influential Subahdar, or Viceroy of Bengal. On his death, Shujah Khan, by the address of two brother adventurers, obtained possession of the viceroyalty, and in gratitude for their services, he bestowed the administration of the province of Bahar on the younger of the two, Alverdi Khan. On the death of Shujar, his son and successor, Sereffraz Khan, ill-treated the brothers to whom his father had been so largely indebted, upon which Alverdi Khan, having obtained a patent for the viceroyalty from the court of Delhí, marched against Sereffraz, and slew him in battle. Alwerdi had reduced the whole country to obedience, and was rapidly increasing its prosperity by the wisdom of his administration, when the Mahrattas of Berar, having forced the passes of their mountain frontier, began to ravage the rich provinces of Bengal, Bahar and Orissa. During the fifteen years of his administration, or rather reign, for his obedience to the court of Delhí was merely nominal, Alverdi was engaged in almost incessant wars with the Mahrattas and his own Patan or Afghan mercenaries, who seized every opportunity of attempting to coerce him into gratifying their cupidity. These circumstances prevented him from paying all the attention to the character and education of his family which he might otherwise have bestowed; as he had no children, he selected for his heir the eldest son of his youngest nephew, on whom he bestowed the title of Suraj-ad-dowla. A worse choice could hardly have been made; Suraja indulged himself in all the vices of an oriental prince, and allowed nothing to interfere with the gratification of his passions.

The first act of Suraj-ad-dowla was to plunder his uncles and aunts of all the treasures they had accumulated under the government of Alverdi; while thus employed, he learned that the finance minister of his second uncle had escaped to Calcutta, and his demand that the fugitive should be sent back was peremptorily rejected. Suraja had always disliked the English; he knew that Calcutta was badly governed, and he believed it to be immensely rich; to gratify, therefore, at once his rage and his avarice, he directly marched against the town, nor could all the remonstrances and submissions of the governor and council divert him from his purpose.

After a hurried consultation, the governor and council of Calcutta resolved that the place was untenable, and prepared to make their escape on board the shipping. This was effected with such disgraceful precipitation, that one hundred and forty-six persons were left behind, exposed to the doubtful humanity of the Subahdar. Suraj-ad-dowla did not meditate cruelty, he promised the prisoners that not a hair of their heads should be touched, and then gave orders that they should be secured for the night. The Hindú guards placed them in a small, ill-ventilated chamber, called "The Black Hole," where one hundred and thirty-one of them died from heat and suffocation before the morning. Intelligence of this calamity was conveyed to Madras, where Clive and Admiral Watson were fortunately present, and the forces intended to be sent to Salabat Jing were ordered to be got ready for the recovery of Calcutta.

Clive had gone to England, where he was rewarded for his services by the rank of lieutenant-colonel in the royal army, and the appointment of deputy governor of Fort St. David. On his arrival at Bombay, where it was arranged that he should act in concert with the Mahrattas, in attacking Salabat Jing and expelling the French from the Dekkan, he found that the peace of Southern India had been restored by the events recorded in the conclusion of the preceding chapter, and he therefore resolved to reduce the pirate Angria, whose depredations had inflicted severe injuries on the English trade. Watson commanded the fleet, and Clive the land forces in this expedition; they sailed to Gheriah, Angria's capital, which was situated on a rocky promontory nearly surrounded by the sea, and defended by a fort of extraordinary strength. Notwithstanding these advantages, Gheriah was taken after a very ineffective resistance. The fort was retained by the English, in contravention of the terms under which they were engaged to co-operate with the Mahrattas, whom they contrived to anticipate in a mutually-projected scheme of deception.

Notwithstanding the fame which he deservedly obtained by this exploit, Clive found some difficulty in obtaining the command of the expedition designed to recover Calcutta. After two months had been spent in dispute, his appointment was finally sanctioned; his authority was declared to be independent of that of the Presidency of Calcutta, and he received strict orders to return to Madras as soon as the objects of his mission should be accomplished. Clive found little difficulty in retaking Calcutta; the garrison scarcely resisted the cannonade from the shipping for two hours, when they evacuated the place. The merchandize belonging to the Company was found mostly untouched, because it had been reserved for the Subahdar, but the houses of individuals were totally plundered. This success was followed by the capture of Hoogly, a wealthy city about twenty-five miles higher up the river, an event which so enraged the Subahdar that he returned to besiege Calcutta. Clive resolved to surprise him in his camp, and though this bold attempt failed, it produced such an effect on the mind of the Subahdar, that he concluded a treaty with the English, and two days after, entered into an alliance with them, offensive and defensive. An attack was next made on the French settlement at Chandernagore, which was taken after a brief resistance, before the Subahdar, who had prohibited such an attempt, could effectually interfere. Clive had now effected more than what had been originally intended, and the time had come when, according to his instructions, he was bound to return with the army to Madras.

But Clive had now formed plans for establishing the British influence in Bengal on a permanent basis. Mir Jaffier, who had married the sister of Alverdi Khan, had organized a conspiracy against Suraj-ad-dowla, and by a promise of immense bribes to the English generals and members of council, he secured their co-operation in his traitorous attempts. The war with the Subahdar was renewed, and Clive took the field; as he advanced he was surprised at not being joined by Mir Jaffier, but he received a letter from that nobleman, stating that he could not move in consequence of the awakened suspicions of the Subahdar, but that, if the English proceeded and hazarded an engagement, he would desert to them on the day of battle.

Clive called a council of war, in which it was resolved not to hazard a battle, but after the council had separated, further reflection led him to change his mind; he crossed the river, and at about one o'clock in the morning of the 22nd of June, took up his position in the grove of Plassy.

Clive's forces amounted to little more than three thousand men, about one-third being Europeans; his artillery consisted of eight six pounders and two small howitzers. The Subahdar advanced against this handful of men, with fifty thousand foot, eighteen thousand horse, and fifty pieces of cannon, At eight in the morning the battle commenced, and continued until five in the afternoon, but was nothing more than a distant and irregular cannonade. Mir Jaffier was seen moving off with his troops, at the moment that Clive was advancing to charge; both events so terrified the Subahdar, that he fled from the field on a fleet camel, accompanied by his attendants: no further resistance was made, and the English took possession of the hostile camp, having lost no more than eighty men in killed and wounded. Never, perhaps, before had the fate of a mighty kingdom been decided in so feeble an engagement.

On the following morning, a message was received from Mir Jaffier, declaring that he and many of the Omrahs waited for the commands of the conqueror. Clive invited him to his quarters, whither the Mir went rather reluctantly, as he feared that the English general might reproach him, for not having joined him with the promised aid previous to the battle. His apprehensions were soon dispelled, Clive received Mir Jaffier with the greatest kindness, and entrusted him with the charge of proceeding to the capital, in order to prevent the escape of Suraj-ad-Dowla and the removal of his treasure.

The unfortunate Subahdar had fled from the field of battle to Moorshedabad, and sought shelter in his palace. He found himself

> "Deserted at his utmost need,
> By those his former bounty fed,"

no friend or partisan appeared to join him, so that when Mir Jaffier approached, he fled in disguise from the city, hoping to make his escape to the French in Bahar. The rowers of his boat were soon worn out by fatigue; they stopped at Raj Mahl, where the unfortunate Suraj-ad-Dowla was recognized by a man whom he had formerly treated with great cruelty; he was seized and delivered over to Mir Jaffier, who placed him under the custody of his son. The son, a brutal and ferocious prince, caused him to be assassinated.

Clive arrived at Moorshedabad on the 25th of June; a meetting was held, to confer about the sums which Mir Jaffier had consented to pay in restitution to the Presidency, and in presents to the civil and military officers, but the chief officer of finance declared that the whole of the late Subahdar's treasures were inadequate to meet the demand. This intelligence was equally painful and unexpected, but the most stringent enquiry only confirmed its truth. It was at last agreed that one half of the money should be paid immediately, and the remainder in three equal payments in three years. In this partition of plunder, a piece of consummate, but not unmerited, treachery was practised upon a Hindú merchant, which must not be passed over without notice. One of the principal agents in the plot against Suraj-ad-Dowla, was Omichund, the owner of a large property in Calcutta, but who had attached himself to the court of Moorshedabad. He was the principal agent in conducting the negociations between Mir Jaffier and the English; he was thus master of the secrets of both, and he resolved to profit by his position. When every thing was prepared for action, he waited on Mr. Watts, the Company's agent at the factory of Casimbazar, and threatened to reveal the whole secret, unless he was assured of a donation of thirty lacs of rupees, equivalent to about £350,000. It was necessary to promise compliance with this exorbitant demand, for the rejection of it would have been followed by the murder of all the Company's servants at Casimbazar, the destruction of Mir Jaffier with all his family and adherents, and the frustration of all the great projects which the English had formed. Lured by the expectation of so large a bribe, Omichund continued to divert the suspicions which the unfortunate Subahdar had formed of Mir Jaffier's fidelity, and thus led him blindfold to his ruin. Omichund now claimed the stipulated reward of his treachery, but he learned to his great surprise, that two treaties with Mir Jaffier had been drawn up and signed; one in which satisfaction should be provided for Omichund, and which he should see; another, and that which should be really executed, in which he was not named.* When Omichund, at the final settlement, was informed of the trick that had been played upon him, he fainted away. It is added, that he lost his reason, and was from that moment insane; but this statement is probably exaggerated.

After the arrangements with Mir Jaffier had been concluded, Major Coote was sent with a strong detachment to expel the French from Bahar, and to reduce the governor of that province to the obedience of the Subahdar. The troops were forwarded in boats, so wretchedly manned and equipped that their progress was both slow and hazardous; Coote disembarked, and attempted to push forward by land, but the European portion of his forces broke out in a dangerous mutiny. The result of these delays was that, long before Coote could reach Patna, the French having been amply supplied with every thing necessary to their convenience, retired to Oude, where they met a ready reception, and fresh instructions arrived from Clive, which led to an amicable arrangement with the Governor of Bahar.

Although Mohammed Alí, whom the English had made nabob, was without a rival in the Carnatic, he received but a very small share of its revenues, and was, consequently, unable to pay the stipulated subsidies to the government of Madras. The forces of that presidency had been greatly diminished by the sending of the armament to Calcutta, and Clive refused to send any of the soldiers back, though war now raged between France and England, and a fleet was daily expected with reinforcements to the French in Pondicherry. Under these circumstances, the president and council of Madras adopted a general resolution to remain inactive, from which, however, they soon swerved, by directing Captain Calliaud, the governor of Trichinopoly, to attempt the reduction of Madura and Tinevelly, which were supposed to be capable of yielding large pecuniary supplies. Calliaud, who was a brave and enterprising officer, made the best preparation his inadequate means would admit, for the reduction of both places, but when he came before Madura, he

* To the honour of Admiral Watson it should be recorded, that he refused to be a party to this treachery. He would not put his name to the false treaty, and the committee forged his signature.

found the place much stronger than he had anticipated, and after an ineffectual attempt to take it by storm, he resolved to wait for his battering cannon. An expedition against Vellore was similarly circumstanced, but before artillery could be furnished, it was necessary to recall the detachment to Madras.

The government of Pondicherry had resolved to wait for the arrival of the forces which they expected from Europe, but when they saw the English so largely employed, and their small army dispersed over so wide a space, they resolved to avail themselves of the advantages offered them by fortune. Carefully masking their intentions, they collected all their available strength, and when they were least expected, presented themselves before Trichinopoly. The garrison, deprived of the troops which had been sent against Madura, were insufficient to guard the walls, and they had five hundred French prisoners in the fort. Intelligence of the danger to which Trichinopoly was exposed, reached Calliaud before Madura. He immediately raised the siege, and marched for Trichinopoly, where an army five times the number of his own, waited his approach. On one side of the town was a large plain, seven miles in extent, consisting of rice-fields covered with water, which the French had neglected, believing it to be impassable. But nothing could daunt the spirit of Calliaud's troops, wearied as they were by their forced march from Madura, they made their way through the rice-fields, up to their knees in mud, and formed a junction with the garrison. The French commander, astonished at the news of their entrance, and despairing of success, marched away from Pondicherry on the following day.

Several petty operations were undertaken by the French and English, with little advantage to either side. Colonel Aldercron was sent with a detachment against Wandewash; he took the town, but was unable to capture the fort, before the return of the French from Trichinopoly compelled him to retreat. At his departure he set fire to the defenceless town, an outrage which the French revenged by burning Conjeveram. A third power soon appeared to claim a share in the plunder of the Carnatic; a powerful Mahratta army passed the frontiers, to claim payment of the *chout* or annual tribute which they levied on the chief princes of India, and the English government found it necessary to comply with their demands. Calliaud renewed his attack on

Madura, but, finding himself unable to take it by storm, he purchased its surrender by a large bribe to the garrison. The French and English troops, without engaging in any great enterprize, continued to make incursions upon each other, and to devastate mutually the unhappy country. "These operations," says Mr. Orme, "being always levelled at defenceless villages, carried the reproach of robbery more than the reputation of war." Events, however, were in progress, which soon changed the character of the war, and rendered it, on each side, a desperate struggle for existence.

Upon the breaking out of the war between France and England in 1756, the French ministry resolved to strike an important blow in India. The Count de Lally was appointed to the chief command; he was descended from one of the Irish families, which had been compelled to emigrate at the revolution in consequence of their having adhered to the cause of the Stuarts, and he was therefore animated by a bitter hatred of British ascendancy, which had crushed both his country and his creed. At the battle of Fontenoy he took several English officers prisoners with his own hand, and was raised to the rank of colonel by King Louis himself on the field of battle. He was accompanied to India by his own Irish regiments, composed of the best troops in the service of France, by fifty of the royal artillery, and by several officers of great distinction. Although he lost more than four hundred men during the voyage, by a malignant fever caught at Brest, he was so confident in his strength that he resolved to open the campaign with the siege of Fort St. David, before which he left his fleet, while he proceeded to Pondicherry in order to collect and bring up the land forces of the Presidency. Here he found his first great difficulty in the deplorable ignorance of the French governor and council; they could give him no information of the condition of the English, nor of the state of the towns along the coast; they furnished him with unskilful guides, and an inadequate supply of provisions, so that his forces, when he arrived before Fort St. David, were quite worn down with hunger and fatigue. This gave them a motive and an apology for commencing a system of plunder and insubordination, from which they could not be easily recalled. A more serious interruption to his plans was the arrival of an English squadron under Admiral Pococke, which, though inferior in force, at once proceeded to attack the French at their station off Cuddalore. The engagement terminated to the advantage of the English, but, as their ships were superior in sailing, they all escaped with the exception of one which was driven on shore.

Notwithstanding these disadvantages, Lally commenced the siege of Fort St. David, which he pushed forward with the most ardent spirit. The place was wretchedly defended; the greater part of the ammunition was wasted in a distant cannonade, and the fleet, notwithstanding its success, made no attempt to throw in any relief. At length, after a month's siege, the English capitulated on the 1st of June, 1758. The officers and soldiers remained prisoners of war, but the fortifications were destroyed and levelled to the ground. Lally then sent a detachment against Devi-Cotah; at its approach the garrison evacuated the place, and retired in the utmost trepidation to Trichinopoly.

In the meantime the judicious policy of Bussy had established the temporary supremacy of the French in the Dekkan. After having forced the Nizam and his Omrahs to submit to his terms, by his brilliant defence of his position at Hyderabad in 1756, Bussy proceeded to the Northern Circars, for the purpose of collecting the revenues of these provinces at the point of the bayonet. Few of the Polygars, or local chiefs, ventured to resist his progress. The Polygar of Bohilee, however, defended his fort to the last extremity; and when no further hope of protracting resistance remained, he set fire to the fortress, the garrison of which slew themselves rather than yield to the enemy. The English establishments in the Circars, including the important settlement of Vizagapatam, surrendered almost at discretion, but it is creditable to Bussy that he treated his prisoners with the greatest kindness and consideration. From these labours he was called to protect the Nizam from the results of a revolution which threatened him in his capital. Contrary to the prudent advice of Bussy, Salabat Jing had entrusted his two brothers with the government of important provinces, and in particular had bestowed upon Nizam Ali, the younger and more dangerous of the two, Berar, the most extensive province of the Dekkan. Taking advantage of a dangerous mutiny of the troops, Nizam Ali presented himself before his humbled brother, Salabat Jing, and offered to ensure his safety, provided he were recognized as heir to the government, and entrusted with the custody of the Nizam's great seal. Salabat Jing was forced to comply, and Nizam Alí transferred the seal to his brother, Bassalat Jing, having first taken security that it would be used agreeably to his directions.

On receiving intelligence of these events, Bussy made a forced march to Aurungabad by a road which had never before been travelled by European troops; his presence disconcerted the plans which had been formed for the dethronement of Salabat Jing, and Bussy having soon after secured himself by obtaining possession of the celebrated fortress of Dowlatabad, assumed the complete dictation of the Nizam's policy. One of the turbulent brothers was slain in a scuffle, and Nizam Alí was so alarmed that he fled northwards, leaving Salabat Jing in full possession of his recovered authority. Both the Nizam and Bussy were equally aware that the permanence of this state of things could only be ensured by the continuance of the French at Aurungabad: they were therefore equally surprised and annoyed when Lally sent an imperious order, that Bussy and his troops should immediately join him to carry out the schemes which he had formed for the complete overthrow of the British empire in India.

Lally's gigantic plans were impeded by want of money, and he adopted the most desperate courses to obtain an immediate supply. The government of Pondicherry had a dubious claim on the King of Tanjore for five millions of rupees; Lally resolved to enforce payment, and as there were not sufficient numbers of the lower caste in Pondicherry to perform the servile operations necessary in a camp, he pressed all the citizens without distinction, or regard to Hindu prejudice, and compelled them to carry burdens and perform whatever labour might be required. Nor was he less harsh in his conduct to the Europeans; he attributed their refusal to supply his large demands for funds and supplies, to dishonesty and misconduct, displaying so little prudence as incessantly to declare these opinions in the most pointed and offensive terms which his language could supply. Such proceedings rendered him in a short time odious to every class of men in the colony, precluded all possibility of cordial co-operation, and destroyed all chance of a tolerable management of their common concerns.

From the terror of the Natives, the alienation of the Europeans, and the want of money, no part of the equipment of the expedition against Tanjore, was complete in any one of its particulars.

During its progress the Pagoda of Kiveloor was stormed, but none of the wealth it was reputed to contain could be found, which so enraged Lally that he ordered six of the Brahmins belonging to the temple to be seized, and as if they had been convicted spies, to be blown to pieces from the muzzles of his cannon. The siege of Tanjore was commenced, but want of ammunition prevented the French from making a rapid progress, and Calliaud twice relieved the place by detachments from Trichinopoly. Still a vigorous assault might have been successful, but before it could be attempted, intelligence was received that an English fleet had arrived off Carical, whence the besiegers derived their supplies. A council of war was held, and a resolution taken to raise the siege. This was soon discovered by the garrison of Tanjore; they sallied out, and severely harassed the rear of the retreating French, who had great difficulty in reaching Carical, where they found the English fleet anchored at the mouth of the river. Lally's hopes now rested on the French fleet, which was numerically stronger than that of the English, but in an engagement off Carical, which lasted about an hour, the French admiral was so roughly handled, that he was forced to sheer off and make all sail for Pondicherry; and thence, in spite of the most urgent remonstrances, he departed to the Mauritius.

Still resolved to besiege Madras, Lally made himself master of Arcot, where he failed to procure the supplies which he had expected, and what was scarcely less injurious to his cause, he neglected to sieze Chinglapet while it lay defenceless, thus giving his adversaries time to fortify a possession essential to the supply of the garrison. After many vexatious delays, he arrived before Madras, and took possession of the Black Town. The unity wanting in the councils of the besiegers, was maintained in Madras by the abilities of Governor Pigot and the veteran Lawrence; still the weak defences might probably have yielded to the vigorous efforts of Lally, who, though opposed and impeded by his officers, was zealously supported by the soldiery, had not a reinforcement arrived from Bombay at a most critical moment, February 16th, 1759. "Words," says Lally, "are inadequate to express the effect which the appearance of these reinforcements produced. The officer who commanded in the trenches deemed it even inexpedient to wait for the landing of the enemy, and two hours before receiving orders, retired from his post. So precipitate was the retreat, that the sick and wounded were abandoned to the English, who treated them with all the care which the laws of war and humanity imperatively prescribe.

Reinforcements to both parties arrived from Europe, but the French fleet having been defeated in an indecisive naval engagement, returned to the Mauritius. Colonel Coote, who had come out with the new armament to take the command of the English, opened the campaign with the capture of Wandewash. Lally hastened to recover this important place, and Coote permitted him to exhaust the strength of his men in constructing approaches, until everything was ready for an assault. The English then advanced by a rapid march, which gave them the great advantage of being able to choose their ground before Lally could form his lines. At the very commencement of the action, the French cavalry, after having advanced a few paces, fled as if seized by a sudden panic, without striking a blow. Lally brought up his infantry, but permitted his men to exhaust themselves by opening fire at such a distance that their shot was ineffectual. As the column approached, it was received by the opposite English regiment with a close and murderous discharge; but pressing forward by its own weight, it broke through the opposing battalion. This apparent success was fatal; the severed ranks of the English overlapped the flanks of the assailing column, and completely destroyed it by close and repeated volleys. A panic seized the whole French line; their entrenchments were carried at the point of the bayonet; Bussy, who attempted to recover them, was dismounted and made prisoner; it was no longer a battle, but a rout. The cavalry, which had behaved so badly in the action, protected the retreat with great gallantry, so that Lally was enabled to carry off his wounded and his light baggage, but his artillery, munitions of war, and heavy baggage, were abandoned to the victors. Had Coote immediately advanced against Pondicherry, the settlement would probably have fallen, so disheartened were the French and so divided were their councils.

The English marched from Wandewash to besiege Arcot, taking Chettapet on their road. Arcot made but a feeble resistance; it capitulated when two breaches, neither of them practicable, had been made. Gingee was abandoned at the same time, and Lally took up a position at Valdore, in order to keep open the communications of Pondicherry with the southern districts, from which alone provisions could be obtained. The French army was absolutely without equipments, stores, and provisions; Lally repaired to Pondicherry to obtain supplies, but the council of the presidency were unwilling, or unable, to afford him any effectual relief, and their mutual recriminations increased the distracted state of their affairs. Coote steadily pursued his victorious career. Timery surrendered after a feeble resistance; Devi-Cotah was abandoned; the Forts of Trincomalee, Pennacoil, and Alamparva, were taken with little difficulty. It was expected that Carical, the chief naval possession of the French, would have made a very obstinate defence, but it was surrendered almost on the first summons; Valdore, Chillambaram, and Cuddalore were taken about the same time, so that on May the 1st, 1760, the French were confined to the bounds of Pondicherry, and the English encamped within four miles of the town. Large reinforcements arrived from England, increasing the fleet to the amount of seventeen sail of the line, and adding greatly to the European part of Coote's army. Lally, as a last resource, applied for assistance to Hyder Ali, who had at this time become master of the resources of the kingdom of Mysore; Hyder sent an auxiliary force to his aid, which defeated an English detachment that attempted to intercept their march. But the Mysoreans were soon discouraged by the wretched condition in which they found the affairs of the French, and having received information that their presence was required by an emergency at home, they quitted their camp in the night, and returned to Mysore.

Eight months had now elapsed since the total discomfiture of the French at Wandewash, during which time the intrepid Lally had contrived to deter the English from forming the siege of Pondicherry; even now, abandoned by the Mysoreans, and thwarted by his own countrymen, he formed a plan for surprising the English which displayed great judgment and sagacity. Four bodies were formed to attack the English camp in the night, and had they acted in complete concert, the issue would have been very doubtful; but one of the divisions fell behind its time, and disconcerted the operations of the remainder: the French were repulsed, and their condition rendered worse than ever.

At this critical moment, a commission arrived from England, giving the command of the forces to Monson and superseding Coote, who was ordered to Bengal. The council of Madras wished to delay the execution of these orders, but Coote at once resigned the command to Monson, and even permitted him to retain the services of his own regiment. Monson's first operation was to force the bound-hedge of Pondicherry; the plan was badly executed, and a considerable loss was incurred. Monson himself was so severely wounded as to be rendered incapable of active exertion, he, therefore, united with the council in soliciting Coote, who had not yet sailed for Bengal, to resume the command of the army.

Coote's return gave the greatest pleasure to the soldiers; under his guidance they executed all the fatiguing operations necessary to complete the investment of Pondicherry, while Lally made the best use of his post, in the Fort of Ariancopang, to annoy the besiegers and obtain provisions for the town. The blockade was rigidly maintained during the rainy season, at the termination of which, batteries were erected for an active siege. On the night of the 30th of December, all the labours of the English were nearly frustrated by one of the most terrific hurricanes remembered in India. Three ships of war foundered, by which eleven hundred lives were lost; the tents were rent to fragments, the works blown down, and the whole camp thrown into confusion. Fortunately the tempest was accompanied by an inundation, which prevented the French from profiting by the disasters of the English; and Coote used such diligence in repairing the works, that the trenches were opened on the 12th of January, 1761. Two days afterwards, the place capitulated, the whole garrison and civil establishment remaining prisoners of war. The English were so much astonished at their own success, that they did not well know what to do with their new acquisition; Coote and the military officers claimed Pondicherry for the crown; Governor Pigot asserted that it belonged of right to the Company, and declared that no money should be advanced for the troops, until the Company's officers received possession of it. Coote, after solemnly protesting against the measure, gave way: possession was taken of Pondicherry in the names of the Directors; and, according to orders previously received from home, all its fortifications were destroyed.

The capture of Theagur, Gingee, and Mahè, completed the total annihilation of the French empire in India; the intelligence excited great commotion in France, and the Directors had the art to turn the whole of the popular indignation against the brave, but unfortunate, Lally. On his arrival in Europe he was seized and thrown into the Bastille, from whence, as a place too honourable for him, he was removed to the common prison. He was granted the mockery of a trial before the parliament of Paris, convicted, and sentenced to an ignominious death. With indecent precipitation he was executed that very day. He was dragged through the streets of Paris in a common dung-cart, and, to prevent him from addressing the people, a gag was forced into his mouth, so large that it projected beyond his lips. At a later period, full justice was done to the memory of this calumniated victim; his persecutors derived little advantage from the crime,—the French East India Company did not long survive this last display of imbecility and injustice.

CHAPTER VII.

FROM THE ESTABLISHMENT OF THE BRITISH EMPIRE IN INDIA TO THE FIRST WAR WITH HYDER ALI.

When Mir Jaffier had obtained the great object of his ambition, the viceroyalty of Bengal, he found that he was in a far more difficult and unpleasant position than that which he had occupied before his elevation: his treasury was exhausted; he had promised immense sums to the English which he was altogether unable to pay; the chiefs whom he had seduced from their allegiance to Suraj-ad-dowla, were indignant because their rebellion had not produced such rich fruits as they had expected; and the pay of his troops was in arrear. Under such circumstances, it was impossible for any man to give perfect satisfaction to all parties, and Mir Jaffier's character was not the best suited to the difficult circumstances in which he was placed. In fact, had it not been for the guiding influence of Clive's superior mind, and the judicious manner in which he employed the authority which Mir Jaffier's failure to pay his debts had placed in the hands of the president and council, the viceroy must soon have effected his own ruin. In nothing was Clive's sagacity more clearly displayed, than in his preventing the viceroy from effecting the destruction of the Hindú agents of his government, who were the best ministers he could have procured, though he viewed them with jealousy and suspicion.

Alverdi Khan, aware of the turbulent spirit of the adventurers from Persia and Afghanistan, who were usually the chief ministers and officers under the Mohammedan princes of India, adopted the wise policy of promoting the Hindús, who, though less enterprising, were also less dangerous. He entrusted Ramnarain, one of this race, with the important government of Berar; another Hindu, Dooloob Ram, held the office of Dewan, or superintendent of the finances; while the celebrated family of the Sets of Moorshedabad, who by merchandize and banking had acquired the wealth of princes, shared in his councils, and influenced the operations of his government. Mir Jaffier resolved to change this policy, and though he had been under the deepest obligations to Dooloob Ram, he resolved to commence with the destruction of that minister. His preliminary steps, however, provoked insurrections on every side, and he had no means of averting the danger with which he was threatened, but by invoking the aid of the English. On his arrival at Moorshedabad, Clive effected at least a formal reconciliation between Mir Jaffier and Dooloob Ram; the insurgents were reduced to obedience, and the viceroy hoped that he might be able to remove Ramnarain from the government of Berar. Clive did not directly oppose this project, but he accompanied the viceroy's army into Berar, and prevented the commission of any act of hostility. The Subahdar of Oude, a French auxiliary force under Mr. Law, and a body of Mahratta marauders, being about to invade the province, Clive convinced the viceroy that a reconciliation with the Ramnarain was essential to his safety, and induced him, though very reluctantly, to abandon his machinations against that chieftain. At the same time he obtained for the English a lease of the saltpetre monopoly, which formed a principal part of the commerce of Bengal. He offered, indeed, the highest rent which the government had ever yet received, but Mir Jaffier was very unwilling to lose his chance of extorting presents from a tenant placed at his mercy, and would not have signed the lease, but for the pressing necessity of his circumstances.

On his return to Moorshedabad, Clive received intelligence of the indecisive engagement between the English and French fleets on the Coast of Coromandel, and the investment of Fort St. David. Concealing the latter circumstance, he spread a report that the English had won a decisive victory, and then hastened to Calcutta, where the critical state of affairs required his presence. He found there that a new instrument of government had arrived, nominating a council of ten, and appointing four governors, each to preside three months in rotation. Clive's name was not mentioned in the new arrangements, but the gentlemen to conduct the administration, unanimously resolved that he alone had sufficient authority to compel Mir Jaffier to perform his obligations. They invited Clive to accept the office of President, and soon found that by so doing they only anticipated the fresh instructions which were sent out when intelligence of the battle of Plassy reached England.

The intrigues of Mir Jaffier and his son Meeran, for the destruction of Dooloob Ram were renewed; they were seconded by Nuncomar, a Hindu, who had risen into high employments under the government of the Subahdars, and at length Clive was obliged to give Dooloob Ram shelter in Calcutta to save him from destruction. More active interference in behalf of the injured minister, was prevented by intelligence of the disasters which the English had met in the Carnatic, where Fort St. David was taken and Madras threatened with a siege. Clive resolved not to send any of his forces to Madras, but, at the same time, he engaged in an enterprize likely to effect a diversion in favour of that presidency, and, at the same time, highly advantageous to the government of Bengal.

Rájá Anumderaz, one of the Polygars in the northern Circars, was greatly displeased at the conditions on which Bussy had granted him the investiture of his government, and, on the departure of that gentleman to support Salabat Jing against his rebellious relatives, the Rájá attacked and took the French settlement at Vizigapatam. He then sent to the Presidency of Madras, offering to surrender his new acquisition to the English, provided that they would send him a body of troops to aid in the reduction of the Circars. The authorities of Madras were, at the time, too seriously alarmed by the progress of Lally to undertake any distant enterprize, and the Rájá next made application to Clive. In spite of the unanimous opposition of the council, Clive at once concluded a treaty with Anumderaz, and despatched a large armament under Colonel Forde to his assistance. The Rájá was in the condition of most Indian princes at the time; he was believed by the Europeans to be immensely rich, but, in reality, was miserably poor. Forde's operations were, therefore, much retarded by want of money, and he found great difficulty in obtaining a moderate supply. Being joined by the Rájá, Forde advanced against the French, who, with superior forces under M. Conflans, occupied a strong position at Rajamundri. Forde, who was worthy to be joined with Clive, gave orders for an immediate attack, and though he was deserted by Anumderaz, who remained during the battle cowering in a hollow tank, protected from shot, he defeated the French completely, took possession of their camp, and drove them from Rajamundri. The reluctance of the Rájá to fulfil his pecuniary engagements, prevented Forde from immediately profiting by his distinguished success. After a long and vexatious delay, the English again began to move, and M. Conflans, afraid to meet them in the open field, threw himself into the strong fort of Masulipatam. Forde summoned the place, but the French treated his pretensions with ridicule; the defenders within were more numerous than the besiegers, both in their European and native force; a considerable army of observation was left in the field; Salabat Jing was on his march to their aid with the grand army of the Dekkan; and a large reinforcement was expected from Pondicherry. Under all these disadvantages, Forde resolved to attempt a siege, though his troops were in mutiny for want of pay, and his store of ammunition very scanty. He kept up a hot fire from the 25th of March to the 6th of April, 1759, when his engineers reported that there was not enough of ammunition left to supply the batteries for two days, and, at the same time, intelligence was received that the French army of observation was on the point of effecting a junction with the approaching forces of the Dekkan. Under these apparently desperate circumstances, Forde resolved to hazard an assault. The batteries were directed to keep up as hot a fire as possible during the entire of the day, and the troops were directed to be under arms at ten that night. Forde divided his little force into three divisions, and led them at midnight under the walls of the fort. As no such enterprize had been expected, the assailants gained the palisades of the ditch before they were discovered; a heavy fire was then opened on them which sadly thinned their ranks, but they pressed forward with undaunted energy, until they gained the ramparts, when, wheeling to the right and left, they stormed bastion after bastion with an impetuosity which bore down all opposition. Surprised, confused, and terrified by the sound of firing in different and opposite quarters, the French surrendered at discretion just as dawn began to appear. When the sun rose they found, to their mortification, that in Europeans and disciplined Sepoys they considerably outnumbered their captors.

The effect of this, the most brilliant achievement of the war, was great and immediate. Salabat Jing at once entered into a treaty with Forde, ceding Masulipatam to the English, and consenting to banish the French for ever from his dominions; the reinforcement from Pondicherry arrived too late, and having vainly endeavoured to perform some useful service, returned back, after having endured very severe privations.

A new danger in the mean time menaced Bengal; Alumgír II. Emperor of Delhí, instigated by those who were dissatisfied with the government of Mir Jaffier, granted to his son the investiture of Bengal, Bahar, and Orissa, and the young prince assembled a powerful army to assert his rights. Had Ramnarain, the crafty ruler of Berar, joined the imperial forces, the power of Mir Jaffier and of the English would have been greatly endangered, but the cunning Hindú temporized until he could discover which party had the fairer chance of success; a visit to the imperial camp convinced him that the prince was not suited to the struggle he had undertaken, and he therefore closed the gates of Patna. The imperial forces besieged the place; Clive hastened to its assistance, but before he arrived the prince's allies had turned their arms against each other; the Subahdar of Oude having seized the fortress of Allahabad, and afterwards murdered its rightful owner, whom he had invited to trust himself to his generosity. The desertion of one ally and the murder of another, reduced the heir of the once mighty empire of Delhí to such distress, that he was induced to write a letter to Clive, requesting a sum of money for his subsistence, and promising in requital to withdraw from the province. The terms were granted, and all danger was removed. Mir Jaffier was so grateful for his deliverance, that he conferred upon Clive the rank of a chief Omrah of the empire, and bestowed upon him, as a jaghire, or estate, the rent which the Company was bound to pay for the lands round Calcutta. This splendid grant amounted to the enormous sum of thirty thousand pounds a-year.

Clive returned to Calcutta, where he was joined by Forde just in time to meet the danger of another emergency. Although there was peace between England and Holland, the Dutch were exceedingly jealous of the progress which the English had made in Bengal; an armament was prepared in Batavia, destined to form a counterpoise to the English power in that province. It consisted of seven ships, having on board seven hundred Europeans and eight hundred Malays. Clive obtained an order from Mir Jaffier, that the Dutch should not land, but this they disregarded; they entered the Hoogley, and put their forces on shore within a few miles of Calcutta, to commence their march to the Dutch settlement of Chinsura. Forde received orders to intercept their progress, and three of the Company's ships were prepared to attack the Dutch East Indiamen. It was not without some hesitation that Forde attacked the troops of a nation in amity with England,* but he, nevertheless, acted with such dexterity and promptness, that only fourteen of the Europeans ever reached Chinsura, the rest being either slain or taken prisoners. The seven Dutch ships were forced to surrender to the Company's cruizers, and thus the entire armament was destroyed; and, to complete the matter, the Dutch, in order to avert their total expulsion from Bengal, were forced to pay the expenses of the war. After this exploit, Clive and Forde returned to Europe, leaving the command of the army to Colonel Calliaud, who had just arrived with reinforcements from the Carnatic.

Calliaud was not long permitted to remain idle; the emperor's son again attempted to dethrone Mir Jaffier. Scarcely had he commenced operations, when he received intelligence of his father's murder, and he immediately caused himself to be proclaimed emperor, under the title of Shah Alum. The reverence which still attached to the imperial majesty, and the influence of the Nabob of Oude, whom he wisely appointed his vizier, procured him large additions to his forces, and he advanced to besiege Patna. Contrary to the advice of his most prudent counsellors, Ramnarain resolved to hazard a battle; he was completely defeated, and the small English detachment which had been left for his protection, was cut to pieces. Calliaud immediately marched to save Patna, accompanied by Mir Jaffier's son, Meeran, whose cowardice, incapacity, and treachery nearly frustrated every arrangement made by the English leader. Notwithstanding these disadvantages, Calliaud gained a signal victory over the imperialists, which would have put an end to the war, had not Meeran refused to countenance a vigorous pursuit, preferring to enjoy an interval of ease and pleasure at Patna. This neglect suggested to Shah Alum an enterprize of

* He wrote for more explicit instructions; Clive received the letter while playing a game of whist, he tore a slip from it, and wrote with a pencil,

"Dear Forde,

"Fight them immediately, and I will send an order of council to-morrow."

great promise, to push forward to Moorshedabad and secure the person of Mir Jaffier. Had he shown the same promptitude in the execution of the plan, as there was vigour in its conception, he would assuredly have succeeded, but he delayed until Calliaud and Meeran arrived; on their approach to attack him he set fire to his camp and fled. The imbecile Meeran again prohibited pursuit, and the emperor, having been joined by Mr. Law with his small body of Frenchmen, renewed his attack on Patna. Law twice attempted to storm the town, and was with very great difficulty repulsed. A third assault was expected, and scarcely a hope entertained of its being withstood, when Captain Knox, who had performed the journey from Moorshedabad to Patna in thirteen days, entered the walls with a strong reinforcement. Knox belonged to the same class of officers as Clive and Forde. Scarcely allowing his soldiers any time for rest and refreshment, he attacked the imperial camp during the hour of afternoon's repose, surprised his enemies in their sleep, and drove them from their works, to which they never returned.

This victory had scarcely been achieved, when intelligence arrived that the Naib, or deputy-governor of Poorania, was approaching to join the emperor with twelve thousand men and thirty pieces of cannon. Knox, whose forces consisted only of two hundred Europeans, one batallion of Sepoys, five field-pieces, and about three hundred irregular horse, perfectly astounded the people of Patna, by declaring his resolution to cross the river and give battle to the Naib. Ramnarain's soldiers unanimously declared that they would have nothing to say to such an act of madness; an auxiliary rájá, who had about three hundred men in his pay, was, however, so charmed with Knox's valour that he volunteered his aid, which was accepted. Knox's first design was to surprise the enemy's camp at night, but his guide missed his way, and this plan was abandoned. His troops were preparing to take a little repose when the Naib's army was seen approaching. Knox promptly took his ground, and though surrounded by his enemies, defeated them at every point, drove them from the field, and pursued them until his men were sinking from sheer exhaustion. Colonel Calliaud and his precious ally, Meeran, soon got on the track of the retreating Naib, and continued the pursuit for several days. At length, on the night of the 6th of July, 1760, Meeran's tent was struck by lightning, and that prince with all his attendants perished. The death of their leader, is to an Indian army the signal to disband, and Calliaud, aware of this danger, returned with the English forces to Patna.

Clive's departure for England produced injurious changes in the government of Calcutta. According to the usual routine, the government should have devolved on the senior member of council, but the court of directors conferred it upon Mr. Vansittart, who had acquired an unmerited reputation for financial talents, and who possessed an imposing gravity of demeanour, which some believed to indicate steadiness of purpose, and others supposed to be the result of obstinate stupidity. His appointment gave great and not unjust offence to many of the members of the Calcutta council; parties were formed at the board, and state affairs were discussed, with a heat and violence which led to very disgraceful results. Vansittart found the treasury at Calcutta empty, the troops at Patna ready to mutiny for want of pay, Mir Jaffier's allowance to his auxiliaries several months in arrear, and very little hope of obtaining either that or the large balance due to the Company from his first arrangement. Mr. Vansittart instead of consulting the council, discussed his plans with a secret and select committee; the result of their deliberations was a determination to compel Mir Jaffier to place the entire administration of his affairs in the hands of his son-in-law, Mir Casim, and a detachment of troops was sent to Moorshedabad, to enforce the viceroy's compliance. Mir Jaffier acted with unexpected spirit, he refused to yield to any thing but force, and when he found he had no reasonable chance of defending himself, he refused to retain an empty title, and came to reside as a private individual in Calcutta. Men remembered the high price which Mir Jaffier had paid for his elevation; it was reported and believed, that Mir Casim had similarly purchased the viceroyalty from Vansittart and his select committee, and many condemned the impolicy of the transaction, because they despaired of obtaining any share of the bribes.

Mir Casim exerted himself to pay the sums for which he had contracted, as the price of his elevation, the English lending him military aid to enforce the collection of revenues in the provinces. About the same time, Major Carnac, who succeeded Calliaud in the command of the troops at Patna, defeated the imperial forces, and compelled Shah Alum to abandon the province of Bahar. In this battle Mr. Law was taken prisoner, and the respect with which the English officers treated their gallant enemy, produced a very favourable impression on the minds of the Hindús and Mohammedans.

The payments to the English and the expenses of reducing some insurgent chiefs who were aided by the Mahrattas, exhausted Mir Casim's resources; he resolved to recruit his finances by the plunder of Ramnarain, the Hindú governor of Berar. Major Carnac and his sucessor Colonel Coote, aware of the false pretences which were brought forward, for injuring so old and faithful a friend of the English, as Ramnarain, steadily protected him against the artifices of Mir Casim, but Mr. Vansittart was resolved to support the viceroy of his choice, and he recalled both Coote and Carnac from Patna. Mir Casim made that use of his opportunity, which Mr. Vansittart was unable or unwilling to foresee. Ramnarain was immediately seized and thrown into prison; his house was plundered; his friends tortured to obtain confession of hidden treasures, and his life was only spared for the moment, lest the indignation of the English should be too strongly roused. He was eventually put to death with circumstances of great barbarity.

The intelligence of these events, excited a violent spirit of opposition against Mr. Vansittart's government, both in the presidency and the factories; the natives of rank lost all confidence in English protection, when they saw so steady a supporter of the English interests as Ramnarain, sacrificed without scruple; and many of the Europeans, both in the military and civil service, did not scruple to assert, that such partiallity to Mir Casim was the result of corruption, or of a blind determination to support the viceroy at all hazards. At this critical moment, Mr. Vansittart's chief friends in the council were recalled to Europe, for having signed, conjointly with Clive, a letter in which the policy of the court of directors was condemned in very severe, or rather very intemperate terms. The president was thus left in a minority, and Ellis, the most violent of his opponents, was appointed resident at Patna. Ellis treated Mir Casim with the most insulting airs of authority; he seized several of his collectors for interfering with the transit of goods to and from the stations, and he took forcible possession of a quantity of nitre which had been purchased for the viceroy's private use. In these acts of violence, Mr. Ellis was supported by the whole body of the Company's servants. Since the elevation of Mir Casim, they had insisted that the Company's passport, which was only entitled to protect the goods of actual exportation, or importation, from the payment of transit duties, should protect the private trade of the Company's agents, of all descriptions, in every part of the country. Thus protected, the English were fast engrossing the entire trade of the provinces, to the ruin of the native merchants, and to the annihilation of the customs' duties, which were the chief source of the viceroy's revenues. Vansittart honourably exerted himself to check this glaring abuse; but it afforded vast emoluments to the majority of the council; Warren Hastings alone supported the projected system of reform. An arrangement was made with the viceroy, by which private English traders were bound to pay the same transit duties as his own subjects, and no more. These equitable conditions were instantly and ostentatiously violated by the Company's servants. Mir Casim then published an edict abolishing all transit duties in his dominions, in order that his own merchants should participate in the spoils of their sovereign. It will scarcely be believed that peculation had rendered the majority of the council of Calcutta so dead to every feeling of justice, shame and ordinary decency, as to induce them to declare that this abolition of duties was an act of hostility against the Company, and to menace war, unless the edict was recalled. Mir Casim paid no attention to so iniquitous a requisition, and both sides prepared to decide the dispute by force of arms.

Some boats, laden with muskets for the use of the troops in Patna, arrived at Mongheer; the viceroy, aware that the resident, Mr. Ellis, meditated the seizure of that city, stopped the boats, and it was with great difficulty that Messrs. Amyatt and Hay, who had been sent to remonstrate with him by the party opposed to Vansittart, could obtain leave for the convoy to pass. After some discussion, he granted permission for Amyatt to return to Calcutta, but retained Mr. Hay as an hostage. Intelligence of Amyatt's departure having reached Ellis, he laid aside all moderation, and by a night-attack surprised and took the city of Patna. Mir Casim, justly enraged at such an outrage, sent a party to overtake and bring back Mr. Amyatt; that gentleman resisted and was slain, with several of his attendants. The enterprize on Patna, was as unfortunate in its termination, as it was unjust in its conception; the troops after entering the town, were allowed to disperse in search of plunder; the governor, who had only retreated a few miles, when he was joined by a reinforcement from Mongheer, returned and attacked them unexpectedly; the English were driven into their factory, which after a feeble defence, they evacuated and attempted to make their escape in boats. They were interrupted, forced to surrender and sent prisoners to Mongheer, and their fate was shared by the English belonging to the factory of Casimbazar, which was stormed and plundered by the natives.

When the news of these unexpected events reached Calcutta, the council was thrown into the utmost confusion. After much angry crimination and recrimination, it was resolved, in opposition to Vansittart and Hastings, that no proposals of accommodation should be received from Mir Casim, and that the imbecile Mir Jaffier should be invited to resume the authority of which he had been recently deprived. Mir Casim's administration had been on the whole beneficial to the provinces; he paid off the heavy arrears due from his predecessor to the English; availing himself of the services of Sumroo, a German adventurer, who had been a serjeant in the French army, he trained several battalions of Sepoys in European discipline, and he had adopted many wise plans, to encourage the industry and trade of his native subjects. Such merits were, in the East, sufficient to counterbalance the original crime of usurpation, but in the view of the council of Calcutta, his very virtues afforded sufficient ground for his dethronement.

On the 2nd of July, 1763, the English army commenced the campaign; their first engagement was with the van of the viceroy's army, which had taken up a strong position to protect Moorshedabad; the Indians were defeated, but they fell back upon Gheriah, where they were joined by Mir Casim himself with all his forces. On the 2nd of August he was attacked, and, after a fierce engagement which lasted four hours, totally routed, with the loss of all his cannon, baggage, and one hundred and fifty boats laden with provisions. The beaten army then entrenched itself in the strong ground supplied by the range of hills at Oodiva; the English were detained nearly a month before the lines, but on the 5th of September they made a successful assault on the viceroy's position, and drove the viceroy's troops from their entrenchments, in the utmost confusion. They then laid siege to Mongheer, which the viceroy had made his capital; a practicable breach was made, and the garrison, amounting to two thousand Sepoys, surrendered themselves prisoners of war. Each successive defeat inflamed the fears and rage of Casim to renewed acts of cruelty; when routed at Gheriah, he commanded the execution of Ramnarain with several chiefs and persons of distinction; after the rout of Oodiva, he put to death two of the Sets of Moorshedabad; and now, driven almost to insanity by the loss of his capital, he commanded all his European pursuers to be butchered, with the single exception of Dr. Fullerton, who had won his favour by the exercise of his professional skill. The execution of this barbarous command was entrusted to the renegade Sumroo, who fulfilled it to the very letter. Patna was taken by storm on the 6th of November, and Mir Casim, losing all hopes, fled to Oude, where he placed himself under the protection of the Nabob-vizier. Though unable to compete with the English vizier, his disciplined Sepoys enabled the vizier to gain an easy victory over the revolted inhabitants of Bundelcund, who had refused to pay their quota of taxation.

The English remained in cantonments on the frontiers of Oude, partly in hope that the Nabob-vizier could be induced to surrender Mir Casim, Sumroo, and the other deserters, but principally in consequence of the mutinous dispositions of the troops, three hundred of whom, principally French and Germans, marched off in a body to Benares. Sumroo, aware of the insurrectionary spirit in the English camp, suddenly attacked it near Patna, May 3rd, 1764, but was repulsed with great loss; Carnac, the English commander, was too weak to follow up his advantages, and the war lingered until the arrival of Major, afterwards Sir Hector Monro, with a strong reinforcement from Bombay.

Monro had hardly taken the command when the spirit of mutiny raged fiercer than ever; a whole battalion of Sepoys, with their arms and accoutrements, went off to join the enemy. They were, however, overtaken and captured by some troops which remained faithful, and twenty-four of the ring-leaders were sentenced by a court-martial to be blown from the mouths of cannon. The whole army was drawn out to witness this fearful execution; four of the unhappy men were blown away, when the officers of the Sepoys came to the Major, and declared that their men would not allow the execution of any more. Monro at once ordered his field-pieces to be loaded with grape, and the Europeans to form in line, having the guns at proper intervals; he then directed the Sepoy officers to return to their men and command them to ground their arms, declaring that if a single man stirred he would give immediate orders to fire. The Sepoys, daunted by his firmness, instantly obeyed, and the execution proceeded.

After this exhibition of resolute determination, Monro marched against the Nabob-vizier of Oude, and completely routed his army near Buxar. The emperor Shah Alum himself now sought the protection of the English, declaring that he had been held in captivity by his ambitious vizier. Mir Casim fled to Rohillas, believing that he was no longer safe in Oude, and the emperor concluded a peace on terms which left the English supreme in Bengal. These advantages were counterbalanced by the dilapidated condition of the finances in Calcutta. It was utterly impossible for Mir Jaffier to pay the sums due to the Company, and at the same time, to gratify the rapacity of individuals who claimed exorbitant compensations "for losses sustained, or said to be sustained, in an illicit monopoly of the necessaries of life, carried on against the orders of the Company, and to the utter ruin of many thousands of the Indian merchants." These demands were urged, too, at a time when half of his provincial revenues had been ceded to the Company, and when the abuses of private trade had completely deprived him of the income derived from transit duties. His embarrassments proved too much for his feeble health, and he died a victim to care and vexation, in January, 1765.

The Company's servants, without even going through the form of consulting the emperor or his vizier, took upon themselves to invest Mir Jaffier's second son with the viceroyalty, stipulating at the same time that the military defence of the country should be placed in their hands. They also appointed Rez-Khan to be the viceroy's prime minister and deputy—a wise choice, though one which was far from being acceptable to the new potentate. Vansittart, finding that he was in every instance overborne by the majority of the council, resigned his office and was succeeded by Mr. Spencer, under whose auspices the treaty with the new viceroy was completed.

The East India proprietors in England, had been hitherto inactive spectators of the proceedings of their servants in India, but, alarmed at the intelligence of renewed wars in India, of the mutinous spirit of their troops, and the disturbed condition of their finances, they proposed to the court of directors that Clive, who had been elevated to the peerage, should be appointed governor, as the only man capable of retrieving their disordered and almost desperate affairs. This was far from an agreeable proposal to the directors ; Clive's last act, before leaving India, had been a direct insult to their authority ; he had commenced a Chancery suit to recover from them the proceeds of his jaghire, which they attempted to withhold, and he undisguisedly was the strenuous opponent of Mr. Sullivan, the deputy chairman, and the most influential member of the court. After a violent contest, thirteen of the directors voted for his appointment, which was resisted by eleven. The high powers which he demanded were given with less difficulty ; he was invested with the authority of Commander-in-chief, President, and Governor of Bengal; and, together with a committee of four, nominated by the directors, empowered to act without consulting the council, or being subject to its control.

Bengal was not the only part of India whose condition excited uneasiness; the capture of Pondicherry enabled the English to secure the sovereignty of the Carnatic for their creature, Mohammed Alí, and they soon began to show the Nabob that they expected him to rule for their profit. He was forced to raise large sums at an usurious interest to defray the expenses of the late war, and was, at the same time, defrauded of his share of the stores which had been taken from the French. Assistance was given him to reduce his revolted vassal at Vellore ; but they refused to aid him in the subjugation of Tanjore, and took upon themselves to act as mediators in the contest. They compelled the King of Tanjore to pay a large sum to the Nabob as a composition for arrears, but, in return, they obtained for him permission to repair the mound of the Cavery, an embankment which, by preventing the chief branch of that river from re-uniting with the Coleroon, supplies Tanjore with the means of irrigation, and thus contributes to the fertility of the country. They also joined him in no very justifiable attack on the governor of Madura, who made so obstinate a resistance, that his capture, which was finally effected by treachery, is said to have cost a million sterling. Finally, the English resolved to take the entire administration of the revenues of the Carnatic into their own hands. The Nabob was very unwilling to consent to such an arrangement, but resistance was useless, and he submitted.

Lord Clive had two monstrous evils to correct: the custom of receiving presents, which were in fact arbitrary extortions; and the abuses of the private trade. To remedy the first, he insisted that the servants of the Company, both civil and military, should sign certain covenants, in which it was stipulated that they should not accept presents from the native princes under any pretence whatever. General Carnac delayed signing these regulations until he had received two lacs of rupees from the emperor; but this present was fairly earned, and was subsequently sanctioned by the East Indian authorities. The subject of trade presented far greater difficulties; Clive knew very little about commercial principles, and he felt strongly the necessity of giving some emoluments to the servants of the Company, as a compensation for the miserable and inadequate amount of their salaries. Instead of abolishing the private trade, he created a monopoly of the trade in salt, betel-nut, and tobacco, to be carried on exclusively for the benefit of the superior servants of the Company; the profits to be divided in shares proportioned to their respective ranks. No statesman in the present day would defend such an arrangement, but a century ago, few persons understood the real nature of trade; the East India Company was itself a monopoly, and its servants could not suspect that they were wrong in acting on the principles of their masters.

The war against the Nabob-vizier of Oude had been so vigorously prosecuted, that he was compelled to throw himself on the mercy of the English, and submit to whatever terms they were pleased to dictate. He was permitted to retain his dominions, with the exception of Korah and Allahabad, which were resigned to the emperor, and he engaged not to molest his vassal, Bulwant Sing, Rájá of Benares, who had joined the English during the war, and rendered them important services. Warned by the abuses, which under the name of free trade, the Company's servants had perpetrated in Bengal, Bahar, and Orissa, he refused to entertain any proposals on the subject, and the name of trade was not so much as mentioned in the treaty. The unfortunate emperor was obliged to abandon his claim to all the arrears of revenue due to him from the Bengal provinces, and, on the condition of receiving twenty-six lacs of rupees annually, to assign over to the Company, the *Dewanee*, or right of receiving and collecting all the public revenues in Bengal, Bahar, and Orissa.

During the war, the Company had made an allowance to their officers, called *Batta*, to cover the heavy expenses which service in the field entails in India. When the army was sent to support Mir Jaffier, he agreed to give the officers twice the usual amount, under the name of *double batta;* and the practice had been continued by Mir Casim. When the revenues of Bengal were transferred to the Company, the *double batta* was found to be a very serious charge, which the finances could ill bear, but no party had courage to propose, much less enforce a reduction. Lord Clive resolved to remedy the evil, and having first established a new system for regimenting the troops, he issued an order, that from and after January 1st, 1766, double batta should cease, and that, with some few exceptions in favour of distant and expensive stations, officers in the field should receive single batta only, and when in garrison or cantonments, that they should have no allowance in addition to their pay.

The officers entered into a conspiracy to resign their commissions in a body on a certain day, unless the double batta was restored, at a time when the province was menaced by an invasion of the Mahrattas. Clive received early intelligence of the danger; he sent expresses to Calcutta and Madras for a supply of fresh officers, arrested the chief movers of the conspiracy, and took effectual care to prevent them from debauching the minds of the men. A number of the ringleaders, and among others, General Sir Robert Fletcher, were tried, convicted of mutiny, and dismissed the service. This leniency was probably caused by some doubt of the Company's power to punish Europeans capitally; but Clive would probably have gone much farther, could he have foreseen that, by family interest and political intrigue, Sir Robert Fletcher would not only be restored to his rank, but appointed at no distant period to the command of the forces in the presidency of Madras.

The court of directors repeatedly disallowed the trading company which Clive had formed for the monopoly of salt, betel-nut, and tobacco; finding their remonstrances disregarded, they sent out orders so direct and positive as to leave no room for disobedience, and it was arranged that the company should be dissolved, so soon as existing contracts were fulfilled and accounts settled. With this event Clive's administration terminated; he left his authority in the hands of a committee, at the head of which was Mr. Verelst.

The intelligence of the great acquisitions which Clive had made, raised the most extravagant expectations in the minds of the proprietors of East India stock; forgetting the vast expense incurred in making these conquests, and the heavy charge which their retention involved, they carried, in opposition to the proprietors, a vote that the dividends should be increased to twelve-and-a-half per cent.; as this could not be done without borrowing money at a ruinous rate of interest, the interference of the British ministry and parliament was invoked, and thus, to the annoyance of both parties, the question was brought before the public, of permitting a trading company to exercise sovereignty over a great and extending empire. The delusion of the enormous riches to be obtained from India, continued during the successive administrations of Mr. Verelst and Mr. Cartier, though even under their peaceful rule the revenues were scarcely adequate to meet the ordinary expenses of the government, and an expedition undertaken to restore the Rájá of Nepaul, who had been dethroned by his neighbour, the Ghoorka, was abandoned for want of funds, it being necessary to husband all the resources which British India could afford, in order to meet the imminent dangers which menaced the presidency of Madras.

CHAPTER VIII.

THE FIRST WAR WITH HYDER ALI: ADMINISTRATION OF WARREN HASTINGS.

THE East India Company was transformed from a trading association into a sovereign power, without its consent, and almost without its knowledge. Hence it happened that many advantages, which could have been obtained with little difficulty at critical moments, were abandoned, to be afterwards recovered with no small expenditure of blood and treasure. Many writers have assailed the Company and its servants for acts of questionable prudence, and still more questionable morality, in utter forgetfulness that Asia is not Europe, and that in the period when such an extensive empire as that of Delhí is crumbling into ruins, and when its fragments are placed to reward the cupidity of the first daring adventurer who can muster sufficient to proclaim his independence, it is impossible to adopt any uniform and consistent course of conduct. The most perfect beings that ever existed, must have been obliged to regulate their conduct by existing circumstances, which they could neither command nor control. When the conquest of Pondicherry gave the English the supremacy in the Carnatic, they little imagined that they would be involved in the complicated politics of the entire Dekkan, and that their efforts to obtain the tranquil possession of the Circars, would lead to the most perilous war in which they had ever been engaged in India.

The Subahdar of the Dekkan, Salabat Jing, had not been mistaken in his belief that the departure of Bussy and the French, would compromise his safety; he was murdered in September, 1760, by command of his brother, Nizam Alí, who resolved to assert the rights of his viceroyalty over the Dekkan, with greater stringency than his victim, and particularly to establish the ancient supremacy of his viceroyalty over the Carnatic. He invaded the country, and devastated it with more than the usual barbarity of Indian warfare, but on the approach of the English army, made a precipitate retreat. When the English obtained from the emperor the investiture of the northern Circars, which had been always considered part of the viceroyalty of the Dekkan, Nizam Alí resisted their attempts to take possession of the country, until they purchased his permission by stipulating to pay an annual tribute, and to assist him when necessary by the aid of an auxiliary force. The latter stipulation involved the presidency in hostile relations with Hyder Alí, the Governor of Mysore.

Hyder Alí, during the wars between the French and English in the Carnatic, had risen from being the captain of a petty band of marauders to the rank of commander of the army of Mysore, by prudently watching opportunities to sell his services at the moment when they were most wanting, and would bring the highest price. At the same time he acquired an independent principality for himself, by the conquest of the Nairs in Malabar, and by seizing several small districts, which in the distracted condition of Southern India, seemed to be left without a master. The English had joined with the Nizam, pursuant to their unwise stipulation in the invasion of his acquisitions; he made peace with that faithless prince, and prepared to attack the allies whom he had abandoned.

Colonel Smith having received intimation that it was the intention of the Nizam to betray the English to Hyder, retreated to Trincomalee, after having sustained a smart action against the forces of his faithless ally and open enemy. In several engagements of little moment, the English maintained their wonted superiority over Indian troops, and the Nizam, alarmed at his danger, hastily broke off his connection with Hyder, and renewed the treaty with the Presidency of Madras.

This change of policy on the part of the Nizam, filled the minds of the council of Madras with perilous dreams of conquest; they looked upon Mysore as an easy acquisition, and actually conferred upon Mohammed Alí the title of its sovereignty; they recalled Colonel Smith, who was too experienced an officer not to understand the danger which was thus wantonly provoked, and conferred the chief command upon Colonel Wood, who was devoid of experience in Indian warfare.

Hyder defeated Wood, who was unable to save his baggage, and then by a pretended show of timidity drew the English army to a distance from Madras. He then made a rapid march of one hundred and twenty miles in three days; at the head of six thousand horse, he appeared suddenly on the Mount of St. Thomas, in the immediate vicinity of the English capital. The Presidency were filled with consternation. The fort might undoubtedly have held out till the arrival of Smith; but the open town, with its riches, the adjacent country and the garden-houses of the President and Council, would have been ravaged and destroyed. Peace was therefore made with Hyder on his own terms; a mutual restitution of conquests, and a treaty of mutual alliance in defensive wars.

In the meantime the British government was compelled to interfere in the concerns of the Company; a bill was introduced into parliament, vesting the government of Bengal in a governor-general and four councillors, whose authority extended over the two other Presidencies, and establishing at Calcutta a supreme court of judicature, consisting of one chief and three puisne judges. The patronage of these officers was placed in the court of directors, subject to the approbation of the crown; the Company's correspondence of every kind, was obliged to be laid before the ministry; presents were strictly prohibited; and the governor-general, the councillors and judges, were excluded from all commercial profits and presents. Finally, the qualification for a vote in the court of proprietors was raised to one thousand pounds, and instead of an annual election of the whole of the directors, it was enacted "that only one-fourth of the number should go out every year." These changes were strenuously resisted by the Company, but the ministerial projects were supported by large parliamentary majorities, and in due course of time became law.

Mr. Warren Hastings succeeded Mr. Cartier, in the government of Bengal, early in 1772; great expectations were formed of his financial and administrative powers, from the improvements which he had effected, when employed in a subordinate station on the coast of Coromandel. The directors had been sadly disappointed in the amount of treasure derived from Bengal; they first blamed their European servants, and then turned their wrath against the native agents; orders were issued for the arrest of Mohammed Reza Khan, whom the English had themselves appointed chief minister to the viceroy of Bengal; and Rájá Shitab

Roy, who held the same office in the court of Patna, was similarly treated. After a long detention both were acquitted, but they were not restored to their offices. That portion of Reza Khan's duty, which consisted in the guardianship of the Rájá's family, was conferred on Munny Begum, a second wife, or rather concubine of Meer Jaffier, and the administration of the finances was entrusted to Rájá Goordass, the son of Rájá Nuncomar.

In the meantime, Shah Alum became impatient to be restored to his throne in Delhí, and urged the English to fulfil the promises they had made of assisting him in effecting that object. His requests and remonstrances being disregarded, he entered into an alliance with the Mahrattas; an army of these adventurers easily opened for the monarch a way to his capital, but they insisted that their services should be rewarded by the plunder of the country of the Rohillas. The emperor joined them in an expedition against Zabita Khan, whom he had deprived of the government of Delhí, and whom he therefore suspected of hostile designs. Zabita Khan made a spirited defence, but was unable to withstand the united forces of the imperialists and the Mahrattas; he was completely defeated, his wife and children fell into the hands of the enemy, and his country, which had long flourished under a beneficent government, was laid waste by the Mahrattas in spite of the remonstrances of the emperor. The other Rohilla chiefs were filled with alarm; in their terror they applied for aid to their old enemy, the Subahdar of Oude, who was exposed to equal danger with themselves from the Mahrattas, and they entered into a treaty, by which they engaged to pay him thirty lacs of rupees, on condition of his expelling the Mahrattas from the Rohilla country. In the meantime, the Mahrattas, having quarrelled with the emperor, returned to Delhí, forced an entrance into that capital, and made Shah Alum, in all but name, a prisoner. Having extorted from their captive a grant of the districts of Korah and Allahabad, in which he had been established by the English, they returned to the banks of the Ganges, which they made preparations to cross. The Rohillas urgently requested the Subahdar of Oude to lend them effective assistance; he evaded their applications, but, when the Mahrattas retired in consequence of events in their own country, he demanded payment of the promised subsidy though he had never granted the stipulated protection.

A meeting took place between the Subahdar and Mr. Warren Hastings, at Benares, in the beginning of September, 1773, and it led to a treaty in which the Emperor of Delhí and the Rohillas, were deliberately sold and sacrificed to the ruler of Oude. From the time that Shah Alum had thrown himself into the arms of the Mahrattas, the English had made his conduct a pretext for withholding the stipulated tribute from Bengal, though it was their refusal of their promised aid, which had caused the unfortunate sovereign to take this course. Mr. Hastings now went farther; he sold to the Subahdar of Oude, for the sum of fifty lacs of rupees, the districts of Korah and Allahabad, which the English occupied under pretence of preserving them for the emperor. Still more indefensible was the conduct pursued towards the Rohillas; Mr. Hastings agreed to aid the ambitious ruler of Oude in the "extermination" of this innocent people, on condition of his paying forty lacs of rupees into the Company's treasury, and defraying the expenses of the corps employed in his service.

No opposition appears to have been made to the withholding the stipulated payment from Shah Alum, and the alienation of the territories which had been placed under the guardianship of English honour; but the destruction of the Rohillas was so inconsistent with the plainest dictates of common justice, and even sound policy, that Mr. Hastings for some time concealed this part of the treaty of Benares from his council. The Subahdar, however, demanded the promised aid, and an English brigade, under the command of Colonel Champion, was sent to join in the projected invasion. The brunt of the war fell upon the English, who totally routed the Rohillas and slew their gallant leader, Hafiz Rahmet Khan; but all the advantages of the victory were seized by the cruel and rapacious followers of the Subahdar. Never was triumph more fearfully abused; every one who bore the name of Rohilla, was either butchered or forced to seek safety in flight and exile. The Emperor of Delhi had been induced to favour this enterprize by a promise of a share in the conquered territory, but, as his troops arrived too late to take an active part in the war, Suja-ed-dowla refused to fulfil his engagements, and was supported in his breach of faith by the English. In the end, the Subahdar acquired possession of the whole of Rohilcund, with the exception of a small district, which, at the entreaty of the English, he assigned to one of the Rohilla chiefs named Fyzollah Khan, after receiving full assurance of his fidelity and allegiance.

On the 1st of August, 1774, the new constitution which the British parliament had framed for the government of India, came into operation, and, on the 19th of the following October, three new councillors arrived from England, who, together with Messrs. Hastings and Barwell, were to form the board of administration. The subject of the Rohilla war was the first discussed by the council, and the three councillors who had just arrived, severely censured its justice and its policy. They also complained that the correspondence of Mr. Middleton, whom the governor-general had sent as political agent to the court of Oude, was withheld from them, and, in their indignation, they voted that the agent should be recalled, that the British forces should be withdrawn from the Subahdar, and that immediate payment should be demanded of the sums stipulated for their services. At this crisis, Suja-ed-dowla died, and the council insisted that his son and successor should not only fulfil his engagements, but cede to the Company the territory of the Rájá Cheyte Sing, Zemindar of Benares, and raise the allowance for the service of the European brigade. Mr. Hastings protested against this extortion to no purpose; the policy of his opponents in the council, was warmly approved by the court of directors at home.

While the territories of the Company in Bengal and the Carnatic had been gradually enlarged, little or no addition had been made to their possessions in western India. Bassein and Salsette, which commanded the entrance into the harbour of Bombay, remained in the possession of the Portuguese until the year 1750, when they were occupied by the Mahrattas, by whom they were highly valued. An opportunity of acquiring these valuable posts appeared to be offered by a cruel war among the Mahrattas, arising out of a disputed succession to the office of Peishwa, which, though nominally a subordinate dignity, had for some time included all the real sovereignty of the state. A similar dispute at the same time distracted Gujarát, which had been wrested from the empire of Delhí by Pillagee Guccowar, or "the herdsman," who rendered the sovereignty hereditary in his family, and rendered the epithet by which he was distinguished, the title of royalty. The Presidency of Bombay supported Ragonat Ras, or, as he is more commonly called, Ragoba, as lawful claimant of the office of Peishwa, stipulating to receive Salsette, Bassein, and some other cessions as the price of their services. After some delay these terms were ratified, and these important stations were occupied by English garrisons. An army was at the same time sent to put Ragoba in possession of Poonah, the Mahratta capital, which would, no doubt, have succeeded had not orders arrived from the Supreme Council of Calcutta, disapproving the entire course of policy pursued by the Presidency of Bombay, and peremptorily commanding that the cause of Ragoba should be abandoned. A treaty was concluded with that chieftain's rivals, which deprived the English of Bassein and all their acquisitions in Gujarát, but which, at the same time, secured them the possession of Salsette and the adjacent islands. To complete the confusion, this arrangement had scarcely been made when letters arrived from the court of directors, approving, in the strongest terms, the previous proceedings of the Presidency of Bombay, which had just been condemned and overthrown by the council of Calcutta.

In the meantime, the majority of the council had begun to receive grave charges of corruption and peculation against Mr. Warren Hastings, while he exerted all his authority and influence as governor-general to stifle enquiry. The principal witness on the most serious charge, was the Rájá Nuncomar, who exhibited the particulars of a sum amounting to 354,105 rupees, which he asserted that his son Goordass and Munny Begum, had paid for their elevation to the offices mentioned in a preceding page. So great was the effect produced on the council by this evidence, that Mr. Hastings was commanded to refund the money which he had thus illegally received. But he refused to acknowledge the majority as a council, and returned no answer.

A suit was instituted against Nuncomar, for conspiring with others to get up a petition against the parties to the prosecution, but it proved a complete failure. An obscure native was brought forward to indict Nuncomar for perjury, and on this charge he was arrested and thrown into prison. He was then tried before the supreme court, by a jury of Englishmen, convicted and hanged. The crime for which he was made to suffer, was not capital by the laws of Hindustan, whether Mohammedan or Hindú; the date of its alleged commission was

1770, while the law which gave jurisdiction to the supreme court, was not passed until 1774; it had been expressly declared, that all civil disputes between native and native, should be decided in their own courts, and it was the obvious design of the framers of the statute to extend the same regulation to penal cases; finally, there were said to have been marks of precipitancy and unfairness on the part of the judge, which shewed that Nuncomar was a predestined victim. The impeachment of Sir Elijah Impey, the judge who tried the case, subsequently failed, and the execution cannot therefore be fairly stigmatized as a judicial murder, but there can be no doubt that it was a case in which the rigours of the law were extended to their very utmost range, in order to remove an individual whose inconvenient disclosures rendered him dangerous to persons in power.

The necessity of new arrangements for collecting the revenues, led to fresh disputes between Mr. Hastings and Mr. Francis; the former proposed that the districts should be farmed to the Zemindars on leases for life; the latter recommended that the Zemindars should be recognized as proprietors of the soil. After a long dispute, both projects were rejected by the court of directors, who ordered that the settlements should be made only from year to year, on an average of the collection raised during the three years preceding. At this time, the death of one of his opponents, gave Mr. Hastings a majority in the council, but he had previously deputed a gentleman of the name of Maclean, to convey his resignation to England, where it had been accepted by the court of directors. Mr. Wheler was named as his successor, presented to the king for his approbation, and accepted. General Clavering, as senior member of the council, was empowered to administer the government until Mr. Wheler should arrive.

When this intelligence arrived in Bengal, it produced a scene of confusion, which nearly led to fatal consequences. Hastings disavowed the proceedings of his agent, and refused to resign; Clavering insisted that he should be recognized as governor. An appeal to arms seemed inevitable; Hastings was ready to abide the result, but Clavering fortunately had either less courage or more prudence, and he referred the matter to the courts of law, which decided in favour of Hastings. No sooner was his authority thus recognized, than he began to reverse the proceedings of the former majority of the council. Mr. Bristow was recalled from Oude, and the governor's creature Mr. Middleton was sent to take his place; Mr. Fowke was deprived of his office in Benares, under the pretence that the purposes of his mission were accomplished, but in a few days after another resident was appointed. Both these transactions were condemned by the court of directors, but Hastings paid no regard to their remonstrances.

The interference of the supreme council in the affairs of the Mahrattas, had left the minds of the rulers of Poonah and those of the presidency of Bengal, in a state of mutual jealousy and dissatisfaction. Certain French emissaries made their appearance in Poonah, and there was reason to fear that they would obtain from the Mahrattas, permission for their countrymen to establish a station on the coast of Malabar. Some of the council proposed to conciliate the Mahratta chiefs by yielding up Ragoba, but Mr. Hastings espoused the policy of the Bombay presidency, which he had so recently condemned, and ordered forces to be prepared to aid in restoring Ragoba to his office as Peishwa. Six battalions of Sepoys, one company of artillery, and a corps of cavalry, marched from the station of Calpee, under the command of Colonel Leslie, to act in concert with the Bombay army, which was entrusted to Colonel Egerton and two civilians, who acted as field deputies. Never, perhaps, were any expeditions worse managed; Egerton contrived, after wasting much precious time, to reach a post within sixteen miles of Poonah, where he found the Mahrattas prepared to dispute his progress. He and the other deputies lost what little sense or courage they possessed; in spite of the remonstrances of the military men, who felt assured of an easy victory, orders were given for an immediate retreat. It was as wretchedly conducted as it had been imprudently commenced. The Mahrattas overtook the retiring soldiers, and harassed them very severely; the cowardly committee then proposed to enter into a convention, and concluded a bargain for their own safety on the most humiliating terms.

Colonel Leslie's conduct was equally disgraceful; he advanced very slowly, wasting his time in negociations and transactions with various local chiefs, which exposed him to the suspicion of selfish and dishonourable motives. The supreme council, finding that he disregarded their urgent commands to accelerate his march, sent orders that he should be deprived of his command, but he escaped this disgrace by death; he was succeeded by Colonel Goddard, an officer of a very different character. Goddard advanced into the very heart of the Mahratta country, in the hope of being able to co-operate with the Bengal army; fortunately, he received timely notice of the disgraceful convention which had been concluded; he peremptorily refused to accede to its terms, and led his forces to Surat, after having marched three hundred miles in nineteen days, and baffled the efforts of twenty thousand Mahratta horse, sent to intercept his retreat. Here he was joined by Ragoba, who had contrived to make his escape from Poonah.

The supreme council disavowed the convention which the committee had concluded, and appointed Goddard to the command of the army. It required all that officer's firmness and prudence to overcome the paltry jealousy of the Bombay authorities, but he finally succeeded, and took the field in the beginning of January, 1780. With little difficulty he obtained possession of Dubhoy, and carried Ahmedabad by storm; the Mahrattas attempted to overreach him in diplomacy, by opening protracted discussions which would have detained him until the season for operations was past, but he refused to listen to their proposals, and on the morning of April 3rd, surprised Scindiah and Holkar in their camp, routing their numerous forces with the utmost facility, and almost without loss.

Sir Eyre Coote, who had been appointed to the vacancy in the supreme council produced by the death of Colonel Clavering, arrived in Bengal just as a treaty had been concluded with a Hindu prince, called the Rana, who possessed a hilly country of considerable extent, lying on the Jumna, between the territories of the Mahratta chieftain, Scindiah, and the kingdom of Oude. Intelligence arrived that the territory of the Rama had been invaded by a body of Mahrattas, which his want of resources made it impossible for him to resist. A small body of troops which had been prepared, under Captain Popham, to reinforce Goddard, was sent to the assistance of the Rana. Though he had only a single battalion under his command, Popham greatly distinguished himself by his enterprise and talents. He expelled the Mahrattas from Gohud, pursued them into their own territories, where he took the fortress of Lahâr. But a much more memorable exploit was the capture of Gualior, which had always been regarded as impregnable by the princes of Hindustan. This fortress is built on the summit of a stupendous rock, scarped round to the depth of about twenty feet, having a precipitous ascent of about one hundred feet from the scarp to the wall; the rampart wall itself being thirty feet high. It was garrisoned by a thousand picked men; yet Popham attacked it by escalade on the 3rd of August, and carried it by sheer valour. This brilliant exploit struck so much terror into the Mahrattas, that they abandoned the surrounding country, and conveyed the alarm to Scindiah in his capital.

Out of this war arose a new series of disputes in the supreme council. Mr. Hastings and Mr. Francis mutually accused each other of profligate fraud and falsehood; their disputes at last led to a duel, in which Mr. Francis was wounded, upon which he quitted the council, and returned to Europe.

CHAPTER IX.

AFFAIRS OF THE CARNATIC; SECOND WAR WITH HYDER.

The position of the Company's affairs in the Carnatic, was very different from their relations to the country in Bengal. By the avowed possession of the dewannee in the latter province, they obtained for themselves and their officers, the direct discharge of the principal offices of internal government; but in the Carnatic, they had recognized the Nabob, Mohammed Alí, as the undoubted sovereign of the country, and the rightful possessor both of military and financial power. On account of the Nabob's notorious imbecility, the presidency of Madras found it necessary to employ a British force for the protection of the country, and to insist that Mohammed Alí should defray the expenses of its maintenance out of his revenues. It was soon found that his income was inadequate to his expenditure; he was forced to have recourse to loans; money was advanced to him on exorbitant interest, by the servants of the Company, secured by mortgages on the revenues of particular districts, which they were entitled to draw direct from the collectors. By this course, the Nabob's embarrassments were greatly increased, while the exactions of the English merchants, his creditors, became more proportionately severe. It was the obvious interest of the Company to check the Nabob in his pernicious career, and particularly to prevent his alienating his revenues to rapacious usurers; but these money-lenders were able to represent such interference as an unwarrantable restriction on the freedom of an independent prince, and to excite angry feelings against the prudent conduct of the Madras presidency, both in the parliament and cabinet of England.

At this crisis, Admiral Sir John Lindsay, arrived at Madras, July 26, 1770, invested with the power of a king's minister plenipotentiary, to maintain the arrangements which had been made in India, by the eleventh article of the treaty of Paris. He at once adopted a course of policy, directly contrary to that which had been pursued by the presidency of Madras and sanctioned by the court of directors, and he formally recognized the Nabob as a fellow sovereign with the king of Great Britain, declaring that he had come to afford him the protection of the British monarch against all his enemies. The Nabob at once described the president and council of Madras as his worst enemies, averring that they had deprived him of the greatest part of his revenues and power.

At this moment the presidency was on the brink of a dangerous war, arising out of the following circumstance. At the conclusion of the treaty with Hyder Alí in 1769, it was agreed "That in case either of the contracting parties shall be attacked, they shall, from their respective countries, mutually assist each other to drive the enemy out. Hyder soon applied to the English to unite with him in supporting the insurrection of a Mahratta chief against the Peishwa, but this proposal was prudently declined. Early however in 1770, the Mahrattas invaded Mysore, and Hyder again applied for aid, pursuant to the conditions of the treaty, proffering to pay three lacs of rupees, if he could obtain effectual assistance. It was not easy for the English to find any pretext for a refusal, but they evaded, procrastinated and withheld, resolving not to take arms until the last extremity. The Nabob on the other hand was anxious to enter into an alliance with the Mahrattas: he had a personal dislike to Hyder; the Mahrattas stimulated his ambition by the promise of splendid gifts of territory; and finally, he believed that his alliance with them would render his government independent of the English. Sir John Lindsay warmly adopted the Nabob's views, with respect to the Mahratta alliance, and spared neither reproach, exhortation, nor threat, to compel the presidency to embrace the same course of policy. Intelligence of these disputes reached England, Sir John Lindsay was recalled, and Sir Robert Harland, with an additional naval force, was sent to exercise the same powers in his stead.

Sir Robert Harland warmly advocated the expediency of a Mahratta confederacy, but the presidency of Madras firmly refused to form such an alliance. The Nabob was thus obliged to content himself with mediating between the belligerents; a peace was concluded with the Mahrattas, on terms extremely unfavourable to Hyder, who thenceforth began to detest the English, for not only abandoning him in the hour of his need, but also for listening to projects which menaced his very existence.

But though the president and council refused to gratify the Nabob's desire for the Mahratta alliance, they tendered him ready aid, to subdue the Rájá of Tanjore. This petty sovereign had furnished a smaller contingent, both of money and troops, during the late war with Hyder, than he had been expected to supply, and had even opened secret communications with the enemy. Both the Nabob and the English, were eager to punish him whenever an opportunity offered ; a pretence for war was afforded by the Rájá's attack on the Polygars or chieftains of the districts called the Marawars, whom the Nabob claimed as his subjects, and he demanded that the Tanjore prince, should not attack his vassals. This remonstrance was disregarded, an appeal was made to the English, and an army was assembled at Trichinopoly, under the command of General Smith, to combine with the forces of the Carnatic, headed by the Nabob's son, Omrát-al-Omrah. Having captured several strong intervening places, the allies advanced to the capital of Tanjore, which they immediately invested. A practicable breach was effected and preparations for an assault were made, when on the very eve of the attack, General Smith was informed that Omrát-al-Omrah had concluded a treaty with the Rájá, and that the war was at an end. Great was the indignation of the English authorities at this unexpected termination of the expedition, but rightly foreseeing that this accommodation was not likely to be lasting, they retained possession of the frontier town of Tanjore, and left their forces in the service of the Nabob.

The Nabob immediately requested the service of the English to aid him in subduing those very Polygars of the Marawars, for whose protection he had ostensibly declared war against Tanjore. Notwithstanding the obvious inconsistency in the pretexts of the Nabob, the Presidency, without hesitation, consented to undertake the expedition. The Marawars were conquered, and the innocent inhabitants of the district treated with the most signal barbarity and injustice ; and when this was accomplished, the Nabob resolved to renew his attack on the kingdom of Tanjore, under the false pretence that the conditions of the late treaty had not been fulfilled. The council of Madras having solemnly recognized the injustice of the war, resolved, nevertheless, to assist the Nabob on the ground of policy and expediency. On the 20th of August, 1773, the siege of Tanjore was renewed; on the 16th of December a practicable breach was made, and entered by storm in the heat of the day, when the garrison did not expect an assault, and was unprepared for resistance. The assailants scarcely encountered any resistance; the Rájá of Tanjore and his family remained prisoners. Immediately after this victory, the Dutch were summoned to evacuate Nagore, which they had purchased from the Rájá, and, as they were unable to maintain themselves, they were forced to comply.

The deposition of the Rájá of Tanjore was disapproved by the court of directors, and Lord Pigot, who was appointed Governor of Madras, where he had formerly ruled previous to his elevation to the peerage, brought out orders for the restoration of the deposed sovereign. He was also directed to effect some desirable changes in the financial administration of the Northern Circars. Lord Pigot proceeded at once to the restoration of the Rájá, in spite of the remonstrances of the Nabob and the opposition of Sir Robert Fletcher, who, after having been cashiered for mutiny in Bengal, had been appointed to the chief command of the army of Madras. When this restoration was effected, a claim was made by Mr. Paul Benfield to a large share of the revenues of Tanjore, which, he asserted, had been assigned to him by the Nabob of the Carnatic, in payment of a debt amounting to a quarter of a million of money. Two circumstances of suspicion naturally presented themselves—Benfield was a junior servant of the Company; his salary was small, and the extravagance of his habits great: it was therefore in the highest degree improbable that this enormous debt really existed; and, supposing that it did exist, there was great doubt of the Nabob's right to pay his own debts out of the property of the restored Rájá of Tanjore. In fact, there was every reason to suspect that the whole was a collusion between Benfield and the Nabob, to defraud the Company and the Rájá. Benfield's claims were discussed in the council and rejected, but, after the lapse of a few days, it was voted that they should be reconsidered, and this was followed by a decision in favour of their validity. Lord Pigot, finding himself opposed by the majority, resolved to exert his powers as President to protect the Rájá of Tanjore from demands which he declared to be iniquitous. The disputes between the hostile parties increased in bitterness, until at length the majority of the council took the extraordinary step of arresting Lord Pigot and placing him in close confinement. This insult so preyed upon his high spirit, that his health, which was never very strong, sunk under the shock; he died after a confinement of eight months, and a coroner's jury recorded a verdict which indirectly accused his persecutors of murder. A compromise was effected with the Rájá of Tanjore, but Benfield's exorbitant claims were never realized.

When the intelligence of these events reached England, great indignation was excited, not only in the body of East India proprietors, but in the nation at large. The court of proprietors voted, by a large majority, that Lord Pigot should be restored, and that a rigid enquiry should be made into the conduct of the principal actors in his imprisonment. The court of directors sanctioned these resolutions by the casting vote of the chairman. But the influence of the ministry was exerted to neutralize these votes, and it was finally resolved that both parties should be recalled for the purpose of an enquiry into the whole affair. The death of Lord Pigot, and the important public events which soon followed, diverted attention from this unexampled proceeding; four of the most active members of the council were, indeed, prosecuted by the attorney-general, at the instigation of the House of Commons, after their return to England; they were convicted of a misdemeanour, and sentenced to pay a fine of one thousand pounds each, which, in their case, was but a nominal punishment.

On the death of Lord Pigot, the government of the Presidency of Madras devolved on Sir Thomas Rumbold, Mr. Whitehill, and General Sir Hector Munro. A committee of circuit had been formed to regulate the collection of the revenues in the Northern Circars. Rumbold's first measure was to suspend the proceedings of the committee, and to command the Zemindars, or chiefs who farmed the revenues, to appear personally at Madras and enter into new arrangements. It was asserted that this measure was adopted for the purpose of giving Rumbold and his supporters an opportunity of making a corrupt personal bargain with each of the chiefs, and, in one instance at least, there was abundant evidence to justify such suspicions. Vizeram Raz, the Rájá of Vizanagaram, was compelled to assign over the management of his affairs to his brother, Sitteram Raz, and at the same time agreed to receive from this favoured individual, not more than one half the amount of tribute which ought to have been obtained for the Company. It subsequently appeared that Sitteram Raz had paid very large sums in Madras which never found their way into the Company's treasury, and that Sir Thomas Rumbold and his secretary, Mr. Redhead, had forwarded to Europe more than six times the amount of their respective salaries.

When the arrangements had been made with the Nizam, in 1776, it had been agreed that his brother, Basalat Jing, should hold the Circar of Guntur in jaghire during life, or so long as the Subahdar should remain in friendship with the Company. Some alarm was excited at Madras, by intelligence that Basalat Jing had taken a French force into his service; a negociation was commenced with this prince, which ended in his agreeing to cede Guntur to the Company for a certain annual payment, and his engaging to dismiss his French auxiliaries on condition of his receiving an English force for the protection of his country. His offers were accepted, and a body of troops, under General Harper, was sent to garrison his dominions. The French, however, were only dismissed to pass into the service of the Nizam, who was not a little jealous of the alliance which had been formed with his brother.

The Nizam's indignation was still more justly excited, by the refusal of the Presidency of Madras to pay any portion of the tribute which had been stipulated for the possession of the Northern Circars. His claims were recognized by the supreme council at Calcutta, and this body sent a temperate letter to the council of Madras, remonstrating against the impolicy and iniquity of its proceedings. Sir Thomas Rumbold made an angry and most intemperate reply; in order to evince further his disdain of control, he granted a lease of Guntur for ten years to the Nabob of Arcot, though he was well aware that the court of directors had every reason to be displeased with his exertions in their jaghire and in his own dominions. The patience of the directors was at length exhausted; in their letter of the 10th of January, 1781 after severely censuring the transactions just described, they dismissed Sir Thomas Rumbold and two of his council from their service, deprived two more of their seat in the council, and expressed the strongest displeasure against the commander of their forces, Sir Hector Munro.

But before Sir Thomas Rumbold and his associates were deprived of power, they had been guilty of greater political crimes than those already recorded, the consequences of which were long and severely felt throughout the whole of British India. Hyder Ali had been not unjustly displeased with the treatment which he had received from the government of Madras; he resolved to form a connection with the French, who were on the brink of a new war with the English, and his advances were eagerly met by the Governor of Pondicherry, who supplied him with arms, ammunition, and other warlike supplies, through the French settlement of Mahè, on the coast of Malabar. Information of these transactions was conveyed to Rumbold, but he did not pay them any attention; on the contrary, he continued to treat Hyder with studied disrespect, while he permitted the military and pecuniary resources of Madras to fall into a state of the greatest confusion.

In the beginning of July, 1778, intelligence was received in Bengal which, though somewhat premature, was acted upon as certain, that war had commenced between England and France. A resolution was immediately formed to take possession of all the French settlements in India; Chandernagore, Masulipatam, and Carical, surrendered without resistance, and it was resolved to lose no time in the reduction of Pondicherry. Sir Hector Munro, to whom the conduct of the siege was entrusted, proceeded with a culpable negligence and slowness, for which it is not easy to account, as he was certainly a man of unquestionable courage. Sir Edward Vernon, who commanded the British naval force, displayed great energies; he defeated a French squadron so severely that its commander at once abandoned the Indian Seas, and then landed the marines and a body of sailors to aid in the assault. The Governor of Pondicherry, after a gallant defence, proposed terms of capitulation, which were cheerfully granted; the garrison marched out with all the honours of war, and one regiment was permitted to retain its colours. The defences of Pondicherry were then dismantled, and the fortifications destroyed.

The only place now left to the French in India, was the small fort and settlement of Mahè, on the coast of Malabar. Hyder had formerly intimated to the Madras government, that he would oppose any attack on Mahè, and retaliate by an invasion of the Carnatic ; but, notwithstanding this threat, and the disheartening intelligence of the reverses which the Bombay army, as already mentioned, had suffered in the Mahratta country, the presidency of Madras pursued its designs. Mahè was captured without firing a shot, by Colonel Braithwaite, on the 19th of March, 1779, and retained until the 29th of the following November, when Braithwaite being ordered to join General Goddard at Surat, levelled the fort with the ground.

Before Braithwaite's arrangements for going to Surat could be completed, he received a requisition from the chief and factory at Tellicherry, which was exposed to considerable danger. Hyder, enraged at the protection granted to a Nair chief who had incurred his displeasure, stimulated the neighbouring chieftains to attack the settlement, which would have been exposed to the most imminent danger, had not Braithwaite moved with his whole detachment to its support. These elements of dissention daily assumed a more threatening aspect, until at length, in November, 1779, the Nabob of the Carnatic sent certain information to Madras, that a league, for the total expulsion of the English from India, had been formed by Hyder, the Mahrattas, and the Nizam. Notwithstanding this warning, no measures were taken which had a reference to the war, until the following June, when orders were given that the detachment which had been sent to protect Basalat Jing, the command of which had been transferred from Colonel Harper to Colonel Baillie, should cross the Kistna, to be more in readiness "in case of any disturbance in the Carnatic."

On the 21st of July, intelligence was received, that Hyder had crossed the frontier with an army of one hundred thousand men, including twenty thousand trained infantry, thirty thousand cavalry, and four hundred Europeans who had been in the service of the Nizam. He had more than one hundred pieces of cannon, managed by Europeans and natives trained to the practice of artillery, and he was assisted by the councils of Mr. Lally, the leader of the French force, who was an officer of high reputation. To oppose this force, the English could only muster six thousand infantry, one hundred trained cavalry, in addition to the Nabob's irregular horse, and a few pieces of cannon, for which there were scarcely any means of equipment. To this must be added, the total alienation of the people of the country, who were justly weary of the joint government of the Company and the Nabob.

At this crisis, Sir Hector Munro exhibited the greatest reluctance to assume the command of the troops; he wished to entrust the management of the campaign to Lord Macleod, who had just arrived in India at the head of a Highland regiment; but Lord Macleod did not approve of Munro's plans, and he therefore refused to stake his reputation in executing military movements of which he more than doubted the wisdom. So fierce were the debates on this subject in the council, that Munro actually challenged one of the members. Much precious time was thus lost, but at length, Munro marched from St. Thomas's Mount, after having sent Baillie orders to join him at Conjeveram. Although cattle could with difficulty be procured for the transport of provisions, Munro persisted in encumbering his march with heavy artillery, the use of which, as he had no fortifications to attack, it is not easy to conjecture.

Hyder had now laid siege to Arcot, and Munro was eager to be joined by Baillie, in order to attempt the relief of the place; but, on the 31st of August, he learned that Baillie, who was remarkably deficient in promptitude and decision, had been stopped by the swelling of a small river, about five miles north of Trepassore. On the same day, he learned that Hyder had left Arcot, and was moving on Conjeveram. Baillie had reached Perambaucum, within fifteen miles of the main army, when he when he was attacked by Tippoo Saib, Hyder's son, with a prodigious superiority of force. After a desperate conflict of several hours, the English repulsed their assailants, but Baillie was so weakened, that he declared any onward movement was beyond the strength of his detachment, and urgently requested Munro to push forward to his relief, with the main body of the army. Instead of doing so, Munro sent a detachment to his aid, under the command of Colonel Fletcher. This brave body effected a junction with Baillie, who quitted his ground on the 9th of September, in the full belief that his progress would be facilitated by some movement on the part of the main body. Such also was the persuasion of the Europeans in Hyder's service; they urged that chieftain to retreat, and when his spies brought word that there were no preparations for a movement in the camp at Conjeveram, they insisted that the spies must have been bribed, for that such folly and blindness on the part of the English general were utterly incredible.

In spite of the opposition made by Tippoo's forces, Baillie continued his march during the night of the 9th, but early on the morning of the 10th, he was informed that the entire host of Hyder was approaching to overwhelm him. Nothing ever exceeded the steadiness and determination with which Baillie's handful of men sustained the attack of their enemies; had Munro made the slightest exertion to create a diversion in their favour, by attacking the enemy in the rear, Hyder's hosts would have been irretrievably defeated, but he did not move until late in the day, and he then returned after a short march, under the mistaken notion that Baillie was victorious. Strange to say, the gallant band would probably have achieved a triumph had not two of their tumbrils blown up in the midst of the action, by which accident they were at once deprived of ammunition, and their lines were thrown into confusion. Though exposed to a heavy fire of rockets and cannon, charged home by masses of cavalry, and pressed by close volleys of musketry from bodies of infantry on their flanks and in their front, the Europeans maintained the fight after the Sepoys had been annihilated, and still demanded to be led on, and to cut their way through the enemy. But Baillie, perceiving that his forces were reduced to about four hundred men, and despairing of receiving any assistance from Munro, held up a flag of truce. Quarter was promised on condition of an immediate surrender, but no sooner had they laid down their arms, than the savages rushed upon them with unbridled fury, and they would all have been massacred, but for the prompt and generous interference of Lally and the French officers. About two hundred Europeans were spared, but they were reserved for the horrors of a captivity which was worse than death.

Munro was now forced to make a speedy retreat; he reached St. Thomas's Mount on the evening of the 13th of September, with an army thoroughly dispirited and exhausted. The presidency began to tremble for Madras itself; the place was destitute, not only of provisions, but of supplies of every kind, and had Hyder followed the English with his usual impetuosity, he would probably have overthrown their sovereignty in the Carnatic. At this calamitous period, the Governor-General of India, Warren Hastings, acted with a promptitude and wisdom which might well atone for many delinquencies. He at once proposed that fifteen lacs of rupees, and a large detachment of European infantry and artillery should be sent to Madras; that Sir Eyre Coote should have the command of the army, and the sole management of the money transmitted, and that the Governor of Fort St. George should be suspended until further orders. To these mandates the presidency of Madras very reluctantly submitted. On the 7th of November, Sir Eyre Coote took his seat in the council at Madras, produced the decree deposing the governor, and had the satisfaction of finding it sanctioned by the majority of the members.

Arcot had by this time fallen; the first efforts of Sir Eyre Coote were therefore directed to protect Vellore and Wandewash, which were closely besieged but gallantly defended by feeble garrisons. The siege of Wandewash was abandoned on the approach of the English, but, instead of pursuing their advantages, they were obliged to direct their course to Pondicherry, in consequence of the arrival of a French fleet on the coast. The flattering prospect of retrieving the influence of their country in India, induced the Frenchmen of Pondicherry to forget the clemency with which they had been treated by their conquerors; they applied coercion to the English resident, enlisted Sepoys, and began to collect provisions at Carangoly. Sir Eyre Coote hasted to disarm the inhabitants, to remove the provisions from Carangoly, and to destroy the boats. He then marched to protect Cuddalore, which was menaced by Hyder, making the most strenuous exertions to bring that leader to an action. Having failed in forcing a battle, the army next moved to protect Trichinopoly, which was threatened; and on its road, attacked without success, the fortified Pagoda of Chillingbram. The failure was fortunate; it gave Hyder courage to hazard a battle, at a time when want of provisions and means of transport threatened to force the English to coop themselves up in Madras. The fight was furious; it lasted six hours, and ended in the complete defeat of the enemy. Had the English possessed cavalry and other means of active pursuit, they might have deprived Hyder of his artillery and stores, and, possibly, reduced him to the necessity of evacuating the province.

In consequence of this victory, Tippoo raised the siege of Wandewash, and Coote, being joined by a body of Sepoys which had come overland from Bengal, resolved to attempt the recovery of Madras. Hyder prepared to resist them on the ground where he had defeated Baillie. "His position," says Munro, whose description of the battle is brief but authentic, "was such that a stronger could not have been imagined. Besides three villages which the enemies had occupied, the ground along their front, and on their flanks, was intersected, in every direction, by deep ditches and water-courses; their artillery fired from embrasures cut in mounds of earth, which had been formed from the hollowing of the ditches, and the main body of the army lay behind them. The cannonade became general about ten o'clock, and continued, with little intermission, until sunset, for we found it almost impossible to advance upon the enemy, as the cannon could not be brought up without much time and labour over the broken ground in front. The enemy retired as we advanced, and always found cover in the ditches and behind the banks. They were forced from all before sunset, and, after standing a short time a cannonade on open ground, they fled in great hurry and confusion towards Conjeveram." From this account it appears that Hyder's army was only saved from a total rout by the difficulty of getting at it, and that Hyder concealed his defeat by pretending that it was only a drawn battle. Soon afterwards Hyder marched to prevent the relief of Vellore. Coote followed, surprised him in his camp, and inflicted upon him a severe defeat; Hyder could only save his guns by the sacrifice of his cavalry, which was almost annihilated in covering his retreat. After this exploit the army returned to St. Thomas's Mount, having lost nearly one-third of its members in this perilous campaign.

Lord Macartney had now come out as Governor of Madras, and Sir Eyre Coote, aware that his lordship was not likely to allow him so much independence of command as he had previously possessed, began to exhibit a sensitive jealousy which rendered the position of all parties peculiarly painful. Lord Macartney brought out intelligence of the commencement of war between England and Holland, in consequence of which he resolved to take possession of the Dutch settlements in India. He commenced by attacking Sadras and Pulicat, both of which surrendered with little opposition. The President next resolved on the attack of Negapatam, but was much annoyed by the strenuous resistance of Sir Eyre Coote, who would neither march to the attack himself nor spare any of his troops for the purpose. Lord Macartney collected the remaining forces of the presidency, and entrusted the command of the expedition to Sir Hector Munro. That officer displayed, on this occasion, more activity, zeal, and enterprise than he had manifested on former expeditions. In less than three weeks from the landing of the soldiers and marines, the Governor of Negapatam was forced to surrender, though his garrison was more numerous than the besieging force. A large quantity of warlike stores, together with a double investment of goods, no ships having arrived from Holland for the investment of the preceding year, was found in the place. Nor was this all; a detachment was embarked and sent against the Dutch settlement of Trincomalee in Ceylon, which was added to the English conquests, so that the Dutch were expelled from every one of their stations in the Indian Seas.

The fall of Negapatam, in spite of his opposition, and contrary to his predictions, did not tend to soothe the irritated feelings of Sir Eyre Coote. Lord Macartney had great difficulty in preserving even the appearance of harmony while he conducted a difficult negociation with the Nabob, which ended in the surrender to the English of the financial administration of the Carnatic, on condition of paying the Nabob one-sixth of the revenue. Intelligence of the fall of Chittore, and of the danger to which Vellore was exposed, produced a more beneficial effect on the general than entreaties and remonstrances; he immediately took the field, though he was so ill as to be able to travel only in a palanquin, and he did not turn back though he was attacked by an apoplectic fit on the road. In spite of Hyder's opposition, which was, however, confined to a distant cannonade, supplies for three months were conveyed to Vellore, and the general then led back his army in safety to the Mount.

After the capture of Mahè, the Madras detachment remained at Tillicherry, besieged by the Nairs, until it was relieved by Major Abingdon with a force from Bombay. The fortress was again invested by one of Hyder's generals, and the major applied to the presidency of Bombay for reinforcements; in reply he received orders to evacuate the place, but he concealed the letter from his soldiers, and sent such strong representations to his superiors that they supplied him with a considerable force. Thus strengthened, Abingdon resolved to confine himself no longer to defensive measures; he sallied forth on the night of the 7th of January, 1782, suddenly attacked the enemy's camp, threw the besiegers into such confusion, that they dispersed without making any resistance, wounded their leader and made him prisoner. Having demolished the enemy's works and improved the fortifications of Tellicherry, Abingdon marched against Calicut, which surrendered after a short siege, and was occupied by an English garrison.

In the meantime, a secret expedition was prepared in England which occupied much of the public attention; it was generally believed that the armament was designed to act against some part of Spanish America, but its real destination was the Cape of Good Hope, and subsequently the Indian Seas. M. de Suffrein, who commanded a French squadron, which had been prepared to support the cause of France in the east, discovered the secret of the English designs. He followed in close pursuit, and found the English squadron anchored in Praya Bay, in the Cape de Verd Islands, utterly unsuspicious of the approach of an enemy. Though thus attacked at a disadvantage, the English beat off their foes, but so much time was wasted in refitting, that Suffrein reached the Cape long before them, and so strengthened its fortifications as to render an attack hopeless. Commodore Johnstone, however, made prize of the greater part of a fleet of Dutch East Indiamen, which were at anchor in Soldanha Bay; he then returned to Europe with his prizes and most of his squadron, leaving the rest to proceed with troops to India. Why he should thus have abandoned the Indian Seas, when he knew that Suffrein had sailed thither, we are unable to explain, but at this unhappy period of the American war, the English arms were destined to suffer disgrace in every quarter of the globe, from the obstinacy and incapacity of those entrusted with the direction of affairs. While the principal ships of war, having on board General Meadows and Colonel Fullarton, with the chief part of the army, went in search of Admiral Hughes, on the Coast of Coromandel, the remainder sailed for Bombay with a detachment entrusted to Colonel Humberstone Mackenzie. After his arrival, Humberstone hearing of the dangers to which Madras was exposed, resolved to make a diversion on the coast of Malabar, and for this purpose joined Abingdon at Calicut, whence he made incursions into Hyder's dominions, and gained several advantages.

In the mean time, Suffrein having obtained reinforcements at the Isle of France, sailed for the Coast of Coromandel, and narrowly missed intercepting the English squadron, before it could effect a junction with Admiral Hughes. Twenty-four hours after this junction was effected, Suffrein appeared in Madras roads, and Hughes immediately prepared for action. The engagement was indecisive; after a distant cannonade, Suffrein proceeded to Porto Novo, where he landed an army of three thousand men, including a regiment of Caffres, under the command of M. Bussy. Drury sailed for Trincomalee, to refit his ships.

Hyder's son, Tippoo, hastened to join his French auxiliaries. He had just inflicted upon the English one of the heaviest losses which they had endured in the entire course of the war, by the destruction of Colonel Braithwaite's detachment in Tanjore. Braithwaite, whose force consisted of one hundred Europeans, one thousand five hundred sepoys and three hundred cavalry, had encamped on an open plain, near the banks of the river Coleroon, believing that he was exposed to no danger from a distant enemy. In this position he was surrounded and attacked by Tippoo, at the head of ten thousand cavalry, an equal number of infantry, four hundred European troops, and twenty pieces of cannon. During twenty-six hours of incessant conflict, Braithwaite's gallant little troop repulsed the hordes brought against them by Tippoo; at length, Lally with his Europeans advanced against them, the courage of the Sepoys failed, and they fell into confusion. Lally had the utmost difficulty in obtaining quarter for these brave men, but it must be added, that Tippoo subsequently treated his prisoners with great humanity.

The arrival of such large reinforcements from France, gave alarming strength to Tippoo; he laid seige to Cuddalore, which surrendered on the 3rd of April, and became a convenient station, both naval and military, for the French. This loss might have been prevented by the English admiral, Sir Edward Hughes, but the king's officers, both on sea and land, disdained to receive orders from the Company's servants, and we shall subsequently see, that several opportunities of performing essential service which the sagacity of Lord Macartney pointed out, were wantonly thrown away by the naval and military commanders.

Sir Eyre Coote took the field on the 17th of April, having delayed the army in cantonments, partly for want of proper supplies, but principally in consequence of his disputes with the civil authorities. His object was to protect Parmacoil, but on arriving at Carangoly, he found that the place had already surrendered. He then made an attempt to surprise Arnee, where Hyder's treasures were deposited, but Hyder engaged the attention of the English, with a distant cannonade, while Tippoo with a strong detachment removed the treasure, after which he retired, affording the English no opportunity of coming to a decisive engagement. On his return to Madras, after this indecisive campaign, Coote had the misfortune to lose a regiment of European cavalry, which was drawn into an ambuscade and cut to pieces.

Hyder contrived to amuse Sir Eyre Coote with pretended negociations, while he prepared to combine with the French fleet, in recovering Negapatam. Fortunately, Sir Edward Hughes met Suffrein as he was steering towards the place, and brought him to action. The engagement was close, warm and general; the French were beginning to fall into disorder, when a sudden change of wind enabled Suffrein to withdraw his shattered ships, with which he sailed to Cuddalore. Here he made the most vigorous and successful efforts to repair his vessels, and in a short time was again at sea in as good a condition as ever. Intelligence of this event was conveyed to Madras; Lord Macartney sent the most pressing instances to Sir Edward Hughes, to put to sea and protect Negapatam and Trincomalee, which were both menaced, but the jealousy of the admiral rendered him obstinate; he refused to put to sea until it pleased himself, and he delayed until the 20th of August, nearly three weeks after the departure of Suffrein from Cuddalore. The consequences of this lamentable folly may easily be anticipated; when Hughes arrived off Trincomalee, he found that the fortress had surrendered to the French three days before. Hughes, burning to revenge this loss, engaged the French fleet on the 3rd of September, and notwithstanding the inferiority of his force, gained a victory, of which he did not know how to take advantage. One French ship was disabled, and two others so severely injured, that it was ten days before they could be got into harbour. Suffrein justly described these vessels as presents received from the English admiral, who made no attempt to take advantage of their defenceless condition, but returned to Madras.

The dissensions between the English authorities were soon renewed; Sir Edward Hughes announced his intention of abandoning the Coast of Coromandel, and seeking shelter in Bombay during the season of the monsoon. He persevered in this design though information was received that Negapatam was already attacked, and that Sir Richard Bickerton was on his way to join him with five sail of the line. Bickerton arrived in Madras roads on the fourth day after the departure of Hughes, but, on learning the proceedings of the admiral, he followed him to Bombay. At the same time, Sir Eyre Coote, whose health had been long declining, surrendered the command of the army to General Stuart, who inherited all the obstinacy, but few of the better qualities of his predecessor.

No military operations of any consequence were undertaken during the winter months, but Madras suffered all the horrors of a dreadful famine. A dreadful hurricane, which came on soon after the departure of the fleet, wrecked the store-vessels, which were laden with rice, no supply could be obtained from Bengal, and war had exhausted all the resources of the Carnatic. The multitude of the dead and dying superadded the horrors of pestilence; fifteen hundred bodies were burned weekly in the trenches, and not less than half a million of persons perished in the Carnatic.

We must now turn our attention to the war waged against the Mahrattas by the Presidencies of Bombay and Bengal. General Goddard, having received information that Holkar and Scindiah would be attacked from the upper provinces of Bengal, and thus prevented from interfering with his operations, resolved to lay siege to Bassein, while, at the same time, he sent Colonel Hartley into the Conkan to secure the revenues of that country for the British authorities, and also to cover the besieging army. Hartley expelled the Mahrattas from the Conkan, and took up a position near the Bhore Ghaut, whence he retreated to Doogaur on the approach of an enormous hostile force. Here he was attacked, on the 10th and 11th of December, 1780, by twenty thousand Mahrattas, whom he completely defeated, with the loss of their general. Bassein surrendered at discretion about the same time. Goddard then made an advance upon Poonah, but soon returned, and suffered severely from the pursuit of the Mahrattas as he descended the Ghauts. On the Bengal side, Colonel Carnac, who had superseded Captain Popham, was on the very brink of ruin, when he adopted the bold resolution of surprising Scindiah's camp by night. The enterprise was completely successful; the enemy dispersed and fled in disorder, leaving several guns and elephants, with a quantity of ammunition, in prize to the victors. Colonel Muir soon afterwards joined Carnac, and, as senior officer, assumed the command. He opened negociations with Scindiah, whose resources were now exhausted, and finally, a treaty was concluded with the Mahrattas at Salbye, on the 17th of May, 1782.

Colonel Humberstone, who commanded at Calicut, having received reinforcements, took the field early in September, and captured several forts, though he was obliged to leave his heavy artillery behind, for want of draught cattle. The capture of Palacatcherry was necessary to the complete success of his operations, but finding that it would be impossible to take the place without artillery, Colonel Macleod, who had been sent by Sir Eyre Coote to take the command, resolved to occupy a camp at several miles distance, until his battering cannon should arrive. The officer entrusted with the conduct of the retreat gave wrong orders, so that the baggage and stores were thrown into the rear, an error which did not escape the notice of the watchful enemies. When the army had passed a narrow defile, with the exception of the rear-guard and baggage, the enemies suddenly made an attack, by which they obtained possession of all the provisions, and nearly all the ammunition. It now only remained for the English to make their retreat to the sea-coast with the utmost expedition, and on their road, they received information that Tippoo was hastening after them with twenty thousand men, which Hyder had detached from the army of the Carnatic. Tippoo soon appeared; the English continued their retreat, fighting at every step, and at length succeeded in occupying Paniani. Here they were assailed with desperate fury, and had great difficulty in repelling the attack. They were preparing to meet a second assault, with some misgivings as to the result, when, to their utter astonishment, they saw Tippoo's army in full retreat, and in a few hours not one man of the Mysore forces could be seen.

This unexpected movement was caused by the death of Hyder, intelligence of which had been secretly communicated to Tippoo. Though great pains were taken to conceal the event, the news was conveyed to Lord Macartney, who urged General Stuart to take advantage of the crisis, and attack the Mysorean army. Stuart peremptorily refused obedience, first pretending to disbelieve the intelligence, and then asserting that the army was deficient in equipments for marching at that season of the year. Hyder died on the 7th of December, 1782, General Stuart did not commence active operations until the 5th of the following February, when the opportunity of striking a decisive blow was irrecoverably lost. Stuart withdrew the garrisons from Wandewash and Carangoly, which it was held impossible to maintain, and blew up the fortifications of both. He then marched towards Vellore, where he received information that Tippoo was retreating from the Carnatic, and had given orders for the evacuation of Arcot.

Tippoo was recalled to the western side of India, not only by the necessity of establishing his authority in his hereditary dominions, but also for the purpose of repelling a very formidable invasion. After his departure from Paniani, the English army divided, the Sepoys proceeding by land to Tellicherry, and the Europeans by sea to Merjee. Here they were joined by General Matthews, from Bombay, with a considerable army, which he increased by collecting all the troops along the coast. Thus strengthened, he forced the passes of the Ghauts, took possession of Bednore, carried Ananpore by storm, and compelled Mangalore to capitulate. It was proposed that the treasure found in these places should be applied to pay the large arrears due to the army, but Matthews refused to listen to any such proposition. Suspicions of his rapacity were spread, but he severely punished all refractory proceedings. Three of the principal officers, Colonel Macleod, Colonel Humberstone, and Major Shaw, quitted the army to lay their complaints before the governor and council of Bombay. So flagrant did the conduct of the general appear to these authorities, that they ordered him to be superseded, transferring the command of the army to Colonel Macleod, who was next in rank. Unfortunately, Macleod, on his return to the army by sea, fell in with a Mahratta squadron, ignorant of the recent peace; Shaw was killed, Humberstone was mortally wounded, and Macleod, who was also wounded, remained a prisoner.

While the army of Matthews was dispersed in detachments, Tippoo suddenly concentrated his forces and invested Bednore, which was unprepared for resistance. The English made a brave defence, but were finally forced to capitulate. In this extremity, Matthews distributed the public treasure among his soldiers, and Tippoo availed himself of this breach of faith to violate the terms of the capitulation. Matthews, after having suffered the most cruel tortures, was assassinated in prison; his unfortunate companions were subjected to the horrors of a most rigorous captivity. Tippoo, immediately after this success, proceeded to invest Mangalore, a seaport town, to the possession of which both he and his father attributed a very inordinate importance.

While the army of Madras remained inactive, Suffrein, whom the English admiral had not yet returned to oppose, landed Bussy with a reinforcement of French troops at Cuddalore. Urgent requests were made to General Stuart by Lord Macartney, to prevent the French from establishing themselves in this important post, but neither reproaches nor remonstrances could induce him to move for several weeks, and then he marched at less than the rate of three miles per day. In the meantime, the fleet, greatly augmented, returned to Madras, whence it was sent to aid in the operations designed for the recovery of Cuddalore.

When General Stuart arrived before Cuddalore, he found that the French had already thrown up several fortifications. He hazarded an attack upon their lines, which was partially successful, but the English suffered so severely, that they made no attempt to improve their victory. The hostile fleets arrived nearly at the same time off Cuddalare; an engagement ensued with the usual result. Suffrein was defeated, but remained near the scene of action to repair his losses, while the victorious English admiral, returned to Madras with as much precipitation as if he had been beaten. Suffrein landed as many men as could be spared from the fleet, and Bussy, thus reinforced, made an attack upon the English lines, which was repulsed with great difficulty. It deserves to be remarked that Charles John Bernadotte, the present king of Sweden, then only an humble serjeant in the French service, was wounded and taken prisoner in this engagement. Bussy was preparing for a renewed attack, which in all human probability would have been successful, had not intelligence arrived that peace had been concluded between France and England. A cessation of arms was instantly agreed upon, and Bussy sent an invitation to Tippoo, to join in the treaty, at the same time recalling the French battalions engaged in his service. The same messenger who brought intelligence of the peace to the camp, conveyed to General Stuart a peremptory summons to appear before the Governor and Council of Madras. After some delay he obeyed; a new series of disputes followed, and at length, the governor and council resolved that Stuart should be dismissed the Company's service; he refused to obey, and was supported in his refusal by Sir John Burgoyne, the second in command. Lord Macartney adopted the decisive measure of arresting Stuart and bringing him a prisoner to the Fort, whence, in a few days, he sailed for England.

Amid all these errors and disgraces the honour of the English arms was nobly maintained by Colonel Fullarton, who had the command of the army in the southern provinces. In the midst of a career of conquest, he was stopped by orders from General Stuart, requiring him to join the troops at Cuddalore, and when he resumed his march, he received information that an armistice had been concluded. Learning, however, that Tippoo had renewed hostilities against Mangalore, he pushed forward to make a dash upon Seringapatam without waiting for further orders. He reduced the strong fortresses of Palacatcherry and Coimbatore, and had made every arrangement for moving on Seringapatam, when he received orders, on the 28th of November, to suspend all operations, and restore the places he had taken. Fullarton, aware of the treacherous character of Tippoo, retarded the execution of these commands, and had reason to be proud of his foresight when, on the 26th of the following January, he received directions to re-assemble his army, and renew the war. Tippoo was resolved not to listen to any terms of peace, until he had completed the reduction of Mangalore, which he had besieged at great loss for more than a year. General Macleod, who had been sent with a squadron to relieve the place, instead of landing, entered into a negociation with Tippoo, and agreed to return to Bombay, on condition of being allowed to throw a month's provision into the garrison. The supply was drawn from damaged stores purchased of a navy agent, and was so bad that not one in twenty of the pieces of beef and pork could be eaten even by the dogs. At length the gallant Campbell, by whom and his garrison the place had been so nobly defended, proposed to capitulate. Tippoo granted them the most favourable terms, and they marched to Tellicherry with arms, accoutrements, and the honours of war.

In the negociations for peace with Tippoo, the English commissioners submitted to many humiliations, which showed that their spirit was broken by the numerous disasters of the war. A treaty was at length concluded, March 11th, 1784, on the basis of a mutual restitution of conquests; it was ratified by the supreme council at Calcutta, in the absence of Mr. Hastings, and an additional clause, which, contrary to every rule of equity, that gentleman, at a subsequent period, wished to introduce, was rejected by the honourable firmness of Lord Macartney.

During the entire of this period, there was an incessant struggle between the presidencies of Bengal and Madras. Hastings lost no opportunity of mortifying Lord Macartney, whom he viewed with jealousy on account of his rank as a peer, and still more for being the first person chosen from the king's service to fill one of those high offices which had been previously restricted to the Company's servants. After Sir Eyre Coote had returned to Bengal, Hastings sent him back with powers to resume the military command, exempt from dependence on the Madras government. It is probable that Lord Macartney would have resisted such a subversion of his authority, and thus the presidency might have been involved in civil war; but the danger was averted by the death of Coote, who expired three days after his landing in Madras, April 26th, 1784.

CHAPTER X.

CONCLUSION OF THE ADMINISTRATION OF WARREN HASTINGS.

During the Mysorean and Mahratta wars, the Governor-general and council were involved in other affairs of no ordinary importance. A contest arose between the council and the supreme court of judicature which virtually involved the Company's right to sovereignty over the provinces which it had acquired, though it apparently was a mere struggle between the judicial and executive authorities. The supreme court created by Act of Parliament in 1773, consisted of one chief and three puisnè judges. Its civil jurisdiction extended to all claims against the Company and against British subjects, and to all such claims of British subjects against the natives, as the party in the contract under dispute had agreed, in case of dispute, to submit to its decision. In criminal cases, its powers extended to all British subjects, and to all persons directly or indirectly in the service of the Company, or of any British subject at the time of the offence. Parliament, however, did not define what it was that constituted a British subject, and the judges adopted a wide interpretation of the phrase, which not only included all the subjects of the Company, but even the subjects of the native powers over whom the Company exercised an immediate control. The judges had not been long in the exercise of their functions, when the effects of their pretensions began to appear, writs were issued at the suit of individuals against the Zemindars, in ordinary actions of debt; the Zemindars were ordered to Calcutta, to enter an appearance; if they neglected the writ, they were taken into custody; or if on their arrival at Calcutta, they were unable to find bail, which if they were strangers and the sum more than trifling, it was nearly impossible that they should do, they were consigned to prison for all the time which the delays of English judicature might interpose between this calamitous stage and the final termination of the suit.

It had been the immemorial practice in India, for that branch of the administration connected with the collection of the revenue, to exercise a power of summary jurisdiction in all disputed matters connected with taxation. This power was vested in the provincial councils and the courts, called Dewannee Adaulut, established under their authority. The supreme court soon began to interfere with the Dewannee Adaulut; when any coercive process was issued by the latter, the defaulters were taught to sue out a writ of habeas corpus in the supreme court, where it was held competent and was in practice customary, for the judges to set them at liberty upon bail. As the inhabitants of India are even more reluctant to pay taxes than those of England, the members of the government justly dreaded that it would become impossible to realize any revenue in India, if the payment could only be enforced by the tedious and expensive forms of English law. The Company had reserved to the Nabob of Bengal, Mobarek-al-Dowla, the Nizamut or administration of justice in civil cases; to this government of the Nabob, the judges of the supreme, or, as they loved to call it, the King's Court, declared that they would pay no regard. "The act of parliament," said Mr. Justice Hyde, "does not consider Mobarek al-Dowla as a sovereign prince; the jurisdiction of this court extends over all his dominions." Mr. Justice Le Maistre went farther: "With regard to this phantom," he said, "this man of straw, Mobarek-al-Dowla, it is an insult to the understanding of the court to have made the question of his sovereignty; but it comes from the Governor-general and council: I have too much respect for that body to treat it ludicrously, and I confess I cannot consider it seriously." He further added, that "the Nabob was a mere empty name, without any real right, or the exercise of any power whatever." That the recognition of such pretensions would have transferred the entire of the government to the hands of the judges of the supreme court, is too obvious to require any illustration.

Mr. Hastings, in order to remedy this condition of affairs, instituted a new court of appeal from the provincial courts, which he named the Sudder Dewannee Adaulut, at the head of which he placed the king's chief justice, Sir Elijah Impey, with a salary of about £7000 annually. As both the place and the pay were held during the pleasure of the governor and council, it appears to have been presumed that Impey would no longer set the jurisdiction of the king's courts in opposition to the Dewannee Adauluts, and that he would become an instrument of conciliation between the council and the court." The English House of Commons strenuously condemned these proceedings, and finally, Sir Elijah Impey was recalled to answer criminal charges founded on his conduct. Some important changes were at the same time made in financial affairs; a board of revenue was formed at the presidency, to superintend the collection of taxes, and to lease the revenues to the Zemindars, without the aid of any intermediate agency.

Having completed these arrangements, Mr. Hastings set out on his celebrated tour to the Upper Provinces; the government was distressed for money, and he resolved to obtain it from the Rájá of Benares and the Nabob of Oude. Cheit Sing, Rájá of Benares, had been received into the protection of the Company on condition of paying a certain amount of tribute; a large subsidy was now demanded in addition; the Rájá paid it for one year, with a stipulation that it should not be again required. It was demanded the following; he remonstrated; an army was sent to enforce compliance, and he was compelled to pay, not only the original demand, but £2000 as a fine for delay, under the title of expense of the troops employed to coerce him. In the third year the same remonstrances were repeated; the Rájá's agent paid the Governor-general two lacs of rupees as a present, but the contribution was nevertheless enforced, and a new fine of £10,000 imposed. Mr. Hastings resolved to treat the Rájá as a refractory Zemindar; he proceeded to Benares, refused to admit Cheit Sing into his presence, and finally gave orders that he should be arrested as a delinquent. The people of Benares rose in defence of their ruler, forced a way into the palace, and destroyed the greater part of the Sepoys and officers who had him in charge. During the confusion, Cheit Sing escaped by a wicket which opened upon the river, and with some difficulty, made his way to the opposite side. An attempt to recover the palace was defeated with great loss; Mr. Hastings, destitute of men and money, was exposed to great personal danger, but he effected his escape from Benares to Chunar. The war that ensued was of brief duration; the forces which Cheit Sing collected, when all his offers of submission were rejected, made but a feeble resistance; after a severe defeat, they disbanded themselves, and the Rájá fled to Bundelcund, leaving his wife and treasure in the fort of Bijygur. This place was soon captured, but the treasures were divided among the soldiers, who refused to yield any part of it up to the government, even as a loan. Cheit Sing's deposition was formally announced, a grandson of the late Rájá Bulwant Sing, by a daughter, was selected as the new Rájá; the amount of tribute was raised to forty lacs of rupees, and the administration of justice in Benares was subjected to the control of the Company's officers.

The attention of the Governor-general was next directed to the case of the Vizier-nabob of Oude, whose stipulated payments to the Company had fallen greatly into arrear, in consequence of the heavy expenses he incurred in supporting the English brigades which he had been compelled to maintain. "It is notorious," says Mr. Francis, "that the English army had devoured his revenues and his country, under the pretence of defending it." The debt with which the Nabob stood charged, amounted to £1,400,000; previous to adopting the measures on which he had resolved in order to obtain payment, Mr. Hastings superseded Bristow, the resident at Lucknow, and appointed his creature, Middleton, to the vacancy, in defiance of the express orders of the court of directors. There were two princesses, known by the name of Begums, the mother of the late Nabob, and his widow, who was also the mother of the present Nabob; they had been left in possession of large jaghires, to provide, not only for their own support, but for the maintenance of the numerous families of preceding nabobs, and Suja-ad-Dowla had bequeathed them at his death the greater part of the treasure which happened to be in his hands. The riches of the Begums appeared to Mr. Hastings an admirable resource; he agreed to relieve the Nabob of the expense of maintaining the English troops and gentlemen which he was unable to bear, provided that he would strip the princesses of their treasures and jaghires, delivering the proceeds to the Governor-general. The reasons which Mr. Hastings adduced for this extraordinary proceeding were, that the Begums had endeavoured to excite insurrections in Oude in favour of Cheit Sing, and that they had employed their power and influence to embarrass and disturb the Nabob's administration.

The resumption of the jaghires was effected with little difficulty; after which the Nabob, accompanied by Middleton, the English resident, with a body of English troops, proceeded towards the abode of the princesses at Fyzabad. After a short time had been spent in demands and negociations, the English were ordered to storm the town and castle; but as no opposition was made, little blood was shed; the troops took possession of all the outer enclosure of the palace of one of the princesses, and blocked up the other.

It was deemed imprudent to shock oriental prejudices by violating the sanctity of the female apartments; Middleton, however, seized upon the principal agents and favourites of the Begums, placed them in irons, and ordered that they should be kept without food until the princesses had surrendered their treasures. By these means more than half a million of money was extorted from the Begums by the Resident, for the use of the Company. More, however, was required; the prisoners were detained several months in close confinement, and, at least, menaced with torture, if corporeal punishment was not actually inflicted. At length, when it was evident that no more money could be had, the prisoners were set at liberty, and the joy which they naturally evinced at their deliverance, was actually quoted as a proof of their having had no reason to complain of the treatment which they had received.

One more circumstance connected with these transactions remains to be mentioned; Mr. Hastings accepted a present of one hundred thousand pounds from the Nabob, of which he informed the directors, and in very plain terms requested their permission, as a reward for his services, to make the money his own. But his proceedings began now to excite much dissatisfaction in England; several of his measures were reprobated by the Court of Directors, and, at length, on the 8th of February, 1785, he resigned his office, and embarked for England. Few rulers of any country have had to encounter more difficulties, and meet so many extraordinary temptations as Mr. Hastings during his administration in Bengal. His government was, on the whole, popular both with the English residents and the Natives; nor must it be forgotten, whatever may have been his defects, that he was the first, or among the first servants of the Company, who attempted to acquire any language of the Natives, and who set on foot those liberal enquiries into the literature and institutions of the Hindús, which have led to the satisfactory knowledge of the present day.

CHAPTER XI.

LEGISLATIVE PROCEEDINGS IN ENGLAND RESPECTING INDIA. WAR WITH TIPPOO SULTAN.

As the exclusive privileges of the East India Company were to expire on three years notice after the 25th of March, 1780, great anxiety was created in the beginning of that year respecting the terms on which the Charter should be renewed. The contests between the supreme council and the supreme court in Calcutta—the loud complaints which Mr. Francis made of the conduct of Mr. Hastings, and the intelligence of the dangers to which the Carnatic had been exposed by the irruption of Hyder Alí, created a great excitement throughout the nation, and led many to fear that the English interests in Asia were brought to the verge of ruin by the misconduct of the persons entrusted with their management. Lord North, who was then prime minister, deemed it a fixed principle of constitutional law that the crown had an absolute and indefeasible right to all territories acquired by subjects, while the Company boldly asserted that the Indian provinces they had gained, belonged of right to themselves. With this abstract question another of more practical importance was joined, namely, what proportion of the proceeds from their Indian territories, the Company should be compelled to pay over to the nation.

Lord North's administration was, at this period, tottering to its fall; the American war, unwisely provoked and miserably conducted, had ended in the establishment of the independence of the United States, and the consequent loss to the nation of the most valuable colonies which had ever belonged to any empire. Ireland had taken advantage of the minister's weakness to demand freedom of trade and legislative independence; a growing party in England began to agitate for parliamentary reform, and many who had been zealous supporters of the minister in the House of Commons, went over to the ranks of opposition. These circumstances induced the Company to resist the minister's proposals for a new arrangement, and an extension of the charter was finally obtained, with only one additional condition, the recognition of the minister's right to inspect all despatches relating to financial, civil, and military affairs, received by the directors from their servants in India. Select committees of the House of Commons were appointed to investigate various matters connected with the state of Indian affairs, and the valuable reports which they published, put the legislature and the country in possession of a vast fund of information, illustrating the true condition of the British empire in the East.

Lord North was driven from office in 1782; his successor was the Marquis of Rockingham, who was the leader of a party notoriously hostile to those who at this period managed the affairs of India. A bill of pains and penalties against Sir Thomas Rumbold was introduced, but it was conducted very slowly through the several stages of legislation, and was finally abandoned. On the death of the Marquis of Rockingham, the Earl of Shelburne, afterwards Marquis of Lansdowne, became premier. This gave great offence to Mr. Fox, who not only seceded from the cabinet, but formed a coalition with his old political opponent, Lord North. To their united parliamentary strength, the Shelburne cabinet was forced to yield, and the coalition ministry was formed, to the great vexation of the king, and the secret discontent of the nation. In due time Mr. Fox introduced his plan for the better government of India; he proposed to entrust the power and patronage possessed by the court of directors and proprietors, to seven commissioners chosen by the legislature; and, at the same time, regulations were proposed for preventing the evils which had arisen in the local government of India. This plan was the signal for the fiercest strife of parties ever witnessed in England; it was said that the minister aimed at engrossing all the power and patronage of India, through the means of commissioners, who would only be his nominees, and that he thus designed to make himself independent both of the king and the people. The ministerial measure, notwithstanding this clamour, passed the Lower House by large majorities, but, when it reached the Lords, the king empowered Earl Temple to declare that he would consider every one who supported the measure as personally his enemy; the bill was, consequently, lost on the second reading by a majority of eighty-seven against seventy-nine. The coalition-ministry was soon after dismissed, and a new cabinet formed under the auspices of Mr. William Pitt.

Parliament having been dissolved, the result of the consequent election gave Mr. Pitt's cabinet a decisive majority, and enabled him to carry, triumphantly, his bills for the government of India. The most important innovation he introduced, was the creation of a board of control, composed of six members of the privy council, chosen by the king, with power "to check, superintend, and control all acts, operations, and concerns, which in anywise relate to the civil or military government, or revenues of the territories and possessions of the said united Company in the East Indies." This vague and indefinite phraseology left the relations between the board of control and the court of directors in a very unsettled state, and soon led to angry collision between these bodies. The power of the court of directors was increased, and that of the court of proprietors greatly decreased; the directors were at the same time empowered to elect a committee of secresy, which could transact business with the board of control, without making any inconvenient communications in open court. It was enacted that all servants of the Company should give an exact inventory of the amount of property which they brought from India; and a new tribunal was constituted "for the prosecuting and bringing to speedy and condign punishment British subjects guilty of extortion and other misdemeanours while holding offices in the service of the king or Company of India." As this tribunal has never since been called upon to act, it is not necessary to enquire into its constitution or efficacy.

Mr. Macpherson, the senior member of council, assumed the government of India immediately after the departure of Mr. Hastings; he made no change in the policy of his predecessor, to whom he imputed the blame of the large and dangerous accession made to the Mahratta power when Scindia took possession of Delhí, and of the person of the unfortunate emperor. This, however, attracted less attention than the affairs of the Carnatic; the board of control decided that all the debts which the Nabob of the Carnatic had contracted, or was said to have contracted with private individuals, should be recognized as legitimate claims, without any investigation or enquiry, and that means should be taken for their payment with interest. There was little doubt that many of these debts were collusive and forged, for when similar claims were investigated in 1805, out of claims amounting to twenty millions, little more than one million of the sum was found by the commissioners to be true and lawful debt; but the persons who now urged their claims, had acquired considerable parliamentary interest by purchasing the representation of corrupt boroughs, and they formed a phalanx of supporters, with whose services the ministers were unwilling to dispense. Through their influence, also, it was directed that the Nabob should resume the management and collection of his revenues, which he had been induced to resign to the presidency of Madras.

Lord Macartney strenuously resisted these proposed changes, and went to Calcutta to impress their pernicious tendency upon the minds of the supreme council. While thus engaged, he received information of his appointment to the office of Governor-general, but, previous to his acceptance of it, he resolved to return to England for the purpose of consulting with the ministers and the court of directors. On coming home, he found that he was likely to encounter a very bitter opposition from the friends of Hastings and Macpherson; he therefore asked to be raised to the British peerage, in order that his opponents might be daunted by such a signal mark of ministerial favour. No answer was vouchsafed to this request, and, three days after it was made, Lord Cornwallis was appointed Governor-General of India. This was soon after followed by the impeachment of Mr. Warren Hastings by the House of Commons, at the bar of the House of Lords. The trial commenced on the 13th of February, 1788, and ended on the 23rd of April, 1795, in the acquittal of the accused. The circumstances connected with it belong to the history of England rather than of India; we need only say that Mr. Hastings was mainly indebted for his escape to the eloquence of his accusers; they over-stated their case so monstrously that they excited public sympathy for the criminal, and the applause bestowed on their flights of oratory placed them before the public in the light of very graceful actors, not as persons engaged in a grave and serious transaction.

Lord Cornwallis assumed the administration of Indian affairs in the month of September, 1786; his first attention was directed to the affairs of Oude, in consequence of the complaints made by the Nabob-Vizier of the heavy expenses imposed upon him for the maintenance of the Company's brigades. The Governor-general, however, firmly refused to remove any portion of the troops, though he granted the Nabob some alleviation of his pecuniary burthens. The Guntoor Circar was obtained from his highness the Nizam, on very favourable terms, but the close alliance which was formed in consequence, between the Nizam and the Company, gave great offence to Tippoo Sultan, and he showed his resentment by espousing the cause of the Rájá of Cherika, who had quarrelled with the English respecting the payment of his debts, for which they held the customs of the port of Tellicherry as a security. Some negociations ensued, which shewed distinctly the hostile designs of the Sultan of Mysore, but all doubts were removed when Tippoo blockaded Tellicherry, and led an army to invade the dominions of the Rájá of Travancore, a faithful ally of the English. The territories of Travancore were defended by a line of works about thirty miles in length; they consisted of a ditch about sixteen feet broad and twenty deep, a strong bamboo hedge, a slight parapet, and good rampart, with bastions on rising grounds, which almost flanked each other. On the 24th of December, 1789, Tippoo appeared before the lines of Travancore, and on the 29th, he turned the right flank of the works and introduced a portion of his army within the wall; before, however, he could open the gates, his troops were thrown into confusion by an unexpected resistance, and driven, with great slaughter, across the ditch, Tippoo himself effecting his escape with considerable difficulty.

After his defeat, the King of Mysore disavowed the outrage, and described it as the unauthorized act of his troops; but Lord Cornwallis was not easily deceived, and he immediately entered into treaties with the Nizam and the Mahratta authorities, at Poonah, to restrain the ambition of Tippoo. In the meantime, the sultan again assailed the lines of Travancore, and forced an entrance on the 7th of May, 1790; he then razed the lines, and spread desolation over the surrounding country. On the other hand, General Meadows, with the Madras army, advanced to invade Coimbetore, and thence penetrate into the heart of the Mysore country, while General Abercrombie, with the army of Bombay, attacked Tippoo's territories on the Malabar Coast. The first operations of the English were very successful; a line of communication was established; an enemy's country was obtained for the supply of the troops; and nothing remained but to ascend the Gujelhutty Pass, and make Tippoo contend for his throne in the centre of his dominions. Before the attempt could be made, Tippoo descended with his army by this very pass, and nearly succeeded in surprising Colonel Floyd, who commanded a large division of the English army. By a very rapid and fatiguing march, Colonel Floyd effected a junction with the main army, while Tippoo made an unsuccessful attempt to surprise another English detachment commanded by Colonel Maxwell. But though disappointed in these enterprizes, the sultan captured several of the English depôts, and obtained considerable booty, both in provisions and stores. The remainder of the campaign was spent in indecisive operations; Meadows was unable to bring Tippoo to fight a pitched battle, and from deficient intelligence, was unable to take advantage of the sultan's desultory movements.

Lord Cornwallis had not been long in India, before he became convinced of the necessity of once more taking the collection and management of the revenues of the Carnatic out of the hands of the Nabob of Arcot. The court of directors sanctioned this course of policy, which Lord Macartney had been so severely condemned for pursuing; but it was, at the same time, declared that the arrangement was only temporary, and that the Nabob should be restored to perfect independence at the conclusion of the war. Having completed these financial arrangements, Lord Cornwallis prepared to open the second campaign in person, and successfully masking his movements, arrived at the Pass of Mooglee, before it was in the power of the enemy to offer any obstruction to his march. On the evening of the 5th of March, 1791, the English arrived before Bangalore; the following morning Colonel Floyd, with a strong detachment, unexpectedly encountered Tippoo's entire army, and rashly gave orders for an immediate attack. His hardihood would, in all probability, have been crowned with success, had he not been severely wounded by a musket ball, when the soldiers, being left without orders, fell into some confusion. Fortunately, Major Gowdie covered the retreat with a body of infantry and a few guns, which effectually checked the pursuit. On the night of the 21st of March, Lord Cornwallis hazarded the assault of Bangalore, though the breaches were yet incomplete, and the sultan with his whole army lay in sight of the town. The valour of the assailants bore down all opposition; the enemies, attempting to escape, crowded and choked the gate, a deplorable carnage ensued, and the bodies of more than one thousand of the garrison were buried after the assault. The capture of Bangalore did not bring the English all the advantages they had expected; provisions were scarce; the draught cattle were reduced to skeletons, and scarcely able to move their own weight, and the auxiliary force sent by the Nizam was utterly worthless. Notwithstanding these disadvantages, the Governor-general advanced to besiege Seringapatam, having previously sent orders to the Bombay army to invade Mysore on the Malabar side. But though a victory was gained over Tippoo, the want of necessary supplies, and the increasing sickness in the English camp, compelled Lord Cornwallis to retreat, after having sacrificed his battering train and all his heavy stores. A few days after this loss had been incurred, his lordship was joined by the Mahrattas, with a supply of provisions and draught cattle, but the season was now too late for resuming military operations, and the army continued its retreat to Bangalore.

Immense preparations were made for the ensuing campaign, and before it opened, detachments from the English army captured several of the hill-forts which protected the passes into Mysore. The most important of these strong fortresses was Savendroog, a name which signifies "the rock of death;" it was built on a rock computed to rise above half a mile in perpendicular height, and was surrounded by a close forest, or jungle, several miles in depth, having its natural impenetrability heightened by thickets of planted bamboos. The strength of the mountain had been increased by enormous walls and barriers, which defended every accessible point; and to these advantages was added the division of the mountain, by a great chasm, into two parts at the top, on each of which was erected a citadel; the one affording a secure retreat, though the other were taken, and, by that means, doubling the labour of reduction. Yet this formidable fortress was taken by storm on the 21st of December, with no other casualty to the assailants than one private soldier slightly wounded. Ootadroog, a fortress scarcely less important than the preceding, shared its fate a few days afterwards.

The detachment sent to aid the Mahrattas, under the command of Captain Little, performed many eminent services without obtaining any effective assistance from the allies, who were, indeed, rather an impediment. With only seven hundred men, Captain Little attacked ten thousand Mysoreans, strongly posted in a fortified camp, put them to the rout, and captured the whole of their guns. This brilliant exploit was followed by the reduction of the fortress of Lemoga, which opened to the allies a portion of Tippoo's territories which had hitherto escaped the ravages of war. Instead of advancing to aid General Abercromby, who had reached the top of the Ghauts on the Malabar side, the Mahrattas made a fruitless attempt on Bednore, tempted by the hope of its rich plunder; and they thus materially deranged the governor's plan for the campaign, and led to the loss of Coimbetore, which was forced to capitulate to a Mysore army. The terms of the capitulation were atrociously violated, and this outrage prevented Lord Cornwallis from listening to Tippoo's overtures for peace.

Having been joined by reinforcements from Hyderabad, the Governor-general advanced to undertake the siege of Seringapatam, and, on the 5th of February, 1792, arrived within sight of that capital. Seringapatam is situated on an island formed by two branches of the river Cavery, which, after separating to a distance of about a mile and a half, again unite about four miles below the place of their separation. The fortress is erected in the western angle of the island, and the eastern part was fortified with redoubts and batteries connected by a strong entrenchment with deep ditch; the fort and the out-works were provided with three hundred pieces of cannon, and formed a second line, on which Tippoo could retire if driven from his fortified camp. This camp was placed in an enclosure between the bound hedge and the river—it was protected in front by a large tank or canal, and was further secured by six redoubts, mounted with more than one hundred pieces of heavy artillery. The Sultan's army consisted of about six thousand cavalry and fifty thousand infantry, commanded by Tippoo in person.

On the evening of the 6th of February, the British troops,

after having been dismissed from parade, were ordered to fall in again with their arms and ammunition. By eight o'clock the arrangements were completed for surprising Tippoo's fortified camp, and the army marched forward to the assault in three columns. The series of operations which followed is the most brilliant in the annals of Indian warfare; two of the strongest redoubts were taken; Tippoo's routed army was driven in confusion across the river into the island; pursued thither by their assailants, several of their batteries stormed, and a defensible position secured in the island before the morning dawned. Vast numbers of Tippoo's troops took advantage of the confusion to desert their standard, and one body, ten thousand strong, which consisted of persons forcibly enlisted in Coorg, wholly disappeared, the men having sought shelter in their native woods.

The conflict was renewed at break of day; the guns of the fort opened a tremendous fire on the redoubts, of which the English had gained possession, and desperate attacks were made on every part of their position. Tippoo's soldiers were, however, defeated on every point, and, on the evening of the 7th, the battle was at an end. The English loss amounted to five hundred and thirty-five in killed and wounded, but more than four thousand of the Mysoreans are calculated to have fallen. Nine days afterwards Lord Cornwallis, who had, in the meantime, narrowly escaped from a sudden attack made by the enemy's cavalry, was joined by General Abercromby with two thousand Europeans, and about double that number of Native troops.

On the evening of the 18th, while a small detachment beat up the enemy's camp, and threw the entire army into confusion, ground was broken on the northern side of the fort, and the first parallel completed before day-light without the loss of a man. Everything promised a favourable termination of the siege; but on the morning of the 24th, to the great grief of the army, it was announced that Tippoo had signed the preliminaries of peace. The conditions of the treaty were that he should cede one-half of his territories to the allies, pay three crores and two lacs of rupees to defray the expenses of the war, and give up two of his sons as hostages for the due performance of these stipulations. Such was the ascendancy gained by Lord Cornwallis over his Indian allies, that they confided the entire negociation to his discretion, declaring their willingness either to go on with the war or conclude a peace, and to agree to any terms which should meet with his approbation.

Though Tippoo had sent his sons to the English camp, where they were most honourably received, he exhibited great reluctance to complete the negociations, particularly objecting to the article which secured the independence of the Rájá of Coorg. Some preparations were made for renewing the siege, but the Sultan finally submitted on the 19th of March, and the hostage princes performed the ceremony of delivering the definitive treaty to Lord Cornwallis and the allies. Immediately after the conclusion of this treaty, the Governor-general took possession of all the French settlements in India, the Revolution in France having precipitated that country into war with England.

CHAPTER XII.

ADMINISTRATION OF SIR JOHN SHORE AND LORD MORNINGTON, AFTERWARDS MARQUIS OF WELLESLEY.

Lord Cornwallis introduced many important changes in the administration of the financial and judicial affairs of India, which were not so successful as his military operations. He resolved to erect the Zemindars or collectors of the land-revenue into a body of landed proprietors, renting their Zemindaries as estates from the Company, and paying the land-tax as a species of rent. This unfortunate project, which shewed utter ignorance of the peculiar tenure of land in India, brought ruin on the Zemindars, and inflicted severe injury on the Ryots or cultivators of the soil. Many of the judicial reforms were inapplicable to the socialcondition of India, and, therefore, failed to produce the beneficial results which had been too eagerly anticipated. In 1793, the Charter of the East India Company was renewed with very little opposition, and, about the same time, Lord Cornwallis was succeeded by Sir John Shore, a civil servant of the Company, whose knowledge of the revenue system of India was held in particular esteem.

The alliance, offensive and defensive, which had been concluded between the English, the Nizam, and the Mahrattas, included a mutual guarantee against their common enemy, the King of Mysore, but had no stipulations for the possible case of hostilities arising between two of the allies. This, however, was a contingency against which it was necessary to make some provision, for the Mahrattas were jealous of the enlarged and growing power of the English; and they were impatient to reap the spoils of the feeble Nizam—an acquisition to which they regarded the connection of that prince with the English as the only obstruction. Scindia, the most powerful of the Mahratta chiefs, was the foremost in proclaiming his dissatisfaction, and he did not disguise his anxiety to see the power of Tippoo strengthened, as a counterpoise to the still more formidable power of the English. The death of Scindia induced the Nizam to precipitate a war; he advanced into the Mahratta territories, hoping to profit by the confusion which he believed to exist in the court of Poonah; but the Mahrattas were on the alert, and sent a powerful army to intercept his march. The armies met near Kurdla, and a sharp engagement took place. In the very heat of the fight, the Nizam and his officers were seized with a sudden panic; they fled from the field, and their army was totally routed. The Nizam sought shelter in the little fort of Kurdla, where he was closely besieged by the Mahrattas, and, in two days, compelled to beg a peace on whatever terms his enemies pleased to dictate. It is not wonderful that this prince should have been much displeased by the refusal of the Company to allow the British battalions which he had in his service, to accompany him in this campaign; he dismissed them immediately after his return, and directed his attention to strengthen his own regular infantry, which had been disciplined by a French officer named Raymond, who had acquired great experience in Indian warfare. The existence of this force was viewed with great jealousy by the English, especially as some French officers, who were prisoners at Madras, were detected in a project of escape, and as some of the Madras Sepoys had actually gone over to the French. The death of the Peishwa, and the intrigues in Poonah, which ended in the elevation of Hajèe Ras, the son of Ragoba, to the supreme power, enabled the Nizam to obtain more favourable terms from the Mahrattas than he had previously expected, and particularly a relaxation of the severe conditions which had been imposed upon him by the convention of Kurdla.

When the treaty of Seringapatam had been fully executed, Sir John Shore sent back the sons of Tippoo, and took the opportunity of restoring these hostages, to make some effort for establishing friendly communications with the sultan. But Tippoo's pride had been too severely hurt to allow of friendship, and he disdained to act the hypocrite; he received the officer who brought back his sons with cold civility, and declined entering into any conference.

The affairs of Oude had fallen into great disorder from the

extravagance and incapacity of the Nabob-Vizir: his death threatened to superadd the horrors of a disputed succession, for his brother asserted that the reputed children of the late nabob were not really his offspring. At first the Governor-general decided in favour of the young Vizir Alí, but, having subsequently visited Lucknow, he became convinced that this prince's claims were unfounded, and he therefore transferred the throne to Sadat Alí, the brother of the late nabob. As the military force of Oude was entirely English, Vizir Alí was forced to submit, and, on the 21st of January, 1798, Sadat Alí was proclaimed without any opposition.

The administration of the affairs of the Carnatic was even worse than that of Oude. Following the example of Lord Macartney, Lord Hobart, the Governor of Madras, endeavoured to obtain from the Nabob a renunciation of his powers; but, being prevented by the governor-general from having recourse to any effective measures of intimidation, he was unable to succeed. Some fame accrued to Lord Hobart, from his promptitude in seizing on the Dutch settlements so soon as he received intelligence of the commencement of war between England and Holland; their establishments in Ceylon, Malacca, Banda, and Amboyna were reduced almost without a struggle. Soon afterwards, Lord Clive superseded Lord Hobart as governor of Madras, and Sir John Shore, who had been raised to the peerage, by the title of Lord Teignmouth, resigned the government of India and sailed for England.

Lord Mornington arrived in Calcutta to assume the office of Governor-general on the 17th of May, 1798; he had been for some time previously, one of the commissioners for the affairs of India, and, during his short stay at the Cape of Good Hope, he obtained much valuable information respecting the state of the country he was to govern. About three weeks after his arrival in Calcutta, he received what purported to be a proclamation, issued by the French Governor of the Mauritius, importing that two ambassadors from Tippoo Sultan had arrived in the island to propose an alliance, offensive and defensive, with the French, and to request the aid of a body of troops for the expulsion of the English from Southern India; the proclamation then invited the citizens to volunteer their services on the very liberal terms which the Sultan's ambassadors were prepared to offer. The

Governor-general was at first disposed to treat this extraordinary publication as a forgery; naturally supposing that no man in his senses would make such a transaction the subject of a proclamation, but subsequent enquiries confirmed its authenticity, and it was resolved to anticipate danger by immediately proclaiming war against Tippoo.

The condition in which the presidency of Madras was placed by the ruinous state of its finances, did not allow General Harris, who was then the acting governor, to act with the promptitude which Lord Mornington desired. Several of the most influential men in the presidency condemned the war altogether, as both unjust and impolitic, nor was it until the arrival of Lord Clive that any active measures were taken to prepare for hostilities. Another object of English policy was effected with little difficulty; the French corps in the service of the Nizam was disbanded; the officers who commanded it were compelled, by a mutiny of the troops, to seek shelter in the English lines, and they were treated with that generosity which a gallant mind is ever prompted to bestow. Their place was supplied to the Nizam by four battalions of British troops, in addition to the two which had been formerly in his service.

The intelligence of Napoleon's invasion of Egypt, though followed by the account of Sir Horatio Nelson's destruction of the French fleet at the mouth of the Nile, induced the Governor-general to accelerate his preparations. Early in November, he addressed a letter of remonstrance to the sultan, and soon after, he went in person to Madras. All the preparations and arrangements were speedily completed; General Harris took the command of the army of the Carnatic, and General Stuart was appointed to lead the Bombay army, which was to join that of General Harris when he approached Seringapatam. The army of the Carnatic, including the Nizam's auxiliary force, did not fall very far short of thirty thousand men; and "an army," says the governor-general, "more completely appointed, more amply and liberally supplied in every department, and more perfect in its discipline, and the acknowledged experience, ability, and skill of its officers, never took the field in India."

On the 6th of March, General Harris entered the Mysore territory, and captured several hill forts. The Nizam's contingent, strengthened by an European regiment of the line, was placed under the command of the Hon. Colonel Arthur Wellesley, then entering on the illustrious military career which has immortalized his name as the Duke of Wellington. Tippoo's first efforts of stratagem were directed against the Bombay army; having circulated a report that he was about to march against General Harris, he suddenly proceeded, with all possible secresy and despatch, two hundred miles in the opposite direction, hoping to cut off Colonel Montrésor, who was stationed with a brigade of three Sepoy battalions at Sedaseer. He would, in all probability, have succeeded, but for the accidental discovery of his encampment, on the evening of the 5th of March, by the Rájá of Coorg, and some English officers whom the Rájá had conducted to the top of Sedaseer, the highest hill in the country, for the purpose of looking into the Mysore territory. Montrésor made immediate preparations for defence; he was attacked on the following morning by Tippoo's numerous hordes, but he held them at bay until near three o'clock in the day, when General Stuart came to his relief with a reinforcement of European troops. The general found Montrésor's men exhausted with fatigue, and their ammunition almost expended. Tippoo made a desperate effort to prevent a junction, but his troops gave way before the European soldiers; after many of the Mysoreans had fallen, the rest threw down their muskets, swords, and turbans, and fled in confusion. Tippoo waited five days in the neighbourhood, but did not venture to renew the attack; he then returned to Seringapatam.

After having lost several opportunities of attacking the army of the Carnatic with advantage, Tippoo resolved to hazard a battle at Mallavelly. The plan of attack which was arranged between him and his able adviser, Poorniah, was very judicious. A force of three hundred men, commanded by Poorniah, was designed to break through the English line of the right wing, and Tippoo was then to pour his whole force of cavalry into the gap, and cut through the army. Fortunately, General Harris discovered Poorniah's detachment before an attack could be made; he instantly ordered the Scotch brigade to make ready, but not to fire until the enemy came close. The troops had scarcely formed, when the three hundred horsemen, who had been infuriated by stimulating liquors, burst from the jungle. General Harris gave the word so opportunely, that about forty men and horses rolled on the ground within twenty yards of the line, one horseman was bayoneted by the grenadier company, and another cut his way through. The right wing then advanced, but Tippoo's soldiers were so disheartened by the failure of the first charge, that they instantly retreated, and the English were too deficient in means of transport for their artillery and stores to attempt a pursuit. Colonel Wellesley was still more successful on the left wing; the close fire of his infantry threw the opposing column into confusion; the cavalry charged at the critical moment, destroyed great numbers of the enemy, and took their six standards. This battle cost the British army only a loss of sixty-six men killed, wounded, and missing, whilst that of Tippoo was nearly two thousand, amongst whom were many of his bravest men and best officers.

General Harris now prepared to execute the intention he had formed of crossing the Cavary, near Soosilly, if it should appear practicable, and of attacking Seringapatam on the western side, in order to facilitate the juncture of the Bombay army, and of the supplies of grain which were expected to come through the western passes. This movement was wholly unexpected by Tippoo, and when he heard that it had been successfully accomplished he was filled with despair. Having assembled the whole of his principal officers, he said to them, "We have arrived at our last stage; what is your determination?" "To die along with you," was the universal reply.

On the 5th of April, the English army appeared before Seringapatam, and the same evening, Colonels Shawe and Wellesley were ordered to attack a watercourse, and tope or clump of trees, in which the enemy had formed an outpost. Some confusion arose from the darkness of the night, and Colonel Wellesley was repulsed; through some neglect of the proper officer he was nearly too late to take the command when the attack was renewed next morning, but General Harris delayed for his arrival; the tope was again assailed, and taken in less than twenty minutes.

The labours of the siege proceeded steadily until the 4th of May, which was chosen for the assault. The time fixed was one o'clock, when the orientals usually take some repose during the heat of the day. Syed Goffhâr, Tippoo's ablest officer, sent word to the sultan that the English were about to make an attack, but Tippoo, misled by astrological predictions, refused to credit the report, and while the Syed was deliberating on forcing the sultan to the breach, he was killed by a cannon-shot. Nearly at the same moment, Tippoo received information that his bravest general had fallen, and that the assault was commenced. At half-past one o'clock, General Baird stepped out of the trenches, drew his sword, and gave the signal to advance. In less than seven minutes after, the English colours were planted on the summit of the breach. The companies of the two storming divisions wheeled to the right and left as they ascended, fighting their way along the northern and southern ramparts, where every inch of ground was fiercely contested. Thousands fell before the victorious soldiers, and the carnage did not cease until the two divisions met on the eastern rampart. Nothing now remained to be taken but Tippoo's palace, the surrender of which was only delayed by the uncertainty that prevailed respecting the fate of the sultan. Tippoo had fallen in the heat of the fight, severely wounded by three musket balls; whilst he lay on the ground, an English soldier attempted to tear off his embroidered sword-belt, but the sultan, who still retained his sabre, made a cut at the man, and wounded him in the knee. The soldier immediately shot him through the head, and his death must have been instantaneous. It was late in the evening before the sultan's body was found and recognized, but in the mean time his family had been taken under the protection of the British officers. The body was buried the next day, with military honours, in the mausoleum of Hyder Alí; and a violent storm of thunder and lightning, which destroyed several Europeans and Natives, gave an awful interest to these last solemn rites.

The months of July and August were spent by General Harris in obtaining and securing possession of the various districts and forts belonging to Mysore, and in checking the ravages of Dhoondiah, a plundering chieftain whom Tippoo had confined, but who was imprudently released by the English. With some difficulty, the banditti collected by this adventurer, were dispersed, and he was forced to seek shelter among the Mahrattas. Some discussion was excited in the army by the appointment of Colonel Wellesley to the government of Seringapatam in preference to General Baird, who had commanded the assault, and was besides the senior officer; but for this preference, a very sufficient and honourable reason may be assigned; Colonel Wellesley relieved General Baird the morning after the capture of the place, and won the confidence of the inhabitants by his exertions to put a stop to plunder, and other military outrages.

The Governor-general had now to dispose of a kingdom; he resolved that no part of it should be given to the family of the late sovereign, but he assigned them a residence in the fort of Vellore, and made a very liberal allowance for their subsistence. Part of the kingdom of Mysore, in the immediate vicinity of its ancient capital, was erected into a principality for the family of the original Hindú Rájás, whom Tippoo had deposed; some rich districts were assigned to the Nizam, others of equal value were retained by the English, and finally, a small portion of the conquered territory was given to the Mahrattas, although they had taken no part in the war.

After the conclusion of the Mysore war, the Governor-general planned an expedition against the Isle of France; this island had been for some years the resort of a number of armed vessels, which, with singular activity and boldness, carried on a predatory warfare against British commerce in the Eastern seas. The losses sustained by the merchants and Company from the depredations of those daring privateers, were estimated at two millions sterling; and the existence of such a rallying point for any armament which might be equipped in France against the British possessions in India, was deemed, not unjustly, as disreputable to the national reputation as it was injurious to the national commerce. Lord Mornington took prompt measures to put an end to this evil. A military armament was prepared to be placed under the command of Colonel Wellesley, and a communication was made to Admiral Rainier, who commanded the British squadron in the Indian Seas, requesting that he would proceed to Trincomalee to meet the forces and transports assembled there, and co-operate in the attack upon the Isle of France. To the surprise of every body, the admiral peremptorily refused to take any share in such an expedition without express orders from home. As no imputation has ever been made against Admiral Rainier's courage, we are left to conclude that he was influenced by that jealous tenacity of authority, which frequently led naval officers in the Indian Seas to refuse obeying orders from the Governor-general of India; but whatever may have been his motives, the results of his decision were most disastrous; for the privateers of the Isle of France continued, during several subsequent years of the war, to harass and plunder with impunity the commercial navigation of the Indian Seas.

The Governor-general next resolved to send the troops which he had collected in Ceylon against the Dutch settlements in Batavia, but from this project he was diverted by instructions from England, directing him to send a force from India to Egypt in order to assist in the expulsion of the French from that country. The forces assembled at Ceylon were therefore despatched to Bombay, to be joined there by a body of native infantry which had been held in readiness there for foreign service. The united force was placed under the command of General Baird, and was sent by the Red Sea to Egypt. It arrived too late to be of any service, the French having capitulated before it could commence any active operations.

While this expedition was absent, the Governor-general, anticipating hostilities from the Mahrattas, and aware that the Nizam was unable to defend his territories against them without an English auxiliary force, while the vacillating politics of his court might induce him to dismiss that force as he had done before, entered into arrangements by which the Nizam ceded to the English some rich districts, the revenues of which were to be applied to the payment of the auxiliary brigade. This arrangement was, of course, inconsistent with the act of parliament, which forbade the acquisition of a new territory, but its obvious policy prevented any objection being raised. Indeed, many would have rejoiced if the Nizam had been induced to surrender all his power for an adequate pension, in order that an end might be put to the corruption and profligacy of the court of Hyderabad. Dangers, however, menaced the Company from another quarter, and withdrew attention from the Nizam.

CHAPTER XIII.

CONTINUATION OF THE ADMINISTRATION OF THE MARQUIS OF WELLESLEY.

The Governor-general had long been dissatisfied, not unreasonably, with the arrangements which Lord Teignmouth had made for administering the affairs of Oude. The Nabob-Vizir was irregular in the payment of his subsidies; the armed rabble, which constituted his military force, was calculated to invite rather than deter enemies, and his civil administration was little better than a system of legal profligacy. During the Mysore war, and for some time previously, India was menaced with an invasion of the Afghans, whose enterprising sovereign, Shah Zemán, was tempted to such an enterprize by the solicitations of Tippoo Sultan, and by a fugitive prince of the imperial family, who persuaded him that his efforts would be supported by all the Mohammedans throughout India. His first invasion of the Punj-áb was commenced at the close of the year 1795, but he had not been more than a fortnight beyond the Indus when he was obliged to return home to quell a dangerous rebellion. In the January of 1797, he renewed his attempt, and advanced to Lahore, where he made some attempts, not wholly unsuccessful, to reconcile the Sikh chieftains to his dominions. The Sikhs were originally a peaceful religious sect, not unlike the society of Quakers; their creed was a strange compound of Hindú and Mohammedan doctrines; it spread rapidly through the Punj-áb and the countries bordering on the tributaries of the Indus, and, at first, attracted little notice. The bigoted advisers of the emperors of Delhí persuaded these princes to commence a cruel persecution of this harmless sect. They were hunted down by a licentious soldiery, and at length took up arms in self-defence. A few years sufficed to change this patient race into hardy and independent warriors, able to defy the declining power of the empire of Delhí.

Shah Zeman's efforts to conciliate the Sikhs, were resisted by the bigoted train of Mohammedan priests, which followed with his army, by the rapacity of his vizier, and by the licentiousness of his soldiers, which he was unable to restrain. Still, he was so far successful as to have a reasonable prospect of retaining the Punj-áb, and thence attacking the ancient empire of Delhí. The advance of the Afghans and the occupation of Lahore, did not fail in creating a strong sensation throughout India. The weakness of the Mahrattas, the whole of whose forces were drawn to the southward by their own dissensions; the feebleness of the government of the Nabob-Vizir, and the disposition of the greater part of his subjects to insurrection and revolt, together with the anxiety of all the Mohammedans for the establishment of their ancient religious supremacy, prepared scenes of disorder and anarchy which would, doubtless, have opened so soon as the Shah had advanced to Delhí. Many of the Rohilla chieftains, remembering the cruel injustice with which their race had been treated by Warren Hastings, were already in arms. Fortunately, the rebellion of his brother, Prince Mohammed, compelled Zemán to return home in the summer of 1797, but not until he had announced his intention of renewing the invasion on the earliest opportunity. He came back to Lahore the next year, but was soon compelled to abandon India in order to protect his own dominions from the Persians. This induced the Governor-general to send rather an expensive embassy to the King of Persia, for the purpose of negociating an offensive and defensive alliance with that monarch; a treaty was concluded, but it never came into operation, for, early in 1801, Shah Zemán was dethroned by his brother Mohammed, who made him a prisoner, and deprived him of sight.

Another circumstance besides the dread of Shah Zemán, rendered Lord Wellesley anxious to accelerate his meditated reforms in Oude. Vizir Alí, after having been deposed by Sir John Shore, was permitted to reside in Benares, but as this place was too near his former dominions, it was resolved that he should be removed to Calcutta. He viewed this change with the utmost aversion, and remonstrated against it most strenuously. On the 14th of January, 1799, he visited the President, Mr. Cherry, and complained of the hardship of his removal in very intemperate language. Mr. Cherry remonstrated with him on his imprudence, when the young man started from his seat and struck at the president with his sword. This was the signal to his attendants, they rushed upon the unfortunate gentleman, and murdered him on the floor. Four other Englishmen fell victims to these assassins; but a fifth made so vigorous a defence, that time was given for the arrival of a body of horse, upon which Vizir Alí and his attendants took to flight. Though Saadat Alí believed that his old rival was about to make an attempt upon his throne, his timidity was too great to allow of his making any vigorous exertion to overtake the criminals; he pleaded an excuse, that he could rely neither on the discipline nor the fidelity of his troops. Vizir Alí's career was, however, brief; he at first assembled a numerous body of adventurers, but, meeting with some reverses, he was abandoned by his followers, and forced to seek refuge with a Rajput chief, by whom he was soon surrendered to the British government.

The Governor-general now insisted that the Nabob Vizir of Oude should disband, as speedily as possible, the whole of his military force, and replace it by an army exclusively British. He was, however, to retain that kind of troops which had been employed to collect taxes. Colonel Scott was entrusted with the conduct of this negociation, which the Nabob Vizir protected with all the delays which oriental diplomacy could suggest. At length the Nabob intimated a wish to resign the throne of Oude, a proposition which the Governor-general hesitated to accept, unless the abdication was made in favour of the Company. It soon appeared that Saadat Alí's object was merely delay; he had great and natural objections to dismiss his own army, and entrust the defence of his dominions to the British troops, believing that his power would be thus reduced to a mere shadow, and that he would sink into an empty pageant of royalty. The vigorous measures of the Governor-general soon forced the Nabob into compliance, and on his representation that he was unable to meet the expenses of the British brigade, he was required to transfer the exclusive management of the civil as well as the military government of his country to the Company, under suitable provisions for the maintenance of his court and his family; and, at the same time, he was informed that he must surrender, in absolute sovereignty to the English, so much territory as would afford a revenue adequate to pay the subsidy stipulated with Lord Teignmouth, and defray the expenses of the military establishment besides.

Saadat Alí had again recourse to all the delays which his ingenuity could suggest, but the Governor-general inflexibly adhered to his demands, and threatened to employ force unless they were accepted. The Nabob waited until he heard that troops were actually on the march, and then, being incapable of resistance, he yielded a reluctant consent. Lord Wellesley proceeded to execute his plans with the same promptitude which he had displayed from the beginning; on the very day that the treaty was signed, he issued a commission for the provisional government and settlement of the ceded districts, placing his brother, Mr. Henry Wellesley, at the head of the board. During the negociations, Lord Wellesley made a tour to the Upper Provinces, and visited Saadat Alí at Lucknow, where he seems to have in some degree soothed the irritation of the Nabob for the sacrifices he had been compelled to make.

The court of directors was far from being satisfied with these arrangements; it was whispered that the great object of the Marquis of Wellesley's policy, was to provide lucrative places for his numerous brothers, and the appointment of Mr. Henry Wellesley was particularly condemned, as he did not belong to the class of Company's servants, to whom, by act of parliament, the filling up of vacancies in the civil service was limited. The board of control refused to sanction the order of the court of directors for the immediate removal of Mr. Henry Wellesley, declaring that the appointment was only temporary, and, therefore, not within the restricting rules. In the meantime, a new necessity was created for continuing Mr. Henry Wellesley's services by the conclusion of an arrangement with the subordinate Nabob of Furruckabad, similar to that which had been already made with his superior, the Nabob of Oude. A Rájá named Rugwunt Sing refused to submit to the alterations which were made; it became necessary to employ force, and his two forts, Sasnee and Bidgeghur were besieged and taken. Some other refractory Zemindars, who had profited by the anarchy which formerly prevailed in the Doab, were compelled to submit to the British government, and, when the tranquillity of the ceded districts was established, Mr. Henry Wellesley resigned his office.

On the other side of India, misgovernment and neglect of payment afforded a pretext for adding the dominions of the Nabob of Surat to the Company's territories. Surat had been the most flourishing commercial mart in India, when first the trade of that country was opened to European enterprize; it was the usual port of embarkation for Mecca, and was generally called by the Mohammedans "the Gate of the Holy City." Many of the Parsees, or Persians who adhered to the ancient religion of Zoroaster, had settled in the city, and enriched it by the active trade which they conducted with the Arabian and Persian Gulphs. In the doctrine of the Delhí empire, the Nabob of Surat, like many other of the imperial feudatories, became virtually independent, and rendered the succession to his government hereditary. Disputes arose respecting the inheritance, which were decided by the interference of the English government, and the sovereigns of Surat gave further proofs of their weakness by consenting to pay *chout*, or tribute, to the Mahrattas. A disputed succession in 1799 afforded an opportunity for reducing the Nabob of Surat to the same condition as the Nabob of Oude; he was induced to surrender the civil and military administration of his dominions to the English, on condition of receiving a pension, and enjoying the empty title of sovereignty. The great difficulty remaining was to obtain deliverance from the misery of the Mahratta *chout*. The Guicowar prince expressed the greatest readiness to compliment the Company, to whom he looked for protection, with the share which belonged to him. But the business was not so easily arranged with the Peishwa, for the party opposed to the English was at this period very influential in the court of Poonah.

The Rájá of Tanjore was about the same time reduced to the condition of a mediatized prince. Some time previously, there had been a dispute respecting the succession to the throne of this country; the Rájá Zuljajee, on his death-bed, bequeathed his kingdom to his adopted son, Sarbojee, whom he entrusted to the care of the celebrated missionary Swartz, but the validity of the act of adoption was doubted, and the English government decided in favour of Zuljajee's brother, Amar Sing. There soon appeared many valid reasons for doubting the propriety of this decision, and they were strongly urged on the consideration of the government, when Sarbojee was forced to seek refuge at Madras from the tyranny of Amar Sing. Finally, Sarbojee was placed upon the throne on condition of assigning over to the English the civil and military administration of his kingdom. However mortifying this arrangement may have been to the sovereign, there is no doubt but that the better system of government which the English introduced, was attended by the most beneficial results to the Rájá of Tanjore.

Great inconveniences had arisen from the state of the relations between the government of Madras and the Nabob of Arcot; his independence had been preserved by the sinister influence of those who had led him to contract debts at exorbitant rates of interest, and had absorbed to themselves nearly all the revenues of his country. But the impoverishment produced by this drain on his resources, soon exhausted the supply; not only were the means of parliamentary corruption wanting to the peculators, but even the Nabob's subsidies to the Company fell heavily into arrear, and his neglect to pay the promised arrears at the commencement of the Mysore war, had very nearly produced the most fatal consequences. Soon after the capture of Seringapatam, documents were discovered among the secret records of the sultan, containing very strong evidence of a treacherous intercourse having been maintained by the late Nabob Wallajah and the reigning prince, Omdát-al-Omrah, with Tippoo Sultan, for objects hostile to the interests of the Company. Preparations were made for assuming the civil and military administration of the Carnatic by force, when Omdát-al-Omrah died, and was succeeded by his reputed son, Ali Hossein, under the guardianship of two noblemen of the court. Lord Clive went in person to conduct the negociation with the young prince, who at first expressed his readiness to comply with the proposed terms, but, subsequently, retracted all his concessions. Not unreasonably offended at such vacillation, Lord Clive, with the concurrence of the Governor-general, resolved that Ali Hussein should be deposed, and the nabobship transferred to his cousin, Azím-ed-Dowlah. Alí Hussein protested against this change, and declared his willingness to accede to the terms offered by Lord Clive. No regard was paid to his remonstrances; he soon after fell a victim to dysentery, and Amar Sing, the deposed Rájá of Tanjore, died nearly at the same time. The arrangements for the future administration of Tanjore and the Carnatic, were therefore completed without interruption.

Lord Wellesley was very eager to establish the same relations with the Mahratta states which he had completed with the Nizam, namely, to procure their assent to the establishment of an English subsidiary force in their dominions, and an assignment of a portion of territory sufficient for their support. The obvious recommendations of this plan were, that the troops of the native princes were little better than hordes of banditti, subsisting on plunder rather than pay, and that the existence of such armies was utterly inconsistent with the maintenance of peace in India. On the other hand, the presence of a subsidiary disciplined force was sure to deliver the Indian princes from the dread of insurrection, which was the only check to their habits of cruelty and oppression; under such circumstances the English necessarily appeared to themselves and others, little better than hireling supporters of tyranny, and thus, after having taken the military administration, they were frequently compelled, and in all cases were tempted to seize the civil government likewise.

The Governor-general commenced his negotiations with the Peishwa, who, by the Mahratta constitution, was the legal sovereign of all the Mahratta chieftains. But his authority, though nominally recognized, was virtually rejected by several of the powerful feudatories who held under him by military tenure, and particularly by Holkar and Scindia. The latter, indeed, held the reigning Peishwa, Bajee Rao, in such a state of control that Lord Wellesley believed he would gladly embrace the proposal of receiving an English subsidiary force, in order to deliver himself from a degrading dependence upon his own vassal. Circumstances arose within the Mahratta states, which seemed to favour the Governor-general's design. The powerful family of the Holkars, which had for more than three-fourths of a century been settled in the northern Mahratta states, had not only established their virtual independence, but had acquired an extent of power and dominion not inferior to that of the peishwa himself. A disputed succession gave Scindia a pretext for interfering in the affairs of the Holkars; he conferred the sovereignty on Cashee Rao, put his rival and brother, Mulhar Rao, to death, but preserved the posthumous son of the latter as a hostage for the fidelity of his uncle. Jesswunt Rao, the son of the late Holkar by a concubine, escaped from Scindia's search, and soon appeared in the field at the head of a numerous army of adventurers. He was severely defeated by Scindia, in an engagement near Indore, the capital of Holkar's dominions, on the 14th of October, 1801, and fled, with the loss of his artillery and baggage. In the course of the next year, however, he had assembled a still more considerable force, and marched to attack the united forces of Scindia and the Peishwa, in the vicinity of Poonah. A battle was fought on the 25th of October, 1802. After a warm cannonade of about three hours, the cavalry of Holkar made a general charge. The cavalry of Scindia gave way, when that of Holkar cutting in upon the line of infantry, put them to flight and gained a decisive victory.

The Peishwa, not doubting of success, had quitted his palace with some intention of joining in the action, but being frightened by the noise of the firing, he turned off to the southward of the town, in order to wait the result. When he learned the result, he fled to the fort of Singurh, having previously sent to the British Resident, Colonel Close, the preliminaries of a treaty by which he bound himself to subsidize six battalions of British Sepoys, and to cede twenty-five lacs of rupees of annual revenue for their support. During the engagement, the British flag floating over the Residency, ensured the respect of both parties, to which the high estimation in which Colonel Close was held by the Natives not a little contributed.

On the day following the battle, Holkar sent a message requesting an interview with the Resident, which was, of course, accepted. Colonel Close found the victorious chieftain in a small tent, ankle-deep in mud, wounded by a spear in the body, and by a sabre in the head. His conversation was polite and frank, he spoke lightly of his wounds, and expressed himself in the most friendly terms towards the resident and the British government. He seemed extremely desirous of obtaining the mediation of the resident in settling with Scindia and the Peishwa, and solicited Close, whom he detained about a month in Poonah, to act as arbitrator. Holkar's moderation, whether real or affected, was lost on the Peishwa; he retreated from place to place, sent letters to the Bombay government requesting that ships might be sent to convey him to that island, and actually proceeded in an English vessel to Bassein.

We have already mentioned, that the Guicowar abandoned to the Company his share of the *chout*, which had been levied on Surat; he also surrendered to them the district of Chourassy, and employed other means to obtain their alliance. The death of this prince, in September, 1800, exposed his country to mutinous disturbances. Anund Rao, his son and successor, was a prince of weak intellect, unable to control the intrigues of the various factions which divided the court of Baroda. These intrigues soon led to an open war between the illegitimate brother of the Guicowar and Nowjee Appajee, who had been the chief minister under the late sovereign. The English government sided with the latter, and sent him a small detachment of troops. A decisive victory was gained over Mulhar Rao, the cousin of the late Guicowar, and the most powerful enemy of the minister.

Rowjee was thus left free to pursue the schemes of economical reform which he had formed; the most important of these was the dismissal of the Arab mercenaries in the Guicowar's service, but these fierce soldiers refused to disband until their demands of enormous sums as arrears had been complied with; they broke out into mutiny, seized Baroda, and detained the Guicowar a prisoner in his capital. Baroda was immediately invested by the English, and forced to surrender, after a siege of ten days. Many of the garrison, contrary to the articles of capitulation, went to join the rebel Kanhojee, but they were closely pursued, defeated them in two smart engagements, and ultimately drove Kanhojee from Gujarát.

Holkar resolved to treat Bajee Rao's flight to Bassein as a formal abdication of his sovereignty, and in conjunction with several other Mahratta chiefs, he proclaimed Amrut Rao the legitimate Peishwa. Thenceforth all appearance of moderation was laid aside; the ministers of the fugitive prince were tortured with the most dreadful cruelty, to force them to reveal the secret of their treasure; and every respectable householder of Poonah, possessed of property, was seized and forced by every wicked means to give up his wealth. At the commencement of these cruelties, Colonel Close quitted Holkar's court, and proceeding to Bassein, concluded with Bajee Rao a treaty on the basis of the preliminaries which had been transmitted to him at Poonah. By this treaty, the Peishwa bound himself to receive an English subsidiary force, and provide for its subsistence; to exclude from his territories Europeans of all nations hostile to the English; to relinquish his claims on Surat; and to submit to the arbitration of the English all points of dispute between him and the Guicowar.

It is not to be supposed that Bajee Rao very willingly signed a treaty which virtually deprived him of independence; it was no sooner concluded than he commenced secret intrigues with Scindia and Raghojee Bhonslay to frustrate its execution; and these chieftains willingly combined to prevent arrangements which threatened to destroy the power they had hitherto possessed in the court of Poonah, and over the Mahratta states generally. The Governor-general was prompt to fulfil his part of the engagement in restoring the Peishwa; Colonel Stevenson, at the head of the Hyderabad subsidiary force, accompanied by fifteen thousand of the Nizam's troops, approached on the Peishwa's eastern frontier; while Major-general Wellesley marched direct on Poonah, from the borders of Mysore, with a strong detachment from the Madras army. General Wellesley made a forced march on Poonah, in order to save the city, which, it was said, Amrut Rao intended to burn; but both Holkar and he had evacuated the place previous to the arrival of the British troops. We may mention that Amrut Rao eventually entered into engagements with General Wellesley, and joined him during the progress of the war, with a body of horse. The Company rewarded his services by a liberal pension, and a residence at Benares.

After Bajee Rao's restoration, the efforts of the Governor-general were directed to obtain the acquiescence of the leading Mahratta chiefs in the treaty of Bassein. Raghojee Bhonslay, Rájá of Berar, opposed the conditions of the treaty with all his might, and laboured to reconcile Scindia and Holkar, that they might unite in frustrating the English policy. General Wellesley having been vested with full powers as political agent of the Governor-general, as well as military commander of the army of the Dekkan, soon grew weary of the vexatious delays and protestations of the chieftains; he therefore demanded as a test of their sincerity, that Raghojee should withdraw with his troops to Berar, and Scindia to Hindostan. This plain and distinct proposal, so characteristic of its author, perplexed the Mahratta chiefs; they were obliged to give a decisive answer, and that being a refusal, was regarded as a declaration of war.

An army was collected in Hindustan, under General Lake, to act against the northern Mahrattas, where Scindia had large bodies of troops commanded and partially disciplined by French adventurers. General Wellesley, assisted by Colonel Stephenson, directed the operations in the Dekkan, which was the first theatre of war. Wellesley commenced by besieging Ahmednugur, which had the reputation of being almost impregnable, but which only held out four days. He then went in pursuit of the Mahrattas, who were anxious to avoid an engagement, and on the 21st of September, 1803, formed a plan, by which, he moving in one direction and Stephenson in another, should unite and attack the Mahrattas on the morning of the 24th. On the evening of the 23rd however, having learned that the Mahratta army amounting to more than fifty thousand men, with a hundred pieces of cannon, had encamped in his neighbourhood, the general resolved to attack them, without waiting for Colonel Stephenson, though his whole force did not exceed four thousand five hundred men.

The Mahrattas were formed in a long line on the bank of the Kailna river, near its junction, having their left flank resting on the fortified village of Assaye, near which their infantry and guns were posted. General Wellesley crossed the Kailna, a little below Assaye, and by thus placing his troops on the tongue of land between the two rivers, compelled the enemy to narrow their front, and thus deprived them of some of the advantages which they might have obtained from their immense superiority of force. The battle commenced with a heavy fire of round and grape from the Mahratta artillery, which did terrible execution. The English line, though destitute of artillery, still pressed forward, when a large body of Mahratta horse, charged the 74th regiment, which had suffered very severely. The English cavalry, consisting of the 19th light dragoons, and the 4th Madras horse, received the order to charge with a joyous shout, to which the infantry responded, the very wounded cheering them as they passed. Their onslaught was irresistible; the enemy's first line fell back upon the second, and the British infantry pressing forward, drove both into the Juah at the point of the bayonet. Every attempt which the fugitives made, to form beyond the river, was defeated by the headlong charges of the British cavalry; the last body of infantry at length was broken; the battle was completely decided, and ninety-eight pieces of cannon remained in the hands of the victors. Many of the Mahrattas, however, who had thrown themselves on the ground as if dead, when the British advanced, rose after they had passed and turned their guns on the British rear; after the more important parts of the victory had been secured, it was some time before the firing thus occasioned could be silenced. The loss of the victors was severe; upwards of one-third of their forces were killed or wounded, but they had achieved one of the most splendid victories recorded in Indian history.

Colonel Stephenson did not join the main army until the evening of the 24th, when he was sent in pursuit of the fugitives. He did not overtake them, but he reduced the city of Burhanpore and the strong fort of Aseerghur. At the same time a detachment from the Gujarât army, captured Baroach and some other fortresses of less importance.

In the mean time, General Lake, who had been invested with the same powers in Hindustan, which General Wellesley possessed in the Dekkan, advanced from Cawnpore against Scindia's northern armies, which were commanded by M. Perron, a French officer of some ability and unquestioned valour. The first operation of the campaign was the storming of Aligurh, a fort which might easily have been made impregnable. It was taken by the heroism of the assailants, but they suffered a severe loss, principally caused by General Lake's want of foresight, a want which unfortunately was conspicuous on more than one occasion. The British cantonment at Shekoabad was surprised by a detachment of Mahratta cavalry, under a Frenchman named Fleury, and the garrison compelled to capitulate, the detachment which Lake sent to its assistance, arriving too late to be of any use.

Perron, at this crisis, received information, that Scindia had resolved to supersede him and transfer the command to one of his personal enemies. He therefore addressed a letter to General Lake, requesting to be allowed to pass through the Company's territories with his property, family and the officers of his suit, to Lucknow; by the direction of the Governor-general, the necessary safe-conduct was promptly granted.

From Ahgurh, General Lake advanced upon Delhí, but when within six miles of the city, his advanced guard of cavalry was suddenly exposed to a heavy and destructive fire of artillery.

Louis Bourquin, the French officer next in command to Perron, assembled a powerful Mahratta force, and concealing his guns by high grass, completely took the English by surprise. Lake saw that it was necessary to draw the Mahrattas from their strong position; he therefore commanded the cavalry to retire, and the enemy, mistaking the movement for a retreat, rushed after them in full assurance of victory. The cavalry, however, retired in good order, until it reached the head of the advancing column, when opening from the centre, they permitted the British infantry to pass to the front. The battalions moved forward under a tremendous fire of grape, round and cannister from the Mahratta guns, until within a distance of one hundred yards, when they fired a volley and then charged with the bayonet. Scindia's infantry could not withstand the onslaught; they abandoned their guns and fled. The English battalions then broke into open columns of companies, and the cavalry charging through the intervals, made dreadful havoc of the fugitives, many of whom only escaped the sabre to perish by drowning in the Jumna. The consequences of this victory, were the immediate possession of the imperial city of Delhí, and the deliverance of the emperor Shah Alúm, from the degrading and painful captivity, in which he had long been held by the Mahrattas.

General Lake then marched against Agra, which was in a state of the greatest anarchy. Before the breaking out of the war, the garrison had been commanded by English officers, who had been confined by their own troops, on the commencement of hostilities. Seven battalions of Scindia's regular infantry, were encamped on the glacis; but the garrison were afraid to admit them into the fort, lest they should plunder a rich treasury which they wished to reserve for themselves. These battalions were attacked by General Lake, and defeated with the loss of twenty-six of their guns. A few days afterwards, the garrison liberated their officers, and capitulated on condition of being permitted to retire with their private property; the treasury, the arsenal and one hundred and sixty-two pieces of cannon, fell into the hands of the victors.

General Lake next marched against the battalions sent by Scindia from the Dekkan, which had been reinforced by the relics of Bourquin's army. After a tedious pursuit, he came up with them at sunrise on the 1st of November, and believing them to be in full retreat, ordered his cavalry to intercept their flight. But the Mahrattas, instead of retreating, had taken up a very strong position; their right resting on the fortified village of Laswaree, their left on the village of Mohaulpore, and their front lined with seventy-five pieces of cannon chained together, so as to resist the charge of horse. The cavalry were driven back, and the infantry with the brigade of guns came forward to the attack. Scindia's horse behaved in the most cowardly manner, but the battalions which had been trained by the French officers, fought with a desperate determination, which nothing could subdue. The greater part of them refused to surrender, but fell where they stood, with arms in their hands. The battle of Laswaree, cost the English more than eight hundred men in killed and wounded, but it completely destroyed Scindia's power in northern India; and at the same time English divisions completely subdued the districts of Kuttack and Bundelcund.

In the Dekkan, General Wellesley, after many harassing operations, arising from the celerity with which the enemy moved from place to place, succeeded in bringing the confederates to an action at Argaom, on the evening of the 29th of November, and routed them with very little difficulty. This success being followed by the capture of Gawelgurh, terrified the confederates into peace. The Rájá of Berar, was the first to yield; he ceded a large portion of his territories to the English and their allies, abandoned all claims of *chout* upon the Nizam, and consented that no European should be admitted into his dominions, without the permission of the British government. Accredited ministers from each of the contracting parties, were to reside at the court of the other, and the Rájá very reluctantly received a resident at Nagpore, Scindia held out a fortnight longer, but finally yielded to similar terms; but he had to sacrifice a much larger portion both of territory and influence than his ally.

During the progress of hostilities, Holkar remained in Malwa, levying enormous contributions from friend and foe, scarcely crediting, or affecting to disbelieve, the accounts of the rapid victories of the English. When it was too late he determined to make an effort for retrieving the independence of the Mahrattas; he sent ambassadors to Scindia, urging him to break the treaty which he had just concluded, but that chieftain was, or pretended to be, so exasperated against Holkar that he immediately communicated the fact to the British authorities. General Lake believed that Holkar was amicably disposed; he invited the chieftain to send ambassadors in order that a treaty might be negociated, but he was mortified when the Mahratta deputies urged the most extravagant demands, and supported them by a letter from Holkar stating that, in case of a refusal, "his country and his property were on the saddle of his horse, and to whatever side the reins of his brave warriors should be turned, the whole of the country in that direction should come into his possession." The Governor-general having been made acquainted with Holkar's demands, resolved not to temporize any longer; orders were issued directing General Wellesley and General Lake to attack Holkar's troops and possessions in every direction. Scindia at the same time professing the utmost readiness to co-operate with the British.

After some trifling operations, General Lake placed his main army in cantonments, but sent Colonel Monson with a strong detachment, to co-operate with Colonel Murray, who was to attack Holkar's dominions on the side of Gujarát. Monson advanced with great spirit, but, hearing that Holkar was coming to meet him in force, he resolved to retreat. This movement, injudicious in itself, was conducted with a most lamentable want of skill, judgment, and discretion; Monson had no confidence in the Sepoys, nor they in him; the officers and men desired for nothing so much as a halt and a fair fight; their leader's determination was to seek shelter under the guns of some fortress. But the governors of forts on his line of retreat, declared against the English; the troops, dissatisfied, weary, and starving, burst through all bonds of discipline, and fled to Agra in broken parties. In consequence of this success, Holkar's fame spread through the country, and greatly increased the number of his followers.

General Lake immediately took the field to repair these disasters, but, instead of making a dash on Holkar's infantry and guns, he wasted his energies in fruitless efforts to bring the Mahratta cavalry to action, and, when these failed, remained inactive at Mutha. This delay afforded Holkar an opportunity of attempting an important enterprize, the surprise of Delhí and the possession of the emperor's person, in which he very nearly succeeded. His failure must chiefly be attributed to the skill and valour of Colonels Ochterlony and Burn, who, with a small body of Sepoys, made a successful assault, repelled a sortie, and, under incessant fatigue, defended a city ten miles in circumference. General Lake marched to the relief of the capital, but Holkar's infantry had gone, five days before his arrival, towards the states of the Rájá of Bhurtpore, who had broken his engagements to the English government. General Frazer undertook the pursuit, and, on the 13th of November, came up with the Mahratta infantry strongly posted, near the fortress of Deeg. Frazer headed the charging battalions in person; he drove the enemy from their first range of guns, and was advancing on the second when he fell mortally wounded. The command now devolved on Colonel Monson, who was eager to avenge his late disastrous retreat; under his guidance, the enemy were driven successively from each of their lines of battery until they got under the walls of the fort; one body which attempted to make a stand, was driven into the lake, and many of them drowned. Eighty-seven pieces of cannon were taken, and among them, Colonel Monson had the satisfaction to find fourteen of those he had lost during his retreat.

Four days afterwards, General Lake, after a most persevering pursuit, overtook Holkar's cavalry at Furruckabad. The surprise would have been complete had not the accidental explosion of a tumbril, just before the onset, roused the Mahrattas to a sense of their danger. Holkar and his immediate followers escaped, but three thousand of his troopers were put to the sword. Deeg was immediately invested, and stormed after a siege of ten days. Holkar now appeared on the verge of ruin, his territory in the Dekkan was reduced; his principal forts in

Malwa, including his capital, Indore, were in the possession of the English, and the reduction of Bhurtpore was alone wanting to reduce him to the condition of a helpless fugitive.

The town of Bhurtpore, eight miles in extent, was everywhere surrounded by a mud wall of great thickness and height, and a very wide and deep ditch filled with water. The fort was situated at the eastern extremity of the town ; and the walls were flanked with bastions at short distances, mounted with a numerous artillery. The Jhats had crowded in from the surrounding districts to the defence of their capital, and the broken battalions of Holkar had entrenched themselves under the walls of the place. General Lake arrived before Bhurtpore January 2nd, 1805, with a very insufficient battering train, and without taking the ordinary precaution of reconnoitring the place, commenced a siege. Four desperate assaults were made, and repulsed with dreadful slaughter; the two first failed, from the breadth of the ditch and the depth of its waters, not having been ascertained by the assailants. The two others were baffled by the unexpected strength of the defences, and the vigorous resistance of the besieged. All four were honourable to the valour of the troops, but not very creditable to the military skill of their general. The Rájá of Bhurtpore was, however, disheartened by the preparations for continuing the siege; he made proposals for peace, and was allowed to negociate on very favourable terms, although every one of the British authorities felt the disadvantage of leaving Bhurtpore to be a monument of their failure ; but it was deemed expedient to grant favourable terms to the Rájá, at a time when there was every appearance of a renewal of hostilities with Scindia.

Scindia had actually advanced towards Bhurtpore with an intention of taking part in the war, and had permitted the camp of the British President, to be attacked and plundered without making any attempt to discover and punish the offenders, when he heard that the Rájá had concluded a treaty with the British. Even then he allowed Holkar to join his camp, but could not be again induced to encounter the perils of war. His negociations were protracted, until a change in the government of British India, was followed by the adoption of a course of policy by which most of the advantages gained in the Mahratta war were thrown away.

CHAPTER XIV.

ADMINISTRATION OF THE MARQUIS CORNWALLIS AND SIR GEORGE BARLOW.

Lord Wellesley's government of India had been very brilliant but very expensive; his system of policy aimed at placing the entire military arrangements of India under the control of the British, by inducing or compelling the principal native princes to substitute a disciplined subsidiary force for their own undisciplined and turbulent hordes, leaving them, however, the power of administering the civil government at their pleasure. Such an arrangement would clearly have given the Company an absolute control over all the foreign relations of the Indian princes, and rendered that body the guardian of general tranquillity. The subsidiary treaties with the Peishwa and the Nizam enabled the Governor-general so to dispose the forces supplied to both these powers, that they formed a complete chain of defence against any possible attack, not only covering the frontiers of both princes, but giving permanent security and tranquillity to all the southern parts of the Peninsula. Scindia, to whom such an abridgement of the Mahratta power, which prevented the levying of *chout* on the feeble states of the south and west, was peculiarly obnoxious, had been so humbled that there was very little fear of his venturing to renew hostilities. Holkar was little better than leader of a body of cowardly banditti; his troops being so disspirited that they would not venture themselves within fifty miles of an English army. Great expenses, indeed, had been incurred, but it was certain that the pressure would only be temporary, for the revenues were beginning to improve, the conquered and ceded districts began to grow profitable after tranquillity had been restored, and the economic reductions, which were commenced as the war drew to a close, gave promise of a large and early surplus revenue from our possessions.

The court of directors from the beginning took a very harsh view of Lord Wellesley's policy, and thwarted him in every particular where they were not checked by the interference of the Board of Control. Even the conquest of Mysore was very ungraciously recognized by the authorities in England, and sixteen years elapsed before General Harris received any public reward for his services at Seringapatam. But this hostility was mainly owing to an act of justice towards the merchants of Calcutta, which was deemed injurious to the interests of certain monopolies in England, and which certainly diminished the unfair profits which accrued to certain parties possessing great influence in the direction. On the renewal of the Charter, in 1793, it had been stipulated that 3,000 tons of the Company's shipping were to be allotted annually to private merchants. The rate of freight, however, was not specified, and of course the Company's agents, with the usual impolicy and injustice of monopolists, fixed so high a rate that the British merchants and manufacturers were deterred from engaging extensively in the trade. Thus the exports to India were very limited in amount; whilst there was an increasing amount of exports from India, which was liable to serious checks and hindrances from the uncertainty and cost of the means of conveyance. This was so strongly felt by the court of directors, that in 1798, they authorized the government of Bengal to take up ships on account of the Company, and re-let the tonnage to the merchants of Calcutta. Lord Wellesley refused to act on this notable plan, which would have superadded an immense quantity of fraud and jobbing to the previous evils of expense and delay; he, therefore, permitted the merchants and ship-owners to make their own arrangements for the extent and rate of the freight, subject only to such regulations as would prevent any interference with the Company's privileges. Not a word need be said in favour of this policy, it was obviously nothing more than establishing a principle of common honesty in commercial affairs, by placing the merchant and ship-owner on an equal footing. But common honesty, or freedom of trade, which is the same thing, was the most inconvenient thing in the world to those who profited by exorbitant profits; and the arrival in the port of London of Indian produce, in India-built ships, created a sensation among the monopolists, which could not have been exceeded if a hostile fleet had appeared in the Thames.

The ship-builders of the port of London took the lead in raising the cry of alarm; they declared that their business was on the point of ruin, and that the families of all the ship-wrights in England were certain to be reduced to starvation. The connection between ship-building and the maintenance of a rate of freight, so high as to prevent shipping from being employed, was not, indeed, very obvious, but it suited the convenience of the monopolists to keep their own delinquencies of exorbitant charge out of sight. The interest of the consumers, that is, of the people of the three kingdoms, in obtaining a more certain supply of London produce at a cheaper rate than before, was, of course, more studiously concealed, and persons were allowed to declare that the trade of England would be ruined, because that trade with India had been greatly facilitated and increased. Fortunately, the President of the Board of Control, backed by nearly the entire of the independent mercantile interest of India, took the same view of the question as the Governor-general, and all the efforts of the monopolists to set aside the new arrangements were defeated. Their disappointment on the occasion was far from increasing their admiration of the government of the Marquis of Wellesley.

The view which Lord Wellesley took of the shipping question, was the calm and deliberate result of his investigation of a measure, concerning which he felt no particular solicitude. Any man of ordinary talents, who viewed the question without the bias of private interest, must have arrived at the same conclusion; had his arrangements been set aside, he would only have lamented the strength of sordid interest and prejudice, but personally, would have felt no annoyance. He shewed less indifference in his efforts to maintain the College of Fort William—an institution of which he was the creator and fosterer—but which encountered the most strenuous opposition from the court of directors. His exertions, however, were so far successful that a college was maintained for the instruction of Bengal writers in the oriental languages used in that part of India, and, some years later, a college was founded in England for the education of the junior civilians of all the presidencies in the usual objects of

European study, and in the principal languages of the East. This institution has proved of so much service that it is to be hoped its basis may be enlarged, and that it may extend instruction to those who are intended for official and mercantile situations in other oriental countries, particularly Turkey and the Levant.

But the question by which Lord Wellesley's administration must finally be judged, is the policy of the subsidiary alliances which it was his great object to establish throughout India. There can be no doubt that their universal acceptance would have established the supremacy of the Company, and secured the general tranquillity of India; but Lord Wellesley does not appear to have made sufficient allowance for the natural reluctance of princes to resign the military defence of their dominions into the hands of foreigners, and their dislike to the subjection which the nature of the subsidiary connexion necessarily imposed. Attempts to shake off such fetters ought to have been anticipated, and when they occurred there was no alternative between the restoration of the prince to complete independence, or the utter annihilation of his power. But the East India Company had now succeeded to the central power, which had been anciently possessed by the Emperors of Delhí, and, upon the exercise of its controlling authority, the tranquillity of the whole Peninsula depended. If the Company ceased to assert and exercise supremacy, all India must have fallen into anarchy. Indeed, this result followed to a very great extent when the policy of Lord Wellesley was abandoned.

The Marquis of Cornwallis, in spite of his accumulated years and infirmities, was appointed the successor of Lord Wellesley. He arrived at Fort William in July, 1805, just as Lord Lake had intimated to Scindia, that no further delay in the liberation of the British president, whom he insolently detained a prisoner, would be permitted. Lord Cornwallis commenced his career by relaxing in this preliminary, and consenting to treat with Scindia on his own terms. Fortunately, for the honour of the British name, Lord Lake succeeded in obtaining the president's liberation before the degrading concession of the Governor-general was made known. By the new treaty with Scindia, the numerous Rájás west of the Jumna, who had been taken under the protection of the British government, were to be abandoned to their own resources, and to be compensated by cessions of the territories we had conquered, which they were manifestly unable to defend. The Rájá of Jypore had entered into an alliance with the English against Scindia, and, though he had on many occasions deviated both from the letter and spirit of his engagements, yet, when Holkar's army approached his frontiers, he was induced by Lord Lake to take an active part in the war, and his services greatly contributed to its final success. Notwithstanding these services, and Lord Lake's remonstrances against the breach of the public faith, which he had plighted, the alliance with Jypore was dissolved; the Rájá's representatives boldly protesting that the English had made their honour subservient to their convenience.

In the midst of his exertions, Lord Cornwallis sunk under the increased fatigue which he had imposed upon himself by a journey to the upper provinces. He was succeeded by Sir George Barlow, a civil servant of the Company, who had filled several subordinate situations creditably, but who did not possess the qualifications necessary for a post of so much importance and responsibility as that of Governor-general of India. Sir George Barlow not only adopted Lord Cornwallis's policy of non-interference, but carried it to a greater extent than his lordship ever contemplated. Treaties were concluded with Scindia and Holkar, which left those chieftains free to form new schemes of dangerous ambition; he exerted himself to dissolve the intimate alliances which had been formed with some of the principal Native states, and to free the English from the obligations and protection contracted with minor chiefs; it has even been said that both he and the Marquis of Cornwallis contemplated abandoning all the British possessions west of the Jumna, as likely to prove sources of expense, trouble, and danger.

But circumstances soon occurred, which led Sir George Barlow, not only to doubt, but to depart from his policy of non-interference. Meer Alum, the able minister of the Nizam, whom the English had for many years supported, by his attachment to their interests lost the confidence of his feeble sovereign. Intrigues were detected at Hyderabad, not only for removing the minister, but for destroying the subsidiary alliance with the British government. The nature of this conspiracy and the character of those associated for its execution, which included all the discontented soldiery, required prompt decision. The necessary orders were sent to the resident and the commander of the troops, by whose promptitude the conspiracy was disconcerted. The Governor-general displayed equal wisdom, in opposing the recommendations of the court of directors to modify the treaty of Bassein, which their persevering hostility to the Marquis of Wellesley led them to regard as the great source of all their difficulties; but every hour brought evidence from the Mahratta territories of the increasing importance and value of the arrangements made at Bassein.

The policy of the Marquis of Wellesley had made an immense change in the condition of the Mahrattas; their perilous power was broken, their marauding expeditions checked, and their claims to *chout*, or payment for forbearance, which they had been accustomed to exact from their neighbours, were utterly annihilated. The Peishwa had ceded a large tract of country to the English; he was controlled in his foreign relations and supported on the throne by a British force. The territories of the other Mahratta chiefs had been dismembered; the Emperor of Delhí had been taken under the protection of the English; and they sat down exhausted and dismayed, sensible of some of their own errors when too late; but with no plan, or even sentiment of union, except hatred to that nation by which they had been subdued.

When Jesswunt Rao Holkar was restored to his dominions, he intimated to his army that he was under the necessity of dismissing about twenty thousand of his cavalry, most of whom were natives of the Dekkan. Large arrears being due to these men, they mutinied, and were only pacified by receiving Holkar's nephew, Khondee Rao, as a pledge for payment. The possession of the legal heir to the Holkar family, induced the mutineers to revolt, and proclaim their prisoner the legitimate sovereign. But the firmness of Holkar's infantry overawed them, and their arrears being soon after paid, by a sum of money extorted from the unfortunate Rájá of Jypore, the sedition was quelled. The innocent instrument of the mutineers fell a sacrifice to his enraged uncle, who put both him and his brother to death. Not long after Holkar fell into a state of insanity, from which he never recovered until the day of his death, Oct. 20th, 1811.

The regency of Indore, when it was found necessary to place Holkar under restraint, was divided between one of his concubines, Toolzee Rye, a woman of profligate habits and most vindictive disposition, and Ameer Khan, who was nothing better than a chieftain of banditti. They administered the government in the name of Mulhar Rao Holkar, a boy about four years of age, the son of Jesswunt Rao, by another concubine. This deplorable government, if such anarchy can be called a government, was alternately swayed by two factions, the Mahrattas and the Patans, who were constantly intriguing against each other, and nothing could exceed the miserable condition of the country. At the court, bribery, executions and murders; in the provinces, violence, rapine and bloodshed.

Scindia's territories were in a state scarcely less deplorable than Holkar's. His army was far too numerous for his finances, and in order to appease the clamours of his troops, he was obliged to allow them to subsist at free quarters in his provinces. The burthen of their exactions became in many places intolerable, and districts which had previously been cultivated and profitable, were fast running to waste and wretchedness. The Peishwa was more fortunate; his troops, commanded by Bappoo Gokla, who had been recommended to this station by General Wellesley, united with the English subsidiary force, quelled every appearance of insurrection in his dominions.

CHAPTER XV.

ADMINISTRATION OF LORD MINTO.

Lord Minto reached India in July, 1807; he had previously acquired a high character as a statesman, and was remarkable for his reluctance to be fettered by mere precedent, and for his determination to judge in all things for himself. If he had shared in the erroneous views which many persons in England had formed of the administration of the Marquis of Wellesley, he found soon after his landing, that the system which had been devised by the Marquis Cornwallis, and pursued by Sir George Barlow, was pregnant with the most injurious consequences to all the Native states, and perilous to the existence of the British empire in the East.

The Pindarries, a class of the lowest freebooters, had been long known in the Dekkan; they were early employed in the Mahratta wars, and numbers of them engaged in the service both of Scindia and Holkar. They were in general more attached to their immediate commander than to the prince who hired their services; they not unfrequently changed sides, and plundered their masters whenever they found an opportunity. So soon as the tide of Mahratta conquest was turned, the Pindarries were obliged to plunder the territories of their former masters for subsistence; the very desolation they carried along with them brought them recruits, and their numbers were greatly augmented by the bodies of irregular horse which Lord Lake disbanded at the termination of the war.

In every thousand Pindarries about four hundred were well armed and mounted; of that number about every fifteenth man carried a matchlock, but their favourite weapon was the Mahratta spear, which is from twelve to eighteen feet long. The remaining six hundred were common plunderers and followers, armed like the Bazar retainers of every army in India, with any sort of weapon which chance supplied. Before the Pindarries set out on an expedition, a leader sent notice to the inferior chiefs, and hoisted his standard on a particular day after the cessation of the rains, generally about the period of the Dusserah, a Hindú feast in honour of the return of spring. As soon as the rivers were fordable, and a sufficient number had assembled, they moved off by the most unfrequented routes towards their destination. Commencing with short marches of about ten miles, they gradually extended them to thirty or forty miles a-day, until they reached some peaceful region against which their expedition was intended. Terror and dismay burst at once on the helpless population; villages were seen in flames; wounded and houseless peasants flying in all directions, fortified places shutting their gates, and keeping up a perpetual firing from the walls. The plunderers dispersed in small parties, and spread themselves over the whole face of the country; all acting on a concerted plan, they swept round in a half circle, committing every sort of violence and excess,—torturing to extort money, ravishing, murdering, and burning in the defenceless villages; but seldom venturing on danger unless the prospect of a booty was very certain. When they approached a point on the frontier, very distant from where they had entered, they united and went off in a body to their homes. Whilst they continued their excesses, marauders of all descriptions sallied out to join them, or profit by their presence, and whole districts became a scene of rapine and conflagration.

The ordinary modes of torture inflicted by these miscreants, were heavy stones placed on the head or chest; red-hot irons applied to the soles of the feet; tying the head of a person into a *tobra*, or bag for feeding horses, filled with hot ashes; throwing oil on the clothes and setting fire to them; besides many others equally horrible, which could not be named with decency. The awful consequences of a visit from the Pindarries, can scarcely be imagined by those who have not witnessed them. For some time their ravages were chiefly confined to Malwa, Rajpootana, and Berar; a few of them, however, ventured almost every year into the dominions of the Nizam and the Peishwa, though little notice of them was taken by the British government, while they refrained from molesting its own subjects and territory.

The situation of the ancient Rajpoot states of Odepore, Joudpore, Jypore, and other principalities, became at this period truly deplorable; but their condition and sentiments cannot be painted in more striking colours than by using the terms of a despatch from Sir Charles Metcalfe, the enlightened resident at Delhí, who, adverting to their repeated applications for the aid of the British government, observes :—"When I reply to these various applications, I find it difficult to obtain even a confession that the moderate policy of the British government is just. People do not scruple to assert that they have a right to the protection of the British government. They say that there always has existed some power in India to which peaceable states submitted, and, in return, obtained its protection ; that then their own governments were maintained in respectability, and they were secure against the invasions of upstart chiefs and armies of lawless banditti. That the British government now occupies the place of the great protecting power, and is the natural guardian of the peaceable and weak ; but, owing to its refusal to use its influence for their protection, the peaceable and weak states are continually exposed to oppressions and cruelties of robbers and plunderers, the most licentious and abandoned of mankind." Nor were the Rajpoots alone exposed to danger ; the Sikh chieftains west of the Sutlej, from whom our protection had been withdrawn, were in a state of alarm and disturbance, dreading to be reduced under the sway of Runjeet Sing, who had founded a kingdom in the Punj-áb, which daily increased in strength.

The court of directors expressed some dissatisfaction at the extent to which the policy of non-interference had been carried by Sir George Barlow ; they censured the abandonment of the Rajá of Jypore, expressing a hope that "the supreme government in India would take care, in all its transactions with the Native princes, to preserve our character for fidelity to our allies from falling into disrepute, and would evince a strict regard in the prosecution of its political views, to the principles of justice and generosity." The government in India had also shewn that it was alive to the evil impressions which might result from Sir George Barlow's having rescinded the article of the treaty concluded by Lord Lake, which precluded Scindia from ever again employing his profligate minister, Sirjee Rao Ghatkia, the author of the treacherous attack on the British residency. While bestowing a very qualified approbation on the altered treaty, the court of directors expressed a hope that neither in the motives by which the supreme government was actuated, nor in the communications with Scindia, any just ground was afforded for a suspicion on the part of the Mahratta chieftains, that the British government entertained any dread of the consequences which might possibly result from insisting on a scrupulous adherence to the stipulations of treaties." But, notwithstanding the justness of these views, there still existed in the Directory a strong desire to avoid, by every possible means, any further extension of political connexions. It was hoped that peace might be preserved without our being compelled to assume that paramount power, which seemed to be the more dreaded, the nearer that it was brought within our grasp. So Lord Minto was entrusted the trial of the experiment, how far it was possible for us with safety to stop short of taking into our hands the supremacy, if not the sovereignty of England.

Sir George Barlow had been obliged to make the court of the Nizam an exception to his policy of non-interference, and to take active steps to support that prince's prime minister, Meer Alúm. On the death of that nobleman, there were several competitors for the vacant office, but after some time it was arranged between the Nizam and the Governor-general, that the office should be divided, the name of minister being given to the Nizam's favourite, Moneer-al-Mulk, and, its active duties being entrusted to an English partisan, Chand-u-Lal, under the title of Dewan.

Chand-u-Lal was a Brahmin, but this circumstance did not prevent him from being taken into the service of a Mohammedan prince. The Brahmins of the Carnatic are generally men of education, acquainted with at least the principles of mathematical science, and remarkable for their skill in commercial and financial affairs. On the other hand, the Mohammedan Omrahs, to which class Moneer-al-Mulk belonged, are generally conspicuous for their conceit and their ignorance, unable to keep an ordinary account, and yet ready to undertake the most complicated affairs of the exchequer. Chand-u-Lal clearly saw that he would not long be permitted to retain his office as Dewan, unless English interest continued paramount at the court of Hyderabad; he therefore exerted himself with all his might to forward those schemes of military reform, which had been originally suggested by the Marquis of Wellesley. Corps were disciplined by British officers, and a regular army sprung up, organized in all its branches by the British resident.

The Dewan, who personally derived great support from this force, implicitly acquiesced in every proposition which the resident made for the appointment of officers, and for the pay and equipment of the new battalions. In return for this, and his steady adherence to the engagements of the defensive alliance, he was protected by British influence and power from the attacks of his numerous enemies, and left to control, as he thought best, the internal government of the country, the prosperity of which began early to decline, under a system which had no object but revenue, and under which, neither regard for rank nor desire for popularity existing, the nobles were degraded and the people oppressed. The Nizam (of whose sanity very reasonable doubts were entertained) lapsed into a state of gloomy discontent; and while the Dewan, his relations, a few favorites, and money-brokers flourished, the good name of the British nation suffered; for it was said, and with justice, that our support of the actual administration freed the minister and his executive officers from those salutary fears, which act as a restraint upon the most despotic rulers. The unhappy result of those arrangements which the fear of greater evils had led him to confirm, appears to have been felt and deplored by Lord Minto, but the remedy was most difficult without over-stepping the limits prescribed for his observance; and, in fact, no effectual effort was made to check these evils during his lordship's administration.

Bajee Rao had scarcely been restored to his authority by the treaty of Bassein, than he began to evince the distrust and duplicity of his character towards his new allies; and openly avowed, in regard to many persons subject to his authority, that revenge was his principal motive for entering into alliance with the English. The Peishwa was, in fact, a profligate sensualist; his favour was reserved for those who pandered to his passions and his crimes, and his ministers were chosen from his agents in lust and murder. Through these unscrupulous agents, he kept up a correspondence with the chief confederate against the British power, and ascribed his connexion with that government, which to them he reprobated and deplored, to necessity, occasioned by their absence, and to the treachery of the southern Jaghiredars. General Wellesley (since, Duke of Wellington) had early appreciated the character of Bajee Rao, and had anxiously urged upon the government the necessity of speedily arranging the relations between the Peishwa and the southern chieftains. In fact, these powerful lords, though calling themselves the subjects of the Peishwa's family, had for ages shewn it a very lax obedience, submitting to its orders or usurping upon its rights, according to the character and means of the sovereign upon the throne. These Jaghiredars also had established a strong claim on the consideration of the English by their conduct during the war against Scindia and Holkar, so that, while the Peishwa was to be supported in the assertion of all his just rights as lord paramount, it was obviously desirable that he should be prevented from effecting, what he earnestly sought, their utter ruin.

The terms proposed by the resident at the court of Poonah, for adjusting the difference between the Peishwa and the Southern Jaghiredars were:—The mutual oblivion of past injuries—the abandonment of all pecuniary claims on either side—the guarantee to them of the *Serinjamny* lands, that is, lands granted to support a specific number of troops for the service of the paramount prince, so long as they served the Peishwa with fidelity—the relinquishment, on their part, of all former usurpations—their attendance, when required, with the whole of their contingents—and of a third part at all times—under the command of a relation. So long as the Jaghiredars adhered to these terms, the British government agreed to guarantee their personal safety, and that of their relations. Lord Minto sanctioned this departure from the policy of non-interference, which, from this time forward, may be said to have been virtually abandoned, and he sent orders to Madras, Mysore, and the Dekkan, to have a sufficient force assembled to compel the submission of any chieftains who might prove refractory.

Bajee Rao and the Jaghiredars were equally unwilling to submit their claims to the arbitration of the British government. The Peishwa would not at first listen to any proposition which did not comprehend the entire resumption of the lands held by the southern chieftains, and their being compelled to submit to his authority by force of arms. The Jaghiredars were equally unwilling to resign their old usurpations, and enter into fixed stipulations of allegiance; but the presence of a large British force compelled obedience; they all joined the Peishwa at Panderpore, whence they accompanied him to Poonah, where all matters were finally arranged under the mediation of the British resident.

Though these arrangements greatly increased the Peishwa's influences and resources, Bajee Rao never forgave the English for not having given him the aid of their troops to execute his meditated scheme of vengeance on the Southern Jaghiredars.

We have already mentioned Ameer Khan, as one of those who had seized on the regency of Holkar's dominions when the insanity of Jesswunt Rao, rendered him incapable of conducting the government. He soon quitted Indore, and placing himself at the head of a large body of Pindarries, began to levy exactions, sometimes in Holkar's name, and sometimes in his own. One of his first acts, was to threaten the territories of Berar with invasion, under the pretence that the Rájá owed large sums to Holkar. Lord Minto could not contemplate with indifference an army of Pindarries and other military adventurers, encamped on the banks of the Nerbudda, under an ambitious Mussulman chief, whose conquest of Berar would bring them into immediate contact with the territories of the Nizam. Community of religion would no doubt have induced a powerful party in those dominions, including most probably the Nizam himself, to join in schemes for the establishment of Mohammedam supremacy in southern India, and the consequent overthrow of British power. Under such circumstances it would have been ruinous to adhere to the policy of non-interference. Lord Minto abandoned it without hesitation, and tendered to the Rájá of Berar the gratuitous protection of the British government. Ameer Khan was driven from the frontiers of Berar, but Lord Minto would not sanction the pursuit of the freebooter into his own dominions, and Ameer Khan escaped with an unbroken army to prosecute new schemes of conquest and oppression.

Though the influence of the French in India was virtually annihilated, by the destruction of Tippoo and the dispersion of the armies which Perron and other French adventurers had found amongst the Mahrattas, yet Napoleon frequently exhibited a settled purpose to contest with the English the empire of the East, and early in the year 1808, he sent ambassadors to Persia, who were said to have been most favourably received by Futteh Ali Shah, the reigning sovereign, and to have concluded a treaty very menacing to the English interests. This intelligence excited much alarm, both in London and Calcutta; missions without any apparent concert, were sent to Persia by the

Governor-general and the British ministry; the envoys took very different views of the course of policy which ought to be pursued, and that which was most absurd in itself and most pernicious in its consequences, was eventually adopted. Captain Malcolm, Lord Minto's envoy, proceeded to Abanshir, but on the king of Persia refusing him leave to advance to Teheran, and insisting on his negociating with his son, the Viceroy of Shirar, he declined going any further, as unbecoming the dignity of the English nation, that its representative should treat with a prince at a provincial capital, while the French ambassador, who had been received in direct violation of an existing treaty, enjoyed the distinction of residing at the court and carrying on his negociations with the king. These reasons and many others for not complying with his majesty's desire, were embodied in a memorial and sent to Teheran; but producing no effect, the representative of the supreme government sailed for Calcutta. On his arrival there, orders were given to prepare an expedition, which was meant to occupy one of the Bahrein islands, in the Persian Gulph; and as the early failure of the French promises was anticipated, they being quite inconsistent with the arrangements made between Napoleon and the Emperor of Russia, there existed no doubt that the Persian government, would soon be reduced to the necessity of asking that friendship which it had slighted; and until it should be in this temper, it was obvious to every person with the slightest pretensions to statesmanship, that the alliance, would never take a shape which merited confidence or promised benefit.

Sir Harford Jones, the ambassador from the court of London, took a very different view of affairs; he was a weak man, intoxicated by the pride of directly representing his sovereign, and anxious in every way to prove himself independent of the council of Calcutta. It was the fashion of the day, for England to pay people for protecting themselves, and to subsidize every power which seemed willing to accept a subsidy, almost thanking those who did us the honour to accept our money. Persia could not be treated less liberally than others; a treaty was concluded in March 1809, by which Great Britain was bound to pay the king of Persia, an annual subsidy of one hundred thousand pounds, so long as he should be at war with Russia, to supply sixteen thousand stand of arms, with twenty field-pieces complete, and such numbers as could be spared of artillery-men and officers, to instruct the Persian army; on the other hand, Persia agreed to assist Great Britain in repelling any attempt on the part of the French, to invade the Company's territories in India.

The pecuniary loss which it inflicted, to purchase the most worthless of guarantees, was the least of the evils resulting from this disgraceful treaty; it was studiously circulated through the East, that England had been forced to purchase the protection of the Persian monarch, and the Asiatic princes, who well knew the feebleness of Persia, felt and expressed their contempt for those who stooped to accept of such protection. The treaty was concluded when Russia was an ally of France; it seems not to have entered into the ambassador's head, that such a contingency was possible, as Russia becoming at some subsequent period the ally of England. When this event took place, England was rather awkwardly situated, by having made opposite engagements with Persia and Russia, but Persia as being the weaker power, was of course sacrificed.

The same alarm of a French invasion which had caused these missions to Persia, suggested one to the court of Kabul, then governed by the late Shuja-al-Mulk, who had just conquered his brother Mohammed. An alliance was concluded with Shah Shyrja, and though he was soon afterwards driven from the throne, and became a pensioner on the bounty of the British government, the favourable impression made by the embassy on the minds of the Afghans, was not effaced until our late attempt to restore Shah Shuja to his kingdom after he had been thirty years an exile.

We have mentioned in a former page, that the Marquis of Wellesley's wise plans for the reduction of the islands possessed by the French and Dutch in the Indian Seas, had been frustrated by the unaccountable obstinacy of Admiral Ranier. The weakness of the French marine, for several years prevented the enemy from availing themselves of their positions in the isles of Bourbon and Mauritius on one side, and the harbours of Java and its dependencies on the other, to annoy our commerce. But in the winter of 1808, a squadron of French frigates sailed from different ports of France and Holland, eluded the vigilance of the British cruizers, and reached the Indian Seas in the following spring.

Great injury was done to English commerce by these unexpected enemies; consequences still more disastrous were not unreasonably anticipated, so that Lord Minto was universally applauded when he declared his resolution to reduce those islands, and deprive the enemy's ships of any harbour where they could find shelter. A large army was assembled in the Carnatic, and was almost ready for departure, when an unexpected event menaced the whole fabric of British power in the East with complete ruin.

Sir George Barlow, on resigning the supreme authority had been appointed governor of Madras, where he employed himself in devising plans for the reduction of the heavy expenses of the army. An order was issued, that the allowance hitherto made to the officers commanding native regiments, for the purpose of providing camp-equipments for their soldiers, should immediately cease. The abruptness of this order, and the want of consideration for the feelings of the persons whose interests were concerned, gave general, and not unjust, dissatisfaction. A dangerous spirit of mutiny spread abroad through the army, which was greatly increased by Sir George Barlow's sending round a test of allegiance to the existing government, for signature, to the whole of the officers, in order that he might ascertain the names of those who would support or oppose his acts. Those who refused to sign, amounting to more than two-thirds of the officers of the Native army, were menaced with dismissal—a threat partially carried into execution. Some of the mutineers seized Seringapatam, and two battalions of Sepoys had rather a smart skirmish with the king's troops that besieged them. Every thing threatened a most perilous crisis, when the fortunate arrival of Lord Minto, who was universally respected, led to the restoration of tranquillity. Obedience was cheerfully tendered to his mild firmness, which the blustering violence of Sir George Barlow had failed to obtain. A general amnesty was published, excluding only those who had taken a leading part in the disaffection, and most even of these were subsequently restored.

Very little difficulty was found in reducing the islands of Bourbon and Mauritius, but as the conquest of Java seemed to be a more perilous enterprize, the Governor-general made corresponding exertions, and actually accompanied the expedition, which was commanded by Sir Samuel Auchmuty, serving as a volunteer. On the 4th of August, 1811, the Java troops disembarked at a village about twelve miles from the capital of Batavia, and the landing of the whole was effected in twenty-four hours, without a single accident. After some minor operations, Sir Samuel Auchmuty marched against the Dutch forces, which were strongly posted at Cornelis, occupying an entrenched camp, having each flank protected by a river, with a chain of redoubts and batteries in front, mounted with three hundred pieces of cannon. Batteries were raised against two of these redoubts, which maintained so heavy a fire that the guns of the enemy were silenced. An assault was ordered on the morning of the 26th; the outworks were carried at the point of the bayonet, and the fugitives were so hotly pursued that they had not time to remove the bridges of planks which joined the works to the camp. Although the Dutch fought well on the outworks, they lost all courage when their camp was stormed; numbers fell without any attempt to resist, and five thousand surrendered themselves prisoners of war. Notwithstanding this decisive defeat, Governor Jansens, with the characteristic obstinacy of his nation, continued to protract the war; but garrison after garrison was yielded to the English, and at length, on the 16th of September, this valuable island was surrendered. We need only add, that it was retained until the end of the French war, when the English having just held it long enough to learn its great value, and to win the affections of the native inhabitants, restored it to the Dutch.

The policy of non-interference prevented Lord Minto from taking any steps to check the tyranny which the Nabob-vizier practised on his subjects in Oude; but he exerted himself to secure Travancore and Bundelcund in their allegiance to the country, restoring to the latter country a tranquillity of which it had been for a long time deprived. Great alarm continued to be excited by the Pindarries, who no longer abstained from violating the British territories, a party of them having burst into Mirzapore, and left behind them at their departure, the usual traces of their ravages, villages burned, fields laid waste, and the cultivators murdered. Dread of exciting a new Mahratta war, which was likely to be viewed with displeasure by the court of directors, prevented Lord Minto from taking effectual steps to punish these barbarous marauders, but his despatches showed how erroneous was the course of policy which had been pursued since the departure of the Marquis of Wellesley, and prepared the way for a return to the vigorous measures of that enlightened statesman.

The Pindarries were not the only marauders who menaced the tranquillity and security of British India. The Ghoorkas, a warlike race, on our north-eastern frontier, had, by dexterously availing themselves of the disputes and distress of their neighbours, extended their sway from the limits of their native hills over the entire province of Nepaul. They next turned their views to the adjoining plains, most of which were tenanted by Rájás depending either on the Company or its allies, and committed several depredations in the districts of Gurruckpore and Sarun. These excesses seem, at first, to have been considered more as the irregular and unpremeditated acts of individual officers on the frontier, than as evincing any hostility in the nation. At length their frequency and increased boldness became intolerable, so that Lord Minto was induced to address the Ghoorka Rájá of Nepaul in very decided language. "I cannot believe," said his lordship, "that while an amicable inquiry into disputed points concerning lands, is going on in the district of Gurruckpore, the unprovoked and unpardonable outrage just described to have taken place in the adjoining district, can have had the sanction of your government; on the contrary, I am convinced it will excite your severe displeasure. It is impossible for me, however, to suffer it to pass, without bringing it distinctly to your notice, and calling on you to disavow and punish the perpetrators of this act, and to cause the people who have been forcibly carried away to be released, and the plundered property to be restored; complaints have also reached me of encroachments committed by your subjects in the district of Zeyhoot, which cannot be permitted to continue.

"If redress is not afforded, and similar proceedings in future not prevented, the British government will be obliged to have recourse to its own means of securing the rights and property of its subjects, without any reference to your government. But I will not relinquish the hope that your immediate compliance with the requisition contained in this letter, and a strict control over your officers and subjects in future, will prevent the recurrence of circumstances which cannot fail to render nugatory any attempt to adjust the disputed points by amicable enquiry and discussion, and to produce consequences which it must be the wish of the government to avoid."

This document amply shows that Lord Minto was prepared to take active measures for checking the insolence of the Ghoorkas, if it should be found that moderation and forbearance had no effect except to increase aggression. But he left India before an answer to this despatch could be received, and on his successor devolved the duty of checking the encroachments of this proud and warlike people, and of vindicating, by their punishment, the insulted honour of the British government. "The administration of Lord Minto," says Sir John Malcolm, "differs essentially from that of every Governor-general who preceded him. It was impossible for a man possessed of such clear intellect, and so well acquainted with the whole scheme of government, to be long in India without being satisfied that the system of neutral policy which had been adopted, could not be persevered in without the hazard of great and increasing danger to the state. His calm mind saw at the same time, the advantage of reconciling the authorities in England to the measures which he contemplated. Hence, he ever preferred delay, where he thought that it was unaccompanied with danger, and referred to the administration at home, whom he urged, by every argument he could use, to sanction the course he deemed best suited to the public interests. But this desire to conciliate and carry his superiors along with him, did not result from any dread of responsibility; for wherever the exigency of the case required a departure from this general rule, he was prompt and decided."

In 1813, Lord Minto returned to England, where he had been but a few weeks, when a sudden illness terminated the useful life of this virtuous and distinguished public servant. His loss at this juncture was a very serious misfortune, for no one was ever more calculated to succeed in impressing others with a just idea of the true condition of our Indian empire, or to give wiser counsel on every point connected with its future government.

CHAPTER XVI.

ADMINISTRATION OF THE MARQUIS OF HASTINGS.

THE Marquis of Hastings arrived in Calcutta October 13th, 1813, with the authority of Governor-general. The authorities in England, had been for some time fully aware that it would soon be necessary to resort to strong measures, for the protection of our subjects and allies from the inroads of those large hordes of freebooters, whose excesses appeared to increase with our forbearance. It seems, however, to have been expected that hostilities might be avoided, and tranquillity maintained, by forming alliances with such states as had not become predatory. At such a time, it was fortunate that the government of India was entrusted to a nobleman equally distinguished for his diplomatic and military attainments, and who had given many signal proofs of his talents as a soldier and a statesman.

It was not until late in December, that an answer was received to the despatch which Lord Minto had sent to the Rájá of Nepaul; the Ghoorka's reply to the complaints of the English was obsequious even to servility, but it evaded every one of the points in issue. Commissioners were appointed to meet those of the Nepaul prince, but the discussions led to no useful result. Points which had been adjusted on apparently incontrovertible evidence, and, with the assent of both parties, were revived by the Nepaulese commissioners; and on the Governor-general refusing to enter anew into discussions which he had been led to believe were already adjusted, his agent was warned to quit the frontier, and the representatives of the Ghoorka government were recalled to Katmandu, the capital of Nepaul. The Governor-general then addressed a letter to the Rájá, reviewing the late negotiations, and requiring that orders should be sent for the peaceable surrender of the districts which the Nepaulese had seized, and of which they retained possession, though they had themselves confessed that these lands were the property of the British government. The Rájá was distinctly informed that unless these districts were restored, possession of them would be taken by the British troops, and that all those villages which had been conditionally surrendered pending the negotiations, should be permanently annexed to the dominions of the Company. No notice being taken of these communications, Sir Roger Martin, the magistrate of Gurruckpore, took possession of the Turaee country, which skirts the base of the Nepaulese hills, and, at the same time, the villages on the Sarun frontier were occupied without resistance, the Nepaulese troops retiring as the English advanced. Such was the state of affairs when the setting in of the periodical rains, which in these districts is a most unhealthy period, made it expedient to withdraw the troops, and commit the charge of the disputed lands to the Native officers who had been appointed to their management.

The Nepaulese had retired with a deliberate purpose; no sooner did they perceive that the civil officers and police were left defenceless, than they rushed upon them from their fastnesses in the hills: after killing eighteen, and wounding six of the police establishment stationed at Butwal, they murdered the superior officer, who had been left in charge of the place by the British government, with circumstances of great barbarity. This atrocious murder, which was perpetrated in the presence of the Foujdar, or commander-in-chief of the Nepaulese on that frontier, was followed by several other insults and outrages. Remonstrances were again made to the Prince of Nepaul, but the Rájá avowed and supported the outrages committed by his officers; and refused to make any reparation for the injury and insult offered to the British government.

All hopes of an amicable adjustment of the differences with the Ghoorkas were now at an end, and the Marquis of Hastings prepared for war. At this time the finances of Bengal were in a very unsatisfactory condition; the treasury had been drained almost to its last rupee, so that it was difficult to find means for defraying the ordinary expenses of government. The young Nabob of Oude, who had recently succeeded his father, was induced, by his personal respect for the Governor-general, to lend large sums at a lower rate of interest than was usual in India, and thus a sufficiency was obtained to meet the immediate emergencies of the war.

Although the Pindarries had not repeated their predatory visits, it was well known that they were only watching for a favourable opportunity of renewing their incursions; and the Marquis of Hastings had represented to the government in England, in the strongest terms, the necessity of their immediate and specific sanction to a course of measures calculated to remedy this alarming and impending evil. As a precautionary means of effecting this object, negociations had been commenced for concluding a subsidiary treaty, and defensive alliances, with the Rájá of Berar, or, as he is more frequently called, of Nagpore. But, after long delay, Rhagojee Rhonslah broke off the treaty in 1814, and even entered into a league with Scindia to reduce Vizir Mohammed, the Nabob of Bhopaul, a gallant chief, who had long maintained himself against the Hindú states, by whose combined arms he now appeared on the point of being overwhelmed. The position of the Nabob's territories, his personal character, and the friendship he had shewn to the English in the former Mahratta war, pointed him out, on the failure of the negociations with Nagpore, as a valuable ally, whose assistance was almost essential to the success of the operations contemplated for the suppression of the predatory system.

A treaty, offensive and defensive, was concluded with the Rájá of Bhopaul, and also with Govind Rao, the hereditary lord of Sagur. By these alliances the British stations in Bundelcund were connected with those of Berar, and means were provided for watching the intrigues of the various Mahratta princes, as well as of Runjeet Sing, the ruler of Lahore, and Ameer Khan, the principal leader of the Pindarries. This alliance gave great offence to Scindia, who affected to look upon the Rájá of Bhopaul as one of his dependents, but his remonstrances were unheeded; a communication was made both to him and the Rájá of Nagpore, that any attack on Bhopaul would be resented as an act of hostility against the English government, and, in order to give effect to the menace, a body of troops was formed in Bundelcund, while the subsidiary force with the Nizam, was advanced to Elichipore, the capital of Berar. Having nearly completed these arrangements, the Governor-general directed all his attention to the Nepaulese war.

The frontier of Nepaul consisted, in addition to the Sal Forest, which separates it from the plains of the Turaee, of a series of mountain ridges, intersected in various places by narrow valleys and rugged defiles; it extended about six hundred miles from east to west. It was resolved that this great frontier should be penetrated by four armies at the same time. General Ochterlony was directed to lead a force of six thousand Sepoys from Laodiana, through the passes of the hills which overlook the Sutlej: General Gillespie moved from the Doab to the west of the Jumna, arriving ultimately at the important town of Nahir; General Wood was ordered through Bootwal to Palpa; and the principal army, under General Morley, received orders to force the passes of Gunduck, and march directly upon the Ghoorka capital, Katmandu.

General Gillespie was the first in the field; he crossed the frontier on the 22nd of October, 1814, and captured Dera, the principal town in the extensive valley of Dera-Daun, without opposition. Balbhadar Sing, who had been entrusted with the defence of the town, retreated to a steep hill called Nalapanee, where having enlarged the works of an old fortress which stood on the summit, he determined to make a stand. Gillespie, who underrated both the strength of the position and the courage of its defenders, resolved to carry Nalapanee by assault. He led the storming party in person, but scarcely had he reached the foot of the wall, when he was struck dead by a musket bullet, which penetrated his heart. The troops immediately fled in confusion to the lines, leaving many of their comrades behind them. Intimidated by this result, Colonel Mowbray retreated to Dera, where he remained until he obtained a train of heavy artillery, for the purpose of reducing Nalapanee. Having procured a fine battery of eighteen-pounders, he again advanced, and after two days of heavy fire, succeeded in effecting a breach. An assault was then hazarded, but the Ghoorkas made a desperate resistance, and finally drove back the storming party with immense loss, particularly in officers. So disheartened were the Sepoys, that they could not be got to renew the attempt, and Mowbray was forced to have recourse to bombardment, which finally compelled the gallant garrison to evacuate the place, after it had been reduced from six hundred to seventy persons. Some indecisive operations followed, Mowbray being probably unwilling to risk any great effort until he was joined by General Martindell, Gillespie's successor.

General Martindell having reached the camp, the army advanced against Nahir, which the Ghoorkas evacuated on their approach, taking their post round Jythuck, a mountain fortress, built on the crest of a ridge, nearly four thousand feet above the level of the plain. Having reconnoitred the position, Martindell resolved to turn it on both flanks, concealing his real designs by a false attack in front. Unfortunately, the grenadiers who led the southern column, despising their enemies, precipitately attacked a stockade which was flanked by rocks on either side. The stockade was bravely defended; a heavy fire of musketry from the rocks on either flank, thinned the ranks of the assailants, and the grenadiers were driven back in great confusion. The Sepoys, who ought to have supported them, were found not to be formed into line; the Ghoorkas therefore pushed forward, driving the British troops in confusion before them, and chasing them with great slaughter to the very verge of their camp. This unfortunate event rendered nugatory the successful exertions of the northern column, which was however withdrawn in comparative safety. General Martindell immediately retreated to Nahir, where he remained for some time inactive.

Ochterlony's cautious movements with the second army, which he led from the banks of the Sutlej, to the north-eastern hills, formed a complete contrast to the rash enterprizes we have just described. He was opposed to Ameerah Sing, the bravest and best leader of the Ghoorkas; instead of risking an engagement, he compelled the enemy, by a series of masterly manœuvres, to abandon one strong post after another, until he obtained possession of the hilly tract between Plassea and Belaspore. General Wood was less fortunate; in passing through the Sal forest, which extends in front of the Bootwal pass, his troops unexpectedly encountered a stockade, and received a volley which did great execution. Colonel Hardyman, of the 17th royal regiment, restored order and turned the position of the Ghoorkas on both flanks; but General Wood was so disheartened by the surprise, that he ordered the retreat to be sounded, much to the astonishment and indignation of the officers and men, who were thus obliged to relinquish a certain victory. The rest of Wood's campaign corresponded with this inauspicious commencement; it was wasted in a series of timid movements, which showed an equal want of skill and courage in the commander.

General Morley's career was scarcely less calamitous and was rather more discreditable, than that of General John Wood. Having injudiciously left three large detachments at posts, twenty miles distant from each other and from all support, he was thrown into a state of pitiable consternation, on learning that two of them had been cut off by the Ghoorkas. Such an effect did this calamity produce, that he suddenly quitted the camp, without leaving any instructions behind him, and made the best of his way to Calcutta. General George Wood, who succeeded him, adopted the cautious or timid policy of his mamesake, already mentioned, and the campaign was spent in idleness.

So unexpected, and we may add, so disgraceful a termination of a campaign, for which such ample preparations had been made, inspired confidence in all the enemies of the English throughout India. A marked change was observed in the tone assumed by the Peishwa and Scindia; Runjeet Sing and Ameer Khan made several suspicious movements, showing that they were in readiness to act, so soon as an opportunity should offer. The Marquis of Hastings was not disheartened, he learned that the district of Kumaoon, in the north of Nepaul, was nearly destitute of troops, and as he could not spare any of the army to take advantage of its condition, he determined to entrust the service to an irregular force. For this purpose he empowered Lieutenant-colonel Gardiner and Captain Hearsay, who had been formerly in the Mahratta service, to raise a force among the warlike Patans of Rohilcund, who readily enlisted under the English banners.

Captain Hearsay possessed more bravery than skill; he unfortunately spread his troops over too wide a surface, and while a portion of them blockaded Koolulgurh, he was forced to give battle with the remainder, to a very superior army coming to relieve the place. The Rohillas fought bravely, but were finally defeated; Hearsay was wounded and taken prisoner. The Ghoorka conqueror, Hasta-Dal, conveyed his captive to Almora. This disaster was more than compensated by the distinguished success of Gardiner's Patans; the colonel advanced from post to post, with equal celerity, caution and skill, availing himself so skilfully of the peculiar mode of fighting adopted by the Patans, that they proved superior to their antagonists in every engagement. He appeared before Ahnora, a little after Hearsay's defeat, where he was fortunately joined by two thousand regular infantry and a small train of artillery, under the command of Colonel Nicholls. Hasta-Dal, attempting to throw relief into Ahnora, was intercepted by a detachment, and slain in the skirmish which ensued. This so disheartened the Ghoorkas, that they surrendered Ahnora after a very feeble defence, and Captain Hearsay was restored to his friends without ransom.

It was not until he had received repeated orders from Calcutta, that General Martindell could be induced to move, and then his operations were so utterly destitute of plan or object, that he might just as well have remained inactive. He spent the entire season before Jythuck, sometimes trying the effect of an active siege, but failing in nerve when the time for an assault arrived; sometimes trying the effect of a blockade, without effectually closing the enemy's communications.

In the meantime, General Ochterlony prepared to follow up the advantages which he had obtained. The Ghoorkas retiring before him, fell back upon a most formidable position, on a mountain ridge of abrupt connected peaks, all of which but two were carefully stockaded, and were further protected by the stone redoubts of Maloun and Seringhar. Ochterlony seized the two peaks which had been neglected, confident that the efforts of the Ghoorkas to recover them would lead to a decisive action. He was not disappointed; the Ghoorkas, headed by one of their bravest chiefs, assaulted the English position with desperate heroism, and, for more than two hours, maintained the closest combat which had ever been witnessed in India; they were, at length, driven back, after having lost their leader and about one-third of their bravest men, and the entrenchments they had so carefully erected were rendered useless. Ameera Sing was anxious to protract resistance, but the other chiefs were so disheartened that they abandoned him one by one, and he could only procure safety for himself and his few faithful followers, by agreeing to a convention, according to the terms of which all the country west of the Kalee was surrendered to the English. The fortress of Jythuck was included in this cession, and thus Ochterlony's success made some compensation for the errors of Martindell.

Proposals for peace were now made and entertained, but the Nepaul prince refused to accept the terms on which the English insisted, and the war was renewed. General Ochterlony, who was now deservedly placed at the head of the main army, advanced, in February, 1816, into the midst of those forests that guard the entrance into Nepaul, which had so long baffled the enterprize of his predecessors. He soon reached the first of the great series of fortifications which guarded the chief pass through the hills of Nepaul. A brief examination was sufficient to shew that the stockades could not be carried by assault, and he was, therefore, compelled to seek means by which they could be turned. Fortunately, a water-course was discovered by which it was barely possible to reach an eminence commanding the pass. Sir David Ochterlony himself took the lead of the column destined to thread this perilous labyrinth; it had to encounter the greatest perils and privations, but the summit was finally gained, and the enemies abandoned the entrenchments, which were thus rendered useless. The Ghoorkas, in revenge, attacked, with their whole force, a post which the English had established at Makwanpore, but, after a severe contest which lasted several hours, they were completely defeated. Another victory was obtained by a detachment under the command of Colonels Kelly and O'Halloran, which so disheartened the court of Katmandu, that the Rájá and his council intimated their readiness to comply with the terms which they had so recently rejected.

At this crisis a third power was invited to take a part in the contest; the Ghoorkas were nominally the subjects of the Chinese empire, and their Rájá applied for assistance to the sovereign power. The Chinese assembled an army, but, with their usual procrastination, delayed their march until the war was over, and the terms of the treaty partially carried into effect. On receiving a statement from the English authorities of the causes of the war, and the purposes for which it was prosecuted, they at once declared that the Ghoorkas were in the wrong, upbraided them for their treachery, derided them for their weakness, and then abandoned them to their fate. The Governor-general was, however, not disposed to encumber the Company with distant and unprofitable possessions; he confined the Ghoorkas within the limits of Nepaul Proper, but required no sacrifice of their ancient dominions.

The reverses which the English met in the early part of the Nepaulese war, gave a fresh stimulus to the Mahratta intrigues; Scindia was the chief of the secret confederacy, the stationary camp which he had established under the protection of the fort of Gwalior, had, in a few years, become a very thriving town, almost deserving the name of a city, and his pride was greatly increased by witnessing such a proof of his growing greatness. He not only intrigued with the Peishwa's court in Poonah, and with Holkar's regency at Indore, but entered into close alliance with the Rájá of Berar, obtained promises of aid from Runjeet Sing and the Rajput princes, and even tried to gain over the Rájá of Mysore. Had the storm burst forth when the British were engaged in the Nepaulese war, the consequences might have been very disastrous; but the Mahratta powers were jealous of each other; they were equally conscious of their own perfidy, and suspicious of the faith of their allies; it consequently required a long time to organize such a confederacy as would have the remotest chance of inspiring mutual confidence. Before the confederates states were prepared to act, the fortunes of the war in the hills had completely changed, and the peace concluded with the Ghoorkas of Nepaul, enabled the British to turn their undivided attention to Central India.

It was fortunate that, during this season of doubt and anxiety, Messrs. Elphinstone and Jenkins, the residents at the courts of Poonah and Nagpore, were gentlemen of unrivalled skill in diplomacy, possessing great firmness of mind and decision of character, and intimately acquainted with the varied relations between the Native states. The Honourable Mountstuart Elphinstone was placed in a situation of peculiar difficulty at Poonah. Even when the Peishwa formed a treaty of defensive alliance with the British at Bassein, the Marquis of Wellesley foresaw that jealousy would rankle in his mind, and that he would, at some future period, manifest his hostility. "It was manifest," as this distinguished nobleman observed, "that the Peishwa had only entered into the defensive alliance with the British government, because his highness was convinced he had no other way of recovering any part of his just authority, or of maintaining tranquillity in his empire. The state of his affairs taking a favourable turn, his highness, supported by the different branches of the Mahratta empire, would be desirous of annulling the engagements he had made with the British government."

The Peishwa was also far from being pleased with some decisions of the English governors, when called upon to act as mediators or arbitrators between him and some of his nominal feudatories. He thought, and perhaps not altogether without reason, that the English adjudicated on conflicting claims with a greater regard to their own interests than his rights. He was particularly annoyed at being obliged to renounce his claim to supremacy over the petty states of Kolapore and Sawant Warree. These little states on the coast of the northern Concan had been, for more than a century, the scourge of the western seas. They fitted out piratical vessels of small size and light burthen, which easily baffled the vigilance of our cruisers, by keeping closer to the shore than would be safe for European vessels.

In the year 1812, Lord Minto compelled these states to enter into certain engagements, by which their principal ports were placed in our hands, and, consequently, the continuation of their piracies prevented. This, however, gave great offence to the Peishwa, who expected to derive the same advantages from the pirates that Scindia did from the Pindarries. We need not repeat what has been already said of the character of Bajee Rao, the reigning Peishwa; like most Asiatic princes, he was equally timid and ambitious; daring in intrigue, but cowardly in action; his inordinate desires were restrained by his inordinate fears. Mr. Elphinstone knew him well, and, by uniting firmness with discretion, kept him in check until, as we shall hereafter see, the influence of a profligate favourite led him through a disgraceful course of crime and treachery, which ended in the annihilation of his dynasty.

In March, 1816, the Rájá of Nagpore died, and was succeeded by his son Pursajee Bhonslah, who was blind, paralytic, and almost an idiot. Two factions contended for supremacy in the court, and the British resident entered into a secret alliance with Appa Sahib, the next heir to the *musnud*, or throne, to secure him the regency, provided that he would support British interests. This arrangement gave a sudden shock to the Mahratta confederacy, for, though Appa Sahib eventually proved faithless, his withdrawal from the Mahratta alliance, in the first instance, was of the greatest importance to the British interests.

Although the Nizam was a Mohammedan prince, and therefore odious to the Mahrattas, efforts were made to engage him in the confederacy, which were defeated by the energy of the resident, Mr. Russell. But the close connexion between the British government and the obnoxious *Dewan*, Chand-u-Lal, exposed the English to great unpopularity. Although the Nizam's sons were young men of the most profligate and dissolute habits, the general dislike of the Dewan gave them considerable influence at Hyderabad. They maintained about their persons bands of ruffians, ready to perpetrate the most revolting crimes. On one occasion they seized a person in the employment of the British resident, threw him into prison, and put him to the torture, in order to extort money. Justly indignant at such an outrage, Mr. Russell made a very strong representation on the subject to the Nizam, and with his sanction sent a detachment of regular troops, under Captain Stone, to arrest the culprits. The princes stood on their defence, and repulsed the Sepoys with some loss. A serious struggle seemed impending; but the resident immediately sent for reinforcements, and directed Colonel Doveton, who commanded the mass of the auxiliary forces concentrated at Elichipore, to march upon Hyderabad. These prompt measures disconcerted the enemies of British power; the princes having laid down their arms, were sent prisoners to a distant fortress, and Colonel Doveton returned to his cantonments. This incident, though not attended with any important consequences, sufficiently proved that the inhabitants of Hyderabad were by no means favourably disposed towards the English alliance, which they associated with the unpopular administration of Chand-u-Lal.

We have already noticed the readiness of Bajee Rao to give his confidence to unworthy ministers; but by far the most pernicious of his advisers was Trimbuckjee-Danglia, whose career is a lamentable exhibition of the low state of morals in oriental courts. Trimbuckjee commenced life as a runner, or messenger, to some of the lowest officers in the Peishwa's service, but having manifested great activity and intelligence, he was soon employed as a *Jasoos*, or spy. His exertions in this degrading office were very important, and the Peishwa took him into his personal service. Though Bajee Rao was of a most suspicious temper, the diligence and unscrupulous obedience of Trimbuckjee won his confidence, and he trusted him with the secret management of his illicit amours. By pandering to the vicious indulgences of the Peishwa, and never hesitating at the commission of any crime which would facilitate the gratification of his depraved desires, the favorite acquired great influence over his master's mind, and was promoted to the command of the artillery, and finally to the rank of prime minister. Trimbuckjee, like most of the Mahrattas, mortally hated all Europeans, but for whose presence, he believed, his nation would obtain the supremacy in India. His whole course of policy was directed to maturing a combined movement for the expulsion of the English, and at his instigation, Bajee Rao revived his claims upon the Nizam and the Guicowar. He also seized upon the estates of the principal jaghiredars, or landholders, and caused their revenues to be paid into the treasury, thus ensuring a plentiful supply of money for the ensuing struggle. By his oppression and violence he collected an enormous sum: it has been ascertained that the Peishwa, at the commencement of the war, possessed fifty crores of rupees, or about five millions sterling.

It might be supposed that the rapacity and debauchery of Bajee Rao would have provoked an insurrection among his subjects, but he was supported by the influence of the Brahmins, whose favour he won by large largesses to themselves and their temples. He was, indeed, a slave to the grossest superstitions: one of his *Gooros*, or spiritual advisers, once told the Peishwa that the ghost of a Brahmin, unjustly slain by the Peishwa's father, had appeared to him in a dream, and required the murder to be expiated by giving a dinner to one hundred thousand Brahmins. This expensive entertainment was actually given by Bajee Rao. A more useful result of his superstition was the planting of more than a million of mango trees, in the vicinity of Poonah, as an expiation for his crimes.

Mr. Elphinstone was soon aware that the outstanding demands on the Guicowar and Nizam, were urged chiefly as pretences for maintaining communications between the courts of Poonah and those of Baroda and Hyderabad; he, therefore, strenuously exerted himself to have them arranged, but was baffled by the delays and pretensions of the Peishwa and his crafty minister. The Guicowar was equally anxious to have the pecuniary relations between himself and the Peishwa definitely settled, and he therefore sent Gungadhur Shastree, a Brahmin of great reputation at Baroda, to be his representative at Poonah, with full power to conclude a final treaty. So great was the dread inspired by the violence and unprincipled conduct of Trimbuckjee, that the Guicowar deemed it necessary to have his minister's safety formally guaranteed by the British government. The Shastree, after the delay of more than a year at Poonah, finding that the negotiations were not likely to be brought to a conclusion, resolved to return to Baroda, and to leave the entire affair to the arbitraticn of the British government.

Such a determination filled Trimbuckjee and his master with alarm, the departure of the Shastree would have interrupted their communications with Baroda, and they therefore resolved to use every artifice for conciliating his favour. The Shastree was a man of inordinate vanity ; he was consequently easily duped by the affectation of respect for his talents, which Trimbuckjee craftily manifested. It was stated, by some of the parties who actually participated in the intrigues, that Trimbuckjee went so far as to propose resigning his own place to the Shastree, in order that the Peishwa might avail himself of the services of so able a minister. Mr. Elphinstone had proposed that the Shastree should be sent home in honour and safety, but he was disconcerted by the refusal of that personage to quit Poonah, and soon after he was surprised to find that a marriage was proposed between the Shastree's son and the Peishwa's sister-in-law. But this alliance was disconcerted, by the refusal of the Guicowar to sanction some cessions of territory proposed by his minister. The marriage was broken off, and Bajee Rao was further offended, by the refusal of the Shastree to permit his wife to visit at the palace. Indeed, no one who respected the honour of a female relative, could allow her to witness the series of gross debauchery and licentious profligacy, which formed part of every-day life, at the court of Poonah.

Trimbuckjee saw that the Peishwa's quarrel with the Shastree, rendered a change in his own policy absolutely necessary, and as he was far too deeply committed, to extricate himself by ordinary means, he resolved to have recourse to assassination.

The Shastree was invited to accompany Bajee Rao and his minister, on a pilgrimage to the temple of Pinderpore, which is highly venerated by all the Mahrattas. Mr. Elphinstone and the Shastree's colleague accompanied the pilgrimage to Nafik, where they were induced to remain, by a series of ingenious devices, while the rest proceeded to Pinderpore. On the night after their arrival, the Shastree was persuaded by Trimbuckjee to join the Peishwa in performing some ceremonies of peculiar sanctity in the temple; he complied, although suffering at the time from fatigue and indisposition; the devotions were performed, and both Bajee Rao and his minister were lavish in their protestations of esteem and friendship. Scarcely, however, had the Shastree quitted the temple, when he was attacked by a body of hired assassins and almost literally cut to pieces. This atrocious crime excited general indignation, the murder of an ambassador, for whose safety the British faith had been pledged, was aggravated by the facts; the victim was a Brahmin, and that the crime had been committed in a place of extraordinary sanctity.

Mr. Elphinstone instituted a minute and strict inquiry, which was conducted with great ability, under the obvious disadvantage of the criminals being the sovereign of the country and his powerful minister. Their guilt was incontrovertibly established, but the Peishwa was informed that he would be permitted to throw the blame upon the special perpetrator, if he would surrender his unworthy minister to British custody. Bajee Rao at first seemed resolved to protect his favourite, but the speedy assembling of a British force at Poonah, so alarmed him, that he delivered up Trimbuckjee to the resident, having first received an assurance, that his life would be spared.

Trimbuckjee was sent to Bombay, and was confined in the fort of Tannah, on the island of Salsette. During his captivity, he frequently admitted to British officers, his share in the murder of the Shastree, but asserted that he had merely obeyed his master's orders. The garrison of Tannah was composed entirely of Europeans, and this circumstance enabled Trimbuckjee to open a communication with his friends abroad, through some of the Native servants in the fort. His principal agent was a horse-keeper, who passed and repassed the window of the place where Trimbuckjee was, daily, while airing his master's horse. He with apparent carelessness, sung the information he had to convey in the monotonous recitative, which forms the staple of Mahratta singing, and the sentries ignorant of the language, never felt the least suspicion. When all was prepared, Trimbuckjee made some excuse for quitting his apartments, and throwing on the disguise of a servant, gained an embrasure, whence he lowered himself into the ditch by a rope, which one of his accomplices had fastened round a gun. His friends were ready outside, and long before his flight was detected, he was safe from all danger of pursuit.

The Peishwa denied all knowledge of Trimbuckjee's movements, but Mr. Elphinstone discovered that he not only supplied the adventurer with money to levy troops, but had even granted him an audience. A singular scene of fraud and evasion followed. Trimbuckjee and other partisans organized large bodies of Mahrattas and Pindarries, while the Peishwa, having first attempted to deny that any such assemblages were made, when this monstrous falsehood could be no longer maintained, disavowed their proceedings and affected to treat them as insurgents. Finally, he issued a proclamation, setting a price on the head of Trimbuckjee Danglia, and sequestrated the property of some of his adherents.

Before entering on the history of the important consequences which resulted from the transactions we have just recorded, it will be necessary to cast a glance at some other parts of our Indian possessions. The reputation which the British arms had acquired by the successful issue of the war against Nepaul, was increased in the following year by the reduction of Hatrass, the stronghold of Diaram, a chieftain tributary to the Company. Trusting in the extraordinary strength of his fort, which was regarded as inpregnable by the Hindús, Diaram exhibited a spirit of contumacy and disobedience which it was resolved to punish in an exemplary manner. The vicinity of the great military depôt at Cawnpore, enabled the British to bring a train of artillery against Hatrass, equal, if not superior, to any that had ever been seen in India; a few hours of its tremendous fire breached that boasted fortification. Its demolition was completed by the explosion of the principal magazine, which destroyed all that remained of its buildings. This achievement, which was attended with no loss to the British, made a most salutary impression where it was much wanted, on their subjects in Hindustan Proper, and also on that turbulent class of feudatories to which the chieftain of Hatrass belonged.

The boldness and number of the Pindarries seemed to increase with the successes of the British. Immediately after the peace with Nepaul and the reduction of Hatrass, a strong body of these freebooters invaded and devastated part of the Madras territories; and both in that and the succeeding year, they repeated their incursions in the Dekkan, which all our troops, and those of the Nizam, could not protect from their merciless ravages. The Governor-general, confident that the continued recurrence of these aggressions, and his repeated representations, would early draw the attention of the authorities in England to the consideration of this intolerable evil, limited himself to a defensive system, whilst he proceeded in making every preparation for that early contest, which the treacherous proceedings of the Mahratta powers showed to be inevitable.

He was cheered in this prudent course, by perceiving that the authorities in England had at length become convinced that the policy of absolute non-interference could not be maintained, and that they were disposed, in some degree, to adopt a course different from that which had been pursued by the Marquis of Cornwallis and Sir George Barlow. Immediately after the renewal of the Company's charter in 1813,—an event which attracted a very small share of the public attention,—instructions were sent out, to take the state of Jypore, which had been abandoned in 1806, under our protection, whenever an opportunity should offer. The war in Nepaul prevented the Marquis of Hastings from acting on these instructions, but soon after its termination, he was induced, by the imminent danger in which the capital of Jypore was placed by the attack of Ameer Khan and his Pindarries, to make an overture for an alliance with its prince. The offer of this alliance, which had been so sedulously courted when the British government withheld its protection, was now received coldly; and it was discovered that the negociations for its accomplishment were protracted, in order that Ameer Khan might be induced to abandon his views, from a knowledge that the Jypore prince could at any time he pleased secure the protection of the British government. The Governor-general, disgusted at such conduct, and seeing no immediate prospect of impending danger, deferred the prosecution of the overture, to the period of making the more extensive arrangements which he now contemplated.

Although the Peishwa continued to protest in the strongest terms that his attachment to the English was unabated, the Resident was enabled to forward to the supreme government at Calcutta, incontrovertible proofs that he was in secret league and correspondence with Trimbuckjee Danglia, and that he was, in fact, the principal promoter of a rebellion which was ostensibly directed against his own government. Other facts proved that he was preparing for war; his treasures were removed from Poonah; his forts were repaired and garrisoned; his adherents began to levy troops in every direction. It was decided by the governor in council, that Bajee Rao had violated his engagements, and placed himself in the relation of an enemy; it was, therefore, resolved that he should be compelled to give us satisfaction for his past conduct, and security for the future, by a new treaty, which should increase our means of checking those dangers to which we had been exposed by his weak and treacherous proceedings. As some of his strongest forts had been placed in the possession of the British, when he was restored to the *musnud* by the treaty of Bassein, Bajee Rao was reduced to the alternative of hazarding an immediate contest, for which he was not prepared, or of signing the treaty dictated to him by the British government. After a severe struggle, in which shame, fear, pride and despair, had alternate sway over his irresolute mind, he signed a treaty on the 18th of June, 1817, by which he abandoned his claims to be regarded as the head of the Mahratta confederacy, and ceded several districts to the English, including the important fortress of Ahmednagar.

The southern Jaghiredars were by this engagement rendered more dependent on the British government than on the Peishwa, though the latter continued to be their nominal head. Some of their lands, of which Bajee Rao had taken possession, were restored; and the whole of the Jaghire of Rastea, which had been resumed, was, at the recommendation of the English government, given back to that once powerful Mahratta family. The Peishwa was thus deprived of that power which his perfidious conduct and hostile dispositions, shewed that he was likely to employ in counteracting or opposing the plans then in progress for the destruction of the Pindarries.

The consequence of the treaty with Bajee Rao was the negociation of a supplementary engagement with the Guicowar, to whom the events at Poonah were of the greatest advantage, as all the claims of the Peishwa were compounded for the trifling sum of four lacs of rupees annually. The object of a new settlement with the court of Baroda, was to effect such a change in our relations as would benefit both states, and put an end to those recurring discussions and differences among local officers, resulting from governments administered on very opposite principles, having mixed territories and claims upon tributaries. The negociation to accomplish this desirable object was protracted till November, 1817, when a treaty was concluded, which adjusted all points in a satisfactory manner, by mutual cessions of rights and interchanges of lands. The most important stipulations were those which gave to the British government the possession of the city of Ahmedabad. This city was the Mohammedan capital of Gujarát; it is situated on the banks of a small navigable river which falls into the sea near the city of Cambay, and was a valuable acquisition, both on account of its political and commercial importance.

These arrangements having been completed, the Marquis of Hastings prepared to execute his great plans for the extirpation of the Pindarries. "What I contemplated," he says, describing these operations, "was the pushing forward, unexpectedly, several corps, which should occupy positions opposing insuperable obstacles to the junction of the army of any one state with that of another, and even expose to extreme peril any sovereign's attempt to assemble the dispersed corps of his forces within his own dominions, should we see cause to forbid it."—"The success of this plan," his lordship adds, "depended on the secresy with which the preparations could be made, the proper choice of the points to be seized, and the speed with which we could reach the designated stations."

One of the first results of this prudent policy, may be said in a great degree to have decided the success of the future war. Scindia, to whom the chiefs both of the Pindarries and the Mahrattas looked for aid, was so circumstanced by the position of a large division under the Governor-general's personal command, and a corps under Major-general Donkin, that he was reduced to the necessity of acceding to a treaty dictated by the Marquis of Hastings, or of exposing himself to defeat and ruin. Scindia preferred the former course, however contrary to his inclination, and repugnant to all his cherished feelings as a member of the Mahratta confederacy. His public defection from a cause, the success of which rested chiefly on his efforts, was a fatal blow, not only to the Pindarries, but to that more general combination against our power, the designs of which were so ably anticipated.

Referring to this critical period, and the local situation of Scindia, Lord Hastings observes, "Residing at Gwalior, he was in the heart of the richest part of his dominions; but independently of this objection, that those provinces were separated from our territories only by the Jumna, there was a military defect in the situation, to which the Maha-rájá, (great chief, or king, a title assumed by Scindia,) had never adverted. About twenty miles south of Gwalior, a ridge of very abrupt hills, covered with the tangled wood peculiar to India, extends from the little Scind to the Chumbul, which rivers form the flank boundaries of the Gwalior district and its dependencies. There are but two routes by which carriages, and perhaps cavalry, can pass that chain; one along the little Scind, and another not far from the Chumbul. By my seizing, with the centre, a position which would bar any movement along the little Scind, and placing Major-general Donkin's division at the back of the other pass, Scindia was reduced to the dilemma of subscribing the treaty which I offered him, or of crossing the hills through bye-paths, attended by the few followers who might be able to accompany him, sacrificing his splendid train of artillery, (above one hundred brass guns,) with all its appendages, and abandoning at once to us his most valuable possessions.

"The terms imposed upon him were, essentially, unqualified submission, though so coloured as to avoid making him feel public humiliation. Their intrinsic rigour will not be thought overstrained or unequitable, when it is observed that I had ascertained the Maha-rájá's having promised the Pindarries decisive assistance, and that I had intercepted the secret correspondence with which he was inciting the Nepaulese to attack us. Nothing, in short, but my persuasion that the maintenance of the existing governments in Central India, and the making them our instruments for preserving the future tranquillity of the country, were desirable objects, could have dictated the forbearance manifested under the repeated perfidies of that prince. He closed with the proffered conditions, and was saved by that consequence. The advantage in another quarter could only be a transient ebullition. To the more distant states, this non-appearance of a formidable force, with which they were to co-operate, was an event which absolutely incapacitated them from effort."

The terms of the treaty dictated by the Governor-general, were, in substance, that Scindia should contribute his best efforts to destroy the Pindarries; that he should furnish a specified contingent to act in concert with the British troops, and under the direction of a British officer, against these freebooters; that the contingent should be kept in a state of complete efficiency; that to provide for the pay of these troops, Scindia should resign for three years his claims upon the British government, which had been recognized in the treaty he had concluded with General Wellesley (now Duke of Wellington) in 1804; that the amount of annual sums hitherto paid as pensions to his family and ministers, should be applied through British officers, to the regular payment of the bodies of cavalry he was to send to co-operate with the British troops; and it was arranged, that, with the exception of these corps, all the divisions of Scindia's army should remain stationary at the posts assigned by the British government, without whose concurrence none of them should move.

It was further stipulated that Scindia should admit British troops to garrison the fort of Aseerghur and Hindia, during the war, as pledges for the faithful fulfilment of his engagements; and he consented to the eighth article of the treaty, unwisely concluded with him under the sanction of the Marquis of Cornwallis, which left the Rajput states at his disposal. By the new arrangements, the English government was placed at liberty to conclude treaties with the Rajput states of Jypore, Joudpore, Odipore, Khottah, Bhondee, and others on the left bank of the Chumbul. This article, however, secured to Scindia, under the guarantee of the British government, his established tribute from these principalities, but restricted him, in the event of their forming engagements with the Company, from any future interference in their concerns.

However contrary such a treaty was to the inclinations of Scindia, it had the effect of rendering him inactive, if not neutral, throughout the operations that immediately ensued; and much effort was necessary to bring into action even those parts of his army which we had obtained the means of paying. The strong fortress of Aseerghur was not delivered over to the English troops. The pretext was the disobedience of its governor, Jesswunt Rao Lar, who, on the subsequent war, openly espoused the cause of Bajee Rao. When the same chief subsequently gave protection to Appa Sahib, the fugitive Rájá of Nagpore, he was summoned to surrender, and orders were sent by Scindia requiring prompt obedience. With these he refused to comply, and the fort was regularly besieged by the British troops. After its capitulation, accident brought to light a letter from his prince, directing him to obey all commands which he might receive from the Peishwa.

When Mr. Close, the resident at the court of Scindia, shewed this letter to the Mahar Rájá, he at once admitted its authenticity, and the violation of faith of which it was an evidence; but he pleaded in palliation those friendly relations which had, for several generations been established between his family and that of the Peishwa. This fair plea was not rejected. Lord Hastings, with politic liberality, limited his demand consequent on this discovery, to the perpetual cession of the fortress of Aseerghur, which, from its position, became, in our hands, a check upon robbers and freebooters. Before the cession it was occupied with robbers and freebooters, and it would have continued to be a place of refuge and protection for them, so long as it remained in the possession of a Mahratta prince.

These arrangements being completed, the Marquis of Hastings arranged the plan of operations against the Pindarries; their settlements being chiefly in Malwa and the valley of the Nerbudda, it was resolved to act upon them simultaneously by the armies of the Dekkan, Bengal, and Gujarát. Sir Thomas Hislop commanded the Dekkan forces, which amounted to fifty-three thousand men, in six divisions, communicating with the Bengal force at one extreme, and the Gujarát army, commanded by Sir

William Grant Keir, at the other. The Bengal army, amounting to thirty-four thousand men, was divided into four divisions, with two corps of observation; and there were besides several bodies of irregulars engaged, amounting altogether to about twenty-four thousand soldiers. The whole disposable force of the Pindarries did not much exceed thirty thousand men, and the dissensions between their principal chiefs, Cheetor, Kurrum Khan, and Wasil Mohammed, prevented them from forming any plan of united action. Ameer Khan, imitating the policy of Scindia, had entered into a treaty with the English, and all the minor states had formed stipulations engaging themselves to prevent the Pindarries from obtaining shelter in their dominions. At this crisis, events occurred at Poonah which changed the entire plan of the campaign, and placed us at war, not only with the freebooters, but with the acknowledged lord of the Mahratta confederacy.

It could not be supposed that Bajee Rao would have been satisfied with the treaty of Poonah, which had been forced upon him at a moment when his secret preparations for war were incomplete, and to which he never would have submitted but from the most imperious necessity. In the month of July, 1817, he proceeded on his annual visit to the temples of Punderpore; he was not accompanied by the resident, for Mr. Elphinstone believed that an abatement of vigilance would have a good effect, and be received as a mark of the restoration of confidence on the part of the British government. At the same time the Peishwa apparently reduced his military establishment, by dismissing a large number of his cavalry; but it was subsequently discovered that he had given each of his officers seven months pay, with orders to remain at his village, and to hold himself in readiness to return when summoned, with as many followers as he could collect. Every exertion was made by the British to raise the stipulated number of horse, but the Peishwa's emissaries resisted the recruiting by every means they could devise.

After having performed his pilgrimage to Punderpore, the Peishwa, instead of returning to Poonah, proceeded to Maholy, a village near Satara, at the junction of the Yena and Kistna, which was regarded by the Hindús as a place of peculiar sanctity. During his stay there he was visited by the political agent of the the Governor-general, Sir John Malcolm, who had just made a tour through the Dekkan, for the purpose of instructing the different residents in the nature of the operations about to be commenced against the Pindarries in Malwa. Sir John Malcolm was generally an able diplomatist, and had displayed much skill in various negociations with the Mohammedan powers, but he was unable to compete with the craft of the Hindús, being easily duped by their protestations of personal admiration and regard. The Peishwa's professions were most cordial, and communicated with such an appearance of earnestness and candour, that Sir John Malcolm was completely deceived, and returned to Poonah in the full conviction that Bajee Rao would now heartily engage in the British cause; and that, by encouraging him to raise troops, and treating him with perfect confidence, he would prove a faithful ally. Mr. Elphinstone took a much wiser view of Bajee Rao's character; he expressed, in plain terms, the little reliance which could be placed on Mahratta promises: but Sir John Malcolm was not to be convinced; he gave orders that the hill-forts which had been pledged for the execution of the treaty should be restored to the Peishwa, and that General Smith's force, which occupied a position to overawe Poonah, should march to the frontiers of Candeish, leaving a mere handful of troops for the protection of the residency.

The Peishwa did not return to his capital until the end of September. During his stay at Maholy, he was actively engaged in maturing the schemes which he had long meditated against the British government. Bappoo Jokla, an able leader, possessing more of a chivalrous character than is usual in the Hindú warriors, strenuously urged Bajee Rao to commence open war instead of the secret plots to which he was attached. As neither Gokla nor any of the Mahratta chieftains confided in the Peishwa's firmness, it was required that he should bind himself on oath to be implicitly guided by Gokla's counsels, and, at the same time, nearly a million of money was placed at the disposal of that able general.

Sir John Malcolm, in his exuberant confidence, had recommended the Peishwa to recruit his army for the purpose of aiding the English in suppressing the Pindarries, and this afforded him an excellent plea for all his suspicious movements. His recruiting went forward with remarkable activity; his forts also were garrisoned, stored, and repaired; and orders were issued to prepare his fleet. Many Bheels, Ramoosies, and other plundering hordes, were engaged in his service by Trimbukjee Danglia; and special missions were despatched to Nagpore, and the camps of Scindia, Holkar, and Ameer Khan. At the same time he took upon himself the direction of the plans he had formed for the assassination of the resident, and the seduction of the Native troops.

The reports of corrupting the troops were brought from all quarters; some of the Sepoys indignantly refused what to them were splendid offers; and others, pretending to acquiesce, communicated the circumstances to their officers; but the extent of the intrigues could not be ascertained, and they at last became alarming, even to those who knew the fidelity of the Bombay Sepoys, from the circumstance of the Peishwa's having many of their families and relations in his power, against whom he commenced a system of persecution, which he threatened to perpetuate if the Sepoys refused to desert the British service. Gokla resisted all the attempts which were made to engage him to sanction Mr. Elphinstone's assassination, and secret notice of his danger was sent to that gentleman; he was not, however, to be induced to abandon his post; a European regiment was on its march to join him, and the notorious indecision of Bajee Rao gave hopes that his heart might fail him at the critical moment.

As the position of the British cantonments was very unfavourable, Mr. Elphinstone moved the few forces he had at his disposal to the village of Khirkee, which had been early pointed out by General Smith as the best post that could be occupied in case of the apprehended rupture. The Mahrattas believed that the British had withdrawn through fear, and were much encouraged in consequence. The abandoned cantonment was plundered; an officer on his route to Bombay was attacked, wounded, and robbed in open day; the language of the Peishwa's ministers became menacing and insulting; and parties of horse pushed forward to the British lines as if in defiance. It was evident that hostilities could not long be delayed, and, on the 3rd of November, Mr. Elphinstone directed the light battalion, and a body of auxiliary horse, stationed at Sewar, to march upon Poonah. When this intelligence reached the Peishwa, he resolved that hostilities should be delayed no longer.

No part of the Mahratta army was visible from the British residency, excepting bodies of infantry which were assembling along the tops of the adjoining heights, with the intention of cutting off the residency from the camp. "On ascending one of these eminences, on which they were forming," says Captain Grant Duff, the able historian of this war, "the plain beneath presented at that moment a most imposing spectacle. This plain, then covered with grain, terminates on the west by a range of small hills, while on the east it is bounded by the city of Poonah, and the small hills already partially occupied by the infantry. A mass of cavalry covered nearly the whole extent of it, and towards the city, endless streams of horsemen were pouring from every avenue." The additional description given by this intelligent writer, is too graphic a picture to be omitted. "Those only who have witnessed the bore in the gulf of Cambay, and have seen in perfection the approach of that roaring tide, can form the exact idea presented to the author, at sight of the Peishwa's army. It was towards the afternoon of a very sultry day; there was a dead calm, and no sound was heard except the rushing, the trampling, and the neighing of the horses, and the rumbling of the gun-wheels. The effect was heightened by seeing the peaceful peasantry flying from their work in the fields, the bullocks breaking from their yokes, the wild antelopes startled from sleep, bounding off, and then turning for a moment to gaze on this tremendous inundation, which swept all before it, levelled the hedges and standing corn, and completely overwhelmed every ordinary barrier as it moved."

Perceiving that efforts were being made to intercept his communication, Mr. Elphinstone retired with his family to Kirkhee, not without having been exposed to some danger from the fire of the Mahrattas on the opposite side of the river. At the same time he sent orders to Lieutenant-colonel Burr, the officer in command, to move down and attack the Peishwa's army, while the irregulars, under Major Ford, were directed to second his efforts. Both officers promptly obeyed, and Colonel Burr, though suffering under a severe and incurable attack of paralysis, advanced to the attack. The Mahrattas, who had sent on their skirmishers, some of whom had already suffered from the fire of the light infantry, were surprised by this forward movement of troops, who, they had been led to believe, were cowed and dispirited. Gokla, however, cheered them on; he rode from rank to rank, employing exhortations, praises, taunts, as he thought most effectual; but the Peishwa's heart failed him, and after the troops had advanced, he sent a message to Gokla, "not to fire the first gun." At this moment the British troops were halting; their guns were unlimbering;—it was the pause of preparation and anxiety on both sides; but Gokla, observing the messenger from the Peishwa, and suspecting the nature of his errand, instantly commenced the attack by opening a battery of nine guns, detaching a strong corps of rocket-camels to the right, and pushing forward his cavalry to the right and left. The British troops were soon nearly surrounded by horse; but the Mahratta infantry, owing to this rapid advance, were left considerably in the rear, except a regular battalion under a Portuguese named De Pinto, which had marched by a shorter route, concealed for some time under cover of the hedges and enclosures. De Pinto's men were forming with great steadiness, when they were suddenly charged by the English Sepoys, who by this impetuous movement became detached from the line. Gokla led forward a select body of six thousand horse, to take advantage of their imprudence. Colonel Burr fortunately perceived the moving mass, in time to stop the pursuit of De Pinto's routed battalion; he called upon the men to reserve their fire, as there was no opportunity to dress them in line. Unknown to either party, there was a deep slough immediately in front of the British left; the foremost of the Mahratta horses rolled over in the marsh, and many others, before they could be pulled up, tumbled over those in front. The Sepoys poured in their reserved fire on this mass with dreadful effect; they fell into confusion, the force of the charge was checked, and the few horsemen who came into contact with the bayonets, were easily repulsed. Some had galloped round to plunder the camp, but were driven off by a few shots from two iron guns at Khirkee. A company of Europeans coming up to support the Sepoys, the British line advanced, and the Mahrattas fled from the field. This decisive victory was won by the British, over more than ten times their number, with a loss of only eighty-three in killed and wounded; the Mahrattas lost more than five hundred men, and a still greater number of horses.

Hostilities were no sooner commenced, than the ferocious and vindictive character of Bajee Rao's previous orders became apparent. The residency was plundered and burned; the families and followers of the troops, who fell into the hands of the Mahrattas, were robbed, beaten and frequently mutilated; the gardens were destroyed, the trees torn up by the roots, and the very graves violated. An engineer-officer on survey, was attacked and killed. Two brothers of the name of Vaughan, one of them a captain in the Madras army, were taken while travelling between Bombay and Poonah, and though they made no resistance, were both barbarously hanged. A stop, however, was put to these atrocities, when Mr. Elphinstone communicated to Gokla, his determination to exact a severe retaliation for the murder of any British prisoner.

So soon as the communications from Poonah ceased, General Smith judiciously conjecturing that something was wrong, prepared to return. From the time his division quitted Seroor, he was followed by flying parties of the Mahrattas, who severely harassed his march, for want of cavalry prevented him from pursuing them when repulsed. He joined the force at Kirkhee on the evening of the 13th of November, and made preparations for the attack of the Peishwa's camp, but Bajee Rao was afraid to hazard another engagement; he fled to Sattara, abandoning his capital to the mercy of the English. General Smith took every possible care to ensure the protection of the peaceable part of the community; order and tranquillity were soon re-established, and, after a halt of a few days, preparations were made for an active pursuit of the fugitive Peishwa.

We must now turn our attention to Nagpore, where events had occurred very similar in their character to those which we have just described at Poonah. Although the Rájá Appah Sahib was mainly indebted to the English for his elevation to the *musnud*, he early evinced a disposition as inconsistent with the gratitude which he owed them as with the obligations of good faith. He dismissed from their situations Nagoo Pundit and Narrain Pundit, the two ministers who had been instrumental in forming the subsidiary alliance, and he entered into an active and secret correspondence with Bajee Rao, at a period when that prince was occupied in plans known to be hostile to our interests. This correspondence was an infraction of the stipulations of the treaty; but the English government winked at the delinquency, having no desire to press a point of this nature to an unpleasant issue. Every allowance was made for Mahratta habits, and for the weak character of a young prince exposed to artful intrigue.

The court of Nagpore was at this period divided into two parties, one of which was decidedly adverse to the English interests. The influence of this party had latterly much increased, but still the Rájá appeared so open and sincere in all his personal communications with the resident, that a gentleman, less acute and vigilant than Mr. Jenkins, would have been lulled into fatal security. He, however, attended to action rather than words; the additions made to the Nagpore army—the increased activity of the correspondence with Poonah—the public reception of a *Khelat*, or dress of honour, from the Peishwa, and some other circumstances of the same kind, though palliated by plausible excuses, were clear evidences of a spirit of hostility. It was hoped, however, that the intelligence of Bajee Rao's defeat at Poonah, and of the treaty which the Governor-general had concluded with Scindia, would teach the Rájá a lesson of moderation; still it was necessary to be prepared for the worst, and a requisition was sent for immediate reinforcements.

Notwithstanding the amicable professions and protestations which the Rájá continued to make, Mr. Jenkins had obtained positive information that he intended to attack the residency and British cantonments; and the movements of his army coincided so exactly with the reports of his intended proceedings that no doubt remained of the course he meant to pursue. Preparations for defence were therefore made with the greatest activity, and the brigade, which was commanded by Colonel Hopeton Scott, was removed from its inconvenient cantonments to occupy the residency and the adjoining heigths of Seetabuldee. Here the British force, which did not amount to fifteen hundred in all, were attacked on the night of the 26th of November, by an immense force of eighteen thousand men, including four thousand Arabs, and, after an action which lasted eighteen hours, gained a decisive victory over this immense disparity of force. It will be necessary to give as full an account as possible of an engagement which is generally believed to have done more to establish the moral supremacy of the British in Southern India than any other on record.

The residence of Nagpore is separated from the city by a

rocky ridge on the north, and immediately over the residence is a considerable eminence capable of being turned into a strong position. The side facing the continuation of the rocky ridge is, however, exposed to a second and lower eminence on the south side of the ridge, at the foot of which is a considerable village, surrounded with shrubs and trees, extending to the suburbs of Nagpore. This village affords every facility for concealing the approach of an irregular force, and also good cover for an assaulting party.

Colonel Scott, who commanded the British forces, did not make the most judicious of all possible arrangements; a body of three hundred men occupied the south hill, where the brunt of the attack was to be expected; the main body was posted on the northern eminence, which was a very convenient spot for spectators; the three troops of cavalry were posted in the enclosures surrounding the residency, that being the spot where cavalry could be of least service.

On the night of the 26th of November, the Mahrattas opened a heavy fire of matchlocks on the south hill, which they maintained until past midnight, and then gradually slackened until morning. When daylight appeared, the attack was renewed with great fury, and the defenders of the hill assailed with cannon and musketry. Small reinforcements were sent to repair the losses sustained in the repulse of the frequent attempts made to carry it by storm, but at length the British were thrown into confusion by the explosion of a tumbril; the Arabs charged up the hill, sword in hand, drove back the detachment with great loss, and having captured a six pounder, directed a harassing fire on the northern hill. Encouraged by this success, the Mahrattas assailed the British lines in every direction; the huts where the British had been encamped were seized, and the Sepoys were appalled by the shrieks of their wives and children, to whom they could render no assistance. The enclosures where the cavalry stood were menaced, and guns brought up to assail them; Captain Fitzgerald, who held the post, repeatedly sent for permission to charge, and was forbidden by his commanding officer. To his last request Colonel Scott replied, "Let him do so at his peril." "At my peril be it," replied Fitzgerald, and leading his men out of the enclosures, he formed them into line, and charged the main body of the Mahratta horse with irresistible fury. The ease with which the British squadrons cut their way through the Mahratta lines was subsequently compared, by one of the vanquished, to the burning of a thread by the flame of a candle. Fitzgerald not only dispersed the enemy's horse, but cut to pieces a body of infantry advancing to their support, and captured two guns. The defenders of the north hill saw this brilliant exploit with feelings of the highest admiration, they gave vent to their enthusiasm in loud cheers, and proposed immediately to recover the south hill. At this instant, the accident which led to its temporary loss was repeated; the Arabs in their turn were thrown into confusion by an explosion of ammunition; the British troops could no longer be withheld; the orders of the commanding officer were not waited for, or not heard; men and officers rushed forward, mingled together by one common impulse, drove the Arabs down the hill, pursued them to its base, and spiked two of their guns. The Arabs once more rallied, and prepared to advance, but they were charged in flank by a troop of the cavalry, thrown into confusion, and dispersed over the field. Before noon the battle was at an end, and the victory of the British over the Mahrattas—and, it may be added, over the blunders of their own commander—was complete.

The complete defeat of the enemy at all points, and the approach of the reinforcements which had been ordered to advance, put an end to all hope of success in the mind of Appah Sahib; he commenced a negociation for a renewal of friendship, with a solemn declaration, that the late attack upon the British troops, had been made without his will or consent. He was ordered to withdraw his army from the vicinity of the scene of action, before any answer could be returned to his communication. He immediately complied with this demand, and during the period which intervened between the removal of his troops and the arrival of Brigadier-general Doveton's army, the advance of which reached Nagpore on the 12th of December, this infatuated prince continuated making protestations of submission, but pursuing at the same time a weak and vacillating course of conduct.

Soon after General Doveton's arrival, preliminary terms were offered to Appah Sahib; he was required to deliver up his ordnance and military stores, to disband his Arabs immediately and the rest of his troops in a reasonable time, to allow Nagpore to be occupied by the British, and to repair to the residency until the terms of the treaty were finally arranged. Although these conditions greatly limited his power, they still left to him the name and functions of sovereignty, of which it was the wish of the Governor-general that he should be deprived. Local circumstances, however, induced Mr. Jenkins to continue, if possible, the rule of Appah Sahib, and he therefore urged upon that prince, a speedy acceptance and agreement to the proffered terms. After many evasions and efforts to obtain delay, he accepted them and repaired to the British residency, attended by some of his ministers. The troops, who made a weak attempt at resistance, were attacked and routed. The horse dispersed in every quarter, a great part of them retiring to their homes; a large corps of Arabs, however, retreated to the palace, which they defended for some days, and then capitulated.

The Marquis of Hastings directed that the provisional engagements made with Appah Sahib, should be embodied in a treaty; but before the instructions for the final arrangements could reach Nagpore, another revolution had taken place in that capital. The refusal of the governors of several of the forts in Berar, to surrender their positions, gave rise to suspicions, which were soon confirmed by the most indisputable evidence, that their treacherous prince had given them orders not to obey his reluctant summons. Ere long his correspondence with the disaffected part of his troops, and with those ministers who had instigated his former conduct, was detected, and it was distinctly established that he continued, in spite of the moderation with which he had been treated, to cherish designs of renewed hostility. It was also discovered at this period, by proofs deemed conclusive, that he had murdered his predecessor Bala Sahib, in order to obtain that elevation which he had so disgraced. These plots and crimes, although enormous, might have admitted of the resident waiting the result of a reference to the Governor-general; but the information, that the Rájá intended making his escape from his capital, and the renewed activity of his communications with Bajee Rao, who, as we shall have occasion presently to show, made a demonstration about this time in the direction of Nagpore, left Mr. Jenkins no time to deliberate. He ordered a detachment of troops to take possession of the palace, and seize Appah Sahib, who was brought immediately to the residency, where he continued in confinement, till orders were received, that he should be sent under a strong escort to the Company's dominion in Hindustan. While on his journey to Benares, the place appointed for his future residence, the Rájá effected his escape, by feigning illness and bribing some of his guard.

The stratagem was contrived and executed with great skill and cunning. When the officer in charge came to visit the Rájá at the usual hour of the night, he found him to all appearance fast asleep in his bed, and the attendants requested that he would not disturb their master, as great repose was absolutely necessary in his present exhausted condition. The officer, instead of making any minute examination, contented himself with casting a hasty glance round the apartment, and thus failed to discover, that his prisoner's place was occupied by a long bolster. In fact, the Rájá was at that moment many miles off, attended by some Sepoys, whom he had induced to desert. It appears that the troops appointed for his escort, were selected by Appah Sahib himself, the British authorities being anxious to soothe his irritation at the loss of his dominions. But yielding to this particular request was very injudicious, for the troops selected, were men who had been favourably disposed towards the Rájá; indeed, there is good reason to believe that they had not only been tampered with, but won over, previous to their departure from Nagpore. Appah Sahib, fled first to the Mahadeo hills, and thence to Aseerghur, where, as we shall subsequently have occasion to relate, he joined Cheeto, the leader of the Pindarries, just before he was routed by a British detachment.

The Peishwa fled before General Smith's active pursuit, and led the English a long and wearisome chase through the Ghauts. General Smith's army having pushed too far northwards, Bajee Rao retraced his steps and declared his intention of recovering Poonah. Colonel Burr immediately ordered the detachment at Seroor to march to his assistance. It set out on the last day of the year, under the command of Captain Francis Staunton; the troops consisted of one battalion of Native infantry, three hundred irregular horse, and two six-pounders of the Madras artillery, manned by twenty-four Eurpoeans, under the command of a lieutenant and a serjeant. After having marched all night, Captain Staunton, on reaching the high grounds overlooking the village of Korigaum, on the Beema, suddenly found himself in the presence of the Peishwa's whole army, amounting to twenty-five thousand men.

The battle which ensued was one of the most remarkable in the history of British India; our soldiers, fatigued by a long march, without food or water, and exposed to the heat of a burning sun, had to maintain themselves against this immense disparity of force until nine o'clock at night. The British officers conducted themselves most nobly. Lieutenant Patinson, a gentleman of herculean frame, though mortally wounded, led the grenadiers in a desperate charge, and recovered a six-pounder which the enemy had seized. A choultry, where some of the wounded officers had been placed, was seized by the Mahrattas, who murdered Surgeon Wingate; but his fall was avenged and his companions rescued, by Lieutenant Jones and Dr. Wylie, who retook the choultry in spite of superior numbers and desperate resistance. The artillery-men, who were at first disposed to surrender on terms, no sooner saw the mutilated body of their officer, whose head the savages had cut off when he fell mortally wounded, than they declared that they would conquer or die, and they nobly maintained their resolution. The Peishwa, Lokla, and Trimbuckjee Danglia witnessed the conflict, and directed the attacks. On every successive repulse the Peishwa bitterly reproached those officers whose vaunts had induced him to engage in the war, and, when night approached, he not only ceased from attacking Korigaum, but made a precipitate retreat.

The pursuit of the Peishwa was actively resumed after his defeat at Korigaum, but was productive of nothing important except the political effect of exhibiting him as a fugitive. Whenever he was hard-pressed, Gokla, with all the light troops, hovered round the pursuing divisions, firing long shots with their matchlocks, throwing rockets in favourable situations, and cutting off cattle and baggage. Some skirmishes took place in consequence, and the Mahrattas frequently suffered from the shrapnell shells of the horse artillery; but these affairs were attended with no advantageous result to either party.

General Smith, having united all his forces, laid siege to Satara, which surrendered on the 10th of February. A manifesto was then published, stating all the particulars of Bajee Rao's conduct, pronouncing his deposition, and declaring that all his territories, with the exception of a small tract to be reserved for the Rájá of Satara, should be annexed to the dominions of the Company. Equitable regulations were promulgated for regulating the taxation and rental of the country, and many flagrant abuses which had prevailed under the Mahratta government were abolished. In the mean time, Bajee Rao had retreated to Sholapore, where he was joined by a body of horse, under Gunput Rao, from Nagpore. Thus reinforced, Gokla persuaded the Peishwa to make a movement to the westward. General Smith having received information of the plan, immediately commenced an active pursuit with the cavalry and the horse-artillery, and, on the 19th of February, overtook the Mahrattas at Ashtab, just as they were preparing to move off the ground. Bajee Rao sent Gokla a taunting message, intimating that it was to his negligence the exposure of the Mahratta movements to the English had been effected. Gokla replied that the Peishwa's rear should be effectually guarded, and then advanced with a strong detachment of horse, to check the progress of the English. In the slight skirmish which ensued, Gokla was cut down by a dragoon ; the Mahrattas instantly fled, leaving behind them several elephants, a quantity of baggage, and the Rájá of Sattara, whom they had detained as a captive and hostage. Bajee Rao then moved towards Nagpore, where he expected to be joined by Appa Sahib, but, learning that the treachery of the Rájá had been detected and foiled by the English, he fled back again to the northern districts.

The Pindarries, in three separate bodies or *durras*, under their leaders, Cheetoo, Khareem Khan, and Wasil Mohammed, occupied positions between Indore and Sagur, when the Marquis of Hastings had completed his combinations for their destruction. The mutual animosities of these chiefs prevented them from combining in self-defence, or taking any advantage of the events in Poonah and Nagpore. The only enterprise attempted by the Pindarries was to send a detachment from the *durra* of Wasil Mohammed, which got into the rear of General Marshall's division of the Bengal army, and committed some ravages in Bundelcund; the Marquis of Hastings sent a small body of troops, which drove these marauders back to Malwa, and General Marshall's advance was not interrupted. Sir John Malcolm and Colonel Adams, with their divisions acting in concert with Marshall, soon drove the Pindarries from their accustomed haunts, and either took possession of their lands or restored them to the agent of Scindia and the Nabob of Bhopaul. Wasil Mohammed, and Khareem Khan, uniting their *durras*, took the road to Gwalior, whither they had been secretly invited by Scindia; Gheetoo went off to the north-west, in hopes of receiving support from Holkar.

When these movements were ascertained, the Marquis of Hastings sent a detachment across the Sindh, so as to cut off the Pindarries from Gwalior, and, at the same time, brought his own division within thirty miles of Scindia's camp, which had the effect of completely overawing that chieftain. The Pindarries, unable to penetrate to Gwalior, or to return to the southward, directed their flight westwards into Meywar. Many of them were left behind, who were cut off either by the troops or the exasperated villagers. One considerable body, however, got clear off to the southward, and, after traversing the whole Dekkan, entered the Company's provinces in the Carnatic, where they were annihilated or dispersed before the end of the ensuing January.

Cheetoo, in the meantime, being closely pursued by Sir John Malcolm, found refuge in Holkar's camp, in the vicinity of Meludpore or Maidpore. Gunput Rao, the paramour of Toolsee Bye, was at this time the chief director of Holkar's agency, and, as he was a bitter enemy of the British, it soon became evident that hostilities could not be avoided. Indeed, so resolved were the Patans on war, that, suspecting the regency of an intention to open negociations, they put Toolsee Bye to death, and placed Gunput Rao in confinement. Sir Thomas Hislop, who had now arrived with his division and taken the supreme command, finding that his detached parties were severely harassed, resolved to bring matters to a crisis.

Shortly after daylight on the morning of the 21st of December, 1817, the English troops came within sight of the enemy's camp. They found Holkar's army strongly posted near the town of Mahedpore, within a bend of the Supra river, which covered the left flank, the right being protected by a deep ravine. Its front was protected by a formidable park of artillery, consisting of seventy heavy guns ranged in the form of a crescent. These guns being admirably served by the Patans, overpowered the light English field-pieces, and occasioned a heavy loss before the British troops had time to form and advance, after crossing the fords of the Supra. The ford was steep and narrow, the ascent on the opposite bank, naturally difficult, was further obstructed by several guns, carriages, &c., which had been disabled and rendered useless by the enemy's fire, when the head of the advancing column first appeared from the river. When the whole of the infantry had obtained their footing on the opposite bank, they deployed by columns, diverging by the right into line, and took up their respective positions in front of the enemy, each regiment lying on the ground, until the whole line was completed, as Sir Thomas Heslop had directed. At a preconcerted signal, they rose, advanced, and fired a volley; orders were then given to charge; the soldiers at once pushed forward, broke Holkar's battalions, and made themselves masters of his artillery. The Patans fought desperately in defence of the cannon; many of these brave and devoted men refused to abandon their guns, and were bayonetted or sabred where they stood. A few, who saw that any further resistance would be useless, took up their swords and shields, and quietly retreated; but they were overtaken and cut to pieces by the British cavalry. Holkar's horse and infantry had fled on the first onset, and their camp was found standing, but with very few articles of any value in it: at some distance in its rear, five guns, which had been left to cover the retreat, were discovered and taken. The victory was complete, and it lowered the vaunting boasts of Holkar's troops, who, it appears, prided themselves much on a trifling advantage which they had formerly gained over a detachment of the Bengal army, when attacked under unfavourable circumstances.

A heavy fall of rain took place at the close of the action, which greatly aggravated the sufferings of the wounded, and afforded opportunities for plunder to the marauders, who wandered over the field, robbing the living and the dead, and assassinating those who attempted to make any resistance. A large quantity of military equipments and stores, were found upon the field. Among the enemy's supply of ammunition for their heavy ordnance, a large quantity of balls was discovered which, from the private marks of manufacturers, and the names of gunners upon them, must have been obtained, by some treacherous means, from British arsenals. The enquiries instituted on the subject led to no satisfactory result.

From the field of battle the English advanced to Mundisore, where they met envoys bringing offers of peace from young Holkar. A treaty was concluded on terms more favourable than that chieftain had a right to expect, and an English residency was established at Indore. Scindia's court was rendered perfectly tractable by the victory over Holkar, but one of his feudatories having afforded a refuge to Cheetoo and his Pindarries, General Browne was sent to punish his delinquency. This service was performed promptly and efficiently; Jesswunt Rao's camp was surprised, his guns captured, and his principal town stormed. The district which he had governed, was then transferred to another ruler.

In the meantime, Cheetoo with his *durra* of Pindarries, fled in a north-westerly direction, when the pursuit was taken up by the Gujarât division with considerable effect. His *durra* was now the only one at all formidable, the rest had either been destroyed or dispersed, and their chiefs had yielded themselves prisoners. At length, Cheetoo's division was completely surprised and dispersed by a detachment from the fort of Hindia; he escaped with about two hundred followers, and sought refuge with the Nabob of Bhopaul, but the terms which he offered to that chieftain being rejected, he continued his flight until he joined the fugitive, Appa Sahib, to whom his habits of vigilance and activity rendered him a valuable ally. The Pindarries, thus dispersed, without leaders and without homes, soon ceased to be formidable; they were finally absorbed in the agricultural population of Malwa and the Dekkan, where many of them became active and improving farmers.

Sir Thomas Heslop now prepared to return to Madras, resolving on his way to take possession of the severals forts to the southward, which had been ceded by Scindia or Holkar. No resistance was made until the army approached the Fort of Talnier, situated on the right bank of the Tapti river, when a fire was suddenly opened from the walls on the advance and the quarter-master-general's department. The aggression was equally unprovoked and unexpected, being obviously an infraction of the treaty by which Talnier and the other forts south of the Nerbudda were ceded to the English. Information of these stipulations was sent to the Killidar or governor of the fort, together with a sharp remonstrance on his breach of the treaty, and a threat to treat him as a rebel if he persevered; but he met these representations with an evasive and rather hostile reply.

One six-pounder and two small howitzers, the largest guns present with the army, were hastily formed into a field battery, and brought to bear on the gateway of the fort from a neighbouring eminence. The fire of the enemy was soon overpowered and silenced, the parapets destroyed, and the defences dismantled, but, from the small calibre of the artillery employed, no material damage was done to the main wall. It was resolved to force an entrance at the gateway, but, as the storming party advanced, a flag of truce was displayed from one of the bastions; soon after the Killidar and the commander of the garrison came out, declaring that the gates of the fort should be opened so soon as terms of capitulation could be arranged. The English officer in command, replied that the surrender of the place must be unconditional, and directed that this reply should he communicated to the garrison. No one seemed willing to convey the message, and hostilities were resumed. The storming party pushed forward into the traverse, through the broken masonry on each side of the gateway, and advanced with little order, finding all the gates but the last open before them. Here, after a brief delay, a wicket was opened, through which Major Gordon entered with a small party. A short parley followed, when the wicket was suddenly and treacherously closed; the Major and his few followers, hemmed in on every side by ferocious enemies, and cut off from all possibility of relief, were overpowered and slain.

When the first effects of the surprise were abated, the English soldiers rushed forward to the assault, with equal fury and desperation; a party of pioneers broke through the fastenings of the wicket, and opened a passage; the Arabs, who formed the garrison, made a vigorous effort to defend the entrance, but they could not resist men, almost maddened by the unexpected resistance, and by the base treachery practised on their beloved officer and his followers. Under the circumstances, no quarter could be given; about one hundred and fifty Arabs fell beneath the hands of the avengers. Some fugitives, in the hope of escape, concealed themselves in haystacks, but their places of refuge were discovered and fired; the helpless wretches, driven out by the flames, were shot down like beasts of prey by the enraged soldiers. The extermination of the garrison was all but complete; a woman and two Arab boys, who had secreted themselves in a dry well, were the only persons saved.

Nor was this all; the Killidar and the Arab commandant, being considered as rebels by Sir Thomas Heslop, were ordered to be immediately hanged. Many of the officers vainly remonstrated against this unnecessary execution. Even if the Killidar deserved his fate, which is rather questionable, it was obviously unjust to make a victim of the Arab commandant, who acted entirely under the orders of his superior, a civil officer, for whose acts he could not be amenable or held responsible. He was of course innocent of all share in the treachery that occurred at the gate-way, for both he and the Killidar were prisoners in the hands of the English at the time.

The fall of Talnier, and the fate of its governor, ensured the quiet surrender of the remaining fortresses. The keys of the strong hill-forts of Chandore, Unktunky, and Galna, were sent to the English camp by their respective Killidars, who did not wait to be summoned, and these important posts were immediately secured by British troops. Nothing now remained to bring the war to a conclusion, save securing the persons of Bajee Rao, Cheetoo, and Appa Sahib.

After wandering about for some time, with an army daily diminishing by desertion, the Peishwa was surprised and routed by an English detachment under Colonel Adams, who followed up his victory by besieging and capturing the important castle of Chandah. General Putzler, about the same time, made himself master of Wusota, where two English officers were found, who had been made prisoners in the beginning of the war, and had been kept ever since in ignorance of the movements of their countrymen, even when they had opened a fire on the place in which they were confined. Bajee Rao now saw that his affairs were desperate; he made many overtures to Mr. Elphinstone, but as they always implied an ability to treat, he was distinctly told that his unconditional submission only could be accepted. At length, he sought shelter with about eight thousand men under the guns of Asseergurh, whence he sent agents to General

Sir John Malcolm, the nearest of his pursuers, to treat of a surrender.

Sir John Malcolm's better judgment was lulled by the flattery of the Peishwa's envoys, and he was besides anxious to have the glory of bringing the war to a conclusion; he, therefore, opened negociations, though contrary to the directions which had been issued by the Governor-general. It must, however, be confessed that the ready shelter afforded to the Peishwa at Asseergurh—a fortress which Scindia had agreed to surrender to the English, but which its Killidar retained by the secret directions of his sovereign,—gave reasonable ground for believing that the Peishwa might rely on the aid of Scindia if he protracted the war. After some negociation, Bajee Rao surrendered to Sir John Malcolm; he agreed to abdicate the throne; to spend the rest of his life within the English territories, but it was stipulated that the Company should make him an annual allowance of one hundred thousand pounds; while, at the same time, he was permitted to retain all that he had preserved of his treasures. Terms so utterly disproportioned to the Peishwa's position and claims, were with very great reluctance confirmed by the Governor-general, and on many occasions he condemned in the most pointed terms the impolitic concessions made by Sir John Malcolm. Trimbuckjee Danglia escaped for a time, but after many perilous adventures, he was made prisoner by a party of irregular horse, and confined for life in an English fortress.

Appa Sahib and Cheetoo, after having been closely blockaded in the hills, made their escape to Asseergurh, and that celebrated fortress was immediately invested by General Doveton; Sir John Malcolm co-operating, with a force from Malwa. Cheetoo's Pindarries had been received into the fort, but he was himself excluded by the jealousy of the Killidar. Great uncertainty prevailed respecting his fate, but, at length, it was discovered that he had fallen a victim to a tiger, in the jungle where he sought shelter; his body when found, was so mangled that it could not have been identified, but for the fragments of his dress which lay near. Asseergurh made a vigorous defence, but was at length surrendered on the 9th of April, 1819, when it was found that Appa Sahib was not in the fort, but had fled to some other place before its investment was completed.

It required some vigorous management to compel the surrender of several of the forts which their Killidars retained; but one after another was surrendered or taken, and the Governor-general was enabled to develop his plans for the regulation of the conquered country. In general, the rights of the possessors of property were treated with great respect, and the administration of law was very little changed from the Mahratta form of proceedure, but the greatest vigilance was introduced into the criminal courts, for the purpose of putting an end to the organized system of plunder which had previously prevailed.

The only place where any resistance was made to the changes which the Marquis of Hastings introduced, after establishing British supremacy in India, was at Bareilly, in Rohilcund. A tax had been introduced for the support of the police force, unpopular in itself, and levied in a way very offensive to the prejudices of the people. The magistrate of Bareilly entrusted the collection to the *Cutwal*, or Native head of the police, against whom popular indignation was vehemently excited, on account of his harshness, cruelty and venality. He was particularly detested by the higher class of Patans in Rohilcund, who are feelingly alive to every thing which concerns their personal honour, and to whose prejudices the coarse language of a vulgar Hindú villager, as the *Cutwal* is described to have been, was peculiarly offensive. Several tumultuous meetings were held at Bareilly, and a petition against the tax was presented to the magistrate, through the Mufti, who, according to Mohammedan usage, combined the functions of a judge and a priest. No notice was taken of this address; the popular discontent continued, and the bad feeling which existed in the town, was greatly increased by the circumstance of a woman being wounded by some police officers while in the act of levying the tax, by distraining a trifling article equivalent to its amount. This female was carried to the Mufti, who advised that she should be taken to the magistrate. He refused to interfere, directing that a complaint should be formally lodged in the courts if any wrong had been done. The dissatisfied mob brought the woman back to the Mufti, who exclaimed, "If such is the magistrate's justice, no person's life or honour is safe in the town, and it is high time for me to leave it." He then quitted his house, with the avowed intention of making a complaint to the judge of circuit, who was in the neighbourhood, but, unfortunately, he encountered the magistrate, accompanied by a few troops, on the road. The Mufti believed that the magistrate was coming to arrest him; an affray ensued, in which several lives were lost.

The mob, which from the first had shewn no disposition to resist authority, soon dispersed, but the Mufti, who had been slightly wounded, and who was still persuaded that it was intended to make him prisoner, took refuge in a mosque at the outskirts of the town, and caused the green flag of Mohammed to be displayed from its minaret, as a signal that he required his friends and adherents to assemble for his protection.

On the morning of the 18th of April, 1816, Captain Boscawen, with two companies of Sepoys and two guns, took post close to the mosque, a circumstance which confirmed the general belief that it was intended to arrest the Mufti; who, in addition to that veneration in which, from his age and the sanctity of his character and office, he was before held, was now viewed as a popular victim, in whose defence it was the duty of all ranks and classes to unite. Negociations were begun with the multitude, but their irritation and fanaticism were encreased by the arrival of aid from different towns in the vicinity, until the crowds were no longer under the control of those who had first called them into action. A desperate attack was made upon Captain Boscawen's detachment, but after a fierce struggle, which lasted several hours, the infuriated insurgents were repulsed, with the loss of two thousand in killed and wounded.

When the insurrection was quelled, and the excitement so far abated as to allow of an investigation in legal form, a number of persons supposed to have been most active were taken up, and brought to trial before the criminal court. It is a significant and remarkable fact, that they were all acquitted from want of evidence, except one ignorant youth, who was pardoned. A general amnesty was extended to all the inhabitants, with the exception of some of the principal instigators, who, however, provided for their safety by an early flight.

At the close of the administration of the Marquis of Hastings, the situation of the British power was very different from what it had been when that nobleman first assumed the reins of government. The Company's territories were greatly enlarged, and their revenues increased; the Pindarries were annihilated; the power of the Mahrattas, the most formidable enemies of the

British, was annihilated; and Scindia, the only ruler whose resources were undiminished, had shown by all his acts that he had ceased to cherish any plans of ambition. In 1823, Lord Hastings returned to England, after having filled the station of Governor-general for nine years. Differences of opinion may exist regarding some minor points of his government, but none of these points are of a character which can in any degree affect that admiration which is given to all the great measures of his political administration.

CHAPTER XVII.

STATE OF INDIA AT THE CLOSE OF THE MAHRATTA WAR.

The Marquis of Hastings, on his departure from India, left many points unsettled which required the early attention both of the government at home and of his successor in Calcutta. At the peace of 1814, the insular possessions of the Dutch in the Indian Seas, were restored by the English negociators at Vienna, with a facility, or rather a precipitancy, which prevented any stipulations being made in favour of the growing and lucrative trade which the British merchants had opened with the Spice Islands. It was, in fact, virtually recognized that the old Dutch monopoly of the spice trade, and their preponderating influence in the Indian Archipelago, should be restored and maintained, until such time as the government of the Netherlands should think fit to relax in their pretensions of their own accord. Sir Stamford Raffles, the governor of the English settlement of Bencoolen, in the island of Sumatra, soon saw the necessity of adopting some efficacious remedy, to redress the wrongs which the Dutch, from the very first moment of their restoration, began to inflict on the British trade, and he resolved to occupy some place which might in some degree compensate his countrymen for the abandonment of their former conquests. Animated by these views, he took possession of Singapore, off Point Romania, on the Malacca coast, in the direct route to China. The wisdom of his selection soon became apparent; in a very few years Singapore, from a mere cluster of huts, became one of the most thriving commercial cities in the Eastern Seas, and its prosperity still continues progressively increasing.

Though supported by the Marquis of Hastings, Sir Stamford Raffles received no encouragement from the British ministry, and there was some reason to fear that the representations of the Dutch would lead to the frustration of his prudent measures. Fortunately, Mr. George Canning, who was then President of the Board of Control, suggested the nomination of a select committee, with whom he could hold confidential communications, to enable him to meet the Commissioners of the Netherlands. The more the subject was investigated, the more clearly was it seen that the Dutch had completely overreached the English negociators at Vienna, and that some new arrangements were necessary to preserve the British trade in the Indian Archipelago, and even to secure British commerce with China. The negociations were greatly protracted, from the necessity of reference on various points to India. At length the whole terminated in the treaty of 1824, by which the Dutch settlements on the continent of India, with Malacca, and the undisputed right to Singapore, were ceded to the British government, the Dutch acquiring in exchange, Bencoolen and all the Company's rights in the island of Sumatra.

The affairs of Hyderabad exposed the Marquis of Hastings to considerable odium, and led to the refusal of the pension from the Company which his eminent services deserved. In the year 1811, Messrs. W. Palmer and Co. formed a mercantile establishment and bank at Hyderabad, for which they did not obtain the necessary allowance from the Governor-general until after a lapse of two years and four months. During this time the house had dealings with Chand-u-Lal, on behalf of the Nizam's government, to the extent of more than £700,000, with a balance in favour of the former, amounting to about £100,000. This was contrary to the act of parliament passed in 1797, which declared all pecuniary transactions with Native princes, unless sanctioned by the court of directors or the supreme council of Calcutta, to be illegal. On the commencement of the Pindarree war, the Messrs. Palmer were empowered to advance money on two separate accounts to the Nizam, for the purpose of enabling him to send his stipulated contingents to take a share in the Dekkan war. This loan was granted at a very exorbitant rate of interest, but it must be remembered that the Messrs. Palmer had themselves to borrow the greater part of the sum required, and that the raising of money in India is a far more difficult operation than in Europe. It is also necessary to take into account the state of society in Hyderabad, which is thus forcibly pourtrayed by Major Henry Bevan.

"Hyderabad is of very great extent, and very densely populated; the inhabitants are Patans, Indian Mussulmans, and Hindús, but the followers of the prophet greatly preponderate. The Mohammedans of Hyderabad are the most disorderly, turbulent, and ferocious set of ruffians within the limits of India. They are descended from the Jagatay Turks, absurdly called Moguls, who conquered northern India under Baber, and established the empire of Delhí; and they are not one whit less haughty, bigoted, and ferocious than their ancestors were in the days of Timúr. It has never been forgotten by them that they were once the lords of India, and therefore they regard us as the usurpers of their heritage, with a hatred not the less intense because they are compelled to keep it concealed. No European can venture to pass through the city unprovided with a suitable escort; were he to make the attempt he would not escape insult, and perhaps personal injury. No specimens of their abusive and insolent language to British travellers, can be given without grossly offending decency. The state of morals in Hyderabad is execrable; unnatural crime is so common that it forms a topic of ordinary conversation, and is never attempted to be denied or concealed. An officer, who resided a short time in the city, declared that, compared with Hyderabad, Sodom would be found innocent, and Gomorrah the perfection of purity. The lives and properties of the nobles, the merchants, and the bankers, would not be safe for a single day if the British forces were withdrawn. The crowds of half-starved bullies that infest its streets would plunder the place, but for the awe in which they are held by the garrison.

"The *Soucars*, or bankers at Hyderabad, are far from being so respectable a class as in other parts of India. Loans are obtained from them by mortgaging property or giving a deposit of jewels or other valuables. It is a general rule that the value of the deposit should exceed that of the loan by at least one-half. In these transactions the *Soucars*, by the exorbitant interest which they charge, and the frauds they use in depreciating the value of the deposits, far transcend the worst class of pawnbrokers in England."

We have already referred to the weakness of the Nizam's character, and to the support which his profligate *Dewan*, Chand-u-Lal, received from the English government. In fact, when the Nizam proposed, in 1811, to investigate the accounts of that minister, the resident, Mr. Russell, interfered to shelter Chand-u-Lal, and prevented any of his subordinate agents from being examined. When the debts claimed by the Messrs. Palmer, on their three accounts against the Nizam, had amounted to an immense sum, Chand-u-Lal declared that he was anxious to introduce a thorough reform into the financial affairs of the Nizam, and for this purpose he required the command of money to a considerable extent. He applied to the Messrs. Palmer for the loan of sixty lacs of rupees, on the condition that the Nizam should mortgage a portion of his revenues as a security both for the principal and the interest, and that Mr. Palmer should appoint his own collectors to receive the revenues assigned to him. This arrangement was warmly opposed in the supreme council, and was only carried by the casting vote of the Governor-general. It soon appeared that the loan was a mere fiction, and was, in fact, merely a means for capitalizing all the old demands of the house upon the Nizam. Matters remained unsettled when the Marquis of Hastings returned to Europe; but scarcely had his temporary successor, Mr. Adams, been installed in office than he condemned the whole affair as fraudulent and usurious. Furthermore, he peremptorily ordered the assigned revenues to be restored to the Nizam, without making any reservation whatever for the payment of anything beyond the principal of the loan. Palmer's house was, of course, ruined, and many meritorious officers, who had lodged their savings in their hands, were involved in their fate.

One of the most remarkable events in the brief administration of Mr. Adams, was the struggle in which he became involved with the newspapers of Calcutta. For some years previously, various efforts had been made to establish a free press in the presidencies, but the Governors-general had invariably assumed the right of censorship, and sent the authors of obnoxious articles back to Europe. The Calcutta Journal, established by Mr. Buckingham, had on more than one occasion given offence by the freedom of its strictures, until at length Mr. Adam, provoked by some very trifling observations, banished Mr. Buckingham from India. This exertion of authority provoked much discussion, and though it received the sanction of the court of directors, it was generally reprobated by the British nation.

A brief reference to the state of public affairs in England, is necessary to explain the circumstances under which the Earl of Amherst became Governor-general of India. On the accession of his Majesty George IV. the Queen's name was expunged from the Liturgy, and on her return to England a bill of pains and penalties was introduced into the House of Lords, and a long investigation into her conduct commenced. Mr. Canning took no share in this transaction, and separated himself from his colleagues by withdrawing from England. When the bill against the Queen was abandoned, Mr. Canning resigned his office as President of the Board of Control, and in March 1820, he was unanimously chosen Governor-general of India, by the court of directors. The death of the Marquis of Londonderry, however, opening a new career for his brilliant talents in Europe, he resigned his Indian appointment, and became Secretary of State for Foreign affairs. Two candidates were then offered, Earl Amherst and Lord William Bentinck. The claims of the latter arose from circumstances, which require us to go a little further back in Indian history. Lord William Bentinck had been appointed Governor of Madras in 1804, and had commenced introducing a variety of economic and military reforms, which were very acceptable to the court of directors. By some inadvertence, a regulation was introduced respecting the Sepoy uniform, which gave great offence to the prejudices of the Native soldiers, who forthwith broke out into a most dangerous mutiny, at Vellore, and massacred a European detachment. It is, however, now generally believed that the regulations respecting dress, were merely a pretext, and that the mutiny was chiefly caused by the intrigues of the family of the late king of Mysore, who were confined in Vellore. The mutiny was promptly suppressed, but the greatest alarm continued to prevail, and considerable discussion arose respecting the course of conduct which ought to be pursued towards the prisoners, whose numbers exceeded six hundred. The military officers were disposed to have them shot in detachments, as fast as they should be found guilty, in front of the several divisions of the Madras army. This wholesale butchery was reprobated by the council, but they proposed the scarcely less harsh measure, of transporting all the mutineers to some penal settlement. Lord William Bentinck zealously advocated measures of leniency, though many around declared that he was perilling the safety of the Presidency, by the dangerous example of extending mercy to mutineers. The wise and benevolent measures of Lord William Bentinck were, however, adopted to some extent; but before their efficacy was decisively established, a strange event caused him to be recalled from his government.

The commanding officer at Palamcottah, seized by some inexplicable panic, adopted the resolution of disarming his whole corps, separating the Mussulmans from the Hindús, putting arms into the hands of the latter, and expelling the former from the fort. He then sent expresses to the commanding officer at Travancore and to General Maitland, governor of Ceylon, requesting European aid with all possible promptitude, as he had detected a desperate conspiracy, which had taken deep root along the coast. General Maitland promptly dispatched the required aid, and also sent an account of the affair direct to England, without making any communication to the government of Madras. When the reports of the Palamcottah affair came to be invested, the alleged plot proved to be a mere phantom of the imagination. The arms were restored to the Mohammedan troops, who returned to their duties, without showing the least symptom of disaffection. The panic wore away; the Sepoys forgot their fears of an attack upon their religion; and the European officers were no longer in apprehension for the safety of their lives, and ventured to sleep without pistols under their pillows. At this critical moment, Lord Minto, as has been already mentioned, reached Madras on his way to Bengal as Governor-general. His lordship gave his sanction to the lenient course of policy, and agreed with Lord William Bentinck, setting the prisoners gradually at liberty.

General Maitland's despatch arrived in England, a little after the directors had received accounts of the mutiny at Vellore, with more than a usual proportion of misrepresentations and exaggerations. The testimony of the Governor of Ceylon seemed decisive, and a vote was passed for the recall of Lord William Bentinck, under circumstances of haste and precipitancy which implied the harshest censure on his character. It had been usual to allow the superseded governor the nominal possession of his office until the arrival of his successor, or until he could meet an opportunity of returning to England; his lordship's functions, however, ceased immediately on the arrival of the orders; no measures had been taken to enable his lordship to return home, and but for the voluntary kindness of Sir Edward Pellew, he would have been obliged to remain, stripped of authority, till the departure of the homeward-bound fleet; circumstances which produced an impression unfavourable to his lordship's character, both on the public mind at home, and in that of the community over which he had presided as governor.

In the interval between 1807 and 1822, Lord William Bentinck had acquired a well-earned reputation by various military and diplomatic services in various parts of Europe; and the court of directors had learned to appreciate his policy in Madras, and to lament their own precipitancy. He felt that he had strong claims on the consideration of the East India Company: he had rendered them good and faithful service, and had been unceremoniously dismissed from office, when in the act of following out principles admitted to have been sound and judicious. The claims of Earl Amherst were, however, supported by ministerial influence, and on him the appointment was finally conferred.

The war with Ava, like that of Mysore in 1799, and with Nepaul in 1814, was devolved upon the Governor-general as a legacy from his predecessor. Hostilities had commenced and outrages been perpetrated for a series of years before war was actually commenced. Indeed, it will be necessary for us to go back in the history in order to explain distinctly the causes of the Burmese war, the first which the Company waged beyond the limits of India.

The power of the Burmese over the countries to the east of the Bay of Bengal, took its rise nearly at the same time that the English began to acquire supremacy in India, and the progress of both was equally rapid. Conquests on each side brought the two powers into nearer contact, until, at length, the acquisition of Arracan, Assam, and Cachar, placed the Burmese as our neighbours on our north-eastern frontier. The consequence was, that instead of having to deal in this quarter with petty Rájás, who had neither the power nor the inclination to make encroachments, we were brought into a collision with a race flushed by recent conquest, too ignorant of British power, and too vain of their own, to give much importance to the preservation of friendly relations.

During the administration of Lord Teignmouth, a Burmese general advanced into the province of Chittagong in pursuit of three criminals. Some forces were sent to repel this violation of territory; but the Burmese general prevented hostilities by waiting upon the English officer who commanded, and explaining all the circumstances of the case, exhibiting his instructions and pleading his motives. On his retiring, the criminals were surrendered to the Burmese authorities; two of them were put to death by the most cruel tortures, but the third again effected his escape into the British territories.

The Mughs, an agricultural race settled in Arracan, were subjected to the most cruel oppression and tyranny by their Burmese masters. Some of their brethren had been long settled in Chittagong, and had learned to appreciate the superior mildness and equity of the British rule; they invited the sufferers of Arracan to join them, and during the years 1797 and 1798, thousands of the Mughs emigrated to the British territories. Their numbers created some alarm, the offence which our harbouring the fugitives would give to the Burmese authorities was foreseen, and orders were sent to prevent any more from crossing the frontiers. It was impossible that these orders could be obeyed; the emigrants were resolved to die rather than return. On one occasion, when the British authorities required a body of Mughs to go back to their homes, the leader boldly replied, "We will never return to the Arracan country: if you choose to slaughter us here, we are ready to die; if by force you drive us away, we will go and dwell in the jungles of the great mountains which afford shelter to wild beasts."

About the close of the year 1798, not fewer than ten thousand of the Mughs rushed to the frontier, in a state of the utmost agony and distress. This body was followed by another still more numerous. It is, indeed, believed that two-thirds of the Mughs of Arracan forsook the province, the capital of which was at this period nearly depopulated. The fugitives are described, by an eye-witness, as "flying through wilds and deserts without any preconcerted plan, numbers perishing from want, famine and fatigue. The road to the Naaf river (which forms the boundary between the Burmese province of Arracan and the British district of Chittagong) was strewed with the bodies of the aged decrepit, and of mothers with infants at their breasts." Policy became enlisted on the side of humanity, in dictating that, at least, a temporary asylum should be granted to such numbers of despairing fugitives: it would have been hazardous to try coercive measures, and these, if successful, would have consigned thousands of unoffending individuals to the cruel vengeance of a barbarous government. When the question came under the consideration of the government of Calcutta, it was resolved to assign to the refugees grants of waste lands, of which there were vast tracts in Chittagong. In the mean while, however, hundreds were perishing daily, as they were constrained to feed upon leaves and reptiles. The case was urgent, and the government came to the generous determination of relieving their immediate wants, by providing them with food, and with materials for constructing huts to shelter them from the approaching rains.

Captain Hiram Cox, an officer who had been previously employed on a mission to the court of Ava, and who was well acquainted with the Burmese language and customs, undertook the onerous duty of carrying these arrangements into effect. His character and experience pointed him out as the most eligible person, and his success fully equalled the expectations of those by whom he was appointed.

When the last emigration of the Mughs from Arracan took place, there were no more than three hundred Burmese troops in the metropolis of that province; and these were too much intimidated by the extent of the disaffection, to attempt opposition to the movement or pursuit of the fugitives, most of whom were thus enabled to cross the Naaf without molestation. Their oppressors, however, were not disposed to lose their victims so easily; they made vigorous exertions, and, collecting an army of about four thousand men, followed the emigrants into Chittagong, and fortified themselves in the dense woods of that province, by stockading their position: they maintained themselves several weeks in this entrenched camp, carrying on a petty warfare with the British troops. The commander of these invaders addressed a letter to Mr. Stonehouse, the civil magistrate of Chittagong, in which he observed, "If you, regarding former amity, will deliver us up all the refugees, friendship and concord will continue to exist. But, if you persist in keeping in your country the slaves of our king, the broad path of friendship and intercourse between the states must be blocked up. Our disagreement is only about these refugees: we wrote to you to deliver them, and you have been offended thereat. We again write to you, who are in the province of Chittagong on the part of the king of the Company, that we will take away the whole of the Arracanese; and further, in order to take them away, more troops are coming. If you will keep the Arracanese in your country, the cord of friendship will be broken."

To this threatening demand Mr. Stonehouse replied, that no negociations could be entertained so long as the Burmese troops remained within the British territories, and that the commander must abide by the consequences should he disregard this admonition. They continued, however, to maintain their post, where they were successful in repelling an attack made upon them by a detachment of British Sepoys, July 18th, 1799. Soon afterwards they retired within their own frontiers, and Lieutenant Hill was deputed, by the supreme government, to the Governor of Arracan, that he might endeavour to effect an amicable settlement.

Such was the state of affairs when Captain Cox reached Ramoo, on the banks of the Naaf, and entered upon the performance of his duties. He reported, that since the orders of government had arrived for the admission of the Mughs, they had necessarily, for the sake of subsistence, widely dispersed themselves; that some time would elapse before their numbers could be accurately ascertained; but that they were generally computed at from twenty-five to thirty thousand persons, of all ages and both sexes; and that, notwithstanding the relief extended to them by their countrymen, who had been long settled in Chittagong, and by the native inhabitants who had hired several of them, the mortality continued to be very great, especially among the children, of whom not less than twenty perished daily.

"I anticipate," said Captain Cox, "the sensations of the honourable board on perusing this statement, so afflicting to humanity, and dismiss all fear of being deemed improperly importunate in earnestly entreating their early decision on the means of terminating the sufferings of the emigrants. The good of the state demands the encouragement of cultivation in this fair, fertile, and hitherto neglected district. I am decidedly of opinion that the whole of the emigrants should be settled together: collected, they will materially assist and comfort each other; they may more easily be protected from the injuries to which their ignorance exposes them. Governed by their own laws and customs, they will soon be naturalized to the soil, increase rapidly in strength and numbers, and become a useful and flourishing colony, while, if dispersed, individuals, indeed, might derive temporary benefit, but the majority would probably drag out a wretched, vagabond life, and, at no distant period, become extinct.

"The situation which I should recommend for their settlement is the district between the Mars Callis or Ramoo river, and the Naaf. My reasons for this choice are as follows:—

"1st.—The emigrants themselves prefer it.

"2nd.—The lands are almost entirely unoccupied, and nearly free of legal claims, so that their settlement on them will be less difficult or expensive.

"3rd.—They are, for most the part, under forest, and being so remote a frontier, hitherto subject to incursions of an active and audacious enemy, no other description of persons would choose to undertake the arduous task of clearing them.

"4th.—The former refugees, being already settled on the borders of this district, will render material assistance to this infant colony.

"5th.—The vicinity of the sea, and three navigable rivers, will prove an abundant resource in the article of provisions, as the natives of Arracan are very expert fishermen.

"6th.—The great and, indeed, the only objection that I know of to the settling of the emigrants in this district is, that it will be an eternal cause of jealousy to their former masters, and that their predatroy incursions into Arracan may provoke an inextinguishable rupture with the Burmah government.

"In respect to the first branch of this objection, I have to reply that the rupture was not of our seeking, and humanity has already decided the choice of our alternative. In respect to the second, assuredly every irregularity may be prevented by the establishment of a proper post on the Naaf, and the vigilant administration of the person who may be appointed to govern this district."

On the 18th of April, 1799, Captain Cox reported to the

Governor-general that he had registered thirteen thousand of the emigrants, and that he had every reason to believe that there were between forty and fifty thousand in the province, who would come forward as soon as he had ground enough for their subsistence, and he reported, before he left Chittagong, in the middle of the year, that he had settled ten thousand four hundred and sixty Mughs in the district which he had recommended. Their principal settlement was named after him, Cox's Bazaar.

Soon after the return of Captain Hill from his mission to Arracan, the Burmese monarch sent an envoy to Calcutta, who was received in a very friendly manner by the Marquis of Wellesley, who was then the Governor-general. The ambassador made very strong remonstrances respecting the encouragement which had been given to the emigrants. The Marquis of Wellesley replied, that the British government was willing to surrender any of the Mughs who could be found to have been guilty of crimes which might render them unworthy of protection, and make it the common interest of nations to bring them to punishment, and that all emigrants, without distinction, who might be so disposed, should be at perfect liberty to return to their native country. A proclamation was issued at the same time, declaring that any subjects of the Burmese king, who might thereafter emigrate, should not be received within the British territories.

Towards the close of the year 1800, the governor of Arracan peremptorily demanded the unconditional surrender of the Mughs, and addressed a letter to the magistrate of Chittagong, conveying threats of invasion if there were not an immediate compliance with the terms of the requisition. The Governor-general, in remarking on this communication, states, that he would have considered himself justified in resorting to arms for the purpose of obtaining reparation for this insult, if he had not believed that the governor of Arracan had acted without the authority of his court. To ascertain this point, and to improve our commercial and political relations with the Burmese government, Lieutenant-colonel Symes was sent as ambassador to Ava in 1802, and, in the meantime, a respectable detachment, under Lieutenant-colonel Fenwick, was posted on the frontier of Chittagong.

It is stated in a despatch reporting the result of this mission, that Colonel Symes received general assurances of the friendly disposition of the Burmese court, which he impressed with full confidence in the good faith and amicable views of the British government. Several years elapsed, during which the question of the emigrants appears to have lain dormant; but when Captain Canning was at the Burmese court in 1809, he ascertained that the king had long entertained the design of conquering the provinces of Chittagong and Dacca.

During the course of the year 1811, the British government began to experience the evil consequences of establishing the Mugh refugees in a situation which might be said to have afforded them a constant view of their native country, and which was too well calculated to keep alive the memory of their wrongs, and to inspire them with a restless desire to recover their ancient rights and former homes. Some bold adventurers belonging to the colony of Mughs, which had settled in Chittagong, formed themselves into a band under the command of a chieftain named Kingberring, and commenced predatory attacks on the exposed country of Arracan. The Burmese troops entrusted with the defence of that province, retaliated by incursions into the Company's territory; these acts of hostility were resented, and much complaint and recrimination took place between the officers on the British and Burmese frontiers.

In 1813, a mission from the Burmese Viceroy of Pegu reached Calcutta. The deputies were preceded by a person charged with a commission from the Burmese sovereign, professedly to purchase some of the sacred books of the Hindús at Benares. Although there was reason to suspect that this person had other designs, he was permitted to proceed; but, instead of purchasing books, he spent his time in intrigues of a character hostile to the British government. Another officer of the Burmese government solicited permission to visit Delhí, on the same pretext of collecting manuscripts; but, as it was discovered that his real object was the forming a confederacy among the Native powers for the expulsion of the English from India, the supreme government refused him permission to travel through the British provinces, and apprised the viceroy of Arracan that, on his furnishing a statement of the sacred writings and other articles required, they would be procured and transmitted to him, without his having the trouble of deputing agents. As this offer was not accepted, the insincerity of the pretext was at once rendered apparent.

It appears from the despatches sent home from the government of Calcutta to the court of directors in England, that the attention of the supreme council during the year 1813, was frequently engaged by the rumours of active and extensive preparations being made by the Burmese government for the invasion of the British territories. It was stated that the King of Ava had been ascertained to cherish plans for the conquest of the provinces of Chittagong and Dacca; and that he suspected the British government of encouraging the repeated incursions of the fugitive Mughs. On the other hand, there was reason to suspect that Kingberring and his followers persevered in their predatory enterprizes, notwithstanding many severe defeats and failures, in the hope of precipitating a rupture between the British government and the court of Ava. They believed, and subsequent events showed the accuracy of their calculations, that the intolerable conceit of the Burmese would lead them to provoke a war, by committing acts which must of necessity be resented; and they entertained no doubt that in such a contest the British would be victorious. As a final consequence of the war, they anticipated the conquest of Arracan, and their restoration to their homes under a government of their own.

The death of Kingberring in 1815, and the efforts made to preserve the peace of the frontier, seemed to have averted the threatened war; it was therefore not without astonishment that a letter was received in April, 1816, from the Rájá of Ramere, Governor of the Burmese frontier provinces, written in a style of more than ordinary bombast, and containing a demand for the surrender of all the Mugh emigrants, with a very plain menace that a refusal to comply with this demand must produce immediate hostilities.

"The English government," says this singular document, "does not try to preserve friendship. You seek for a state of affairs like fire and gunpowder. The Mughs of Arracan are the slaves of the King of Ava. The English government has assisted the Mughs of our four provinces, and has given them a residence. There will be a quarrel between us and you, like fire. Formerly the government of Arracan demanded the Mughs from the British government, which promised to restore them, but at length did not do so. Again the Mughs escaped from your hands, came and despoiled the four provinces, and went and received protection in your country. If at this time you do not restore them according to my demand, or make delays in doing so, the friendship now subsisting between us will be broken."

This letter was brought to Mr. Pechell, the magistrate at Chittagong, by the son of the Rájá of Ramere, who declared that the contents of the letter had been dictated by the king himself, and were therefore not open to discussion. On communicating with the Governor-general, Mr. Pechell was directed to answer the Rájá of Ramere in a firm and conciliatory manner, and at the same time a letter was sent to the viceroy at Pegu, stating the reasons which induced the government to refuse the surrender of the Mughs.

In this letter the Governor-general stated "that the British government could not, without a violation of the principles of justice on which it invariably acts, deliver up a body of people who had sought its protection, and some of whom had resided within its territories for thirty years; but that no restraint was imposed on the voluntary return of the people to their native country, although no authority would be exercised for the purpose of effecting their removal from the British territories: more especially, when there appeared to be less cause than ever for such a measure, the exertions of the British government having restored tranquillity: the death or captivity of Kingberring and his principal associates, and the return of the Mughs in general to industrial pursuits, having rendered the renewal of disturbances a matter of great improbability." The viceroy was assured that the vigilance of the British officers would be continued, and that any persons who might engage in criminal enterprizes would be punished with the utmost severity. After the full explanation which had been made of the principles, views, and resolutions of the British government, the Governor-general expressed himself persuaded "that the enlightened mind of his Burmese majesty, would perceive the inutility of agitating a question, the further discussion of which could lead to no result advantageous to either state."

In 1817, the chief magistrate of Chittagong issued a proclamation, threatening the emigrants, that if their incursions into the Burmese territories were renewed, the perpetrators should be delivered over to the authorities of Arracan, to be dealt with as they thought fit. Soon after the issuing of this proclamation,

Charipo, one of the most daring leaders of the Mughs, committed a desperate robbery beyond the frontiers; he was seized, with a number of his followers, and Mr. Pechell recommended that this incorrigible offender, with the most guilty of his associates, should be instantly delivered over to the Burmese government, as the only measure which would deter others from such guilty proceedings. The Marquis of Hastings was at this period absent from Calcutta, but the matter was taken into consideration by the vice-president and council. After an attentive consideration of the course recommended by Mr. Pechell, they rejected it as equally cruel and impolitic, admitting, however, the force of his reasoning, and stating their conviction that such an example would produce a salutary and permanent impression. Their reasons for dissenting from his recommendations, were thus stated in a letter from the chief secretary of the supreme government to Mr. Pechell; "that when the vice-president in council contemplated the barbarous punishments, which the Burmese might be expected to inflict on the wretches delivered up to their vengeance, he felt that it would be repugnant to the merciful character of the British nation, to expose so many persons to the vindictive resentment of their enemies, exasperated, as they justly were, by repeated aggressions. In resolving to abstain from delivering up the prisoners, the vice-president in council was influenced by the consideration that it would probably constitute an encouragement to a repetition of demands, on the part of the Burmese authorities, for the surrender of fugitives, and form a precedent which on such occasions would create a considerable degree of embarrassment."

A judge of circuit was appointed to assist Mr. Pechell, in the trial of the offenders, but from the difficulty of obtaining the kind of evidence required by the Mohammedan law, Charipo and his party escaped conviction, though their guilt was their boast, and notorious to the whole country. Such a result naturally gave great dissatisfaction to the Burmese, and their determination to retaliate on the British provinces was loudly and frequently expressed.

In 1818 the son of the Rájá of Ramere arrived on a second mission at Chittagong; from whence, he informed Mr. Pechell, that he desired to proceed to Calcutta, in order that he might deliver to the Governor-general, a letter, which he declared that his father had written under the direct orders of the young King of Ava. An authenticated copy of this letter was communicated by the young Rájá to Mr. Pechell. The following is a summary of its contents: "The countries of Chittagong and Dacca, Moorshedabad and Cassimbazar, do not belong to India. Those countries are ours. The British government is faithless; this was not formerly the case. It is not your right to receive the revenues of these countries; it is proper that you should pay the revenues of these countries to us; if you do not pay it, we will destroy your country."

There can be no doubt that the Rájá of Ramere, from the very beginning of the Nepaulese war, had urged his sovereign to declare war against the British government, influenced probably by a knowledge of the various intrigues and machinations against the Company's power, which were rife through the interior of India. It is probable that the Burmese monarch believed that the moment was favourable to his views, and that he had opened some secret negociations with the Mahrattas. Before, however, the mission could reach its destination, the British arms had gained a decisive triumph over the Mahratta powers, and the Burmese troops had sustained a reverse in a contest with the Siamese. Under these circumstances, the Marquis of Hastings resolved to treat the obnoxious communication as a forgery, or, at least, as an unauthorized proceeding on the part of the Rájá of Ramere. This course was probably not disagreeable to the Burmese monarch, when he found that the grounds on which he based his confidence had slipped from under his feet. "By this procedure," said his lordship, "I evaded the necessity of noticing an insolent step, foreseeing that his Burmese majesty would be thoroughly glad of the excuse to remain quiet, when he learned that his secret allies had been subdued."

The history of the Mugh emigration and its consequences, is not only in itself an interesting episode in the annals of British India, but also a necessary preliminary to an account of the Burmese war—the first, as we have already said, waged by the Company beyond the proper limits of India. We have seen that the dreadful cruelties which were inflicted by the Burmese on the inhabitants of Arracan, after their conquest of that country, drove the unfortunate people to seek shelter within our territories from intolerable oppression. They came in a condition which put it out of the power of the British authorities to deny them shelter; and local circumstances recommended that they should be located in a position favourable for their future subsistence. Unfortunately, the spot selected was one well calculated to exasperate and keep alive the angry passions of exiles; the objections to such a location were, as we have seen, very strongly stated; but the agent employed conceived that they might be obviated, and his opinions were adopted by government.

From the day that the Mugh emigrants were permitted to colonize so near the frontier, the natural passions and patriotic resentment of this tribe, the feelings of British humanity, and the principles of internal government established throughout the Company's dominions, came into violent collision with the arrogant pretensions, the offended pride, and the indignant jealousy of the Burmese government, which a long series of successes had rendered one of the haughtiest in Asia. When, in comparatively recent times, the exertions of the Lords Wardens of the English and Scottish Marches, even though they acted in concert, were insufficient to preserve peace on the borders, it could not be expected that the magistrate of Chittagong, who could obtain no co-operation from the impracticable Burmese authorities, should have been able to prevent the aggressions and retaliations which it was easy to foresee must soon terminate in war.

The Burmese would never have consented to the establishment of a joint court, for the trial of what our ancestors used to call "March-treason," or marauding crimes on the borders, and if they had consented, it is not easy to see how such a court could have been constituted. British and Burmese rules of justice are too decidedly opposite to admit of their being united in one administration. We have already quoted from the letter of the supreme council to Mr. Pechell, the strong objections which existed against surrendering real or suspected offenders for trial to the Burmese authorities. A similar view of the question had been taken by the authorities in England. So early as the 6th of January, 1815, the court of directors, in a letter to the supreme government at Calcutta, observed, "We earnestly hope that you have not been driven to the necessity of delivering up Kingberring, because we observe that every Mugh who is suspected of being a partisan of Kingberring is put to death, and that a whole village, containing about two thousand five hundred souls, was massacred on this account, when neither men, women nor children were spared. If, therefore, for the sake of avoiding hostilities with the King of Ava, you should have been compelled to the adoption of this measure, we trust that Kingberring has been the single person surrendered, and that none of his infatuated followers have been included in such surrender. Should Kingberring not have been delivered over to the Burmese government when you receive this letter, we should prefer his being kept in strict confinement, agreeably to the assurance given by the Governor-general to the Viceroy of Pegu." And in another letter, dated in the May of the same year, after noticing in terms of approbation the proposal of uniting the Burmese troops with the British, in the pursuit of the marauding insurgents, the court remarked, "We are pleased to observe, that the magistrate was cautioned to avoid using language which might be interpreted by the Rájá of Arracan into a promise, on the part of our government, to deliver the chiefs of the insurgents into the hands of the Burmese authorities, in the event of their surrendering themselves to the British troops."

The reasonable grounds which the Burmese had for discontent, certainly received no aggravation during the administration of the Marquis of Hastings. No serious incursions of the Mugh emigrants into Arracan had taken place subsequent to the death of Kingberring; nevertheless, the tone of the communications and the letters of the high officers of that state, became every day more insolent, and an evident desire on the part of the British authorities to avoid a rupture, seemed only to inflame their proneness to hostilities. They had grossly miscalculated their relative strength, and had formed plans of conquest which rendered war inevitable.

We have had frequent occasion to mention Runjeet Singh, the founder of the kingdom of Lahore, who had rapidly risen into notoriety by his union of the Sikh tribes into an organized state, and his establishment of a compact monarchy in the Punjáb, long the most distressed part of Asia. As it was during the administration of the Marquis of Hastings, that this chieftain completed his task of organizing a nation and a monarchy, it will be no useless task to give here a sketch of the life of this extraordinary man, and the rise and progress of his power.

We have already mentioned the Sikhs of the Punjáb as an extraordinary sect, driven by persecution to exchange a creed of oatience and submission, for a religion of violence and the sword. When the power of the court of Delhí, so long paramount in Northern India, had fallen into hopeless decay, the landholders of the Punjáb, driven to desperation by the extortions and cruelties of their viceroys, had recourse to plunder for the support of themselves and their families, and they adopted the Sikh religion, more military than that of the Hindús, as a bond of union amongst themselves, and a means of producing popular excitement against their oppressors. The disunion between the Mussulmans, the invasions of the Afghans, and the rebellions in every part of the Delhí empire, favoured the growth of their power; and about the year 1770, not only the Punjáb, but the country east of the Sutlej, as far as the Jumna, was subjected to twelve *Misuls*, or associations of confederate Sikh chiefs, whose united forces amounted to about seventy thousand cavalry, or rather, what is called in India "irregular horse." The smallest of these *Misuls* was governed successively by the grandfather and father of Runjeet Singh, both of whom being men of valour and ability, possessed a moral power which compensated for the weakness of their military force.

Runjeet Singh was born 2nd of November, 1780, at a time when his father's influence was daily acquiring fresh strength. He was attacked by the small pox at a very early age, was badly treated by the Native physicians, and having narrowly escaped death, recovered with the loss of an eye, and with a countenance terribly disfigured. In his twelfth year he lost his father; his mother acted as regent, and preserved the minor's inheritance from the rapacity of his neighbours, but she designedly neglected the boy's education to prevent him from becoming the rival of her power. He was never taught to read or write; ample means were supplied to him for gratifying every youthful passion, and his early years were spent in the indulgence of debauchery, or in following the sports of the field. On attaining his seventeenth year, Runjeet assumed the reins of government in person, and one of his earliest acts was to sanction the assassination of his mother, whose profligacy is said to have excited such universal indignation, that her death was necessary to the stability of the throne.

Between the years 1795 and 1798, the Punjáb, as we have already mentioned, was three times invaded by Shah Zemán, king of the Afghans; the Sikh chieftains fled before him, and he entered Lahore, the capital city, without opposition. But the expense of retaining the country being greater than its advantages, and the Persians having threatened an invasion of Afghanistan, Shah Zemán returned home, leaving twelve of his guns in the bed of the Ghilem. Ere this, Runjeet had begun to carve out a kingdom for himself east of the Sutlej, but, hearing of the retreat of the invaders, he hastened to the Punjáb, which, he justly believed, would afford him more favourable opportunities for the exercise of his ambition. He recovered eight of the guns which the Afghans had abandoned, and forwarded them to Shah Zemán; the monarch was highly gratified with this mark of attention, and, in return, granted to the chieftain the investiture of the province of Lahore. The Mussulmans of the town readily yielded obedience to the mandates of the Afghan monarch; they proffered their aid to Runjeet Singh, who, by their assistance, expelled the rival Sikh chieftains from the city. His efforts were now directed to forming the Siks into a united body, ready to assert their independence, and, while under his guidance, they rapidly acquired a national organization, the Afghans were distracted by a series of sanguinary civil wars. After asserting his independence, and assuming, with the general consent of the Sikhs, a royal title, the King of Lahore resolved to seize all the Afghan provinces east of the Indus. Towards the close of 1805, their reduction was all but complete, when Runjeet was re-called to Lahore by intelligence of the approach of the Mahratta chieftain, Holkar, closely pursued by a British army under Lord Lake. Holkar hoped to secure the co-operation of the Sikhs, or, in case of failure, to continue his retreat into the Afghan dominions; but, being baffled by the steadiness of Runjeet, he yielded to the difficulties of his situation, and concluded a peace with the British. Friendly messages passed between Runjeet and Lord Lake, but no regular treaty was formed.

After a lapse of two or three years, the efforts of the King of Lahore to add to his dominions the territories of the independent Sikh chieftains between the Sutlej and the Jumna, brought him into hostile collision with the British government. Runjeet, however, was unwilling to risk a war; he agreed to limit his dominions on the east by the boundary of the Sutlej, and he ever afterwards cautiously avoided everything which could give offence to the Company or its officers. The excellent discipline of the Sepoys, who accompanied the British envoy sent to conclude this treaty, attracted the notice of the Sikh monarch; he thenceforth became anxious to have an army instructed in European tactics, and offered large rewards to the deserters that would enter his service. His success was rapid; in a few months he had formed several regular battalions, whose drill and evolutions might have satisfied any but the most rigid in military discipline. In 1810, he tried the effect of his new soldiers, in invading the province and besieging the city of Mooltan, but was forced to retire with loss, He was, however, more successful in reducing to obedience the chieftains in the hills north of the Punjáb. The civil wars of the Afghans still continued, and Runjeet took advantage of them to extend his dominions to the south and west.

In 1812, Runjeet celebrated the marriage of his son, then only ten years of age, and invited Colonel Ochterlony, the British resident at Loodiana, to witness the festivities. Though the colonel must have been viewed with some distrust, and perhaps dislike, as being the official protector of the independent Sikh tribes on the east of the Sutlej, he was treated with great courtesy, and his opinion sought respecting the discipline of the Sikh battalions, and the merit of the fortifications erected around Lahore. Soon after, a revolution in Afghanistan compelled the dethroned monarch, Shah Sújah, to seek shelter in Lahore. Runjeet made the unfortunate exile a prisoner, and compelled him to surrender all his jewels, including the celebrated *Koh-i-nur*, or "mountain of light;" Shah Sújah would, indeed, have been stripped of all his property, had he not found means to escape into the British territories, where he and his blinded brother, Shah Zemán, were long supported by pensions from the East India Company.

As we shall have occasion to refer again to this period of Afghan history, it will be sufficient to state here, that the revolution was effected chiefly by the abilities and influence of Futteh Khan, who became the vizier of the successful candidate for the throne of Afghanistan. This celebrated minister applied to Runjeet for assistance in reducing the province of Kashmír, the governors of which had pretended to embrace the cause of the exiled monarch, but were, in reality, anxious to establish their own independence. On the other hand, the agents of Shah Sújah, in the court of Lahore, made large promises to engage Runjeet in supporting that monarch's restoration. The politic rulers of the Sikhs negociated with both parties, and deceived both. While Futteh Khan was engaged in reducing the turbulent chieftains of Kashmír, Runjeet bribed the governor of Attock to yield him that important fortress, by which he at once secured his own dominions, and opened for himself a passage to the Afghan provinces west of the Indus. Futteh Khan returned hastily from the mountains, and attempted to recover a fortress which, ever since the time of Alexander the Great, has justly been regarded as the key of India, but he was defeated with loss, and forced to retire beyond the Indus.

Kashmír now became a tempting object to the Sikhs; it was invaded in the beginning of the year 1814, but the Afghans were in possession of all the mountain passes, and the army of Lahore was forced to make a very precipitate and ruinous retreat. The fatigues of this very difficult campaign, united to disease, produced by the malaria of Kashmír, and an uninterrupted course of sensual indulgence, broke down the health of the Sikh monarch, and reduced him, for a time, to a state of inactivity. But, on his recovery in 1818, his army again took the field, and he subdued the province of Moultan, which rounded and secured his southern frontier.

The close of that year was productive of events still more favourable to the growing ambition of the king of Lahore. In consequence of the murder of Futteh Khan, the able Afghan vizier, by the son of that monarch whom he had placed upon the throne, the numerous brothers of that minister dethroned Shah Mohammed, and parcelled out the kingdom into petty principalities, which they divided amongst themselves. Runjeet took advantage of their weakness and mutual jealousies; he crossed the Indus, and made himself master of Peshawar. In the following year he renewed his attack upon Kashmír, and the Afghans, no longer supported by the abilities of Futteh Khan, fled over the mountains and abandoned this beautiful valley.

During the administration of the Marquis of Hastings, the supreme authority of the Company had been established over the entire peninsula of India; but the British dominions were thus placed nearly in close contact with the frontiers of the Afghans, the Sikhs, the Chinese, and the Burmese nations, requiring great tact and delicacy of management, and which might expect, in case of a war, to be favoured by the insurrections of the discontented throughout the interior of India. On this account, and also because the empire possessed by the Company had already acquired an inconvenient size, the Marquis of Hastings earnestly deprecated any war beyond the frontiers of India, which was not absolutely necessary to the maintenance of British supremacy within the peninsula itself.

CHAPTER XVIII.

THE ADMINISTRATION OF EARL AMHERST.

Lord Amherst had been an unsuccessful ambassador to China in 1815, and, beyond what he might have learned incidentally on his voyage, knew nothing whatever of the East. He found India in a state of perfect tranquillity; the country, indeed, had recently suffered severely from the cholera, and a famine had produced much evil in the presidency of Madras, but the country generally acquiesced in the establishment of British supremacy, and the wise measures which the Marquis of Hastings had adopted for tranquillizing the conquered provinces, had produced the happiest effects. The Mahrattas were tranquil, the Pindarries had disappeared, and the services of the troops were only required occasionally to pursue some band of robbers, composed of men who found it difficult to abandon their old military and predatory habits, or to check some refractory Zemindar, who was discontented with the regularity and punctuality which had been introduced into the financial administration. This calm, however, was suddenly interrupted by the breaking out of the Burmese war, of which the causes have been explained in the preceding chapter.

Hostilities were commenced by the Burmese; their chiefs, without any previous attempt at explanation or negociation, made a night attack on the island of Shaporee, a small piece of land, or rather sand-bank, at the entrance of the Tek-Nauf or arm of the sea which divides a part of the province of Chittagong from Arracan. It had been customary to keep a small guard on this islet, for the purpose of watching the frontier and checking any predatory expedition of the Mughs, but the slightest danger from the Burmese was not anticipated by the Sepoys; they were, consequently, easily defeated, several lives were lost, and the Burmese took the formal possession of what was indisputably

British property. When an explanation of this conduct was demanded from the governor of Arracan, he vauntingly declared that it was the determination of his government to retain possession of the island, and intimated that, unless the right of the court of Ava to Shaporee was distinctly admitted, the sovereign of that country would invade the British territories. In a very short time after this attack, the commanding officer and some of the crew of the Company's cruiser, *Sophia*, were detained on shore by the Burmese, and carried into captivity; they were ultimately released, but no explanation or apology was offered for so harsh and unjustifiable a proceeding. Other hostile acts were committed at the same time by the Burmese governors, on the frontiers of Assam and Munnipore; they crossed the frontiers, drove off many elephant hunters, and plundered several villages. The local authorities, finding that all their remonstrances were disregarded, drew together some companies of infantry, and resolved to repel the invaders by force; but the Sepoys, being scattered over a wide surface, were sometimes out-numbered and severely handled by the invaders. Daily increasing in confidence, the Burmese advanced into the province of Sylhet, and took up a position within five miles of its capital, and only two hundred and twenty-six from Calcutta. Here they were attacked by Colonel Brown with a very inadequate force, when the British were repulsed with the loss of five officers and more than a hundred men. This slight success so emboldened the Burmese, that they called upon the Rájá of Jurteea to withdraw his allegiance from the Company, and acknowledge himself a subject of the King of Ava.

Great alarm was excited in Calcutta by this intelligence; the Governor-general felt that such repeated aggressions ought not to be endured; he therefore issued a manifesto, by which the Burmese were declared to be public enemies; the causes of complaint against them were stated at full length, and all British subjects, both European and Native, were prohibited from holding intercourse with them until the differences were terminated. "The deliberate silence of the court of Ava," said this document, "as well as the combination and extent of the operations undertaken by its officers, leave it no longer doubtful that the acts and declarations of the subordinate authorities, are fully sanctioned by their sovereign. The Governor-general in council, therefore, for the safety of the subjects and the security of our districts, already seriously alarmed and injured by the approach of the Burmese armies, has felt himself imperatively called on to anticipate the threatened invasion. The national honour no less obviously requires that atonement should be had for wrongs, so wantonly inflicted, and so insolently maintained; and the national interests equally demand that we should seek, by an appeal to arms, that security against future insult and aggression, which the arrogance and grasping spirit of the Burmese government have denied to friendly expostulation and remonstrance."

The most extraordinary want of information prevailed among the authorities at Calcutta regarding the Burmese nation and country. Little or nothing was known of the geographical aspect of the land, its military resources, its capability of furnishing provision, or the nature and amount of its population. It was a mere matter of conjecture whether the Burmese were good or bad soldiers; no one appeared to have the slightest acquaintance either with their tactics or their mode of warfare. In this state of things, the supreme government wavered for some time in determining whether it would be preferable to commence the war by land or by sea. It was, at one time, intended to have marched into Ava through Arracan; while a subsidiary force, acting simultaneously, was to proceed from Cachar; but, on further enquiry, it appeared probable that Arracan would be found too unhealthy for such a plan of operations, and the expedition was abandoned.

A second plan for the campaign was arranged, and somewhat hastily adopted. It was resolved that an army, composed of detachments from the Bengal and Madras presidencies, should proceed under convoy of a considerable squadron, and take possession of Rangoon, the chief sea-port of the Burmese empire, at the mouth of the Irrawaddy river. It was supposed probable that the mere seizure of this great emporium, would daunt the King of Ava, and induce him to offer terms of peace: but, in case of his refusal, it was intended to make Rangoon a depôt for ammunition and military stores; to seize the boats, which were known to be abundant; and to ascend to the capital of the empire, six hundred miles up the river; a second army being prepared to co-operate by an overland march upon Amerapoora. We shall soon see that all these expectations were destined to be disappointed.

Port Cornwallis, a convenient harbour in the Andaman Islands, was chosen as the place of general rendezvous, and thither the Bengal division was transported in the month of April. It was principally composed of royal troops, for the Bengal Sepoys have a religious aversion to the sea, which, fortunately, is not shared by the Native army of Madras. While detained in Port Cornwallis, waiting for the troops from Madras, the British officers made several attempts to open an intercouse with the few inhabitants of this sequestered island. Every effort proved ineffectual, the Andamanners were, as they still continue to be, savages in the fullest sense of the word; they shun the approach of civilized man, and if at any time they are discovered in the dense jungle which covers the entire island, and reaches to the very margin of the sea, never fail to evince the hostile feelings with which they regard a stranger's visit to their shores, by shooting flights of arrows at the boats, and flying to the interior as soon as a landing is effected. It was already suspected that the inhabitants of the opposite coast of Pegu, belonging to the same race, might be found equally reluctant to enter into friendly communications.

Early in May the Madras troops arrived in the Bay; owing to the exertions of Sir Thomas Munro, the able governor of that presidency, they were in the highest state of discipline and efficiency. The united forces were placed under the command of Sir Archibald Campbell, an officer who had served with much distinction in the Spanish campaigns, but who had little knowledge of Indian warfare, or of the peculiar habits of Sepoy soldiers. Commodore Grant commanded the naval part of the armament, which consisted of the royal ships Liffy, Larne, Sophie, and Slaney, several of the Company's cruisers, and a steam-vessel called the Diana, which was then a novelty in naval architecture.

On the 10th of May, the squadron and transports anchored within the bar of the Rangoon river; its arrival was totally unexpected by the Burmese authorities, who were thrown into alarm and consternation. Beacons were kindled at the different *Chokies*, or guard and custom-houses at the mouth of the river, which were repeated during the night by signal fires, which were seen blazing from every prominence in the surrounding country. The British officers resolved at once to push forward to Rangoon, hoping that the town would at once capitulate on terms of protection, and thus at once place at their disposal the resources of the country, in cattle, boats, drivers, and boatmen, with all of which the expedition was wholly unprovided.

Every necessary arrangement having been made with the utmost expedition, the fleet sailed up the river on the morning of the 11th, with a fair wind; that remarkably fine frigate, the Liffy, leading the way. Some harmless shots were fired from the *Chokies* or guard-houses, but these were the only impediments offered to the progress of the armaments, although, from the intricate navigation, and narrow channels through which the ships had to steer, each of them successively passed within a few feet of a thickly-wooded shore, where a few marksmen would have had perfect command of the vessels, and might have committed fearful havoc upon the crowded decks. Precisely at noon the Liffy anchored close to the principal battery at the king's wharf, in Rangoon, the other vessels and transports taking their stations successively in her rear. No interruption was offered to these arrangements, and, when they were completed, a pause of some minutes ensued, during which not a shot was fired. The Burmese seemed daunted, and the British officers hoped that the proclamations, and assurances of success which had been sent on shore the preceding day, would induce the people of the town to make an offer of capitulation. At length, the Burmese chiefs forced their followers to open a feeble fire on the shipping. The Liffy replied with a smart cannonade, which soon silenced every gun on shore; the enemy, unable to withstand her powerful broadside, fled in confusion from their works, and, the troops being landed, took possession of a deserted town.

It now appeared that, so soon as the intelligence of the appearance of the British on the coast had reached Rangoon, the governor, aware that the place could not be defended, directed the whole of the inhabitants to be assembled, and, under the officers and slaves of government, to be driven in a mass to the inmost recesses of the jungle. This system is invariably adopted by the tyrannical government of Ava; the men are in such cases regimented into divisions, and their unfortunate families are strictly guarded, in order that the women and children should be hostages for the good conduct of their fathers, brothers, and husbands, whose desertion or misconduct in the field is punished by the slaughter of their nearest relations.

The pity and regret which the invaders naturally felt for the unhappy citizens of Rangoon, expelled from their homes to endure the agonies of famine, and the barbarous cruelties of their chiefs, during the inclement rainy season which was approaching, soon gave way to anxiety for their own position; they were deserted by the people of the country, from whom alone they could expect supplies; they were unprovided with the means of moving either by land or water, and, during the coming monsoon, no prospect remained but that of a long residence in the miserable and dirty hovels of Rangoon, trusting to the transports for provisions, with such partial supplies as foraging parties might procure from time to time, by distant and fatiguing marches into the interior of the country.

Rangoon itself was no very desirable residence. "Its shape," says the author of 'Two Years in Ava,' "is oval; and round the town is a wooden stockade, formed of teak planks driven a few feet into the ground, and, in some places, twenty feet high. The tops of these are formed of beams transversely placed, and at every four feet is an embrasure at the summit of the wall, which gives it a good deal the appearance of an ancient fortification. A wet ditch protects the town on three sides, the other is on the banks of the river."

The interior of the city was scarcely more creditable to Burmese architecture, than the fortifications. "It consists of four principal streets intersecting each other at right angles, on the sides of which are ranged, with a tolerable degree of regularity, the huts of the inhabitants. These are solely built of mats and bamboos, not a nail being used in their formation; they are raised invariably two or three feet from the ground, or rather swamp, in which Rangoon is situated, thereby allowing a free passage for the water, with which the town is inundated after a shower; and at the same time affording shelter to fowls, ducks, pigs, and pariah dogs, an assemblage which, added to the inmates of the house, place it on a par with an Irish hovel. The few brick houses to be seen are the property of foreigners, who are not restricted in the choice of materials for building, whereas the

Burmese are, on the supposition that, were they to build brick houses, they might become points of resistance against the government.

"But even these buildings are erected so very badly, that they have more the appearance of prisons than habitations. Strong iron bars usurp the place of windows, and the only communication between the upper and lower stories is by means of wooden steps placed outside. Only two wooden houses existed much superior to the rest, and these were the palace of the Maywoon, and the Rondaye, or hall of justice. The former of these, an old dilapidated building, would have been discreditable as a barn, in England, and the latter was as bad."

There were no stores in Rangoon, and nothing was found in the neighbourhood beyond some *paddy*, or rice in the husk; the careful policy of the Burmese authorities, had removed far beyond reach everything that was likely to be useful to an invading army; and through the entire history of the war, we shall have occasion to remark with how much vigilance they followed up the only system which could have rendered the situation and prospects of the invaders seriously embarassing, or have afforded to themselves any reasonable hope of ultimate success. Great anxiety was felt, for the fate of the few British merchants and American missionaries who were known to be residing in Rangoon; they had disappeared from Rangoon, and it appeared but too probable that they had been sacrificed by the barbarians. On enquiries being made, it was found that when the first alarm of the approaching armament had been given, all the foreigners in Rangoon were seized, chained, and confined in the king's *Godown*, or custom-house. They were repeatedly brought up for examination to the hall of justice, where they were rigidly interrogated by the governor and his assistants. But, as they were utterly ignorant of the intention of the British government to send any expedition from India, they were incapable of giving any information on the subject. Their silence was attributed to treachery by the governor and his colleagues; the prisoners were accused not only of having been aware of the invasion, but also of having concerted measures for the attack of Rangoon with the British officers. They vainly pleaded their innocence, representing the improbability of their remaining in the country if they had known that war was at hand, and that the very town in which they resided would be the first object of attack. These excuses were disregarded; the Burmese chiefs declared that the captives should be put to death, and they were sent back to the custom-house to undergo their sentence. The guards who surrounded them in their prison, took a savage pleasure in parading and sharpening their instruments of execution before their eyes, in strewing the sand, and in making the necessary preparations for the work of death. The prisoners remained for many hours in this terrible state of suspense; at length the fire of the Liffy brought matters to a crisis; a thirty-two pound shot struck the *Godown*, where the authorities were assembled, and speedily broke up their meeting. The chiefs lost no time in leaving the city, and marched with their prisoners some miles into the country. The advance of some British troops, sent to reconnoitre, so alarmed the Burmese escort, that they left their prisoners behind them in a house, where they were found and liberated by the British patrols.

Sir Archibald Campbell's first operation, was to take possession of the Shoedagon, or Golden-Dagon Pagoda, about two miles and a-half from Rangoon; a magnificent structure, which is thus graphically described by the intelligent author from whom we have already quoted. "The approach to it, on the southern face, is through a fine row of mango, cocoa-nut, and other beautiful trees, leading from the town, and shading a capital road, at each side of which are monasteries or kioms, of great antiquity, and carved all over with curious images and ornaments, whilst here and there the attention is attracted by huge images of griffins and other hideous monsters, guarding the entrance to different pagodas. At the end of this road rises abruptly the eminence on which the Golden Dagon stands. It is encircled by two brick terraces, one above the other, and on the summit rises the splendid pagoda, covered with gilding, and dazzling the eyes by the reflection of the rays of the sun. The ascent to the upper terrace is by a flight of stone steps protected from the weather by an ornamental roof. The sides are defended by a balustrade representing a huge crocodile, the jaws of which are supported by two colossal figures of a male and a female Palloo, or evil genius, who with clubs in their hands, are emblematically supposed to be guarding the entrance of the temple.

"After ascending the steps, which are very dark, you suddenly pass through a small gate, and emerge into the upper terrace, where the great pagoda, at about fifty yards distance, rears its lofty head in perfect splendour. This immense octagonal gilt-based monument is surrounded by a vast number of smaller pagodas, griffins, sphinxes, and images of the Burmese deities. The height of the Tee, three hundred and thirty-six feet from the terrace, and the elegance with which this enormous mass is built, combine to render it one of the grandest and most curious sights a stranger can notice. From the base it assumes the form of a ball or dome, and then gracefully tapers to a point of considerable height, the summit of which is surmounted by a Tee, or umbrella of open iron work, from whence are suspended a number of small bells, which are set in motion by the slightest breeze, and produce a confused, though not unpleasant sound."

For some days after the disembarkation of the troops, it was hoped that the British proclamations of protection would induce the inhabitants to return to their homes, and afford some prospect of local supplies, during the period that the invaders were obviously doomed to remain stationary; but the removal of the people from their houses, was only the preliminary to a concerted plan, of laying waste the country in front of the British army, in the hope that famine would drive it from the shores. To this system the Burmese authorities adhered long and steadily, with a skill and unrelenting indifference to the sufferings of the poor inhabitants, which too clearly marked to what extremes a barbarous government and its chiefs, would have recourse in defence of their country.

The policy of the Burmese was to blockade the invaders, but avoid the hazards of a pitched battle; their troops, levied from all parts of the kingdom, formed a cordon around the British cantonments, capable, indeed, of being forced in any direction, but admirably calculated to harass and wear out the patience of regular troops, whether Indian or European. "Hid from our view," says Colonel Snodgrass, "on every side, in the darkness of a deep, and, to regular bodies, impenetrable forest, far beyond which the inhabitants and all the cattle of the Rangoon district had been driven, the Burmese chiefs carried on their operations and matured their future schemes, with vigilance, secresy, and activity. Neither rumour nor intelligence of what was passing within his posts, ever reached us. Beyond the invisible lines which circumscribed our position all was mystery, or vague conjecture."

These circumstances baffled all the previous calculations of the English commander; he had been led to hope that the mere occupation of Rangoon, would induce the court of Ava to accede to the very moderate demands of the Governor-general. If the Burmese persevered, he had been taught to hope that the people of Pegu, living under the tyrannical sway of a government with which they had for centuries waged a war, not always unsuccessful, would embrace the opportunity of asserting their independence, and humbling the tyrant under whose arbitrary rule they had so long suffered every species of degradation. It was forgotten that the crushing despotism of the court of Ava, had taught the Peguers to look upon their masters as irresistible, and that a small European force could inspire little confidence into men, who had witnessed the unchecked conquests of the Burmese for nearly half a century. The hope of finding Native boats, to carry the invaders six hundred miles up the river, to assail a metropolis which no subject of Ava ever mentions or hears mentioned without awe and reverence, ought never to have been entertained. From the particular constitution of Burmese society, the boatmen of the Irrawaddy are more closely attached to the crown, and more immediately dependent on royal authority, than any other class of the community. "Every town on the river," says Captain Cox's journal, "according to its size, is obliged to furnish a gilt or common war-boat, and to man and keep it in constant readiness; of these his majesty can muster from two to three hundred; they carry from forty to fifty men each, and are, I think, the most respectable part of his force. As they live chiefly by rapine, and are in a state of constant hostility with the rest of the people, they are audacious, and prompt to execute any orders, however violent and cruel." On this occasion, the boatmen proved their devotion to their king, by removing every boat that was likely to be useful to the invading force. Such was the unpleasant and hazardous condition of the British at the commencement of the rainy season, the longest, perhaps, that is experienced in any part of India, and during which no troops could keep the field for twenty-four hours together.

"To form a correct idea," says Colonel Snodgrass, "of the difficulties which opposed the progress of the invading army, even had it been provided with land carriage, and landed at the fine season of the year, it is necessary to make some allusion to the natural obstacles which the country presented, and to the mode of warfare practised by the Burmese generally. Henzawaddy, or the province of Rangoon, is a delta formed by the mouths of the Irrawaddy, and, with the exception of some considerable plains, or rice-ground, is covered by a thick and tenacious jungle, intersected by numerous creeks and rivers, from whose wooded banks an enemy may, unseen and unexposed, render their passage difficult and destructive.

"Roads, or anything deserving that name, are wholly unknown in the lower provinces. Footpaths, indeed, lead through the woods in every direction, but requiring great toil and labour to render them applicable to military purposes; they are impassable during the rains, and are only known and frequented by the Carian tribes, who cultivate the land, are exempt from military service, and may be considered as the slaves of the soil, living in wretched hamlets by themselves, heavily taxed and oppressed by the Burmese authorities, by whom they are treated as altogether an inferior race of beings from their countrymen of Pegu. Those Carians, generally residing in the interior, at a distance from the large rivers, in their intercourse with one another, and in their continual visits to the provincial towns, travel by the footpaths of the jungle; but, except by these scattered tribes, the trade and communication between the different parts of the lower province, are almost wholly carried on by water.

"The Burmese, in their usual mode of warfare, rarely meet their enemies in the open field. Instructed and trained from their youth, in the formation and defence of stockades, in which they display great skill and judgment, their wars have been for many years a series of conquests; every late attempt of the neighbouring nations, to check their victorious career, had failed, and the Burmese government, at the time of our landing on Rangoon, had subdued and incorporated into their overgrown empire, all the petty states by which it was surrounded, and stood confessedly feared and respected even by the Chinese, as a powerful and warlike nation. When opposed to our small but disciplined body of men, it may easily be conceived with how much care and caution, the system to which their owed their fame and reputation as soldiers was pursued—constructing their defences in the most difficult and inaccessible recesses of the jungle, from which, by constant predatory inroads and nightly attacks, they vainly imagined that they would ultimately drive us from their country."

The court of Ava had expected and prepared for war, but it had never imagined that the British forces would invade their frontiers, and still less that hostile operations would commence on the distant shores of the Pegu and Tenasserim. On the contrary, they had begun to make arrangements for invading Chittagong from the frontiers of Arracan, and thus spread reports that, unless all claims to the island of Shaporee were immediately relinguished, an army of thirty thousand men, would invade Bengal and march direct on Calcutta. It was not until the English expedition had actually landed in Pegu, that the possibility of such an attempt obtained belief in the enemy's capital; but, when the intelligence arrived, no time was lost in making the most vigorous preparations for the expulsion of the invaders. Every town and village within three hundred miles of the seat of war, sent in its contingent of armed men under the local chief; the Irrawaddy was covered with fleets of warriors from the towns upon its banks, proceeding, with all possible haste, to join the general rendezvous of the grand army of Henzawaddy; and it was not doubted, that prompt destruction would overtake the intrusive strangers, who were supposed to be shut up and surrounded in a distant corner of the empire.

About the end of May, the Burmese became more daring as their troops increased in number; they gradually approached the British position, and commenced stockading themselves in the jungle, within hearing of the advanced posts. Sir Archibald Campbell gave every possible encouragement to these operations, believing that the natural and increasing annoyance of the enemy might afford him abundant opportunities of making such an impression upon their forces, as might induce the court of Ava to sue for peace. At length, the Burmese having stockaded an advanced corps within a very short distance of the piquets, the British commander resolved to lead out a reconnoitring party in person, especially as it had been reported that the governor of Shudaung was stationed there with a considerable force, both for the purpose of harassing the English outposts by desultory attacks, and also for preventing the inhabitants of Rangoon, who were said to be in the jungle in his rear, from returning to their homes and assisting the invaders.

As the troops advanced, the stockade, being incomplete, was abandoned; the enemy retired slowly before the British column, through a dense jungle, and, as the reconnoitring party wound its way through a narrow and broken track, unfinished breastworks and stockades hastily abandoned, proved that this forward movement had not been anticipated. As the soldiers emerged from the jungle into some rice fields, a violent storm of rain, such as is only witnessed in tropical climes, burst suddenly over them; but, though obliged to leave their field-pieces behind, the troops advanced to a narrow gorge of the plain, leading to some villages which the Burmese had occupied in force. On approaching the villages, it was observed that they were protected by two stockades, and the shouts of defiance issuing from these defences, shewed that they were occupied by warriors confident in themselves and in the strength of their position. The rain had so wetted the muskets, that the British troops could not return the heavy fire which was opened on them by the enemy; no time was therefore lost in closing on the hostile line; three companies rushing forward, soon forced their way into the interior, and as the Burmese would neither give nor take quarter, a fearful butchery ensued of the defenders of the stockade, driven from their ramparts into an unmanageable mass of confusion. The Burmese general made no movement to the assistance of the stockaders until the English were seen to be in possession of the works; his whole line then moved forward with horrid yells, but, daunted by the firm front of the British soldiers, they again retired, leaving the assailants to carry off their killed and wounded.

Though successful in this affair, and in previous reconnoisance up the river, where the stockaded village of Kemmadure was stormed by a small detachment, the English had learned to respect the obstinate gallantry of the Burmese, who generally allowed themselves to be cut down at their posts rather than fly. It was particularly remarked, that at Kemmadine a female warrior had exhibited extraordinary courage; she was the young wife of the governor of Rangoon, and was found expiring of an agonizing wound, the torture of which she endured with exemplary fortitude, after the close of the action. Still the British had won a victory with very disproportionate means, and had every reason to anticipate a favourable result from a general engagement.

This skirmish had the effect of impressing the Burmese with such respect for British valour, that they resolved to have recourse to their favorite system of intrigue and cunning, hoping to lull the invaders into inactivity by professions of friendship, while they completed the fortification of their entrenchment, and the equipment of their army. Sir Archibald Campbell duly appreciated the value of these professions, and did not relax in his arrangements for an attack upon Kemmendine, an important position, which the Burmese were labouring day and night to strengthen and secure. "The village of Kemmendine," says Snodgrass, "situated on the river only three miles above Rangoon, was a war-boat station, and chiefly inhabited by the king's war-boat men. The ground behind the village, elevated and commanding, is surrounded by a thick forest in its rear. The heights had been already strongly stockaded and abatised in front; the approach on the land-faces was also rendered difficult by a thick and extensive jungle, and the swampy nature of the ground towards the river, strengthened the works on that side." Arrangements were made for attacking this important post on the morning of the 9th of June, when it was announced that two men of rank, desirous of conferring with the English general, requested passports to visit Rangoon by water. Leave was granted, and two war-boats soon made their appearance, from which the deputies landed, and proceeded to the house where the British commissioners were waiting to receive them. The two chiefs assumed at their entrance all the ease and familiarity of old friends, but it soon appeared that they were either unwilling or unauthorized to enter into any discussion respecting the points at issue between the two powers; they asked that a delay of a few days might be granted, but the motives of this request were too obvious, and it was peremptorily refused.

At two o'clock on the morning of the 10th of June, the British army advanced towards Kemmendine by a road which lay parallel to the river, and at no great distance from its brink. About nine, the advancing column found its progress checked by a formidable stockade, protected on three sides by the jungle, and the visible part being fourteen feet high, protected in front by piles of branches and palisades driven diagonally into the ground. Two eighteen-pounders were brought up to breach the work, and they opened with such effect that a great gap was soon apparent in its outward defences. The troops were then ordered forward to the assault, and, in a few minutes obtained complete possession of the work; the enemy in their retreat leaving two hundred men dead on the ground. "At the rear gate of the fort," says Snodgrass, "the gilt chattah (umbrella), sword, and spear of the Burmese commander were found, the chattah much shattered by a shower of grape, and the body of the chief was found a few yards farther in the jungle. He had apparently received his death-wound where the emblems of command were dropped, and had, probably, been carried off by his attendants until their own safety rendered it expedient to leave their burden behind them. The chief was said to have been recognized as the elder deputy of the day before, whose pacific tone had so much amused us."

It was five in the evening when the British force came in front of the great Kemmendine stockade, which the enemy seemed resolved to defend with the greatest obstinacy. On reconnoitring the works, General Campbell found them much stronger than he had anticipated. It was resolved, therefore, to try the effect of a bombardment on the following morning, the troops taking up their position for the night, within a hundred yards of the enemy's stockade. The night was wet, the rain pouring down in torrents, but the English were kept too much on the alert to be conscious of all the misery of their uncomfortable situation. The author of 'Two Years in Ava' gives the following graphic description of this extraordinary bivouac:—"The shouts of the Burmese had a curious effect, much heightened by the wild scenery of the dark gloomy forest that surrounded us: first a low murmur might be heard, rising, as it were, gradually in tone, and followed by the wild and loud huzza of thousands of voices;—then again all was silence, save now and then a straggling shot or challenge from our own sentries, and soon afterwards another peal of voices would resound through the trees. This they continued all night; but, towards morning, the yells became fainter and fainter, and at daybreak they totally ceased." At dawn the mortar batteries opened, and, after a short bombardment, the columns of attack moved forward, but they only arrived in time to witness the last of the Burmese retreating with the utmost rapidity. The effect of shells in a crowded stockade was terrific to persons unused to these implements of war, and they prudently commenced the evacuation of the place soon after the batteries were opened.

The victory of Kemmendine induced the Burmese to keep at a more respectful distance from the British lines, but it produced no desire for peace in the court of Ava, nor did a single native inhabitant return in consequence to his home. The chiefs, fully confident in the ultimate success of their plans, pursued their desolating system with unrelenting rigour, and with a success which rendered the invaders wholly dependent on India for the means of prosecuting the war. Towards the end of June, the Burmese seemed to have recovered from their panic; intelligence was received that Sykia Woongee, third minister of state, had received positive orders to drive the English into the sea. About mid-day on the 1st of July, the threatened attempt was made; large bodies of the enemy appeared issuing from the jungle to the right and left of the great Dagon Pagoda, which might be considered the key of the British position. They moved towards Rangoon, in a line nearly parallel to the British front, and commenced a spirited attack on that part of the position nearest to the town. Two field-pieces, served with grape and shrapnel, soon checked their advance, while the regiment of Madras Native infantry, advancing to the charge, compelled them to seek for safety in a rapid flight. The first part of the Sykia Woongee's plan of retreat having thus failed, he did not think it expedient to persevere, but gave orders for a general retreat. When the news of his defeat reached Ava, he was recalled in disgrace, and the command of the army was conferred upon Soomba Woongee, the second minister of state.

The war now lingered for a season; the English troops suffered severely from the want of vegetables and fresh meat, multitudes sickened every day, and the mortality of the army became alarming. Though the Burmese did not prove very formidable soldiers, they were found to be the most expert thieves in existence, as the following ludicrous account of a plundering incident in the Great Pagoda, abundantly testifies:—

"The soldiers, for several nights previous, had missed some arms, although a sentry was before the door, and they generally slept with their firelocks by their sides. This evening every one was on the alert, extra sentries were posted, and every precaution taken to secure the marauders, when on a sudden, the alarm being given, the officer on duty, who was reposing in one of the little temples, ran to the door, and inquired what had occurred; but hearing that only a knapsack had been found in the grass, and that no other traces existed of the depredators, he turned round to lie down again, and, to his infinite astonishment, found that his bed had vanished! A light was in the room, and a servant sleeping near it, yet, notwithstanding, the impudent thieves had also ransacked every basket, and escaped with the contents. We afterwards learned that the robbers were Burman soldiers belonging to the camp at Kummeroot, whither they carried their spoils."

Kummeroot, where the new Burmese commander had stockaded his army, was a strong position in the most difficult part of the forest, within five miles of the great Dagon Pagoda. A commanding point on the river above Kemmendine, was also fortified in communication with the stockaded camp, by which the Burmese chief not only obstructed the navigation of the river, but obtained an excellent position for the construction of fire-rafts for his contemplated destruction of the British shipping. Sir Archibald Campbell resolved to attack both positions simultaneously, leading, personally, the column designed to assail the enemy's position on the river, while General M'Bean led the division destined to attack Kummeroot. The enemy's position above Kemmendine was found to be truly formidable; this principal stockade was erected on a bold projecting point, where the river divides into two branches; it was provided with artillery, and defended by a numerous garrison. On the opposite banks, stockades were erected, enfilading the principal work, and all mutually defending each other. A naval force was sent to clear the way, consisting of a brig and three Company's cruizers, under the command of Captain Marryat. The Burmese guns were soon silenced by the superior fire of the shipping, and a preconcerted signal having announced that the breach was practicable, the storming party pushed acros the river in boats, soon surmounted every difficulty, and carried the stockade with comparatively little loss. Great numbers of the Burmese were killed, and many more drowned while attempting to escape by the river.

Similar success crowned the operations of the land column;

on approaching Kummeroot, General M'Bean found himself surrounded with stockades of great extent and strength, occupied by vast numbers, who viewed his approach with ridicule and contempt. Unprovided with guns, he resolved to hazard an immediate assault on the principal works, which consisted of three stockades, one within the other; the last being the head-quarters of Soomba Woongee, the Burmese commander-in-chief. He was sitting down to his forenoon repast, when the approach of the British troops was first announced to him, but, confident in the imagined strength of his position, and the valour of his men, he merely directed his chiefs to proceed to their posts, and "drive the audacious strangers away." His repast, however, was soon interrupted, when the nearer approach of the rapid volleys of musketry shewed that the assailants had forced his outer line of defence. He hasted to place himself at the head of his men, whom he found crowded into the centre stockade, a confused and helpless mass, on which the unremitting fire of the British did fearful execution. At length Soomba Woongee himself fell; none of the other chiefs could restore order, and the Burmese finally fled, leaving more than eight hundred men dead on the field, while the jungle and the surrounding villages were crowded with wounded wretches, left to perish for want of proper food and care.

The capture of ten stockades, protected by thirty pieces of artillery, and garrisoned by vastly superior numbers, disheartened the Burmese, but General Campbell had no means of taking advantage of their panic, for he was unable to advance a single day's march into the country. Under these circumstances, an expedition was sent against the maritime province of Tenasserim. Its principal cities were reduced with little difficulty, and, in addition to obtaining possession of several excellent harbours, it was found that the climate of Tenasserim was so salubrious to European constitutions, that those who had been prostrated by the pestilential climate of Rangoon, rapidly recovered their health and efficiency.

Towards the end of July, the king of Ava, who seems to have been sorely perplexed to account for the continued success of a handful of British troops over his innumerable hordes, sent down two of his brothers to superintend the operations of the war, accompanied by numerous astrologers, who were to point out the moment when the aspect of the stars was most favourable to the success of their plans. A more formidable, but scarcely less ludicrous portion of the princely train, was a detachment of the king's Invulnerables. These warriors were distinguished by the short cut of their hair, and by the peculiar manner in which they were tattooed, having the figures of elephants, tigers, and a great variety of ferocious animals indelibly and even beautifully marked upon their arms and legs; they had also gold, silver, and sometimes precious stones, inserted in their arms, probably introduced under the skin at an early age.

"These men," says Snodgrass, "are considered by their countrymen as invulnerable; and, from the absurd exposure of their persons to the fire of an enemy, they are either impressed with the same opinion, or find it necessary to show a marked contempt for danger in support of their pretensions. In all the stockades and defences of the enemy, one or two of these heroes were generally found, whose duty it was to exhibit the war-dance of defiance upon the most exposed part of their defences, infusing courage and enthusiasm into the minds of their comrades, and affording much amusement to their enemies. The infatuated wretches, under the excitement of opium, too frequently continued the ludicrous exhibition, till they afforded convincing proof of their claims to the title they assume."

The Burmese princes were warned by their astrologers to wait for the first lucky moon, and, as this was not very near, Sir Archibald Campbell, who had received information of the enemy's arrangements, resolved, in the interval, to attack some strong posts on the rivers, by which fishermen and others were prevented from bringing provisions to Rangoon. Syriam, a fort originally erected by the Portuguese, had been strongly stockaded, and all its defences repaired. A party was sent in boats to attack the place, and it was found that neither the great numerical superiority of the enemy, nor their formidable preparations, could enable them to withstand British enterprize. The Burmese, after a brief resistance, were driven from the fort on the Pagoda, leaving behind them eight pieces of cannon and a considerable quantity of ammunition. From the fort the English proceeded to the Pagoda, which was still more easily captured. Among the plunder was found an edict, issued by the Prince of Sarrawaddy, which deserves to be inserted as a precious specimen of Burmese arrogance and ignorance.

It is addressed to Semeboon, *Mayoon* and *Attawoon*, that is governor and collector of the district, and is couched in the following terms:—

"In order that not one of the wild foreigners may escape from being destroyed and slain, they must be apprehended by covering the face of the earth with an innumerable host, to accomplish which effectual measures are in progress.

"Should you, from observation, judge the place and preparations going forward at Syriam to be ineligible or inadequate, you will make such alterations as you may consider necessary, that the strength and stability of the post may be fully established.

"On the people of Syriam strict authority must be enforced, for there are some among them who slight your orders. You will place guards at the entrances of all the creeks connected with the river, where they must constantly watch.

"(Signed) "SHOEMANDOGEE MANDOUN."

Among other affairs of posts, the attack of a stockade on the Dolla river deserves to be mentioned. The detachment sent on this expedition was suddenly exposed to a heavy fire of grape and musketry, from concealed enemies. Great loss was sustained before the troops could land and form; but then, though three officers and fifty men had fallen, the survivors forced their way into the redoubt, which was deserted on their entrance.

At length, information was received that the astrologers had fixed a propitious time for the attack of the British position. Sir Archibald Campbell took the necessary precaution to resist the attempt, which was made at midnight on the 30th of August. The Invulnerables rushed boldly up the road leading to the great Pagoda, shouting out threats and imprecations against the impious strangers whose presence defiled that sacred place. The English remained perfectly still, until the dense multitude had agproached the gateway; then the guns opened with heavy discharges of grape, followed by volleys of musketry, which did fearful execution in their crowded ranks. In a short time the Invulnerables lost all courage, and fled back to the jungle, leaving the plain strewed with the dead and dying. An incident in another part of the line, recorded by an eye-witness, deserves a passing notice:—"A piquet of one hundred Sepoys was likewise attacked, and, while the men were drawn up to receive the Burmahs in front, some of these latter contrived to creep to the rear, and enter the house which the piquet occupied, from whence they carried off the Sepoys' knapsacks!"

General Campbell resolved to follow up his success, by driving the Burmese from all their posts in the vicinity of Rangoon. For this purpose, Major Evans was sent with about three hundred men, to ascend the Lyne river, while Colonel Smith with the light division, consisting entirely of Sepoys, made an advance on the road to Pegu. After clearing several stockades, Colonel Smith learned that a large division of the enemy, with some cavalry, elephants and guns, had established themselves in a fortified pagoda at Kykloo; he therefore sent to General Campbell, for an European re-inforcement, which he considered necessary to infuse courage into the Sepoys. This reasonable request was refused, with something like an imputation on the motives by which it was dictated. The colonel, thus taunted, resolved to hazard an assault. All the officers displayed great courage and conduct, but it was impossible to induce the Sepoys to advance against the Burmese, whose physical strength is greater than that of any other Asiatic nation. It was at length necessary to give the signal for retreat, after a severe loss had been incurred in killed and wounded. This unhappy result, which was clearly owing to the want of a European detachment to cheer and support the Sepoys, was made the subject of injurious and unworthy comment. Although Colonel Smith completely exonerated himself in the minds of all fair and honourable men, competent to pronounce an opinion upon the subject, yet the circumstance weighed so heavily on his high-spirited and sensitive mind, that he never held his head up afterwards, but gradually sunk into an early grave, the victim of unmerited imputations.

We must now turn our attention to Arracan, where the Burmese had begun to make preparations for invading Bengal. Maha Bandoola, their leader, advanced with a strong corps to Ramoo, which surrounded and attacked a small British detachment left to defend that post. After a gallant resistance, the British were overwhelmed by numbers and almost totally destroyed. On hearing of this disaster, the commanding officer, who was marching to the relief of Ramoo, retired on Chittagong, which he supposed would be the next place attacked. The Burmese, however, made no effort to follow up their success, and before Bandoola could prepare for any fresh enterprise, he was recalled to take charge of the defence of his country.

This trifling affair excited a most extraordinary alarm throughout Bengal; the peasants on the frontiers, fled from the fields, reports were circulated that the Burmese were invincible, and the Native merchants of Calcutta, were with difficulty dissuaded from removing their families and property. It subsequently appeared probable that these alarms, and the unhappy mutiny at Barrackpore, were in some degree excited by the Peishwa and the other Mahratta chiefs at Benares, who had been left in possession of wealth and power by the unhappy policy of Sir John Malcolm.

At the end of the rainy season, the British in Rangoon, began to entertain more favourable views of their situation, than they had ventured to indulge since their first occupation of the place. A great improvement in the health of the troops was manifest at the beginning of November, and the promise of an early movement in advance, had its influence even upon the hospitals, inspiring the sick with an ardent desire to be able to join their comrades in the approaching operations. Five hundred Mugh boatmen had arrived from Chittagong, and were busily employed in preparing boats for river-service, and a re-inforcement had arrived, consisting of two British regiments, some battalions of Native infantry, a squadron of cavalry, a troop of horse artillery and a rocket-corps. Transports with draught-cattle were beginning to arrive, and the men were busily preparing for march, when their attention was directed to the near approach of Maha Bandoola and his army.

Bandoola was the best general in the Burmese service, and his army was the most formidable that the court of Ava had ever sent into the field. Notice of the enemy's approach was fortunately obtained, by an intercepted letter from the new general to the ex-governor of Martaban, in which he notified having left Prome at the head of an invincible army, with horses and elephants, and all manner of warlike stores, for the purpose of capturing, or expelling, the English from Rangoon. On the 30th of November, the Burmese army was assembled in the extensive forest in front of the Shoedagon Pagoda; their lines, extending from the river above Kemmendine in a semicircular direction, towards the village of Puzendown, could be distinctly traced by the columns of smoke rising above the forest from the watch-fires of the different bivouacs. A distant hum of voices was heard from this multitude, as if they had established themselves for the night, but darkness scarce set in when it ceased; and there was heard in its room a sound as of heavy columns marching, which drew onwards till it seemed to approach to the very edge of the jungle. The utmost degree of watchfulness, it will readily be imagined, prevailed within the Golden Pagoda, where both officers and men anticipated a furious assault as soon as the dawn should return; nor was there any disposition to relax, notwithstanding that the woods began to resound ere long, with blows of the axe and hammer, and the crash of falling trees. Yet, the day broke without realizing, in this quarter at least, the expectations which men had formed. The enemy continued perfectly still, under cover of the forest, contenting themselves, as it appeared, with watching the manœuvres of the English, and hindering them from detaching to support the point against which their first efforts were directed.

"The day had scarcely dawned on the 1st of December," says Colonel Snodgrass, "when hostilities commenced with a heavy fire of musketry at Kemmendine, the reduction of that place being a preliminary to any general attack upon our line. The firing continued long and animated; and from our commanding situation at the Great Pagoda, though nearly two miles distant from the scene of action, we could distinctly hear the yells and shouts of the infuriated assailants, occasionally returned by the hearty cheer of the British seamen, as they poured in their heavy broadsides upon the resolute and persevering masses. The thick forest which separated us from the river, prevented our seeing distinctly what was going forward; and when the firing ceased, we remained for a short time in some anxiety, though in little doubt, as to the result of the long and spirited assault. At length, however, the thick canopy of smoke, which hovered over the fierce and sanguinary conflict, gradually dissolving, we had the pleasure of seeing the masts of our vessels lying at their old station off the fort, a convincing proof that all had ended well on our side."

Six or seven different divisions of the Burmese were discovered in the course of the forenoon, marching across the plain of the Dalla river. As they advanced towards Rangoon, the appearance of the chiefs on horseback, with their gilt chattahs or umbrellas glittering in the sun, produced a most imposing effect, which would, probably, have been dissipated by a closer inspection of the disorderly mob of their followers—a crowd rather than an army. Later in the day, several very dense columns were seen issuing from the forest, about a mile in front of the east face of the great Pagoda, their lines being decorated with an extraordinary profusion of flags and banners. The several divisions took up their position on the crest of a sloping woody ridge in front of the Pagoda, resting on the river at Puzendown, which was strongly occupied by cavalry and infantry. "These," says Snodgrass, "formed the left wing of the Burmese army. The centre, or the continuation of the line from the great Pagoda up to the Kemmendine, where it again rested on the river, was posted in so thick a forest as to defy all conjecture as to its strength or situation. In the course of a few hours we thus found ourselves completely surrounded, with the narrow channel of the Rangoon river alone unoccupied in our rear, and with only the limited space within our lines which we could still call our own. The line of circumvallation taken up by the enemy obviously extended a very considerable distance, and divided as it was by the river, injudiciously weakened his means of assailing us on any particular point; but, as far as celerity, order, and regularity are concerned, the style in which the different corps took up their stations in the line, reflected much credit on the arrangement of the Burmese commander.

"When this singular and presumptuous formation was completed, the soldiers of the left columns also laying aside their spears and muskets, commenced operations with their entrenching tools, with such activity and good will, that, in the course of a couple of hours, their line had wholly disappeared, and could only be traced by a parapet of new earth, gradually increasing in height, and assuming such forms as the skill and science of the engineers suggested. The moving masses which had so very lately attracted our anxious attention, had sunk into the ground; and to any one who had not witnessed the whole scene, the existence of these subterranean legions would not have been credited:

the occasional movement of a chief, with his gilt chattah (umbrella) from place to place, superintending the progress of their labour, was the only thing that now attracted notice. By a distant observer, the hills covered with mounds of earth, would have been taken for anything rather than the approaches of an attacking enemy; but to us, who had watched the whole strange proceeding, it seemed the work of magic or enchantment."

In the afternoon, a strong English detachment under Major Sale, made a sortie in order to discover how the hostile force was arranged. As this movement was wholly unexpected by the Burmese, they were unprepared for resistance; they were taken in flank, and driven from their cover with considerable loss, and a great quantity of their arms and tools were destroyed before they could muster their forces to drive back the daring assailants. This successful enterprize obtained for the British some new information respecting the Burmese mode of warfare, and the manner in which they push forward their approaches. Their trenches were found to be a succession of holes, capable of containing two men each, and excavated so as to afford shelter, both from the weather and the fire of an enemy; even a shell lighting in the trenches, could only kill two men at the most. "As it is not the Burmese system to relieve their troops in making these approaches, each hole contained a sufficient supply of rice, water, and even fuel, for its inmates; and under the excavated bank, a bed of straw or brushwood was prepared, in which one man could sleep while his comrade watched. When one line of the trench is completed, its occupiers, taking advantage of the night, pushed forward to where the second line is to be opened, their place being immediately taken up by fresh troops from the rear, and so on progressively, the number of trenches occupied varying according to the force of the besiegers, to the plans of the general, or to the nature of the ground."

In the evening, the Burmese returned to their trenches and recommenced their labours. Soon after sunset a fierce attack was made upon the post of Kemmendine, while, on a sudden, the heaven and the whole surrounding country, became brilliantly illuminated by the flames of several tremendous fire-rafts, which had been set to float down the river for the purpose of destroying the shipping in Rangoon; and these were followed by war-boats, ready to take advantage of any confusion which might ensue should some of the vessels be fired. The skill and intrepidity of the British seamen averted the danger; entering their boats, they grappled with the fire-rafts, and ran them ashore upon the banks of the river, where they were harmlessly consumed. The attack upon Kemmendine was repulsed at the same time, with heavy loss to the assailants.

"The fire-rafts, upon examination, were found to be ingeniously contrived and formidably constructed, made wholly of bamboos firmly wrought together, between every two or three rows of which a line of earthen jars of considerable size, filled with petroleum or earth-oil, and cotton, were secured. Other inflammable ingredients were also distributed in different parts of the raft, and the almost unextinguishable fierceness of the flames proceeding from them, can scarcely be imagined. Many of them were considerably upwards of a hundred feet in length, and were divided into many pieces, attached to each other by means of long hinges, so arranged that when they caught upon the cable or bow of any ship, the force of the current would carry the ends of the raft completely round her, and envelop her in flames from her deck to her main-topmast-head, with scarcely a possibility of extricating herself from the devouring element." Kemmedine was a point from which these formidable rafts could be launched almost with a certainty of reaching the shipping in the harbour, and hence arose Maha Bandoola's great anxiety to become master of that important post.

For three or four days, Sir Archibald Campbell allowed the Burmese to push forward their approaches until they had come within half musket-shot of the British lines. So soon, however, as the enemy had brought their munitions and warlike stores from the jungle into their entrenchments, it was resolved to make a decisive attack. Two columns were mustered for this service, under the command of Majors Sale and Walker, while a flotilla of armed boats, under the direction of Captain Chads, proceeded up the Puzendown creek, and opened a heavy fire on the rear of the enemy's entrenchments. On the morning of the 5th, the columns advanced; that commanded by Major Walker at first encountered a spirited resistance, and its leader fell; but the troops pressed forward, and drove the Burmese from trench to trench at the point of the bayonet. Major Sale's column forced the centre with great ease, and the British columns uniting, drove the Burmese from every part of the works into the jungle, leaving the ground behind them covered with the dead and wounded, with all their guns, entrenching tools, and a vast quantity of small arms.

Notwithstanding his repeated failures and defeats, Bandoola shewed that he was resolved to persevere, and his troops laboured with unabated zeal in making their approaches to the Great Pagoda. On the morning of the 7th, four columns of attack emerged from the British lines, and, after sustaining a heavy fire, forced their way into the trenches; the Burmese immediately gave way, they were precipitately driven from their numerous works, curiously shaped, and strengthened by many strange contrivances, into the thick forest in their rear. On the evening of the same day, a British detachment proceeded from Rangoon to attack the enemy's position at Dalla, which had, hitherto, enabled them to keep Kemmendine in a state of siege. They succeeded with very little loss, and thus the Burmese were driven from their entire position, with the loss of all their guns and the whole materiel of their army. It was impossible to ascertain the number of the slain, as it was the practice of the enemy to remove and conceal the dead, which they could effect the more easily on account of the thick forest in their rear. Notwithstanding the exertions and threats of Bandoola, hundreds of his men deserted him after his reverses; he had also reason to fear that his tyrannical sovereign would take vengeance on him for a series of defeats, rendered more disgraceful by his former vaunts, and he resolved, if possible, to maintain his ground.

About four miles in rear of his scene of operations for the reduction of the Golden Pagoda, Bandoola had established an army of reserve, which was busied all this while in stockading and otherwise rendering defensible, a position of which the village of Kokien formed the key. To it he now retreated, where considerable reinforcements meeting him, he found that he could still muster five-and-twenty thousand men under arms, with which he determined to risk another action, should the English venture to attack. Not content, however, to rely upon the valour of his soldiers, he bribed some of the few inhabitants which had returned to Rangoon, to set fire to the city; under the idea that, amid the confusion attendant on such event, an opportunity might present itself of acting again on the offensive.

The fire, however, was speedily extinguished, and on the 15th, the army advanced for the purpose of attacking, at three different points, the intrenchments at Kokien. Never was movement attended with more perfect success. The enemy maintained a heavy fire so long as the troops were rushing on, but fled whenever the heads of the columns began to penetrate the works; and the line of entrenchments was carried with comparatively little loss to the assailants, the slaughter among the fugitives being absolutely appalling. It is computed, indeed, that, from the 1st to the 15th of December, there fell of the Burmese not less than six thousand men, of whom many were chiefs and officers of rank, while the total of the British killed and wounded, did not exceed forty officers and five hundred rank and file.

We have already mentioned the preposterous alarm which was produced in Calcutta, when intelligence was received of the slight successes obtained by the Burmese in Chittagong. Unfortunately, this panic spread farther, and a report was studiously circulated among some of the Sepoy regiments, that the Burmese were in possession of certain charms which rendered them invulnerable, and that the spell could not be dissolved by lead or steel. This strange rumour was very generally believed by the credulous Natives of Bengal, and, added to their superstitious hatred of the sea, made many of them secretly resolve not to form part of the reinforcements which were about to be sent to Rangoon. Their reluctance to embark, was greatly increased at this critical moment, by the appearance of an order for curtailing the extra allowances which had been previously made to troops about to take the field. Several minor causes of dissatisfaction existed, and the discontent of the Sepoys was secretly aggravated by the machinations of some of the Native inhabitants of Calcutta, and by religious impostors, who were believed to have been hired by some of the state prisoners at Benares. All these causes combined to produce a most formidable mutiny, of which the following summary account is given by Mr. Gleig:—"In the cantonments of Barrackpore, there were quartered the 26th, the 47th, the 62nd, and the 10th regiments of Bengal infantry. They were all under orders for service, some being directed to march upon Arracan, others to prepare for embarkation; but, when directed to parade on the morning of the 31st of October, in order that their appointments might be inspected, the 47th positively refused to turn out. Every exertion was made by the European officers to overcome the spirit of disaffection, but without effect. Portions of the 62nd and of the 10th joined the mutineers; and, for a few hours, matters wore an extremely unpleasant appearance. But the Royals, and the King's 49th, which had not yet quitted Calcutta, were promptly moved to the scene of difficulty, and a brigade of guns was planted, so as to command the rear of the malcontents when drawn up upon the esplanade. Another effort was then made to lead them into submission; they rejected it, and the guns immediately opened. Nearly two hundred men were cut to pieces where they stood; and the remainder being disarmed, the ringleaders were put to death, the No. 47 erased from the Army List, and the mutiny effectually suppressed. There was no longer the slightest reluctance manifested to proceed either to Arracan or Pegu; nor was any bad impression left upon the minds either of soldiers or people, by the act of terrible but necessary severity, which had been perpetrated."

After the defeat of Bandoola at Kokien, many of the inhabitants of Rangoon returned to their homes, and the population of the city was further increased by multitudes of deserters, who brought with them numerous articles of provision and conveyance, which proved eminently useful to the invaders. Still, there was a sad lack of means by which to move an army of ten thousand men, through a country where it was felt that no reliance could be placed on the aid of the inhabitants; and where any deficiency of provisions, or interruption of the line of communication, might be attended with the worst consequences. As it was manifest, however, that the war would be protracted for ever, unless an attempt were made to penetrate into the interior, Sir Archibald Campbell resolved to march against Prome with one column, while General Cotton proceeded in boats with another division, to the same destination. A detachment under the command of Major Sale, was, at the same time, directed to reduce the important town of Bassein. On the 11th of February, 1825, the march was commenced; no enemy appeared, but miles upon miles of stockading, proved that the Burmese had, at one time, resolved to check the progress of the invaders; while numerous tracks of elephants, and other marks of extensive bivouacs, shewed that they were not deficient in numbers to dispute a passage. The few villages of the district through which the route of the land-column lay, had been destroyed, the inhatants driven into the interior, and every vestige of their dwellings swept away. The wild-hog and tiger had alone escaped the general persecution, and now retained undisputed possession of the woods and the once fertile plains. The cultivators of the soil belong to a tribe called the Carians; one of their villages escaped the general ruin, and it offered an extraordinary spectacle to the British troops. "The houses of these strange people are of the most miserable description—mere pigeon-houses perched in the air on poles, with a notched stick as the sole means of egress and ingress to the dwelling; they are, however, well adapted for protecting their inmates from the ravages of the periodical deluge, the still more destructive inroads of prowling tigers, in which the woods abound. The Carians, although the quietest and most harmless people in the world, are, nevertheless, of the strongest and most robust frame. The cultivation of the land in Pegu and the lower provinces, is in a great measure left to them; and, although their numbers are very limited, such is the fertility of the soil, that they not only keep up the consumption of their own districts, but annually send large quantities of grain to the royal granaries, for the use of the less fertile provinces of Upper Ava. They pay heavy taxes to government, but are free from the conscription laws, and are never called upon for military service. The women generally bear the marks of premature old age, probably from a too liberal share of the hard work falling to them, which, in more civilized countries, devolves wholly upon the male inhabitants. These people appeared heartily glad to see us, and cheerfully assisted in repairing the roads; they also brought ducks, fowls, and other articles for sale, for which they found a ready and most profitable market. They willingly undertook to carry letters and communications from one corps of the army to another, and no instance occurred of their having disappointed or deceived their employers."

At Mophee was found the splendid mansion of Maha Bandoola, built for him when coming down to Rangoon in all the pomp of state; it had not been inhabited since he left it, for the Burmese laws punish with death, any person who inhabits a house of a higher order of architecture than that to which he is entitled by his rank. The town of Lain, prettily situated on the banks of the river of the same name, was found uninjured, but nearly deserted; those peasants who remained in their houses were found favourably disposed; they willingly brought buffaloes and other necessaries into the camp. On the 2nd of March, the invaders reached Sarrawah, a large and populous town on the Irrawaddy, a place of considerable trade, and the depôt for the war-boats of the Burmese monarch.

The troops appear to have been greatly struck with the magnificence of the river, which now, for the first time, rolled its mass of waters before them. Of great depth, and exceedingly rapid in its course, it is described as measuring, even during the droughts, about eight hundred yards in width; nevertheless, the admiration with which all ranks were disposed to regard it, suffered a serious interruption, when it was discovered that the population had hastened to place its channel between them and the strangers. Sarrawah, indeed, like Rangoon, when first approached, was entirely deserted. It was evident, moreover, that the migration had only now been completed, inasmuch as crowds still lingered on the opposite bank, whom all the efforts of the general, though exercised through the agency of one or two old priests, failed to bring back to their homes.

"At Sarrawah," says the author of 'Two Years in Ava,' "were many handsome kioums, or monasteries, containing large collections of Gaudinas, of different sizes and materials; these were ranged on stands, richly ornamented with stained glass and gilding fancifully disposed in several grotesque shapes, and surmounted by canopies, on which the same species of ornament bore a conspicuous part. About the apartments were numerous offerings of the pious; and in one of the houses a book was found, which may be considered as of great importance, as showing the estimation in which this nation was held by a very insignificant power in Europe, at a time when we, its immediate neighbours, must have been enveloped in shameful ignorance of everything concerning it. This was a plain and simple exposition of the Christian faith, in the Latin and Burman languages, and printed at the press of the Society for the Propagation of the True Faith at Rome, in 1785." The same authority goes on to inform us, that "on inquiry, I found that about that period some Italian priests were settled near Ava, and taught Latin to several people, and among others, to Mr. Gibson."* "For many years past, no persons of the Roman Catholic persuasion have visited Ava as missionaries; but the religion is still followed by a few individuals, and is represented by priests of that race miscalled Portuguese, who, from their intermarriage with the natives of India, now retain but little trace of their origin, except the dialect, which still remains to them, of the language of their forefathers."

The sound of cannon in the direction of Donoobew showed the falsehood of the report that this place had been evacuated by Maha Bandoola, but, as no one believed in the possibility of a repulse, Sir Archibald Campbell continued to advance for the purpose of occupying Prome and cutting off the retreat of the Burmese. He had not, however, proceeded two days journey beyond Sarawah, when he received the unwelcome intelligence that the attack on Donoobew had failed. It was, therefore, necessary to make a retrograde march, for the purpose of obtaining possession of a place so important to the success of the plan of operations which had been formed for the campaign.

Late on the evening of the 24th, the column, after an exhausting march, reached a village, from whence the position which Bandoola occupied at Donoobew became, for the first time, visible. The spectacle was very striking, for the works were extensive, and apparently full of troops; while the river was crowded above the stockade by swarms of Burmese war-boats. As the army approached, bodies of cavalry hovered along its flank, and the war-boats, starting from their anchorage, came in close to the brink of the river, and opened their fire. Nevertheless, no check was made: and, on the 25th, a position was taken up within cannon-shot of the stockades; while General Campbell, attended by his chief engineer, proceeded to reconnoitre. He found that they embraced an oblong square, which measured

* A remarkable personage, a native of Madras, the son of an English father and a low-caste mother, called Gibson, who had spent all his days in Ava, and stood high in the confidence of the government. He joined the British army at Rangoon, and astonished the heads of departments by his knowledge of general history, and his acquaintance with the English, the Portuguese, the French, and a whole host of Eastern languages; he also added a little, by means of a rude map, to the information of which Colonel Symes's work had already made them masters.

about a thousand yards in length, by five hundred in breadth; and that they masked the brick walls of an old Pegu fortress, round three sides of which a moat was drawn, the river washing the fourth. It was therefore quite impracticable to accomplish, with his limited means, even an imperfect investment; and the camp was, in consequence, pitched so as to rest one flank on the river, and leave the other to be protected, as it best might, by the piquets.

The day passed over quietly enough; for an occasional attempt to annoy by a fire from the war-boats, scarcely sufficed to disturb the tranquillity of any one. The piquets, too, were strong and well posted: and as the night brought with it a bright and cloudless moon, both men and officers lay down to rest without any apprehension of danger. Considerable uneasiness had, indeed, prevailed since morning, not because of the proximity of the enemy, but because, as yet, no intelligence of General Cotton's approach had been received, and the exhausted stock of the Commissariat threatened, in the event of his protracted absence, to occasion little short of famine in the lines. But these causes of care and care itself were alike forgotten, when the rapid discharge of thirty or forty muskets, and the immediate running in of the piquet on the right flank, suddenly called the men to their guns, and caused them to prepare for battle. In a moment there arose a discordant yell, while a crowd of Burmans rushed towards the camp, and began a desultory fire on all sides. It was a bold manœuvre on Bundoola's part, and well worthy of his established reputation; but it failed to produce any effect. The latter part of the night was very dark, and enabled the enemy to carry off their killed and wounded, which could not be few. The loss of the British was three killed, and about twenty wounded.

On the morning of the 27th, the flotilla conveying the marine column, was seen in full sail up the river. The Burmese made the most desperate efforts to resist its progress, opening a heavy fire on the vessels from their war-boats and their batteries; but thirteen of the former were soon captured by the steam-vessel, while to the latter an effective reply was made, both by the guns of the flotilla and the field-pieces on shore. In like manner a sortie, in which seven elephants took a part, was repelled with great slaughter; the body-guard charging both elephants and cavalry, and overthrowing them in quick succession. The result was, that mortars, battering guns, and all things else of which the army stood in need, were landed that night, and that a heavy bombardment was immediately commenced, with the most destructive effect. This was followed by the erection of batteries, which opened a steady fire on the 1st of April, and on the 2nd, dispositions were made, as soon as the breaches should be deemed practicable, to carry the place by assault. But the day had scarcely dawned, when a couple of prisoners, escaping from the fort, came in with intelligence which excited no trifling degree of astonishment. It appeared that Bundoola had been killed on the previous day by a fragment of a shell; that the troops refused to obey any other officer, or to remain in Donoobew, and that the works were evacuated in the dead of the night, with a degree of regularity which set the vigilance of the besiegers at defiance. Nothing, therefore, now remained but to take possession of the abandoned redoubt; and, after making such fresh arrangements as the altered condition of the army required, to recommence, with as much celerity as possible, the march to Prome.

As the troops advanced, various efforts were made by the Burmese to delay their march, by engaging the general in treacherous negociations, and, when these proved ineffectual, the Prince of Sarrawunty burned and laid waste the villages on the route, driving thousands of helpless, harmless people from their homes into the woods. Prome was abandoned as the English advanced, and cantonments were provided for the troops in its neighbourhood, as the setting in of the rainy season, early in June, put an end to the operations of the campain. Every encouragement was now held out to the terrified inhabitants, who had either fled to the jungle, or been driven away by their police to return to their homes. Their houses were left unoccupied; their little property scrupulously guarded and preserved; while proclamations, inviting them to return to their former residences, and promising protection, and liberal payment for the fruits of their industry, were distributed as much as possible throughout the country.

The happy result of these measures exceeded the most sanguine expectations. The persecuted inhabitants poured in from every quarter; some from the woods, bringing their families, cattle, waggons, and other property belonging to them; but by far the greater number returned in a most miserable and starving condition, having lost, or been plundered by their guards of all that they possessed. The tide of the population so long receding before the invaders, having once over-leaped the barriers which restrained it, now flowed back towards the deserted provinces; the Natives retiring from the vicinity and approach of their own armies, to seek for safety and protection under the British flag. Plentiful bazaars at every station, soon bore ample testimony to the confidence of the inhabitants in the justice and good faith of their invaders; the troops lived in the midst of comfort and abundance, rendered more delightful by their sufferings at Rangoon in the preceding year. To the Burmese, unused to receive anything but stripes from their rulers in payment for their labour, the liberal conduct of the British was equally novel and pleasing. They worked diligently so soon as they found that they were certain of receiving liberal payment. Large fleets of canoes, so constructed as to stem the torrents of the Irrawaddy, were soon placed at the disposal of the commissariat, and such a stock of provisions conveyed to, and kept up at Prone, as was judged adequate for the support of the British force, in advance on the Burmese capital.

Some subordinate operations from the frontiers of Bengal, against the Burmese provinces of Assam, Cachar and Arracan, are thus briefly but accurately described by Mr. Gleig. "On the 1st of February, Rungpore, the capital of Assam, submitted by capitulation to Colonel Richards; and the whole province became reduced under the authority of the English. In like manner, General Shuldham, though retarded in his progress by the jungly nature of the country, pushed forward some way through Cachar in the direction of Munnipore; while General Morrison, after a series of brilliant affairs, which occupied the 26th, 27th, 28th, and 29th of March, succeeded in clearing Arracan entirely of the Burmese. He then detached a force under Brigadier-General McBean, which occupied without resistance the islands of Rameree and Sandowey. Had he found it practicable to cross the hills, so as to winter anywhere rather than amid the swampy forests of Arracan, the results of his campaign would have been as satisfactory as they were honourable. Unfortunately, however, this was not the case; and hence an army, which had carried all before it in the field, became so thoroughly disorganized by disease, that, in order to preserve the lives of the survivors, it was of necessity broken up."

While the British were preparing their magazines in Prone, the court of Ava was making the most zealous and persevering exertions to recruit a new army, to check the progress of the invaders and weary them out in the protracted contest. Men were levied in every part of the country, and for the first time in its history, the Burmese government offered large bounties to induce men to enlist. The tributary Shan tribes bordering on China, were ordered to furnish their quotas in this emergency; and an armed contingent of fifteen thousand men was embodied and disciplined in these distant states. Unacquainted with the progress of the war, and filled with extravagant ideas of the power of their masters, these wild tribes, under the command of their *Chobwas*, or chiefs, hastened to take a share in the defeat of the presumptuous strangers who had dared to profane the sacred soil of Ava. Before the end of September, the Burmese had organized a force of about seventy thousand men, better armed and disciplined than any army which they had yet brought into the field.

Negociations were not neglected, but the Burmese ministers were found so full of treachery and falsehood, that the conferences were very unsatisfactory; the armistice, which was granted in order to afford them an opportunity of consulting with the court of Ava, was flagrantly violated by the Burmese, and no notice was taken of the urgent remonstrances against this breach of faith. At length, the final answer arrived from the court, it was couched in the following laconic terms:—"If you desire peace, you may go away; but, if you ask either money or territory, no friendship can exist between us. This is Burmhan custom."

In obedience to the most peremptory orders received from their sovereign, to surround and attack the rebel strangers on all sides, the Burmese army began on Prone in three divisions. Sudda Woon led the right division along the western bank of the Irrawaddy; Kee Woongee, the prime minister, took the command of the centre on the other side of the river, accompanied by a large fleet of war-boats, conveying stores and provisions for the army; and the left, under the command of Maha Nemiow, moved by a route about ten miles distant from that of the central division, from which it was separated by a forest so impervious as completely to destroy the possibility of mutual co-operation. There was, besides, an army of reserve under the king's brother at Melloone; a corps destined to repel any invasion from the side of Arracan; and another, which watched the English garrison in Rangoon. On the 10th of November, Maha Nemiow's army took post at Watty-goon, about sixteen miles from Prome, with the intention of pushing forward to the British rear. Colonel M'Dowal, with two brigades of Native infantry, was sent to prevent these operations, but the Burmese, receiving information of his advance, came to meet him half-way. The British centre, driving the enemy before them, penetrated to the stockades of Watty-goon; unfortunately, at this moment, Colonel M'Dowal was slain, and the Sepoys were so disheartened at the loss of their leader, that it was necessary to retreat. This movement was conducted with great order and regularity, but not without severe loss. The effect of this slight advantage gave such courage to the Burmese, that they resolved to advance direct upon Prone, still, however, pursuing their cautious plan of approach, moving slowly, and stockading themselves at every mile. Maha Nemiow's corps at Simbike, had come within a short morning's walk of the English lines. Eight thousand of his men were Shans, who had not yet come in contact with British troops, and they were accompanied by three young and handsome women of high rank, who were believed to possess the miraculous power of rendering bullets harmless by sprinkling them with enchanted water as they passed through the air. These Amazons, dressed in warlike costume, rode constantly amongst the troops, inspiring them with courage, and ardent wishes for an early meeting with the foes, as yet only known to them by the deceitful accounts of their Burmese masters.

The last day of November was spent by the British in making arrangements for a dashing movement on the enemy's stockades, beginning with the left. Sir Thomas Brisbane, with the flotilla, was directed to cannonade the positions of the other Burmese divisions, while a body of Sepoys drove in Kee Woonghee's outposts, so as to prevent any suspicion of the real attack on Maha Namiow. Early on the morning of the 1st of December, two columns marched against Nemiow; one, commanded by General Cotton, proceeded direct to Simbike, while the second, under the personal superintendence of Sir Archibald Campbell, crossed the

Nawine river, and moved along its right bank for the purpose of attacking the enemy in the rear. Sir Thomas Brisbane's cannonade so completely deceived the enemy, that General Cotton's division reached the first line of palisades before their approach was suspected. The storming parties were soon formed, and moved forwards with their usual intrepidity; the Shans, encouraged by the presence of their veteran commander, who, unable to walk, was carried from point to point in a handsomely gilded litter, and further, cheered by the exhortations and example of the fearless Amazons, offered a brave resistance to their assailants. At length, however, a lodgment was made in their crowded works; they fell into confusion, and were mowed down by the close and rapid volleys from the troops who had gained their ramparts. "The strongly-built enclosures of their own construction everywhere preventing flight, the dead and dying soon blocked up the few and narrow outlets from the works. Horses and men ran in wild confusion from side to side, trying to avoid the fatal fire; groups were employed in breaking down and trying to force a passage through the defences, while the brave, who disdained to fly, still offered a feeble and ineffectual opposition to the advancing troops. The gray-headed Chobwas of the Shans, in particular, showed a noble example to their men; sword in hand, singly maintaining the unequal contest, nor could signs or gestures of good treatment induce them to forbearance—attacking all who offered to approach them with humane or friendly feeling, they only sought the death which too many of them found. Maha Nemiow himself fell, while bravely urging his men to stand their ground, and his faithful attendants being likewise killed, by the promiscuous fire, while in the act of carrying him off, his body, with his sword, Wonghee's chain, and other insignia of office, were found among the dead. One of the fair Amazons also received a fatal bullet in the breast, but the moment she was seen, and her sex recognized, the soldiers bore her from the scene of death to a cottage, where she soon expired."

Sir Archibald Campbell's column had pushed rapidly forward, and it soon met the defeated and panic-struck fugitives as they emerged from the jungle to make their escape over the Nawine river. The horse-artillery was instantly unlumbered, and a heavy fire opened upon the crowded ford; here another of the

Amazons fell, with numbers of her countrymen. Such was the consternation of the Burmese, that they no longer thought of continuing their retreat, but dispersed in small groups into the jungle, whence they endeavoured to find their way back to their own home. "Few of the Shans assembled again in arms; but obliged, in order to escape their Burmese pursuers, to follow a route through insalubrious forests and unpeopled deserts, numbers whom the sword had spared, perished from famine and disease in their journey to their distant country."

The victors encamped that night on the banks of the Nawine river, in order to be ready to attack Kee Woongee's division at Napadee, early the next morning. On the morning of the 2nd of December, the first English division, after a march of two hours, through a thick forest, debouched into a plain upon the river-side, opened a communication with the flotilla, and drew up in front of the stockaded heights of Napadee. "Nothing," says Colonel Snodgrass, "can exceed the natural obstacles opposed to an advance upon those heights, independent of the artificial means which the enemy had not failed to employ, to render his situation, in every respect, secure; the range of hills he occupied, rise in succession along the banks of the Irrawaddy, the second commanding the first, and the third the second; their base is washed by the river on one side, and they are covered by the forest from the approach of any force upon the other. The only road to the heights lay along the flat open beach, until checked by the abrupt and rugged termination of the first hill, up the sides of which the troops would have to scramble, exposed to the fire of every gun and musket upon its summit; and, in addition to these difficulties, the enemy had a numerous body of men stockaded along the wooded bank, which flanks and overlooks the beach, for the distance of nearly a mile in front of the position, and whom it was necessary to dislodge before the main body could be attacked."

There was a considerable pause, as Sir Archibald Campbell had resolved to wait for the appearance of a detachment which had been sent to force, if possible, a passage through the jungle, and turn the enemy's right; but every effort to penetrate the forest having failed, it was resolved to assail Napadee in front. The flotilla moved forward, and opened a spirited cannonade on each side the river; a detachment under Colonel Elrington stormed some flanking outworks, while the main body of attack marched steadily up the hill, without returning a shot to the continued volleys of their opponents; the crest of the hill was at length won, the British pressed forward with the bayonet, and, in the course of an hour, the whole position, nearly three miles in extent, was completely mastered. A prodigious carnage ensued, as the fugitives, crowding upon one another, strove vainly to escape from their own inclosures; while the loss by desertion, which immediately began to take place, proved enormous. Thus, in the course of two days, was the main body of the Burmese army, which it had taken four months to assemble, entirely destroyed; while of artillery, between forty and fifty pieces, with ammunition and stores to a large amount, remained in possession of the conquerors. During the attack, the flotilla, pushing rapidly past the works, succeeded in capturing all the boats and stores which had been brought down for the use of the Burmese army; in this service the steam-vessel was particularly useful. Her unusual appearance excited the more alarm, as the Burmese had a tradition that their capital would remain invincible, until a vessel should advance up the Irrawaddy without oars or sails!

On the morning of the 5th of December, a strong detachment was sent against the remaining division of the Burmese on the west bank of the Irrawaddy, under the command of Sudda Woon. The troops being landed at some distance above the stockades, commenced the attack in flank and rear, while the batteries and men-of-war's boats cannonaded them in front; and the enemy, already disheartened and panic-struck, evacuated, after a feeble resistance, their line upon the river, retreating to a second line of stockades which they had prepared in the jungle in their rear. The British, following up their first success, and not aware of the existence of any second line, came suddenly upon the crowded works, whose confused and disorderly defendants, unable to retreat through the narrow gates of their enclosure, and too much alarmed to offered effectual opposition, became an easy conquest to the assailants; hundreds fell in the desperate effort to escape, and the nature of the country alone prevented the whole corps from being taken; which, now dispersed and broken, fled in all directions through the woods.

Sir Archibald Campbell, though disappointed in his hope of co-operation from the side of Arracan, resolved to bring the war to an immediate conclusion, by marching with the army of the Irrawaddy direct on the enemy's capital, which was still three hundred miles distant; and nothing was wanting in the troops, or forgotten by their leader, which could tend to ensure success. On the 9th of December, the army advanced. A storm of rain on the third day of the march, caused considerable suffering, and was followed by the breaking out of malignant cholera in the camp. The army, however, pushed forward, and, on the 19th, reached the enemy's abandoned stockades at Meaday, where a most frightful scene was presented, which is thus forcibly described by Colonel Snodgrass:—"Within and around the stockades, the ground was strewed with dead and dying, lying promiscuously together, the victims of wounds, disease, and want. Here and there a small white pagoda, marked where a man of rank lay buried; while numerous new-made graves plainly denoted that what we saw was merely the small remnant of mortality, which the hurried departure of the enemy had prevented them from burying. The beach and neighbouring jungles were filled with dogs and vultures, whose growling and screaming, added to the pestilential smell of the place, rendered our situation far from pleasant. Here and there a faithful dog might be seen, stretched out and moaning over a new-made grave, or watching by the side of his still breathing master; but by far the greater number, deprived of the hand that fed them, went prowling with the vultures among the dead, or lay upon the sand, glutted with their foul repast.

"As if this scene of death had not sufficed, fresh horrors were added to it by the sanguinary leaders of these unhappy men. Several gibbets were found erected about the stockades, each bearing the remains of three or four crucified victims; thus cruelly put to death, for perhaps no greater crime than that of wandering from their post in search of food, or, at the very worst, for having followed the example of their chiefs in flying from the enemy."

From this horrid place, the army pursued its course towards Melloone, meeting similar examples of suffering and cruelty almost at every step. At length they reached Patanagoh, a town upon the river, exactly opposite Melloone, "The Irrawaddy, at this place, is six hundred yards broad, and the fortifications of Melloone, built upon the face of a sloping hill, lay fully exposed to view, within good practice of our artillery. The principal stockade appeared to be a square of about a mile, filled with men, and mounting a considerable number of guns, especially on the water face; and the whole position, consisting of a succession of stockades, might extend from one to two miles along the beach. In the centre of the great stockade, a handsome new gilt pagoda was observed, which had been raised to the memory of Maha Bandoola, as a testimony of his Burmese majesty's distinguished approbation of the services of that chief, and with a view to incite the present leaders and soldiers of the army, by whom he was much admired, to emulate the noble example he had set them at Donoobew, in preferring death to the loss of his post. . . . . Under the stockade, a large fleet lay at anchor, consisting of war-boats, commissariat-boats, accommodation-boats, and craft of every description."

Soon after the British had reached their ground, their attention was suddenly excited by the clang of gongs, drums, and other warlike instruments. Its purpose was soon apparent; crowds of boatmen, with their short oars across their shoulders, were seen running to the beach; in an instant, every boat was manned and in motion up the river. As the flotilla and steam-vessel had been detained below by the intricacy of the river, the artillery was ordered to open fire, upon which the boatmen either jumped into the river, or returned, with all speed, to their former situations. In the meantime, the steam-vessel and flotilla got under weigh, and, passing close to the enemy's works, without a shot being fired on either side, anchored at some distance above the place, thus effectually cutting off all retreat from it by water.

Offers of negociations having been renewed, a large accommodation was moored in the middle of the river between the two armies, and the first diplomatic meeting fixed for January 1st, 1826. After a long discussion, the treaty was accepted and signed, fifteen days being allowed for sending it to receive the king's ratification. Long before that period elapsed, the British had reason to believe that some treachery was intended, and when the armistice expired, a formal notice was sent that hostilities would be renewed at the midnight of the 18th. When the specified hour arrived, the English began to erect batteries and land their heavy ordnance; so heartily did they labour, that, before ten o'clock on the following morning, twenty-eight pieces of artillery were in position, and ready to open on the enemy's defences. Shortly after eleven the batteries opened and maintained a heavy fire, without intermission, for two hours, during which time the troops intended for the assault were mustered and embarked in boats, forming four brigades. Notwithstanding every previous arrangement, the first brigade arrived at its point of attack before the others were ready to co-operate, but the soldiers, notwithstanding, moved forward to the assault with steadiness and regularity, and soon established themselves in the interior of the works. No exertions of the Burmese officers could induce their dispirited soldiers to make any effort for defence; they abandoned one position after another, until the other brigades, cutting in upon their line of retreat, completed their ruin; they were driven with severe loss from all their stockades, leaving behind them the whole of their artillery and military stores. The booty included eight gilt war-boats, three hundred other boats of different descriptions, forty thousand rupees in money, with gold chains, gilt umbrellas, and swords without number. In Prince Memiaboo's house, a decisive proof of the dishonesty of the Burmese in the late negociations was discovered—the identical treaty which the Commissioners had signed on board the barge, and which it was now evident had never been sent for approval to the Burmese monarch.

Memiaboo and his beaten army retired from the scene of their disasters with all possible haste, and the British commander prepared to continue a close pursuit; before, however, commencing his march, he sent the unratified treaty to Kee Woongee, merely telling him that, in the hurry of his departure from Melloone, he had forgotten a document, which he would probably find more useful and acceptable to his government, than he had considered it some days previously. The Burmese did not appreciate the irony; in reply, the Woongee and his colleague politely returned their best thanks for the paper, but observed that the same hurry which had caused the loss of the treaty, had compelled them to leave behind a large sum of money, which they also much regretted, and which, they were sure, the British general only waited an opportunity of returning.

On the 25th, the army resumed its march, over the worst roads which had been met since leaving the frontiers of Hemzawaddy. They passed through a barren but an exceedingly interesting country, abounding, among other curiosities, with "oil wells"—

in other words, with numerous reservoirs of petroleum. As had been the case in approaching Melloone, however, every village and cabin was in ruins; while here and there, along the road-side, the bodies of men and women were attached to gibbets—terrible proofs of the ferocity of those who seemed determined on waging war even to extermination. Occasionally, too, the advanced guard fell in with the enemy's rear, when a skirmish more lively than destructive ensued; and on the 30th, the wreck of the body-guard, now reduced to thirty troopers, was so fortunate as to surprise five hundred men in bivouac, and to overthrow them by a brilliant charge.

On the 31st, a boat was seen coming direct from Ava, having on board Dr. Price, an American missionary, Surgeon Sandford, of the Royals, three European soldiers, and the master of a little gun-boat, who had been made prisoners in the course of the war. "Such uncouth figures as these poor fellows were, have seldom been exhibited, with their hair uncut and beards unshorn, ever since they had been taken." These were accompanied by one or two Burmese of rank, who came with full powers to negociate and conclude a peace, and who, on Sir Archibald Campbell's positive refusal to abate one jot of his former demands, assured him, without hesitation, that they would be granted. Not all their entreaties could, however, prevail upon him to suspend his march. Sir Archibald Campbell, however, consented not to pass Pagham Mew for twelve days, which he could do very safely, as the army was not within ten days march of that city.

About this time, unpleasant news was received from the small British force which had been left in Pegu; part of it had been repulsed with heavy loss, in an attack upon the strong stockade of Sitoung, the commanding officer, Colonel Comoy, and another officer killed, and several wounded. No time was, however, lost in remedying this unfortunate failure. Colonel Pepper, who held the chief command in Pegu, immediately advanced upon Zitoung with a stronger detachment than that which had been defeated, and, after some sharp fighting, routed the enemy with great loss.

As Sir Archibald Campbell advanced towards Pagham Mew, he received intelligence that the Court of Ava had resolved to renew hostilities, at the instigation of a savage warrior of mean birth, who had boasted, that with thirty thousand men, he would utterly annihilate "the rebellious strangers." The Burmese monarch, influenced by his queen, who was a zealous supporter of the war-faction, accepted the offer of this arrogant boaster, and conferred upon him the singular title of Neewoon Breen, which signifies, "Prince of Darkness," or rather, "King of Hell." A new levy was speedily made, and the soldiers were honoured with the flattering appellation of Gong-to-Doo, or "Retrievers of the King's glory." Though the British army was much diminished by the absence of two brigades, and did not amount to two thousand fighting men, Sir Archibald Campbell pressed forwards to Pagham Mew, and on emerging from a tangled jungle, he saw the Burmese army, amounting to more than sixteen thousand men, drawn up in an inverted crescent, the wings of which threatened the little body of assailants on either flank. Undismayed by the strength or position of the enemy, the British pushed boldly for their centre, which was instantly overthrown, leaving the unconnected wings severed from each other, so that it required the utmost activity on their part to reach the second line of redoubts, under the walls of Pagham Mew. The British column, following up in the enemy's retreat with the greatest celerity, afforded them little time for rallying in their works, or in the city; into both of which they were closely followed, and again routed with great slaughter; hundreds jumped into the river to escape their assailants, and perished therein. "Out of the army which thus endeavoured to protect the capital," says Mr. Gleig, "only thirteen hundred men, with their leader, 'the King of Hell,' returned to Ava. The fate of the latter was a very tragical one. Notwithstanding his disaster, he had the audacity to present himself before his sovereign, and to assure him, that if his Majesty would grant him a thousand more men, and allow him again to try his fortune, he would positively defeat us. The king heard him with patience, and allowed him to finish his tale; but it was no sooner concluded, then making a motion with his javelin to his surrounding attendants, they seized the unfortunate chief and dragged him off to punishment. He was instantly hurried forth, and whilst on his way to the place of execution, suffered every indignity which the infuriated guards could inflict. Yet even at this awful moment, a fine sentiment of loyalty burst from him; for when on the point of losing sight of the imperial palace, he suddenly turned round, and inclining his head, said, 'Let me make one parting obeisance to the residence of my sovereign.' A few moments more terminated his existence: he was thrown under the feet of horses and elephants, and trampled to death."

The army continued to advance until it reached Gandaboo, only forty-five miles from the Burmese capital; but the king of Ava was now quite humiliated and dispirited. He consented to accept peace on any terms which the British commander pleased to dictate, sent back the prisoners, and commissioned two ministers of state to sign the articles of treaty.

"At four o'clock on the 24th," says the author of 'Two Years in Ava,' "the commissioners finally assembled, and immediately signed and sealed the Treaty of Yandaboo, the Burmahs affixing, as their signet, the impression of a peacock. This event was announced to the army by a royal salute, and immediately afterwards the Burman chieftains proceeded with Sir A. Campbell and Mr. Robertson, to view some of our troops and artillery. The thirteenth and thirty-eighth regiments chanced to be on parade at the time, and were directed to perform two or three evolutions, and charge, a manœuvre that exceedingly astonished our visitors, who, on finding themselves thus surrounded by the 'rebel English strangers,' did not appear quite at their ease, particularly when a large crowd of soldiers had assembled to look at the chieftains, amongst whom they ridiculously supposed was the King of Ava. Some field-pieces were then brought out, and fired fifty rounds, to show the rapidity with which we could load and reload; and finally several shells and rockets were thrown across the river. During the latter part of the exhibition one of the rockets exploded at the moment it left the tube, and scattered the shot around us, but fortunately without doing any injury; when Sir A. Campbell, seeing that the Burmahs were rather discomposed, informed them that they might now perceive we could make our shells explode at any distance we pleased. After this exhibition ended, one of the Burmahs was quietly asked what he thought of it? 'Oh,' said he, 'we can do all this much better ourselves, at Ava!'

"Dinner awaited the principal men in the general's tent, and they partook of almost every dish on the table, but not one of them would commence eating until the Woonghee set the example. We were obliged to cut their meat for them, as they did not know how to use a knife, and were too polite to eat with their fingers, seeing it was not our custom. Not one of the party would take a glass of wine, probably fearful lest it should be misrepresented to the king; but they entered into conversation with much ease and spirit, and the Attweynwoon declared that really the English and Burman nations were very similar to each other, being equally possessed of bravery, wisdom, talent, and every other good quality.

"At half-past nine, the Woonghee and Attweynwoon departed from Ava, leaving the Woondock and inferior chieftains to arrange the money transactions. Two war-boats also were left, to convey a deputation of three of our officers, whom it was intended should proceed to the capital, bearing a few presents to the king, as a proof that sincerity and confidence were established between us.

"On the morning of the 26th, Captain Lumsden, of the horse-artillery, Lieutenant Havelock, Deputy-Assistant Adjutant-general, and Dr. Knox, proceeded up the river and reached the Burman camp at Yeppandine, when they were stopped in consequence of the king having expressed his determination not to receive the British officers, as he considered it an humiliating act, in his present humbled state.

"His majesty had remained secluded in his palace since the signature of the treaty, and was so much annoyed with the two Burman commissioners for having authorized the visit of our officers, that he threatened to behead them, should he be obliged to receive the deputation. A great sensation also was created amongst the inhabitants of the capital, when they heard that the chief of the flying artillery was on his way up, as they concluded he was followed by the whole army, and, so much did they dread our approach, that the Woonghee sent a message to Ava, on the signature of the peace, to desire the population not to be alarmed when our salute was fired.

"On this conduct of the king being made known to Sir A. Campbell, he immediately sent to recall the deputation, but, in the interim, the Golden Foot had changed his mind, and sent a handsome gilt war-boat to convey the officers to Ava.

"It was quite dark before they arrived, yet, notwithstanding, the king was particularly anxious to receive them; but Menzaghee and others having dissuaded him from this fancy, the audience was fixed for the morrow. In the interim the gentlemen were conducted to the house of Monshoeloo, Maywoon of one of the quarters of the palace, where an excellent repast in the English style, with a profusion of wine, was prepared for them; and, on the following morning, they prepared to wait on his majesty, when a discussion arose whether they should wear their swords, a point which was conceded to the Burmahs, as being in direct contradiction to the established etiquette of the court. At three o'clock the officers were summoned to proceed to the Rondaye, where another dispute arose, respecting the place at which they were to take off their shoes; but it was agreed, after some demur on the part of the Burmahs, that they should not do so till at the steps of the palace.

"The officers then entered the outer gate of the palace, preceded by the presents to the king; and, marching through a line of soldiers, passed under three other gateways, the last defended by several pieces of cannon. Directly opposite to this was the entrance to the hall of reception, where, at the upper end, the royal throne was placed; but, the etiquette not permitting them to march straight up to it, they were obliged to advance in a semicircular direction, in front of the troops which were drawn up in a crescent on each side. At the entrance of the hall the shoes were taken off, and during this time bands were playing, and dancing girls exhibiting their graces to the strangers, who then entered the hall, and seated themselves on the ground at about fifty feet from the vacant throne. Above them, were several members of the royal family; and the rest of the assembly was composed of the different high officers of the crown, the whole dressed in white muslin. Pickled tea, garlick, and betel, were then presented to the officers, in crystal cups, as a particular mark of favour; and shortly afterwards, the music suddenly ceased, and a dead silence pervaded the assembly. This was succeeded by a distant chaunting, which approached nearer and nearer, until the folding doors behind the throne were thrown open by invisible hands, and disclosed to view the king advancing with slow and measured steps, and dressed in a white jacket and turban, with a splendid gold chain thrown over his shoulders. His majesty took possession of the throne, and remained perfectly motionless, except that he now and then applied to his betel-box, and occasionally lifted his eyes to look at the foreigners.

"A list of the presents from the British commissioners having been read, the three officers were invested with Burman titles,* which the Golden Foot had been pleased to grant, and the ceremony consisted in binding on the forehead a piece of gold, on which their new rank was written; a ruby ring, a piece of silk, two lackered boxes, and as many cups, were also presented to each of them; and the king then, in an almost inaudible tone of voice, said something to those next him, who immediately asked aloud, whether the foreigners had any petition to prefer, and, Captain Lumsden having replied that 'he hoped the peace and friendship between the two great nations might be lasting,' the audience finished by the king's retiring in the same manner that he advanced.

"Captain Lumsden remained at the house of Monshoeloo during the next day, but had no opportunity of seeing much of the city, as he had received intimation that it was not according to the wishes of the king, that the English should stray far from their habitation. From the slight view the officers had of the metropolis, it struck them as being well-built, but at that moment not containing the usual population.

"On the 4th of March, Captain Lumsden and his companions left Ava, and on their way down, had a good view of Chagain, a large city opposite, which, many years ago, had been the capital, and now appeared very populous. Captain Lumsden brought with him, as a present from the king, for Sir A. Campbell and Mr. Robertson, two shabby ruby rings, a few pieces of silk, and some boxes; but even this paltry gift was handsomer than the first peace-offering made in the royal name to Sir A. Campbell, and which consisted of cocoa-nuts, sugar-canes, honey, patates, walnuts, palmyra-tree sugar, bad sweetmeats, two jars of ghee, and some nuts,—a curious sample of royal magnificence."

By this treaty, which included eleven articles, besides a twelfth or supplementary clause, explanatory of one or two which had gone before, the King of Ava renounced his right of sovereignty over Assam, Cachar, and Jylna; permitted Munnipore to be

* Captain Lumsden was styled, "renowned and valiant Knight."

erected into an independent kingdom, recognized the mountains of Arracan as the boundary between his dominions and those of the Company, and gave up the whole of Tenasserim to his conquerors. He pledged himself to pay in four instalments one crore of rupees; engaged not to molest any of his subjects on account of any part which they might have taken against him during the war; agreed to include the King of Siam in the general pacification, and granted to British vessels, trading or otherwise, which might visit his ports, the same privileges which were enjoyed by his own ships. The English, in return for all this, undertook to fall back to Rangoon immediately; to evacuate the country altogether, as soon as the second instalment should have been paid; and to send in all the prisoners taken during the war, with as little delay as might be compatible with their removal from a distance. It deserves to be recorded that the Burmese promptly and honourably discharged all the conditions to which they had engaged themselves, and that, while the monarch who signed it held the sceptre, there was no reason to complain of the infraction of a single article.

It was discovered that the breaking off of the former treaty, which had been concluded at Melloone, was owing to the perfidious conduct of a priest called Raj Goroo, who had been intrusted with a pacific message from the British commander to the King of Ava. Instead of executing this commission, he persuaded the weak monarch that the English were a mere handful of desperate adventurers, anxious only to extort money. Ample evidence was also obtained that the Burmese monarch had not only sanctioned but commanded the outrages of the Arracan chieftains, which had been the original cause of the war, and that twelvemonths before hostilities had commenced, his majesty had been engaged in devising plans and making arrangements for the conquest of Bengal. Maha Bandoola, then high in favour, was the great projector of the plan, and, with a hundred thousand men, a number which it was believed that the king could easily assemble, pledged himself for its execution. So high were the hopes of conquest entertained by the court, that when Maha Bandoola went to commence his campaign in Arracan, he was furnished with golden fetters, in which he was to bring the Governor-general of India a captive to Ava.

On the 5th of March, Sir Archibald Campbell began his retrograde march, which was marked by no important incident. But all the troops did not come home by way of Rangoon. A battalion of Sepoys, with a few elephants, being supplied with Burmese guides, received orders to penetrate across the country of Arracan, and it accomplished the service with comparatively little trouble, and a total absence of all suffering. While this proved that Ava was accessible over land, it also showed that the misfortunes which overwhelmed General Morrison's army, might have been avoided by a little more knowledge of the country on the frontiers, and a greater exertion of promptitude and enterprize. The march of that division of the army passed over the mountains of Arracan, and brought the English acquainted with the Kieaans, one of the most singular races in Asia; they are thus described by the author of 'Two Years in Ava':—

"The origin of the Kieaans is lost in fiction; and of their early history the present race know little, except by vague tradition, which states them in former days to have been the possessors of the plains of Ava and Pegu, until a horde of the Tartars, from the north, made an irruption into their territory, and settled there, under the authority of the Kieaan king. In the course of time, the strangers became very powerful, and, having elected a sovereign amongst themselves, threw off the yoke of the Kieaan king, declared their chief supreme, and asserted, at the same time, that 'it was incompatible with nature to have two kings and two races of people in one land.' Seizing, then, the Kieaan chieftains who disputed his authority, the new king put them to death, and, prescribing their friends and followers, left them no alternative but flight or submission to his authority. In consequence of this tyrannical conduct, the Kieaan chieftains preferring a free life, in a strange land, to slavery in their own country, collected all their followers and herds of cattle, in which their principal wealth consisted; and, taking advantage of the first opportunity of escaping, regained their independence by taking refuge in the lofty remote mountains on the frontiers of China, Siam, and Arracan, where they considered themselves safe from the persecutions of their powerful neighbours. With them fled some members of their former royal family, but, in the course of time, deaths and frequent changes of residence destroyed all traces of them, and the Kieaans of this part of the country know not whether the descendants of their ancient princes still exist.

Divested as they were of a common head, under whom they might rally, the inhabitants of each village selected from amongst themselves, one who, either from age or experience, was deemed worthy to be their chief; and in this independent state they have since continued, each little community considering itself perfectly distinct from those adjoining.

"The small republics have since resisted all attempts at much intercourse with the adjoining nations, and have preserved, unsullied, their innate love of liberty and independence. Repeated efforts have been made by the Burmahs to reduce the mountaineers under their sway, but without any lasting success, though it would appear that, at a very distant period back, the Kieaans had been obliged to pay tribute. It is related that, shortly after the expulsion of the Kieaans from the plains, the despotic sovereigns of Ava demanded an annual tribute from the persecuted mountaineers, who, when unable to comply with the demand, were forced to deliver all the pretty women of their families into the hands of the tyrant's satellites, by whom they were carried to court, and then selected to adorn the seraglio of the king. To such an excess was this at last carried, that the Kieaans, in order to save their race from extermination, persuaded all the nubile women to sacrifice their beauty at the altar of freedom, an act which they cheerfully complied with; and tatooing their faces in the manner before described, rendered themselves so hideous, that the monarch was quite disgusted, and directed others to be sought for, when none but children could be found who had not undergone this operation. Foiled in his endeavours to transport the mountain beauties to his harem, the Tartar dropped the practice, and, the necessity for tatooing no longer existing, that custom is now optional, and seldom undergone by the women until they are twenty-five or thirty years of age.

"Only one trace of supreme authority still exists among the Kieaans, and this in the person of the Passine, or head of their religion. This situation was formerly held by a man who resided on a mountain called the Poijou, near the source of the Moh river, and united in his person the two offices of soothsayer and priest, which are now held by his descendants in the male and female line.

"Writing and books being unknown to the Kieaans, the mandates of the Passines are verbal, but irrevocable; to them every dispute of importance is referred for arbitration, and in cases of marriage or sickness they are consulted.

"The tenets of the Kieaan faith are most simple, and of the supreme Deity they appear to have no conception; for to my question on the subject, my informer answered, that 'they were the offspring of the mountains, and of nature;' and nature alone appears to have any claims on their feelings.

"A thick bushy tree, bearing a small berry, by the Burmahs called subri, is the principal object of their adoration. Under its shady branches they, at certain seasons of the year, assemble with their families, and offer up sacrifices of pigs, oxen, and grain, on which they afterwards revel. Their cattle of every kind accompany them during these excursions, and participate in the devotion offered to the tree; the principle of the Kieaan religion being to adore everything that is of use, or conduces to the luxuries of life. They also put implicit faith in the supernatural qualities of the aërolite, which is considered a certain charm against every evil. Whenever a thunder-storm occurs, the Kieaans search among the trees to find those which may have been scathed, or their branches broken by lightning. When one is discovered, they immediately commence digging underneath the broken branch in search of this stone, which they state to be about the size of a man's hand, and to have fallen from heaven; and if they are successful, a hog and a bullock is instantly sacrificed and devoured. The stone is then deposited with the Passine, who preserves the precious talisman with the greatest care.

"The Kieaans have no idea how the world was formed, and their distinction between good and evil, consists in supposing that those who honour and respect their parents, take care of their children and cattle, eat most meat, and drink spirits to the greatest excess, will be sure of being well provided for hereafter, by their souls entering the bodies of cows, oxen, or pigs; whereas those people whose sensual appetites are not so great, and do not enjoy to the utmost those benefits which are thrown in their way, will be disregarded and contemned."

It was found that an excellent road, far from discreditable to the engineering abilities of the Burmese, had been made over the mountains of Arracan, and, as this pass must become of great importance in the very possible case of any future war with the court of Ava, we shall insert a description of it from the same intelligent author:—

"In early times, the Kieaans used to prowl about this road in search of plunder, and attack and murder any traveller they might chance to meet with; but as their numbers were never very great, the merchants who formerly passed this way united their forces, and forming little caravans of from thirty to three hundred men, placed themselves beyond the power of these savage marauders.

"A great trade was carried on before the war with Arracan and Ava, in which it is said forty thousand people were annually employed: the former country exported Indian and European manufactures, such as velvets, broadcloths, piece goods, silks, and muslins; and betel-nuts, salt, and other articles, the produce of its own soil; receiving in return, ivory, silver, copper, palmyra sugar, tobacco, oil, and lackered boxes. It was principally to further this intercourse that the late King of Ava, Minderaghee Prah, caused this superb road to be made—a work which reflects the greatest credit, not only on him who planned it, but also on those who carried it into execution. The labour bestowed upon it has been immense, as, for nearly twenty miles, the road is cut out of the hill side, to the width of between ten and twelve feet, and that with the most judicious attention to the falls of the ground. The remains of a parapet, formed of trunks of trees, are visible in many places; and it would be very advantageous if something of the kind still existed, the precipices off the road being most terrific, and of such a depth, that if an animal lost its footing and fell over, his death would be almost inevitable. An accident of this kind occurred to the pony of one of the officers. In leaping a tree which had been felled across the road, the poor beast trod on some loose earth and rubbish, which immediately gave way with him, and, to our infinite horror, he was precipitated down the height, crushing, by his fall, the slight bushes that grew on the side of the hill; fortunately, at about one hundred and fifty feet descent from the road, he was stopped by a bushy tree, and, in a short time afterwards, resumed his footing, when he proved, most miraculously, to be unhurt. It was impossible to bring the animal back to the road whence he started; but we succeeded in leading him up about half a mile further on, by gradually edging along the hill.

"The Aeng road was first commenced in 1816, under the superintendence of the Sandowey Woon and other chieftains, through whose territories it passed, the whole plan, in the first instance, having been laid out by the engineers of the king. During the first two years only five hundred workmen were employed; but when the road had been completed nearly up to the summit of the mountain, two hundred more were added, each man receiving seven rupees per month wages, who finished it as far as Shoechatoh. But what contributed more than anything to the completion of the road, was a most sensible rule enforced by the Burman government, by which, in lieu of taxes on their merchandize, it obliged all the travellers to carry with them working tools, and repair those parts of the road which might require it, or facilitate the access to the water. In this manner, constant use, instead of spoiling the road, only improved it; and it was solely owing to the stagnation of commerce during the last two years, and the consequent encroachment and ravages of the monsoon, that any part of the route was bad; for, as the communication is closed between May and January, the havoc committed during that period must be annually repaired."

Throughout the whole course of the Burmese war, the Madras government, which was then administrated by Sir Thomas Mann, gave the most powerful and efficient support to the operations of the army. His exertions were the more valuable on account of the deplorable ignorance which prevailed at Calcutta, respecting the country, the habits and the resources of the enemy. In England a strong feeling was raised against Lord Amherst, on account of the length to which the war was protracted, and the strange errors in the commissariat department, by which the advance of the troops was delayed, and the men were exposed to a series of sufferings at Rangoon, which would have demoralized and destroyed any but a British army.

In the early part of 1825, during the operations against the Burmese, the attention of the Bengal government was called to certain proceedings, where Durgoon Sal, aided by his brother Mundoo Sing, attempted to usurp the rights of their cousin

Bulwunt Sing, a minor and rightful heir to Buddoo Sing, the late Rájá. The failure of Lord Lake before Bhurtpore, had filled the inhabitants with the most extravagant pride, and had produced a very strong impression, not only on the neighbouring principalities but throughout India. "It is really strange," said the late Bishop Heber, "how much importance has been attached to the fortress of Bhurtpore; even in the Carnatic, Sir Thomas Munro tells me, the native princes would not believe that it ever could be taken, or that the forts were not destined to be the rallying point of India. The expression in fact had become a sort of proverb, that India was not yet conquered, for Bhurtpore had never been taken." Under these circumstances, it is not surprising that a strong Anti-English party had been formed in Bhurtpore, and that the reluctance of the Rájá to engage in hostilities, gave great offence to the ambitious and enthusiastic portion of his subjects, but especially to his nephew, Durgoon Sal, who for some time had been regarded as his probable successor.

Time passed, and in his extreme old age, the Rájá, who had hitherto been childless, was made happy by the birth of a son. Aware of the ambitious temper of his nephew, and foreseeing that the child would receive at his hands no fair play, Buddoo Sing made haste to secure for him the especial protection of the English, by soliciting from them, while he was yet alive, the *Khelat* or robe of inauguration for his son, and proclaiming him, under their sanction, heir to the throne. He had not long done so, when a mortal disease overtook him, and he died, leaving the prince Bulwunt Sing in his sixth year, surrounded by enemies.

Scarcely was the Rájá dead, when Durgoon Sal usurped the throne; the guardians of the young prince fled with him to Calcutta, and besought the assistance of the Governor-general, to restore him to his rights. Independent of all considerations of right, it was so obviously desirable to remove the unfavourable impression produced by our former failure before Bhurtpore, and to destroy the delusion respecting the impregnability of any Indian fortress, that orders were given to make such extensive arrangements as would afford a moral certainty of success. Just as they were completed, Lord Combermere arrived in India, to take the command of the army. That the enterprize was one of some difficulty and danger, will at once appear from the following description of Bhurtpore at this period, for which we are indebted to Mr. Gleig.

"The city stands in a plain, and is begirt by an extensive forest, of which, till the summer of 1824, the trees extended to the crest of the glacis. That forest constituted, in former times, a sort of preserve for the Rájá's game, but on the first threatening of hostilities, care was taken to level a considerable portion of it, so as to leave an open space of six or seven hundred yards on all sides round the ditch. The ditch again, as has been already stated, is enormously wide and deep; and there is a jhul or lake hard by, on piercing a narrow embankment on the side of which, the whole may be filled with water to the depth of many feet. A wall surrounds the town, flanked at proper intervals by towers and bastions, but the curtains are low, while the bastions, by reason of their circular form, stand more exposed to the fire of a besieging artillery, than they would be were their construction such as the rules of modern science require. Finally, there is a citadel, kept apart from the town by a ditch and ramparts, distinct from those which form the *enceinte* of the whole, of which the position is such as to hold the town completely at its mercy."

On the 10th of December, Lord Combermere appeared before the walls with an army of upwards of twenty thousand men, and a field of more than a hundred pieces of artillery. During the night the enemy had cut the embankment to the northward, for the purpose of filling the broad and deep ditch. But they had delayed this operation too long; the British troops arrived in time to make themselves masters of the embankment and repair the breach, before a sufficient quantity of water had flowed into the fosse to render it impracticable. The following days were occupied in reconnoitring the works and determining the points of attack, until the battering train and its appurtenances should have come up, the fortress occasionally firing upon the reconnoitring parties, and skirmishes taking place between small detachments and the enemy's cavalry encamped under the walls.

Lord Combermere, desirous to save the women and children from the horrors of a siege and of a bombardment, like that which must follow from such a battering train as he was about to employ, addressed a letter to Doorjun Sal on the 21st, calling upon him to send them out of the fort, promising them a safe conduct through the British camp, and allowing four and twenty hours for that purpose, before he should open his fire on the town. Having received an evasive answer, his lordship again sent to him allowing a further extension of the time for twelve hours, but the humane offer was not accepted.

On the 23rd therefore, everything being in readiness to commence operations, and the north-east angle of the works having been fixed upon as the point of attack, the besiegers, under a heavy fire, took possession of a ruined village called Kuddum Kundee, and of Buldeo Sing's garden, and completed their first parallel at the distance of about eight hundred yards from the fort. On the morning of the 24th, two batteries erected at these two points, opened upon the town, and on the 25th, another more advanced battery between them, having likewise begun its fire within two hundred and fifty yards of the north-east angle, the defences of the east side of that part of the works were in a great measure destroyed. A battery was then constructed, bearing on the north face of the same angle, at a distance of about two hundred and fifty yards. The rest of December was employed in a similar manner, in strengthening the old batteries, erecting new ones and pushing forward the works; a constant fire, which left scarcely a roof uninjured, being kept up against the town; while the enemy seemed to be reserving their resources to the last, and the operations of the besiegers were exposed to no material interruption. On the 3rd of January 1826, the artillery began to breach the curtains, the ditches in front were found to be dry, and from the raggedness of the counterscarp, offered fewer obstacles than had been expected. Such however was the tenacity of the tough mud walls, that they resisted the effects of shot better than masonry would have done; it was found that the batteries were insufficient to reach them, and recourse was had to mining. On the evening of the 6th, a mine was commenced in the scarp of the ditch on the northern side-face of the work, with the purpose of improving the breach; but the engineers, fearing that they might be discovered if they continued their operations during the day, sprung it at daylight on the following morning, when it was not sufficiently advanced to have any material effect upon the wall; in making a second attempt the miners were driven away, having been countermined from the interior before they had entered many feet, and the gallery was subsequently blown, it being discovered that the enemy was keeping watch in it. On the 14th, another mine, under one of the bastions, was exploded too precipitately and failed of its effect. Two more mines were immediately driven into the same work, which were sprung on the 16th so successfully, that with the aid of a day's battering, they effected an excellent breach, which was reported to be practicable. On the 17th, the mine under the north-east angle was completed, and the following day was fixed for the storm.

Early in the morning of the 18th, the troops destined for the assault, established themselves in the advanced trenches, unperceived by the enemy. The left breach was to be mounted by the brigade of General Nicholls, headed by the 59th regiment; that on the right by General Reynell's brigade, headed by the 14th regiment, the explosion of the mine under the north-east angle, was to be the signal for the attack. At 8 o'clock the mine was exploded with terrific effect; the whole of the salient angle, and a part of the stone cavalier in the rear, were lifted into the air, which for some time was in total darkness; but from the mine having exploded in an unexpected direction, or from the troops having been stationed, in consequence of mis-calculation, too near it, the ejected stones and masses of earth, killed in their fall several men of the regiment at the head of the column of attack, and severely wounded three officers.* They fell so

* An eye-witness has given the following description of this fearful scene :—" The general had departed but a few minutes, and we were all in that state of breathless excitement which our situation was calculated to produce, when a spectacle was presented to us, to which I have never beheld, and shall probably never behold, any thing akin. I had fixed my eyes intently on the angle of the bastion, beneath which I was aware that the mine had been formed, when, suddenly, the ponderous wall heaved as if shaken by the power of an earthquake. There was no noise, no explosion, and, as it happened, the very firing had for the instant ceased, but the wall rocked like a ship lifted upon a wave, and then sunk down again. This occurred twice, and then, with a sound, to which the loudest thunder were soft music, stones, earth, logs of wood, guns and men, flew into the air. Of more I cannot speak, except that shrieks and groans burst upon the ear, as soon as that tremendous crash was over, giving evidence, but

thickly about Lord Combermere himself, that Brigadier-general M'Combe, who was standing next to him, was knocked down, and two Sepoys who were within a few feet of him, were killed on the spot. The troops immediately mounted to the assault with the greatest order and steadiness, and, notwithstanding a determined opposition, carried the breaches. The left breach was the more difficult of the two; the ascent was very steep, but the troops passed on and quickly surmounted it, the grenadiers moving up it slowly and resolutely, without yet drawing a trigger, in return for the volleys of round shot, grape and musketry which were fired upon them. Some of the foremost of the enemy, defended the breach for a few minutes with great resolution, but as the explosion of the mine had blown up three hundred of their companions, they were compelled to give way, and were pursued along the ramparts. Whenever they came to a gun which they could move, they turned it upon their pursuers, but they were immediately killed by the grenadiers, and the gun upset. In two hours the whole rampart surrounding the town, although bravely defended at every gateway and bastion, along with the command of the gates of the citadel, were in possession of the besiegers, and early in the afternoon the citadel itself surrendered. Brigadier-general Hugh, commanding the cavalry, having been entrusted with preventing the escape of the enemy's troops after the assault, made such a disposition of his forces, that he succeeded in securing Doorjum Sal, who with his wife, two sons, and one hundred and sixty chosen horse, attempted to force a passage through the 8th Light Cavalry.

The loss of the enemy could not be computed at less than four thousand killed; and owing to the disposition of the cavalry, hardly a man bearing arms escaped. Thus, as by the surrender of the town, all the stores, arms, and ammunition fell into the possession of the victor, the whole military power of the Bhurtpore state might be considered as annihilated. The fortifications were demolished; the principal bastions, and parts of several

too decisive, that the engineer's assurances as to the safety of our position were groundless; but as to seeing the objects from whence they came, that was out of the question. A dense cloud of smoke and dust was over us: to breathe, far less to command the sense of sight, amid which was no easy matter."

curtains, were blown up on the 6th of February; it being left to the rains to complete the ruin. The Futty Bourg, or "Bastion of Victory," built, as the Bhurtporeans vaunted, with the bones and blood of British soldiers who fell in the assault under Lord Lake, was now laid low, and among its destroyers were some of those very men, who, twenty years before "had been permitted," in the boasting language of the Natives, "to fly from its eternal walls." In fact, the fort, in a military point of view, was in a state of complete ruin, open in every direction, and would demand as much expense or nearly so, to render it again formidable, as would raise another in a new position. All the other fortresses within the Rájá dominions immediately surrendered, the inhabitants returned to their abodes, and the Rájá was reinstated in his authority.

Lord Combermere broke up his camp to return to Calcutta, on the 20th of February, and arrived there early in April.

Thanks were voted by Parliament, and by the East India Company; the prize-money arising from the capture, granted to the Company by the King, was ordered by the court of directors, to be distributed among the army.

In January 1826, the Bombay presidency was involved in a discussion with the Rájá of Calapore, a small independent Mahratta state in the province of Bijapoor. The British government, anxious to avoid a rupture, endeavoured through the resident to adjust the difference which had arisen, without having recourse to extreme measures.

The Rájá, deaf to all remonstrance, and blind to the real interests of his state, continued to disregard the advice offered to him; he raised additional levies of troops, and at once placed himself in a hostile attitude, which rendered it incumbent on the government to prepare against aggression. Their remonstrance not only remained unanswered, but the Rájá, at the head of large bodies, commenced plundering the properties and territories of his own dependant chiefs, and those under the especial protection or guarantee of the British Government, extorting money from the inhabitants, by means of excessive cruelties. Thus forced into active operations, Colonel Welsh marched from Belgaum, with the whole of the disposable troops of that station, crossed the Gutpurba river, on the 12th of September, and subsequently took up a position in the vicinity of Katabughee, in the Colapore territories, the inhabitants of which flocked in numbers to Colonel Welsh's camp, soliciting protection. These measures had the desired effect; the questions pending with the state of Colapore, were brought to a satisfactory conclusion without recourse to actual hostilities; arrangements were entered into for securing the peace and tranquillity of the country, and to prevent, on the part of the Rájá, any violation of his engagements. The articles of agreement were confirmed by the Governor-general, on the 24th January, 1826.

Lord Amherst proceeded to the Upper Provinces, in 1837. On his lordship's visit to Delhí, a final settlement took place, of the relations in which the British government in India stood towards the king of Delhí. It terminated the implied vassalage previously rendered, or which was supposed to exist towards the royal family, by the British government. The event created very naturally a strong sensation at the time, as it was the first instance of our openly and decidedly asserting the independence of the British power; it was generally believed, that the crown of Hindostan bad been transferred to the British nation.

The event is said to have been viewed with deep melancholy by the royal family and their dependents. They felt, whatever privations they might have suffered from the Mahrattas, their title to the sovereignty of India had been invariably acknowledged. They were now for the first time divested of it. The feeling of the public, however, corroborated the opinion expressed by General Wellesley, that the Natives were the most indifferent people, as to their governors, of any he had met with. They seemed on the present occasion to be unconcerned in the matter; and contemplated without surprise our assumption of a character "which had been purchased with the talents, treasure and blood of our nation."

Lord Amherst having returned to the presidency, embarked in H.M.S. *Herald* at the close of March, for England, resigning the provincial government into the hands of W. B. Bayley, Esq.

CHAPTER XIX.

ADMINISTRATION OF LORD WILLIAM BENTINCK AND LORD AUCKLAND, TO THE BEGINNING OF THE AFGHAN WAR.

LORD WILLIAM BENTINCK entered on the arduous duties of Governor-general of India, under circumstances of peculiar delicacy and difficulty. The expenditure in the Burmese war and in the reduction of Bhurtpore, had added thirteen millions to the registered debt of the Company; there was an increasing expenditure in every branch of the administration, and the outlay of the government far exceeded the resources from which it was to be defrayed. The necessity of retrenchment was earnestly urged by the court of directors, and the new Governor made his appearance in Calcutta, under the unpopular character of a financial reformer. Two committees were formed, one charged with the reduction of the civil, and the other of the military expenses, but the resistance to the latter was so great that its functions were soon suspended. More general discontent was excited by the imposition of a stamp duty; all the Europeans in Calcutta, of every party, were unanimous against the justice and expediency of the measure; they even questioned its legality, and counsel were heard for three days against the registration of the act. Public meetings were summoned to prepare petitions to the court of directors and the English parliament; these assemblies were prohibited by the council, but were nevertheless held in defiance of their authority, and the petitions were unanimously adopted.

Great opposition was also made to the restrictions which had been placed on the press; the regulations prohibiting the publication of any periodical work, without an express license from the supreme council, were resisted by a strong party in Calcutta, and were absolutely rejected in Bombay, three of the judges refusing to register the act, as being contrary to law. While the Europeans were thus agitated, not a little excitement was produced among the Natives, by the publishing of a proclamation, strictly forbidding the practice of *Suttee*, that is of burning or burying alive, the widows of Hindus. It was feared that this interference with the religious usages of the Natives, might provoke a general insurrection; but Lord William Bentinck was not to be daunted in enforcing obedience to the laws of humanity, and in a very short time, the Hindus themselves expressed their satisfaction at the abolition of so detestable a practice.

The Emperor of Delhí began to feel very sensibly the degradation of his condition, and after he had make some representations on the subject to the authorities in Calcutta, he resolved to send an ambassador to represent his case to the government of England. He chose for his envoy the Rájá Rammohun Roy, a Hindu of very distinguished literary attainment, and well acquainted with the English language and literature, in addition to his own. The mission was of course unsuccessful; indeed, during the tour which the Governor-general made in the Upper provinces, he found the Natives universally contented with the Company's government, and the readiness with which he afforded access to any who had a real or imaginary cause of complaint, greatly increased these feelings of loyalty.

After having carefully examined the provinces of Bengal, Lord William Bentinck embarked on board the Enterprize steamer, to examine the condition of Penang, Singapore, and the other eastern settlements, for the purpose of further extending his measures of economical reform. He recommended that the government of these provinces should be placed under the council of Calcutta, and that many other reductions should be made in offices, which entailed a needless expense on the administration. While he thus exerted himself to improve the affairs of the Company by judicious retrenchments, he was not negligent of the improvement of the people committed to his charge; his exertions to promote the diffusion of education and sound knowledge among the native Hindús, were incessant; he not only founded schools, but used every means in his power to procure proper teachers, and encouraged by personal distinction any young students who were remarkable for their industry. He also laboured with considerable success to suppress the practices of Thuggism and Dacorty, or the associations for murder and robbery, which prevailed extensively in India.

The three Presidencies enjoyed universal tranquillity, when the approaching termination of the Company's Charter, rendered it necessary that the British parliament should take into consideration, the principles on which the government of the British dominions in the east, should be conducted for the future. On the 13th of June, 1833, Mr. Charles Grant, (now Lord Glenelg,) introduced the subject to the reformed parliament, and developed the ministerial arrangements in a series of resolutions, which were with little difficulty sanctioned by both houses. It was determined that the government of India, should be entrusted to the Company for a term of years, on the ground that its administration during the last forty years, had, with all its faults and imperfections, proved of the greatest benefit to the people of that country. It was next resolved, that the trade with China should be thrown open to the public, and that the Company should abandon all its exclusive privileges as a commercial body.

Although the tranquillity of India, was not at this period disturbed by foreign wars, some petty disturbances were excited in various quarters, which required the prompt exertions of the authorities. The Rájá of Mysore was deprived of his authority, and the administration of his territories assumed by the Company. Several other changes were made in various places, but none which involved any serious operations, save the expedition against the Rájá of Coorg. His father has already been mentioned, as a zealous ally of the English, during the war with Mysore, and the memory of the services he had then performed, induced the British to tolerate many equivocal acts of the reigning prince. His cruelties and oppressions, rendered him very unpopular amongst his own subjects, whilst his haughty demeanour was very offensive to all his neighbours. At length, he behaved so violently towards his sister and her husband, that they were forced to seek refuge in the British territory. The Rájá, indignant at the escape of his intended victims, addressed letters to the Governor-general, couched in the most insulting terms; he assumed an attitude of defiance, instigating and encouraging others to pursue the same course. Many of his excesses had been passed over, or only noticed with gentle remonstrance, but this forbearance served only to increase his pride, and intoxicate him with the belief that he was dreaded by the British government. At length, the Governor-general was convinced that further endurance was equally impracticable and impolitic; a large force was assembled, under the command of Colonel Lindesay, and a proclamation issued, announcing that Verr Rejundi Woodier, should no longer be considered Rájá of Coorg, and that his territories were about to be occupied by British troops. All British subjects in his service, were ordered immediately to withdraw, under pain of being treated as traitors.

On entering the Coorg territory, the British troops at first met but little resistance, but upon approaching the capital, they found that strong stockades had been erected, within which the Rájá had concentrated his forces. These defences were spiritedly, and save in one instance successfully, attacked by the British divisions. The attack on the Buck stockade was repulsed, with the loss of seventy men and four officers. It was however a work of considerable strength, having ramparts of masonry, together with a ditch and a stockade, and was memorable, as the spot where Hyder Ali was routed in the preceding century, with prodigious loss. Mudkerry, the Rájá's capital, however, having been captured by another division, that prince lost all courage and voluntarily surrendered himself a prisoner, "He entered Mudkerry," said a spectator, "attended by two thousand unarmed men, and preceded by fifty pelanquins, said to contain the females of his establishment; in front of the procession were two fiddlers (!) who struck up the '*British Grenadiers*' on passing the guard at the Fort-gate." Notwithstanding this musical compliment, he was sent off under an escort to Bangalore, and the province of Coorg was annexed to the dominions of the Company, by the unanimous desire of its inhabitants.

The expeditions which had been previously undertaken against the Chooars, in the eastern districts of Bengal, and the Filloorydars, in the hill-country behind the Circars, were not regarded as wars, for they were in truth rather expeditions to break up gangs of robbers, than hostilities against an avowed enemy. The robbers were hunted from place to place, and their fastnesses destroyed; such of their leaders as were not slain in battle, were taken and executed, by which prompt measures tranquillity was restored. But the conquest of Coorg was regarded as entitled to be dignified as a war, on account of the difficulty of the country and the approved valour of its inhabitants. Accordingly, prize-money to the amount of thirteen lacs of rupees was distributed to the victorious troops.

Dowhit Rao Scindia was the most powerful of the Mahratta princes who had been permitted to retain their independence, and his administration of his dominions greatly added to his strength. The stationary camp, which he had established at Gwalior, in process of time became a considerable city. Experience had taught him his inability to cope with the English, he therefore avoided anything which would excite their jealousy or hostility ; but his success in consolidating his power naturally produced some anxiety, and a close watch was kept on the interior movements of the court of Gwalior. Scindia's death without male heirs, placed the regency in the hands of his widow, the Baiza Bye ; but she felt the difficulty of maintaining a female administration, over such turbulent subjects as the Mahratta chiefs, and to ensure a male successor, she adopted a youth, who took the name of Jhundkoo Rao, and was invested with the title of Maharájá. During the minority of this favoured young man, Baiza Bye administrated the government with great ability, but when he came of age, he aspired to the actual possession of supreme power, which the Bye was by no means willing to grant. The intrigues and disputes of their several partizans, filled the court of Gwalior with confusion ; those who favoured the maintenance of tranquillity being anxious to continue the regency, while the youthful and ardent, wished to enforce the claim of Jhundkoo Rao, who, without any regard to his obligations to his benefactress, determined to enforce his claims by every means in his power. Such was the condition of affairs, when Lord William Bentinck, in one of his tours, visited the Mahratta capital ; the young prince immediately applied to the Governor-general to place him upon the *musnud*, promising in return, a faithful adherence to the policy of the British government. Lord William intimated in reply, that Gwalior being an independent state, the British government could not interfere with its internal arrangements ; he then reminded him of what he owed to his patroness, recommended him to pay the utmost deference to her wishes, and to wait patiently for the time when she would voluntarily surrender the reins of government to his hands. Jhundkoo Rao, though he feigned acquiescence, was by no means disposed to follow this advice, and in July 1833 made an attempt to seize the reins of power. This being frustrated, he repaired to the mansion of our resident, who, unwilling to interfere, had left it fast locked. The young prince sat the whole day in the court of this official dwelling, without food, and under a burning sun; but having at last obtained an audience, and being refused all support, he made his submission to the Bye. Meantime, however, a large body of the military, impatient of a female government, discontented with Baiza, and perhaps desirous of change, applied a ladder to the Mahárájá's apartment, brought him out, and proclaimed him their sovereign. The lady took refuge with some troops who still adhered to her; but they were unequal to contend with the opposite party, who were more numerous, and possessed all the artillery. An agreement was made, under the mediation of the resident, that Jhundkoo Rao should be placed on the musnud, and acknowledged by Britain; while the regent should retire unmolested to Dholapoor. There she still attempted to make a stand; but being closely invested and reduced to great distress, she at length surrendered, was allowed a revenue of ten lacks of rupees, and took up her residence near Futtyghur.

There were many persons who condemned the course of policy pursued by the Governor-general at this crisis, believing that it approached too closely to the mischievous system of non-interference adopted by Sir George Barlow. They deemed it dangerous to have the sovereignty of the most powerful of the Mahratta states transferred from the hands of a female of pacific habits, to a young and ambitious man, surrounded by warlike and violent chiefs, ready to lead him into the most perilous and desperate enterprizes. In fact, there were some threatening appearances both in the court and army of Gwalior, which at one time seemed to menace a renewal of hostilities, or, at least, such an interference with British interests as would render some military demonstrations necessary. Jhundkoo Rao was, however, too prudent to gratify the warlike inclinations of his chiefs; he vigorously exerted himself to suppress their demonstrations of discontent, and finally compelled them to acknowledge his uncontrolled sovereignty. Although it cannot be said that the Mahratta powers are perfectly reconciled to British supremacy, yet they seem to feel that if they provoked a contest it would end in their utter ruin ; they are even doubtful of the fidelity of their own subjects, who feel, very sensibly, the difference between their condition, and that of the industrious classes in the territories subject to British sway.

The Rajput princes, although they never possessed such authority as the chieftains of the Mahrattas, are far more haughty ; so great is their pride of birth, that they generally murder their infant daughters through fear, that if they were permitted to attain maturity, they might degrade their families by marriages with persons of inferior caste. When the Mahratta power was at the summit of its prosperity, the Rajputs would gladly have availed themselves of British protection, to escape the heavy impositions of *chout*, or tribute, exacted from them by the marauding chiefs ; but their offers having been rejected by Lord Cornwallis, it was subsequently found very difficult to prevail upon them to accept the terms of protection which they had once so earnestly solicited. Even when they had concluded subsidiary treaties, they looked upon themselves as persons who had granted a favour, and were generally reluctant to fulfil the obligations they had contracted. During his tour through the Upper Provinces, in the year 1832, Lord William Bentinck convoked a congress of the Rajput princes at Ajmere, where he exerted himself with considerable success, to impress upon their minds the necessity of observing the faith of treaties. Promises of obedience were lavishly made, but, as their sincerity was rather questionable, it was resolved that an example should be made of the first Rájá who failed to fulfil the conditions of his tenure. Maun Sing, Rájá of Joudpore, had been restored to power by the Governor-general on the usual terms of subsidiary dependence. It soon appeared that he had no intention of discharging his obligations ; he absented himself from the conferences at Ajmere, he allowed his stipulated tribute to fall two years into arrear, and he afforded shelter to bands of marauders who had been chased from the British provinces. It was also believed that he had engaged in intrigues to induce other Rajput princes to imitate his contumacy, if not to join in a confederacy for the purpose of recovering their former independence. When remonstrances were made against these equivocal proceedings, Maun Sing evinced no desire to comply with the requisitions of the Governor-general, or to act according to his professed obligations; his answers were not only equivocating, but seemed to insinuate menaces of hostility. It was at length resolved that a force should be assembled to invade his territories, sufficiently numerous to compel him to an unqualified submission, or, if he continued obstinate, to deprive him of his throne. For this purpose an army of ten thousand men was ordered to assemble at Nusserabad, on the 10th of October, 1834, and the greatest activity was displayed in preparing the field-equipments necessary for the force. Maun Sing was far from expecting such promptitude; no sooner had he learned that matters were coming to so serious a crisis, than he sent a deputation of thirty of his principal courtiers, with a gorgeous train of attendants, to Ajmere, for the purpose of holding an amicable conference with the British residents in that city, Major Alves and Captain Trevelyan. The envoys made the most lavish professions of their master's attachment to the British government; they protested that he never had any intention of giving offence, and that it was with equal surprise and regret he learned that offence had been taken. These protestations were received by the residents for just so much as they were worth; indeed, it was perfectly obvious that Maun Sing was only anxious to gain time by protracted negociations; in reply to such hollow declarations, the residents informed the envoys that words were of no value without actions, and that the hostile demonstrations must proceed, unless Maun Sing immediately proved his sincerity by delivering up the criminal refugees to whom he had given shelter, and paying down a sum of money sufficient to defray his arrears and the expenses of the forces collected at Nusserabad. This plain dealing perplexed the envoys; they made many apologies, pleading their master's inability to fulfil such conditions, and making use of every evasion to escape compliance. But when the residents informed them, that the only alternative would be the immediate dethronement of the Rájá, they showed the utmost consternation, and humbly requested a delay of three days that they might consider the proposals. At the end of that time a second conference was held;

the envoys again made every exertion to evade yielding to the conditions demanded, but, finding that the residents were inexorable, they finally acceded to an unqualified submission.

This was not the only danger which menaced the peace of Western India. A rude tribe called the Shekhawattees occupied the almost desert territory west of Rajpootana, and were divided into marauding hordes, under a number of petty chiefs. They had long been accustomed to subsist by plundering the neighbouring districts, and the Native powers regarded their depredations as almost a matter of course. Acquiring courage from continued impunity, they at length began to extend their incursions into the British territories. A portion of the force levied to punish Maun Sing was sent against these freebooters, under the command of General Stevenson. Very little resistance was made to the invasion; the bands of the Shekhawattees did not venture to meet the regular troops in the open field, and their forts were either abandoned, or surrendered almost at the first summons. Finally, the district of Sambhur was retained as a security for the expenses of the war, and a detachment was left to overawe the rude natives.

A tragical and distressing event, which occurred about the same time in the Rajput state of Jypore, is thus described by a writer in the 'Edinburgh Cabinet Library':—"The Rájá, a thoughtless and voluptuous youth, had left the whole administration in the hands of Jotaram, originally a banker, an able man, but believed to bear that unprincipled character too common among Indian statesmen. The prince died suddenly, leaving an infant as the heir; and as the inspection of his body was refused to the public, a strong suspicion arose that the minister, finding his master about to shake off his influence, had secretly murdered him. Amid the ferment thus occasioned, the British residency interposed, and procured the removal of Jotaram, and the transference of the government to a regency,—measures which appeared entirely accordant with public feeling. Soon, however, a jealousy was entertained, that public affairs were placed entirely under the dictation of a few foreigners, and a feeling of enmity arose, which broke forth fatally on the following occasion:—On the 4th June, 1835, Major Alves, the resident, with Mr. Blake, Cornet M'Naghten, and Lieutenant Ludlow, had an interview with the Myesaheb, or dowager-princess. After taking leave, as the first-mentioned gentleman was mounting his elephant, a man rushed out of the crowd with a drawn sword, and inflicted three wounds, one in the forehead; but, these being immediately dressed, he was placed in a palanquin, and conveyed home in safety. The assassin having been seized, Mr. Blake undertook to conduct him to the place of confinement; but as he proceeded, the cry was raised, 'The Feringees have shed blood in the palace!' A crowd instantly assembled, who are said to have been joined by many of the police; stones were thrown, and attempts made to stop him by maiming his elephant. He reached the city gate, which was found shut, whereupon he turned back, and sought shelter in a mundur or temple, which was then fastened on the inside; but the multitude burst in, and he fell pierced by numerous wounds. He is said to have been a very promising officer, and generally popular among the Natives. M'Naghten, by galloping in another direction through the crowd, though assailed by stones and other missiles, reached the residency in safety. The government disowned all knowledge of this outrage, though five individuals, whose guilt was clearly proved, were condemned and executed. Suspicion, however, soon fell upon Jotaram, the late minister, and, after long preparation, he and several grandees connected with him were brought to trial before a Native jury. Being found guilty of instigating and abetting the crime, sentence of death was pronounced upon them; but it was commuted to exile and imprisonment."

Rammohun Roy's mission to England excited little attention in Europe, but in India, and particularly in Delhí, it made a considerable impression in favour of the imperial family, and tended greatly to revive the hereditary respect felt for the house of Timúr. The emperor's reviving popularity was not a little increased by the conduct of the acting resident at Delhí. He insulted and beat the passengers in the open streets whenever they omitted to make obeisance to him. This treatment naturally gave great offence to the people, and even excited an angry sensation throughout Northern India. The injured Natives had no means of redress; there was no law to which an appeal could be made; no regular process by which they could procure relief from such intolerable oppression; they were subject to the arbitrary will of the acting resident, whose distance from all authority by which he might be controlled, left him at liberty to follow his own inclinations. At length, a general resolution was taken by the Natives, to abstain from appearing abroad when the acting resident was expected to take his daily rides. None but the emperor himself was free from the caprice of this gentleman; and, though the monarch sensibly felt his dependence, he long abstained from such a confession of inferiority as appeared to be involved in an appeal to the Governor-general. When, however, the appeal was made, it was received by Lord William Bentinck, with the respectful attention due to fallen majesty: the resident was removed by the Governor-general, and this circumstance tended to strengthen the growing opinion of the influence, which of right belonged to the emperor of Delhí, being acknowledged by the English authorities, since so high an officer had been removed through his interference.

These occurrences, and some others, scarcely less annoying, showed the necessity for erecting Delhí into a fourth presidency, and the introduction of a regular system of law and judicial administration, as in the rest of the British territories. Until this was done, the situation of acting resident at Delhí, was one of great difficulty, and even danger, for he had to act in direct opposition to the prejudices and feelings of all by whom he was surrounded. Even the greatest exertion of caution and prudence was insufficient to overcome these perils. In March, 1835, Mr. Fraser, the acting resident and commissioner at Delhí, was shot dead by a hired assassin, who fired three balls into the body of the unfortunate gentleman, and galloped off before he could be seized by the escort. It would have been perilous to the security of British power, if such a crime had been allowed to have passed unpunished; a very strict enquiry was made, and it was discovered that this atrocious crime had been contrived by a Native chieftain, the Nabob of Ferozepore, who had hired Kurreem, the actual murderer. Both were brought to trial, condemned, and executed. So unpopular were the English at this time, in Delhí and its neighbourhood, that the greatest sympathy was shown for the assassin, and songs eulogizing the deed were composed in honour of his memory.

The general tranquillity of India during Lord William Bentinck's administration, afforded an opportunity for the prosecution of two great projects, the consequences of which have not been yet fully developed; the opening of communications with the countries west of the Indus, between that river and the Caspian Sea; and the establishment of a steam communication between England and India. The primary object in forming any connection with the countries west of the Indus, was the extension of British commerce. It was believed that it would be possible to open markets for the sale of British manufactures in the great trading cities of Central Asia; the goods being conveyed in steam-boats up the Indus, and then transported by Native merchants across the mountain-passes of the Indian Caucasus. In order to facilitate this desirable object, Lord William Bentinck, during his northern progress, had an interview with Runjeet Singh, the ruler of Lahore, which was one of the most gorgeous displays of oriental magnificence that can be imagined. The King of Lahore expressed himself favourable to such an extension of intercourse, and, with rather greater difficulty, the Ameers of Scinde were induced to adopt the same course of policy. Lieutenant, afterwards Sir Alexander Burnes, was encouraged by the Governor-general to undertake an exploring tour through the countries of Central Asia, then almost unknown. This enterprising traveller collected very important information respecting the political condition, the commercial relations, and the geographical features of the countries between the Caspian and the Indus; and his subsequent publication of his travels excited a considerable share of public attention in England.

But these countries were interesting in a very different and important point of view. It had been, for some time, suspected that the Russians, adopting the policy of Napoleon, looked with a jealous eye on the supremacy which the British had acquired in India, and that plans for destroying the English power in that peninsula, had been discussed in the cabinet of St. Petersburgh. It was, therefore, part of the instructions given to Lieutenant Burnes, that he should examine the military capabilities of the countries between the Caspian and the Indus. It appears to be the general result, from his enquiries, that no danger can reasonably be dreaded from a Russian invasion proceeding through the desert countries east of the Caspian, which are totally destitute of the provisions necessary to support a large army, and which present almost invincible obstacles in the nature of their surface, to the transport of a commissariat and military stores. The wild tribes of the Desert were found to be exceedingly jealous of strangers, but more especially of the Russians, as they have been long in the practice of kidnapping Russian peasants from the frontiers, and reducing them to slavery. The investigations of Lieutenant Burnes have not been so fruitful in beneficial results as it was at first supposed that they would have been, and it is not easy to see how a beneficial trade can be opened with the Natives of Central Asia, until they are so far civilized as to produce some commodity which they can offer in exchange for British manufactures.

Three routes were proposed for steam-communication with India; the first was the usual course taken by sailing-vessels round the Cape of Good Hope; this was tried by a vessel called the *Enterprize*, in 1825, and, though she made the voyage in safety, yet so little appeared to have been gained in the saving of time, that this plan was abandoned. The second route was from Bombay, through the Red Sea to Suez, and thence through Egypt to the Mediterranean. The experiments by this route were decisive, and a monthly line of packets has been established. A third route by the Euphrates and Persian Gulph, was examined by an expedition under the command of Colonel Chesney; he demonstrated the practicability of navigating that river, and the tractability of the Arabs; but before further enquiries could be made, the feasibility of the passage by the Red Sea was so fully established, that it was deemed unnecessary to search for any other route.

The navigation of the Ganges, by river-steamers, early occupied the attention of the Governor-general, and under his patronage the system was commenced. It has had the most complete success, both in affording security and rapidity to communication; but it will probably be long before the system can be safely applied to the other great rivers of Asia.

Financial derangements threw a gloom over the close of Lord William Bentinck's Indian administration. The fluctuations to which the government loans were liable, induced many persons to invest their capital or their savings, in the houses of agency established at Calcutta. Unfortunately, the command of money induced many of these houses to enter into ruinous speculations, which soon led to a commercial crisis. One house after another became bankrupt, until the last failed in January, 1834, inflicting a fearful loss on the commercial community of Calcutta, and reducing many worthy officers to a state of the greatest distress, as they lost, in the crash, the accumulated savings of their lives. Instead of adding any comments of our own on this portion of Indian history, we shall quote 'Mr. Auber's Closing Remarks on Lord William Bentinck's Administration,' as they are equally distinguished by their force and truth :—

"It is impossible to do more than to briefly and imperfectly advert to the leading points of an administration, which extended over a period of seven years, and which comprised such a variety of measures, carried forward under novel and peculiar circumstances.

"There had scarcely been a preceding government, in which some prominent event had not thrown comparatively into the shade the less attractive matters, intimately connected with the welfare and happiness of the people, and with the internal government of the country.

"It was the fortune of Lord William Bentinck to enter upon the office of Governor-general, at a time when antecedent events had given a tone to the several branches of the service, by no means calculated to diminish the onerous duties imposed upon the head of the Indian administration.

"To carry into execution measures of economy and retrenchment, on points irritating to the feelings of the body constituting our main hold upon our eastern empire, was not only an unwelcome but a difficult task, requiring much firmness, tempered with judgment and discretion. The Governor-general discharged his duty, at much cost to his personal feelings ; at the same time contending with unflinching determination against indiscretions, emanating in quarters where the Government would naturally have expected to meet with aid and support, in the performance of a great public trust.

"Measures relating to the civil branches of the service, but not more palatable to its members, were imperatively called for: but their introduction infused a spirit of energy and zeal, where supineness or laxity of control, had suffered inertness or apathy to creep in. The difficulties of the Governor-general's position were enhanced by a variety of reports, calculated to unsettle the public mind regarding the future system for governing India. An extensive enquiry, instituted by parliament, had been prosecuted amidst fluctuating ministers, each entertaining, so far as could be gathered, opposite views of the principles upon which a future settlement should be made between the public and the Company: a state of things, materially influencing the whole frame of Indian society, but more particularly that portion at the seat of government. Publications emanating from members high in the service, evinced little respect for the authority in whose name the affairs were administered, whilst an unbridled freedom of comment was indulged on the conduct of their representative in India. Much of the feeling was to be traced to the effects of the overwhelming ruin caused by the universal failures of the agency houses: havoc and dismay were spread throughout all branches. Savings had been deposited by the servants, in the cherished expectation that they would enable them to return to close their lives in their native land; but at one fell swoop they saw their little all swallowed up, their prospects blasted, and themselves left to prolong an unwilling and cheerless service, with broken spirits, and minds soured by severe and unexpected disappointment.

"Amidst a state of things so little calculated to make a favourable impression upon the Indian community, Lord William Bentinck, nevertheless, received a series of addresses, bearing the strongest testimony which could be offered to the valuable services of a high public functionary, on retiring from the scene of his labours. The value of such testimonies was enhanced by the qualified terms in which they were expressed.

"It was not an indiscriminate eulogy, but the honest avowal of men who were sensible that the Governor-general had conferred benefits on India which demanded a public acknowledgment. The address from the mercantile community declared, that they felt themselves impelled by a strong sense of duty to contribute their humble testimony in approval of numerous measures, completed or in preparation, having for their object the general improvemant of the country, the moral and social advancement of its vast and varied population, and the development, in particular, of its commercial and agricultural resources. They well observed, that in many respects his lordship's administration had necessarily been of a character widely different from those of his predecessors. Theirs were days of war and diplomacy, and profuse expenditure; to his lordship had fallen the more painful task of consolidating, preserving and organizing;

of repairing the deep wounds in public finances; of contending with an alarming deficit, and of enforcing the remedy of severe economy and retrenchment, by which the charges of India had been very greatly reduced, and the Company's treasury considerably relieved.

" The Native population, meeting at the Hindu College, declared that his lordship had done every thing kind for them; the only act of unkindness was parting with them. They expressed their veneration for his lordship's person and character, and their gratitude for the enlarged spirit of justice and benevolence with which the Natives had been treated, under his administration.

" At a public meeting at the Town Hall, a resolution was passed, requesting his lordship to permit his statue to be erected in some conspicuous part of Calcutta, to be of bronze, and equestrian, and to be executed by Chantrey.

" Lord William Bentinck quitted Calcutta in March, 1835.

" The Court of Directors, on learning that his lordship's health constrained him to relinquish the government, passed the following Resolution on the 26th September, 1834:—

" Resolved, That this Court deeply lament that the state of Lord William Bentinck's health should be such as to deprive the Company of his most valuable services; and this Court deem it proper to record, on the occasion of his lordship's resignation of the office of Governor-general, their high sense of the distinguished ability, energy, zeal and integrity, with which his lordship has discharged the arduous duties of his exalted station."

Immediately after the intelligence of Lord William Bentinck's resignation had been received, the court of directors appointed Lord Heytesbury Governor-general of India by an unanimous vote. Their choice was cordially approved by Sir Robert Peel and the Duke of Wellington, who were then ministers; but, before his lordship could sail to his destination, the Whigs returned to power, and an early intimation was conveyed to the court of directors, that the restored ministers felt themselves obliged to annul the appointment of Lord Heytesbury, and to have so responsible an office as that of Governor-general of India, confided to a statesman whose views accorded with their own. Although this announcement was anticipated, it did not fail to produce some dissatisfaction in the court of directors, and long discussions between them and the government. In the meantime, the supreme authority at Calcutta devolved on Sir Charles Metcalfe, whose brief administration was marked by several concessions to popular opinion, particularly by the abolition of all restrictions on the freedom of the press. After some delay, the court of directors finally concurred in the nomination of Lord Auckland, who was perfectly acceptable to the ministers. On the 4th of July, 1836, his lordship landed at Calcutta, and assumed the reins of government.

Everything seemed to promise that the administration of Lord Auckland, would not be less pacific than that of his predecessor. The Governor-general was known to be a consistent supporter of pacific policy, and eager to carry out those schemes of social improvement, which can only be effected in a period of perfect tranquillity. His earliest attention was devoted to the promotion of the schemes which had been formed for the advancement of Native education, and the communication of so much knowledge to the Mohammedans and Hindús as they were willing to receive. But circumstances occurred, which induced Lord Auckland to enter deeply into the troubled politics of Central and Western Asia, and to involve his government in a struggle of which the final issue is as yet uncertain. Before entering on the history of the Afghan War, which is so important as to require a chapter to itself, we shall briefly notice the principal occurrences within the limits of India, which were connected with Lord Auckland's administration.

About the time of his lordship's accession to power, the Rájá of Gúmsúr, a mountainous tract, inhabited by a peculiar race called the Rhoonds, of whom very little was known, displayed such a refractory spirit that a considerable force was sent to reduce him to obedience. The troops experienced some difficulties in ascending the rugged mountain chain which fenced the frontiers of Gúmsúr, and, when they reached the summit, they were surprised to see, expanded beneath them, an extensive and fertile tract of country, covered with flourishing villages, and richly cultivated. At first they encountered but little resistance; Gúmsúr and the principal forts were occupied without difficulty; the Rája and, afterwards, his son submitted to the English. Several subordinate chieftains, however, continued to resist, confiding in the strength of their fastnesses and jungles. Two campaigns were spent in this desultory warfare; the troops suffered very severely from sickness in this marshy and unhealthy country, and several casualties were sustained in desperate skirmishes. At length the fierce Khoonds were subdued, and their chief fortresses demolished.

The kingdom of Oude is the most important dependency of the government of Bengal, and its internal condition, ever since the conclusion of the subsidiary treaty, has been a constant source of anxiety to the government of that presidency. Such anarchy and confusion were produced in Oude during the administration of Lord William Bentinck, by the misgovernment of the monarch, that the Governor-general was induced to make some preparations for transferring its management, at least for a a time, to the English authorities; but the court of Lucknow took the alarm, and averted the danger by the introduction of several salutary reforms. In the year 1837, the king's growing infirmities showed that the throne was soon likely to become vacant. A little before his death, he acknowledged as his sons two youths, Rywan Jah and Moonah Jaun; but it was generally believed that they were not his children, and that he had been induced, by undue female influence, to recognize them. His family interfered, and obtained from him a formal declaration of the fraud; on his death, the question of succession was referred to the British authorities. After a long and anxious consideration, it was resolved to set the two young men aside, and, according to the laws of succession peculiar to Mohammedan law, to confer the crown on Nasseer-ed-Dowlah, the eldest surviving uncle of the dying monarch. In the mean time, however, the queen-mother, a bold and ambitious princess, had espoused the cause of Moonah Jaun, whom she treated as her adopted child.

The remaining transactions with the court of Oude may be best told in the words of a writer already quoted:—" On the night of the 7th of July, 1837, Colonel Law, the resident at Lucknow, received a message that the king was taken suddenly ill, and believed to be dying. This officer having ordered his troops to be in readiness, obeyed the summons, when he found that his majesty had just expired. Having, in this crisis, obtained from Nusseer-ood-Dowlah an engagement to sign such a treaty as the Governor-general should dictate, he led him to the royal residence, where preparations were made for his immediate installation. Suddenly, however, a great noise was heard, and it soon appeared that the Padsha, with an armed force of about 2,000 men, was approaching the palace, which, as our soldiers were not yet come up, was very slightly guarded. In spite of a warm remonstrance, the Natives burst open the gates, filled the edifice with shouts and clamour, seized both the prince and the Company's servants, in presence of whom Moonah Jaun was placed on the throne, the Begum being seated in a palanquin beneath him. The insurgents, after some violent proceedings towards the resident, allowed him to retire, when, upon finding his men assembled, he sent repeated messages to the Begum, calling upon her to surrender. As she returned evasive answers, a battery was opened, and, in a short time, she and her minions were made prisoners. The old prince, whom, though he had endured many insults, they found safe, was immediately seated on the throne, and his accession announced by a royal salute to the inhabitants of the capital.

"All these proceedings were approved by the Governor-general; but of the promise extorted from the king relative to a new treaty, it appears that no advantage has been taken.

"Claims were advanced by two nephews, sons of a deceased elder brother, who urged that, as their father, if alive, would have succeeded, they ought to inherit in his stead. This question, however, had early attracted the attention of the Indian government, who, after much consideration and reference to high authorities, as well as precedents (among which was that of the present King of Delhí), had concluded that, according to the principles of the Soonee sect, a son cannot succeed to rights or property to which his father was heir, if he died before coming into actual possession. In this case, the inheritance goes to a brother. A curious contest also arose between the two princes, which was the eldest; but, as both were excluded, there was no need to discuss this question. One of them spent a considerable time in England, but without being able to obtain any attention either from Parliament or the Company."

CHAPTER XX.

THE AFGHAN WAR.

In the preceding chapters we have briefly noticed the revolutions in Afghanistan, which terminated in the dethronement and exile of Shah Shujah, who, after a brief residence at the court of Lahore, became a pensioner on the bounty of the English government, and made the frontier town, Loodiana, his principal abode. Shah Mahmood, or Mohammed, was unfit for the throne, to which he was elevated by the vizier Fatteh Khan, but the beginning of his reign was successful beyond the highest expectations of his partizans. The only quarter from which he was menaced with danger, was from the side of Persia. The monarch of that country claimed tribute from Herat, and when it was refused, he advanced to besiege that city. The Afghan minister sent his able vizier, Futteh Khan, to aid in the defence of that place; his operations were so far successful that the Persians were defeated with loss, but the Afghans gained more advantage than honour from their success, for being seized with a sudden panic they abandoned the field, after having achieved the victory. Futteh Khan effaced the memory of his services by seizing the person of the Governor of Herat, although he was the brother of his sovereign, depriving him of the whole of his wealth, and violating his harem in searching for concealed treasure. Prince Kamran, Shah Mohammed's eldest son, vowed revenge for the insult offered to his uncle; he watched his opportunity, seized the unfortunate vizier, and deprived him of sight. After a lapse of five or six months, Shah Mohammed followed up this cruelty, by putting to death the minister to whom he owed his crown, with circumstances of great atrocity.

"The tragedy," says Sir A. Burney, "which terminated the life of Futeh Khan, Barukzye,* is, perhaps, without parallel in modern times. Blind and bound he was led into the court of Mahmood, where he had so lately ruled with absolute power. The king taunted him for his crimes, and desired him to use his influence with his brothers, then in rebellion. He replied without fear, and with great fortitude, that he was now but a poor, blind man, and had no concern with affairs of state. Mahmood, irritated at his obstinacy, gave the last orders for his death, and this unfortunate man was deliberately cut to pieces by the nobles of the court; joint was separated from joint, limb from limb, his nose and his ears were lopped off; nor had the vital spark fled, till the head was separated from the mangled body. Futeh Khan, bore these cruel tortures without a sigh; he stretched out his different limbs to those who thirsted for his blood, and exhibited the same cool indifference, the same reckless contempt for his own life, which he had so often shown for that of others. The bloody remains of this unfortunate person, was gathered in a cloth and sent to Ghuznee, where they were interred."

Mohammed Azeem Khan, the eldest brother of the murdered vizier, at once had recourse to arms, and as we are informed by Sir Alexander Burnes, his first intention was to restore Shah Shujah. Shujah after all his misfortunes, might have now reascended the throne of his ancestors; but before Azeem Khan had reached Peshawer, he (Shujah) prematurely displayed his notions of royal authority, by insulting some friend of his benefactor, whom he considered to be encroaching on his dignity, *by using a palanquin.* The whole Barukzye family took offence at such ill-timed pride; and Azeem Khan determined to place a more compliant master on the throne." "A favourable opportunity presented itself in the person of *Ayub* (or Job,) a brother of Shujah. He entered the camp of Azeem Khan, and sued for the throne as the most abject of slaves, 'Make me but king,' he said, 'permit money to be coined in my name, and the whole power and resources of the kingdom may rest with yourself; my ambition will be satisfied with bread, and the title of

* The Barukzye, or Barak Zai tribe, to which the vizier belonged, had long been regarded as the rivals of the Dooranee, or royal tribe, from which the Afghan monarchs were descended.

king.' This was just the person the Barukzyes wanted, and his conditions were accepted."

Ayub, however, was a mere puppet; Azeem Khan really possessed the supreme, but on his death in 1823, the country fell into complete confusion: a series of civil wars arose between his children and his numerous brothers, which ended in their parcelling out the empire into petty principalities. One of these principalities however, Herat, remained in the possession of Shah Mohammed, and is still retained by his son Kemran. Ayub was forced to become an exile, and was supported by a pension from Runjeet Singh.

Although the Barukzye brothers never formed a perfect confederacy, they for the most part recognized the supremacy of Dost Mohammed Khan, who after having overthrown his nephew, took possession of Kabúl. Next to him, the most important rulers were Shere Dilkhan, who took possession of Candahar, and Sultan Mohammed Khan, who established himself in Peshawer. Cashmire, as we have already stated, together with the province of Balkha, was seized by the Sultan of Bokhara, and the Ameers of Scinde proclaimed their independence.

Dost Mohammed Khan was the son of an inferior wife, and was therefore not regarded as of equal rank with the rest of his twenty brothers. His education was neglected in his youth, and he is said not to have learned reading and writing until after his accession to power. When the death of Senafráz Khan left his mother without a protector, and Dost Mohammed a young orphan, she destined the boy to a menial situation in the mosque erected to the Afghan saint, Lamech. He took no share in the several revolutions organized by his active brother, Futteh Khan, which ended in the dethronement of Shah Zemán, the expulsion of Shah Shujah, and the elevation to royalty of Shah Mahmood, with Fatí Khan as vizier, or rather "as viceroy over him." The first circumstance which brought Dost Mohammed into notice is thus related by Mr. Masson. "On the second assumption of power by Sháh Máhmúd, he was advancing in youth, and was always about the person of his brother the Vazír, rather as a dependent than a relative, performing even menial offices, such as serving him with wine, and preparing his chillam. The course of events led the court to Peshawer; when Dost Máhomed Khân first brought himself into notice by an atrocious deed, which well marked his reckless and daring disposition. Amongst the many brothers of the Vazír, Máhomed Azem Khân, of nearly the same age, was distinguished by his dignified deportment and propriety of conduct. He was also very attentive in the administration of his affairs. The Vazír, so indifferent to his personal matters that frequently no dinner was prepared for him, and his horses were standing without barley, was piqued at the better management of his brother, and felt annoyed when he heard him lauded. He imputed the prosperous condition of his establishment to the ability of the sáhibkár, or steward, Mírza Alí Khân, who, he used to observe, had made a 'shaks,' or man of his brother. One day, exhilarated by wine, he exclaimed, 'Would to God that some one would kill Mízra Alí, and deliver me from the dread of Máhomed Azem Khân.' Dost Máhomed Khân, present, asked if he should kill the Mírza; the Vazír replied 'Yes, if you can.' Next morning, Dost Máhomed Khân placed himself on the road of the mírza, in the bazar of Peshawer, and as he proceeded to pay his respects to his employer, accosted him with 'How are you, Mírza?' placed one hand upon his waist-shawl, and with the other thrust a dagger into his bosom. He immediately galloped off, not to the quarters of the Vazír, but to the tent of Ibráhím Khân Jemshídí, a Sirdár of note, and in favour with Shâh Máhmúd. Here he was within the circle of the royal tents, and it would have been indecorous to have removed him: perhaps his reason for seeking refuge there. Máhomed Azem Khân was naturally incensed upon hearing of the catastrophe, and vowing that nothing but Dost Máhomed Khân's blood could atone for that of his ill-fated Mírza, in violent anger sought the Vazír. That profligate man expressed his contrition, that an accidental remark made by him, in his cups, should have caused the perpetration of so foul a crime; but pointed out, that the Mírza could not be recalled to life; that Dost Máhomed was still a brother; that if it were determined to punish him he could not be taken from his asylum; that the impure habits of Shâh Máhmúd and his son Kámrân were known to all, and if Dost Máhomed, a beardless youth, was left in their power, fresh causes of ridicule and reproach were likely to arise to the family,—what had been done, could not be undone: it was prudent, therefore, to forget the past, and avert the evil consequences of the future. By such representations and arguments, Máhomed Azem Khán suffered himself to be persuaded, the Mírzar was forgotten, and Dost Máhomed Khân was brought from the protection of Ibráhím Khân, Jemshídí. The youth had developed talent of high order, and his retinue was increased by the Vazír from three or four horsemen to twenty."

We shall next give a specimen of the means employed by Dost Mohammed to obtain supreme power during the distractions that followed the dissolution of the Afghan monarchy :—

" The sturdy leaders of the Kohistân, were successively circumvented and disposed of. One of the most potent and cautious, Khwoja Khânjí, of Kárrézaí, was nearly the only one who remained, and he had rejected every overture, and refused to attend upon any consideration the camp of the Sirdár. It was felt by Dost Máhomed Khân, that nothing was done while Khwoja Khânjí remained in being, and he redoubled his exertions to ensnare him. He sent Korân after Korân ; engaged to marry his daughter ; but he could not entice the old chieftain from his castle. The Khwoja, like every man in the Kohistân, had enemies. The chief most inimical to him, was in attendance upon Dost Máhomed Khân. This Sirdár, as a last means of winning the confidence of the Khwoja, put his enemy to death, claiming the merit of having proved the sincerity of his desire to become friendly with him, at the risk of incurring disgrace in the eyes of the world. The murder took place at Baiyân, and Dost Máhomed Khân invited the Khwoja to meet him, and cement their friendly understanding, at the castle of his former foe. The Khwoja was now overcome, and to fulfil his destiny, repaired to Baiyân. He came, however, with a most numerous retinue. Dost Máhomed Khân received him with all politeness and humility ; a thousand protestations of friendship and service flowed from his lips ; he addressed the old man as his father, and, it may be, lulled his suspicions. At night, Dost Máhomed Khân took the hand of the Khwoja, and led him within the castle, that he might witness the preparation of an inventory of the effects of the slain, observing, that it was necessary, as the Khwoja knew what a particular man the Vazír was. As soon as the castle was entered, the gates were closed, and as the Khwoja passed into an apartment, said to be the Tosha Keâna, Dost

Máhomed Khân gave the signal, in Túrkí, to his Kazilbash attendants, who cut their victim down. His head, severed from his body, was thrown from the battlements amongst his followers. In the first transports of their indignation they commenced an attack upon the castle, but disunited and disconcerted, they retired before morning. Dost Máhommed Khân was left at leisure to rejoice in his victory, and the triumph of his dexterity."

In the year 1832, when Dost Mohammed's power was firmly established, Mr. Masson reached Kâbul, and he thus sketches the character of the ruler and the state of the country:

" Dost Máhomed Khân might have an accomplice, he could never have a friend, and his power, erected on the basis of fraud and overreaching, was always liable to be destroyed by the same weapons. Many of his vices and errors were, undoubtedly, those of his countrymen, and of circumstance. His fortune had placed him in an age in which honesty could scarcely thrive. Had he been born to legitimate power, he would have figured very respectably; his talents would have had a fair field for their developement and exercise, and he would have been spared the commission of many enormities, then unnecessary. It has been remarked, that he never acted wantonly, or perpetrated mischief for the mere sake of mischief, and that he was open to shame, but it was doubtful whether for having done evil, or because he had gained nothing by it. It is fair to notice the conduct of Dost Máhomed Khân in his new capacity of supreme chief of Kâbal, especially as it did him much credit in many respects. From his youth upwards he had been dissipated, and prone to all the vices of the country. Master of Kâbal, he abjured wine and other unlawful pleasures. The chief of the community, it was due that his example should not be questioned. Of his application and aptitude for business, there could be but one opinion.

" In all matters where no political questions had force, he was fair and impartial, and free from haughtiness; and accessible to all classes. Vigilant in the administration of the country, crimes became few. People ceased to commit them, conscious they should be called to account."

But it was not in the power of Dost Mohammed Khan to repress the jealous ambition of his brothers, or the turbulence of the Afghan chiefs, especially as he was prevented from having recourse to vigorous measures, by the war with the Sikhs, and the repeated attempts of Shah Shujah to recover his crown. In fact, at the beginning of the year 1836, Kabul was in a state of complete anarchy, and Dost Mohammed could think of no better mode of insuring tranquillity, than by treacherously seizing all the chiefs whom he suspected of intriguing against his person. This notable design was defeated by his taking for adviser the chief agent in these very intrigues, who, of course, revealed his intentions to the chiefs, and placed them on their guard. It would be tedious to enter on any investigation of Dost Mohammed's plans for the destruction of his brothers, or their machinations against him ; it would be a mere record of treachery, weakness, and vacillation. The following brief extract, from Mr. Masson, will shew what was the melancholy condition of Afghanistan in 1836 :—

" The large military force the Amír deemed it advisable to keep up, and to which he was in some measure compelled, pressed heavily upon his finances, and a multitude of expedients were put into practice to meet the extraordinary expenses it involved. No opportunity was neglected of seizing property, and although a pretext, more or less valid, was generally urged, extreme dissatisfaction prevailed, and the popularity of the Amír diminished daily. An effort made to increase the revenues derived from the Ghiljí districts of Ghazní, threw them into insurrection, and the Ghiljí districts of Kâbal were on the verge of revolt for the same reason. In both instances the Amír gained a trifle, notwithstanding the Ghazní Ghiljís defeated his troops. In the autumn, Máhomed Akbar Khân marched into Taghow, and after some severe fighting, in which men of consideration were slain, possessed himself of the valley. Here also tribute was enforced. Many of the troops employed in this expedition, went provided with barâts, or orders for their pay, drawn out in anticipation. Such orders are described as being on the stag's antlers, meaning that the stag must be first caught."

In such a state of affairs, it was difficult to resist such active enemies as the Sikhs, and Runjeet Sing having crossed the Indus, made himself master of Peshawer, which had belonged to Sultan Mohammed Khan, an elder brother of Dost

Mohammed Khan. Events still more perilous to the peace of central Asia, occurred about the same time in other quarters.

We have mentioned that one branch of the royal family of Afghanistan had retained possession of Herat. When Kemran assumed the sceptre in that city, he was so daunted by the successes of the Persian prince, Abbas Mirza, that he consented to become a tributary to the Shah of Persia, and to raze his strong fortress of Ghorian on the frontiers of Khorassan. The death of Abbas Mirza, which was soon followed by that of his father, Futteh Alí Shah, exposed Persia to the hazard of civil war, which, indeed, was only averted by the prompt interference of the English; the confusion appeared to Kemran a favourable opportunity for evading the fulfilment of his engagements; he refused to restore Ghorian; to permit the Persian families in Herat to return to their homes; or to pay the promised tribute. He even went farther, and allowed his vizier to invade Khorassan, and carry away twelve thousand persons, whom he sold as slaves. Such was the aspect of affairs when the English envoy, Mr. Ellis, arrived at Teheran on a mission of condolence to the King of Persia. He found the young king, Mohammed Shah, bent on attacking Herat, to punish the perfidy of Kemran, and inclined to extend his claims to Ghuzni and Kandahar, which had formed part of the Persian monarchy in the time of Nadir Shah.

The causes of war against the Prince of Herat were too obvious to be denied, but, at the same time, it was felt that very serious interests would be endangered by the approach of the Shah of Persia, either in the way of direct conquest, or by the admission of his right of dominion to the frontiers of India. Such an event would, doubtless, have unsettled the minds of the Mussulman population throughout the peninsula, and awakened a dangerous fanaticism, which it would have been very difficult to control. There were, however, some considerations still more serious; Mr. Ellis found the Russian influence predominant in the councils of Persia, and the Russian ambassador, Count Sunovich, suspiciously anxious to precipitate the march of the Shah's army on Herat. In fact, there was reason to believe that the Persians would only be the advanced guard of the Russians, who would thus be brought into dangerous proximity with the most exposed frontier of British India.

The Barukzye brothers were at this time much alarmed by the rapid progress and repeated victories of the Sikhs, and they equally feared and hated Shah Kemran, who was the most bitter enemy of their family. They were, therefore, anxious to secure the friendship of Persia, though they professed that they would rather gain their objects by the intervention of the British government. It does not appear that, at this period, any effort had been made to mediate between the Sikhs and Afghans on the part of the authorities in India; the war was waged at a distance from the English frontiers, and, therefore, excited a very small share of attention. The hatred, however, which the Afghans and the Mohammedans generally bear to the Sikhs, is so intense, that the war between them ought to have been very carefully observed, lest it might lead to some outburst of Mohammedan enthusiasm. Dost Mohammed Khan's inclination to form an alliance with Persia, though mainly, was not wholly caused by his dread of the Sikhs; by his mother's side he was descended from the Persian tribes, which had been sent to colonize Afghanistan in the reign of Nadir-Shah; they were called Kuzzilbashes, that is, "Red-heads," from their retaining the cap, which formed part of their national costume; and they retained the Shíah form of the Mohamedan faith, in opposition to the Afghans, who are strongly attached to the Sonnete creed. His connection with these tribes, naturally disposed Dost Mohammed to form a Persian alliance, and, in the existing state of the court of Teheran, it was scarcely possible to negociate such an alliance, without also entering upon some diplomatic relations with the Russians.

The attempt which Shah Shujah made to recover his throne, in 1834, was believed at Kabúl to have been indirectly favoured by the English authorities. Its failure was certainly unpleasant and unexpected at Calcutta, and there is no doubt that many subordinate officers gave the Shah secret assistance. But, notwithstanding these causes of suspicion, Dost Mohammed sought the interference of the British to prevent the encroachments of the Sikhs, and made a strong application to Lord Auckland on the subject, immediately after his lordship's arrival in India. The Governor-general resolved to embrace the opportunity of opening commercial negociations with the countries west of the Indus, and securing to British merchants the free navigation of that river; he therefore sent Captain (afterwards Sir Alexander) Burnes, on a mission to Kabúl, from whence, it was hoped, that great advantages might result to British trade with Central Asia.

This mission has been very severely criticized, and Mr. Masson's remarks upon it are, at least, entitled to attention :—

"The main, and great aim of government, is declared to be to open the Indus. Was the Indus ever closed, or farther closed than by its dangerous entrances and shallow depth of water? Another object was to open the countries on and beyond the Indus to commerce. Were they also ever closed? No such thing: they carried on an active and increasing trade with India, and afforded markets for immense quantities of British manufactured goods. The governments of India and of England, as well as the public at large, were never amused and deceived by a greater fallacy, than that of opening the Indus as regarded commercial objects. The results of the policy concealed under this pretext, have been the introduction of troops into the countries on and beyond the river, and of some half-dozen steamers on the stream itself, employed for warlike objects, not for those of trade. There is, besides, great absurdity in commercial treaties with the states of Central Asia, simply because there is no occasion for them. From ancient and prescribed usage, moderate and fixed duties are levied; trade is perfectly free; no goods are prohibited; and the more extensive the commerce carried on, the greater advantage to the state. Where, then, the benefit of commercial treaties?"

Although this criticism displays too great a tendency to judge from actual results rather than original purpose, it must be confessed that the crisis was ill chosen for commencing negociations, Afghanistan being at the time distracted internally by the feuds of the Barukzye brothers, and menaced externally by the Persians on one side, and the Sikhs on the other. Indeed, the Afghans did not and could not appreciate the advantages of a commercial treaty; they were, however, willing that the English should mediate between them and the Sikhs, and they felt grateful for the acknowledgment of the independence of the Barukzye chiefs, which had been obtained from Shah Kemran, in return for his being secured against the attacks of Persia. Dost Mohammed, in fact, from the beginning looked upon the mission as political, and for this the British government was clearly unprepared.

In September, 1837, Captain Alexander Burnes reached Kabúl, at a time when recent events appeared to give him the power of accomplishing the objects of his mission with little or no difficulty. Dost Mohammed was anxious to recover Peshawer from the Sikhs, and Runjeet Singh was just as anxious to get rid of a useless and expensive acquisition.

"It appears," says Mr. Masson, "that the Máhárájá was so confounded at the death of Hárí Singh (his favourite general), that he informed Captain Wade that he should be glad to give up Pesháwer, preserving his pardah, or his honour. Nothing could be clearer than that the Máhárájá was willing, at the request of the British government, to have abandoned his unjust conquest, —such request would have saved him the appearance of having been forced to give it up, and have preserved his pardah. Farther, no person acquainted with the state of the country and its relations, could have doubted but that he intended to restore it to Súltàn Máhomed Khán, who already enjoyed half the revenues—and from whom it was taken. Its restitution to Dost Máhomed Khân was a measure neither to be conceived with any propriety, nor to be demanded, with any justice, from the Máhárájá. The disposition of the Máhárájá was so unhoped for, and so favourable to the success of the mission, that it is no less extraordinary than unfortunate that Captain Burnes should not have seen the matter in the light every one but himself did."

In justice, however, to Sir Alexander Burnes, it must be remarked that Dost Mohammed, at this period, was secretly negociating both with the Persians and the Russians, and that the Persian king, Shah Mohammed, was slowly advancing on Herat, with every reasonable project of being joined by the Barukzye brothers. In the December of 1837, the Persian army crossed the frontier and laid siege to Herat, and, at the same time, a Russian emissary made his appearance in Kabúl, where he was received with studied attention. Mr. M'Neill, the English ambassador in Persia, offered himself as a mediator between the Persian monarch and the sovereign of Herat, but the Russian ambassador counteracted his exertions, and the siege was continued. Herat, however, was vigorously defended; the Persians lay several months before the walls, and did not hazard an assault until they had battered the city for six days with an incessant fire from forty pieces of cannon. When the signal of attack was made, the Persians advanced with great gallantry, and planted their standards three several times upon the breach, but were unable to maintain their position. The Afghans attacked them energetically, sword in hand, with a vigour which was irresistible, and drove them across the ditch. The loss of the assailants amounted to nearly two thousand men, including a great number of officers of the highest rank. More than three-fourths were found to have fallen by sabre wounds. The preservation of Herat was owing, in a great degree, to the distinguished abilities and valour of Lieutenant Pottinger, who happened accidentally to be present; he taught the Afghans how to resist the military arts of the besiegers, and he thwarted the attempts of the Russian agents to excite dissensions in the garrison.

Such was the situation of affairs in Persia and Kabúl, when the Indian government deemed it necessary to interfere in the affairs of Afghanistan. The principles by which such an interference was justified are laid down in a manifesto issued by Lord Auckland from Simla, and, as this document is one of the highest importance, we shall publish it at full length :—

"1. The Right Honourable the Governor-general of India having, with the concurrence of the Supreme Council, directed the assemblage of a British force for service across the Indus, his lordship deems it proper to publish the following exposition of the reasons which have led to this important measure.

"2. It is a matter of notoriety that the treaties entered into by the British Government in the year 1832, with the Ameers of Sinde, the Nawab of Bahawulpore, and Maharájá Runjeet Singh, had for their object, by opening the navigation of the Indus, to facilitate the extension of commerce, and to gain for the British nation, in Central Asia, that legitimate influence which an interchange of benefits would naturally produce.

"3. With a view to invite the aid of the *de facto* rulers of Afghanistan to the measures necessary for giving full effect to those treaties, Captain Burnes was deputed, towards the close of the year 1836, on a mission to Dost Mahomed Khan, the Chief of Kabúl. The original objects of that officer's mission were purely of a commercial nature.

"4. Whilst Captain Burnes, however, was on his journey to Kabúl, information was received by the Governor-general that the troops of Dost Mahomed Khan had made a sudden and unprovoked attack on those of our ancient ally, Maharájá Runjeet Singh. It was naturally to be apprehended that his highness the Maharájá, would not be slow to avenge this aggression; and it was to be feared that the flames of war being once kindled in the very regions into which we were endeavouring to extend our commerce, the peaceful and beneficial purposes of the British government would be altogether frustrated. In order to avert a result so calamitous, the Governor-general resolved on authorizing Captain Burnes to intimate to Dost Mahomed Khan that, if he should evince a disposition to come to just and reasonable terms with the Maharájá, his lordship would exert his good offices with his highness for the restoration of an amicable understanding between the two powers. The Maharájá, with the characteristic confidence which he has uniformly placed in the faith and friendship of the British nation, at once assented to the proposition of the Governor-general, to the effect that, in the meantime, hostilities on his part should be suspended.

"5. It subsequently came to the knowledge of the Governor-general, that a Persian army was besieging Herat; that intrigues were actively prosecuted throughout Afghanistan, for the purpose of extending Persian influence and authority to the banks of, and even beyond, the Indus; and that the court of Persia had not only commenced a course of injury and insult to the officers of her Majesty's mission in the Persian territory, but had afforded evidence of being engaged in designs wholly at variance with the principles and objects of its alliance with Great Britain.

"6. After much time spent by Captain Burnes in fruitless negociation at Kabúl, it appeared, that Dost Mahomed Khan, chiefly in consequence of his reliance upon Persian encouragement and assistance, persisted, as respected his misunderstanding with the Sikhs, in using the most unreasonable pretensions, such as the Governor-general could not, consistently with justice and his regard for the friendship of Maharájá Runjeet Singh, be the channel of submitting to the consideration of his highness; that he avowed schemes of aggrandizement and ambition, injurious to the security and peace of the frontiers of India; and that he openly threatened, in furtherance of those schemes, to call in every foreign aid which he could command. Ultimately, he gave his undisguised support to the Persian designs in Afghanistan, of the unfriendly and injurious character of which, as concerned the British power in India, he was well apprised, and by his utter disregard of the views and interests of the British government, compelled Captain Burnes to leave Kabúl without having effected any of the objects of his mission.

"7. It was now evident that no further interference could be exercised by the British government, to bring about a good understanding between the Sikh ruler and Dost Mahomed Khan, and the hostile policy of the latter chief showed too plainly that, so long as Kabúl remained under his government, we could never hope that the tranquillity of our neighbourhood would be secured, or that the interests of our Indian empire would be preserved inviolate.

"8. The Governor-general deems it in this place necessary to revert to the siege of Herat, and the conduct of the Persian nation. The siege of that city has now been carried on by the Persian army for many months. The attack upon it was a most unjustifiable and cruel aggression, perpetrated and continued, notwithstanding the solemn and repeated remonstrances of the British envoy at the court of Persia, and after every just and becoming offer of accommodation had been made and rejected. The besieged have behaved with gallantry and fortitude worthy of the justice of their cause, and the Governor-general would yet indulge the hope that their heroism may enable them to maintain a successful defence, until succours shall reach them from British India. In the meantime, the ulterior designs of Persia, affecting the interests of the British government, have been, by a succession of events, more and more openly manifested. The Governor-general has recently ascertained, by an official despatch from Mr. M'Neill, her Majesty's envoy, that his excellency has been compelled, by the refusal of his just demands, and by a systematic course of disrespect adopted towards him by the Persian government, to quit the court of the Shah, and to make a public declaration of the cessation of all intercourse between the two governments. The necessity under which Great Britain is placed, of regarding the present advance of the Persian arms into Afghanistan, as an act of hostility towards herself, has also been officially communicated to the Shah, under the express order of her Majesty's government.

"9. The chiefs of Candahar (brothers of Dost Mahomed Khan

of Kabúl) have avowed their adherence to the Persian policy, with the same full knowledge of its opposition to the rights and interests of the British nation in India, and have been openly assisting in the operations against Herat.

"10. In the crisis of affairs consequent upon the retirement of our envoy from Kabúl, the Governor-general felt the importance of taking immediate measures for arresting the rapid progress of foreign intrigue and aggression towards our own territories.

"11. His attention was naturally drawn, at this conjuncture, to the position and claims of Shah Soojah-ool-Moolk, a monarch who, when in power, had cordially acceded to the measures of united resistance to external enmity, which were at that time judged necessary by the British government, and who, on his empire being usurped by its present rulers, had found an honourable asylum in the British dominions.

"12. It had been clearly ascertained, from the information furnished by the various officers who have visited Afghanistan, that the Barukzye Chiefs, from their disunion and unpopularity, were ill fitted, under any circumstances, to be useful allies to the British government, and to aid us in our just and necessary measures of national defence. Yet, so long as they refrained from proceedings injurious to our interest and security, the British government acknowledged and respected their authority. But a different policy appeared to be now more than justified by the conduct of those chiefs, and to be indispensible to our own safety. The welfare of our possessions in the East requires that we should have on our western frontier, an ally who is interested in resisting aggression, and establishing tranquillity, in the place of chiefs ranging themselves in subservience to a hostile power, and seeking to promote schemes of conquest and aggrandizement.

"13. After a serious and mature deliberation, the Governor-general was satisfied that a pressing necessity, as well as every consideration of policy and justice, warranted us in espousing the cause of Shah Soojah-ool-Moolk, whose popularity throughout Afghanistan had been proved to his lordship by the strong and unanimous testimony of the best authorities. Having arrived at this determination, the Governor-general was further of opinion, that it was just and proper, no less from the position of Maharájá Runjeet Singh, than from his undeviating friendship towards the British government, that his highness should have the offer of becoming a party to the contemplated operations. Mr. M'Naghten was accordingly deputed in June last to the court of his highness, and the result of his mission has been the conclusion of a tripartite treaty, by the British government, the Maharájá, and Shah Soojah-ool-Moolk, whereby his highness is guaranteed in his present possessions, and has bound himself to co-operate for the restoration of the Shah to the throne of his ancestors. The friends and enemies of any one of the contracting parties, have been declared to be the friends and enemies of all. Various points have been adjusted, which had been the subjects of discussion between the British government and his highness the Maharájá, the identity of whose interests, with those of the honourable Company, has now been made apparent to all the surrounding states. A guaranteed independence will, upon favourable conditions, be tendered to the Ameers of Scinde; and the integrity of Herat, in the possession of its present ruler, will be fully respected; while by the measures completed, or in progress, it may reasonably be hoped that the general freedom and security of commerce will be promoted; that the name and just influence of the British government will gain their proper footing among the Natives of Central Asia, that tranquillity will be established upon the most important frontier of India; and that a lasting barrier will be raised against intrigue and encroachment.

"14. His majesty Shah Soojah-ool-Moolk, will enter Afghanistan surrounded by his own troops. and will be supported against foreign interference, and factious opposition, by a British army. The Governor-general confidently hopes that the Shah will be speedily replaced on his throne by his own subjects and adherents, and when once he shall be secured in power, and the independence and integrity of Afghanistan established, the British army will be withdrawn. The Governor-general has been led to these measures, by the duty which is imposed upon him of providing for the security of the possessions of the British crown; but he rejoices that, in the discharge of this duty, he will be enabled to assist in restoring the union and prosperity of the Afghan people. Throughout the approaching operations, British influence will be sedulously employed to further every measure of general benefit; to reconcile differences; to secure oblivion of injuries; and to put an end to the distractions by which, for so many years, the welfare and happiness of the Afghans have been impaired. Even to the chiefs, whose hostile proceedings have given just cause of offence to the British government, it will seek to secure liberal and honourable treatment, on their tendering early submission; and ceasing from opposition to that course of measures, which may be judged the most suitable for the general advantage of their country.

"By order of the Right Honourable the Governor-general of India,

"(Signed) "W. H. M'NAGHTEN,
"*Secretary to the Government of India,*
"*with the Governor-general.*"

A tripartite treaty was concluded, between the British government, Runjeet Singh and Shah Shuja, whereby the Mahárájá of the Sikhs, was confirmed in his present possessions, and bound to co-operate in the restoration of the Shah. It was also resolved to tender a guaranteed independence to the rulers of Scinde, and to leave Herat under the government of Kemran. Shah Shujah was to levy an army of his own, but was to be supported by a British force, until his restoration was effected and the security of his dominion established. Two armies prepared; that from Bombay was to ascend the Indus, and enforce if necessary, the co-operation of the rulers of Scinde, while the Bengal army was to descend by the left bank of the Sutluj, so as to form a junction with the Bombay division, at Shikarpore. The following description of Shikapore, by Major Hough, will explain the reasons why it was chosen as a place of rendezvous, and the causes of the importance it acquired during the subsequent operations of the war.

"The town of Shikarpore contains about 6,000 houses and 30,000 inhabitants, the houses are all built of mud, and it is a dirty place. It is a place of much resort, and the first of importance between Rohree and Dadur, near the entrance to the Bolan Pass. It has some pretensions to trade, but none to consideration from its buildings. There are a number of Jews here, from whom bills can be obtained or negociated, on any place in India, or even on Constantinople, China, or any place almost in the world: in fact, money transactions are the chief employment of the wealthy people of the place, and the merchants will contract to furnish large quantities of grain. Being so near the Indus, whenever the free navigation of the river increases the commerce of Scinde and Afghanistan, Shikarpore will become a place of great commercial importance."

The news, however, of the raising of the siege of Herat, and the retreat of the Shah of Persia, which reached the Governor-general about this time, led to some changes in the military operations. It was resolved, that only a portion of the Bengal force should be sent forward, and that the command of the entire expedition, should be given to Sir John Keane, the chief of the Bombay division. At the same time, a personal interview took place between the Governor-general and Runjeet Singh, which was conducted with extraordinary magnificence, and greatly tended to secure for the expedition, active aid from that energetic sovereign.

It soon appeared that the rulers of Scinde were unwilling to fulfil their stipulations, and permit the march of an European force through their territory; it was therefore necessary to force a passage. A strong division marched upon Hyderabad, which was taken without any effectual resistance. This was followed by the capture of Kurrachee, the richest city in Scinde, which so terrified the rulers of that country, that they submitted to a new treaty, agreeing to make an immediate payment of £300,000; to maintain an auxiliary force of 4,000 men, under the command of British officers; to pay a tribute amounting to nearly one half of their revenue; and to acknowledge the sovereignty of the Company over their country.

In the meantime, the Bengal division pursued its course along the Sutluj, until it reached Bhawulpore on the Indus. Here, in pursuance of a treaty with the Ameer, possession was obtained of the fortress of Bakkur, which was of great importance to the secure passage of the Indus. Its value may be best understood from the following description given of it, by Lieutenant Leech, in his report to the supreme government.

" It is situated on an island in the Indus, between Rohree on the east bank, and the village of Sukkar on the west near to the latter; it is conveniently situated, and if remodelled, would be an excellent situation for troops: it is built in the usual manner, partly of burnt and partly of unburnt bricks, and its walls are thirty to thirty-five feet high; the elevation of the island on which it stands above the river, is twenty-five feet; it is loopholed, and has a weak parapet; on the east, there is an unfinished *fausse-braye* without a *terreplein*, acting merely as a screen to part of the fort walls; it looks, however, imposing from without, with its turrets and loop-holes; there is a low parapet wall to the west. It is commanded by the city of Rohree, where an enfilading battery would be advantageously erected, to cover the occupation of the island to the north of the fort, well screened by large trees, from which island the escalading party could cross with no difficulty, as there is no current. There is at present a garrison of about ten men, and one gun on the ramparts, which have been partly destroyed by its discharge! The inside is in ruins, there being only a few huts, and a bungalow of the Ameer of Khypore, the magazine in time of siege."

At this place, a bridge of boats was constructed, for the passage of the Bengal army over the Indus, and upon the 14th of February, General Nott had the honour of leading the first body of disciplined troops, to the opposite banks of this noble river, with all the "pride, pomp and circumstance" of military triumph. The whole of the troops, baggage and cattle, passed over by the 18th without the occurrence of a single accident.

Towards the beginning of March, the whole army had assembled at Shikarpore, and soon afterwards it began to thread its way through the difficult country leading to the Bolan Pass. Here their sufferings may be said to have commenced; the wild tribes of Belooches, who could never be got to attack them in front, hung upon the flanks and rear of the army, sweeping off the camels and the baggage, with the provisions. These marauders were in general well-mounted, and carried sometimes a sabre in each hand, in addition to their daggers, bucklers and guns. One of their means of defence, was to inundate the country, by damming up the rivers, so that the troops were forced to march through the water, until they came to the dykes. Their progress was also impeded by the dense jungles which they were obliged to clear for their encampments; and the dead camels which they abandoned by the way, emitted an odour that was almost insupportable. The men, however, proceeded in excellent spirits, for they had as yet felt no inconvenience from the want of provisions.

It was in the passage of the defiles of the Bolan Pass, that their real hardships began; they were entered by the Bengal column, on the evening of the 18th of March. Although the heat in the plain which the troops had left, was intolerable, a hurricane of snow swept over their heads in Bolan, and the way was so encumbered with great fragments of rock, that they were compelled to abandon their tents, together with the greater number of their camels, to the wild robbers who hovered on their flanks day and night. The principal promoter of these outrages was Mehrat Khan, the chief of the strong fortress of Khelat, who instigated the plundering tribes to assault and murder the followers of the army, at the same time that he was negociating a treaty with the representative of the British government.

On the 26th of March, the army reached Quettah, where the want of provisions began to be severely felt, and the soldiers were placed on a limited allowance. As they advanced towards Kandahar, the want of water caused the death of nearly sixty horses, but fortunately, when their distress was at the highest, a supply of water and forage was discovered on the Doree river, at some distance from the line of march.

Those who were present, describe the scene which ensued as most appalling. "The moment the horses saw the water, they made a sudden rush into the river, as if mad; both men and horses drank till they nearly burst themselves. Officers declare that their tongues cleaved to the roofs of their mouths; the water was very brackish, which induced them to drink the more. The river was three feet deep, and more in some places; and was five or six miles off the proper road. Many dogs and other animals died. No officer present ever witnessed such a scene of distress."

Kandahar having been abandoned by the Sirdars, was occupied by the British troops, and the army halted for some weeks in its vicinity, to recover from its recent fatigues. The address of the Commander-in-chief to his soldiers, gives a very lively description of the difficulties which had been encountered, and of the spirit and zeal with which those difficulties had been surmounted:—

"The combined forces of Bengal and Bombay being now assembled at Kandahar, the Commander-in-Chief congratulates all ranks on the triumphant, though arduous, march they have accomplished, from distant and distinct parts of India, with a regularity and discipline which is much appreciated by him, and reflects upon themselves the highest credit. The difficulties which have been surmounted have been of no ordinary nature, and the recollection of what has been overcome, must hereafter be a pleasing reflection to those concerned, who have so zealously, and in so soldier-like a manner, contributed to effect them, so as to arrive at the desired end. The engineers had to make roads, and, occasionally, in some extraordinary steep mountain passes, over which no wheeled carriage had ever passed. This was a work requiring science, and much severe labour; but so well has it been done, that the progress of the army was in no manner impeded. The heavy and light ordnance were alike taken over in safety, by the exertion and good spirit of the artillery, in which they were most cheerfully and ably assisted by the troops, both European and Native, and in a manner which gave the whole proceeding the appearance, that each man was working for a favorite object of his own."

During the delay at Kandahar, the ceremony of Shah Shujah's installation was performed. The whole of the British army (Bengal and Bombay) was drawn up in line, at the dawn of day, in front of the city of Kandahar to the north, amounting to about seven thousand five hundred men. A platform, or throne, was erected in the midst of an extensive plain. At sunrise, the guns of the palace announced his majesty's departure. Lieutenant-general Sir J. Keane, with the Staff, were awaiting the egress of the possession, at the Herat gate, whence the king proceeded on horseback, through a street formed by his own contingent. On his coming near the line, a royal salute (twenty-one guns) was fired, and on his passing down the line, there was a general salute, and the colours were lowered, as in the case of crowned heads. On his ascending the throne, a salvo was discharged from one hundred and one pieces of artillery. Sir J. Keane, and the envoy and minister at this court, offered presents on behalf of the British government, of one hundred and one gold-mohurs each, and then the officers, British and Native, in the king's service, offered *nuzzars* (presents). The "army of the Indus" then marched round, in front of the throne, in review order; this grand ceremony presented an imposing spectacle.

On the 27th of June, the army advanced from Kandahar, to

assail the celebrated fortress of Ghazni, or Ghuznee, but owing to the difficulties which impeded the transport of the artillery, the troops did not arrive before the place, until the 21st of July. We are indebted to Major Hough, for the following description of the day's march, which brought them in sight of the fortress.

"The country over which we marched was undulating, but open; though we crossed some water-courses, still there was nothing to impede our movements, or prevent our acting in concert. Shortly after we had marched, we met a chief* with a few followers, who had been in the fort of Ghuznee, and had left it during the night, with the intention of joining us. The route was nearly in a direct line all the way, except the last three or four miles, when it turned to the left, and then the fort of Ghuznee burst on our view. It looked formidable with its fortifications rising up, as it were, on the side of a hill, which seemed to form the back ground to it, towards the citadel. We observed as yet no hostile movements. The columns were advancing slowly, but steadily, on the wide plain, and no noise was heard, save that of the movement of the guns, the distant sound of the horses' feet, and the steady tramp of the infantry; while, there being a slight breeze, the distant clouds of dust indicated, to those afar off, the approach of an army in battle-array. The advance of the army was observed by Hyder Khan by means of his telescope. As soon as the advance had arrived within a mile of the fortress, it was perceived that preparations were being made by the enemy to stop our advance. The object was, now, to dislodge the enemy from the villages and gardens which they occupied, close to and around the fort."

Sir John Keane found the fortress much stronger than he had anticipated; it was surrounded with a ditch and a high wall, flanked by towers and protected by a citadel. There was no heavy artillery suitable for sieges, with the army, and the garrison had obviously resolved on making a resolute defence,

* A nephew of Dost Mohammed. He was sent to Sir A. Burnes, who was in advance with the Commander-in-chief. From him they learnt that Gool Mahomed, the Ghiljie chief, who had been marching on our right flank all the way from Candahar, had gone into the fort and left it again, but that his horses were there. Also, that the Governor meant to resist, and various other particulars. This chief said he had not been well treated by his uncle."

for a heavy fire was opened on the British troops, as soon as they came within range of the guns. It was resolved to take it by storm, and the whole of the 22nd was spent in reconnoitring and making preparations for the assault. By three o'clock the next morning, the detachments were all at their respective posts, and the guns, chiefly field-pieces, in position at points which commanded the eastern face, as well as the Kabúl gate of the fortress. So secretly were these proceedings conducted, that not a single shot was fired by the Afghans, until they were aroused from their security, by a feigned attack, made upon the opposite quarter. The storming party under Colonel Dennie, then marched up to the Kabúl gate, where they opened a fire upon the ramparts and parapets which commanded the entrance, whilst Captains Thompson and Peat attached the bags of powder to the gates. These exploding, burst the gates open, and before the defenders could recover from their astonishment, Colonel Dennie, at the head of the storming party, rushed into the town. As at Herat, so here, the Afghans disputed the ground, inch by inch, hand to hand, with pistol, dagger and sabre. The darkness was more favourable to the assailants, than to the besieged : every street was strewn with the slain ; out of the garrison, which consisted originally of three thousand five hundred men, more than five hundred were killed within the walls, and fifty men fell in the defence of a single fortified house. "There was a heap of straw here," says an eye-witness, "some stray shot struck it, a moving was observed, a shower of balls was poured in, the straw fired, only one man escaped, and he was shot close to the burning mass. This house was the residence of the Governor, Hyder Khan, and the females of the principal people of the place were collected here. Here, too, were the magazine and granary."

"The centre square," says Major Hough, "exhibited a scene of blood and confusion ; horses, many wounded, were running about in all directions, fighting each other, kicking and biting, and running quite furious at any one they saw ; so dangerous had these animals become, that the men were obliged to be ordered to shoot the horses in self-defence, as they endangered the lives of all, and particularly of the wounded men, while being carried out." Before sunrise, the British banners were waving from the citadel, and all opposition was at an end. Protection was immediately granted to the women, and to such of the garrison as laid down their arms. A son of Dost Mohammed was found among the prisoners, and was entrusted to the charge of Sir Alexander Burnes.

The capture of one of the strongest places in Asia, with such apparent ease, made a deep impression on the minds of the Afghans. Dost Mohammed believing that the fortress would keep the English for some time, was proceeding towards the capital with his cavalry and a park of artillery; but when the news of the fall of Ghuzni arrived, his army broke up and dispersed, apparently in despair.

While Sir John Keane was advancing leisurely towards Kabúl, through the rich valley between that city and Ghuzni, Colonel Wade was making his way forward to that city, through the formidable Khyber Pass. This was a work of great difficulty, as appears from Major Hough's brief account of these terrible defiles. "The Khyber Pass is about twenty-eight miles in extent. From the entrance on the Peshawer side it is seven miles to Ali Musjid, from which it is two miles to Lalabeg Ghuree, a valley which is about six miles long, and one and a quarter broad; hence is the Pass of Lundeekhana; in fact, excepting the valley, the rest of the Pass, or for twenty-two miles, can be commanded by Jingals (wall-pieces), or even by the mountain rifle (Juzzail) fired with a rest, and in many places by the common musket. The road being stony, the movements of troops with guns is necessarily slow. The first four miles, after the entrance to the Pass, the road is contracted, and the hills on each side, are nearly perpendicular; to the left, two miles up the Pass, there is a road which leads up to the top of the hills. It widens after the third mile, but still the road is exposed to a fire from either side. At about five and a half miles is the town of Jaghir on the right, which could fire on any enemy moving by either road. From this tower, Ali Musjid is one and a half mile; on the left is the range of hills by which you move up to the fort; on the right is the hill which runs parallel to, and which is commanded by the fort. The range of hills to the left leads to the cantonment of the Kyberees; that of Choorah is about eight miles from the fort; that of Teerah seven or eight marches off. The tower of Jaghir was filled with the enemy. The fort contained a considerable garrison. There were breastworks thrown up on the hills: so that it was necessary to move on slowly, and at each halt to stockade the troops, as well as to protect the position; and the left was the point which required the most exact vigilance."

The death of Runjeet Singh created some difficulties in the management of the auxiliary Sikhs, who acted under Colonel Wade; but he steadily pressed onwards, and easily made himself master of Ali Musjid. The garrison evacuated it, after a very slight attempt at resistance; they probably were daunted by the intelligence of the fall of Ghuzni.

On the 6th of August "the army of the Indus," after a march of more than fifteen hundred miles, reached its destination at Kabúl, and on the following evening, Shah Shujah made his entry into his capital. Dost Mohammed, abandoned his baggage and artillery, and fled with a few followers over the Hazareh mountains into Bokhara. The conduct of the army on its long and very fatiguing march, through a variety of countries, often presenting the greatest temptations to a breach of discipline, was highly creditable. Major Hough, justly says, "though the troops had much to contend with, owing to various changes of temperature prejudicial to their health; and were for a long time on half-rations; were deprived of many necessary comforts, owing to the harassing hostility of plunderers; no troops in any warfare, perhaps, ever suffered so much with such soldier-like feeling; and never did any army marching in a foreign country, commit so few acts which could prejudice the inhabitants against it; while the people begin to acknowledge the beneficial effects of the change from anarchy to monarchy."

In order to follow out the conquest, Major Outram was sent into certain disturbed districts, between Kabúl and Kandahar, to tranquillize the disaffected Ghiljie tribes, which had not yet acknowledged Shah Shujah, and replace the refractory chieftains with new and more loyal governors. Nor was the treachery of the Khan of Khelat forgotten; General Willshere, led a strong detachment against his fortress. After some smart skirmishes in the neighbourhood of Khelat, the besiegers resolved to adopt the same course of tactics, which had proved so successful at Ghuzni. A storming party succeeded in blowing open the gate, and made their way into the town, the enemy disputing every inch of ground up to the walls of the inner citadel. After a sharp struggle, the troops at length succeeded in forcing an entrance into the last stronghold of the capital of Beloochistan. A desperate defence was made there, by Mehrat Khan in person, and he with several of his chiefs fell fighting, sword in hand. With his death all resistance ceased, and the Belooches were reduced to temporary obedience.

After leaving a detachment for the protection of Shah Shujah, the main body of the troops returned home by the route of the Khyber Pass and Peshawer. The gratitude of the country for the services performed, was evinced by a liberal distribution of honours and pensions. Shah Shujah instituted an order of knighthood on the occasion, but some of the circumstances attended with the degree of precedency in the new order, excited murmuring and dissatisfaction.

During this campaign, there were some menacing appearances on the part of the Nepaulese and Burmese, which seemed to threaten wars on the north-eastern frontiers of India, but the fall of Ghuzni probably induced the chiefs of both nations to abstain from provoking the British powers. Rumours were also rife of a plot having been formed, for a general insurrection of the Native princes throughout India, which excited no small alarm in Calcutta. Whether true or false, they led to the dethronement of a prince who was indebted for his sovereignty to English generosity. The circumstances are thus stated by a well-informed writer. "The Rájá of Sattara," as was mentioned in a former chapter, "had been drawn from the prison in which the other Mahratta chiefs held him, and invested with a certain sovereignty, on condition of his being entirely guided by the advice of the British resident, and holding no intercourse with foreign states through any other channel. He was found to have violated this engagement, and even to have taken a share in hostile negociations. Yet, he was offered a continued enjoyment of power, provided he would renounce such unfriendly measures, and dismiss the minister who was supposed to have prompted them. Having refused to comply, he was seized, confined in a neighbouring fort, and Appa Sahib his brother, placed on the throne. Slight disturbances also took place at Poonah. At Hyderabad, a somewhat serious conspiracy was formed among thirty or forty leading men, headed by the Nizam's brother, a proud and daring chief; but, being discovered, it was baffled, and the prince conveyed to the fort of Golconda. During the investigation which followed, the Nabob of Karnaul, a place situated about one hundred and twenty miles farther south, was found implicated. A force was immediately marched to reduce the town, which was entered without opposition; and the Nabob, who had been carried away by his own troops, was pursued and captured after a sharp conflict. Within the fortress, however, were found a number of well-constructed furnaces, in which cannon and shot had been cast on a large scale, and in forms fitted not for defence only, but for active proceedings in the field. These preparations had been secretly carried on for a considerable time. Again, the Rájá of Joudpore, after yielding in 1834, to all the demands of the Governor-general, had constantly evaded their fulfilment, and now showed himself more than ever refractory. Six regiments, with some cavalry and artillery, were sent against him, on whose approach he abandoned the stronghold, which was entered without resistance, only one British officer being wounded. Thus, the troubles which had brooded in so many quarters were crushed, and our ascendancy appeared thus to be more fully than ever established throughout Hindostan."

The possession of the fortress of Aden, at the entrance of the Red Sea, was deemed necessary to the completion of the plans for a regular steam-communication between England and India, on account of its convenient position as a station; a treaty for its surrender was therefore concluded with the Sultan, which was signed both by him and the Abdallah chiefs. Notwithstanding these arrangements, the Sultan's nephew resolved to resist the English expedition, sent to take possession of the town. The combat which ensued was of short duration, but was very vigorously maintained; it ended in the defeat and dispersion of the Arabs, but it was several months before the tribes in the neighbourhood, could be induced to abstain from desultory and harassing hostilities.

Although the prowess of British arms, and the terror of the British name, had deprived Dost Mohammed of the sovereignty of Afghanistan, and obtained for Shah Shujah possession of the throne, it soon became obvious that it would be impossible for the restored monarch to retain possession of his seat without European protection. The Afghans, who are among the most bigoted of the Mohammedan races, asserted that he had sold his nation to the Feringees,—that he was a traitor to his country, and a renegade to his religion. One influential nobleman, Syed Hossein, chief of Koona, sent an insulting letter to the king, upbraiding him with his apostacy, and declaring that if the Russians were on their march, as was then reported, it was his intention to join them. Such an insult could not be passed over with impunity, and Sir Willoughby Cotton, who commanded one division of the force returning to India, dispatched Colonel Orchard with a strong detachment, to attack the fort of Pooshut, where the Koona chief had taken up his residence. The soldiers engaged in this expedition suffered severely from the weather; rain fell in torrents, and the masses of snow on the neighbouring hills, rendered the cold so intense that the men's limbs became quite benumbed. On arriving before the fortress, the Colonel commenced operations by battering down the gate with cannon; when this was effected, the soldiers were on the point of rushing in, when they discovered that there was a second gate, and a second wall, from which a murderous fire was opened on the advancing column. The British were unable to return this fire with any effect, as their muskets and ammunition had suffered from the rain; they were, therefore, obliged to retire and shelter themselves from the guns of the fort. After some delay, an attempt was made to blow up the inner gate, and powder was laid in great quantities for the purpose; but this was found too damp to explode. It was then resolved to withdraw the troops, and renew the assault on the following morning. Syed Hossein, however, evacuated the place during the night, and on the 18th of January, 1840, it was occupied without opposition. The continued rain, and the deep mud produced by its incessant fall, prevented any pursuit of the insurgent chief, which was rather unfortunate, as his escape gave great encouragement to the disaffected throughout the country.

Dost Mohammed had at first despaired of recovering his ancient power, but the increasing unpopularity of Shah Shujah revived his hopes, and the intelligence that the Russians were advancing upon Khiva, probably led him to hope that he would obtain from them an efficient auxiliary force. He laboured very diligently to form a confederacy of the Mohammedan powers, north and west of Afghanistan, for the purpose of expelling the Feringee infidels from Central Asia. The King of Bokhara affected to enter very warmly into the project, and invited Dost Mohammed to his court. The Khan accepted the invitation, but he soon had reason to suspect the sincerity of the Bokhara monarch, whose object was simply to seize and imprison Dost Mohammed and his family, until he had extorted from them a surrender of their valuable jewels. Dost Mohammed refused to allow his family to follow him, which so enraged the King of Bokhara that he threw his guest into prison, and would have put him to death but for the active interference of the Khan of Kokan, who took up arms to prevent such an outrage. The King of Bokhara, however, refused to relinquish his prisoner, who would probably have been sacrificed at the first opportunity, had he not contrived to make his escape. The manner in which his deliverance was effected is thus described by Mr. Atkinson :—

"Dost Mohammed was confined in a small mosque, near one of the great bazaars. He succeeded in bribing a guide to procure him a good horse, to be posted in a suitable situation, a few miles from the city, and to remain himself close by for the purpose of shewing him the way. He then assumed the Uzbek dress, and finding an opportunity of joining his conductor, an Uzbek, who was ready mounted in the thronged bazaar, jumped up behind him. The Dost and the Uzbek trotted on unnoticed, passed through the city, and reached the spot where the other horse was stationed, without impediment. He then sprung upon his own horse, and eagerly pursued his journey; but in a few days he discovered that the animal had become rather lame, and, dreading the chance of being detected and chased, and unable from that circumstance to accomplish his own deliverance, he thought it more safe to have recourse to even an inferior steed, which was sound in wind and limb, than to continue on his own. Upon the urgency of the occasion, he therefore made an exchange with his guide. Proceeding onwards, the Uzbek began to repent of his undertaking, and, apprehensive of the consequences to himself, considered in what way he might avert the punishment that awaited him, if discovered. He was also anxious to turn the ex-ruler to some account, and was not long in forming the scheme of getting him back to Bokhara, and delivering him up to the king. A favourable moment soon occurred, for next day he fell in with a few horsemen, with whom he entered into conversation about Dost Mohammed and the Feringhees, and finding they were enemies of his charge, his avarice led him to hope for a high reward, not only from them, but from the King of Bokhara. In this spirit he said to them, 'Perhaps you would like to gain a prize. Do you see that horseman? That is Dost Mohammed, who has just escaped from prison at Bokhara,' pointing to the Kabúl chief, a few hundred yards a head of them. 'No! no!' they replied, 'that is impossible; Dost Mohamed would never ride on such a sorry Yaboo* as that, and you, his follower, mounted on this fine horse; no, no! You are yourself Dost Mohammed in disguise. We know you well; so come along with us to Bokhara.' The consternation of the guide at this blow to his cunning project, was strongly depicted on his countenance, which to the horsemen was an additional proof that he was 'the real Simon Pure.' He was thus caught in his own trap, and, in spite of his remonstrances, borne away, Dost Mohammed being left unsuspected to pursue his own course to Kholoom."

During the progress of these events, several disasters were experienced by the British troops in various encounters with the fierce Belooches. Lieutenant Clarke, who was escorting five hundred camels through the dangerous defiles in the hill country of North Cutchee, was surrounded and slain, with the greater part of his detachment. On this and some subsequent occasions, it was observed that the Sepoys did not display their usual firmness and gallantry. It is probable that their physical powers, and, consequently, their moral strength, had been deteriorated by a climate so different from that to which they had been accustomed, and perhaps they were also somewhat disheartened by their old traditions of the prowess and conquests of the Afghans.

A second encounter with the Belooches at a later period, was more successful in its results, but scarcely less disastrous in some of its events. Captain Browne, who commanded the garrison in the fort of Kahun, being closely besieged and rather hard-pressed by the Belooches, Major Clibborn was sent to his relief on the 12th of August, with a convoy consisting of about five hundred infantry, fifty of the Scinde cavalry, and two pieces of cannon. After a very fatiguing march, under a burning sun, for fifteen

* Hack.

days, the troops reached the dangerous pass of Surtof, about eight miles from Kahun, on the 28th.

Two days afterwards, while engaged in defiling through the pass, the enemy appeared in front, and commenced a destructive fire upon the troops. The Beloochees had destroyed the regular road, and obstructed the only path that was left, by breastworks covered with thorny bushes. The guns of the convoy were immediately placed in position to enfilade the pass in front, and the major ordered the left flank companies of the 1st and 2nd Grenadiers, to storm the heights where the enemy were posted. The following account of the contest which ensued, is graphic enough to deserve insertion :—

"The enemy opened a very heavy fire, but our party gallantly advanced and gained the head of the pass, and were ready to push on, when a dense mass of the enemy overwhelmed the storming party with musketry and showers of stones, while others fell on them with sabres, committing a fearful havock on the retreating Sepoys ; the advance companies were ordered to the support of the guns and colours, when the numberless enemy rushed down with the most determined gallantry, and with such impetuosity, that the troops had hardly time to form ; hard fighting on both sides, the enemy yelling and howling like beasts of the forest ; but the well applied rounds of grape from Captain Stamford's howitzers, soon repulsed the enemy with considerable loss, leaving above 200 dead on the field. Our troops suffered severely, above 150 killed and wounded."

Notwithstanding this success, the situation of the convoy was most critical, and the want of water was dreadfully felt by the thirsty and wearied troops. We again quote from a contemporary narration of what occurred :—

"The heat was dreadfully intense, and the suffering of the men and cattle from exhaustion and thirst, had become painfully apparent ; the little water remaining in puckalls from the last halting place was dried up, and no water was procurable unless the pass was carried, and the post of Kahun was distant about six miles. The puckall bheesties and camel puckalls, together with the gun-horses and officers' horses with followers, under an escort of fifty of the irregular horse, went for water. At this time the cries of the wounded and dying, for 'water! water!' were increasing, and gave rise latterly to scenes of frenzy and despair. In this manner they remained, anxiously awaiting the arrival of the water party. Some stragglers came in and reported that the water party was surrounded in a nullah: what was to be done? They had already lost 150 men of the force, the remainder were enfeebled with the thirst and exertions of the two previous days, and, to add to their difficulties, most of the camel drivers, dooley bearers, &c., had absconded during the action, after plundering the commissariat of the load of flour, &c. The gun-horses were gone, and the men of the Golundauze so prostrated from fatigue and thirst, that latterly they could scarcely rise to fire a gun. Major Clibborn, after mature deliberation, found that it would be impracticable to throw provisions into the fort of Kahun, and further, that unless the water party returned, the whole force must perish of thirst; the sad alternative was forced upon this gallant officer, of abandoning the unfortunate garrison at Kahun. No signs of the water-party appearing at 10 P.M., Captain Stamford was ordered to spike his guns, and this enfeebled force moved off with as much quietness as the frantic state of the men would permit. Almost everything was abandoned, owing to the desertion of the camel drivers, and at daylight they had partly descended the pass at Surtef, when the little baggage, stores, and treasure, they were able to bring with them, fell into the hands of the enemy. A great number of followers were here massacred. Without food and tents, and marching in the burning heat of the sun, they were obliged to make one forced march to Poolajee, where they arrived completely famished."

Another account is from its brevity still more striking,—

"We beat the enemy, but heat and thirst killed us—the men were frantic—mad;—Major Clibborn's conduct was capital,—coolness itself, and he only abandoned his materiel to save the lives of the enfeebled and frantic survivors, after all his gun horses, camels, and camel-drivers and followers, had either fled or been killed. We have a nation in arms against us."

The gallant conduct, however, of Major Clibborn and his little band was not without result; for the terror inspired by their courage in the minds of the Beloochees was such that they permitted Captain Browne afterwards to evacuate the fort of Kahun, and retire with all his troops, materiel, and stores, to Shikarpoor without molestation.

Before continuing the history of the operations against Dost

Mohammed, it is necessary to glance at the proceedings of the Russians, who had declared war against the Khan of Khiva in the December of 1839, and were engaged in the prosecution of hostilities during the greater part of 1840. Khiva is a Mohammedan principality, on the eastern side of the Caspian Sea; having on its north the vast steppes traversed by the Cossacks, who are nominally dependent on Russia, and the wild tribes of Turcomans, Bokhara, and Balkh on the east, and Persia on the south. It is sufficiently near Afghanistan to render any movement of Russia towards its acquisition a matter of grave importance, but it was difficult for the English government to remonstrate against the expedition, as the people of Khiva had frequently committed the most atrocious ravages on the Russian frontier. The manifesto issued by the Russian government, describing the situation of Khiva, and the nature of the insults which had provoked the war, is a document of great interest and also of no small political value, from the distinctness with which it sets forth the designs of the Russians on Central Asia. It shall therefore be inserted entire :—

"Khiva, which borders on the Kirgis-Kossacks, the inhabitants of which are Russian subjects, has constantly, for a series of years, shown, by acts of hostility, the little esteem it entertained for a power with which, for its own sake, it should have kept up a friendly intercourse. Our trade with the provinces of Central Asia was a source of prosperity for the inhabitants of Khiva, who drew from it their principal resources, and possessed through it in Russia the rights and privileges granted to the other inhabitants of Asia: but Khiva, far from appreciating advantages and benefits, has been guilty of the most flagrant disloyalty and unparalleled audacity. It daily harasses the wandering tribes that encamp on our frontiers, interrupts the intercourse the other states of Asia keep up with us, detains the caravans of Bokhara on their way to and from Russia, obliges them to pay extravagant duties, and compels them, by main force, to pass through its territory, and there seizes a considerable portion of their merchandize. These insults to foreigners holding commercial intercourse with Russia are, however, of less importance than the attacks which have been made on Russian caravans. Not one of these can now cross the deserts without danger. It was in this manner that a Russian caravan from Orenburg, with goods belonging to our merchants, was pillaged by the armed bands of

Khiva. No Russian merchant can now venture into that country without running the risk of losing his life, or being made a prisoner. The inhabitants of Khiva are constantly making incursions into that part of the country of the Kergis which is at a distance from our lines, although the Kergis recognized the sovereignty of Russia under their khan, Abul Chaix; they destroy their camps, lay them under heavy tributes, excite them to disobedience against the legal authority, give an asylum to those who revolt, and to crown all these insults, they are detaining several thousand Russian subjects in slavery. The number of these unfortunate wretches increases daily, for the peaceful fishermen on the banks of the Caspian are continually attacked and carried off as slaves to Khiva. The unfortunate condition of so many victims has naturally excited the solicitude of our government, which, of course, considers it to be a most sacred duty to protect and insure the lives and tranquillity of all the subjects of the empire. But the generous manner in which it called the attention of the inhabitants of Khiva, to the consequences to which their criminal conduct would infallibly give rise, has unfortunately been disregarded. Deaf to entreaty, they despise the indulgence we have shown, and, confounding in their ignorance moderation with weakness, they have calculated on impunity. In their blindness they have gone so far as to construct two forts beyond the frontiers, on the road of the caravans proceeding to Bokhara, in order to attack our merchants with less danger. Since then their incursions and robberies have daily increased, and, at present, their implacable hatred against Russia knows no bounds. As a last resource to bring these barbarians to reason, the Khiva merchants in Russia were arrested, and the release of the Russian prisoners and the cessation of hostilities, were announced as the condition of their liberty. But this measure was not attended with success, for, after having waited three years, at most 100 persons were sent back, though last spring, on the borders of the Caspian, 200 Russian subjects were carried off as prisoners. But now every means of persuasion has been exhausted. The rights of Russia, the security of her trade, the tranquillity of her subjects, and the dignity of the state, call for decisive measures, and the emperor has judged it to be high time to send a body of troops to Khiva to put an end to robbery and exaction, to deliver those Russians who are detained in slavery, to make the inhabitants of Khiva esteem and respect the Russian name, and, finally, to strengthen in that part of Asia the lawful influence to which Russia has a right, and which alone can insure the maintenance of peace. This is the purpose of the present expedition, and as soon as it shall be attained, and an order of things conformable to the interest of Russia and the neighbouring Asiatic states, shall be established on a permanent footing, the body of troops, which has received orders to march on Khiva, will return to the frontiers of the empire."

A strong Russian force was accordingly, without loss of time, despatched under General Brelowsky, which reached Khiva at the latter end of March in this year. The troops halted on the borders of the Steppes for some weeks, in consequence of the heavy snow that had fallen, and afterwards came down the Sea of Aral to Khiva. Their number was estimated at nearly 30,000 men, with twelve batteries of artillery. In various encounters which they had with the soldiers of the khan, the latter were invariably worsted, but the victors were much annoyed and galled by the species of *guerilla* warfare kept up by their opponents. Captain Abbott was at this time the British envoy at the court of the Khan of Khiva, and the latter wished to make use of his services as a mediator between himself and the Russians, professing his willingness to give up slavery and surrender the Russian slaves within his power, but declaring that he had no means of paying the demands made upon him by way of compensation by that government.

No sooner had Dost Mohammed escaped from the clutches of the King of Bokhara, than he began to levy troops for the avowed purpose of expelling the English and their protected monarch, Shah Shujah, from Afghanistan. Accounts were received at the same time, that Khelat, which had been so gallantly taken by General Willshire in the preceding year, had been retaken by the son of its late ruler, Mehrab Khan, and that the Belooches were every where rising to join in an attack on the English. It was exceedingly difficult to obtain any correct information of the motions of the enemy; indeed, so completely had the insurgents closed up every source of intelligence, that on the night of the 17th September, Dost Mohammed actually slept within three miles of the English camp; and the first knowledge of his proximity was derived from the appearance of some hundreds of Uzbeks on the heights at the dawn of the following morning. Brigadier Dennie, who commanded the detachment at Bamian, though his forces did not amount to one thousand men, consisting entirely of Native corps, resolved at once to attack Dost Mohammed's forces, which were more than eight times his number. The Uzbeks broke at the first charge, and suffered very severely from the active pursuit of the cavalry in their flight. Dost Mohammed lost his tents, baggage, kettle drums, standards, and his only piece of artillery. A series of petty expeditions against the chiefs, who were known to be in correspondence with Dost Mohammed, engaged the attention of the British during the greater part of the summer, until intelligence was received that the Khan had succeeded in assembling a new army, and had taken post at Purwan. On the 2nd of November, a detachment under Colonel Salter advanced against this position; as he proceeded, he was informed that Dost Mohammed was endeavouring to escape by a flank movement through the hills. Two squadrons of cavalry were sent to intercept the fugitives, accompanied by the political agent, Doctor Percival Lord, who had accompanied the late mission to Kabúl, and being personally acquainted with Dost Mohammed, might, as it was hoped, induce that chieftain to a peaceful surrender if any opportunity for opening communications should be afforded. As the cavalry approached the enemy, some unexpected resistance was offered to its advance, upon which the men, seized with an unaccountable panic, galloped back to the rear, leaving their officers without protection. Doctor Lord and three officers were killed on the spot, and some others were severely wounded. Dost Mohammed contrived to escape in the confusion produced by this disastrous affair, and his army dispersed. It was supposed that the khan would throw himself into Kohistan, which was ripe for revolt, but on the evening of the day after the battle, to the great surprise of every body, he surrendered himself to Sir William M'Naghten, the British resident at Kabúl. The particulars of this unexpected event are thus given by Mr. Atkinson:—

"On the evening of the 3rd, whilst taking his ride, the envoy and minister received the alarming communication made by Sir A. Burnes, which naturally produced in him a corresponding impression of gloom.* He was, in this depressed state of mind, proceeding homewards, accompanied by two or three officers, and within fifty yards of the gate of his residence, when a horseman, passing his escort and the gentlemen with him, rode suddenly up to him, and said, 'Are you the Envoy?' 'Yes, I am the Envoy.' 'Then,' rejoined the horseman, 'here is the Ameer.' 'What Ameer? Where is he?' 'Dost Mohammed Khan!' was the reply. The surprise, the amazement of Sir William M'Naghten at this announcement, may be readily conceived, and, in an instant afterwards, he beheld the very ex-chief himself alighting from his horse, and claiming his protection. The whole scene was truly electrical. The Dost was requested to remount and ride on to the gateway, where both alighted. The envoy then took his arm, and led him through the garden up to the house, saying, "Why have you persevered so long in opposing our views, and subjecting yourself to so much vexation and anxiety, aware as you must be of the good faith and liberality of the British government, as well as of its power?' but his only reply was, in the true Asiatic spirit—'that it was his fate! he could not control destiny!' Arrived at the house, and seated in the very room where, a year before, he was 'monarch of all he surveyed,' the voluntary prisoner delivered up his sword into the hand of the envoy, observing, that he had now no further use for it; but the envoy, with becoming generosity, begged him to keep it."

From Kabúl, the khan was sent to Peshawer, where he was joined by his nine wives and the rest of his family; from thence he was removed, with as little restraint as possible, to Laodiana, where he became a resident in the very house which had been inhabited by Shah Shujah during his long and tedious exile.

In the course of the year, several desperate attacks were made on the frontiers of Aden by the discontented Arabs, and, though they were all repelled with great slaughter of the assailants, yet the garrison suffered severely from the incessant vigilance which was rendered necessary by their inveterate hostility. So ferocious were these fanatics, that it was unsafe to give them quarter; in many instances they attempted the lives of those who mercifully endeavoured to rescue them from danger, or even to dress their

* The account of the escape of Dost Mohammed, and the disaster at Purwan.

wounds. Indeed, at this period, a great increase in the enthusiasm and fanatical spirit of the various Mohammedan races, was manifest throughout Asia; they seemed to feel that a time was come when the very existence of their religion was menaced by the rapid progress of the Christian powers, and they therefore prepared to defend it with all the zeal and fury of ignorant bigotry. The appearance of the English west of the Indus greatly increased this feeling, for Christians were thus introduced into the lands where Mohammedanism retained its greatest purity.

Afghanistan had been too long a prey to anarchy, for its chiefs to appreciate the blessings of order and tranquillity; the heads of the Ghiljie tribes had been accustomed to receive a regular stipend from the government for keeping open the roads between Kabúl and Jelallabad, and, as this was nothing better than a payment of "black mail" to marauding hordes, Sir William M'Naghten resolved to diminish and, perhaps, finally abolish the allowance, which was at once a heavy drain, and a great degradation to the government. The chiefs protested vehemently against this curtailment of their accustomed gains, but, finding that their remonstrances were disregarded, they resolved to adopt retaliatory measures and enforce compliance with their demands. A caravan, valued at twenty thousand rupees, was seized at Tereen; the *dáks*, or post-messengers, were intercepted, and all communication with Hindustan was cut off. A large detachment under Sir Robert Sale, was sent to open the passes, but, though the chief pretended to negociate, the column had to fight its way forward during a toilsome march of eight days, and the rear-guard suffered very severely from the desperate attacks of the Ghiljies, who rushed upon the troops from their mountain fastnesses whenever they saw them entangled in the defiles. General Sale's energetic exertions, seconded by the zeal and gallantry of the troops, finally prevailed over the untrained ferocity of the Ghiljies, and there appeared every reason to believe that the tranquillity of the country would soon be re-established, and free communications opened.

In the meantime, while Sale's force was at Gundamuck, on the road to Jelallabad, an alarming insurrection burst forth in Kabúl itself, November 2nd, 1841. It was so wholly unexpected, that letters written by the English resident envoy, on the preceding day, declared that affairs were in a prosperous condition, and that perfect tranquillity reigned in the capital. The causes assigned for this unexpected outbreak were various; some asserted that it was a sudden burst of Mussulman fanaticism; others attributed it to the general indignation produced by what appeared to be a wanton massacre, perpetrated on some insurgent Ghiljies by Lieutenant Lynch; while reports were spread of its having been instigated by the blind Shah Zeman, by the family of Dost Mohammed, and even by Shah Shujah himself. It is not easy to discover which of these conjectures is the most plausible, but there can be no doubt that a general confederacy had been formed for the expulsion of the English, and that the warnings of its bursting forth were incautiously neglected.

The first manifestation of the popular fury was a murderous assault on a party of English officers, returning from Shah Shujah's *durbar*, or audience. Sir Alexander Burnes and three other officers were murdered, one of them in the presence of the Shah himself; and such was the overwhelming force of the insurgents, that the British troops could only secure themselves in their entrenched camp, and in the Bala Hissar, or citadel of Kabúl. The whole city was up in arms, the bazaars were plundered, the houses of the British officers ransacked, and their property destroyed, the public treasury pillaged, and large bodies of troops collected for the purpose of attacking the British position.

From this period to the end of December, the British troops were incessantly harassed by attacks from the hordes of insurgent Afghans, who made desperate efforts to force both the entrenched camp and the Bala Hissar. Akbar Khan, the favourite son of Dost Mohammed, became the leader of the revolt, and his presence gave fresh vigour and bitterness to the assailants. Though generally successful in the repeated engagements which were fought during the six weeks that succeeded the revolt, the English began to despair of the final issue, as their ammunition was exhausted, their commissariat destroyed, and their stock of provision and clothing insufficient for their wants; and their camp annoyed by the effluvia from the heaps of unburied corpses, several thousands in number, which lay around. Under these circumstances, it was resolved to capitulate with the enemy: Sir William M'Naghten, accompanied by four officers, went to arrange the terms with Akbar Khan, but during the discussion some differences arose, which so exasperated the barbarous chieftain that he shot the British envoy dead on the spot with his own hand.

The charge of the mission now devolved upon Major Eldred Pottinger, who accepted the terms to which the unfortunate Sir William M'Naghten had partially assented, and the army prepared to retreat on Jelallabad, through the fearful defiles of the Khoord-Kabúl pass. The camp was evacuated on the 5th of January, but the faithless Afghans broke through the terms of the convention, the retreating troops were attacked with the utmost fury, and their entire march was a continued fight. Under these circumstances, it was deemed prudent to send the ladies back to Kabúl under the protection of Akbar Khan's party, while the army continued its perilous way through the defiles. In a very short time afterwards, the soldiers appear to have lost all confidence in themselves and their officers, they became disorganized, and were cut off in detail by the hordes of mountaineers.

General Nott, who commanded at Kandahar, on the first intelligence of the revolt sent Colonel Maclaren, with a strong brigade, to the relief of Ghazni and Kabúl. Had this detachment executed its mission, the subsequent disasters would have been averted ; but when the brigade had arrived within two days march of Ghazni, without meeting any molestation from the enemy, the snow was found to be so deep, and the cold so severe, that a retrograde movement was deemed necessary. The troops returned to Kandahar in safety, but Kabúl and Ghazni were abandoned to their fate. An army of the insurgents soon afterwards menaced Kandahar, but General Nott at once marched out against the barbarous hordes, and routed them with very little difficulty. On the eastern side of Afghanistan, General Sale maintained his position at Jelallabad, though ordered to evacuate it by his unfortunate superior, General Elphinstone ; but an attempt made by Colonel Wyld, to bring him relief through the Khyber pass, was unsuccessful. Ghazni, like Kabúl, was surrendered to the insurgents by capitulation, but as in the former case, the terms of the convention were flagrantly violated, and the garrison ruthlessly massacred.

The effect produced by the disasters in Afghanistan, both in England and India, was very great, but the general feeling was, that immediate measures should be taken to retrieve the national honour, and punish the perfidy to which so many gallant soldiers had fallen victims. It was resolved that measures should be taken to send prompt relief to General Nott at Kandahar, and to General Sale at Jelallabad, both of whom continued to maintain their posts with equal skill and gallantry, though incessantly exposed to harassing attacks.

While General Nott was engaged in the pursuit of what he believed to be the main body of the western insurgents, the Afghans assembled in force before Kandahar, and, on the night of the 11th of March, made a fierce attack on its diminished garrison. They were defeated with great loss, but, unfortunately, the weak state of the cavalry prevented the possibility of vigorous pursuit, or of forcing the enemy to a general action. It was said that a son of Shah Shujah had commanded the enemy in the attack on Kandahar, and information was at the same time received from other quarters, which proved that the monarch's family evinced little gratitude for his restoration.

In the meantime, Brigadier England was advancing from Scinde to the relief of General Nott, with reinforcements of men, money, and military stores. On the 27th of March, he reached the village of Hykulzie, and was received in the most friendly manner by the chiefs of that place, who did not, however, inform him that the Kajjak Pass, a few miles in his front, was strongly barricaded and secured by stockades. When the impediment was discovered, a storming party was formed, and the men advanced to the attack with great intrepidity; they were, however, driven back with some loss, and the brigadier deemed it prudent to retire on Quettah, until he could make arrangements with General Nott for a combined attack on the passes, both on the eastern and western side.

On the eastern side of Afghanistan, General Sale was contending manfully against the difficulties of his position at Jelallabad. Surrounded by the insurgents, under the command of Akbar Khan in person, this gallant veteran baffled both the force and fraud of his Afghan assailants. As a last resource, Akbar Khan spread a report that General Pollock had been defeated in his attempt to force the Khyber Pass; he even had public rejoicings in his camp for the pretended victory, on the very day that the Afghans were driven from Ali Musjid. But General Sale was neither deceived nor disheartened; on the contrary, he resolved to make an immediate attack upon the Afghan camp, though the enemy had five times his number, and though his own men were much weakened by the severe privations they had endured. This bold enterprize was crowned with the most distinguished success: the Afghans were completely defeated, and four guns, which had been taken from the unfortunate Kabúl army, were recovered. Unhappily, the victory was purchased with the life of the gallant Colonel Dennie, who had distinguished himself so much at the storming of Ghazni; he fell while leading his column to the attack of a fort.

The forcing of the Khyber Pass, by General Pollock, which was effected with great skill and gallantry, brought the relief which was much wanted, to the heroic defenders of Jelallabad. Nearly at the same time, General England retrieved his former disaster, by leading his reinforcement through the Kajjak Pass, and effecting a junction with General Nott. A new revolution took place in Kabúl; Shah Shujah was treacherously murdered by the Barukzye chiefs, and this event appears to have dissolved the confederacy of the Afghan leaders.

Here we must conclude the account of the Afghan War, and the History of British India, simply adding that on the last day of February, 1842, Lord Ellenborough landed at Calcutta, to take the office of Governor-general of India.

CHAPTER XXI.

HISTORY OF BRITISH INTERCOURSE WITH CHINA.

The East India Company possessed, for so many years, the exclusive monopoly of the Chinese trade, and made it so important a part of their administration, that a History of British India would be imperfect without some notice of British intercourse with the Celestial Empire. Before, however, we enter upon this subject, it will be advisable to take a retrospective glance at the early course of trade between Europe and China. Silk was produced exclusively in China until the time of the Emperor Justinian, when two Persian monks conveyed the eggs of the silk-worm, in a hollow cane, to Constantinople, and taught the Byzantines how to rear the insects and manufacture the silk. From Constantinople the culture of silk extended to Sicily and Italy, so that, in the course of a century, Europe no longer depended upon Asia for a supply of that article. In consequence of this change, the trade with China almost wholly ceased, until it was revived by the Mohammedans, who penetrated to that country through Bukaria. The best account we have of this trade, is derived from the relation of the voyages of two Arabian travellers who visited China in the ninth century:—

They remark : " Most of the Chinese ships take in their cargo at Siraf, where also they ship their goods, which come from Bassora, and other ports ; and this they do, because in this sea there are frequent storms and shoal water in many places. When ships have loaded in Siraf, they water there also, and from thence make sail for a place called Maskat. From this port ships take their departure for the Indies, and first they touch at Kau-cammali, and from Maskat to this place is a month's sail with the wind aft. Kau-cammali is a frontier place, and the chief arsenal in the province of the same name, and here the Chinese ships put in and are in safety. Having watered, they begin to enter the sea of Harkand; they sail through it, and touch at a place called Lajabalus, where the inhabitants do not understand the Arabic, nor any other language in use with merchants. From this place, the ships steer towards Kalabar, the name of a place, and kingdom, on the coast, to the right hand beyond India. In ten days after this, ships reach a place called Betuma, where they may water. It is worth notice, that in all the islands and peninsulas of the Indies, they find water, when they dig for it. In ten days from the last-mentioned place, they arrive at Senef; here is fresh water, and hence comes the aromatic wood. Having watered at this place, it is ten days' passage to Sandarfulat, an island where there is fresh water. Then they steer upon the sea of Sanji, and so to the gates of China; for so they call certain rocks and shoals in the sea, between which is a narrow strait through which ships pass. It requires a month to sail from Sandarfulat to China, and it takes up eight whole days to steer clear of these rocks. When a ship has got through these gates, she goes with the flood tide into a fresh water gulph, and drops anchor in the chief port of China, Kanfu, and here they have fresh water both from springs and rivers, as they have also in most of the other ports in China.' We have given this at full length, in order to furnish to the reader an idea of the tedious passages which were made at this time. Kanfu is, perhaps, Kwangchow-foo,—Canton; but some think that it was a port to the west of Canton, which now no longer exists.

" These Arabs do not inform us about the origin of this trade. It is very likely that some Arabs first made the voyage in a Chinese junk, and afterwards piloted their countrymen to Kanfu.

" 'When merchants enter China by sea, the Chinese seize on their cargo, and convey it to warehouses; and so put a stop to their business for six months, till the last merchantman arrives. Then they take thirty per cent. upon each commodity, and return the rest to the merchant. If the emperor wants any particular thing, his officers have a right to take it preferably to any other person whatsoever; and, paying for it to the utmost penny it is valued at, they dispatch his business immediately, and without injustice.'

" They speak of some great revolution, which affected the

trade considerably. An officer named Bai-chu, not of royal extraction, joined to his banner vagabonds and abandoned wretches, and marched against Kanfu. 'This city,' our travellers say, 'is one of the most celebrated in China, and was, at that time, the port for all the Arabian merchants; situated at some distance from the sea, so that the water is fresh. This rebel at last became master of the city, and put all the inhabitants to the sword, A.D. 877. There perished on this occasion 120,000 Mohammedans, Jews, Christians, and Parsees, who were there on account of traffic. The mulberry trees were cut down, and the silk trade began to stagnate. The whole empire was thrown into a state of anarchy. There arose many unjust dealings with the merchants who traded thither; which, having gathered the force of a precedent, there was no grievance, no treatment so bad, but they exercised it upon the foreign Arabs and the masters of ships. They extorted from the merchants what was not due; they seized upon their effects, and behaved towards them contrary to all established law. But God punished them, by withdrawing his blessing from them in every respect, and by causing the navigation to be forsaken, and the merchants to return in crowds to Siraf and Oman, pursuant to the infallible orders of the Almighty Master, whose name be blessed.'

"We must make a few more extracts. They state, that 'the Chinese coin no money besides the little pieces of copper like those we call falus; nor will they allow gold and silver to be wrought into specie, like the dinars and dirhems that are current with us. For, say they, if a thief goes with an evil intent into the house of an Arab, where is gold and silver coin, he may carry of 10,000 pieces of gold, and not be much burdened therewith, and so be the ruin of that man who should suffer the loss. Whereas, if a thief has the same design upon the house of a Chinese artificer, he cannot, at most, take away 10,000 falus, or pieces of copper, which do not make ten miticals, or dinars, of gold.'

"There was formerly a man, of the tribe of Koerish, whose name was Ebn Wahab. He went to the emperor's court; and sent several petitions to acquaint his majesty that he belonged to the family of the prophet of the Arabs. He obtained, finally, an audience; and the emperor asked him how they had destroyed the kingdom of the Persians. Upon this, Ebn Wahab answered, that they did it by the assistance of God; because the Persians were involved in idolatry, adoring the stars, sun, and moon, instead of worshipping the true God. After some further conversation, the emperor turned towards the interpreter, and said, 'Tell him we esteem but five kings: he whose kingdom is of the widest extent, is the same who is master of Irak; for he is in the midst of the world, and surrounded by the territories of other kings: and we find that he is called the king of kings. After him, we reckon our emperor here present: and we find that he is styled the king of mankind; for no other king is invested with more absolute power and authority over his subjects; nor is there a people, under the sun, more dutiful and submissive to their sovereign than the people of this country. We, therefore, in this respect, are the kings of men. After us, is the king of the Turks, whose kingdom borders upon us; and him we call the king of lions. Next, the king of elephants; the same is the king of the Indies, whom we also call the king of wisdom; because he derives his origin from the Indians. And, last of all, the King of Greece, whom we style the king of men; for, upon the whole earth, there are no men of better manners, nor of comelier presence, than his subjects. These,' added he, 'are the most illustrious of all kings; nor are the others to be compared with them.' We question very much the veracity of this whole conversation; but think the principal leading points may be according to truth. The emperor then showed his visitor the images of the prophets; and, finally, the image of Mohammed, riding upon a camel. At the sight of which he wept; and, being asked the cause, he exclaimed: 'There is our prophet and our lord, who is also my cousin.' Ebn Wahab describes the magnificence of Humdan, the capital; which, he says, is two months distant from Kan-fu. As an instance of the justice wherewith all matters were treated, our travellers mention an Arab merchant, who, being oppressed by some eunuch, the intimate confidant of the emperor, went to the monarch to lay his case before him. Though he was a favourite, the emperor rebuked him very sharply, saying: 'I grant thee thy life in consideration of thy former services in the rank thou holdest in my house; but I will confer upon thee a command among the dead, as thou hast not been able to acquit thyself of thy duty which thou holdest over the living.'

"They praise the uprightness and impartiality of the learned

Chinese judges, who devoted their whole lives to the study of the law. They are greatly taken with the ingenuity of the Chinese in all arts and sciences. Whilst they consider the nation as the only wise one on earth, they speak in terms of abhorrence of their idols and vices. It is their opinion, that 'the emperor reserves to himself the revenues which arise from the salt mines, and from a certain herb, which they drink with hot water, and of which great quantities are sold in all the cities to the amount of great sums; they call it sah, and it is a shrub more bushy than the pomegranate tree, and of a more pleasing smell, but it has a kind of bitterness with it. Their way is to boil the water, which they pour upon this leaf, and this drink cures all sorts of diseases. Whatever sums are lodged in the treasury, arise from the poll-tax, the duties upon salt, and upon this leaf.' They speak with the utmost contempt of the vices so prevalent to this day in China. 'There are schools in every town for teaching the poor and their children to write and read, the masters are paid at the public charge. The Chinese have no sciences, and their religion and most of their laws are derived from the Indians; nay, they are of opinion that the Indians taught them the worship of idols, and consider them a very religious nation. The Chinese are more handsome than the Indians. They wear long garments and girdles in form of belts, dress in silk summer and winter; and the women curl their jet hair,' which the travellers greatly admire."

Imperfect as this narrative is, it shews that the Saracens, with their characteristic enterprise, had opened a commercial intercourse with Northern China, and it was probably from them that the Italian republics learned the value of the Chinese trade in the age of the Crusades. The conquests of the Moguls under Jenghiz Khan and his successors, placed Northern Asia for some time under the government of a single race, and the enterprising Marco Polo, took advantage of this circumstance to visit its more remote regions.

Marco Polo was a Venetian merchant, of noble birth; about the middle of the thirteenth century he visited the court of the Mongolian king, Berekè, on the eastern side of the Euxine Sea, where he became acquainted with an ambassador who was about to visit Kublai Khan, the great head of the Mongolian race, who was then completing the conquest of China. Marco and his brother Maffio, were invited to accompany the ambassador, and they gladly embraced the opportunity. Their route lay through Northern Persia and Turkestan, and in the course of their travels they visited Kashgar, Bokhara, Samarcand, and other places which were the depôts of overland-traffic, and thence they penetrated to Kambalu, or as it is now called, Pekin. Kublai Khan received the strangers with great kindness; he professed great anxiety to open a communication with Europe, and empowered the brothers to apply to the pope for a body of missionaries to instruct his people in Christianity. The brothers departed for Europe with these joyful tidings, but such were the perils and difficulties of the journey, that three years elapsed before they reached the port of Giazza, in Lesser Armenia. The pope was much delighted with the intelligence they communicated, and deputed them as ambassadors to the Khan, empowering them to promise compliance with all his requests.

"They entered upon their journey in 1272; their road was beset with dangers, but, being men of great determination, they overcame them all. Marco Polo, who has given us the description, was one of the party. Their progress was tedious; they were three years and a half on their way before they reached Klemen-fu, a magnificent city, where the monarch at that time kept his court. When his majesty heard of their approach, he sent his people to meet them, and issued orders to prepare for their reception in the places they had to pass. By these means, and through the blessing of God, they were conveyed in safety to the royal court. The emperor, aware of their talents, used them in various enterprizes, of which the management required a great deal of skill. After having amassed considerable riches, they felt a great desire to return home. Nicolo Polo accordingly took an opportunity one day, when he observed the emperor more cheerful than usual, of throwing himself at his feet, and soliciting, on behalf of himself and his family, to be indulged with his majesty's gracious permission for their departure. The emperor refused their request.

"In the year 1287, Bolgana, Queen of Persia, and the wife of Arghun, died. In accordance with her dying request, Arghun applied to Kublai, his relation, to receive from his hand a maiden to wife, from among the relations of his deceased spouse. The emperor gladly complied with the request, and chose a damsel of seventeen years old for this purpose. But fresh wars had broken out, and the mission was compelled to retrace its steps to China, after many fruitless attempts to penetrate Tartary. In the meanwhile, Marco Polo returned from a successful voyage to the Indian Archipelago. It was now proposed to send the queen by sea, Marco having made himself thoroughly acquainted with the navigation of the Archipelago. By these means, Kublai was with difficulty induced to let the Italians depart. Fourteen ships were therefore equipped, each having four masts, and capable of carrying nine sails. The khan presented the Italians with many rubies and other valuable jewels; furnished the ship with provisions for two years; gave them a golden tablet, which contained the order for their having free and safe conduct throughout his dominions; and gave them authority to act in the capacity of his ambassadors, to the pope, the kings of France and Spain, and other Christian princes. After a navigation of three months, they arrived at an island, which lay in a southern direction, named Java; from whence they employed eighteen months in searching for the place of their destination. In this time a great number of the crew had died, and when they reached the place, Arghun himself, for whom the bride was destined, had departed this life. They delivered her, therefore, to the son of the deceased; and the Italians now set out, under a strong escort, on their return home. On their way they learned that the great Kublai had died, and therefore abandoned all thoughts of revisiting China. Loaded with riches, they, in 1295, arrived at Venice, after many adventures. On this occasion they offered up their thanks to God, who had been pleased to relieve them from such great fatigues, after having preserved them from innumerable perils."

Marco Polo's travels led to no immediate result; on the one hand, the successors of Kublai Khan were unable to appreciate his enlightened policy in promoting intercourse with foreigners; on the other hand, Europe was distracted by petty wars, immersed in ignorance, and very partially reclaimed from the barbarism of the middle ages.

The discovery of the passage round the Cape of Good Hope was followed, as we have seen, by the establishment of the empire of the Portuguese in the Eastern Ocean. After they had acquired possession of the best trading stations in Molacca they became desirous of reaching China, or as it was then called, Kathai, which vague traditions had described as a land of wealth and marvels.

Raphaël Perestrello, therefore, left Malacca with a junk, and arrived in China in 1516. He was successful in his voyage, and this gave rise to an expedition of greater importance. Fernao Peres de Andrade, who had eight vessels under his command, after having received orders from his sovereign to survey the ports of China, sailed for this country in the following year. The sight of eight large vessels, and the hardy features of the crew, struck the Chinese, who are always, on such occasions, conscious of their own weakness, with utter consternation. They were surrounded by a large imperial naval force, and only two ships, which had on board an envoy, T. Pires, sent by the Viceroy of Goa, were permitted to proceed from Sah-shan, (Sancian, or St. John's), where the others remained at anchor, to the provincial capital of Canton.

Andrade had ingratiated himself with the naval commander of the imperial fleet, by liberal bribes. Money will effect everything in China, and all tribunals and officers are unlocked by its magical influence. Pires, as an envoy from his master, came to conclude a commercial treaty with the emperor, and was friendly received by the governors at Canton. But his journey to the court was deferred, for the imperial council had not yet decided what measures to adopt. The late sultan of Malacca had arrived at Peking, acknowledging himself a vassal of the imperial empire, in order to obtain the countenance of the universal, political father, to reinstate him in his possessions, wrested from him by the Portuguese. This circumstance greatly injured the mission.

But Andrade, anxious to secure success to the trade, was unsparing in promises and bribes. He loaded several vessels, and sent them back to Malacca. But whilst he was successfully negociating for the privileges of trade, he received news that his fleet had been attacked by pirates, and his people reduced by disease. Some of his vessels went with a Loo-choo junk to Fuhkeëm, and from thence proceeded to Ning-po, where they founded a settlement, and carried on for a long time a lucrative trade. The elder Andrade had sailed, and his brother, like himself, always on the alert to effect his purpose, had established a settlement upon St. John's. Here he was attacked by the Chinese fleet; and courage (a scarce commodity), failing the imperial commander, they made a regular blockade of Andrade's squadron, until he made his escape in 1521. He is accused of having joined pirates, which never was proved, but his stubbornness is greatly exposed in a statement forwarded by the local government; the Portuguese are described as a nation which merely came to spy out the land, and afterwards to lay it waste with fire and sword.

Pires had to wait three years, during which time he was treated with the utmost contempt, before he could effect his embassy. When arrived at Peking, he was compelled to worship a wall, behind which the emperor was said to be seated. Unhappily, the emperor died, and his successor, Kea-tsing, wished to sacrifice the ambassador to the manes of the deceased monarch; but, after submitting to the severest humiliations, the ambassador and his suite were permitted to return alive to Canton, under the strictest custody, as if they had been convicted felons. Andrade's measures had greatly contributed to bring on this disagreeable conclusion. The Portuguese were ordered, in haughty terms, to restore Malacca to its rightful owner, and never more to appear in any Chinese harbour. They had been accused of horrible crimes, and it was hinted to them that their ignorance of the laws of the Celestial Empire alone pleaded their exemption from undergoing capital punishment. A squadron, in which was one ship from Lisbon, had likewise arrived in Canton river; two others joined this fleet; they were loaded with ammunition. Such a great number of ships gave umbrage to the suspicious Chinese government, and the acts of the commander were not calculated to conciliate the good will of government. The Chinese admiral blockaded them, until a reinforcement of two other ships arrived. The Portuguese, now in their turn, assaulted the Chinese admiral; whose fleet, after having been defeated, was dispersed by a heavy gale. To retaliate the injury done to the imperial navy, the Chinese government put the Portuguese prisoners to death; and when Pires arrived at Canton, he was, with his whole train, thrown into prison and murdered.

Ignorant of the fate of his countrymen, Melho Coutinho arrived the next year. The Chinese government, actuated by a spirit of dark revenge, killed the greater part of his crew in a scuffle, which ensued at a watering-place at Tam-ao; and thus the trade with foreigners was for some time interrupted. The Chinese government, though pretending to view this paltry affair with the utmost indifference, was very soon sensible of the advantages which the people had foregone.

Like all restrictive laws of China, not founded in justice, the prohibition of foreign trade was without effect. The trade was carried on at Teën-pih (or Teën-pak), to the west of Canton. In 1534, Kwang-king, an officer of that district, influenced by a considerable bribe, requested his superiors to have the trade transferred to Macao (Gaou-mun), a peninsula constituting a part of the Meang-shan island, and joined to it by a small isthmus, in 22° 11′ 30″ N. lat., and 113° 32′ 30″ E. long.; eight miles in circuit, the greatest breadth being one, the length three miles;—a rocky, hilly territory. This had been long ago the resort of many hordes, who wished to escape the oppressions of the mandarins, and the legal duties imposed upon their goods. The Portuguese erected here, in 1537, some sheds, in order to dry goods, destined for tribute, which had been damaged in a storm. These temporary sheds were very soon exchanged for substantial buildings, and the mandarins, prompted by fear, or induced by bribes, connived at this encroachment. Whilst this infant settlement was in progress, their hopes at Ningpo, from whence they had carried on a very lucrative trade to Japan, were finally blasted. The Portuguese adventurers, who at this time crowded to China, were often men of the worst character; even criminals, who were banished from the country. Their misconduct on one side, and the vexatious behaviour on the side of the Chinese, caused a revolt, which ended in their expulsion from Chinchoo and Ningpo.

The unwearied Francis Xavier, had been anxious to introduce Roman Catholicism into China, by an embassy to the court of Peking. A private individual furnished the funds for this undertaking, but the governor at Malacca appropriated the money to the use of government, and the expedition could not proceed.

The Chinese government, viewing this nascent colony with a very jealous eye, the supreme government of Canton cited before them the judge and captain of the place. In consequence of these summons, M. Ruggiero and M. Penella were dispatched to the viceroy. This grandee upbraided them for their wilful disobedience of the celestial laws, by creating for themselves their own laws, and threatened to expel them. This harsh language was very soon smoothed by rich presents, and thus they received permission to remain at the place. As an acknowledgment of their vassalage, they had to pay a ground rent, amounting latterly to 500 taëls per annum. From this moment Macao became the central station for the Portuguese-Chinese trade. Many Chinese flocked thither, and the government appointed a mandarin to govern their natural subjects, without the interference of any foreign power. Moreover, they prohibited, in 1612, the Portuguese from building new houses. This unreasonable prohibition, after full tenure of the island had been granted, was productive of a great income to the local mandarins, who sold their connivance for considerable sums. Even the repair of old houses was not allowed, unless a special permission had been previously obtained. This law was instituted to prove a check upon the insolence of barbarians, who had built better houses than any in the whole empire, and to teach them to depend entirely upon the compassion of the son of heaven.

From Macao they regularly resorted to Canton. The imported goods were valued, and the duties paid in goods, till 1582, when silver was required; on their exports they paid six per cent. They sent annually a deputation to Canton, who were entrusted with the management of business, and paid at their arrival, besides the duties, 4000 dollars as a present to the mandarin, and, at their departure, 8000 dollars. At first the market was open only once a year, but from 1580 twice; in January began the purchase of the goods for the India market, in June, for the Japan trade, which there was carried on to a very great extent. Many ships besides engaged in smuggling, to the great annoyance of the supreme government.

Meanwhile, the Dutch having become very powerful in India, waged an exterminating war against the Portuguese, to drive them out of their Indian possessions, and to engross their trade. Macao was considered one of the best situated places to carry on trade both to China and Japan. In 1622, Reyerszoon anchored in Macao roads, with fifteen ships. He began to disembark, and drove the Portuguese before him. At this sudden appearance of the enemy, the tocsin rang, and the whole population took up arms.

The Dutch had nearly passed the hermitage of Guia, when

a heavy battery was opened upon them from the Monte. Anxious to form a rallying point, they posted themselves at the foot of the Guia, but were attacked with so much violence in the rear, that they were forced to retreat as speedily as possible, with great loss. The slaves had joined in the general fight, and having behaved bravely during the battle, were emancipated by their masters; and the viceroy remunerated their services by presenting them with 200 peculs of rice. This attack was renewed in 1627. On this occasion the Dutch admiral's ship was burnt; and the fleet, apprehensive of succour from Manilla, left the roads, without having effected anything.

By this time, Philip II. had been acknowledged the lawful King of Portugal. He sent from Manilla a friar, to invite the people of Macao, who had created for themselves a republican government, to submit to the Spanish monarchy, 1582. In this proposal the inhabitants of Macao readily acquiesced, and remained annexed to the Spanish dominions till 1641. It was during this period that the unfounded rumours of Cataneo's ambitious views upon the crown of China were spread. This occasioned general consternation amongst the citizens, who had, by degrees, grown rich. The Chinese became afraid of their unbidden guests, and stopped all supplies of provisions until the rumour had subsided. The Jesuits had, at this time, raised a few miserable huts and a chapel on the Ilha-verde, near Macao. A Mohammedan military mandarin mistook this settlement for a fort. He boldly attacked it when the Portuguese were at church, but was afterwards killed in the scuffle which ensued. The matters were compromised by the literary mandarin at Heang-shan, who erected a stone upon the island, on which an inscription was engraved, stating that the island belonged to the Chinese empire, whilst the Jesuits remained in possession of it.

The trade at Canton had, hitherto, been carried on to the mutual interest of both parties, when the Chinese, wearied with the presence of the foreigners in the provincial city, confined the trade solely to Macao, in 1631. A company of merchants appointed by government had to furnish the exports, and to transport them to Macao, where they received, in return, the imports. But this regulation ended in smoke. The Chinese merchants, oppressed by their own government, were constrained to impose upon the foreigners to such a degree, that the trade would entirely have become extinct if the Macao authorities had not applied to the supreme government at Canton. The mandarins wrote, in consequence, to the emperor, saying: "Macao was, formerly, an insignificant place; it is now a kingdom; it has many forts; and a great, insolent population. It would be proper to inquire how much rice and liquor the Portuguese may want, and let them have the supply, and entirely debar them from the commerce at Canton." The emperor assented to this proposition; at the same time the mandarins had been feed, and matters were compromised, trade being carried on just as before.

The Portuguese had been for forty years in the undisturbed possession of the Japanese trade, and gained immense profits; but in 1614 the emperor of Japan proscribed the Christian religion, and restricted the Japanese trade with foreigners. Tanogun Sama finally expelled the Portuguese, and forbade them, under penalty of death, ever to return again. The city of Macao suffered greatly by this new regulation, and therefore sent four very respectable citizens to Japan, in order to bring the matters again to a good train, With the exception of a few black men, the whole crew and ambassadors were massacred by the Japanese. The vessels never returned from this disastrous voyage, 1640. Any other European nation would have revenged this national insult, but the Portuguese had become too weak, and all that John IV., at his accession to the throne of Portugal, could do, was to send an ambassador, in order to signify his exaltation to the throne. They tried the last time, in 1685, to re-establish their trade by sending back a number of shipwrecked Japanese to their own country. The Japanese did not molest them, but strictly prohibited their re-appearance on the coast of Japan.

The most valuable trade for Macao wasthus lost; the English and Dutch entered into competition with the Portuguese in the Chinese market, and, from this moment, Macao began to decay.

By acknowledging the Emperor of China as a liege lord, the Portuguese were sometimes suffered to send an envoy to Peking with tribute, on which occasions they were treated with magnificence and liberality, and enjoyed liberty to range at pleasure over the country. During the decline of the Ming dynasty, they sent, amongst other articles of tribute, three guns, which were afterwards imitated by the Chinese founders. At the approach of the Tartars, Rodrigues, a missionary, was sent to Macao to call in the aid of the Portuguese, who sent, accordingly, four hundred well-disciplined soldiers, with three canons, as far as Nan-chang-foo, the capital of Këang-see; here they received the news that the Tartars had been repulsed, and had to return, without either effecting anything, or receiving the Chinese subsidies. How much soever the Chinese may boast of their power, their application to a small colony for four hundred auxiliaries, fully proves their weakness.

At last, the victorious Mantchoos took possession of Canton, 1650, and the Portuguese were summoned to appear before the viceroy. A deputation of several gentlemen departed for Canton, loaded with presents for their new masters, and found favour in their eyes. The Tartars graciously condescended to receive the homage of their humble vassals.

Kang-he, unable to subdue the Fuh-keën pirates, issued an edict, whereby all inhabitants along the coasts of the maritime provinces, were ordered to destroy their dwellings, and retire for about five leagues into the country, under pain of death. Macao was to have been involved in the general ruin, as a maritime place, and owed its preservation to the influence of Adam Schaal, the missionary, who interceded for them to spare their settlement. A Chinese naval commander, however, anxious to put a stop to the whole trade, was about to confiscate all the Portuguese ships and cargoes, when suddenly his wrath was appeased by enormous bribes. Trade was now recommenced under great disadvantages, for the Portuguese had to obtain a license before they could leave the port.

To remove all these difficulties, and save the colony from ruin, an envoy, Saldanha, was despatched to the court of Peking with rich presents, which the city of Macao had procured. He went by way of Canton, in a boat, which had a flag inscribed, "Tribute-bearer," and arrived in 1667 at the place of his destination. His endeavours to mitigate the sufferings of his fellow-citizens proved fruitless, and he returned with the news that they must trust to themselves. The trade rapidly decreased; there was no commercial enterprize, no vigorous exertion to retrieve the loss; other nations were able to trade at a cheaper and more profitable rate; even the few ships which remained the property of the citizens, and there were finally only two, could not be employed. At this critical juncture, Kang-he declared all Chinese ports open for foreigners, 1685. The Portuguese at Macao had now again tendered their homage to their native king. They might have expected some aid from the mother country, or have tendered their allegiance to Spain; on the contrary, they were most enthusiastic in their loyalty towards the house of Braganza, and sent their new king 200 brass guns and a considerable sum of money.

Kang-he pursued his liberal course for some years; when some of his Canton officers made the most serious representations, that liberal measures were fraught with the utmost danger to the state. They described the Europeans as a daring, unruly race; represented the Chinese who went abroad, as disaffected towards their own government, and ready to join the barbarians in conquering China. Kang-he nominated a commission, to deliberate upon the subject. The result was, that all Chinese subjects were prohibited from going to any country, south of China, either as traders or emigrants. Macao retained the privilege of a free trade. The viceroy even offered to the senate at Macao. to make this place the general emporium of foreign commerce, and grant the city the duties on all imports. Prompted by a narrow policy, lest the foreigners might engross the Chinese trade, the Portuguese rejected this brilliant offer, 1717. Even, when it was again proposed, in 1732, the city rejected it, upon the suggestion of the Viceroy of Goa. What a place would Macao have been by this time, had this offer been accepted? Their shipping, which, in the meanwhile, had increased, was restricted by Yung-ching to the number of twenty-five vessels, of which the names, which, up to the present time, have never changed, were noted down by the Chinese. Macao felt less the consequences of the decay of Portuguese power and trade in Asia, than the other settlements. To conciliate the favour of the Chinese, and to give no umbrage to their jealousy, the Macao government acted the part of mediators between the contending missionaries in China; and by the mediation of John V., King of Portugal, requested the pope to grant the Chinese converts liberty to practise the Confucian rites. There had previously arisen some difficulties between the King of Portugal and the pope, about the right of investiture of Chinese bishops; but this difference was amicably adjusted, by dividing this privilege between the contending parties. When, however, Yung-ching proscribed Christianity, his Portuguese majesty sent De Sousa e Menezes, with Father Magelhaens, to China, (in 1726,) in order to intercede in behalf of his religion. He was urged, by the Viceroy of Canton, to proceed immediately to Pekin; but the ambassador requested the mandarins to forward a letter, wherein he alluded to the distinction between a vassal and an independent monarch; in order that he might be treated by all public officers with due respect. The viceroy waived this request; but assured him that the disgraceful term, "Tsin-kung—tribute-bearer," should by no means be applied to him. In 1727, the ambassador made his splendid entry into the capital; and, in order to show his liberality, scattered a great quantity of crusades amongst the thronging populace. Two court mandarins preceded him when he was about to obtain an audience; the ambassador carried his master's letter with both hands, and was followed by his retinue. Then, entering the western gate, he ascended the steps of the throne, and presented his credentials in a kneeling posture. After having quitted the hall by the same way, he performed the act of obeisance with his whole retinue. When this ceremony was over, he was brought to the foot of the throne, and seated at the head of the grandees. He then was permitted to deliver his speech, which he did upon his knees. Some days after this, he delivered his rich presents; the emperor viewed them as so many tokens of affection from the King of Portugal. He and his people were allowed to walk about in the capital wherever he wished. When he had his audience of leave, at Yuen-ming-yuen, the emperor presented him with a cup of wine, and sent him, from his own table, several dishes. The imperial presents were trifling; but the state sent the King of Portugal thirty chests of various articles. But, though the reception was very friendly, no solid advantages resulted from this mission; which, notwithstanding the reluctance of the envoy, was performed with all the ceremonies of vassalage.

Macao declined less rapidly than the other eastern possessions of Portugal, and is still of some value as a commercial station. It was occupied by the English in 1802, to prevent it from falling into the hands of the French, but the Chinese government energetically protested against this arrangement, and the garrison was withdrawn. The Portuguese trade with China is now all but annihilated, and the revenues of Macao, are not sufficient to defray the expenses of the administration.

The Dutch having shaken off the yoke of Spain about the close of the 16th century, were excluded from all the ports belonging to Spain and Portugal in the Indian and American seas; they were therefore compelled to seek new countries and harbours for their commercial speculations. By means of the Japanese, with whom they had formed amicable relations, which still subsist, they were enabled to form a colony in the island of Formosa.

They easily extended their possessions on the coast. The aborigines are an inoffensive race, easily subdued. China was at that time torn asunder by internal dissensions, and could not oppose the growing power of the usurpers. They established themselves at Ke-lung (or Ke-long), on the north coast, and on the west coast at Tae-wan-foo,—where they built the Fort Zelandia,—at Tam-suy, and at Lo-kang. But they were not merely intruders; the Natives being without religion, and very docile, they instructed many thousands in the truths of Christianity, who were baptized, and attached by the common faith to their masters. Fort Zelandia was by no means a paltry defence to the nascent colony, being a square castle, with large bastions; below which, towards the sea, was another fortification, consisting of two regular bastions, an excellent covered way, and four half-moons; the whole united to the fort by very strong walls, and defended by a great number of cannon, and a numerous garrison. The town was long and large, extremely well peopled. A poll-tax, at the rate of half a guildar a head per annum, furnished the revenue for the maintenance of the place. Being only 24 leagues from the coast of China, and 130 from Japan, it served as an intermediate emporium for both countries.

But this great success rendered the Dutch remiss. The fortifications were neglected, the store-houses emptied. Whilst every individual was anxious to advance his own interest, the state of the colony greatly decayed. Most of the ships, on their way to Japan, touched at Tae-wan. In both their home and return cargoes, the Formosan settlers dealt very advantageously, and amassed considerable property. The Fuh-keën junks also found their way to Formosa; many individuals were driven, by war and rapine, to seek a new home at Tae-wan; and thus trade and population increased, whilst the government lost its influence.

Kok-sing, a native Chinese, who had taken up arms against the Tartar conquerors of his country, being driven from the main-land, resolved to wrest Formosa from the Dutch, and by a rare union of courage and perseverance, succeeded in effecting that object. All the efforts made to retrieve this loss proved ineffectual, and the Dutch were compelled to rest content with permission to establish a factory in Canton. When Holland was annexed to France, during the late European war, the Dutch trade with China ceased, and the attempts made for its revival, since the conclusion of peace in 1815, have been utterly abortive. There is, however, some trade in rice between China and the Dutch settlements in Java.

In the reign of Elizabeth, an effort was made by some English merchants to open a trade with China, but the vessels were lost on the voyage. It was not until the time of Charles I. that a small English squadron appeared in the Canton river. License to trade was refused, but the perseverance of the Company's servants at length overcame opposition, and an English factory was established. The trade was, however, conducted under great disadvantages; the local authorities at Canton treated the merchants and supercargoes with contemptuous insult; the duties paid on merchandize were changed according to the avarice or caprice of the Chinese governor, and every possible impediment was offered to the extension of commerce.

Other great difficulties frequently arose, from the nature of the cargoes which were sent from England. The Company was very anxious to export as many British manufactures, and especially woollens, as were saleable. Yet the consumption in China was comparatively small, and many of the goods found no purchasers.

It was impossible to prevent the affrays which occasionally took place; and in one instance the Chinese interfered, and strangled a French sailor who had killed a Portuguese. On the whole, the trade had considerably improved, notwithstanding the great obstacles; for the consumption of tea increased at home. Some very unjust acts occurred also occasionally. A Captain M'Leary had seized upon a Dutch ship, in 1781, to indemnify himself for the loss he had sustained in a Spanish ship which he had captured, and for which he had to pay a heavy fine of 70,000 dollars to the magistrate at Macao, after having suffered imprisonment for some time. But when he was willing to divide the spoil with the Chinese authorities, the matter was again dropped, and things went on as before.

Besides the heavy exactions, which were constantly renewed, a serious affair occurred, on account of the firing of a salute, whereby a Chinese was killed, in 1784. The supercargo of the ship was decoyed into the power of the Chinese, and marched into the city of Canton under a very strong military guard. The avenues leading to the quay were all barricadoed, and filled with soldiers. The linguists and merchants fled, the hongs were deserted, and the communications between Canton and Whampoa suspended by order of the hoppo. The surrender of the gunner, who was strangled, eventually procured the liberation of the supercargo.

In order to put an end to these annoyances, it was resolved to send a solemn embassy to the court of Pekin, for the purpose of negociating a commercial treaty with the emperor. Lord Macartney was chosen as envoy, and Sir George Staunton was joined with him, as he was well acquainted with the forms of Chinese diplomacy.

An excellent assortment of presents, and a friendly letter from the British government, accompanied this mission, which sailed from Portsmouth in 1792, and arrived in July, 1793, at the Pih-ho. The mandarins, perceiving that the vessels could not cross the bar, thought that they must be very heavily laden with presents intended for his imperial majesty. Provisions were supplied plentifully, and the ambassador treated with the greatest respect. Two mandarins of the highest rank came to congratulate them upon their arrival, and behaved with such civility that they prepossessed the ambassador very much in favour of the Chinese. Whilst himself and his retinue embarked for Pekin, the ships received orders to proceed to Japan, there to endeavour to establish a free trade. Amidst an immense crowd of people, they passed up the river till they arrived at Tung-choo-foo. To their great astonishment, the English were accused of having supported the Tibet rebels; this circumstance made an unfavourable impression, though the ambassador endeavoured to contradict it as a palpable untruth. Though this may be said to have been a splendid embassy, they were, nevertheless, degraded by having written upon the flags, "Tribute-bearers." When arrived at Pekin, where lodgings were assigned them between Hae-teën and Yuen-ming-yuen, they were required to perform their prostrations at the audience. This was entirely against their inclination and orders. But, to remove this difficulty, the ambassadors proposed that a high officer of state should perform the same ceremonies of homage before the picture of his British majesty, which he was required to do. However, the legate who had charge of the embassy showed himself an enemy to Europeans, and endeavoured to thwart all their objects. As the emperor was at Jĕho (Zhehol), in Tartary, they were obliged to repair thither. They passed the Great Wall, and arrived at the place of their destination, a place composed of miserable hovels, beside the dwellings of the mandarins. The subject of the requisite prostrations was again taken up with all due warmth; but the emperor was condescending enough to yield to the request of Lord Macartney, who promised to perform the same genuflexion as he did in an audience to his own sovereign.

On the day of audience, the ambassadors were ushered into the gardens of Jĕ-ho. Tents had here been pitched, the imperial one had nothing magnificent, but was distinguished from all the others by its yellow colour. The imperial family, as well as mandarins of the first rank, had all collected. Shortly after day-light, the sound of musical instruments announced the approach of the emperor. He was seated in an open chair, borne by sixteen men, and seen emerging from a grove in the background. Clad in plain dark silk, with a velvet bonnet and a pearl in front of it, he wore no other distinguishing mark of his high rank. As soon as the monarch was seated upon his throne, the master of the ceremonies led the ambassador towards the steps. The latter approached, bent his knee, and handed in a casket set with diamonds, the letter addressed to his imperial majesty by the King of England. The emperor assured him of the satisfaction he felt at the testimony which his Britannic majesty gave him of his esteem and good will in sending him an embassy, with a letter and rare presents; that he on his part entertained sentiments of the same kind towards the sovereign of Great Britain, and hoped that harmony would always be maintained between their respective subjects. He then presented to the ambassador a stone sceptre, whilst he graciously received the private presents of the principal personages of the embassy. He was perfectly good-humoured, and especially pleased with the son of Sir G. Staunton, who talked a little Chinese, and received as a token of imperial favour, a yellow plain tobacco pouch, with the figure of the five-clawed dragon embroidered upon it. Afterwards, the ambassadors from Birmah and little Bukharia, were introduced, and performed the nine prostrations. A sumptuous banquet was then served up, and after their departure, they had presents sent to them, consisting of silks, porcelain and teas. Upon an application made to the prime minister, respecting a merchant ship which had accompanied the ambassador's frigate, they received the most flattering answer, and every request was fully granted them. Having accompanied the embassy, the ship was to pay no duty. After their return to Pekin, it was intimated to them that his majesty, on his way to Yuen-ming-yuen, would be delighted if the ambassador came to meet him on the road. When the emperor observed him, he stopped short, and graciously addressed him. He was carried in a chair, and followed by a clumsy cart, which could not be distinguished from other vehicles, if it had not been for the yellow cloth over it. On his arrival at Yuen-ming-yuen, he viewed with great delight the various presents which the ambassador had brought with him. A model of the "Royal Sovereign," a ship of war of a hundred and ten guns, attracted much of his notice.

In consequence of this embassy, his imperial majesty called together a council to deliberate what answer ought to be given to the letter. A hoppo from Canton, who had lost his rank, and the imperial legate, strongly opposed any offer of friendly terms. The result of this conference was, that the ambassador was given to understand that, as the winter approached, he ought to think about his departure. At an interview with the minister of state, to which he was invited in the palace, he found the emperor's answer contained in a large roll covered with yellow silk, and placed in a chair of state. From thence it was sent into the ambassador's hotel, accompanied by several presents. News which arrived from Canton, stating the probability of a rupture between England and the French republic, hastened the departure of the ambassador. He had been very anxious to obtain some privileges for the British trade, but the prime minister was as anxious to evade all conversation upon business. The splendid embassy was only viewed as a congratulatory mission, and treated as such.

No practical result followed from this expensive embassy; the relations between the English and Chinese in Canton, continued to be vexatious and unsatisfactory; and the disputes occasionally became so violent that the trade was suspended, or the English ships detained.

About the year 1815, several very offensive measures were adopted by the viceroy of Canton towards the Company's supercargoes: not only was an edict issued, according to which all Native attendants were to be withdrawn, and all Chinese prohibited to communicate with them: but the Company's linguist, who had been employed to carry the picture of the Prince Regent to Pekin, was seized, and their written representations were returned unopened. At the same time, a very offensive edict was published, which said: "Foreigners are not permitted, voluntarily, to present statements to government: they are indebted to the clemency of the emperor for their trade, as also for the permission to tread the ground, and to eat the herbs in common with the Chinese. If, after the publication of this edict, it occurs that foreigners presume, of their own accord, to make applications to government, the viceroy will, on discovery, request his majesty's permission to punish them severely."

In the year 1816, the British ministers, at the request of the Company, resolved to send a second embassy to China, and Lord Amherst was selected as a proper representative of the government. His lordship received from the court of directors, for his guidance in the negociations, an elaborate statement of the causes that had led to the adoption of this measure, and the objects which it was hoped that he might gain. We shall give the abstract of this document from Mr. Auber's work, as it throws much light on the embarrassing nature of the restrictions to which British intercourse with China was subjected.

"The *causes* were, 'the capricious and vexatious proceedings which the local government of Canton had, for some time past, held towards the Company's representatives there, by which they had obstructed and embarrassed the conduct of the Company's commerce, shewed that it was exposed to arbitrary interruption, to uncertainty, and insecurity, all which were highly prejudicial to concerns of such magnitude and importance, to which the idea of permanence was essential. These proceedings had rendered the task of the supercargoes, in upholding the interests of their employers, extremely difficult, and they occasioned a reasonable apprehension lest the wanton exercise of power in such a government as that of China, should lead to an entire stoppage of the trade, either by the immediate act of the local authorities, or by compelling the supercargoes on their part to have recourse to that extreme measure, in order to avoid the still worse alternative of yielding to despotic imposition, which might be expected to derive further encouragement from suspension.

"The *objects* were, a removal of the grievances which had been experienced, and an exemption from them and others of the like nature, for the time to come, with the establishment of the Company's trade upon a secure, solid, equitable footing, free from the capricious, arbitrary aggressions of the local authorities, and under the protection of the emperor, and the sanction of regulations to be appointed by himself.'

"It was observed, if the Chinese were by violence to shut us out from their trade, or by a series of oppressive and vexatious proceedings to force us to abandon it, we might not remain perfectly passive under the great losses and privations that must thus ensue, and they could not but be aware that nothing could be more easy for us than to take possession of their valuable islands to the eastward, which would enable us to intercept the whole of their Asiatic maritime trade, and to carry terror even to the neighbourhood of Pekin itself. It was added, 'Justice forbids, and must ever forbid, that such speculations should be really entertained. Their withdrawing from us the liberty of trading in their country could never be a legitimate cause of hostility against them; but the Chinese government, if they were in an unfriendly, inhospitable spirit, by inequitable conduct, to force to a close a pacific intercourse which has subsisted so long, and in which this country has embarked so great a capital, it could hardly fail to resent such a harsh and injurious proceeding.'

"The admission of an English consul at Canton, as likely to improve the means of communication, and to prevent, or more easily obviate differences and misunderstandings between the local authorities and the supercargoes, was a point to be considered; but if he were to have no other powers than those possessed by other consuls there, they would amount only to such powers as the Company's chief supercargo had always exercised.

"The course of policy pursued by the British nation in India was explained, as calculated to satisfy the Chinese that we are not actuated in our conquests by a desire of national aggrandizement.

"The importance was pointed out, of securing admission to some of the more northern and central parts of China."

This embassy failed even more signally than that of Lord Macartney; the Chinese insisted that the ambassador should perform the degrading ceremony of the *Ko-tow*. Lord Amherst peremptorily refused compliance, and he was therefore forced to return home without having been admitted to an audience.

In a letter from the emperor to the Prince Regent was the following passage: "Hereafter there is no occasion for you to send an ambassador so far, and be at the trouble of passing over mountains and crossing seas;" and in a vermilion edict* the following passage: "I therefore sent down my pleasure to expel these ambassadors, and send them back to their own country, without punishing the high crime they had committed."

The British frigate Alceste, commanded by Captain Maxwell, soon after came into the Bay of Canton, and a threat was made, that she would be prevented by force from anchoring within the Bogue. After some delay, during which the hostility and insincerity of the Chinese were equally apparent, Captain Maxwell resolved to force a passage, and maintain the privileges which, on former occasions, had been conceded to British ships of war.

As soon as the frigate weighed, a signal was made from the boats; lights were displayed at the forts, and a brisk cannonade from ninety or one hundred guns was commenced. One shot fell on board the Alceste, and two lodged in the bows of the ship.

When the frigate was within half musket-shot of the forts, a broadside was poured into them, on which the lights disappeared and the forts on the starboard side were silenced. The forts on the larboard hand, on which the guns could not be

* From its being written on paper of that colour by the Emperor's own hand.

brought to bear, continued firing for some time, and the Alceste anchored at the second bar without further molestation.

This firmness inspired the Chinese with more respect than they had previously felt for British prowess, but they still continued to annoy and insult the servants of the Company. The views which the court of directors entertained on this subject, may be best understood from a statement of their views respecting the result of Lord Amherst's embassy, which they made to the general body of proprietors in April, 1818.

They remarked, that "no expense or trouble were spared that appeared calculated to contribute to the success of the mission to the imperial court. To whatever causes its failure may be ascribed (and it is not to our present purpose to investigate those causes), it may, we think, be clearly inferred that, in the event of future disagreements with the Viceroy of Canton, no dependence can be placed on the efficacy of an embassy, though appointed and commissioned by the crown.

"When we directed that your intercourse with the Chinese should be conducted in a mild and conciliatory temper, it by no means follows that we are in any degree inclined to surrender or abandon the immunities and privileges hitherto enjoyed by our factory, and to which the imperial edicts have recognized our just claims. We no more entertain the opinion that the real interests of British commerce are to be preserved, by a servile and abject submission on the part of those to whose hands such interests are entrusted, than we expect that our particular commerce with China will be best upheld and maintained by the use of strong and threatening language in your intercourse with the officers of the government. Allowance should at all times be made for the known habits of the Chinese in their official correspondence.

"Whenever you recur to remonstrance or complaint, the cause should be first well weighed, and the necessity for the measure clearly established; and when, after due deliberation, you may determine on an address to the local authorities, all harshness of expression should be avoided, and great care taken that no personal feeling be suffered to mix itself with the expression of official remonstrance or complaint."

Adverting to the conduct of the Chinese officers having entered the printing-house at Macao, the court observed, that "it was a very improper act, and formed a fit occasion of remonstrance to the viceroy; but it did not follow that in such remonstrance you were authorized to threaten with summary punishment, the officers of the government in case of the repetition of such an act, on the ground that the laws of England give the right of repelling a forcible and disorderly entrance by force of arms. The laws of England and those of China are very dissimilar in many instances, and, however superior those of the former may be, it cannot be contended that the Chinese should regulate their conduct to Englishmen residing in China, according to the laws and customs of England. All you can justly contend for is, a continuance of the protection hitherto enjoyed, and that the laws of China shall be equally administered to you in common with other foreign residents."

The select committee having suggested to Admiral Sir Richard King, the propriety of a ship of war annually visiting China, &c., the court expressed a strong feeling of disapprobation at that step; and observed, that "the intercourse carried on in the dominions of the Emperor of China by the East India Company, is purely of a commercial nature, and it is our fixed determination to preserve that character inviolate, in the whole of the communications which are made by those acting under our authority with the Chinese. You will, therefore, in future, cautiously abstain from making the officers of his majesty's service parties in any dispute which may arise between you and the Chinese, and you will also be careful, in any differences which may occur between the commanders of the country ships and the Chinese, to carry your interference no further than that of remonstrance or recommendation."

At the beginning of the year 1822, the select committee entrusted with the superintendence of British affairs in Canton, became involved in serious discussions with the local authorities, arising out of the death of two Chinese, killed by the fire of his majesty's ship Topaze, at Lintin, in the month of December preceding. The barge of that frigate had been sent on shore, for the purpose of procuring water and enabling the seamen to wash their clothes. While thus engaged, they were attacked by a mob of Chinese marauders, and some of the men severely injured. Under these circumstances the officer commanding the frigate fired some round shot to disperse the mob, and two of the

Chinese were killed. The viceroy of Canton, demanded satisfaction for their death, but at the same time refused to investigate officially the attack which had been made on the sailors. The captain of the frigate, on the other hand, refused to surrender his men for trial to the Chinese authorities; and under these circumstances, there was a total cessation of trade. The select committee recorded the following remarks, in reference to these circumstances, which deserve attention, as they exhibit the nature of the difficulties with which the Company's servants in Canton had to contend.

"We see our situation, clearly made responsible for the acts of between two and three thousand individuals who are daily coming in contact with the lowest of the Chinese, and exposed to assaults so wanton, and often so barbarous, as well as to robberies so extensive, that self-defence imposes upon them the necessity of attacking their assailants in a manner from whence death must often ensue. A great and important commerce is instantly suspended, whole fleets at times detained, ourselves liable to seizure, and to be the medium of surrendering a man to death whose crime is only self-defence or obedience to orders, or else to lend ourselves to the most detestable falsehoods, in order to support a fabricated statement which may save the credit of the officers of the Chinese government.

"Can the Honourable Company wish their servants and their trade to remain in this degraded, this dangerous situation? Will the British government expect that the captain of his majesty's ship is, upon this occasion to sacrifice every feeling of honour and humanity?

"The captain of his majesty's ship has, in the most decided terms, stated that he never will surrender any of his people to the justice of the Chinese; and, as there is no precedent on record of an honourable adjustment of a case of homicide, we have no ground upon which to remonstrate with his majesty's officer upon the present occasion.

"We shall briefly recapitulate the cases of homicide noted in in our records.

"In 1780, a French sailor who killed a Portuguese in self-defence, was strangled without any form of trial.

"In 1784, the gunner who, in obedience to orders, fired a gun on the occasion of a ship saluting, was put to death. The surrender of this man is considered to have inflicted indelible disgrace upon all parties concerned.

"In 1800, the centinel on the forecastle of his majesty's schooner Providence, was charged with the intended murder of a Chinese, whom, in obedience to orders, he fired at whilst attempting to cut the schooner's cable. The most serious negociations ensued, which were terminated by the wounded man surviving for a period of more than forty days, although he died shortly afterwards.

"In 1806, Edward Sheen, against whom not the shadow of proof existed, was saved by the Chinese officers inventing a most flagrant falsehood as to the manner in which the deceased person came by his death. The form of public trial was, however, gone through; and it must not be forgotten that a most treacherous attempt was made to seize Sheen's person, in violation of the most positive stipulations in writing to the contrary.

"In 1810, an accusation was brought against the English for the murder of a Chinese in the street adjoining our factory. Chinese witnesses attempted to prove the identity of the men, and failed. The form of trial was gone through. A written assurance was given, that if the men could be found they should be punished; which assurance caused a renewal of the discussions at the close of the year 1811. In both the foregoing instances, whole fleets were detained when on the point of sailing.

"In 1820, the fifth mate of the Winchelsea having absconded, the charge was got rid of by a most unworthy subterfuge, to which, for the sake of the trade we were induced to lend ourselves. The Chinese laws will not admit the possibility of a magistrate suffering a criminal to escape; and hence, if the identical culprit is not forthcoming, the danger that results to those whom the Chinese, in order to screen themselves, hold as responsible.

"In 1821, an unfortunate occurrence, from which the death of a woman was likely to have ensued, in which the ship Lady Melville was implicated, was settled, as innumerable others have been, by pecuniary inducements to the relations of the deceased not to lodge complaints with the officers of government.

"A few months ago, Terranovia, a Sicilian belonging to an American ship, charged with throwing a jar at a woman, which is said to have struck her on the head, and to have caused her to fall overboard from her boat, was strangled. He was first examined on board ship, not allowed to call any witnesses, again tried at a commercial hall in the suburbs of Canton, the doors being closed, and not a foreigner of any country allowed to enter. His execution took place within forty-eight hours. It was conducted with illegal secresy. The report to the emperor falsified the material facts, both of proof and mode of conducting the trial.

"The frequent recurrence of our present difficulties must be expected, until some change takes place in the footing upon which our intercourse with the Chinese is carried on. The contempt of foreigners, engendered and fostered by the abusive terms in which they are spoken of by the officers of government, the want of police regulation, and the defenceless state in which we are placed by the difficulty of access to the magistrates, leaves us exposed to assaults of all descriptions, and if self-defence is not received as a plea in cases of homicide, no individual can for one instant be considered safe.

"Whatever may be the distinctions in the Chinese written laws, we see that in the practice, as far as respects Europeans, no discrimination is shown, and, on the present occasion, we see that the plea of self-defence is decidedly rejected.

"The great facility which foreigners have of escaping in ships, and the liability of the whole trade to suspension therefrom, is a consideration of such momentous weight, that we trust that the Honourable Court will use every effort, by negociation with the Chinese, and by laws enacted at home, to put the cases of homicide on such a footing as shall prevent embarrassment to the trade."

In 1832, the court of directors communicated their sentiments to the select committee at Canton, upon the whole of their proceedings. They observed, "The commerce between Great Britain and China is too important to be put to hazard without the most urgent and imperious necessity, and, on no account, upon considerations of a personal nature. It is of essential moment to the Indian as well as to the home revenues, both as regards the state and the East India Company, as well as in the regular supply to the British public, of an article of general consumption.

"We sought that trade originally: the advantages which it has yielded have induced us to exert every endeavour to secure its continuance. Those exertions have been attended with success: and, although late events have led to the expression of opinions in favour of a more decided and less pacific course of policy, we are by no means prepared to adopt or to act upon such opinions.

"To attempt to maintain a purely commercial intercourse, such as that with China, by force of arms, would, in a pecuniary point of view, be anything rather than a matter of profit, even if justice and humanity could allow us for a moment seriously to contemplate such a step."

They condemned the application to the Bengal government for the aid of ships of war, and observed: "It is a notion too commonly entertained and acted upon by you, and encouraged by foreign merchants residing at Canton, that nothing is to be gained from the Chinese by obedience to their laws and edicts, but that much may be obtained by intimidation. You may have succeeded for the moment in setting the government at defiance; but that government has not only taken the first opportunity to assert its dominion, but also, with the view of making you feel the consequences of disobedience, it has almost invariably deprived you of some advantages which it had either tacitly or avowedly yielded to friendly remonstrances." The court concluded their letter in the following terms: "The preservation of the national honour is in the hands of his majesty's government, and it must be for the king's ministers alone to take the responsibility of deciding upon the adoption of extreme measures for vindicating that honour, if insulted. These measures, if resorted to, will most materially affect the valuable interests at present dependent upon a peaceful prosecution of our intercourse with China."

Several abortive efforts were made at this time, to open commercial intercourse with the northern ports of China, and thus provide means of escape from the irritations and perplexities which were constantly arising in Canton; but the obstinacy of the Chinese authorities rendered all these efforts abortive. It was found that the Natives were generally anxious for trade, but the government exhibited the utmost jealousy of foreigners. The Montchews, who have been lords of China for about two centuries, probably fear that their subjects might be induced to attempt the re-establishment of the ancient independence of their nation, if they could obtain foreign aid against the tyrannical Tartars. Another cause of this jealousy, appears to be the rapid progress of British power in India. The emperor and his court are well aware that, two centuries ago, the English sought permission to trade in India from the Emperor of Delhí, in more humble guise than they have ever appeared in Pekin; but now the ancient empire of the descendants of Baber, is a British province, and the last representative of the imperial family, a pensioner on foreign bounty. However much we may regret, we cannot reasonably be surprised at the determination of the Mantchews, to avert from themselves such a fate as that which has befallen the ancient lords of India.

From the accounts we have given, it is manifest that the British trade with Canton, so long as it was under the exclusive management of the East India Company, was barely tolerated but never formally recognized by the Chinese authorities. The Viceroys of Canton assumed and exercised the right of suspending the trade at their pleasure, and always regarded the permission to traffic as an important boon, for which foreigners could never be sufficiently grateful. All efforts to place relations on a more equitable and satisfactory basis, completely failed; the imperial court could never be induced to consent to establishing a commercial treaty and receiving a resident ambassador at Pekin. Two lines of policy were open to the Company; that of submission and concession, which was actually adopted, or the maintenance of such a naval force as would enable the select committee to obtain a redress of grievances by some active demonstration, and compel the Chinese to respect the British power. When the trade with China was thrown open, it became evident that some speedy measures should be adopted to establish equitable relations between the British traders and the viceregal court of Canton. The task of protecting the more extensive traffic which was certain to follow, devolved upon the general government when it was taken from the Company, and it was felt to be a task of considerable difficulty and delicacy.

The British ministers resolved to place the management of the trade, under a special superintendent, appointed by the crown, and consequently recognized as a public functionary. His powers were to extend to the adjustment of all disputes among the merchants themselves, and also to the regulation of the negociations with the local authorities. Here, however, lay an unsuspected difficulty; the Chinese authorities had never sanctioned British commerce, they always acted as if they merely connived at its existence. The intercourse under the Company, had been managed by a *Tae-pan*, or supercargo; for the imperial officers affected to regard all mercantile affairs, and particularly those of foreigners, as matters which it was below their dignity to notice. The appointment of a superintendent, who was to reside at Canton, to exercise a certain jurisdiction, independent of the Chinese government, and who claimed as a right the privilege of treating directly with the deputies of the emperor, was regarded as an outrage on the national dignity, and was certainly a violation of the strictest regulations of the empire.

When intelligence was received at Canton, that Lord Napier had arrived off Macao, in an English vessel of war, the governor of that city sent orders that his lordship should remain at Macao, until the pleasure of the viceroy should be known. Two of the Hong merchants bore this message to Macao, but in the meantime Lord Napier had gone in a boat to Canton, and actually reached that city before they could overtake him. The Governor issued an order, declaring, that in conformity with the Chinese laws, the new functionary could not be permitted to remain in the city; and a second edict declared, that the Hong merchants should be held responsible for his obedience. A long and tedious course of negociations followed; the trade was suspended, and the appearance of two British frigates, which forced their way into the Canton river, failed to overcome the Chinese obstinacy. At length Lord Napier, whose health had given way under fatigue and anxiety, consented to return in a chop-boat to Macao. The Chinese insulted and harassed him all the way down the river, which so increased his illness, that it terminated fatally. On his death, the office of superintendent devolved on Mr. Davis. He was succeeded by Sir George Robinson, who in his turn made room for Captain Elliot; but no effort was made to obtain a recognition of the superintendent's authority from the Chinese government.

A new source of difficulty arose, from the great increase in the smuggling of opium which had followed the opening of the trade; the Emperor and his ministers avowed their determined resolution to prevent the importation of this drug, and a special commissioner, named Lin, was sent to Canton, in order to enforce measures for its exclusion. Captain Elliot foresaw the difficulties which were likely to arise from Lin's appointment and his own anomalous position; he had the title of superintendent, but he was not recognized in any diplomatic capacity by the Chinese Government, and he was invested with no legal authority over British subjects, engaged in an open trade. In fact, the consequences of the opening of the China trade, had not been taken into consideration by the British statesmen; previous to that change, Chinese commerce was nothing more than the traffic between a company of English merchants in London, and the Hong company of Chinese merchants in Canton; this was suddenly changed into a commerce between two nations, without any previous agreement or consultation between the two parties. The Chinese felt, and not unreasonably, that the British government had made most extensive alterations in the general system of commerce, without ever having examined how far these alterations were consistent with the laws and institutions of China. The Company had been represented by its merchants at Canton, and they could of course conduct all their negociations through the Hong merchants, never approaching the Chinese authorities except by a petition; but the superintendent appointed by the British ministers, represented the British nation, not a trading company; he could not, without degrading himself and his country, consent to communicate with the government only through the Hong, and he was equally precluded from using the humiliating character *pin*, which signifies "petition," in his official communications to the Chinese authorities. In India the Company had changed from a trading association into a soveriegn power, but in China, it still remained a company of merchants and nothing more; and it had been the uniform policy of the government of Pekin, while it tolerated commerce with European merchants, to refuse all diplomatic relations with European courts.

The opium question was an additional source of perplexity; the importation of that drug had been long prohibited by law, but it had, nevertheless, been imported so regularly, if not with the express sanction, at least with such connivance on the part of the Chinese authorities, that the trade might be considered virtually recognized. Two circumstances combined to render this trade odious to the court of Pekin; the first was the deleterious effect of the drug; the second was that the opium was purchased with Sycee silver, and, consequently, that its importation drained bullion from the empire. On all sides it was conceded that the Chinese government had a right to prevent the importation of opium, but it had only the right to do so through its own officers, by adopting such measures as all civilized governments adopt to prevent smuggling. Captain Elliott appears to have been scarcely less anxious to put an end to the opium trade than the Chinese themselves, but here, as we have said, he was checked by the want of authorities. In the former condition of the trade, the supercargoes appointed by the Company had a right to remove all unlicensed traders, but this authority of course ceased when the opening of the trade rendered licenses no longer necessary. It must be added that many of the merchants at Canton, after the rejection of Lord Amherst's embassy, had frequently, and in very strong terms, represented to the authorities at home, the necessity of curbing the caprice and insolence of the Chinese rulers by an imposing display of maritime force, and some had gone so far as to recommend the occupation of an island, or some other favourable station on the coast of China. This policy, however, found no countenance from the court of directors; that body had learned to dread nothing so much as an extension of territory, and had scarcely less reason to dread the great derangement of their commercial transactions, which would result from a suspension or stoppage of the tea trade. It was not distinctly seen that the abolition of the Company's exclusive privileges, was virtually a revolution in the entire system of commerce between China and Great Britain; a revolution effected by one party without any attempt to explain it to the other, or to arrange the difficulties and perplexities which must necessarily have arisen from such a change.

Commissioner Lin arrived at Canton impressed with a very high sense of his own personal importance, and with more than the average share of hatred and dislike towards foreigners, usual with functionaries of the Celestial Empire. His national pride was not a little increased by the patience with which the ill-treatment of Lord Napier had been borne, and he resolved to treat the present superintendent with as little respect and ceremony as had been shown to that unfortunate nobleman. As the commercial regulations originally stood, foreigners never came directly before the Chinese tribunals; they were compelled to transact their business through the Hong merchants, who were regarded as their sureties, and to them the government looked in the first instance when there was any violation of the law.

Such was the state of the law when Lin arrived at Canton; he forthwith issued an edict to the foreigners, demanding that every particle of the opium should be delivered up to the government, in order that it might be destroyed; and, at the same time, required the merchants to sign a bond by which their lives and properties would be placed at the disposal of the Chinese government. Captain Elliott peremptorily refused to comply with these conditions, upon which the factories were blockaded, and the merchants at Canton threatened with imprisonment, and even menaced with death. It was necessary, under these circumstances, to surrender the opium in order to prevent any further violence; at the same time, Captain Elliott wrote to Lord Auckland, Governor-general of India, declaring that the Canton trade had been broken by acts of tyranny, and applying for the assistance of as many armed vessels, to protect British life and property, as could be spared from the Indian station.

In the month of August, 1839, an affray took place at Macao, between some English sailors and Chinese villagers, in which, unfortunately, one of the latter was killed. Commissioner Lin immediately demanded of Captain Elliott that the homicide should be delivered up, in order that he might be put to death. This was of course refused, and Lin, in consequence, issued an edict, prohibiting any provisions, or other articles, being supplied to the British at Macao. Captain Elliott then gave public notice to the latter, that he intended to leave Macao for Hong-Kong on the 23rd, and invited all who wished to quit that place, to accompany him on board. Before this, however, a British passage schooner, called the Black Joke, while on her way from Macao to Hong-Kong, was attacked by several Chinese junks, and boarded, when several of the Lascars, who manned the Black Joke, were cut down, and thrown overboard—and Mr. Moss, a young Englishman, who happened to be on board, was most barbarously maltreated. Happily, however, another British schooner came up at the critical moment, and the Chinese made off in their boats. On the 23rd, the chief superintendent left Macao, and took up his residence at Hong-Kong, off which lay the Volage frigate, commanded by Captain Smith.

After a long series of unpleasant discussions, Lin declared that the trade should be suspended until the English merchants had entered into the bonds which he required. He was induced to persevere in this demand by the imprudence of Mr. Warner, who commanded the ship *Thomas Coutts;* this gentleman, without consulting the superintendent, signed the obnoxious bond, and thus supplied Lin with a precedent to which he could appeal. So much was he intoxicated by Mr. Warner's submission, that he threatened to destroy the shipping unless the several masters imitated the example of the commander of the Thomas Coutts, within three days; he made such demonstrations as to show that he intended to act upon this threat, and he thus provoked an encounter which taught him the superiority of the British artillery.

Finding that the Chinese were preparing to attack the fleet, and that Admiral Kwan lay in considerable force near Chuenpee, the chief superintendent recommended to Captain Smith the immediate removal of the Volage and Hyacinth (another English frigate) to that neighbourhood, and prepared a moderate but firm address to the High Commissioner Lin. Captain Elliott himself went on board the Volage frigate on the 28th of October, which took up her station on the 2nd of November, not far below the first battery, where an imposing force of war-junks and fire-vessels was collected. On the 3rd, the Chinese squadron, in number twenty-nine sail, broke ground, and anchored close to the British vessels, while a short correspondence took place, in which the Chinese peremptorily demanded the delivering of an Englishman, and refused to retire. Captain Smith now resolved to compel them to return to their former anchorage, and desist from their menacing attitude. At noon, therefore, the signal was made to engage, and the ships then lying hove-to at the extreme end of the Chinese line, bore away a-head in close order, having the wind on the starboard beam. In this way, and under easy sail, they ran down the Chinese line, pouring in a destructive fire. The lateral direction of the wind enabled the ships to perform the same evolution from the other extreme of the line, running up again with their larboard broadsides bearing. The Chinese answered with much spirit, but the terrible effect of the English fire was soon manifest. One war-junk blew up at pistol-shot distance from the Volage, three were sunk, and several others water-logged. In less than three-quarters of an hour,

Admiral Kwan and his squadron retired in great distress to their former anchorage, and Captain Smith offered no obstruction to their retreat. It is to be feared, however, that this clemency was thrown away upon the Chinese, who have no conception of the true principles of such forbearance, and subsequent facts show that they actually claimed the victory. This they, perhaps, founded on the circumstances of her majesty's ships making sail for Macao, for the purpose of covering the embarkation of the English, who might see fit to retire from that place, and of providing for the safety of the merchant ships. On the 4th November, the Volage joined the fleet at Hong Kong, and the Hyacinth was left at Macao, to watch events in that quarter.

The English government resolved not only to protect its subjects, but to compel the Chinese court to recognize the principles of international law. A powerful naval and military armament was prepared, and placed under the command of Admiral Elliott and General Burrell; and such activity was displayed, that the van of the armament appeared in the outer waters of Canton early in June, 1840. Just before its arrival, the Chinese authorities at Canton had sent some parcels of poisoned tea to be sold to the English sailors, but the boat in which it was conveyed happened to be captured by Chinese pirates, who sold her cargo to their countrymen, many of whom died in consequence, and thus the nefarious attempt was frustrated. At the same time, Lin issued a new proclamation, offering rewards, on a graduated scale, for the destruction of British ships of war, and taking their commanders, whether dead or alive. An abortive attempt was made at the same time to burn the British shipping, which is thus described in the Canton Register:—

"The first alarm was given about two A.M., on Tuesday, the 9th of June. A noise was heard from amongst the small Chinese boats inshore. It appeared, on subsequent inquiry, that some mandarin boats had got in amongst them for the purpose of making captures. They attacked the cutter Devil, and wounded the Lascars on board. Immediately after, distant lights appeared in the direction of the passage of the Capsingmoon, called the Flood Gates; and the commanding officer of the Danish King fired a gun, and hoisted the signal previously ordered by the senior officer of her majesty's ships, for fire-rafts; and instantly almost the fire burst forth from at least fifteen fireboats; the appearance was very beautiful. The wind and tide were then favourable for their course. As they approached they blew up like some beautiful works, what in English pyrotechnical science would be called 'a flower pot.' The beauties of the sight, however, did not dissipate the alarm felt by those on board the ships, who were also fearful there might be other crafty schemes in progress, and that they might be attacked from other quarters; consequently, most of the ships slipped their cables and moved out of danger, each more anxious than his neighbour to get into the rear. The scene and danger caused great excitement; the night was very dark, the wind slackened, and so many vessels being under weigh at once in a small space, caused great confusion, and many consequently came in contact, but we have not heard of any serious damage.

"The boats of the squadron were actively employed towing the rafts clear of the shipping, and anchoring others.

"The junks were first turned adrift chained together two and two; nine of these rafts were counted, which gives eighteen boats. But it was ascertained that some had not ignited, and some had exploded, the wrecks being seen floating about the bay the next morning.

"On examination, the fire-rafts were found to be constructed of what had been very old outside fishing boats; what remains of them will supply the fleet with firewood for a month. They were full of dross, the remains of the combustible matter."

Commodore Sir J. Gordon Bremer arrived off Canton, on the 22nd of June, and issued a proclamation establishing a blockade of the river and port of Canton, and directing that foreign vessels arriving off the coast of China, should anchor in the Macao roads. On the other hand, the chief magistrate of the district in which Macao is situated, published an edict, requiring the people to join heart and hand with the government, for the destruction of the barbarians, and forbidding any Chinese ships to put out to sea, except such as were laden with combustibles for the destruction of the enemy. An extract from this edict is a curious illustration of the feelings which animated the Chinese authorities.

"Fishermen and other seafaring people are called on to go out and destroy foreign vessels, and whilst thus engaged are promised that their families will be housed, clothed, and fed in the public offices at the public expense, and, says his excellency Lin, they will be entitled to even higher rewards than have already been offered them in a former proclamation. The people are again told that rewards will be given them for killing Englishmen, but they are cautioned not to mistake such for Portuguese or individuals of any other nation than English, as such mistake will be punished according to the existing laws against murder. The proof required of having destroyed a ship, is the board with her name; that of having killed an Englishman, his head; either of which, on being delivered to any district magistrate, will entitle the bearer to receive the promised reward. Englishmen sailing or pulling in small schooners or boats, are ordered to be attacked and exterminated. Honours, rewards, and happiness will be the lot of him who kills an Englishman."

In the meantime Sir J. Gordon Bremer, followed by Admiral Elliott, steered northwards, and on the 5th of July reached the island of Chusan, which it was resolved to occupy. A landing was speedily effected, and on the 6th, the city of Ting-hae-heen, was taken almost without opposition. Unfortunately, the troops after their conquest, misconducted themselves by drinking too freely of a spirit distilled from rice, and committed several acts of glaring insubordination. Admiral Elliott reached Chusan the day after its surrender, and immediately proceeded to Ningpo, for the purpose of landing a letter addressed by Lord Palmerston to the Chinese court. The authorities at Ningpo, declined to forward the letter, but they treated the mission with unusual deference and civility. This change of tone, must, however, be attributed to the prompt chastisement which the Blonde frigate inflicted on the fort of Amoy, for firing on a flag of truce; the guns of the frigate soon laid the fort in ruins, and put the troops to flight as well as the war junks, except one which was taken and destroyed.

Admiral Elliott proceeded up the Peeh-ho river, for the purpose of opening negociations with a Chinese minister of high rank, deputed to meet him by the emperor. Keshen was a crafty negociator; he pretended the greatest anxiety to effect an amicable arrangement, and by his earnest protestations induced the admiral to remove the' fleet from Chusan, where its vicinity to the capital overawed the emperor, under the pretence that matters could be more easily arranged at Canton, as that had been the seat of the original quarrel. Soon after the return of the fleet to Canton, Admiral Elliott was obliged by ill-health, to surrender the command to Sir J. Gordon Bremer, and thus the entire conduct of the negociations, devolved upon the superintendent Captain Elliott.

Kesben's insincerity very soon became apparent; his great object was to protract the negociations, and gain time; Captain Elliott's patience was at length worn out, and he directed the Commodore to commence offensive operations. The first attack was made upon the Forts of Chuenpee and Ty-cock-tow, which were vigorously assailed by the shipping, and by a land force under the command of Captain Scott. The forts were taken by storm, and the only incident deserving remark occurred at Ty-cock-tow, where the Chinese had barricadoed their houses, and fired on the soldiers after the gate had been stormed.

"Just at this time," says Mr. Mackenzie, "Mr. Viner of the Blenheim entered the fort, at the head of a party of seamen, and pursuing several Chinese towards the upper end of the fort, observed them retreat into a house, on which he fired his pistol off through one of the windows. In an instant a terrific explosion took place, which we at first attributed to a mine, but it appeared that the pistol had been fired into the magazine, and as all the powder lay loose, it instantly blew up. By this accident Mr. Viner was severely burnt, and many men were injured for life. Had the Chinese submitted on our obtaining possession of the fort, many lives would have been spared; but they continued to wound our men, which so irritated them, that numbers were shot. In some instances during the fight, they took refuge in the water, and discharged their match-locks at the pursuer, and then throwing the weapon away, begged for mercy; a system of warfare which our men did not at all understand.

"The loss on the side of the enemy, was not less than six hundred killed and wounded, while we had not one killed, but thirty wounded; many of these were, however, disabled for life. The tortures which most of the Chinese endured, must have been dreadful, for whenever they were wounded and fell, the match-lock set fire to their cotton clothes, and I saw several instances of their being literally burnt alive. In this affair, the Chinese, neither on the part of officers or men, shewed any want of courage; on the contrary, they displayed many instances of individual bravery, and all defended their positions as long as they were tenable with great devotion."

While the troops were thus engaged, the Nemesis steamer and the boats of the men of war, attacked the Chinese war-junks, in Amoy Bay. Seventeen of the junks, including that of the admiral, were destroyed; the admiral's vessel was blown up by a Congreve rocket, which went through the deck into her magazine; as she was full of men, and laden with money which had been sent down from Canton, to pay the troops, the loss must have been very great. Negociations were again renewed, and after three weeks of inaction, Captain Elliott believing that a treaty was on the point of being concluded, gave orders that the forts should be restored to the Chinese, and that the fleet should remove from the inner waters to the island of Hong-Kong, which had been ceded to the British.

Captain Elliott, in fact, had a personal interview with Keshen, in which all the preliminaries of peace were arranged, and a treaty prepared and sent up to Canton, for the signature and ratification of the imperial commissioners. Keshen, with characteristic faithlessness, failed to fulfil his agreement respecting the treaty, and Captain Elliott, with great reluctance gave orders that hostilities should be renewed. Sir J. Gordon Bremer made immediate preparations to attack the Forts of Upper and Lower Anunghoy, and North Wantong, which defended the Bogue, or entrance to the Canton river. The last account of the operations that ensued, is that given by Mr. Keith Mackenzie, who acted as military secretary to the commander-in-chief. We shall therefore make some extracts from his narrative.

" The capture of the two Anunghoy forts was entrusted to Sir Le Fleming Senhouse, having under his command the Melville 74 and Queen steamer, with a flotilla of rocket boats. About half-past ten A. M., the Blenheim got under weigh; her progress, however, was but slow, owing to the lightness of the wind. She was followed by the Melville, considerably astern. Shortly after, the remainder of the squadron got under weigh, and stood slowly towards the other forts. The day being most lovely, and the river smooth as glass, it was an exciting and superb sight to observe these fine ships all moving majestically onwards towards their work of destruction. The surrounding heights were covered with troops, posted on commanding points, and protected by small sand-bag batteries.

" The action commenced about noon, by the Queen firing at a battery, which as well as the lower Anunghoy fort, opened on her and the Blenheim, before they got within range. The latter ship did not fire a shot till she let go her anchor, about six hundred yards from the fort, when she clewed up all her sails and opened her broadside. In a few minutes, the Melville came to her assistance, and took up her position a short distance ahead of the Blenheim, about four hundred yards from the fort. The Chinese kept up the action here for some time with great spirit, but the terrific broadsides of the two line-of-battle ships, at length drove the Tartars from their guns; on seeing which, Sir Le Fleming Senhouse landed at the head of the marines and small-arm men, and driving all before him, carried these fine forts.

" Upon this occasion, the Chinese did not lose so many men as might have been expected, whilst on our side success had been obtained with but a very trifling loss. If, however, numerically, the enemy had been no great sufferers, that day's encounter cost them the life of their brave old Admiral, for both Kwan and his second in command, fell by bayonet wounds received in their breasts, whilst gallantly leading on their men to an attack. A day scarcely elapsed, before an application was made by the family of the deceased to be permitted to possess all that remained of their departed relative; a request which was followed by an immediate and unhesitating compliance. Eventually the remains of the gallant admiral were borne away by his friends, under a salute of minute guns from the Blenheim, as a token of that respect, which by a generous and civilized enemy is scrupulously rendered to a departed and valiant foe."

The other forts were captured with similar promptitude, and with scarcely any loss to the assailants. This result was so wholly unexpected by the Chinese, that various pictures were found in the forts, representing the total annihilation of the British squadron. Captain Elliott accompanied the ships during their tedious progress up the river, the Chinese having impeded the navigation by rafts, sunken junks and stones. Almost the only opposition encountered was at the first bar, which was defended by an immense raft, a large ship mounting thirty-two guns, purchased from the Americans, a heavy battery of forty-four pieces of cannon, and a body of two thousand men. These defences were forced without any loss of life to the assailants, and on the 4th of March preparations were made to subdue all the other forts which protected the entrance to Canton. An armistice was however again granted, but it expired without leading to any good result, and on the 7th, Sir Hugh Gough, who had arrived from Madras to take the command of the army, stormed the fort which had been named after the unfortunate Lord Napier, the Chinese merely firing one ineffective volley, and then running away. Inscriptions were found on the chase of the guns in this fort, boasting of the brutal treatment of Lord Napier, as if it had been a brilliant victory. On the 18th of March the armament reached Canton, and after encountering a feeble resistance, took possession of the factories and virtually of the city itself, exactly two years after Commissioner Lin had issued his first edict against the opium trade.

A truce was now concluded, during which time the trade was renewed, though in a very unsatisfactory manner, and before the end of May, Captain Elliott had succeeded in getting the teas of the season out of the river. It was however obvious to all, that the Chinese intended some act of treachery. On the evening of the 21st, the British merchants quitted Canton: on the same night hostilities were renewed, by an attack being made on the British shipping, and the next morning the factories were forced and plundered. Sir Hugh Gough immediately resolved to attack Canton, and, the ships having easily cleared the river, a landing was effected, with little loss, on the evening of the 27th of May. Arrangements were made for an attack on the following morning; it was made with equal spirit and success; the principal events of the struggle being thus described by Mr. Mackenzie:—

"At ten A.M., the general advance sounded; and on perceiving our troops advance, a large body of Chinese made a sortie from the eastern fort, as if determined to dispute the heights; the Royal Irish, however, giving one good cheer from right to left, threw in a destructive volley. On this, the Chinese turned and ran, being pursued most gallantly up the hill by the 18th. The 49th had, in the meantime, got possession of the front fort, and had the honour of first hoisting the British colours on the heights.* The 18th regiment, it may be supposed, had a very severe run, but the brave fellows seemed to gather strength as the danger increased, and charging along the ridge which connected the extremities on which the forts were built, exposed to the galling fire of the ramparts of Canton, gallantly captured the fort of 'eternal repose.' As Sir H. Gough came up, he was greeted with hearty cheers from the 49th; but, on his reaching the 18th, his welcome as their leader, but above all, as their countryman,† was most enthusiastic. From this point he had the proud satisfaction of seeing the Union Jack waving over all the forts; for while these operations had been going on upon the left, the gallant naval brigade had nobly done its duty. They, however, had very hard work, and had suffered most severely, for in these two forts the Chinese stood to their guns well; and it was not till our men entered the fort, and cut them down, hand to hand, that we got possession of it. The rear fort was afterwards carried, under a most galling fire from the city walls, not more than eighty yards distant. Many more men were wounded and killed here, after the fort was in our possession, than had been at the storming of it. Among these, were Lieutenant Fox and Mr. Kendall, both of H.M.S. Nimrod, who, while resting after the fatigues of the morning, had each a leg broken by a round shot, and were obliged to submit to amputation. Shortly after this, I regret to add, that Mr. Fox died; Mr. Kendall, however, survived, and next day had the gratification of receiving his lieutenant's commission, dated on the field of battle.

"Thus, in less than one hour after the general advance had been sounded, the British troops looked down on Canton within a hundred and fifty yards of its walls, from which we were only separated by a deep and precipitous glen."

* This fort rejoiced in the name of *Sheting Pow, anglice* "fortress, or asylum, of old age." It may amuse my readers to be informed of the euphonious names which these forts enjoyed. The head-quarters was *Yung-tang-tai*, "fortress of eternal repose." The sailors' forts were *Kung-kik-tai*, "fortress of extreme protection," and *Pou-kik-tai*, "fortress of extreme security." The Marines took possession of *Jin-tun-tang*, or "The Hall of Benevolence." It will be afterwards seen how our gallant tars *kicked* the enemy out of their extreme security.

† Both the general and the regiment are Irish.

The Chinese now began to fire from the walls of the city upon the troops; and they also appeared to make some preparations for attacking the British position from an entrenched camp, separated from the heights by a tract of rice-grounds about a mile in breadth. This was a new call on British enterprize, and the result may be best stated in the woıds of the author already quoted:—

"At about two P.M., some of the principal mandarins left the city on horseback, and proceeded to the camp. As from this it was evident that the enemy meditated a fresh attack, the general, very considerately, to save them the trouble of coming to us, detached the Royal Irish, and one company of the Royal Marines, under the command of Major-General Burrell, to destroy the camp. During our advance, we were much harassed, both by the nature of the paddy ground, which allowed the men to advance only in single file, and also by the very heavy and well-directed fire kept up from the north-east face of the city walls. Nothing, however, could daunt the gallant men, and we succeeded in burning the camp, blowing up the magazines, and dispersing the enemy in all directions. Several of the mandarins' chargers, more properly ponies, being in the camp, broke loose, and, alarmed by the fire and the explosions of the magazines, commenced galloping about in all directions, and by their grotesque caparisons, afforded much amusement. In this affair, many of our men and four officers were wounded.

"In the course of the evening, the out-lying pickets were all strengthened, and inlying ones placed. Sir Hugh Gough also made a reconnaissance of the walls, having determined to take the city by escalade. Thus terminated the evening of the capture of the heights of Canton."

Preparations were now made for an immediate attack upon Canton, with every certainty of success; but on the morning of the 27th, just as the breaching batteries were about to open on the walls, a message was received from Captain Elliott, peremptorily commanding a cessation of hostilities, as negociations were in progress for the ransom of the city. The disappointment and indignation of the army, both officers and men, were extreme, but they felt that their only course was to obey. The ransom for Canton, and the indemnity to merchants for property destroyed, amounted to one million four hundred thousand pounds, but, had Captain Elliott availed himself of his advantages, a much larger sum might have been obtained.

The British armament now returned to Hong Kong, of which formal possession was taken. Here, however, the troops suffered very severely from illness, but not so much as the garrison at Chusan, where the loss of life was dreadful. A period of inaction ensued, during which the Chinese made abundant professions of peace, but, at the same time, vigorously continued their preparations for the renewal of the war. On the 10th of August, Sir Henry Pottinger arrived from England to supersede Captain Elliott, whose frequent suspension of hostilities to enter into delusive negociations with the Chinese, had excited great dissatisfaction. The new superintendent gave immediate orders that the war should be vigorously renewed, and, on the 26th, the city of Amoy, with its formidable line of batteries and war-junks —the whole mounting more than five hundred pieces of cannon —fell into the hands of the British, after a short but animated defence on the part of the Chinese. The following particulars respecting this achievement, taken from Sir Hugh Gough's despatch, will be read with interest.

"Amoy is a principal third-class city of China, and, from its excellent harbour and situation, appears to be well calculated for commerce. The outer town is divided from the city by the chain of rocks I have mentioned, over which a paved road leads through a pass that has a covered gateway at its summit. The outer harbour skirts the outer town, while the city is bounded nearly its whole length by the inner harbour and an estuary, which deeply indent the island, including the outer town and the north-eastern suburb; the city cannot be much less than ten miles in circumference, and that of the citadel, which entirely commands this suburb, and the inner town, though commanded itself by the hills within shot range, is nearly one mile. The walls are castellated, and vary, with the irregularity of the ground, from twenty to thirty feet in height; and there are four gates, having each, in an outwork, a second or exterior gate, at right angles to the inner gate. The citadel contained five arsenals, in which we found a large quantity of powder, with store of material for making it; gingals, wall-pieces, matchlocks, and a variety of fire-arms of singular construction; military clothing, swords of all descriptions, shields, bows and arrows and spears, were also found in such quantity, as to lead to the conclusion that these must have been the chief magazines of the province. Within the sea-defences first taken, there was a foundry, with moulds, and materials for casting heavy ordnance. All these have been destroyed, and so much occupied my time, considering, too, how much the troops were harassed by patrols to keep off Chinese plunderers, and by other duties incident to the peculiarity of our situation, that I abandoned my intention of visiting the interior of the island. These plunderers flocked into the city and suburbs, to the extent, as the Chinese themselves reported, of many thousands; and, I regret to say, that several gangs penetrated into the citadel, and committed much devastation. Indeed, with the prospect of leaving Amoy so soon, I doubt that our marching through the island might rather have frightened away the peaceable householders, and led to further plunder by the mob, than have been of any advantage. Such, indeed, was the audacity of these miscreants, that I was in some cases obliged to fire in order to disperse them; but I am glad to say but little loss of life occurred. I am most happy to be enabled to state that the conduct of the troops has been exemplary; some instances of misconduct have, no doubt, occurred; but when it is considered that they were in the midst of temptation, many of the houses being open, with valuable property strewed about, and many shops in every street deserted, but full of shamshu, it is matter of great satisfaction that these instances were so few."

On the 5th of September, the armament sailed northwards under the command of Admiral Sir W. Parker and General Sir H. Gough. On the 21st they reached Chusan, which had been evacuated in the preceding February, during the delusive negociations with Keshen. The troops were disembarked on the 1st of October, and the place was re-occupied with but little loss. The Chinese suffered severely, and many mandarins were killed.

On the 7th, the troops were re-embarked in order to proceed to the attack of Ning-po. It was, however, necessary first to obtain possession of Chinhae, a city of considerable importance on the mouth of the Ningpo river, thus described by Admiral Parker:—

"The city of Chinhae, which is enclosed by a wall thirty-seven feet in thickness, and twenty-two feet high, with an embrasured parapet of four feet high, and nearly two miles in circumference, is situated at the foot of a very commanding peninsular height, which forms the entrance of the Tahee river on its left or north bank. On the summit is the citadel, which, from its strong position, is considered the key to Chinhae, and the large and opulent city of Ningpo, about fifteen miles up the river; and it is so important as a military post, that I trust I may be excused for attempting to describe it. It stands about 250 feet above the sea, and is encircled also by a strong wall with very substantial iron-plated gates at the east and west ends. The north and south sides of the height are exceedingly steep; the former accessible only from the sea by a narrow winding path from the rocks at its base; the south side and eastern end being nearly precipitous. At the east end of the citadel, outside its wall, twenty-one guns were mounted in three batteries of masonry and sand-bags to defend the entrance of the river. The only communication between the citadel and city is on the west side by a steep but regular causeway, to a barrier gate at the bottom of the hill, where a wooden bridge over a wet ditch, connects it with the isthmus and the gates of the city, the whole of which are covered with iron plates and strongly secured. The space on the isthmus between the citadel hill and the city wall, is filled up towards the sea with a battery of five guns, having a row of strong piles driven in a little beach in front of it, to prevent a descent in that quarter; and on the river side of the isthmus are two batteries adjoining the suburbs, and mounting twenty-two and nineteen guns, for flanking the entrance; twenty-eight guns of different sizes, and numberless ginjals were also planted on the city walls, principally towards the sea.

"The main body of the Chinese forces were posted on the right bank of the river, in fortified encampments, on very commanding and steep hills, field-works and entrenchments being thrown up in every advantageous position, with twenty-three guns and innumerable ginjals mounted in them to impede the advance of the troops. The principal landing-place on this side is within a considerable creek, close to the south entrance of the river, and across this creek we found a row of piles driven. Four batteries, mounting thirty-one guns, were also newly constructed on this side of the river, to flank the entrance; and about half a mile above its mouth a similar obstruction of larger piles was carried completely across, space only being left for one junk to pass at a time. In short, the Chinese had exercised their ingenuity to the utmost to make their defences secure, and a great amount of treasure and labour must have been expended in the execution of these works, fully evincing the importance which they attach to this position."

On the 10th of October, the citadel and city were bombarded by the fleet; while the troops having disembarked, advanced to the attack in two columns, by different routes. The Chinese manifested great firmness, but their fire, though heavy, was ill-directed, and the mines which they exploded failed in their effect. Admiral Parker accompanied one of the columns, and was the first to scale the walls. So impetuous was the assault, that the garrison, though four times more numerous than the assailants, fled through the western gate so soon as they saw the English columns on the ramparts. On the following day, the expedition, greatly aided by the favourable weather, proceeded up the river to Ningpo, a large city, five miles in circumference, and supposed to contain a population of three hundred thousand inhabitants. No preparations were made for resistance; it was said that the troops, since their defeat at Chinhae, had declared that they would not again encounter the British. The gates of the city were, indeed, barricaded, but the walls were soon scaled, and the Chinese themselves assisted in removing obstructions and opening the gates. Several towns in the neighbourhood were captured unresistingly, and Sir Henry Pottinger returned to Hong Kong in order to watch the proceedings of the Chinese at Canton.

On the 10th of March a body of Chinese forces, about twelve thousand in number, advanced upon Ningpo, scaled the walls, and advanced to the market-place in the centre of the town. Sir Hugh Gough made no attempt to resist the enemy until they had fairly entered the city, and were under the necessity of coming to an engagement; he then attacked them so impetuously, that their lines were instantly broken, and they were forced to fly in the greateat disorder. The British guns made fearful havock among the disorganized masses, and the pursuit was close and vigorous. It was remarked that four or five dollars were found in the pockets of every one of the fallen Chinese, from whence it was concluded that they had been bribed into valour on the occasion by their rulers. An attack on Chinghae was repulsed the same night; and about the sametime the junks, which were collected to attack the island of Chusan, were destroyed at Tinghae by the steamer Nemesis. In these engagements there was no casualty on the side of the British, but the loss of the Chinese in killed and wounded was very great, and quite disheartened their armies.

Sir Hugh Gough was anxious to follow up his success, but it was difficult to find out where the Chinese army existed as an organized body. At length he received information that a Chinese force of about four thousand men had encamped at the town of Tse-kee, about eleven miles westward of Ningpo, and that they formed the advance-guard of a much larger force, destined to attack that city. A detachment of eleven hundred men was embarked, and towed by the Phlegethon and Nemesis steamers to the vicinity of the Chinese camp, which was found pitched in a very strong position to the west of the town. The troops occupied Tse-kee without opposition, but when they marched to attack the camp, they were received with a very heavy fire from ginjals and matchlocks. The fire, however, was ill directed, and, when the British closed, their adversaries gave way on every side. The loss of the Chinese exceeded six hundred, that of the English amounted only to three killed and twenty wounded. The Chinese military chest was taken, but its contents were found to be miserably small, not exceeding two thousand dollars.

The operations of the war lingered after these exploits: reinforcements were necessary in order that all the points which it was desirable to embrace in the plan of a decisive campaign, should be acted upon simultaneously. On the 18th of May, however, an attack was made upon Chapoo, the usual port of communication between China and Japan. The town was taken without resistance or opposition: but, after the troops had entered, some Tartar soldiers, who had taken post in a Buddhist temple or Joss-house, fearing that, if they surrendered, no quarter would be given them, unexpectedly opened a severe fire on some British companies, by which one officer was killed and three wounded. The Tartars were, however, soon dislodged, and the greater part of them cut to pieces by the irritated soldiers.

Although Chapoo is not in itself a place of great importance, its occupation by the British is likely to produce a very great effect on the eastern kingdoms of Asia, and particularly on the empire of Japan, which has for some centuries been more exclusive in its policy than that of China itself. Sir Stamford Raffles, before the unwise cession of Java to the Dutch, had formed wise commercial plans which, in all human probability, would have opened the unknown regions of Japan to British enterprize and manufactures, but, unfortunately, the British negociators at Vienna had no means of knowing the value of oriental colonies, except through the directors of the East India Company, and they, deeply interested in the support of their then existing monopoly, were very reluctant to see colonies established in islands which would be directly subject to the crown, and the trade of which would therefore be thrown open to all English merchants. The Chinese war will probably effect, by forcible and expensive means, what the ignorance of the Vienna diplomatists, and the short-sighted and interested policy of the court of directors, prevented from being accomplished by gradual and peaceful methods. There can be no doubt that the appearance of the English in Chapoo, will produce a very lively sensation through the whole of the Japanese empire, and probably induce its court, haughty in the fancied security of ignorance, to reflect upon the danger of persevering in that barbarous course of policy which opposes itself to the progress of commerce and civilization.

The Afghan and Chinese wars differ from all those in which the Anglo-Indian government has been previously engaged, in their not being purely defensive, or at least explicable on grounds of immediate and almost tangible danger. In judging of the progress of British power in Hindústan, it must ever be borne in mind that the East India Company obtained its settlements on the coast, just as the mighty empire of Delhí was crumbling into pieces, and that it was utterly impossible to preserve neutrality in the countless struggles of the Mohammedan and Hindú chieftains to obtain a share of the spoil. Calcutta could not be safe so long as a hostile or rapacious chief was Subahdar of Bengal; though nominally a viceroy, the governor of that province was virtually an independent sovereign, and was, in fact, more closely connected with the Company than with his nominal master, the Emperor of Delhí. From the time that Lord Clive was compelled by the force of circumstances to interfere in the choice of a ruler for Bengal, it was impossible for the Company to recede a step without quitting that part of India altogether. It was not, in the first instance, suspected that the independent existence of a presidency and of a Native state were incompatible, and therefore the Company was compelled to take the *Dewannee*, or collection of the revenues in Bengal, which it did with obvious reluctance. This *Dewannee* was virtually a vice-regal authority, which was changed into absolute sovereignty, not by the ambition of the Company, but by the sheer incapacity of the imperial court to exert its supremacy or even preserve its independence. Allegiance and tribute were due by treaty to the Emperor of Delhí, but not to the Mahrattas, when they became his masters and made him the helpless instrument of their rapacity. In fact, the sovereignty of Bengal fell into the hands of the British by the mere force of circumstances, and had they not taken it, there can be no doubt that the whole of northern India would have fallen into a state of helpless, deplorable, and ruinous anarchy.

But the sovereignty of Bengal involved serious duties and responsibilities, particularly the protection of the minor states, which, together with it, had received the assurances of good government and tranquillity so long as they continued their allegiance to the supreme power. It would have been obviously impolitic to allow them to be devastated by plundering hordes such as the Mahrattas or Pindarries, and there was no injustice in taking them into dependent alliance on the condition of affording them protection. The Company did not seek this responsibility; on the contrary, it made every possible exertion to avoid the discharge of such onerous duties; but experience shewed that sovereignty could not be retained without attending to the responsibilities it involved, and the system of subsidiary treaties, abandoned after the return home of the Marquis of Wellesley, was obliged to be resumed and extended by the Marquis of Hastings. In fact, the Company was forced to constitute itself the heir to the Emperors of Delhí, because no one of the other competitors had even a remote chance of establishing a secure and organized system of government.

In the south of India, the English did not seek territorial aggrandizement until they were forced to do so by the example of the French; it was, in fact, a struggle for existence: had the French presidency of Pondicherry become supreme in the Dekkan, Madras and its dependencies must have been lost to the Company. The first war with Mysore was certainly provoked by Hyder Alí, and besides, he must be rather regarded as an ambitious adventurer endeavouring to found a kingdom, than as a legitimate sovereign established in a state. There is rather more difficulty in the case of the last Mysorean war, which terminated in the death of Tippoo and the abolition of royalty in his family; on that occasion, the Anglo-Indian government, like the authorities at home, were too nervously sensitive to the intrigues of France, and too ready to trace the most indifferent occurrences to republican ambition. The Marquis of Wellesley, in fact, waged war against possibilities, and the causes assigned for a declaration of hostilities in the manifesto which he issued, do not furnish so complete a justification for his precipitancy as could be desired. This, indeed, seems to have been the opinion both of the court of directors and the English people, for, successful as the issue of the Mysore war was, almost beyond all former precedent, the thanks voted to those by whom it was contrived and conducted, were niggardly and cold, nor did the leaders receive any substantial marks of the national gratitude.

The wars against the Pindarries and Mahrattas, stand on a very different ground; the only objection to which they are fairly liable is, that they were too long delayed; it is the duty of every civilized government to put an end to anarchy and marauding upon its frontiers, and to interfere for the protection of peaceful communities from bands of robbers. The Mahratta states were nothing better than organized associations of plunderers; they were superior to the Pindarries, only because their armies were more numerous, their association more complete, and their plundering more systematic. It was as much the duty of the principal established power in India, to put an end to the outrages perpetrated by those confederacies, and to compel them to live in peace, as it is of a leading maritime state to prevent piracy on the high seas. The Nepaulese and Burmese wars were so clearly defensive, that it is not necessary to waste one word upon their justification.

It must be confessed that the present Afghan war is the most questionable, on all the grounds of justice, policy, and prudence, of any in which the Anglo-Indian empire has ever been involved. The rulers of Afghanistan owed no allegiance, direct or indirect, to the authorities in Calcutta, and they had therefore a perfect right to prefer a Russian to an English alliance, if they believed that the former was most conducive to their interests. The contest between the Barukzye brothers and the King of Lahore, afforded but a very poor pretext for interference; it had raged for many years without attracting the slightest notice, and there is evidence than an offer of mediation would have been accepted, if made without any ulterior object than the restoration of peace, for Runjeet Singh was heartily tired of his useless and expensive acquisitions beyond the Indus.

The policy of the war, must ultimately be determined by the reasonableness of the fears which were entertained of the ambitious designs of Russia. It would be obviously insufficient to prove that the cabinet of St. Petersburg, is jealous of the British empire in India, and desirous to witness, or even effect its overthrow; there are few cabinets in Europe, of which the same thing may not be predicated: it is further necessary to establish that the Russians have it in their power to make such a series of complicated combinations with the states of Central Asia, as to render an overland invasion of India, practicable or even possible. When even single travellers have found it a very painful and perilous enterprize, to accomplish the journey from the Anglo-Indian empire to the frontiers of Russia, it seems to be one of the strangest speculations that ever entered the mind, to imagine the march of an organized army through these "wilds immeasurably spread," with the train of artillery, baggage and munitions of war, required by modern tactics. Timúr, Baber and Nadir Shah, had no disciplined troops to encounter, and therefore they had no heavy trains of guns to transport. Their invading armies were composed principally of light cavalry, and they met little or no organized resistance. But what would be the condition of a Russian army when it reached the banks of the Indus, and met there the British troops, fresh, vigorous, and supplied with all the material for making a powerful defence? It is scarcely possible to conceive how the Russians could ever effect such a march; but supposing that they succeeded so far, it is utterly impossible that they could be prepared to encounter the force which would be prepared for their reception.

The Circassian war, which has been far more calamitous and humiliating to Russia, than the Afghan expedition to England, shews that the mountaineers of Asia are very formidable adversaries to European troops, and very difficult to be reconciled to European domination. By no route could the Russians advance, where they would not have to encounter mountainous defiles, to the full as rugged, precipitous and treacherous as those of the Caucasus, and probably not less obstinately defended. Even if an enemy forced or purchased a passage through these mountains, it would always be exposed to have its communications cut off, by the caprice or treachery of barbarians, who are utterly indifferent to the faith of treaties. From the days of the wars between the Romans and the Parthians, to the present hour, it has been invariably found, that though a civilized and disciplined army is sure to triumph over the hordes of uncivilized barbarians in a fair field, it is liable to be worn down by desultory and harassing attacks, especially when the difficulties of country and climate are superadded to the rapacity of plundering tribes, and the ignorant desperation which among barbarians is no feeble substitute for valour. It might be possible indeed for Russian armies to be floated down the Euphrates and the Tigris, but there would still remain the overland march thorough Gedrosia, Carmania, &c. which so nearly proved fatal to the victorious legions of Alexander the Great, and which would assuredly ruin any European army encumbered with the countless requisites of modern war. In fact, the Russians could have no chance of success, except by means of a strong naval armament in the Persian Gulf, and that is not likely to be obtained so long as England remains the mistress of the seas.

The prudence of the Afghan war might be less questionable, if the success of our arms in that country, had been such as to produce a very strong impression of respect and fear on the various sovereigns of Asia. The reverses which we have experienced, however slight and temporary they may be, are likely to produce feelings of a very opposite tendency. The alliance or even acquisition of Afghanistan, can be of very little importance, viewed merely in the light of affording an opening for trade. In fact, the Afghans have very little to give in exchange for European manufactures, and the supplies which they received from Bombay, before the commencement of the war, were probably as great as the consumption of the nation required. The opening of the navigation of the Indus, is not identical with the opening of the trade of Central Asia, because the ranges of mountains to the north are tenanted by savage hordes, whose rate of duties on the transit of goods, will be regulated rather by their blind cupidity, than by any system of enlightened policy. There are two parties to all commercial transactions ; it may be, and doubtless is desirable, that the markets of Central Asia, should be open for British enterprize, but it is very far from being proved that the nations of Central Asia are anxious to become purchasers of our goods.

If in any quarter there seemed a disposition to retain possession of Afghanistan, it would be necessary to point out the disadvantages of its vague and unsettled frontier, compared with so definite and defensible a line as the course of the Indus. This, however, is not necessary ; every one appears to be convinced that the English troops ought to evacuate the country, so soon as their return can be effected without dishonour to the nation. So far as we can see from the documents already published, the war was undertaken to avert contingencies which were very barely within the remotest verge of possibility, but it has led to disasters which are in themselves substantial and real, but which in their remote consequences menace both the tranquillity and the stability of the British empire in India.

On the other hand, the Chinese war may fairly be justified, by a series of insults, annoyances and provocations, which have been continued for the greater part of a century ;—the patient submission of the Company's agents to Chinese insolence, from their fear that any show of resentment would lead to a suspension of the tea trade. An earlier exhibition of spirit would probably have prevented an expensive war, and taught the Chinese, that the laws of nations cannot be violated with impunity.

It is not, however, to be regretted, that the rulers of the Celestial Empire, have been practically taught by our successes the vast superiority of the European system of civilization ; means less forcible would probably have failed to break the torpidity to which the Chinese mind was reduced by the policy of its rulers. Hitherto the efforts made to introduce Christianity into China, have not produced results at all proportioned to the heavy expense incurred, and the zealous labours of the missionaries ; but there is reason to hope, that the delusion which enabled the government to perpetuate ignorance, will be dispelled by the overthrow of the belief, that the government was invincible in strength and unsurpassed in intelligence.

It is scarcely possible to conclude this history without making some reflections on the light which the past throws on the future prospects of Hindústan. Hitherto the British may be said only to have encamped in India ; colonization was long systematically prohibited, and all amalgation between the ruling and the subject races discouraged. A mixed race has indeed been produced by the illegitimate connexions formed by both civilians and military officers ; this race is already numerous, and it must be naturally propelled to claim the privileges of British descent without abandoning its sympathies with its maternal origin. The Anglo-Indian race, must naturally be anxious to see the principle of self-government established in all the colonies dependent on the crown, recognized within the dominions of the Company. Self-government is a principle necessary to the progress of civilization, and the Hindús cannot rise in the social scale while all their laws emanate from Leadenhall Street. Provincial legislatures, would do more to elevate the character of the Hindú and Mohammedan communities, than any other measures which could be adopted ; and they would encrease ten-fold the value of India, as a purchaser of manufacturers, to England. It is not probable that representative assemblies will be conceded to the Presidencies so long as they remain under the exclusive government of the Company, but when the Charter is next renewed, it is probable that the Hindús may obtain some benefit from the principle recognized in every part of the British dominions, that taxation without representation is nothing better than tyranny. The servants of the Company, aided by the honourable policy of the Court of Directors, have successfully exerted themselves to diffuse the blessings of education amoug the Natives ; the rising generation will have learned to appreciate the institutions which produce the well-being of communities, and they cannot fail to be inspired with an anxiety for the establishment of such institutions in their native land.

CHAPTER XXII.

ENGLISH DEPENDENCIES IN THE INDIAN SEAS.

Ceylon.

The fertile island of Ceylon was known to the ancient Greeks by the name of Taprolianè, and to the early Arabian voyagers, under that of Serendil. It is supposed to have been colonized by a body of Singhs or Rajpûts, about five centuries before the Christian era, who were professors of the Budhist creed, which is still maintained by their Singhalese descendants. In the reign of Claudius Cæsar, a Roman publican, who farmed the custom duties of the Red Sea, was driven by an adverse gale from the coast of Arabia, on the island of Ceylon, where he found a flourishing kingdom, and an enlightened sovereign. He induced the monarch to send four envoys to Rome through the Red Sea, for the purpose of negociating a commercial treaty, but we have no evidence that any trading intercourse of importance ensued. There are abundant proofs that the ancient kingdom of Ceylon was both populous and powerful: the ruins of cities and canals, the traces of enormous public works, the artificial Lake of Kandely still existing near Trincomalee, attest the greatness of the Singhalese under the rule of their Native princes. Anorahjapoora, the ancient capital, was sixteen miles square, and a list of the streets in this ruined city is still existence.

In the period between the sixth and thirteenth centuries, the Singhalese had an active trade with China, India, Arabia, and Egypt, in consequence of which Colombo and Galle became flourishing marts of commerce, and among the most celebrated ports of the Indian Ocean. Marco Polo, who visited the island in the course of his travels, described it as "the finest in the world," and the Arab writers vie with each other in celebrating its wealth, fertility, and beauty, both in their history and romance. Some years before the discovery of the passage round the Cape of Good Hope, the coasts of Ceylon were ravaged by piratical adventurers from the shores of Arabia and Malabar; their depredations, united with some intestine commotions, greatly weakened the kingdom; in the year 1153, a Singhalese monarch was able to fit out a fleet of five hundred vessels to resent an insult offered to his ambassadors; in 1505, the reigning sovereign was unable to prevent piratical hordes from seizing his best harbours and plundering his richest cities. Colombo was at this period the royal residence, and the population was divided into two distinct races, the Bedahs, who inhabited the interior of the country, and the Singhalese, or, as they are more usually called, the Cingalese, who inhabit the sea-coast. The Bedahs are supposed to have been the aborigines of the island; they seem to be incapable of civilization, for they continue, to the present day, in the state they were found by the Portuguese, destitute of habitations and clothing, living in inaccessible forests, feeding only on fruits and wild animals, and having no resting-place either by day or night save the branches of large trees.

When the Portuguese admiral, Almeida, appeared off the coast, the King of Colombo was exposed to great danger from the attacks of Arab pirates; the fame of European enterprize and success induced him to place himself under the protection of the crown of Portugal. For this purpose he entered into a treaty with Almeida, stipulating to pay an annual tribute of two hundred and fifty thousand pounds weight of cinnamon, on condition of being delivered from the depredators. The Portuguese being permitted to settle in Ceylon, at first contented themselves with establishing factories in the principal ports; the factories were gradually changed into fortresses; and at length, the Portuguese took formal possession of the principal commercial cities, and expelled the native authorities. Their government was more oppressive in Ceylon than in any other part of their colonies. The Cingalese were excluded from foreign trade with any other nation, and were compelled to accept in payment for their produce, whatever the monopolists pleased to offer. The Native monarchs, compelled to make Kandy, a city in the interior, their residence, could obtain no redress for any injuries that were offered to their subjects, and their representations on the subject were rejected with contumely and insult.

After having long endured these cruelties and oppressions, the Cingalese resolved to apply for aid to the Dutch, who had now become formidable rivals of the Portuguese in the Indian Seas. In 1632, a strong armament was sent from Holland to co-operate with the forces of the King of Kandy, and possession was taken of Trincomalee. A desultory but bloody war ensued; many of the Portuguese were connected by marriage with the Natives, and numbers of the Cingalese had been converted to the Roman Catholic form of the Christian faith by the exertions of the Jesuit missionaries. The Portuguese, though badly supported from home, were thus enabled to protract their resistance for several years; but, on the surrender of their last fortress, Colombo, in 1656, they were compelled to evacuate the island.

The Cingalese gained little by the change; the commercial policy of the Dutch was every whit as exclusive as that of the Portuguese, and their administration of justice equally partial and intolerable. In one respect, however, the policy of the Dutch deserved the highest praise; they established schools in the principal towns, for the purpose of instructing the Native children in the doctrines of Christianity, and the elements of useful knowledge. These schools were, in general, admirably conducted, and they produced very beneficial results. The English government at Madras had long desired to obtain possession of the Dutch settlements in Ceylon, on account of the fine harbour of Trincomalee, which was the only port available in stormy weather for the fleet which protected that presidency. On the annexation of Holland to France, in 1795, an armament was sent against Ceylon, and, after a series of tedious military operations, destitute of the slightest interest or importance, the Dutch possessions in Ceylon were surrendered to the British forces.

Ceylon remained for a short time attached to the presidency of Madras, but it was afterwards rendered independent of the East India Company, and annexed to the empire of Great Britain under the direct government of the crown. A contract, however, was concluded with the Company at the time of the transfer, January 1802, by which the exclusive privilege of exporting cinnamon was leased to that body. It was agreed that the Ceylon government should deliver, annually, 400,000lbs. of cinnamon to the Company, at three shillings per pound, and that the Company should credit the colony with all the clear profits made on the sale of that article, beyond five per cent. Some variations were subsequently made in the contract; but the monopoly proved to be highly injurious to the colony, and not very lucrative to those in whose favour it was established. In 1821, the exclusive privilege of exporting cinnamon was abandoned by the Company, and all persons were allowed freely to purchase and export the spice from the government stores.

The English, like the Portuguese and Dutch, were at first confined to the provinces on the sea-coast, and it was with great reluctance that they were induced to interfere with the interior of the country; they were, however, compelled to do so by the wanton provocations of the Native government. In 1798, the King of Kandy died, and the crown was transferred, by the intrigues of Pelemè Talanè, the chief Adigar, or prime minister, to a young native of Malabar, without birth, talent, or pretensions of any kind. The policy of the Adigar was decidedly hostile to the British government, and he directed the conduct of his creature, the new monarch, at his pleasure; his object was to amuse the British with delusive negociations, until he had completed his plans for their expulsion from the island. After some time had been spent in secret preparations, the English governor, the Honourable Frederick North, provoked by the continued aggressions of the Kandyans, proclaimed war, and ordered two divisions of British troops to proceed into the interior from Colombo and Trincomalee. Little or no resistance was made to the march of these divisions; they united before Kandy, and took possession of that city, which was abandoned on their approach. The Adigar, finding that force was unavailing had recourse to treachery; he lulled the British officers into delusive security by concluding a treaty, in consequence of which the greater part of the troops returned to the provinces, leaving only a small garrison in Kandy under the command of Major Davie. No sooner, however, had the army withdrawn, than the perfidious Adigar blockaded Kandy with all his forces, and compelled Major Davie, whose men were suffering severely from sickness and privations, to consent to a humiliating capitulation. The terms of surrender were, however, atrociously violated; no sooner had the British troops laid down their arms, than they were wantonly attacked and cruelly massacred with the exception of one corporal, who made his escape, though wounded, with the disastrous intelligence to Colombo.

The Kandyan troops advanced to the British frontiers, and carried on a warfare of ravage and spoliation, but their repeated invasions were defeated with great loss. At length, hostilities were suspended as if by tacit consent, in consequence of the weakness of the enemy, and the pacific disposition of the British administration. Meanwhile, the Kandyan monarch provoked the hatred of his own subjects, by many atrocious acts of cruelty and tyranny; we may mention as an instance, that he compelled the wife of one of his chief Adigars, to pound her own children to death in a mortar. Many of his subjects removed from the interior to the British settlements, and some of the chiefs applied for military aid to protect them from oppression, which was not granted. In October, 1814, ten natives of the British province of Columbo, who were engaged in their ordinary traffic with the the people of the interior, were seized by command of the Kandyan monarch, and cruelly mutilated. This outrage, joined with a revolt of the people of the frontier provinces against the tyrant, finally determined the English government to take up arms; the troops were put in motion in the beginning of the year 1815, whilst a proclamation was issued, promising protection and security to the Kandyans, and announcing that the court alone was the object of hostility.

Lieutenant-general Brownrigg, the Governor and Commander-in-chief, arranged the march of the army in divisions, in order to avoid the difficulties connected with the supply of forage and provisions. Rugged roads, rainy weather, and occasional deficiencies of food, were, in fact, the only obstacles against which the army had to contend, for at no part did they meet with armed resistance, and the Adigars were all ready to join them when they found that it could be done with safety to their families. A detachment entered Kandy on the 11th of February, which was found entirely deserted by the inhabitants, and stripped of all valuable property. On receiving promises of protection, however, many of the citizens returned, and the markets were regularly supplied by the people of the adjacent country, so soon as they were assured of obtaining payment for their produce.

The king fled, accompanied by a body of his adherents, chiefly his own countrymen, from Malabar, and some days elapsed before any information respecting the place of his retreat could be obtained. Eventually, he was discovered and surrounded by his own insurgent subjects, and, after a slight resistance on the part of his Malabar guards, was taken prisoner with two of his wives. He was fettered, reviled, and plundered; and every circumstance of his fall denoted the general detestation inspired by a cruel despotism. His life, however, was spared in consequence of the interference of the English general.

This conquest was entirely bloodless on the part of the English, who enjoyed an extraordinary degree of health in the midst of their fatigues. It was resolved that the entire island should be placed under British rule, and a solemn council of the Adigars was held in the audience-chamber of the palace of Kandy, on the 2nd of March. A treaty which had been previously framed, for annexing the Kandyan provinces to the British dominions, was then unanimously accepted; and the result of the convention was declared to the people in a proclamation containing seven articles. The first recited the cruelties of the late Malabar ruler, the Rájá Sri Wilkrenie Rájá Sinha; the second declared the forfeiture of all right to the throne by him and his family; his relatives were prohibited from entering the Kandyan provinces without the express permission of the British government; the dominion of the provinces was vested in the sovereign of the British empire; the religion of Buddha was established, but, at the same time, full liberty was conceded to all other creeds; bodily torture and mutilation were abolished; and it was forbidden to execute any sentence of death, without a warrant from the British governor.

Although, at first, the grants which the Dutch government had made for the support of schools were greatly reduced, a more liberal and enlightened policy has been adopted in Ceylon than in the Company's dominions. In 1811, a charter passed the great seal, granting to every native of Ceylon, not legally disqualified, the right to sit on juries. This mode of trial was accordingly introduced with great advantage, and has produced the most favourable effect on the character of the inhabitants. As a remarkable proof of this, it may be stated that the slave proprietors in the island passed a resolution that, after the 12th of August, 1816, all persons born in slavery should be considered free.

When the treaty was made at Kandy, General Brownrigg intimated that the civil government of the country should be conducted through the medium of the principal Adigars, without any interference on the part of the British army. It was, however, soon discovered that the Singhalese aristocracy was unfit to wield the powers with which it had been entrusted, and the British officers, both civil and military, were frequently compelled to interfere for the purpose of checking the outrages and oppressions perpetrated by a rapacious nobility. The Kandyan chiefs were of course dissatisfied; several of them conspired to overthrow the foreign yoke which they had imposed upon themselves; many of the ignorant Natives were induced to join them, and a formidable insurrection burst forth, in which some of the British authorities were murdered. The prompt measures adopted by the governor soon put an end to the rebellion; the leaders of the insurgents were made prisoners, two of them were publicly executed, and the rest sent into banishment. Since that period the tranquillity of Ceylon has not been interrupted, and its prosperity has rapidly increased since the abolition of the pernicious monopolies by which its commerce was restricted; it bids fair to become one of the most important colonies of the British empire, and it will probably precede all the countries of the East, in accepting from our hands the blessings of Christianity and civilization.

Pulo Penang.

Pulo Penang, or Prince of Wales's Island, is situated on the west coast of the Malacca peninsula, and, though small, is valuable for its excellent harbour, formed by the strait which divides the island from Quedda on the opposite coast. It was long untenanted, or only inhabited by a few miserable fishermen, until it formed part of the marriage portion which Captain Light, the commander of a Company's ship in India, received from the King of Quedda on his union with the daughter of that sovereign. In the following year, Captain Light transferred his acquisition to the Company; under its sanction, a treaty was concluded with the king, by which he confirmed that body in the possession of

Pulo Penang, and added a slip of territory on the adjacent coast of the Malayan peninsula. Commerce soon attracted to Penang a motley population from all the maritime states of Asia ; it serves as an entrepôt for the various produce of China, the eastern islands and straits, the Native merchants from which take back in return British and India goods.

MALACCA.

The British settlement of Malacca is situated at the extremity of the Malayan peninsula, and is about forty miles in length by thirty in breadth. The abriginal inhabitants of the peninsula were a race of oriental Negroes, with woolly hair, jet-black skin, thick lips, and flat nose, like the Africans. About the year 1252, the Malays emigrated from their native country, Palembang in the island of Sumatra, and landing on the peninsula founded the city of Malacca. As they extended their conquests, the Negro-race fled before them into the mountains and forests, where some of their unfortunate descendants still remain. Until the year 1276, the Malays were idolators of the lowest kind, but their spirit of commercial enterprize having brought them acquainted with the Arabs, at that time equally devoted to mercantile pursuits, they adopted the Mohammedan creed, and displayed scarcely less attachment to their new religion, than the Saracens in the first burst of their fanaticism. The Budhist nations around, but particularly the Siamese, resolved to punish the Malays for having adopted the creed of the prophet of Mecca ; a series of sanguinary but indecisive wars ensued, during which the Siamese gained possession of the northern part of the peninsula, but were unable to make any impression on the city of Malacca. The provinces of Tenasserim and Tavoy, were, however, wrested from the Siamese by the Burmese, by whom they were ceded to the British at the conclusion of the late war. The city of Malacca was taken by the Portuguese after an obstinate resistance, in the year 1611. They held it for more than a century, but with great difficulty, as it was repeatedly attacked by the Malayan powers, particularly by the Sultan of Acheen, and the Prince of Jahore, who was descended from its ancient sovereigns. It was attacked in 1605 by the Dutch, who destroyed a Portuguese fleet in the roads, but failed to take the place ; they returned in 1640, and after a close siege, which lasted six months, gained possession of the town, which became one of their principal settlements, and the key of their trade with the seas beyond India. In 1795, it was seized by the British, but was restored to the Dutch at the peace of Amiens in 1801. It was again occupied by the English in 1807, and was one of the unaccountable colonial sacrifices made to Holland, by the negociators of the treaty of Vienna in 1815. In 1825, however, it, together with the fort of Chinsurah in India, were resigned to the English in exchange for our possessions in the island of Sumatra. It is valuable on account of its very healthy climate, and productive tin mines, but its commercial importance has much declined in consequence of the transfer of trade to the rising colonies of Pulo Penang and Singapore.

SINGAPORE.

This island, about twenty-seven miles in length by fifteen in breadth, was formed into a British settlement in 1818, by Sir Stamford Raffles, in order to diminish the evil results which arose from the unwise cession of Java to the Dutch; its possession was confirmed by a convention concluded with the King of Holland and the Rájá of Jehore, a Malay prince, who claimed it as part of his dominions. When first a settlement was formed on the island by Sir Stamford Raffles, the population consisted of only one hundred and fifty Malays, half fishermen and half pirates. Its favourable situation in the Straits of Malacca, attracted such multitudes of settlers, that, in fifteen years, the population exceeded twenty thousand souls, and is still progressively increasing. According to the Malay annals, Singapore was anciently a very flourishing principality; but about the middle of the fifteenth century, its ruler was compelled to abandon the island by an invasion of the King of Majopalut, in Java, since which time its capabilities continued to be neglected, until it was occupied by the English.

THE MAURITIUS.

This fine island more properly belongs to Africa than to Asia, but, as it was part of the possessions of the French East India Company, and is still regarded as an island connected with the

British empire in Hindústan, it will be necessary to give a brief notice of its history. It is about forty-four miles long by thirty-two wide, and lies about six hundred miles to the north-east of Madagascar.

This island was first discovered in the year 1507, by Don Pedro Mascarenhas, an able navigator in the service of the Portuguese government in India, who was sent on an exploring voyage by Almeida, who represented the crown of Portugal in the East. Mascarenhas named the island Cernè, under the false impression, that it was the Cernè Ethiopia mentioned by Pliny; the naturalist probably indicated by that name the island of Madagascar. The Portuguese did not colonize this nor the neighbouring island, which in a later age, received the name of Bourbon; they merely placed some hogs, goats and monkeys on them, to afford a supply of food to any vessel which might be wrecked on the coasts. When Portugal was united to Spain, the gradual decline of the Portuguese empire in the East, prevented the establishing of new colonies, or the undertaking of new enterprizes; Cernè consequently remained unnoticed, and almost unknown until the year 1598, when it was visited by the Dutch Admiral Van Nerk, who took possession of it in the name of his government, and called the place Mauritius, in honour of Maurice, Prince of Orange. The Dutch, however, do not appear to have immediately formed settlements on the island, since it was found to be uninhabited when visited by Captain Castleton, the commander of an English ship, in 1613. Some years afterwards it was seized by some pirates, from whom it was recovered by the Dutch, who placed a small garrison at the Grand Port. In 1712, the Hollanders abandoned the Mauritius, which was then partially colonized by some French settlers from the neighbouring isle of Bourbon. In 1715, Mr. Du Fresne, a captain in the French royal navy, visited the place, and changed its name to the Isle of France; he gave so good an account of it on his return, that the French government resolved to occupy it formally. This was effected in 1721, when the territory was bestowed by the king upon the French East India Company.

The value of this new acquisition was not at first appreciated; no regular colony was sent to the island, and the settlers were, for a long time, composed of adventurers, refugees, and pirates, the outcasts of all nations. The French East India Company, indeed, only regarded it as a refreshing station for their ships, and they found the expense of its maintenance a very heavy burthen on their finances. In 1730, the home government resolved to send out a commission for the purpose of exploring the island, and seeing whether it was worth the cost of its retention. The head of the commission, honoured with the seemingly empty title of governor, was Mr. De la Bourdonnais, who arrived in the island early in the year 1725. He devoted all his energies to the improvement of the colony; he introduced the culture of the sugar-cane, established manufactories of cotton and indigo, laid out roads, erected fortifications and other public buildings, extirpated the Maroon negroes, and laid the foundations of a prosperous colony. Still, the French government thought little of the Mauritius until they witnessed the valuable aid which it rendered to Admiral Suffrein, during the American war, in his exertions to cripple British commerce. It was, indeed, chiefly owing to the possession of this island that a French navy was able to maintain itself in the Eastern Seas.

On the conclusion of peace, in 1782, the attention of the French government was strongly directed to the islands of Bourbon and Mauritius; in 1784, the trade with these islands was opened to all the merchants of France, while the islanders were permitted free traffic with every part of Asia except China. In consequence of this wise measure, the Mauritius became a great commercial depôt; the population rapidly augmented, and many of the most enterprising young men of France hasted to a colony which promised them the means of making speedy fortunes. The administration was entrusted to a governor and intendant, whose rule was perfectly despotic, and their arbitrary conduct excited a dangerous spirit in the colony, which was kindled into action by intelligence of the Revolution in the mother-country.

In January, 1789, the first intelligence of the revolution was brought to the Isle of France by a vessel from Bourdeaux; the captain, officers, and crew wore the tricoloured cockade; they easily induced the colonists to follow their example, and also to institute primary assemblies for the purpose of obtaining a redress of grievances. General de Comreay, who was then governor of the island, attempted to stop these proceedings, and arrested some of the principal leaders; but a tumultuous mob soon assembled in the square of Port Louis, liberated the prisoners, and compelled the governor himself to assume the tricoloured cockade. At this crisis M. de Macnamara, the commander of the French marines in the Indian Seas, arrived in Port Louis, and manifested great indignation at these revolutionary proceedings. He wrote to the minister of marine, condemning the popular movement in the strongest terms, and particularly calling for the punishment of the soldiers of the garrison, who had adopted the cause of the revolutionists. The admiral was betrayed, and a copy of his letter sent to the barracks. Loud cries for vengeance were raised by the infuriate soldiers; they seized upon every boat they could find, and sent their grenadiers to arrest the admiral in his own ship. M. de Macnamara ordered his guns to be loaded and pointed; but when the sailors heard the intelligence of the Revolution, they refused to fire, and surrendered the admiral to the grenadiers. He was brought a prisoner before the newly-elected assembly, the members of which ordered him to be sent to the ordinary place of confinement, until preparations could be made for his trial. On his road to the prison, the admiral attempted, by the aid of his pistols, to extricate himself from his guards, but he was overpowered and massacred by the irritated soldiers. A new governor was appointed, and tranquillity was restored, but the triumph of the Jacobins, and the decree of the French Republic abolishing slavery, threw the affairs of the island into fresh confusion. The appearance of two agents of the French Directory, with eight hundred men of the revolutionary army, and two troops of artillery, in July, 1796, excited the utmost alarm among the white population of an island, where, out of 70,000 inhabitants, no less than 55,000 were slaves. The Whites and the Creoles determined to resist the abolition, which the directorial agents no less resolutely asserted their intention to enforce, threatening that they would hang the governor and his abettors, if any resistance should be made to their arbitrary proceedings.

Fortunately for the white inhabitants, who might otherwise have been involved in the fate of their brethren at St. Domingo, the directorial agents did not promulgate the decree of abolition to the slave population; and before they could do so, they were seized by the colonists, who held them at their mercy. By the prompt interference of the governor and the house of assembly, the lives of the deputies were saved, and they were sent on board the ship *Moineau*, for the purpose of being transported to the Philippine Islands, as the place of exile most remote from France. No sooner was the vessel clear of the harbour, than the Jacobin commissioners resumed their directorial dress, harangued the sailors, and easily persuaded them to steer for France instead of the Philippine Islands. The changes in the republican government, before the commissioners reached home, frustrated their meditated plans of vengeance on the islanders, and, in consequence of the difficulty of communicating with Europe, produced by the vigilance of the British cruisers, the Mauritius, or Isle of France, was, for some years, virtually an independent state.

The republican troops which had accompanied the Jacobin commissioners, were much dissatisfied by the conduct of the governor and the house of assembly. In the beginning of 1798, they conspired to overthrow the colonial government, and to proclaim the emancipation of the slaves. Information of these intrigues was conveyed to the council, and it was resolved that these turbulent troops should be transported to India, as an auxiliary corps to Tippoo Sultan. When the orders for their embarkation arrived, the troops mutinied, and refused to obey. They occupied a position which menaced Port Louis, and threatened to plunder that capital. The Whites and Creoles promptly embodied themselves as a militia, to protect their property; they were joined by bands of volunteers, formed of the planters and farmers in the country, and they were supported by the artillery, a corps which remained faithful to the governor. Every preparation was made for storming the camp of the insurgents, and a sanguinary struggle seemed inevitable. The mutineers, however, were daunted by the extent of the preparations made against them, and they capitulated, on condition of being transported to France. A frigate which lay in the harbour was hastily made ready for sea; they were sent on board, but the taint of Jacobinism which they left behind them, was destined to produce fresh calamities in the island.

In the course of the year 1799, intelligence was received of the measures which the French government had adopted for getting rid of *assignats* and returning to a metallic currency. As these measures were very favourable to creditors, and equally onerous upon debtors, the colonial house of assembly resolved that they should not be promulgated without certain equitable modifications. The money-lenders and capitalists of Saint Louis, who were the creditors of the farmers and planters, were enraged at the delay in promulgating laws which would double their fortunes; they entered into a conspiracy with the lowest rabble, and succeeded in raising a tumultuous mob, which surrounded the house of assembly, and threatened the lives of the members. The governor was forced to dissolve the legislative body, but even this concession nearly proved insufficient, for the populace broke into the place of meeting, and were with great difficulty prevented from perpetrating a general massacre. The planters throughout the island refused to recognize the rule of the populace of Saint Louis, and the citizens themselves soon became weary of the state of anarchy and thraldom, in which they were kept by the Jacobins. A counter-revolution was effected without bloodshed, and the governor took advantage of the crisis, to render the constitution of the island less popular by diminishing the number of the representatives in the house of assembly.

After the renewal of hostilities between England and France, in 1803, the privateers and cruisers fitted out at the Mauritius, severely injured British commerce. Napoleon's usual sagacity, enabled him to appreciate the great advantages derived from the possession of this island, and he intended to send out a strong naval and military armament for its protection. The annihilation of the French and Spanish fleets, at the Battle of Trafalgar, frustrated his designs, and he was only able to send small reinforcements in fast-sailing frigates, which contrived to elude the vigilance of the British squadrons. These additions to the maritine strength of the islanders, enabled them to extend the system of privateering and almost of piracy, by which they harassed the trade between India and China. At length, the losses became so great, that it was resolved to deprive the French of all their naval stations. A naval and military force, prepared simultaneously at the Cape of Good Hope and in India, arrived at the Mauritius in 1810, under the command of General Abercomby and Admiral Bertie; a landing was effected with little loss, upon which the authorities, both of the Mauritius and the Isle of Bourbon, capitulated on honourable terms. At the same time, the stations which the French had established in the Island of Madagascar, were attacked and destroyed, so that no nation hostile to England, remained in possession of a single colony, or harbour, east of the Cape of Good Hope.

At the peace of 1815, the possession of the Mauritius, was confirmed to the English, but the adjacent isle of Bourbon, was restored to France. This was another instance of the incomprehensible policy in relation to the Eastern colonies, adopted by the British negociators at Vienna; a policy which can only be explained by supposing, that the system of free trade which would necessarily have prevailed in Crown colonies, must have early proved fatal to the commercial monopoly of the East India Company.

The colonies of the Cape of Good Hope and St. Helena, are not now so intimately connected with India, as to render it necessary for any notice to be taken of their history; and the Australian colonies have not yet been brought into any close relation with the Asiatic trade. It seems, however, to be the present tendency of Britain to revert to its ancient and wholesome policy of insular colonization, for experience has shewn that continental possessions, compel a civilized nation to enter upon a system of acquisition in self-defence, which seems incapable of being confined within the limits, which both economy and security show to be desirable. The history of Hindústan, contrasted with that of the Crown colonies, in the Asiatic and African islands, bears strong testimony to the truth of the ancient adage—

> "Extended empire, like expanded gold,
> Exchanges solid strength for feeble splendour."

CHRONOLOGICAL TABLE

OF

BRITISH ACQUISITIONS IN INDIA.

Date of Treaty.	Districts gained.	From whom acquired.
1757	Twenty-four Pergunnahs, &c. in Bengal	Nabob of Bengal.
1758	Masulipatam, &c.	The Nizam.
1760	Burdwan and Chittagong	Nabob of Bengal.
1765	Bengal, Bahar and Orissa	Emperor of Delhí.
——	Jaghire of Madras	Nabob of Arcot.
1766	Northern Circars	The Nizam.
1775	Zemindary of Benares	Vizier of Oude.
1776	Island of Salsette	Mahrattas.
1778	Town and Fort of Nagore	Rájá of Tanjore.
——	Guntúr Circar	The Nizam.
1786	Pulo Penang	King of Quedda.
1792	Malabar	Tippoo Sultan.
1799	Canara, Coimbatore, &c.	Ditto.
——	Tanjore	Rájá of Tanjore.
1800	Mysorean Provinces	The Nizam.
1801	The Carnatic	Nabob of the Carnatic.
——	Gurruckpore, Bareilly, &c.	Vizier of Oude.
1802	Bundelkund	The Peishwah.
1803	Kuttack and Ballasore	Rájá of Berar.
——	Territory of Delhí	Scindia.
1805	Part of Gujerat	Guicowar.
1818	Kandeish	Holkar.
——	Ajmere	Scindia.
——	Poonah and the Mahratta Country	The Peishwah.
——	Districts on the Nerbudda	Rájá of Berar.
1824	Singapore	Rájá of Johore.
1825	Malacca, &c.	King of Holland.
1826	Assam, Arracan, Tennasserim, &c.	King of Ava.
1834	Koorg	Rájá of Koorg.
1840	Scinde	Ameers of Hyderabad.

ANALYTICAL AND CHRONOLOGICAL INDEX.

[* Marks events of which the date is uncertain or unknown.]